Aaron Whitaker Guyton of Kosciusko, Mississippi: The Journeys of his African American Children

Dorla A. Evans, PhD

Author of *Joseph Guyton Genealogy: From England to Maryland and across the American South*

Aaron Whitaker Guyton of Kosciusko, Mississippi: The Journeys of his African American Children

Copyright © 2024 by Dorla A. Evans

6303 Central Park Ln NW, Huntsville, AL 35806
Flagview7@gmail.com

All rights reserved. No part of this publication may be reproduced, stored in a retrieval system, or transmitted, in any form or by any means, electronic, mechanical, photocopying, recording, or otherwise, without the prior written permission of the author.

Library of Congress Control Number: 2024920547

ISBN: 979-8-9916062-0-2

To my Guyton Family Members

Acknowledgements

David F. Guyton, an English genealogist of the worldwide Guytons, has been a significant resource and first alerted me to the documents connecting Aaron Whitaker (Whit) Guyton with his African American partners and children. His assistance and documents opened the door to this work. I am grateful to Sam and Jean Guyton for inviting me to the 2022 Guyton Family Reunion in Kosciusko, Mississippi, where the seed for the book was planted.

The reunion was the first meeting of the African American descendants of Whit Guyton and the white descendants of Whit's brother, Joseph Guyton. There I met Karl Glenn Boyd (aka Nykki Lamarr Starr) and his cousin, Rickey Simmons, who encouraged me to add more information about Whit's African American descendants to my previous book, *Joseph Guyton Genealogy: From England to Maryland and across the American South*. Nykki and Rickey's genealogical assistance was invaluable. Moreover, Nykki introduced me to his distant cousin, Channie Brown-Currie, who is the family genealogist for the Artie Rainey branches of the Whit Guyton tree. She shared with me her book prepared for their 2017 Guyton Family Reunion. Rickey introduced me to his first cousin, Rita Murphy McLean, who assisted with the Callie Pairee Gamble line. The photographs, documents, family trees, and family memories are priceless.

As with all practitioners of genealogy who set out to document what they have learned, I recognize the innumerable opportunities for errors. I take full responsibility for these.

Contents

Introduction	25
Possible Origins of the Guyton Name	26
Possible Origins of the Guyton Family	27
Generation #1	30
Samuel GUYTON I (John)	31
Generation #2	39
Samuel GUYTON II (Samuel I, John)	39
Generation #3	43
John GUYTON I (Samuel II, Samuel I, John)	43
Benjamin GUYTON I (Samuel II, Samuel I, John)	54
Generation #4	56
Joseph GUYTON I (John I, Samuel II, Samuel I, John)	56
Generation #5	70
Moses GUYTON I (Joseph I, John I, Samuel II, Samuel I, John)	70
Aaron Steele GUYTON (Joseph I, John I, Samuel II, Samuel I, John)	72
Abraham GUYTON (Joseph I, John I, Samuel II, Samuel I, John)	76
Joseph GUYTON II (Joseph I, John I, Samuel II, Samuel I, John)	77
Hannah GUYTON (Joseph I, John I, Samuel II, Samuel I, John)	84
Generation #6	88
Aaron Whitaker (Whit) GUYTON (Aaron Steele, Joseph I, John I, Samuel II, Samuel I, John)	88
Background Information of Relevant Towns in Attala County, MS	102
Attala County	102
Ethel	103
McAdams	104
McVille	104
New Port	105
Sallis	105
Zemuly	106
Relevant Cemeteries in Attala County	107
Range Maps of Attala County	108

Churches and Cemeteries in Attala County 112
The Great Migration of African Americans to the Industrial North 113
Sharecropping in the South: A Deep Dive into Its Impact on African Americans 116
CHILD OF AARON WHITAKER GUYTON AND SARAH UNKNOWN: CAROLINE'S LINE 119
Generation #7 119
Caroline GUYTON (Aaron Whitaker, Aaron Steele, Joseph I, John I, Samuel II, Samuel I, John) 119
Generation #8 122
William M. TERRY, Sr. (Caroline, Aaron Whitaker, Aaron Steele, Joseph I, John I, Samuel II, Samuel I, John) 122
Joseph Thomas (Joe) TERRY (Caroline, Aaron Whitaker, Aaron Steele, Joseph I, John I, Samuel II, Samuel I, John) 124
John TERRY (Caroline, Aaron Whitaker, Aaron Steele, Joseph I, John I, Samuel II, Samuel I, John) 125
Green TERRY (Caroline, Aaron Whitaker, Aaron Steele, Joseph I, John I, Samuel II, Samuel I, John) 127
Walter G. TERRY, Sr. (Caroline, Aaron Whitaker, Aaron Steele, Joseph I, John I, Samuel II, Samuel I, John) 129
Jacob G. (Jake) TERRY (Caroline, Aaron Whitaker, Aaron Steele, Joseph I, John I, Samuel II, Samuel I, John) 130
Generation #9 131
Mary Emma TERRY (William TERRY, Caroline, Aaron Whitaker, Aaron Steele, Joseph I, John I, Samuel II, Samuel I, John) ... 131
Ethel TERRY (William TERRY, Caroline, Aaron Whitaker, Aaron Steele, Joseph I, John I, Samuel II, Samuel I, John) 134
Nealie Eugene TERRY (William TERRY, Caroline, Aaron Whitaker, Aaron Steele, Joseph I, John I, Samuel II, Samuel I, John) 135
Sarah V. TERRY (William TERRY, Caroline, Aaron Whitaker, Aaron Steele, Joseph I, John I, Samuel II, Samuel I, John) 141
William Vinson TERRY (William TERRY, Caroline, Aaron Whitaker, Aaron Steele, Joseph I, John I, Samuel II, Samuel I, John) 142
Carnes Fred TERRY (Joseph Thomas TERRY, Caroline, Aaron Whitaker, Aaron Steele, Joseph I, John I, Samuel II, Samuel I, John) 143
Stella Mae TERRY (Joseph Thomas TERRY, Caroline, Aaron Whitaker, Aaron Steele, Joseph I, John I, Samuel II, Samuel I, John) 145
Ruth G. TERRY (Green TERRY, Caroline, Aaron Whitaker, Aaron Steele, Joseph I, John I, Samuel II, Samuel I, John) 148
Lockett Joseph TERRY, Sr. (Green TERRY, Caroline, Aaron Whitaker, Aaron Steele, Joseph I, John I, Samuel II, Samuel I, John) 148
Andrew TERRY (Green TERRY, Caroline, Aaron Whitaker, Aaron Steele, Joseph I, John I, Samuel II, Samuel I, John) 150
Romie TERRY, Sr. (Green TERRY, Caroline, Aaron Whitaker, Aaron Steele, Joseph I, John I, Samuel II, Samuel I, John) 150
Generation #10 152
Willie H. EDWARDS (Mary Emma TERRY EDWARD, William TERRY, Caroline, Aaron Whitaker, Aaron Steele, Joseph I, John I, Samuel II, Samuel I, John) 152
Effie EDWARDS (Mary Emma TERRY EDWARD, William TERRY, Caroline, Aaron Whitaker, Aaron Steele, Joseph I, John I, Samuel II, Samuel I, John) 153

Aaron Whitaker Guyton Genealogy

Luria EDWARDS (Mary Emma TERRY EDWARD, William TERRY, Caroline, Aaron Whitaker, Aaron Steele, Joseph I, John I, Samuel II, Samuel I, John) 153

Ulysses (Julious) EDWARDS (Mary Emma TERRY EDWARD, William TERRY, Caroline, Aaron Whitaker, Aaron Steele, Joseph I, John I, Samuel II, Samuel I, John) 154

Ernest EDWARDS (Mary Emma TERRY EDWARD, William TERRY, Caroline, Aaron Whitaker, Aaron Steele, Joseph I, John I, Samuel II, Samuel I, John) 155

Johnnie M. HARMON (Ethel TERRY HARMON, William TERRY, Caroline, Aaron Whitaker, Aaron Steele, Joseph I, John I, Samuel II, Samuel I, John) 157

Jim Roger HARMON (Ethel TERRY HARMON, William TERRY, Caroline, Aaron Whitaker, Aaron Steele, Joseph I, John I, Samuel II, Samuel I, John) 158

Ethel Lavelle CONWAY (Nealie TERRY CONWAY, William TERRY, Caroline, Aaron Whitaker, Aaron Steele, Joseph I, John I, Samuel II, Samuel I, John) 160

Lenard CONWAY (Nealie TERRY CONWAY, William TERRY, Caroline, Aaron Whitaker, Aaron Steele, Joseph I, John I, Samuel II, Samuel I, John) 161

Major Alvin CONWAY (Nealie TERRY CONWAY, William TERRY, Caroline, Aaron Whitaker, Aaron Steele, Joseph I, John I, Samuel II, Samuel I, John) 162

James Welmer CONWAY, Sr. (Nealie TERRY CONWAY, William TERRY, Caroline, Aaron Whitaker, Aaron Steele, Joseph I, John I, Samuel II, Samuel I, John) 163

Leila HARMON (Sarah TERRY HARMON, William TERRY, Caroline, Aaron Whitaker, Aaron Steele, Joseph I, John I, Samuel II, Samuel I, John) 164

Fannie Mae HARMON (Sarah TERRY HARMON, William TERRY, Caroline, Aaron Whitaker, Aaron Steele, Joseph I, John I, Samuel II, Samuel I, John) 166

Walter Alvin HARMON (Sarah TERRY HARMON, William TERRY, Caroline, Aaron Whitaker, Aaron Steele, Joseph I, John I, Samuel II, Samuel I, John) 166

Murie (Murray) HARMON (Sarah TERRY HARMON, William TERRY, Caroline, Aaron Whitaker, Aaron Steele, Joseph I, John I, Samuel II, Samuel I, John) 167

Irma Jean TERRY (William Vinson TERRY, William TERRY, Caroline, Aaron Whitaker, Aaron Steele, Joseph I, John I, Samuel II, Samuel I, John) 167

Yvonne Jacquline TERRY (Carnes TERRY, Joseph TERRY, Caroline, Aaron Whitaker, Aaron Steele, Joseph I, John I, Samuel II, Samuel I, John) 168

Bernice Marie TERRY (Carnes TERRY, Joseph TERRY, Caroline, Aaron Whitaker, Aaron Steele, Joseph I, John I, Samuel II, Samuel I, John) 168

Anetha TERRY (Carnes TERRY, Joseph TERRY, Caroline, Aaron Whitaker, Aaron Steele, Joseph I, John I, Samuel II, Samuel I, John) 170

Velma Ruth GUYTON (Stella Mae TERRY GUYTON, Joseph TERRY, Caroline, Aaron Whitaker, Aaron Steele, Joseph I, John I, Samuel II, Samuel I, John) 170

Joe Frank GUYTON, Sr. (Stella Mae TERRY GUYTON, Joseph TERRY, Caroline, Aaron Whitaker, Aaron Steele, Joseph I, John I, Samuel II, Samuel I, John) 171

Ike Young GUYTON (Stella Mae TERRY GUYTON, Joseph TERRY, Caroline, Aaron Whitaker, Aaron Steele, Joseph I, John I, Samuel II, Samuel I, John) 172

Stellie Rose GUYTON (Stella Mae TERRY GUYTON, Joseph TERRY, Caroline, Aaron Whitaker, Aaron Steele, Joseph I, John I, Samuel II, Samuel I, John) 173

Hubert GUYTON (Stella Mae TERRY GUYTON, Joseph TERRY, Caroline, Aaron Whitaker, Aaron Steele, Joseph I, John I, Samuel II, Samuel I, John) 174

Michael Joseph TERRY, Sr. (Lockett Joseph TERRY, Sr., Green TERRY, Caroline, Aaron Whitaker, Aaron Steele, Joseph I, John I, Samuel II, Samuel I, John) 175

CHILD OF AARON WHITAKER GUYTON AND PATSY GIBSON: PINKNEY'S LINE 177

Generation #7 177

Pinkney (Pink) GUYTON (Aaron Whitaker, Aaron Steele, Joseph I, John I, Samuel II, Samuel I, John) 177

Generation #8 192

Emma GUYTON (Pinkney, Aaron Whitaker, Aaron Steele, Joseph I, John I, Samuel II, Samuel I, John) 192

Patsy J. GUYTON (Pinkney, Aaron Whitaker, Aaron Steele, Joseph I, John I, Samuel II, Samuel I, John) 194

Agnes Isolome (Icy) GUYTON (Pinkney, Aaron Whitaker, Aaron Steele, Joseph I, John I, Samuel II, Samuel I, John) 197

William Amzy GUYTON, Sr. (Pinkney, Aaron Whitaker, Aaron Steele, Joseph I, John I, Samuel II, Samuel I, John) 200

Suegene GUYTON (Pinkney, Aaron Whitaker, Aaron Steele, Joseph I, John I, Samuel II, Samuel I, John) 201

Generation #9 203

Nola J. ALLEN (Emma GUYTON ALLEN, Pinkney, Aaron Whitaker, Aaron Steele, Joseph I, John I, Samuel II, Samuel I, John) 203

Ethel S. ALLEN (Emma GUYTON ALLEN, Pinkney, Aaron Whitaker, Aaron Steele, Joseph I, John I, Samuel II, Samuel I, John) 205

Willie Walter ALLEN (Emma GUYTON ALLEN, Pinkney, Aaron Whitaker, Aaron Steele, Joseph I, John I, Samuel II, Samuel I, John) 207

Earnest Mitchell ROBY (Patsy J., Pinkney, Aaron Whitaker, Aaron Steele, Joseph I, John I, Samuel II, Samuel I, John) 208

Lillie Wardean ROBY (Patsy J., Pinkney, Aaron Whitaker, Aaron Steele, Joseph I, John I, Samuel II, Samuel I, John) 209

Louella ROBY (Patsy J., Pinkney, Aaron Whitaker, Aaron Steele, Joseph I, John I, Samuel II, Samuel I, John) 211

Elmer ROBY (Patsy J., Pinkney, Aaron Whitaker, Aaron Steele, Joseph I, John I, Samuel II, Samuel I, John) 213

Ruth Lee (Ruthie) ROBY (Patsy J., Pinkney, Aaron Whitaker, Aaron Steele, Joseph I, John I, Samuel II, Samuel I, John) 214

Vamis (Vammie) ROBY (Patsy J., Pinkney, Aaron Whitaker, Aaron Steele, Joseph I, John I, Samuel II, Samuel I, John) 216

Fannie B. GAMBLE (Agnes Icy GUYTON GAMBLE, Pinkney, Aaron Whitaker, Aaron Steele, Joseph I, John I, Samuel II, Samuel I, John) 217

Callie Pairee GAMBLE (Agnes Icy GUYTON GAMBLE, Pinkney, Aaron Whitaker, Aaron Steele, Joseph I, John I, Samuel II, Samuel I, John) 219

Nathan Eugene GAMBLE (Agnes Icy GUYTON GAMBLE, Pinkney, Aaron Whitaker, Aaron Steele, Joseph I, John I, Samuel II, Samuel I, John) 224

Aaron Whitaker Guyton Genealogy

Fred (Big Baby) GAMBLE (Agnes Icy GUYTON GAMBLE, Pinkney, Aaron Whitaker, Aaron Steele, Joseph I, John I, Samuel II, Samuel I, John) 225

Nola Mae GAMBLE (Agnes Icy GUYTON GAMBLE, Pinkney, Aaron Whitaker, Aaron Steele, Joseph I, John I, Samuel II, Samuel I, John) 226

Katie D. (KD) GAMBLE (Agnes Icy GUYTON GAMBLE, Pinkney, Aaron Whitaker, Aaron Steele, Joseph I, John I, Samuel II, Samuel I, John) 227

Lovie GAMBLE (Agnes Icy GUYTON GAMBLE, Pinkney, Aaron Whitaker, Aaron Steele, Joseph I, John I, Samuel II, Samuel I, John) 229

Mable Ethel GAMBLE (Agnes Icy GUYTON GAMBLE, Pinkney, Aaron Whitaker, Aaron Steele, Joseph I, John I, Samuel II, Samuel I, John) 232

Lacey GUYTON (William Amzy, Pinkney, Aaron Whitaker, Aaron Steele, Joseph I, John I, Samuel II, Samuel I, John) 234

Emma Evester GUYTON (William Amzy, Pinkney, Aaron Whitaker, Aaron Steele, Joseph I, John I, Samuel II, Samuel I, John) 235

Cherry Mae GUYTON (William Amzy, Pinkney, Aaron Whitaker, Aaron Steele, Joseph I, John I, Samuel II, Samuel I, John) . 237

William Amzy GUYTON, Jr. (William Amzy, Pinkney, Aaron Whitaker, Aaron Steele, Joseph I, John I, Samuel II, Samuel I, John) 239

Pink West (PW) GUYTON (William Amzy, Pinkney, Aaron Whitaker, Aaron Steele, Joseph I, John I, Samuel II, Samuel I, John) 240

Fannie Douglas GUYTON (William Amzy, Pinkney, Aaron Whitaker, Aaron Steele, Joseph I, John I, Samuel II, Samuel I, John) 241

Elizabeth GUYTON (William Amzy, Pinkney, Aaron Whitaker, Aaron Steele, Joseph I, John I, Samuel II, Samuel I, John) 242

Generation #10 243

Samuel Alonzo FORD, Sr. (Nola ALLEN FORD, Emma GUYTON ALLEN, Pinkney, Aaron Whitaker, Aaron Steele, Joseph I, John I, Samuel II, Samuel I, John) 243

Casey Glenn GUYTON, Sr. (Lillie Wardean ROBY GUYTON, Patsy J., Pinkney, Aaron Whitaker, Aaron Steele, Joseph I, John I, Samuel II, Samuel I, John) 245

Rozell J. GUYTON (Lillie Wardean ROBY GUYTON, Patsy J., Pinkney, Aaron Whitaker, Aaron Steele, Joseph I, John I, Samuel II, Samuel I, John) 246

Jimmie Ruth GUYTON (Lillie Wardean ROBY GUYTON, Patsy J., Pinkney, Aaron Whitaker, Aaron Steele, Joseph I, John I, Samuel II, Samuel I, John) 247

Lucy GUYTON (Lillie Wardean ROBY GUYTON, Patsy J., Pinkney, Aaron Whitaker, Aaron Steele, Joseph I, John I, Samuel II, Samuel I, John) 248

Maebell GUYTON (Lillie Wardean ROBY GUYTON, Patsy J., Pinkney, Aaron Whitaker, Aaron Steele, Joseph I, John I, Samuel II, Samuel I, John) 248

Earlene GUYTON (Ruth Lee (Ruthie) ROBY GUYTON, Patsy J., Pinkney, Aaron Whitaker, Aaron Steele, Joseph I, John I, Samuel II, Samuel I, John) 249

Aaron Whitaker Guyton Genealogy

Bernice GUYTON (Ruth Lee (Ruthie) ROBY GUYTON, Patsy J., Pinkney, Aaron Whitaker, Aaron Steele, Joseph I, John I, Samuel II, Samuel I, John) 250

Rubell (Ruby) Bonita MALLETT (Fannie GAMBLE, Agnes Icy GUYTON GAMBLE, Pinkney, Aaron Whitaker, Aaron Steele, Joseph I, John I, Samuel II, Samuel I, John) 253

Katie K. MALLETT (Fannie GAMBLE, Agnes Icy GUYTON GAMBLE, Pinkney, Aaron Whitaker, Aaron Steele, Joseph I, John I, Samuel II, Samuel I, John) 256

Fred MALLETT (Fannie GAMBLE, Agnes Icy GUYTON GAMBLE, Pinkney, Aaron Whitaker, Aaron Steele, Joseph I, John I, Samuel II, Samuel I, John) 258

Alphonzo L. (A.L.) MALLETT (Fannie GAMBLE, Agnes Icy GUYTON GAMBLE, Pinkney, Aaron Whitaker, Aaron Steele, Joseph I, John I, Samuel II, Samuel I, John) 260

Henry (L.C.) SIMMONS (Callie Pairee GAMBLE, Agnes Icy GUYTON GAMBLE, Pinkney, Aaron Whitaker, Aaron Steele, Joseph I, John I, Samuel II, Samuel I, John) 261

Zenolia SIMMONS (Callie Pairee GAMBLE, Agnes Icy GUYTON GAMBLE, Pinkney, Aaron Whitaker, Aaron Steele, Joseph I, John I, Samuel II, Samuel I, John) 264

Vernestine (Susie) JOINER (Katie GAMBLE, Agnes Icy GUYTON GAMBLE, Pinkney, Aaron Whitaker, Aaron Steele, Joseph I, John I, Samuel II, Samuel I, John) 266

Icy Viola NASH (Lovie GAMBLE NASH PARKER, Agnes Icy GUYTON GAMBLE, Pinkney, Aaron Whitaker, Aaron Steele, Joseph I, John I, Samuel II, Samuel I, John) 267

George W. NASH (Lovie GAMBLE NASH PARKER, Agnes Icy GUYTON GAMBLE, Pinkney, Aaron Whitaker, Aaron Steele, Joseph I, John I, Samuel II, Samuel I, John) 270

Lena Mae PARKER (Lovie GAMBLE NASH PARKER, Agnes Icy GUYTON GAMBLE, Pinkney, Aaron Whitaker, Aaron Steele, Joseph I, John I, Samuel II, Samuel I, John) 273

Ilander PARKER, Jr. (Lovie GAMBLE NASH PARKER, Agnes Icy GUYTON GAMBLE, Pinkney, Aaron Whitaker, Aaron Steele, Joseph I, John I, Samuel II, Samuel I, John) 274

Arthur Lee PARKER (Lovie GAMBLE NASH PARKER, Agnes Icy GUYTON GAMBLE, Pinkney, Aaron Whitaker, Aaron Steele, Joseph I, John I, Samuel II, Samuel I, John) 275

Charlene PARKER (Lovie GAMBLE NASH PARKER, Agnes Icy GUYTON GAMBLE, Pinkney, Aaron Whitaker, Aaron Steele, Joseph I, John I, Samuel II, Samuel I, John) 278

Shirley PARKER (Lovie GAMBLE NASH PARKER, Agnes Icy GUYTON GAMBLE, Pinkney, Aaron Whitaker, Aaron Steele, Joseph I, John I, Samuel II, Samuel I, John) 279

Generation #11 281

Edward L. (Eddie) CULPEPPER (Rubell MALLET CULPEPPER, Fannie GAMBLE, Agnes Icy GUYTON GAMBLE, Pinkney, Aaron Whitaker, Aaron Steele, Joseph I, John I, Samuel II, Samuel I, John) 281

Rickey SIMMONS (LC SIMMONS, Callie Pairee GAMBLE SIMMONS, Agnes Icy GUYTON GAMBLE, Pinkney, Aaron Whitaker, Aaron Steele, Joseph I, John I, Samuel II, Samuel I, John) 283

Darlene MURPHY (Zenolia SIMMONS MURPHY, Callie Pairee GAMBLE SIMMONS, Agnes Icy GUYTON GAMBLE, Pinkney, Aaron Whitaker, Aaron Steele, Joseph I, John I, Samuel II, Samuel I, John) 284

Aaron Whitaker Guyton Genealogy

Melvin MURPHY, Jr. (Zenolia SIMMONS MURPHY, Callie Pairee GAMBLE SIMMONS, Agnes Icy GUYTON GAMBLE, Pinkney, Aaron Whitaker, Aaron Steele, Joseph I, John I, Samuel II, Samuel I, John) 284

Marvin Ray MURPHY (Zenolia SIMMONS MURPHY, Callie Pairee GAMBLE SIMMONS, Agnes Icy GUYTON GAMBLE, Pinkney, Aaron Whitaker, Aaron Steele, Joseph I, John I, Samuel II, Samuel I, John) 285

Linda (Carol) MURPHY (Zenolia SIMMONS MURPHY, Callie Pairee GAMBLE SIMMONS, Agnes Icy GUYTON GAMBLE, Pinkney, Aaron Whitaker, Aaron Steele, Joseph I, John I, Samuel II, Samuel I, John) 285

Zenobia MURPHY (Zenolia SIMMONS MURPHY, Callie Pairee GAMBLE SIMMONS, Agnes Icy GUYTON GAMBLE, Pinkney, Aaron Whitaker, Aaron Steele, Joseph I, John I, Samuel II, Samuel I, John) 286

Murriel Delores MURPHY (Zenolia SIMMONS MURPHY, Callie Pairee GAMBLE SIMMONS, Agnes Icy GUYTON GAMBLE, Pinkney, Aaron Whitaker, Aaron Steele, Joseph I, John I, Samuel II, Samuel I, John) 286

Patricia MURPHY (Zenolia SIMMONS MURPHY, Callie Pairee GAMBLE SIMMONS, Agnes Icy GUYTON GAMBLE, Pinkney, Aaron Whitaker, Aaron Steele, Joseph I, John I, Samuel II, Samuel I, John) 287

Tony MURPHY, Sr. (Zenolia SIMMONS MURPHY, Callie Pairee GAMBLE SIMMONS, Agnes Icy GUYTON GAMBLE, Pinkney, Aaron Whitaker, Aaron Steele, Joseph I, John I, Samuel II, Samuel I, John) 287

Sheila MURPHY (Zenolia SIMMONS MURPHY, Callie Pairee GAMBLE SIMMONS, Agnes Icy GUYTON GAMBLE, Pinkney, Aaron Whitaker, Aaron Steele, Joseph I, John I, Samuel II, Samuel I, John) 288

Rita MURPHY (Zenolia SIMMONS MURPHY, Callie Pairee GAMBLE SIMMONS, Agnes Icy GUYTON GAMBLE, Pinkney, Aaron Whitaker, Aaron Steele, Joseph I, John I, Samuel II, Samuel I, John) 288

Felicia MURPHY (Zenolia SIMMONS MURPHY, Callie Pairee GAMBLE SIMMONS, Agnes Icy GUYTON GAMBLE, Pinkney, Aaron Whitaker, Aaron Steele, Joseph I, John I, Samuel II, Samuel I, John) 289

Larry MURPHY (Zenolia SIMMONS MURPHY, Callie Pairee GAMBLE SIMMONS, Agnes Icy GUYTON GAMBLE, Pinkney, Aaron Whitaker, Aaron Steele, Joseph I, John I, Samuel II, Samuel I, John) 289

Vincent MURPHY (Zenolia SIMMONS MURPHY, Callie Pairee GAMBLE SIMMONS, Agnes Icy GUYTON GAMBLE, Pinkney, Aaron Whitaker, Aaron Steele, Joseph I, John I, Samuel II, Samuel I, John) 290

Curtis MURPHY (Zenolia SIMMONS MURPHY, Callie Pairee GAMBLE SIMMONS, Agnes Icy GUYTON GAMBLE, Pinkney, Aaron Whitaker, Aaron Steele, Joseph I, John I, Samuel II, Samuel I, John) 290

Karl Glenn BOYD (Icy Viola NASH BOYD, Lovie GAMBLE NASH PARKER, Agnes Icy GUYTON GAMBLE, Pinkney, Aaron Whitaker, Aaron Steele, Joseph I, John I, Samuel II, Samuel I, John) 291

Felicia Cabrini BOYD (Icy Viola NASH BOYD, Lovie GAMBLE NASH PARKER, Agnes Icy GUYTON GAMBLE, Pinkney, Aaron Whitaker, Aaron Steele, Joseph I, John I, Samuel II, Samuel I, John) 293

Carmelita Sabrina BOYD (Icy Viola NASH BOYD, Lovie GAMBLE NASH PARKER, Agnes Icy GUYTON GAMBLE, Pinkney, Aaron Whitaker, Aaron Steele, Joseph I, John I, Samuel II, Samuel I, John) 293

Rhonda Larita BOYD (Icy Viola NASH BOYD, Lovie GAMBLE NASH PARKER, Agnes Icy GUYTON GAMBLE, Pinkney, Aaron Whitaker, Aaron Steele, Joseph I, John I, Samuel II, Samuel I, John) 295

Thornton BOYD, Jr. (Icy Viola NASH BOYD, Lovie GAMBLE NASH PARKER, Agnes Icy GUYTON GAMBLE, Pinkney, Aaron Whitaker, Aaron Steele, Joseph I, John I, Samuel II, Samuel I, John) 297

Belynda MOORE (Lena Mae PARKER MOORE, Lovie GAMBLE NASH PARKER, Agnes Icy GUYTON GAMBLE, Pinkney, Aaron Whitaker, Aaron Steele, Joseph I, John I, Samuel II, Samuel I, John) 300

Cheryl Penny PARKER (Ilander PARKER, Jr., Lovie GAMBLE NASH PARKER, Agnes Icy GUYTON GAMBLE, Pinkney, Aaron Whitaker, Aaron Steele, Joseph I, John I, Samuel II, Samuel I, John) 301

Chris PARKER (Ilander PARKER, Jr., Lovie GAMBLE NASH PARKER, Agnes Icy GUYTON GAMBLE, Pinkney, Aaron Whitaker, Aaron Steele, Joseph I, John I, Samuel II, Samuel I, John) 302

Sandy D. PARKER (Ilander PARKER, Jr., Lovie GAMBLE NASH PARKER, Agnes Icy GUYTON GAMBLE, Pinkney, Aaron Whitaker, Aaron Steele, Joseph I, John I, Samuel II, Samuel I, John) 302

Tera M. PARKER (Ilander PARKER, Jr., Lovie GAMBLE NASH PARKER, Agnes Icy GUYTON GAMBLE, Pinkney, Aaron Whitaker, Aaron Steele, Joseph I, John I, Samuel II, Samuel I, John) 303

Ollander (Odie) PARKER (Ilander PARKER, Jr., Lovie GAMBLE NASH PARKER, Agnes Icy GUYTON GAMBLE, Pinkney, Aaron Whitaker, Aaron Steele, Joseph I, John I, Samuel II, Samuel I, John) 304

LaTarshe (Toddy) PARKER (Ilander PARKER, Jr., Lovie GAMBLE NASH PARKER, Agnes Icy GUYTON GAMBLE, Pinkney, Aaron Whitaker, Aaron Steele, Joseph I, John I, Samuel II, Samuel I, John) 305

Bernard PARKER (Ilander PARKER, Jr., Lovie GAMBLE NASH PARKER, Agnes Icy GUYTON GAMBLE, Pinkney, Aaron Whitaker, Aaron Steele, Joseph I, John I, Samuel II, Samuel I, John) 305

Natasha PARKER (Shirley PARKER, Lovie GAMBLE NASH PARKER, Agnes Icy GUYTON GAMBLE, Pinkney, Aaron Whitaker, Aaron Steele, Joseph I, John I, Samuel II, Samuel I, John) 306

CHILD OF AARON WHITAKER GUYTON AND PATSY GIBSON: ELIJAH'S LINE 308

Generation #7 308

Elijah GUYTON (Aaron Whitaker, Aaron Steele, Joseph I, John I, Samuel II, Samuel I, John) 308

Generation #8 312

Orlena (Lena) GUYTON (Elijah, Aaron Whitaker, Aaron Steele, Joseph I, John I, Samuel II, Samuel I, John) 312

Doss Ade GUYTON (Elijah, Aaron Whitaker, Aaron Steele, Joseph I, John I, Samuel II, Samuel I, John) 313

Lindsay Ford (Linzy) GUYTON, Sr. (Elijah, Aaron Whitaker, Aaron Steele, Joseph I, John I, Samuel II, Samuel I, John) 316

Wade Harvey GUYTON, Sr. (Elijah, Aaron Whitaker, Aaron Steele, Joseph I, John I, Samuel II, Samuel I, John) 318

Adeline Susannah GUYTON (Elijah, Aaron Whitaker, Aaron Steele, Joseph I, John I, Samuel II, Samuel I, John) 319

Mattie GUYTON (Elijah, Aaron Whitaker, Aaron Steele, Joseph I, John I, Samuel II, Samuel I, John) 321

Shepard GUYTON (Elijah, Aaron Whitaker, Aaron Steele, Joseph I, John I, Samuel II, Samuel I, John) 321

Wiley Leach GUYTON (Elijah, Aaron Whitaker, Aaron Steele, Joseph I, John I, Samuel II, Samuel I, John) 323

Fred L. GUYTON (Elijah, Aaron Whitaker, Aaron Steele, Joseph I, John I, Samuel II, Samuel I, John) 324

Lottie GUYTON (Elijah, Aaron Whitaker, Aaron Steele, Joseph I, John I, Samuel II, Samuel I, John) 325

Generation #9 327

Elige (Lige) Fuller (Orlena (Lena) GUYTON FULLER, Elijah, Aaron Whitaker, Aaron Steele, Joseph I, John I, Samuel II, Samuel I, John) 327

Limmie GUYTON (Doss Ade, Elijah, Aaron Whitaker, Aaron Steele, Joseph I, John I, Samuel II, Samuel I, John) 330

Blanche Gail GUYTON (Doss Ade, Elijah, Aaron Whitaker, Aaron Steele, Joseph I, John I, Samuel II, Samuel I, John) 331

Betty May GUYTON (Doss Ade, Elijah, Aaron Whitaker, Aaron Steele, Joseph I, John I, Samuel II, Samuel I, John) 333

Carrie J. GUYTON (Doss Ade, Elijah, Aaron Whitaker, Aaron Steele, Joseph I, John I, Samuel II, Samuel I, John) 334

Warren Harding GUYTON, Sr. (Doss Ade, Elijah, Aaron Whitaker, Aaron Steele, Joseph I, John I, Samuel II, Samuel I, John) 335

Georgia Lee GUYTON (Doss Ade, Elijah, Aaron Whitaker, Aaron Steele, Joseph I, John I, Samuel II, Samuel I, John) 336

Rosetta GUYTON (Lindsay (Linzy), Elijah, Aaron Whitaker, Aaron Steele, Joseph I, John I, Samuel II, Samuel I, John) 337

Eugene GUYTON, Sr. (Lindsay (Linzy), Elijah, Aaron Whitaker, Aaron Steele, Joseph I, John I, Samuel II, Samuel I, John) 338

Robert Walter GUYTON, Sr. (Lindsay (Linzy), Elijah, Aaron Whitaker, Aaron Steele, Joseph I, John I, Samuel II, Samuel I, John) 339

Magnolia GUYTON (Wade Harvey Sr., Elijah, Aaron Whitaker, Aaron Steele, Joseph I, John I, Samuel II, Samuel I, John) 340

Wade Harvey GUYTON, Jr. (Wade Harvey Sr., Elijah, Aaron Whitaker, Aaron Steele, Joseph I, John I, Samuel II, Samuel I, John) 341

Jodie Mae BURT (Adeline Susannah GUYTON BURT, Elijah, Aaron Whitaker, Aaron Steele, Joseph I, John I, Samuel II, Samuel I, John) 343

Geneva BURT (Adeline Susannah GUYTON BURT, Elijah, Aaron Whitaker, Aaron Steele, Joseph I, John I, Samuel II, Samuel I, John) 343

R.C. BURT (Adeline Susannah GUYTON BURT, Elijah, Aaron Whitaker, Aaron Steele, Joseph I, John I, Samuel II, Samuel I, John) . 344

Madesta GUYTON (Shepard, Elijah, Aaron Whitaker, Aaron Steele, Joseph I, John I, Samuel II, Samuel I, John) 345

Sarah Lee GUYTON (Wiley Leach, Elijah, Aaron Whitaker, Aaron Steele, Joseph I, John I, Samuel II, Samuel I, John) 346

Andy GUYTON (Wiley Leach, Elijah, Aaron Whitaker, Aaron Steele, Joseph I, John I, Samuel II, Samuel I, John) 347

Alma Lee MUNSON (Lottie, Elijah, Aaron Whitaker, Aaron Steele, Joseph I, John I, Samuel II, Samuel I, John) 349

Marie MUNSON (Lottie, Elijah, Aaron Whitaker, Aaron Steele, Joseph I, John I, Samuel II, Samuel I, John) 350

CHILD OF AARON WHITAKER GUYTON AND ARTIE RAINEY: ANDREW'S LINE 352

   Generation #7 352

     Andrew J. GUYTON (Aaron Whitaker, Aaron Steele, Joseph I, John I, Samuel II, Samuel I, John) 352

   Generation #8 353

     Annie Bell GUYTON (Andrew, Aaron Whitaker, Aaron Steele, Joseph I, John I, Samuel II, Samuel I, John) 353

     Letha GUYTON (Andrew, Aaron Whitaker, Aaron Steele, Joseph I, John I, Samuel II, Samuel I, John) 354

   Generation #9 355

     Mable ELLIS (Annie Bell GUYTON ELLIS, Andrew, Aaron Whitaker, Aaron Steele, Joseph I, John I, Samuel II, Samuel I, John) ... 355

CHILD OF AARON WHITAKER GUYTON AND ARTIE RAINEY: JAMES T'S LINE 357

   Generation #7 357

     James T. GUYTON (Aaron Whitaker, Aaron Steele, Joseph I, John I, Samuel II, Samuel I, John) 357

CHILD OF AARON WHITAKER GUYTON AND ARTIE RAINEY: CASE'S LINE 358

Generation #7 358

    Case GUYTON (Aaron Whitaker, Aaron Steele, Joseph I, John I, Samuel II, Samuel I, John) 358

Generation #8 364

    Willie GUYTON, Sr. (Case, Aaron Whitaker, Aaron Steele, Joseph I, John I, Samuel II, Samuel I, John) 364

    Zelma GUYTON (Case, Aaron Whitaker, Aaron Steele, Joseph I, John I, Samuel II, Samuel I, John) 366

    James (Jim) GUYTON (Case, Aaron Whitaker, Aaron Steele, Joseph I, John I, Samuel II, Samuel I, John) 369

    Shelton N. GUYTON (Case, Aaron Whitaker, Aaron Steele, Joseph I, John I, Samuel II, Samuel I, John) 372

    Percy GUYTON (Case, Aaron Whitaker, Aaron Steele, Joseph I, John I, Samuel II, Samuel I, John) 372

    Lula Avery GUYTON (Case, Aaron Whitaker, Aaron Steele, Joseph I, John I, Samuel II, Samuel I, John) 373

    Annie Pearl GUYTON (Case, Aaron Whitaker, Aaron Steele, Joseph I, John I, Samuel II, Samuel I, John) 375

    Fred GUYTON (Case, Aaron Whitaker, Aaron Steele, Joseph I, John I, Samuel II, Samuel I, John) 377

Generation #9 379

    Annie May Guyton (Willie, Sr., Case, Aaron Whitaker, Aaron Steele, Joseph I, John I, Samuel II, Samuel I, John) 379

    Essie Dee Guyton (Willie, Sr., Case, Aaron Whitaker, Aaron Steele, Joseph I, John I, Samuel II, Samuel I, John) 380

    Brazie Guyton (Willie, Sr., Case, Aaron Whitaker, Aaron Steele, Joseph I, John I, Samuel II, Samuel I, John) 382

    Fannie Louise Guyton (Willie, Sr., Case, Aaron Whitaker, Aaron Steele, Joseph I, John I, Samuel II, Samuel I, John) 383

    Willie GUYTON, Jr. (Willie, Sr., Case, Aaron Whitaker, Aaron Steele, Joseph I, John I, Samuel II, Samuel I, John) 384

    Elvie GUYTON (Willie, Sr., Case, Aaron Whitaker, Aaron Steele, Joseph I, John I, Samuel II, Samuel I, John) 387

    Willie Clayton (WC) GUYTON, Sr. (Willie, Sr., Case, Aaron Whitaker, Aaron Steele, Joseph I, John I, Samuel II, Samuel I, John) 388

    Claude GUYTON (Willie, Sr., Case, Aaron Whitaker, Aaron Steele, Joseph I, John I, Samuel II, Samuel I, John) 390

    Mary Lynn GUYTON (Willie, Sr., Case, Aaron Whitaker, Aaron Steele, Joseph I, John I, Samuel II, Samuel I, John) 391

    Vernon T. (Vearn) GUYTON, Sr. (Willie, Sr., Case, Aaron Whitaker, Aaron Steele, Joseph I, John I, Samuel II, Samuel I, John) 391

    Casey Glenn GUYTON, Sr. (James, Case, Aaron Whitaker, Aaron Steele, Joseph I, John I, Samuel II, Samuel I, John) 392

    Lorine RILEY (Annie Pearl GUYTON RILEY, Case, Aaron Whitaker, Aaron Steele, Joseph I, John I, Samuel II, Samuel I, John) 392

CHILD OF AARON WHITAKER GUYTON AND ARTIE RAINEY: MAGGIE'S LINE 394

Generation #7 394

    Maggie GUYTON (Aaron Whitaker, Aaron Steele, Joseph I, John I, Samuel II, Samuel I, John) 394

Generation #8 397

    Herman STINGLEY (Maggie, Aaron Whitaker, Aaron Steele, Joseph I, John I, Samuel II, Samuel I, John) 397

    Louria STINGLEY (Maggie, Aaron Whitaker, Aaron Steele, Joseph I, John I, Samuel II, Samuel I, John) 398

    Lottie STINGLEY (Maggie, Aaron Whitaker, Aaron Steele, Joseph I, John I, Samuel II, Samuel I, John) 400

Mayvell STINGLEY (Maggie, Aaron Whitaker, Aaron Steele, Joseph I, John I, Samuel II, Samuel I, John) 400

Guyton STINGLEY (Maggie, Aaron Whitaker, Aaron Steele, Joseph I, John I, Samuel II, Samuel I, John) 401

Mannie Whitt (Whitt) STINGLEY (Maggie, Aaron Whitaker, Aaron Steele, Joseph I, John I, Samuel II, Samuel I, John) 403

John Ike STINGLEY (Maggie, Aaron Whitaker, Aaron Steele, Joseph I, John I, Samuel II, Samuel I, John) 406

CHILD OF AARON WHITAKER GUYTON AND ARTIE RAINEY: AMANDA'S LINE 409

Generation #7 409

Amanda (Annie B.) GUYTON (Aaron Whitaker, Aaron Steele, Joseph I, John I, Samuel II, Samuel I, John) 409

CHILD OF AARON WHITAKER GUYTON AND ARTIE RAINEY: SIMON'S LINE 411

Generation #7 411

Simon GUYTON, Sr. (Aaron Whitaker, Aaron Steele, Joseph I, John I, Samuel II, Samuel I, John) 411

Generation #8 414

Mary (Maggie) Guyton (Simon, Aaron Whitaker, Aaron Steele, Joseph I, John I, Samuel II, Samuel I, John) 414

Frankie Guyton (Simon, Aaron Whitaker, Aaron Steele, Joseph I, John I, Samuel II, Samuel I, John) 414

Annie Guyton (Simon, Aaron Whitaker, Aaron Steele, Joseph I, John I, Samuel II, Samuel I, John) 415

Joe Dale (Joe D.) Guyton (Simon, Aaron Whitaker, Aaron Steele, Joseph I, John I, Samuel II, Samuel I, John) 416

Hattie Irene Guyton (Simon, Aaron Whitaker, Aaron Steele, Joseph I, John I, Samuel II, Samuel I, John) 417

Robbie Lee Guyton (Simon, Aaron Whitaker, Aaron Steele, Joseph I, John I, Samuel II, Samuel I, John) 418

Steele Guyton (Simon, Aaron Whitaker, Aaron Steele, Joseph I, John I, Samuel II, Samuel I, John) 420

Generation #9 422

Fleming Alexander GUYTON (Frankie, Simon, Aaron Whitaker, Aaron Steele, Joseph I, John I, Samuel II, Samuel I, John) 422

Inez GUYTON (Frankie, Simon, Aaron Whitaker, Aaron Steele, Joseph I, John I, Samuel II, Samuel I, John) 426

Earl Denison Terry, Sr. (Annie GUYTON TERRY, Simon, Aaron Whitaker, Aaron Steele, Joseph I, John I, Samuel II, Samuel I, John) 426

Clinton TERRY, Sr. (Annie GUYTON TERRY, Simon, Aaron Whitaker, Aaron Steele, Joseph I, John I, Samuel II, Samuel I, John) 427

Allie Mae TEAGUE (Robbie GUYTON TEAGUE, Simon, Aaron Whitaker, Aaron Steele, Joseph I, John I, Samuel II, Samuel I, John) 428

Charles Edward Burt (Robbie GUYTON TEAGUE, Simon, Aaron Whitaker, Aaron Steele, Joseph I, John I, Samuel II, Samuel I, John) 429

Fannie Burt (Robbie GUYTON TEAGUE, Simon, Aaron Whitaker, Aaron Steele, Joseph I, John I, Samuel II, Samuel I, John) 430

Erma Jean Burt (Robbie GUYTON TEAGUE, Simon, Aaron Whitaker, Aaron Steele, Joseph I, John I, Samuel II, Samuel I, John) 430

Alice Edna Burt (Robbie GUYTON TEAGUE, Simon, Aaron Whitaker, Aaron Steele, Joseph I, John I, Samuel II, Samuel I, John) 431

Fred Steele GUYTON, Sr. (Steele, Simon, Aaron Whitaker, Aaron Steele, Joseph I, John I, Samuel II, Samuel I, John) 431

CHILD OF AARON WHITAKER GUYTON AND ARTIE RAINEY: IKE'S LINE ... 433

Generation #7 ... 433

Ike GUYTON (Aaron Whitaker, Aaron Steele, Joseph I, John I, Samuel II, Samuel I, John) ... 433

Generation #8 ... 438

Mary Georgia Guyton (Ike, Aaron Whitaker, Aaron Steele, Joseph I, John I, Samuel II, Samuel I, John) ... 438

Isadora Guyton (Ike, Aaron Whitaker, Aaron Steele, Joseph I, John I, Samuel II, Samuel I, John) ... 439

Gus Davis Guyton (Ike, Aaron Whitaker, Aaron Steele, Joseph I, John I, Samuel II, Samuel I, John) ... 442

Joe Frank Guyton (Ike, Aaron Whitaker, Aaron Steele, Joseph I, John I, Samuel II, Samuel I, John) ... 445

Annie Frances Guyton (Ike, Aaron Whitaker, Aaron Steele, Joseph I, John I, Samuel II, Samuel I, John) ... 448

Minnie Guyton (Ike, Aaron Whitaker, Aaron Steele, Joseph I, John I, Samuel II, Samuel I, John) ... 450

Ben Guyton (Ike, Aaron Whitaker, Aaron Steele, Joseph I, John I, Samuel II, Samuel I, John) ... 450

Alice Lee Guyton (Ike, Aaron Whitaker, Aaron Steele, Joseph I, John I, Samuel II, Samuel I, John) ... 451

Claude Guyton (Ike, Aaron Whitaker, Aaron Steele, Joseph I, John I, Samuel II, Samuel I, John) ... 453

Generation #9 ... 455

Charles Willie BROWN (Isadora GUYTON BROWN, Ike, Aaron Whitaker, Aaron Steele, Joseph I, John I, Samuel II, Samuel I, John) ... 455

Emma M. BROWN (Isadora GUYTON BROWN, Ike, Aaron Whitaker, Aaron Steele, Joseph I, John I, Samuel II, Samuel I, John) ... 456

Channie M. BROWN (Isadora GUYTON BROWN, Ike, Aaron Whitaker, Aaron Steele, Joseph I, John I, Samuel II, Samuel I, John) ... 456

Earlene GUYTON (Gus Davis, Ike, Aaron Whitaker, Aaron Steele, Joseph I, John I, Samuel II, Samuel I, John) ... 457

Bernice GUYTON (Gus Davis, Ike, Aaron Whitaker, Aaron Steele, Joseph I, John I, Samuel II, Samuel I, John) ... 458

Curtis GUYTON (Gus Davis, Ike, Aaron Whitaker, Aaron Steele, Joseph I, John I, Samuel II, Samuel I, John) ... 458

Joan GUYTON (Gus Davis, Ike, Aaron Whitaker, Aaron Steele, Joseph I, John I, Samuel II, Samuel I, John) ... 459

Arthur David (Buddy) GUYTON (Gus Davis, Ike, Aaron Whitaker, Aaron Steele, Joseph I, John I, Samuel II, Samuel I, John) ... 459

Katherine RILEY GUYTON (Joe Frank, Ike, Aaron Whitaker, Aaron Steele, Joseph I, John I, Samuel II, Samuel I, John) ... 460

Doris Nell GUYTON (Joe Frank, Ike, Aaron Whitaker, Aaron Steele, Joseph I, John I, Samuel II, Samuel I, John) ... 461

Leander (Lee) GUYTON (Joe Frank, Ike, Aaron Whitaker, Aaron Steele, Joseph I, John I, Samuel II, Samuel I, John) ... 461

Edwin GUYTON (Joe Frank, Ike, Aaron Whitaker, Aaron Steele, Joseph I, John I, Samuel II, Samuel I, John) ... 462

Brenda Dell GUYTON (Joe Frank, Ike, Aaron Whitaker, Aaron Steele, Joseph I, John I, Samuel II, Samuel I, John) ... 462

Linda Bell GUYTON (Joe Frank, Ike, Aaron Whitaker, Aaron Steele, Joseph I, John I, Samuel II, Samuel I, John) ... 463

Bonnie GUYTON (Joe Frank, Ike, Aaron Whitaker, Aaron Steele, Joseph I, John I, Samuel II, Samuel I, John) ... 463

Sarah GUYTON (Joe Frank, Ike, Aaron Whitaker, Aaron Steele, Joseph I, John I, Samuel II, Samuel I, John) ... 464

Willie Edward EVANS (Annie GUYTON EVANS, Ike, Aaron Whitaker, Aaron Steele, Joseph I, John I, Samuel II, Samuel I, John) 464

Terry Leroy EVANS (Annie GUYTON EVANS, Ike, Aaron Whitaker, Aaron Steele, Joseph I, John I, Samuel II, Samuel I, John) 465

Gloria Jean EVANS (Annie GUYTON EVANS, Ike, Aaron Whitaker, Aaron Steele, Joseph I, John I, Samuel II, Samuel I, John) . 466

Bonnie WEBB (Alice GUYTON WEBB, Ike, Aaron Whitaker, Aaron Steele, Joseph I, John I, Samuel II, Samuel I, John) 467

CHILD OF AARON WHITAKER GUYTON AND ARTIE RAINEY: BABY JAMES 468

Generation #7 468

James (Baby James) GUYTON (Aaron Whitaker, Aaron Steele, Joseph I, John I, Samuel II, Samuel I, John) 468

INDEX 469

Figures (Maps and Photos)

Figure 1 City of Norwich on Map of England 30
Figure 2 14th Century Map of Norwich, England 31
Figure 3 St. Paul's Parish Church 32
Figure 4 St. Peter Parmentergate 33
Figure 5 1696 Thomas Cleer Map of Norwich 34
Figure 6 St. Martin at Palace Church in Norwich, Norfolk, England 36
Figure 7 Record of Marriage for Samuel GUYTON II and Margaret UNDERWOOD 39
Figure 8 Completion of John GUYTON I's Apprenticeship as a Dyer 45
Figure 9 Calvert, Baltimore, and Harford Counties, Maryland 47
Figure 10 Robinson's Rest, Home of Benjamin I and John GUYON I in 1740s 48
Figure 11 Guyton Places in Baltimore County, David F. GUYTON 50
Figure 12 Survey of Guyton's Prospect for Samuel GUYTON on 2 Aug 1749 51
Figure 13 Intersection of Guyton Road and Bottom Road in Fallston, Harford Co., MD 52
Figure 14 St. George's Parish Marriage of Joseph GUYTON and Hannah Lyon WHITAKER 58
Figure 15 St. George's Parish Episcopal Church in Perryman, MD 59
Figure 16 Joseph GUYTON I's Survey for Property Called Hit or Miss in Harford Co., MD 60
Figure 17 Joseph GUYTON I's Move from Maryland to South Carolina 61
Figure 18 Map of Old Ninety-Six District, SC in 1785 62
Figure 19 Silver Dollar of Charles III of Spain, 1776 63
Figure 20 Approximate Locations of Joseph GUYTON I and his Children in South Carolina 65
Figure 21 Joseph GUYTON I Gravestone in Guyton Cemetery, Cherokee Co., SC 66
Figure 22 Hannah WHITAKER GUYTON Gravestone in Guyton Cemetery, Cherokee Co., SC 66
Figure 23 County Map of South Carolina 66
Figure 24 Map Showing Location of Gaffney, South Carolina 67
Figure 25 Joseph GUYTON I Transcribed Will 1818 p. 1/2 Union District, SC 68
Figure 26 Joseph GUYTON I Transcribed Will 1818 p. 2/2 Union District, SC 69
Figure 27 Migration of Hannah GUYTON and the Children of Aaron Steele GUYTON 75
Figure 28 Joseph GUYTON II'S 1861 Will p 1/4 80
Figure 29 Joseph GUYTON II'S 1861 Will p 2/4 81
Figure 30 Joseph GUYTON II'S 1861 Will p 3/4 82
Figure 31 Joseph GUYTON II'S 1861 Will p 4/4 83
Figure 32 Alex MARTIN Lands and Martin Cemetery 86
Figure 33 Hannah GUYTON MARTIN's Headstone 86
Figure 34 Alexander MARTIN's Headstone 86
Figure 35 Ellington Cemetery 88
Figure 36 Joseph GUYTON and Zemuely MCCLUSKY GUYTON Headstones in Ellington Cemetery 89
Figure 37 Distant Photo of Joseph and Zemuely GUYTON Area in Ellington Cemetery 89
Figure 38 1850 U.S. Census -- Slave Schedule for Aaron Whitaker Guyton 93
Figure 39 1860 U.S. Census -- Slave Schedule for Aaron Whitaker GUYTON 95
Figure 40 Aaron Whitaker GUYTON Family Schematic from David F. GUYTON 96
Figure 41 Artie RAINEY 97

Figure 42 Artie RAINEY's Family in the 1870 U.S. Census 98
Figure 43 Educable Children's List 1880 Attala Co., MS 99
Figure 44 Karl Glenn BOYD (aka Nykki Lamarr STARR) 101
Figure 45 Diagram of Township, Range, and Sections... 108
Figure 46 Whit Guyton's T13N R6E Location (NE ¼ NW ¼) 40 Acres 110
Figure 47 Section 20 T13N R6E, Whit Owned NE ¼, Upper Right Quadrant 111
Figure 48 Map of Cemeteries and Churches in Attla County, MS in 1976 112
Figure 49 Caroline GUYTON TERRY's Headstone in Russell Cemetery 119
Figure 50 Vinson TERRY's Headstone in Russell Cemetery... 119
Figure 51 1870 Federal Census for Caroline and Vinson TERRY 120
Figure 52 William M. TERRY, Sr... 122
Figure 53 Mary Emma TERRY.. 132
Figure 54 Young James R. (Jim) EDWARDS 132
Figure 55 Older James R. (Jim) EDWARDS 132
Figure 56 John EDWARDS' Sons Johnnie, Tommie, Bill, Ulysses, Ernest, and Walter 133
Figure 57 Nealie TERRY CONWAY 135
Figure 58 Young Nealie TERRY CONWAY 135
Figure 59 William Major CONWAY 135
Figure 60 William Vinson TERRY 143
Figure 61 Marriage Record of Carnes TERRY and Callie McMICHAEL 145
Figure 62 Joe D. and Stella Mae TERRY GUYTON with Babies 146
Figure 63 Obituary of Stella Mae TERRY GUYTON 146
Figure 64 Joe D. GUYTON.. 146
Figure 65 Lockett Joseph TERRY, Sr. 149
Figure 66 Grace HARRISON and Willie H. EDWARDS.. 152
Figure 67 Luria EDWARDS BARTON 154
Figure 68 Ulysses EDWARDS 155
Figure 69 Luegene UNKNOWN EDWARDS.. 155
Figure 70 Ernest EDWARDS.. 157
Figure 71 Jim Roger HARMON's Obituary... 159
Figure 72 Ethel Lavelle CONWAY WARD... 161
Figure 73 Lenard CONWAY 162
Figure 74 Major Alvin CONWAY... 163
Figure 75 Katie Mae HARRIS CONWAY 163
Figure 76 James Welmer CONWAY and Frenetter WHITTINGTON CONWAY 164
Figure 77 Frenetter WHITTINGTON CONWAY 164
Figure 78 James Welmer CONWAY.. 164
Figure 79 Leila HARMON and Otis KERN... 165
Figure 80 Leila HARMON and Otis KERN Enjoying LIfe 165
Figure 81 Curtis Lee BURNSIDE 169
Figure 82 Bernice Marie TERRY BURNSIDE's Obituary 169
Figure 83 Joe Frank GUYTON, Sr.'s Obituary 171
Figure 84 Evell and Stellie GUYTON DOTSON's House in Memphis, TN in 1960..................... 173
Figure 85 The Dotson Home in Ecorse, Michigan.. 173

Figure 86 Headstone of Michael Joseph TERRY, Sr. 175
Figure 87 Fannie SALLIS and Pinkney GUYTON 178
Figure 88 1880 Alabama Census of Males Over 21 179
Figure 89 Deed of Trust Sale of Property Mortgaged by Pink, Fannie, and Amzy GUYTON 180
Figure 90 Blue Pin in Center of Section 23, Township 13N, Range 6E; Section 26 is Immediately South of Section 23 181
Figure 91 Pink, Fannie, and Amzy Land in Section 23 181
Figure 92 Pink, Fannie, and Amzy's Land in Section 26; Section 26 is Immediately South of Section 23 182
Figure 93 Pinkney GUYTON in Mississippi Death Index 182
Figure 94 Mississippi Death Certificate for Pinkney GUYTON 183
Figure 95 Icy Viola NASH BOYD 185
Figure 96 Odell GUYTON DURHAM 185
Figure 97 Nic STARR and Ann BREEDLOVE 185
Figure 98 2005 Guyton Reunion in Kosciusko, MS 185
Figure 99 Google Map Showing Mallett Cemetery's Location (Blue Dot) 186
Figure 100 Mallett Cemetery 1 186
Figure 101 Mallett Cemetery 2 186
Figure 102 Mallett Cemetery 3 186
Figure 103 Rocks Indicating Pinkney and Fannie's Graves 186
Figure 104 Princess STARR and Elisa GUYTON ROTH 188
Figure 105 Ann BREEDLOVE in Red and Rickey SIMMONS in Blue 188
Figure 106 Family Breaking Bread Together after the Dedication... Long overdue! 189
Figure 107 Long Lost Cousins Happy to be Found - Elisa ROTH, Rhonda BALL, Princess STARR, Felicia BOYD 189
Figure 108 Nic and Princess STARR Visit Cousins Sam and Jean GUYTON in Denver, CO 189
Figure 109 Nic STARR and 5th Cousin Dorla COLEMAN EVANS 190
Figure 110 Nic STARR, Ann BREEDLOVE, Princess STARR, William ROTH, Elisa GUYTON ROTH, and Rickey SIMMONS 190
Figure 111 Brothers Nic and Rico STARR'S Visit to St. Louis, MO with our Cousins Elisa GUYTON ROTH and her sister, Annie GUYTON SEAL, and husband, Bob SEAL 190
Figure 112 Guyton Reunion June 2022 in Kosciusko, MS 191
Figure 113 Guyton Reunion in August 2022 191
Figure 114 Addison D. ALLEN, Husband of Emma GUYTON 194
Figure 115 Edna Alma GUYTON 194
Figure 116 Nola J. ALLEN FORD 194
Figure 117 Willie Walter and Willie Mae ALLEN 194
Figure 118 Agnes Isolome (Icy) GUYTON 198
Figure 119 Death Photo of Albert GAMBLE 198
Figure 120 Suegene GUYTON WRIGHT Younger 201
Figure 121 Suegene GUYTON WRIGHT Older 201
Figure 122 Velma Lizzie STINGLEY 208
Figure 123 Louella Roby ROUNDTREE Headstone 211
Figure 124 Othar ROUNDTREE'S Headstone 211

Figure 125 Othar ROUNDTREE 211
Figure 126 Ruth Lee (Ruthie) ROBY GUYTON 214
Figure 127 Gus Davis GUYTON 214
Figure 128 Fannie GUYTON and Dock MALLETT 217
Figure 129 Callie Pairee GAMBLE SIMMONS 220
Figure 130 Henry Porterwood SIMMONS 220
Figure 131 Henry and Callie SIMMONS Tree 222
Figure 132 Everlean SIMMONS LONG 223
Figure 133 Lois SIMMONS 223
Figure 134 Callie Jean SIMMONS 223
Figure 135 S. Thomas (S.T.) SIMMONS 223
Figure 136 Nathan Eugene GAMBLE 224
Figure 137 Nola Mae GAMBLE RILEY 226
Figure 138 Katie D. (KD) GAMBLE 228
Figure 139 Claude (Pretty Boy) JOINER, Sr. 228
Figure 140 Icy GAMBLE PARKER and Natasha PARKER OLGUIN 230
Figure 141 Woodrow Wilson NASH 230
Figure 142 Ilander N. PARKER, Sr. 230
Figure 143 Mable Ethel GAMBLE CLARK 233
Figure 144 Thomas Eugene (Uncle Bud) CLARK, Sr. 233
Figure 145 Obituary of Mabel Ethel GAMBLE CLARK 233
Figure 146 Young Lacey GUYTON 234
Figure 147 Lacey GUYTON in Uniform 234
Figure 148 Emma Evester GUYTON CLAYTON 235
Figure 149 John Wesley CLAYTON 235
Figure 150 Approximate Location of the Clayton Family in 1950 236
Figure 151 Cherry Mae GUYTON PERKINS 237
Figure 152 Andrew PERKINS 237
Figure 153 Cherry GUYTON PERKINS Home in 1995 Detroit 238
Figure 154 Lamar Andrew PERKINS 238
Figure 155 William Henry PERKINS 238
Figure 156 Cherry GUYTON PERKINS, Betty CLARK PERKINS, and William Amzy GUYTON 239
Figure 157 William Amzy GUYTON, Jr. 239
Figure 158 Pink West GUYTON 240
Figure 159 Fannie Douglas GUYTON 241
Figure 160 Young Elizabeth GUYTON SMITH 242
Figure 161 Mature Elizabeth GUYTON SMITH 242
Figure 162 Chandra Valencia SMITH, Daughter of Elizabeth GUYTON 242
Figure 163 Obituary for Samuel Alonzo FORD, Sr. 244
Figure 164 Obituary of Ollie D. RILEY, Sr. 247
Figure 165 Earlene GUYTON LANDINGHAM 249
Figure 166 Bernice GUYTON PHILLIPS 250
Figure 167 Obituary of Bernice GUYTON-PHILLIPS 251
Figure 168 J.C. MALLETT 252

Figure 169 J.C. MALLETT's Headstone 252
Figure 170 Rubell Bonita MALLETT CULPEPPER 253
Figure 171 George Louis CULPEPPER 253
Figure 172 Rubell Bonita (Ruby) MALLETT CULPEPPER's Obituary 254
Figure 173 Daughter Darlene CULPEPPER MORGAN 255
Figure 174 Daughter Mary Jean CULPEPPER McCOY 255
Figure 175 Katie K. MALLETT FAGAN's Obituary 257
Figure 176 William FAGAN's Obituary 257
Figure 177 Obituary of Fred MALLETT 258
Figure 178 Obituary of Vergie Lee NASH MALLETT 258
Figure 179 Fred and Vergie NASH MALLETT Home in Waterloo, IA 259
Figure 180 A.L. MALLET's Headstone in Wright Cemetery 260
Figure 181 Bobbie EVANS MALLET's Headstone at Wright Cemetery 260
Figure 182 Henry (L.C.) SIMMONS 261
Figure 183 Lue Bertha WINDOMS 261
Figure 184 Rickey SIMMONS 262
Figure 185 Vertrishe SIMMONS WILLIAMS 262
Figure 186 Shaneka Latrisha SIMMONS PATTERSON 262
Figure 187 Wakeco SIMMONS 263
Figure 188 Jeannie Mae SIMMONS STRAUSS 263
Figure 189 Diana SIMMONS COTTON 263
Figure 190 Jeanette SIMMONS McKELLAR 263
Figure 191 Tracy SIMMONS 263
Figure 192 Larry Lamar SIMMONS 263
Figure 193 Zenolia SIMMONS MURPHY 264
Figure 194 Ellon MURPHY 264
Figure 195 Ellon MURPHY's Obituary 265
Figure 196 Icy Viola NASH BOYD 267
Figure 197 Thornton BOYD, Sr. 267
Figure 198 George W. NASH Worked with Bands 271
Figure 199 George W. NASH in U.S. Army 271
Figure 200 Karlena L. MOORE 271
Figure 201 George NASH, Jr. 271
Figure 202 Gregory NASH 271
Figure 203 Jeffrey NASH 271
Figure 204 Margo NASH 271
Figure 205 Sherron V. MOORE 271
Figure 206 Gerald L. NASH 271
Figure 207 Sheree Shante NASH 272
Figure 208 Herbert F. MOORE 273
Figure 209 Michael Anthony MOORE 273
Figure 210 Timothy (Tim Man) MOORE 273
Figure 211 Ilander PARKER, Jr. 274
Figure 212 Katherine UNKNOWN PARKER 274

Figure 213 Arthur Lee PARKER 275
Figure 214 Rosemary PINK 275
Figure 215 Barbra Ann NORMAN 275
Figure 216 Keith Anthony PINK 276
Figure 217 Toya N. PINK 276
Figure 218 Cece NORMAN 276
Figure 219 Tyecheia Lynae NORMAN-LOPEZ 276
Figure 220 Christopher Ezriel NORMAN, Sr. 276
Figure 221 Charlene PARKER 278
Figure 222 Buvern FRANCISCO, Jr. 278
Figure 223 Tonya Lashun FRANCISCO 278
Figure 224 Buvern FRANCISCO, III 278
Figure 225 Shirley PARKER 280
Figure 226 Hubert EVANS 280
Figure 227 Obituary of Edward L. CULPEPPER 282
Figure 228 Rickey SIMMONS 283
Figure 229 Rickey ROCKETT 283
Figure 230 Crystal BYNDOM HARMON 283
Figure 231 Colby Von SIMMONS 283
Figure 232 Karl BOYD as a Child 291
Figure 233 Karl BOYD in Classic Rock 291
Figure 234 Karl BOYD in the Army 291
Figure 235 Karl BOYD AKA Nykki Lamarr STARR About 2021 291
Figure 236 Karmeisha Kashaun BOYD 292
Figure 237 Nykkiesha Lavon STARR 292
Figure 238 Tayla Lashae STARR 292
Figure 239 Nykki LaMarr STARR, Jr. 292
Figure 240 Icy Felecia Cabrini BOYD Younger 293
Figure 241 Icy Felicia Cabrini BOYD Mature 293
Figure 242 Carmelita Sabrina STARR 294
Figure 243 Jonte CAMPBELL 294
Figure 244 LaMar JOHNSON 294
Figure 245 Rhonda Larita BOYD 296
Figure 246 Kenyon BOYD 296
Figure 247 Lakeisha BOYD 296
Figure 248 Lakia Icy BOYD 296
Figure 249 Thornton BOYD, Jr. aka Rikki STARR 298
Figure 250 Tiana PETERSON 298
Figure 251 Shaina WHITE 298
Figure 252 Riki STARR 298
Figure 253 Denzel RHONE 298
Figure 254 Amari Monet STARR 298
Figure 255 Kedary STARR 298
Figure 256 Victoria Isabella CHOI 298

Figure 257 Nia STARR 298
Figure 258 Aaliyah Icy STARR 298
Figure 259 Beylynda MOORE HEAD 300
Figure 260 Cheryl Penny PARKER 301
Figure 261 Jerry BOONE 301
Figure 262 Kyler BOONE 301
Figure 263 Eric PARKER 301
Figure 264 Ryan PARKER 301
Figure 265 Chris PARKER 302
Figure 266 Yvette UNKNOWN PARKER 302
Figure 267 Charnelle PARKER 302
Figure 268 Sandy D. PARKER 303
Figure 269 Britteny L. DUNSON 303
Figure 270 Tera M. PARKER 303
Figure 271 Steven S. MORRIS, Sr. 303
Figure 272 Steven S. MORRIS, Jr. 303
Figure 273 Ollander (Odie) PARKER 304
Figure 274 High School Photo of Lishon SEALS 304
Figure 275 LaTarshe (Toddy) PARKER 305
Figure 276 Bernard PARKER 306
Figure 277 Latisha GRANT PARKER 306
Figure 278 S'eance PARKER-TURNER 306
Figure 279 Natasha PARKER 307
Figure 280 Shannon R. SIMMONS 307
Figure 281 De'Avlin V. OLGUIN 307
Figure 282 Shaun SIMMONS 307
Figure 283 1850 U.S. Census -- Slave Schedule for Aaron Whitaker GUYTON 308
Figure 284 1860 U.S. Census -- Slave Schedule for Aaron Whitaker GUYTON 309
Figure 285 Doss and Emma GUYTON with Child 316
Figure 286 Doss GUYTON 316
Figure 287 Millie NASH GUYTON 323
Figure 288 159 York Dr., Jackson, MS (Google Earth) 328
Figure 289 4016 N. State St., Jackson, MS (Google Earth) 328
Figure 290 Elige FULLER Obituary 328
Figure 291 Photo Album of Blanche GUYTON LAMAR WELLS 333
Figure 292 Warren Harding GUYTON, Sr. 336
Figure 293 Twins Rose GUYTON and Ronald GUYTON 336
Figure 294 Georgia Lee GUYTON WELLS PEGRAM 337
Figure 295 Donna Jean GUYTON 342
Figure 296 Martha GUYTON 342
Figure 297 Phyllis GUYTON 342
Figure 298 Julia CORRETHERS BURT 345
Figure 299 Tom Jordan GAMLIN, Sr. 346
Figure 300 Sarah Lee GUYTON GAMLIN 346

Figure	Page
Figure 301 Andy GUYTON's Obituary	348
Figure 302 Marie MUNSON HUNTER	351
Figure 303 Blondean MUNSON	351
Figure 304 Annie Bell GUYTON ELLIS	353
Figure 305 Case GUYTON	358
Figure 306 Map of 1535 Papin St in St. Louis, MO	359
Figure 307 Case GUYTON's Death Certificate	360
Figure 308 Willie GUYTON, Sr.	364
Figure 309 Sunset Memorial Lawns, Northbrook, Cook Co., IL	364
Figure 310 Zelma GUYTON EVANS BURT	367
Figure 311 Young Brittie WILLIAMS EVANS	369
Figure 312 Mature Brittie WILLIAMS EVANS	369
Figure 313 Lovell GUYTON and Albert BEAMON	371
Figure 314 Lula Avery GUYTON on Phone	374
Figure 315 Lula Avery GUYTON Dressed Up	374
Figure 316 Annie Pearl GUYTON	376
Figure 317 Jim Bell RILEY	376
Figure 318 Jim Bell RILEY's Obituary in Chicago, IL	377
Figure 319 Fred GUYTON	378
Figure 320 Fred GUYTON's Obituary	378
Figure 321 Rollie and Essie Dee GUYTON BROWN	381
Figure 322 Ollie BELL, Jr.	383
Figure 323 Frederick Douglas BELL	383
Figure 324 2011 McDougall in Detroit, the BELL Home	384
Figure 325 Willie James GUYTON	386
Figure 326 Tyrone GUYTON	386
Figure 327 Melvin GUYTON	386
Figure 328 Beatrice GUYTON	386
Figure 329 PFC. Melvin GUYTON Killed in Vietnam	386
Figure 330 Willie Clayton (WC) GUYTON, Sr.	388
Figure 331 Vera LaVern TERRY GUYTON	388
Figure 332 Vearn GUYTON, Sr.	392
Figure 333 Lorine RILEY PERKINS	393
Figure 334 James Willie PERKINS	393
Figure 335 Fannie Bea PERKINS	393
Figure 336 Arey PERKINS	393
Figure 337 Bennie Lee PERKINS	393
Figure 338 Maggie GUYTON STINGLEY	394
Figure 339 1701 Spain Street, Home of Herman STINGLEY	397
Figure 340 Louria STINGLEY and Lee Boston TURNER	398
Figure 341 Obituary for Louria STINGLEY TURNER	398
Figure 342 Lottie STINGLEY	400
Figure 343 Mayvell STINGLEY SUDDUTH	401
Figure 344 Obituary of Mayvell STINGLEY SUDDUTH	401

Figure 345 Joe Howard SUDDUTH 401
Figure 346 Death of Guyton STINGLEY in Korea 402
Figure 347 Mannie Whitt STINGLEY 403
Figure 348 Dorotha JENKINS STINGLEY 403
Figure 349 Obituary for Dorotha JENKINS STINGLEY 404
Figure 350 Obituary for Mannie Whitt STINGLEY 404
Figure 351 Woodworth Chapel, Tougaloo College 405
Figure 352 Alcorn State University's Oakland Chapel 405
Figure 353 John Ike STINGLEY's Obituary 406
Figure 354 John Ike STINGLEY 407
Figure 355 Quincy Thelma SUDDUTH 407
Figure 356 John Ike STINGLEY's Memorial Program 408
Figure 357 Metropolitan Missionary Baptist Church 408
Figure 358 Amanda (Annie B.) GUYTON TERRY 409
Figure 359 Simon GUYTON 411
Figure 360 Hattie GUYTON SUDDUTH 418
Figure 361 Obituary of Robbie GUYTON BURT 419
Figure 362 Robbie GUYTON ROBY 419
Figure 363 Minnie GUYTON GUYTON 420
Figure 364 Steele GUYTON 420
Figure 365 Katherine GUYTON ERVIN 421
Figure 366 Fred Steele GUYTON and Fred Steele GUYTON, Jr. 421
Figure 367 Laclain GUYTON 421
Figure 368 Fleming and Emma GUYTON Loss of Land 1963 422
Figure 369 Section 19, Township 13 North, Range 6 East, Choctaw Principal Meridian, Mississippi, Blue Pin (randymajors.org) 423
Figure 370 Section 19, Township 13 North, Range 6 East, Closer view. See Section 19 in Yellow. 423
Figure 371 Illustration of how Townships, Sections, and Quarters are Divided 423
Figure 372 Fleming and Emma GUYTON Land Loss Due to Non-payment of Debt 424
Figure 373 Land Lost for Back Taxes in 1963 424
Figure 374 Land Lost for Loan Default 424
Figure 375 Earl Denison TERRY, Sr. 427
Figure 376 Allie Mae TEAGUE 428
Figure 377 Prince Lamar THURMAN 428
Figure 378 Rickey Nelson TEAGUE with Perhaps Carol LAMBERT 429
Figure 379 Mary THURMAN and Allie Mae TEAGUE THURMAN 429
Figure 380 Charles Edward BURT (with Carolyn?) 430
Figure 381 Fred Steele GUYTON, Sr. and Fred Steele GUYTON, Jr 432
Figure 382 Ike GUYTON 434
Figure 383 Ida RILEY 434
Figure 384 Ida RILEY with Grandchildren, June 1962 434
Figure 385 Map of Zemuly and Thomastown Road Intersection 435
Figure 386 Ida RILEY's Daughters: L to R Alice, Mary, Annie, and Isadora 437

Figure 387 Mary Georgia GUYTON 438
Figure 388 Obituary of Mary Georgia GUYTON 438
Figure 389 An Older Isadore GUYTON BROWN 440
Figure 390 A Young Antney Wesley BROWN 440
Figure 391 Antney Wesley BROWN Plowing the Field 440
Figure 392 BROWN Family in Aug 1963 440
Figure 393 Daughters Eva, Channie, and Emma 441
Figure 394 Shelay BROWN Class of 1960 441
Figure 395 Charles and Eula BROWN 442
Figure 396 Eva BROWN ROGERS 442
Figure 397 Emma M. BROWN EVANS 442
Figure 398 Shelay Mae BROWN 442
Figure 399 Channie BROWN CURRIE 442
Figure 400 Gus Davis GUYTON 443
Figure 401 Ruthie ROBY GUYTON 443
Figure 402 Obituary of Ruth Lee ROBY GUYTON 444
Figure 403 Young Joe Frank GUYTON 446
Figure 404 Older Joe Frank GUYTON 446
Figure 405 Mildred Irene WINGARD GUYTON 446
Figure 406 Obituary of Joe Frank GUYTON 447
Figure 407 Annie GUYTON EVANS 448
Figure 408 Gene Arty (Pie Joe) EVANS 449
Figure 409 Darlene EVANS 449
Figure 410 Allen Leroy EVANS, Jr. 449
Figure 411 Ben GUYTON 451
Figure 412 Genova GUYTON 451
Figure 413 Young Alice GUYTON WEBB 452
Figure 414 Older Alice GUYTON WEBB 452
Figure 415 Oliver Debois WEBB and son Oliver (Butch) WEBB 453
Figure 416 Claude GUYTON and Bonnie WEBB 454
Figure 417 Obituary of Claude GUYTON 454
Figure 418 Charlies Willie and Eula Mae BROWN 455
Figure 419 Channie BROWN-CURRIE 457
Figure 420 Earlene GUYTON LANDINGHAM 457
Figure 421 Bernice GUYTON PHILLIPS 458
Figure 422 Buddy and Juanita FULLER GUYTON 460
Figure 423 Lawanda GUYTON and Kevin HOWARD Engagement Photo 463
Figure 424 Brenda Dell GUYTON CARR 463
Figure 425 Linda Bell GUYTON 463
Figure 426 Willie Edwards EVANS 465
Figure 427 Terry Leroy EVANS 466
Figure 428 Gloria Jean EVANS 466

Introduction

This book documents the family of Aaron Whitaker (Whit) GUYTON (1808-ABT 1882) along with his known ancestors and descendants. The idea for the book originated from my earlier book, *Joseph Guyton Genealogy: From England to Maryland and Across the American South*. I corresponded with David F. Guyton, an English genealogist, who studies the Guyton family worldwide. David gave me invaluable information about the Guytons in England and those who emigrated to America. He also told me about a Kosciusko, Mississippi Guyton family that celebrates with reunions every two years. With David's help, I reached out to the descendants of Joseph A. GUYTON (1805-1880), Aaron Whitaker GUYTON's brother, to wrangle an invitation to their 2022 reunion in Kosciuszko, Mississippi.

Included in my earlier book was the story of Aaron Whitaker GUYTON and his relationships with African American partners and their children together. I was deeply interested in the story. I hoped that African American members of the Kosciusko Guytons would attend the reunion. As attendees were greeted to the reunion, three African Americans entered the room – Karl Glenn BOYD (aka Nykki Lamarr STARR), his wife Princess STARR, and his cousin Rickey SIMMONS. Nic approached the group and was given the floor. Thus began what Nic has called Grace for the Guytons. A time for reconciliation between Black and white; a time to connect and to form new relationships.

Nic and Rickey were anxious to add more of their families to my previous book. Both are descended from Patsy GIBSON and Aaron Whiter GUYTON's son, Pinkney GUYTON. I took notes and began to build the African American tree of Aaron Whitaker GUYTON. Nic sent me a book by Channie BROWN-CURRIE produced for a family reunion. She is descended from Aaron Whitaker GUYTON and Artie RAINEY. As the tree became larger, I was convinced the family needed its own book. The culmination of the work is *Aaron Whitaker Guyton of Kosciusko, Mississippi: The Journeys of his African American Children*. As I was nearing completion of the book, Rickey reached out to his first cousin, Rita MURPHY McLEAN, for the information she might share. The materials offered by Channie, Rita, Nic, and Rickey have been invaluable in identifying family members, securing photographs, specifying relevant dates, and sketching personalities.

It became quickly apparent that there are cultural sensitivities which I will likely never fully appreciate. My writing in the book may upset cultural norms, for which I apologize. I believe it is important to publish the work even if it contains my inadvertent insensitivities. Throughout the book, I use the word marriage for relationships which may or may not have been sanctioned by the church or state. During slavery, marriage for enslaved persons was prohibited.[1] However, in some free northern states, formerly enslaved people could marry. Many enslaved people lived in nuclear families or in what are called by academics as near-nuclear families in which family members lived on adjoining plantations under different ownership. Enslaved people lived with the constant fear of separation caused by being sold, being divided through inheritance, moving of adult children who inherited enslaved people, or

---

[1] Williams, Heather Andrea, "How Slavery Affected African American Families," Freedom's Story, TeacherServe©. National Humanities Center, Accessed 4 Jul 2024, <https://nationalhumanitiescenter.org/tserve/freedom/1609-1865/essays/aafamilies.htm>.

other causes. Many slaveholders encouraged marriage through "jumping the broom," to deter enslaved people from running away. After the Civil War, many previously enslaved individuals sought to find their lost relatives, including placing ads in newspapers and sending inquiries to the Freedman's Bureau. Many people formalized marriages during that time. States often charged high marriage license fees to discourage marriage among African Americans.[2] They also passed miscengenation laws to prevent interracial marriage. The background of such institutions goes far in explaining why we see variation in marriages/partnerships across families.

Where I have U.S. Federal Census data, I have noted information about whether a family owned or rented its own farm (for those who stayed on the farm rather than move to the industrial cities of the north). Approximately 14% of Black farmers were landowners after the Civil War, while the vast majority, around 86%, were either sharecroppers or tenant farmers. From my casual examination of the records, I believe Aaron Whitaker GUYTON's descendants out-performed the national statistics. I suggest the reader do his own analysis. I included information from the Census on the literacy and education levels of the family members. Literacy and education improved over generations and when families moved from rural areas to cities.

Possible Origins of the Guyton Name

There are different derivations of the name Guyton depending upon which spelling one uses – Guyton versus Guiton.[3] Published research shows the Guyton spelling is an English name; whereas, Guiton indicates a name with wide geographical origins, including French.

Guyton is an uncommon surname of Anglo-Saxon origin. It appears to be a name associated with three locations now called Gayton. It was written as Gaitone, Gaituna, and Gettune in the Domesday Book of 1086.[4] Gayton is the name of a parish and village east of King's Lynn (Norfolk); a parish near Towcester in Northamptonshire; and a parish northeast of Stafford in Staffordshire. The ending of the name is common in English names based on the Old English pre-7th Century word tun, meaning an enclosure or settlement. The first part of the name may be Old English for goat or for a personal name or stream. The goat derivation for Guyton would mean basically an enclosure to keep goats. The personal name derivation would mean a farmstead of a man named Gay (Guy). Gayton/Guyton/Gytton (and other variations) is well-recorded in Norfolk Church Registers. The earliest reference is from an undated will sometime between 1469 to 1503 of Thomas Gyton of Great Ryburgh, located about 15 miles northeast of a village called Gayton, England.

Alternatively, Guyton may be of French or continental European origins, with the spelling of Guiton or Guitton. The earliest recorded reference to Guitton appears in Anjou, France in 1172. During this time

---

[2] Holden, Vanessa M., "Slave and Free Black Marriage in the Nineteenth Century," *Black Perspectives*, 19 Sep 2018, < https://www.aaihs.org/slave-and-free-black-marriage-in-the-nineteenth-century/>, accessed 4 Jul 2024.
[3] Guyton, David F., "Origin of the Name Guyton and Close Variants," Guyton Ancestry, <http://guyton.co.uk/wp-content/uploads/Topics/Origin.pdf>, accessed 10 June 2018.
[4] This book is a tax assessment ordered by William the Conqueror in 1086. For more information, go to: <http://www.domesdaybook.co.uk/faqs.html#1>.

of the Norman Conquest, the western part of France (Anjou) belonged to England. In 1342 John de GUITTON was listed in an English patent roll.

I have sometimes found our GUYTON name in the U.S. Federal Census as Guiton. According to the Surname Database [which I can no longer find on the web – 10 June 2018), the name with this spelling usually has French origins. Guyton has over fifty different spelling variants. These range from the traditional Guy, Guye, and Guyon, to Why, Whye and Wyon, to Guido, Ghi, Gyde, Guet, Guidini and Ghidoli, and is recorded in Britain, France, Germany, Italy, and Switzerland.

Guiton may be derived from the occupation as a professional guide (gui is the word for professional guide in the pre-10th century Old French). An example given on the Surname Database of this use of the name is John le GY recorded in the Subsidy Rolls of Essex, England in 1327. The name could be derived from the male personal name, Guy, a French name of the 10th century. Or the surname may be an occupational name from the Old High German word witu and the Old English pre-7th century widu or wudu, meaning a wood. The baptismal name in the forms Wi, Why, and Guy was very popular with the Norman-French.

Possible Origins of the Guyton Family

I have seen references to the Guytons' being French Huguenots.[5] However, there is no concrete evidence for our particular branch of Guytons. For general interest let me first provide some basic information about French Huguenots.[6]

Huguenots were followers of the French Reformed Church, in the Protestant tradition of John Calvin, between the 16th century and the beginning of the 19th century. No one seems to know where the word Huguenot came from but it definitely was a derogatory term. The Huguenots lived primarily in the southern and western parts of France. As they gained in financial and political strength, they more openly displayed their Protestant faith. French Catholics responded with hostility resulting in the French Wars of Religion occurring intermittently between 1562 and 1592 and the beginning of Huguenot emigration to Protestant countries. These wars ended with the Edict of Nantes under Henry IV, which granted the Huguenots religious, political, and military freedoms.

Unfortunately, peace did not last between Protestants and Catholics. Huguenot freedoms were again removed resulting in rebellions in the 1620s leading to continued emigration. Rebellions led to the revocation of Huguenot political and military freedoms. Huguenots retained their religious freedoms

---

[5] For example, see Guyton Rees, Helen. *Guytons Galore: From French Huguenots to Oregon Pioneers*. Portland, OR: Binford & Mort, 1986 and Guyton, G. Monroe; Guyton, Geames W.; and Guyton, Ken, "The Ancestors of John Marion Guyton," July 1984, accessed 27 May 2020, <https://sites.google.com/a/guytonhouse.net/main/geneology-of-john-marion-guyton>.

[6] Here are some good resources. Guyton Rees, Helen. *Guytons Galore: From French Huguenots to Oregon Pioneers*. Portland, Oregon: Binford & Mort, 1986. The Huguenot Society of America, accessed 9 Apr 2020, <https://www.huguenotsocietyofamerica.org/>. "Huguenots," *Wikipedia*, n. d. Treasure, Geoffrey. *The Huguenots*. New Haven and London: Yale University Press, 2013. Treasure's book is an excellent in-depth academic history of the Huguenots.

until King Louis XIV increased their persecution, culminating in the Edict of Fontainebleau in 1685, revoking the Edict of Nantes, and ending the recognition of Protestantism in France. Huguenots had to convert to Catholicism or flee France. And because Huguenots controlled many successful and necessary trades in France, Louis XIV forbade Huguenots' emigration. Hence, much of the Huguenot emigration at this point was done through paying smugglers to gain freedom in Protestant countries, including England, Scotland, Wales, Switzerland, Denmark, Sweden, the English colonies in America, the Dutch Republic (the Low Countries), etc. Persecution officially ended with the Edict of Tolerance in 1787 under Louis XVI and Protestants gained equal rights in 1789.

If our family is French Huguenot, how did the family get to America? There are four major possibilities. First, the Guytons may have emigrated directly from France to America. This is not the case because our first verified Guyton, John GUYTON, lived in Norwich, Norfolk County, England in 1647 when his first child was baptized. Second, the Guytons may have immigrated to England and then immigrated to America. England, as a Protestant country under the rule of Queen Elizabeth I, was the second most popular destination for the Huguenots beginning in 1562. Between 40,000 to 50,000 settled in England, mostly in coastal towns in the southern districts (like Norwich). The largest concentration was in London where they comprised about 5% of the total population in 1700. Their dominant trade was in silk weaving.[7] It is possible the Guytons emigrated from France to England.

Third, the Guytons may have immigrated to the Dutch Republic before they immigrated to Norfolk and then on to America. The Dutch (who were Protestants in the northern provinces of the Low Countries) fought against the Catholics in the southern provinces (present-day Belgium and Luxembourg) in the first years of the Dutch Revolt (1568-1609). Some Huguenots fought alongside the Dutch. Refugees from the Low Countries who fled persecution in their own land found a welcome in the Norwich, Norfolk County, England from 1567 onward. Most of these people were Dutch speakers, but a considerable number were French speakers; the latter are known as Walloons. By the late 1570s, one person in four in Norwich was a refugee who had come into the city within the previous ten years.[8] The mayor of Norwich invited "The Strangers," as they were called, to bring their textile skills and to teach the locals how to make different types of cloth with the goal of shoring up Norwich's dwindling textile industry.[9] Due to their commercial success, the relative tolerance of their Protestant religion in England, and the continued immigration of The Strangers, the textile immigrant population exploded to 6,000 by 1580, making up about 40 percent of Norwich's population. There is no documentation to indicate a Guyton (Guiton) was among the immigrating families but there was a Supplus GEDDON in a tax roll of foreigners in Norwich in 1580.[10] Our earliest documented Guyton family member, John GYTON, lived in

---

[7] "Huguenots," *Wikipedia*, n. d.
[8] elizabethjayne2015. "Strangers-A Brief History of Norwich's Incomers," Norfolk Record Office (blog), 24 Jun 2016 <https://norfolkrecordofficeblog.org/2016/06/24/strangers-a-brief-history-of-norwichs-incomers/>.
[9] *Ibid.* Gidney, Thomas. "The World and a Small Place in England: Norwich's textile industry from the 'Middle Ages' to 'Industrial Revolution'," *World History Connected*, February 2018, <https://worldhistoryconnected.press.uillinois.edu/15.1/gidney.html>.
[10] Guyton, David F., "Origin of the Name Guyton and Close Variants," Guyton Ancestry, accessed 10 June 2018, <http://guyton.co.uk/wp-content/uploads/Topics/Origin.pdf>.

Norwich and was a reeder, or someone who made thatched roofs from reeds. His son, Samuel GUYTON I, was a gardener.

Fourth, the Guytons may not be Huguenots at all! They may have been native to England. David F. GUYTON writes:[11]

> What does appear to be clear from early written records is that initial variants of the name were established in both France and England before the Reformation and the emergence of Protestant and Huguenot churches. There were undoubtedly a number of Huguenot refugees by the name of Guiton and Guitton but all of these arrived a century or more later than the first recorded instances of the names Guyton, Gyton and Gytton in England…. Unfortunately, no conclusive evidence has been found so far to connect early branches of the family in Norfolk, and particularly in Norwich, with French immigrants or with the early Norfolk habitation of Gaituna, now known as Gayton. Both routes are possible and, indeed, both could have occurred in parallel.

---

[11] *Ibid.*

Generation #1

Our documented Guyton family tree begins in the 1600s in Norwich, Norfolk County, England. In 1891 (200 years after our first documented Guyton was buried in Norwich), Norfolk County had the highest concentration of Guyton families in England, although Guyton was not a very common name. As late as 1891 there were only between 26 and 49 Guyton families in Norwich and there were a total of 165 Guyton families in England and Wales.[12] Norwich, Norfolk County is located on the far eastern coast of England as shown on the map in Figure 1.[13] The area is almost directly west of the Netherlands, an early center of the Protestant Reformation.[14]

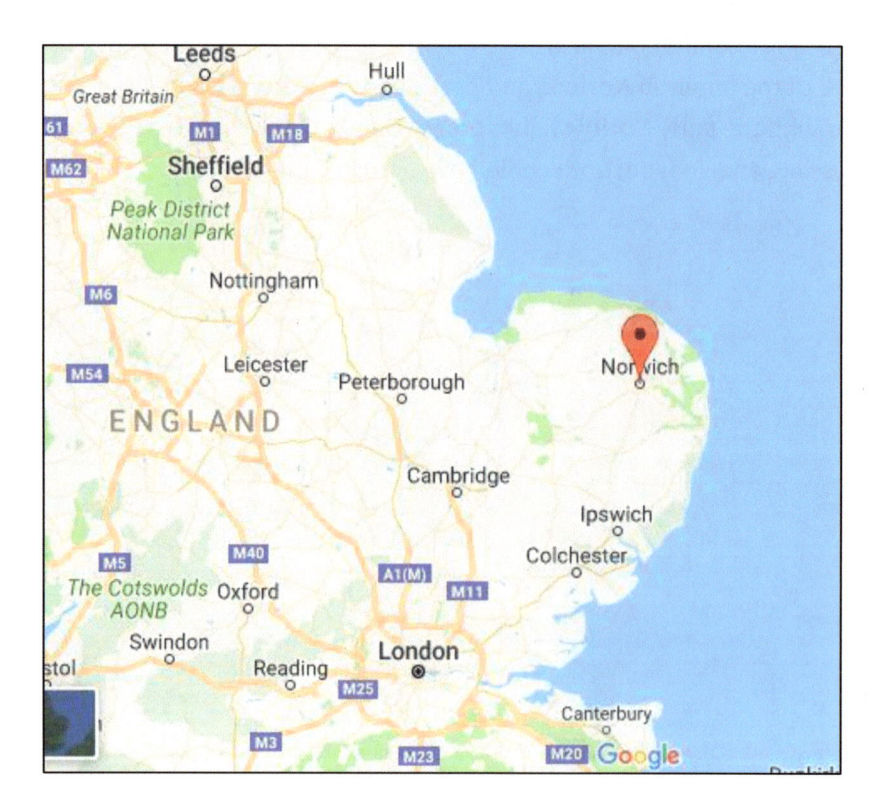

Figure 1 City of Norwich on Map of England

We know at least four generations of the direct line of our Guyton family lived in Norwich, Norfolk County, England. The Guytons moved from living outside the city walls to living in the old city center within the ancient city walls of Norwich. See Figure 2 for a 14th century map of Norwich.[15] Within the ancient walls there were 36 medieval parish churches in addition to the Cathedral of Norwich.[16] The

---

[12] 1891 Census of England and Wales, Norfolk County, England, digital image, s.v. "Guyton," *Ancestry.com*.
[13] "England." Map. *Google Maps*. Google, 9 Oct 2016. Web. 9 Oct 2016.
[14] "History of Religion in the Netherlands," *Wikipedia*, n. d.
[15] George, Martin, "Bold New Vision to Make City Walls among Norwich's Most Prominent Features Again," *Eastern Daily Press,* 14 Sep 2015 <http://www.edp24.co.uk/news/bold-new-vision-to-make-city-walls-among-norwich-s-most-prominent-features-again-1-4231222>.
[16] "List of Churches in Norwich," *Wikipedia*, n.d.

reader can see Norwich Cathedral with the spire in the middle right of the map. Norwich Cathedral survives today as does Norwich Castle, seen on the large mound in the center of the map.

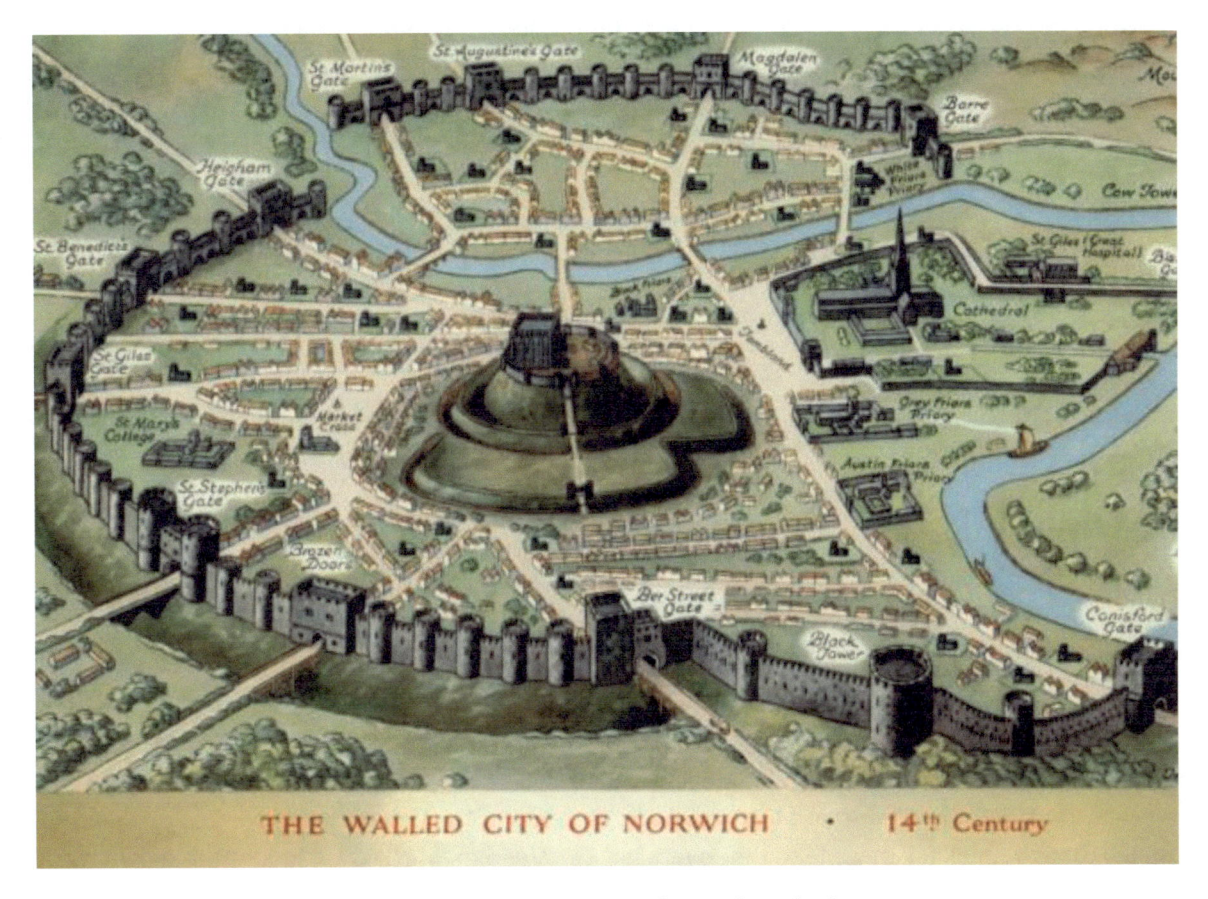

Figure 2 14th Century Map of Norwich, England

Samuel GUYTON I^(John)

Samuel's parents were John GYTON and Margaret UNKNOWN, our earliest known ancestors from Norwich.[17] This section shares the research of David F. GUYTON, who works at developing a world-wide Guyton genealogy.[18] I quote him liberally, with his permission. No early records have been found for John GYTON but he was likely born about 1605 and was married about 1629.

> From later records it is known that he was a reeder, a thatcher using reeds, in Norwich and became a freeman of the city in 1639. He and his family lived initially in the parish of St Paul, a congested and relatively poor area of the city north of the River Wensum known as 'Over the Water' and stretching out beyond the city walls. The parish church was built about 1450 on the site of an earlier Norman church and monastic hospital for

---

[17] Per David F. GUYTON, genealogist of the Guyton family, in a personal communication with the author, July 2020.
[18] Per David F. GUYTON, genealogist of the Guyton family, in a personal communication with the author, 16 January 2021. He is a British researcher who has access to the records at the Norfolk Records Office and the parish churches in Norwich.

the poor dating back another three centuries and it had a distinctive East Anglian low round tower. The church suffered periods of neglect and decay but survived into the twentieth century. It was destroyed by incendiary bombs during a raid on 27 June 1942.

Figure 3 below shows St. Paul's Parish Church before its destruction.[19]

Figure 3 St. Paul's Parish Church

David F. GUYTON indicates above that John GYTON was made a freeman in 1639. The concept of freeman has no parallel in America. A little background can establish the value of being a freeman in Norwich.[20] In 1194 Richard I (Richard the Lionheart) gave towns the right to self-govern in perpetuity in exchange for an annual tax payable to the sovereign. The freemen of Norwich sought the right to self-govern in order to vote for their local administrator, to decide how funds were spent locally, to trade freely within the city, and to eliminate paying tolls while trading throughout England. Non-freemen, or non-citizens, had no rights in the government of the city.

The freemen comprised the governing body of Norwich and were granted special rights to trade freely and conduct business. To become a freeman, a person had to pay rates and taxes, and could qualify in one of three main ways.[21] A father could pass down the right to be a freeman if his son was born after the father became a freeman. Or a man could serve as an apprentice to a freeman for seven years and then pay a fee. Or a newcomer to the city who had apprenticed elsewhere could become a

---

[19] Plunkett, George, "Norwich Mediaeval City Churches," *George Plunkett's Photographs of Old Norwich, 5 Mar 1937*, <http://www.georgeplunkett.co.uk/Norwich/Mediaeval%20City%20Churches/St%20Paul's%20from%20north%20[1553]%201937-05-03.jpg>, n.d., accessed 19 January 2021.

[20] "Freemen of Norwich Timeline," *Freemen of Norwich*, <http://www.norwichfreemen.org.uk/tracing-our-history/>, n.d., accessed 19 January 2021.

[21] "History of Norwich Freemen: 1. Who Were the Freemen?" *Freemen of Norwich*, <http://www.norwichfreemen.org.uk/about/tracing-our-history/1-who-were-the-freemen/>, n.d., accessed 19 January 2021.

freeman by paying a higher fee. The first recorded freeman of Norwich was noted in 1317 in a specially-created book series that continues to this day.

David F. GUYTON continues:

In about 1632 John GYTON and his family moved southwards nearer the city centre to the larger and somewhat more prosperous urban parish of St Peter Parmentergate. Seven of his nine children were baptised at the church including 'Samuel son of John Giton' on 4 April 1647. In 1644 John and Margaret GYTON acquired a property in St Faiths Lane in the parish which they kept until 1662. Hearth tax records indicate that John GYTON was still living in the parish until at least April 1672 although by then he was living on too small an income to pay tax. The parish church is a spacious building with tall Perpendicular windows and a high and wide chancel arch. The church still stands but has been closed for some years and is showing signs of deterioration and decay.

A photo of St. Peter Parmentergate is shown below:[22]

Figure 4 St. Peter Parmentergate

The map, shown in Figure 5 illustrates Norwich in 1696 within the old city walls.[23] David F. Guyton annotated the map to include locations where key Guyton activities occurred. The reader can see St.

---

[22] Plunkett, George, "Norwich Mediaeval City Churches," *George Plunkett's Photographs of Old Norwich*, 3 July 1938, <http://www.georgeplunkett.co.uk/Norwich/Mediaeval%20City%20Churches/St%20Peter%20Parmentergate%20from%20SE%20[2134]%201938-03-07.jpg>., n.d., accessed 19 January 2021.

[23] "1696 Thomas Cleer's Map of Norwich with Annotations." Map. *The National Archives*. Norfolk Record Office. Web. Accessed 11 January 2021, <https://discovery.nationalarchives.gov.uk/details/a/A13531443>. Annotated by David F. GUYTON, genealogist of the Guyton family, in a personal communication with the author, 16 January 2021.

Peter Parmentergate at the lower right with the notation that John GYTON's son, Samuel, was baptized there.

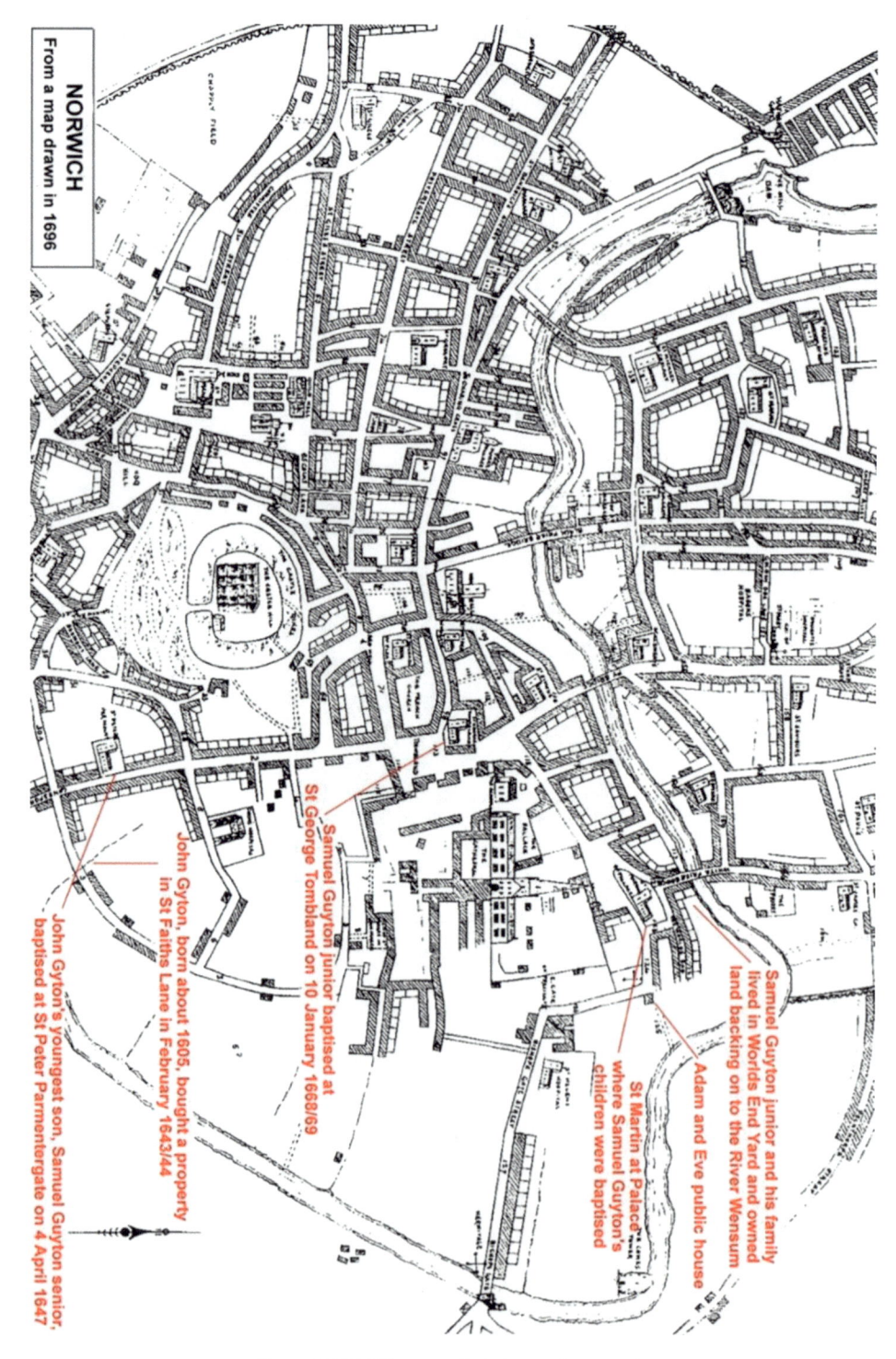

Figure 5 1696 Thomas Cleer Map of Norwich

David F. GUYTON continues his narration of the Guyton story:

Confusingly, there are two records of baptisms on 4 April 1647: 'Samuel son of John GITON' at St Peter Parmentergate mentioned above and 'Sam sonne of Jn GYTTON' at St Michael at Plea. As there was no other family with these names in Norwich at the time, these records are presumed to refer to the same family though it remains a mystery why the event should be recorded twice unless an itinerant clerk mistakenly entered it in both parish registers.

There are no other early records of Samuel GITON/GYTTON (Samuel GUYTON senior) [Samuel GUYTON I, in this book] or his marriage to his wife, Elizabeth, until the baptism of their son, Samuel GYTTON (Samuel GUYTON junior) [Samuel GUYTON II, in this book], at St George Tombland on 10 January 1668/69. The parish church of St George Tombland stands at the north western end of St Faiths Lane facing on to the ancient Saxon market place known as Tombland outside the famous Erpingham Gate and St Ethelberts Gate entrances to the precincts of Norwich Cathedral**Error! Reference source not found.**.. No other family events appear to have been recorded at St George Tombland so the connection with the church may have been through his wife's family rather than Samuel Guyton senior who continues to appear in hearth tax lists with other members of the family in the parish of St Peter Parmentergate from 1671 to 1674.

Samuel GUYTON I and Elizabeth UNKNOWN had three known children:

i   Samuel GUYTON II (bap. 10 Jan 1668/69 St. George's Tombland,[24] Norwich, Norfolk Co., England, bur. 15 Jan 1728) m. Margaret UNDERWOOD (b. Unknown, bur. 16 Jan 1730/1731) on 22 Dec 1691.[25]

ii   Sarah GUYTON (bap. 11 Mar 1676/77 St. Martin at Palace, Norwich, Norfolk Co., England, d. 23 March 1677).[26]

iii   Elizabeth GUYTON (bap. 25 July 1680 St. Martin at Palace, Norwich, Norfolk Co., England).[27]

According to David F. GUYTON, the baptisms of Sarah and Elizabeth GUYTON at St. Martin at Palace marked the first of many Guyton family records found at the parish for the next two centuries.

St. Martin at Palace Church is within the ancient city walls of Norwich, about 200 to 300 yards northeast of Norwich Cathedral. See Figure 6 for a photo of St. Martin at Palace Church.[28] It was largely built in the late 15th century. What seems like a strange name to Americans means the St. Martin Church

---

[24] "England Births and Christenings, 1538-1975," digital image s.v. "Samuell Gytton," (baptized 10 Jan 1668), *FamilySearch.org*.

[25] "Norfolk, England, Transcripts of Church of England Baptism, Marriage and Burial Registers, 1600-1935," digital image s.v. "Samuel Guyton," (1668-Unknown), *Ancestry.com*.

[26] "England, Select Births and Christenings, 1538-1975," s.v. "Sarah Guyton," (1676-1677), *Ancestry.com*; "England Deaths and Burials, 1538-1991," digital image s.v. "Sarah Guyton," (1676-1677), *FamilySearch*.

[27] "Norfolk, England, Church of England Baptism, Marriages, and Burials, 1535-1812," digital image s.v. "Elizabeth Guyton," (1680-Unknown), *Ancestry.com*.

[28] Cmhepworth, "St Martin at Palace Plain Norwich," Family Search, 23 Mar 2010 <https://www.familysearch.org/wiki/en/File:St_Martin_at_Palace_Plain_Norwich.jpg> (10 October 2016).

(there were a number of them in town) that is located by the Bishop's Palace.[29] It currently functions as offices for the Norwich Probation Centre.

More is known about Samuel and Elizabeth GUYTON. According to David F. GUYTON:

> In 1687 'Samuel Geyton of Norwich gardiner & wife Elizabeth' acquired a property known as the 'Angell' together with associated outbuildings, garden and orchard in the rural hamlet of Trowse (pronounced 'Trose') on the southern outskirts of Norwich. From the deeds it appears to have been quite a sizeable property and it is possible that Samuel Guyton senior may have worked it as a market garden. The transition from a family living in the parish of St Peter Parmentergate on incomes too low to pay hearth tax to owning or leasing a reasonably sized property in Trowse remains something of a curiosity. Unfortunately, parish records do not start until 1695 and are largely illegible before 1702 which hinders further investigation. From 1760 to 1878 there was a public house at Trowse called 'The Angel' which may have been the same property.

Trowse is just southeast of Norwich, likely a suburb of today's Norwich. More will be revealed about this property in the section about Samuel GUYTON II in Generation #2.

Figure 6 St. Martin at Palace Church in Norwich, Norfolk, England

An Elizabeth GUYTON was buried 30 Jan 1698 at St. Martin at Palace, followed by a Samuel GUYTON two days later, on 1 Feb 1698. According to David F. GUYTON, these are not our married couple. We know Samuel GUYTON I and his wife, Elizabeth, lived in St. Martin at Palace parish in 1710/11 because he paid window tax in the parish. Taxes were based on glass windows because they

---

[29] Bayne, A.D. *A Comprehensive History of Norwich*. London: Jarrod and Sons, 1869. Made available by Project Gutenberg, 2 Jan 2014, accessed 14 Jun 2018, <http://www.gutenberg.org/files/44568/44568-h/44568-h.htm#page43>.

were a luxury item in homes. Later property deeds indicate Samuel GUYTON I and Elizabeth owned several properties in the parish along Worlds End Lane immediately adjacent to the northern side of the church and stretching back to the River Wensum. Samuel and Elizabeth GUYTON sold properties in Norwich in 1724 so we know they died sometime after that. We do not know their dates of death.

We can put Samuel's story into perspective by looking at national and regional events. Samuel I was born well after the Protestant Reformation of England. King Henry VIII reigned from 1509 until his death in 1547. Desperate for sons to survive him, Henry VIII needed to divorce his first wife, Catherine of Aragon, to marry someone else – Anne Boleyn. The pope refused to grant the needed divorce. So Henry VIII took advantage of the Protestant Reformation that was altering the religious and political face of Europe to convert the country from Catholicism to Protestantism.[30]

The country shifted back and forth between Catholicism and Protestantism with violent repercussions. Samuel I was born around the time that King Charles I was captured and tried for treason against England, and beheaded in 1647. The House of Commons abolished the Monarchy of England, replacing it with the Commonwealth of England. Oliver Cromwell, a leading Puritan, took over as Lord Protector. After Cromwell's death in 1658, the country again shifted between Protestant and Catholic interests. At the time of Samuel I's death (1697), the country was ruled by Protestant William II, who died in 1702.[31]

These national religious events rocked Norfolk County, center for the Protestant Reformation in England.[32] The "nonconformists," as the Protestants were generally called, were known as Presbyterians and Puritans in England. Norwich, being located close to the coast of the Netherlands, became a place of refuge to Protestants fleeing persecution at the hands of the Spanish Catholics in 1567. By 1574 Norwich was notorious for nonconformist Protestant teachings. Queen Mary decreed those ministers of nonconformity in the country beginning with Norwich be punished severely for "prophecyings, and readings, and commenting on the Scriptures." Ministers and Norfolk County's leading citizens, being expelled from their homes by royal intolerance, fled to Protestant areas on the Continent. By 1641, near the time of Samuel I's birth, many of the refugees had returned to Norwich and by 1642 they established an independent church in Norwich. All Samuel I's children were baptized into the Church of England, a conforming Protestant church.

On a lighter note, Norwich was known as a city of some culture. Lord Macaulay, in his *History of England*, described the city in the 17th century:[33]

> Norwich was the capital of a large and fruitful province. It was the residence of a bishop and of a chapter. It was the seat of the manufacture of the realm. Some even distinguished by learning and science had recently dwelt there, and no place in the kingdom, except the capital and the universities, had more attractions to the curious.

---

[30] Johnson, Ben, "Henry VIII," Historic UK (blog), n.d., accessed 11 Jun 2018, <https://www.historic-uk.com/HistoryUK/HistoryofEngland/Henry-VIII/>.

[31] Johnson, Ben, "Henry VIII," Historic UK (blog), n.d., accessed 11 Jun 2018, <https://www.historic-uk.com/HistoryUK/KingsQueensofBritain/>.

[32] Bayne, A.D., *A Comprehensive History of Norwich*, London: Jarrod and Sons, 1869, pp. 241-243. Made available 2 Jan 2014 (accessed 14 Jun 2018) by Project Gutenberg <http://www.gutenberg.org/files/44568/44568-h/44568-h.htm#page43>.

[33] *Ibid.* p. 225.

The library, the museum, the aviary, and the botanical gardens of Sir Thomas Browne were thought by the Fellows of the Royal Society well worthy of a long pilgrimage. Norwich had also a court in miniature. In the heart of the city stood an old palace of the Duke of Norfolk, said to be the largest town house in the kingdom out of London. In this mansion, to which were annexed a tennis court, a bowling green, and a wilderness extending along the banks of the Wensum, the noble family of Howard frequently resided. Drink was served to the guests in goblets of pure gold; the very tongs and shovels were of silver; pictures of Italian masters adorned the walls; the cabinets were filled with a fine collection of gems purchased by the Earl of Arundel, whose marbles are now among the ornaments of Oxford. Here, in the year 1671, Charles and his court were sumptuously entertained; here, too, all comers were annually welcomed from Christmas to Twelfthnight; ale flowed in oceans for the populace. Three coaches, one of which had been built at a cost of £500 to contain fourteen persons, were sent every afternoon round the city to bring ladies to the festivities, and the dances were always followed by a luxurious banquet. When the Duke of Norfolk came to Norwich he was greeted like a king returning to his capital; the bells of St. Peter's Mancroft were rung, the guns of the castle were fired, and the mayor and aldermen waited on their illustrious citizen with complimentary addresses.

Just a reminder of the times in which Samuel GUYTON I and his family lived: Norwich suffered its last epidemic of Bubonic Plague in 1665-1666. The wealthy citizens removed themselves from the city for their safety. Businesses closed, leading to wide-spread unemployment, poverty, and food shortages.[34]

---

[34] "History of Norwich," Norfolk Norwich, n.d., accessed 11 Jun 2018, <http://www.norfolk-norwich.com/norwich/discovering-norwich/history-of-norwich.php>.

Generation #2

Samuel GUYTON II[35] (Samuel I, John)

Samuel GUYTON II's parents were Samuel GUYTON I (bap. 4 Apr 1647 St. Martin at Palace, Norwich, Norfolk Co., England, d. AFT 1724) and Elizabeth UNKNOWN (d. AFT 1724). Samuel II was baptized 10 Jan 1668 at St. George's Tombland,[36] Norwich, Norfolk Co., England and was buried on 15 Jan 1728, most likely in a cemetery of one of the churches in Norwich to which he had family ties. He married Margaret UNDERWOOD on 22 Dec 1691 at St. Gregory's Church, Norwich, just west of the city center.[37] The marriage took place just four years after Samuel GUYTON I acquired the extensive property in Trowse, in the southeast of modern Norwich, outside the old city walls.[38] Margaret was buried 16 Jan 1730/1731, again in an unknown cemetery.

Figure 7 contains the church record of the marriage of Samuel GUYTON II and Margaret UNDERWOOD.

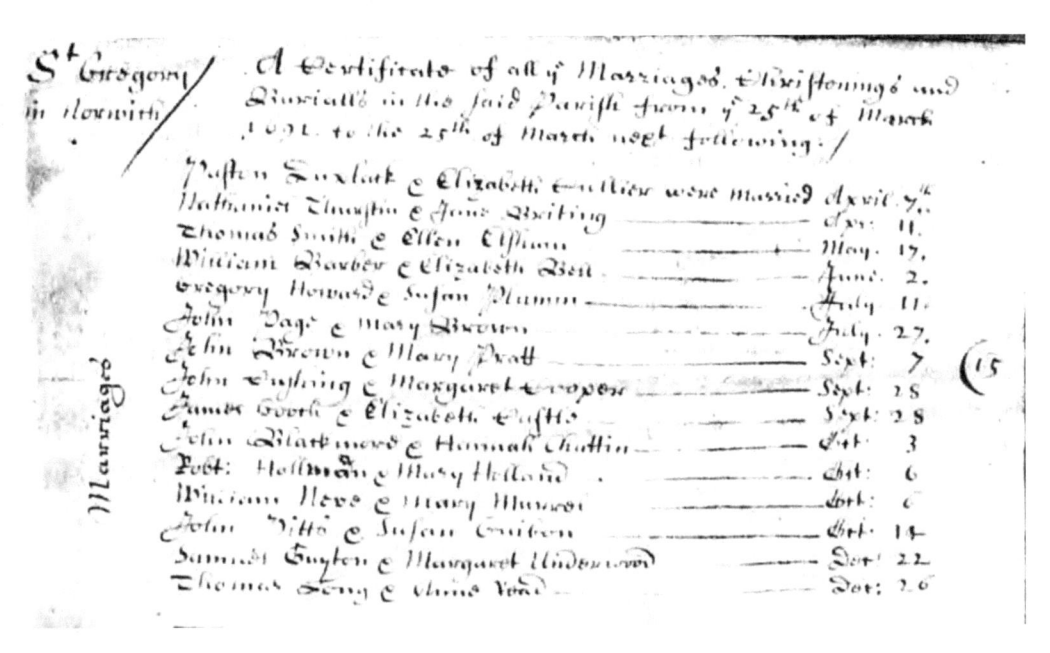

Figure 7 Record of Marriage for Samuel GUYTON II and Margaret UNDERWOOD

---

[35] Much of this section is based on Barnes, Robert William. *Colonial Families of Maryland: Bound and Determined to Succeed*. Baltimore, MD: Clearfield, c2007.

[36] "England Births and Christenings, 1538-1975," digital image s.v. "Samuell Gytton," (baptized 10 Jan 1668), *FamilySearch.org*.

[37] "Norfolk, England, Transcripts of Church of England Baptism, Marriage and Burial Registers, 1600-1935," digital image s.v. "Samuel Guyton," (1668-Unknown), *Ancestry.com*.

[38] Per David F. GUYTON, genealogist of the Guyton family, in a personal communication with the author, 16 January 2021.

David F. GUYTON continues his story of the Norwich Guytons and their property in Trowse:[39]

> Shortly after the marriage of Samuel GUYTON junior [Samuel GUYTON II] and Margaret UNDERWOOD on 22 December 1691, Samuel GUYTON senior [Samuel GUYTON I] and his wife, Elizabeth, entered into an agreement with Margaret UNDERWOOD's mother, a widow also named Margaret UNDERWOOD, and enrolled a deed on 24 November 1692 to grant their property at Trowse to their son and daughter-in-law as part of a marriage settlement. By then Samuel Guyton junior was aged 23, had served his apprenticeship as a Sherman [shearer of woolen garments], and was working as a hot presser in the woollen textile industry in Norwich. The transfer of the property seems to be an unusually generous settlement and no evidence has been found to indicate that Samuel Guyton junior took up residence at the property or continued his father's trade as a market gardener.
>
> The family evidently maintained their residence in the parish of St Martin at Palace and all of the eleven children of Samuel GUYTON junior [Samuel GUYTON II] and his wife, Margaret, were baptised at St Martin at Palace between 1695 and 1711 including the two brothers, John GUYTON [John GUYTON I, in this book] and Benjamin GUYTON [Benjamin GUYTON I], who were baptised on 19 February 1696/1697 and 4 February 1700/01, respectively, and who later emigrated to America. Samuel GUYTON senior and his wife, Elizabeth, were also still living in the parish as Samuel GUYTON senior and Samuel GUYTON junior are both listed as paying window tax[40] in the parish in 1710/11 with Samuel GUYTON junior acting as parish tax collector. It is apparent from later property deeds that Samuel GUYTON senior and his wife, Elizabeth, owned several properties in the parish along Worlds End Lane immediately adjacent to the northern side of the church and stretching back to the River Wensum. Samuel and Elizabeth GUYTON sold these properties in 1724 proving, incidentally, that they were still alive then despite some family histories indicating that they were the Elizabeth GUYTON and Samuel GUYTON who were buried at St Martin at Palace on 30 January 1696/97 and 1 February 1696/97, respectively. It seems more likely that these were infant deaths of children of Samuel GUYTON junior and his wife, Margaret, which might explain the gap between their marriage in 1691 and the baptism of their oldest surviving child, Margaret GUYTON, on 18 October 1695.

Samuel GUYTON II and Margaret UNDERWOOD had eleven known children:

i   Margaret GUYTON (bap. 18 Oct 1695 St. Martin at Palace Church, Norwich, Norfolk Co., England).[41]
ii   John GUYTON I (bap. 19 Feb 1696/7 St. Martin at Palace Church, Norwich).[42] He immigrated to America by 1727 and had a will proved in Harford County, Maryland dated 17 Nov 1782.[43] See Generation #3.

---

[39] Per David F. GUYTON, genealogist of the Guyton family, in a personal communication with the author, 16 January 2021

[40] Glass windows were expensive items during this era. Taxpayers paid a progressive tax based on the number of glass windows their dwellings contained.

[41] "England, Births and Christenings, 1538-1975," digital image s.v. "Margrett Gyton," (baptized 18 Oct 1695), *Ancestry.com*.

[42] "England, Select Births and Christenings, 1538-1975," digital image s.v. "Jn. Gyton," (baptized 19 Feb 1696), *Ancestry.com*.

[43] Barnes, Robert William. *British Roots of Maryland Families*. Baltimore, MD: Genealogical Publishing Co., 2002.

iii		Samuel GUYTON III (b. ABT 1698 St. Martin at Palace Church, Norwich). He was buried on 13 Mar 1785 at St. Martin at Palace.[44]
iv		Lydie (or Lydia) GUYTON (bap. 24 Sep 1699 St. Martin at Palace Church).[45]
v		Elizabeth GUYTON (bap. 4 Feb 1700 St. Martin at Palace Church,[46] bur. 3 Mar 1700 St. Martin at Oak Church, Norwich[47]).
vi		Benjamin GUYTON I (bap. 4 Feb 1701 at St. Martin at Palace Church,[48] d. ABT Apr 1774, Baltimore Co., MD). He immigrated to America in 1719 as an indentured servant[49] and married (second wife) Catherine ADAMS on 26 Sep 1765.[50] His will was proven BEF 7 Jul 1776.[51]
vii		A second Elizabeth GUYTON was born to the couple (bap. 27 Oct 1703 St. Martin at Palace Church,[52] bur. 27 Nov 1783 at St. Martin at Palace Church[53]). She married Benjamin SMITH on 6 Jun 1734 at St. Michael at Coslany Church in Norwich, which is located within the ancient walls of Norwich.[54]
viii		Joseph GUYTON (bap. 17 Aug 1705 St. Martin at Oak Church,[55] bur. 15 May 1757 St. Martin at Palace[56]). He married Ann SMITH on 29 Oct 1727 at St. Laurence's Church in Norwich.[57]
ix		Nathaniel GUYTON (bap. 1 Jul 1707 St. Martin at Palace Church,[58] bur. 30 Aug 1720 at St. Martin at Oak Church in Norwich[59]).
x		William GUYTON (bap. 26 Mar 1709 St. Martin at Palace Church,[60] bur. 26 Mar 1714[61]).
xi		Epaphras GUYTON (bap. 8 Feb 1710 St. Martin at Palace Church,[62] bur. 25 Mar 1712 at St. Martin at Oak in Norwich[63]).

---

[44] "Norfolk, England, Church of England Baptism, Marriages, and Burials, 1535-1812," digital image s.v. "Samuel Guyton," (burial 13 May 1785), *Ancestry.com*.

[45] "Norfolk, England, Church of England Baptism, Marriages, and Burials, 1535-1812," digital image s.v. "Lydia Gyton," (baptism 24 Sep 1699), *Ancestry.com*.

[46] "Norfolk, England, Church of England Baptism, Marriages, and Burials, 1535-1812," digital image s.v. "Elizabeth Gyton," (baptism 4 Feb 1700), *Ancestry.com*.

[47] "England, Select Deaths and Burials, 1538-1991," s.v. "Elizabeth Gyton," (burial 3 Mar 1700), *Ancestry.com*.

[48] "Norfolk, England, Church of England Baptism, Marriages, and Burials, 1535-1812," digital image s.v. "Benjamin Gyton," (baptism 4 Feb 1701), *Ancestry.com*.

[49] "A List of Emigrants from England to America, 1682-1692, 1718-1759" transcribed digital image s.v. "Benjamin Guyton," (departure date 17 Jul 1719), *Ancestry.com*.

[50] "Maryland Marriages, 1655 to 1850," s.v. "Benjamin Guyton," (marriage 26 Sep 1765), *Ancestry.com*.

[51] "Baltimore County Families, 1659-1759," digital image s.v. "Benjamin Guyton," (will 17 Apr 1774-7 Jul 1776), *Ancestry.com*.

[52] "Norfolk, England, Church of England Baptism, Marriages, and Burials, 1535-1812," digital image s.v. "Elizabeth Gyton," (baptism 27 Oct 1703), *Ancestry.com*.

[53] "England, Select Deaths and Burials, 1538-1991," s.v. "Elizabeth Guyton Smith," (burial 27 Nov 1783), *Ancestry.com*.

[54] *"England, Select Marriages, 1538–1973,"* s.v. "Elizabeth Guyton," (marriage 6 Jun 1734), *Ancestry.com*.

[55] "England, Select Births and Christenings, 1538-1975," s.v. "Joseph Gyton," (baptism 17 Aug 1705), *Ancestry.com*.

[56] "England, Select Deaths and Burials, 1538-1991," s.v. "Joseph Gayton," (burial 15 May 1757), *Ancestry.com*.

[57] "Norfolk, England, Church of England Baptism, Marriages, and Burials, 1535-1812," digital image s.v. "Joseph Guyton," (marriage 29 Oct 1727), *Ancestry.com*.

[58] "England, Select Births and Christenings, 1538-1975," s.v. "Nath Gyton," (baptism 1 Jul 1707), *Ancestry.com*.

[59] "England, Select Deaths and Burials, 1538-1991," s.v. "Nathaniel Gyton," (burial 30 Aug 1720), *Ancestry.com*.

[60] "Norfolk, England, Church of England Baptism, Marriages, and Burials, 1535-1812," digital image s.v. "William Gyton," (baptism 26 Mar 1709) *Ancestry.com* (13 May 2020).

[61] "Norfolk, England, Bishop and Archdeacon Transcripts of Parish Registers, 1600-1935," digital image s.v. "William Guyton," (burial 26 Feb 1714), *Ancestry.com*.

[62] "Norfolk, England, Church of England Baptism, Marriages, and Burials, 1535-1812," digital image s.v. "Epaphray Gyton," (baptism 8 Feb 1710), *Ancestry.com*.

[63] "England, Select Deaths and Burials, 1538-1991," s.v. Epahray Gyton," (burial 25 Mar 1712), *Ancestry.com*.

Little is known about the life of Samuel GUYTON II. He did, however, live in quieter times than his father. By 1688 when Samuel II was twenty, the Glorious Revolution resulted in the removal of King James II (the last Catholic king of England), who fled England.[64] A special Parliament (Convention Parliament) met during a brief period when there was no monarch to outline the rights of Parliament and individuals, and to set the limits to rights of the monarch.[65] It approved the Bill of Rights in 1689. Then Parliament offered a joint monarchy to William, Prince of Orange (the Dutch stadtholder), and his wife Mary (daughter of King James II, the unseated king).[66]

During Samuel GUYTON II's lifetime, Norwich reached a population of around 28,000. All of today's principal streets within the ancient walls were constructed by the beginning of the 1700s.[67] The textile industry employed most of the working-class citizens and high demand throughout Europe for these products resulted in good wages. Samuel GUYTON II was likely in the textile trades. His sons, Samuel GUYTON III and Joseph GUYTON, were a hot presser and a worsted weaver/twisterer, respectively, in 1734.[68] Another son, John GUYTON I, completed an apprenticeship as a dyer.[69] According to immigration records, son Benjamin GUYTON I was a hot presser.[70]

Popular and colorful designs, stimulated by the Flemish immigrants combined with the use of worsted wool (a high-quality wool) by itself and later interwoven with silk from Italy, led to Norwich's dominance in textiles in the 17th century. The East India Company introduced colorful cotton fabrics (muslins and calicos) from Bengal at cheaper prices than Norwich could compel in wool. Norwich tried to secure a ban from Parliament against Indian cottons and sought monopoly rights to reduce competition. The East India Company lobbied Parliament into a compromise. Cottons could continue to be imported from India if they were plain and unprinted but forbade the importing or wearing of printed calico fabric. Women's fashion did not always align with the interests of business. In 1719 crowds rioted in Norwich, attacked women wearing imported cloth, ripping their clothes off.[71] Samuel GUYTON II may have witnessed the riots or may have even taken part in them. His livelihood was at stake as were the livelihoods of some of his sons.

---

[64] Bayne, A.D., *A Comprehensive History of Norwich*. London: Jarrod and Sons, 1869, p. 212. Made available 2 Jan 2014 (accessed 14 Jun 2018) by Project Gutenberg <http://www.gutenberg.org/files/44568/44568-h/44568-h.htm#page212>.
[65] "Bill of Rights 1689," *Wikipedia*, n.d.
[66] "Glorious Revolution," *Wikipedia*, n.d.
[67] Bayne, A.D., *A Comprehensive History of Norwich*. London: Jarrod and Sons, 1869, p. 268. Made available 2 Jan 2014 (accessed 14 Jun 2018) by Project Gutenberg <http://www.gutenberg.org/files/44568/44568-h/44568-h.htm#page268>.
[68] "UK, Poll Books and Electoral Registers, 1538-1893," digital image s.v. "Joseph Guyton," and "Samuel Guyton" (poll tax 1734), *Ancestry.com*.
[69] "UK, Register of Duties Paid for Apprentices' Indentures, 1710-1811," s.v. "Amey Dye," (payment date 12 Feb 1718), *Ancestry.com*.
[70] "U.S. and Canada, Passenger and Immigration Lists Index, 1500s-1900s," s.v. "Benjamin Guyton," (immigration 1719), *Ancestry.com*.
[71] Smith, Chloe Wigston. "'Callico Madams': Servants, Consumption, and the Calico Crisis." *Eighteenth-Century Life*, v. 31, no. 2 (March 20, 2007), p. 33.

Generation #3

Two of Samuel GUYTON II's children immigrated to the British Colonies in the early 1700s – John GUYTON I and Benjamin GUYTON I. John GUYTON I is the ancestor of Aaron Whitaker GUYTON and is, thus, the focus of this book.

John GUYTON I (Samuel II, Samuel I, John)

John's parents were Samuel GUYTON II (bap. 10 Jan 1668, bur. 15 Jan 1728) and Margaret UNDERWOOD (b. Unknown, bur. 16 Jan 1730/1731).[72] He was baptized on 19 Feb 1696/7 at St. Martin at Palace Church in Norwich, Norfolk, England.[73] He immigrated to British America by 1727, joining his brother, Benjamin I, who arrived in 1719.[74] John married Mary UNKNOWN before 1726 in Maryland when their son, Samuel, was born. Mary's birth date is unknown; we know she died after 1785 when she was documented selling land she inherited from John I to two of their sons.[75] Different ancestry trees in *Ancestry.com* suggest Mary's name is alternately Mary UNDERHILL or Mary WHITAKER. The two women have completely different ancestries. A Mary UNDERHILL is named as one of John GUYTON I's daughters in his will. Many later male children carried the Whitaker name. John I and Mary's sons, Samuel and Joseph I, married into the WHITAKER family. John I died in 1782 in Harford Co., Maryland. His will, dated 17 Nov 1782, was proven on 25 Mar 1783.[76] John I and Mary may be buried in St. James' Episcopal Church Cemetery, part of My Lady's Manor National Historic Site. There are no headstones to confirm the burial, however.

John GUYTON I and Mary UNKNOWN had at least ten children. John GUYTON II's family Bible contained the birth dates of his siblings, the children of John GUYTON I and Mary:[77]

i   Samuel GUYTON (b. 6 Nov 1727,[78] d. Unknown).
ii Joseph GUYTON I (b. 17 Sep 1732, MD,[79] d. 13 Jul 1818, Cherokee Co., SC[80]). He was buried in the Guyton Cemetery in Gaffney, Cherokee Co., SC. He married Hannah Lyon WHITAKER (b. 26 Mar 1729, Baltimore Co.,

---

[72] Information about John GUYTON I is heavily drawn from Barnes, Robert William. *Colonial Families of Maryland: Bound and Determined to Succeed*. Baltimore, MD: Clearfield, 2007.
[73] "England, Select Births and Christenings, 1538-1975," digital image s.v. "Jn. Gyton," (baptized 19 Feb 1696), *Ancestry.com*.
[74] John GUYTON I's first child, Samuel, was born in Baltimore County, Maryland in 1727. Guyton Rees, Helen. *Guytons Galore: From French Huguenots to Oregon Pioneers*. Portland, OR: Binford & Mort, 1986. His brother, Benjamin, immigrated to British America in 1719 as an indenture servant. "A List of Emigrants from England to America, 1682-1692, 1718-1759" transcribed digital image s.v. "Benjamin Guyton," (departure date 17 Jul 1719), *Ancestry.com*.
[75] Guyton Rees, Helen. *Guytons Galore: From French Huguenots to Oregon Pioneers*. Portland, OR: Binford & Mort, 1986.
[76] *Ibid.* p. 21.
[77] *Ibid.* pp. 30-31.
[78] *Ibid.* p. 19.
[79] *Ibid.* p. 20.
[80] "FindaGrave Index, 1700s-Current," digital image s.v. "Joseph Guyton," (death 13 Jul 1818, Memorial #33147653), *Ancestry.com*.

	MD,[81] d. 1812, Cherokee Co., SC, buried in Guyton Cemetery[82]) on 12 Dec 1754 at St. John's Gunpowder Parish Church, Baltimore Co., MD.[83] This book is devoted to Joseph's family and their descendants.
iii	Nathaniel GUYTON (b. 29 March 1735, MD,[84] d. 1 Oct 1810, Union, Union District, SC[85]).
iv	Sarah GUYTON (b. 3 Jan 1737, MD,[86] d. AFT 1782, when she was named in her father's will[87]). Sarah carried her maiden name in her father's will, suggesting she never married.
v	Abraham GUYTON (b. 8 May 1740, MD,[88] d. BEF 12 Jun 1816) m. Nancy (Ann) UNKNOWN. He wrote his will on 19 June 1812 and his executor filed it on 12 June 1816.[89]
vi	Isaac GUYTON (b. 19 Aug 1742, MD,[90] d. Unknown).
vii	Jacob GUYTON (b. 11 Nov 1744, MD,[91] d. Unknown).
viii	Mary GUYTON (b. 4 May 1747, MD,[92] d. Unknown).
ix	John GUYTON II (b. 1 Sep 1750,[93] d. Unknown, Harford Co., MD, buried in St. James' Episcopal Church Cemetery also known as Manor Chapel) m. Frances UNKNOWN (b. 8 May 1764, d. 17 May 1804).[94] Helen GUYTON REES' book focuses on this branch of the Guyton family.
x	Joshua GUYTON (b. 18 Aug 1757, MD,[95] d. Unknown) m. Sarah MITCHELL on 12 Jan 1781.[96]

We know from the birth records in Norwich, Norfolk Co., England that John I was baptized in St. Martin at Palace Church on 19 Feb 1696.[97] We next see John I in Norwich when he completed an apprenticeship as a dyer in the textile industry. His master (or mistress in this case) was Amey DYE. He completed his apprenticeship when he was 22 years old and paid the taxes due for the privilege of learning on 16 August 1718. Figure 8 is an image of a document recording the taxes collected from

---

[81] "Family Data Collection – Births," s.v. "Hannah Lyon Whitaker," (birth 16 Mar 1729), *Ancestry.com*.

[82] "FindaGrave Index, 1700s-Current," digital image s.v. "Hannah Whitaker Guyton," (death 1812, Memorial #33147887), *Ancestry.com*.

[83] Guyton Rees, Helen. *Guytons Galore: From French Huguenots to Oregon Pioneers*. Portland, OR: Binford & Mort, 1986, p. 20.

[84] *Ibid*.

[85] "FindaGrave Index, 1700s-Current," s.v. "Nathaniel Guyton," (death 1 Oct 1810, Memorial # 163938293), *Ancestry.com*.

[86] Guyton Rees, Helen. *Guytons Galore: From French Huguenots to Oregon Pioneers*. Portland, OR: Binford & Mort, 1986, p. 20.

[87] Guyton, David F., "Wills and Administration: John Guyton in Harford Co., MD," *Guyton Ancestry*, n.d. (accessed 28 May 2020), <http://guyton.co.uk/wp-content/uploads/America/Wills/jg1697_Will.pdf>.

[88] Guyton Rees, Helen. *Guytons Galore: From French Huguenots to Oregon Pioneers*. Portland, OR: Binford & Mort, 1986, p. 20.

[89] Guyton, David F., "Wills and Administration: Abraham Guyton in Pittsburgh, Allegheny Co., PA," Guyton Ancestry, n.d. (accessed 28 May 2020) < http://guyton.co.uk/wp-content/uploads/America/Wills/ag1740_Will.pdf>. Abraham's wife, Ann, was one of the executors of his will.

[90] Guyton Rees, Helen. *Guytons Galore: From French Huguenots to Oregon Pioneers*. Portland, OR: Binford & Mort, 1986, p. 20.

[91] *Ibid*.

[92] *Ibid*.

[93] *Ibid*.

[94] Guyton Rees, Helen. *Guytons Galore: From French Huguenots to Oregon Pioneers*. Portland, OR: Binford & Mort, 1986, p. 39.

[95] *Guyton Rees, Helen. Guytons Galore: From French Huguenots to Oregon Pioneers. Portland, OR: Binford & Mort, 1986, p. 20.*

[96] "Maryland Marriages: 1655-1850," s.v. "Joshua Guyton," (married 12 Jan 1781), *Ancestry.com*.

[97] "England, Select Births and Christenings, 1538-1975," digital image s.v. "Jn. Gyton," (baptized 19 Feb 1696), *Ancestry.com*.

John's apprenticeship. Amey DYE'S name is in the left column of names and John I, son of Samuel II, is in the right column of names.

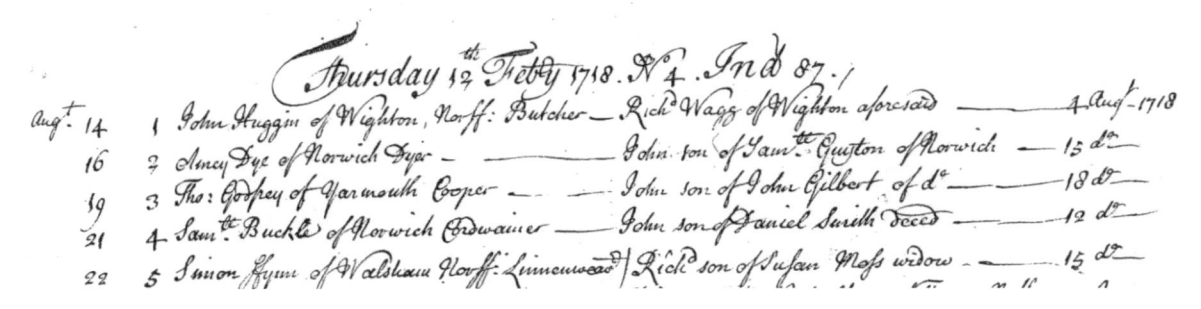

Figure 8 Completion of John GUYTON I's Apprenticeship as a Dyer

We cannot be sure exactly when John GUYTON I came to British America, but it was between 1718 when he completed his apprenticeship and 1727 when his first child, Samuel, was born in Maryland. His brother, Benjamin I, came to Maryland in 1719/1720 as an indentured servant (a 5-year commitment). Perhaps Benjamin I worked off his indenture and then invited John to join him. Or John I may also have come as a servant, but we have no record of it. Nearly all the British immigrants in the colonial period of Maryland arrived as either indentured servants or convicts.[98] Maryland received more indentured servants than any other colony. In 1727 John I and Benjamin I, respectively, were 31 and 25 years old.

Benjamin I and John I probably had little interaction with large groups of American Indians because the Eastern MARYLAND tribes had been pushed out by colonists before either brother arrived in British America. What interaction they may have had would involve trade. Combatants in the French and Indian War, unofficially started by George WASHINGTON in 1754, carried on the war outside of the eastern developed portions of Maryland. Settlers living in Indian territories in today's western Maryland fled back east to the safety of towns, especially Baltimore. The Guyton brothers experienced the influx of people which may have increased the market for their farm goods.

John I's life (1696/7-1782/3) overlapped that of George WASHINGTON (1732-1799) and George's father, Augustine WASHINGTON, Sr. (1694-1743). John I lived a very long life of around 86 years. On today's roads, George WASHINGTON and John I are buried about 65 miles apart.[99] The lives of the Washingtons and the Guytons were hardly similar but they did live through some of the same political and economic events. In 1718 the Virginia Colony fought the Pirates of the Caribbean and killed Blackbeard.[100] In 1720 enslaved people became the majority of the population in South Carolina and around 1730 the majority of enslaved people in Chesapeake, Virginia were born in the Americas. Beginning in the 1720s, a string of laws throughout the South passed dealing with issues of slavery. The Plantation Act of 1740 passed Parliament making it easier for Protestants living in the American Colonies for seven years to become naturalized citizens of the Kingdom of Great Britain. The purpose of the Act

---

[98] "Maryland Emigration and Immigration," Research Wiki, *FamilySearch.org*, n.d., accessed 25 Jun 2018, <https://www.familysearch.org/wiki/en/Maryland_Emigration_and_Immigration>.
[99] *DistanceFromTo: Distance between Cities and Places*, s.v. "Monkton, MD to Mt. Vernon, VA," accessed 15 Jun 2018, <https://www.distancefromto.net/>.
[100] "Timeline of Colonial America," *Wikipedia*, n.d., accessed 15 Jun 2018, <https://en.wikipedia.org/wiki/Timeline_of_Colonial_America>.

was to encourage immigration to British America and to make the naturalization process within the Colonies more workable. The French and Indian War raged from 1754 to 1763. The British Parliament passed the Stamp Act in 1765 to help pay the costs of the French and Indian War but the resistance of the colonists ultimately led to the Declaration of Independence in 1776 and the Revolutionary War (1776-1783). Great Britain formally recognized American independence in 1783, a year after John GUYTON I died.

According to Helen GUYTON REES, John GUYTON I appeared in a list of "taxables" in Upper Hundred Cliffs, located in Calvert Co., MD. She does not say when the list was taken. The Upper Hundred Cliffs are located on a peninsula 100 miles south of Baltimore. There is a Calvert Cliffs State Park in the vicinity of John's place.

Figure 9 highlights the locations of Calvert, Baltimore, and Harford Counties, Maryland where John I and Benjamin I made their homes.

According to a Calvert County website, Captain John SMITH sailed past the cliffs of Calvert while exploring the Chesapeake Bay in 1608. He wrote: "The Western Shore, by which we sailed, we found well-watered, but very mountainous and barren, the valleys were fertile, but extremely thick of small woods, as well as trees, and much frequented with wolves, bears, deer and other wild beasts. The streams were crystal clear and full of fish."[101]

Britain's desire to expand its power and wealth first led to the colonization of Calvert County but there were not enough men to productively run the farms. Mostly single men indentured themselves to servitude in the tobacco fields for five to seven years for a promise of their freedom and fifty acres of land along with the tools, clothing, and supplies to cultivate it.

---

[101] "Founding and Early History," *Calvert County*, n.d., accessed 9 Apr 2020, <https://choosecalvert.com/195/History>.

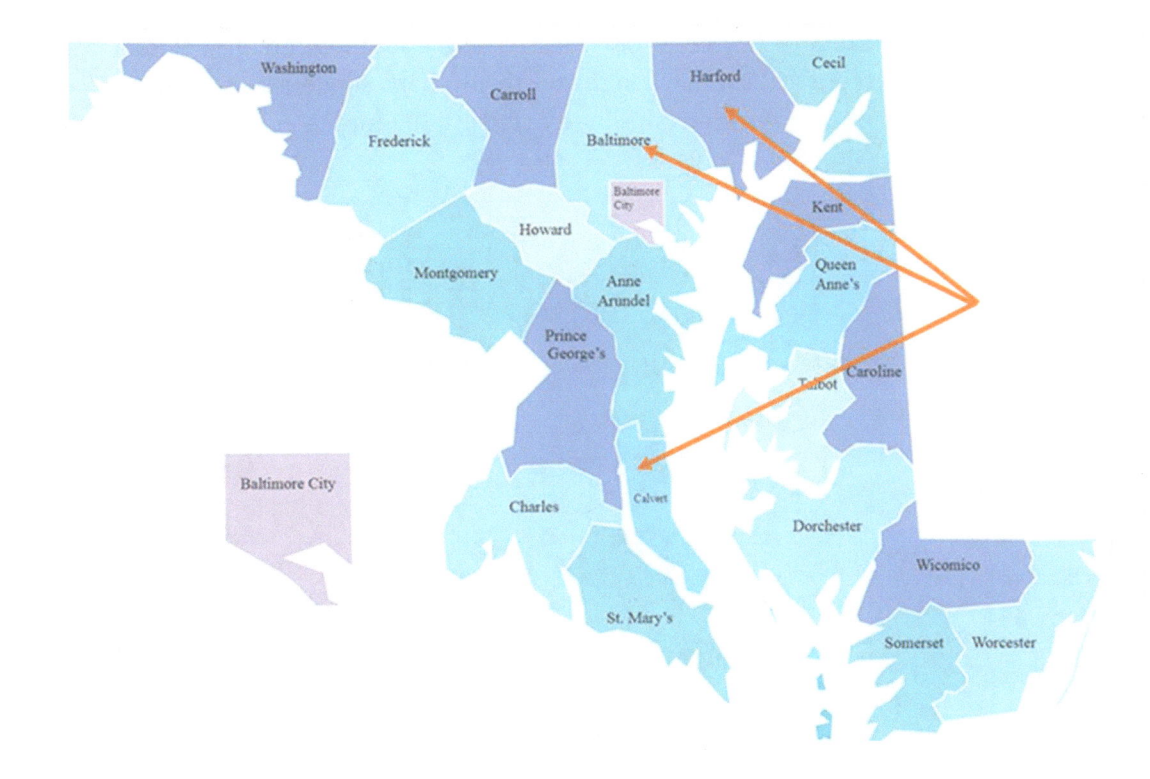

Figure 9 Calvert, Baltimore, and Harford Counties, Maryland[102]

Also colonizing Maryland were Puritans and Quakers seeking to freely exercise their religions. In 1648 Governor William BERKLEY of Virginia expelled Puritans who had first started arriving there in 1611. Governor William STONE of Maryland welcomed them because of the need for more settlers. The Puritans fanned out to the Chesapeake Bay area and down into Calvert County. Quakers first arrived in Southern Maryland in 1655-56 after similarly being expelled from Virginia.[103] Little remains of the Puritans today in Calvert County and elsewhere. Their principal settlement, Providence, returned to its rural roots within five years after the Puritan migration as settlers moved outward to establish their own plantations. In Calvert County, the Puritans were unable to establish any permanent churches and without churches, they had no ministers. Eventually most turned to the Church of England or became Quakers.

Figure 10 illustrates Robinson's Rest, where Benjamin I and John I lived in the 1740s.[104] In 1745 John I and Benjamin I were 49 and 43, respectively. Calvertown at the bottom center of the map was the

---

[102] Map of Present-Day Counties of Maryland. *Maryland Courts: Directory*, Maryland Judiciary, n.d. Web. (c. 2020).
[103] Downing, Cori Sedwick, "What's in a Name: European Roots of Colonial Calvert County Families," *Calvert County Historical Society (blog)*, Jan 2008, accessed 2 Oct 2009, <https://calverthistory.wordpress.com/2009/10/02/whats-in-a-name/>. "History of Quakers in Southern Maryland," *Patuxent Friends Monthly Meeting: Religious Society of Friends,* n.d., accessed 9 Apr 2020, <https://www.patuxentfriends.org/history.htm>. Downing, Cori Sedwick, "Our Puritan Ancestors," *Calvert County Historical Society (blog)*, Mar 2008, accessed 1 Dec 2009, <https://calverthistory.wordpress.com/2009/12/01/our-puritan-ancestors/>
[104] Stein, Charles Francis. "Map of Calvert County in the Colonial Era." *A History of Calvert County, MD*, 3rd ed. Self-published, 1977, p. 224. Adapted by Guyton, David F. "Robinson's Rest," *Guyton Ancestry: Places and Maps,* n.d.,

county seat at the time. A Quaker meeting house was located on the southeastern part of Robinson's Rest with Sunderland All Saints' Episcopal Church in the northwest part. Sunderland's, originally a log structure, is one of the thirty original Anglican parishes created in 1692 for the Province of Maryland.[105]

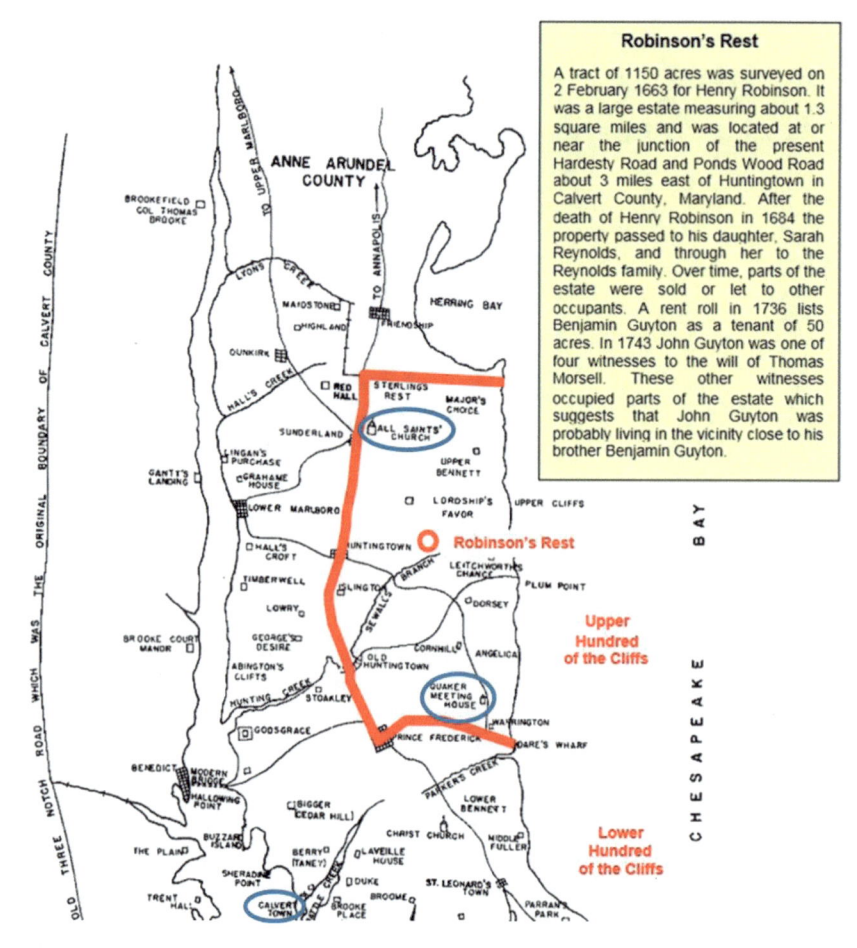

Figure 10 Robinson's Rest, Home of Benjamin I and John GUYON I in 1740s

Robinson's Rest

A tract of 1150 acres was surveyed on 2 February 1663 for Henry Robinson. It was a large estate measuring about 1.3 square miles and was located at or near the junction of the present Hardesty Road and Ponds Wood Road about 3 miles east of Huntingtown in Calvert County, Maryland. After the death of Henry Robinson in 1684 the property passed to his daughter, Sarah Reynolds, and through her to the Reynolds family. Over time, parts of the estate were sold or let to other occupants. A rent roll in 1736 lists Benjamin Guyton as a tenant of 50 acres. In 1743 John Guyton was one of four witnesses to the will of Thomas Morsell. These other witnesses occupied parts of the estate which suggests that John Guyton was probably living in the vicinity close to his brother Benjamin Guyton.

John I and his brother, Benjamin I, moved from Calvert County to Baltimore County in the 1750s and lived near each other.[106] Maryland split Baltimore County, however, in 1774 to create Harford County, resulting in the brothers' living in different counties.

Figure 11 indicates the places where John GUYTON I and Benjamin GUYTON I and their children lived in Baltimore County.[107] One of the highlighted plots is Guyton's Prospect. Mary GUYTON, John I's widow, sold a property in 1785 (referred to as Prospect) to their sons, John GUYTON II and Joshua

---

accessed 29 May 2020, <http://guyton.co.uk/wp-content/uploads/America/Places/Robinson.pdf> Adapted by Dorla Coleman Evans.
[105] "All Saint's Church Sunderland, Maryland," *Wikipedia,* n.d., accessed 4 Apr 2020, <https://en.wikipedia.org/wiki/All_Saints_Church_(Sunderland,_Maryland)>.
[106] Guyton Rees, Helen. *Guytons Galore: From French Huguenots to Oregon Pioneers*. Portland, OR: Binford & Mort, 1986.
[107] Guyton, David F. "Guyton Places in Baltimore County," *Guyton Ancestry: Places and Maps,* n.d., accessed 29 May 2020, <http://guyton.co.uk/wp-content/uploads/America/Places/Gunpowder.pdf>.

GUYTON, in consideration of ten pounds. It measured 135 acres.[108] A surveyor plotted and certified 65-acres of unpatented land (lease) called Guyton's Prospect, completed for Samuel GUYTON (likely John I's son) on 2 Aug 1749.[109] See Figure 12. A survey for an unpatented land certificate (lease) of a 47-acre tract called Guyton's Addition also was conducted for Samuel on 9 Jul 1751.[110]

Both of these properties were part of Lord Baltimore's extensive property in Maryland, making Samuel a tenant. It is not clear on which manor Samuel's leases lay. Based on the boundaries of Gunpowder Manor in Figure 11, the land did not lie there. Nor did it lie in My Lady's Manor, although there are marriage and baptism records for our Guyton ancestors at St. James' Episcopal Church on My Lady's Manor. So when did John I purchase the property? Is Prospect actually a combination of Guyton's Prospect (65 acres) and Guyton's Addition (47 acres)? Lord Baltimore sold off pieces of the property over time but the Maryland Alien Property Commission seized Loyalists' properties during the Revolutionary War. Lord Baltimore's property was resurveyed after the war and put up for public auction, which was conducted 22 Oct 1782. John GUYTON I wrote his will on 17 Nov 1782, only a month after the auction. John GUYTON I must have purchased the land between 1751 and Nov 1782.

The following website allows the user to view the various colonial landholdings of Harford County in Google Earth, including the two properties surveyed for Samuel GUYTON: *map-maker.org/Harford/Harford-leases.kml*. It is not very easy to find specific properties but when you do find them, they are interesting to see superimposed on the land.

---

[108] Signed on 23 Sep 1785 including the mark of Mary Guyton and received and recorded at Harford County Courthouse on 16 Nov 1786. Guyton Rees, Helen. *Guytons Galore: From French Huguenots to Oregon Pioneers*. Portland, OR: Binford & Mort, 1986, p. 21.

[109] Guyton's Prospect Unpatented Land Survey, 10 Nov 1749, for Samuel Guyton, Certificate 653, Baltimore County Circuit Court, Baltimore, Maryland. Maryland State Archives, MSA S1213-666.

[110] Guyton's Addition Unpatented Land Survey, 14 Apr 1752, for Samuel Guyton, Certificate 651, Baltimore County Circuit Court, Baltimore County, Mar. Maryland State Archives, MSA S1213-664.

GUYTON PLACES IN BALTIMORE COUNTY

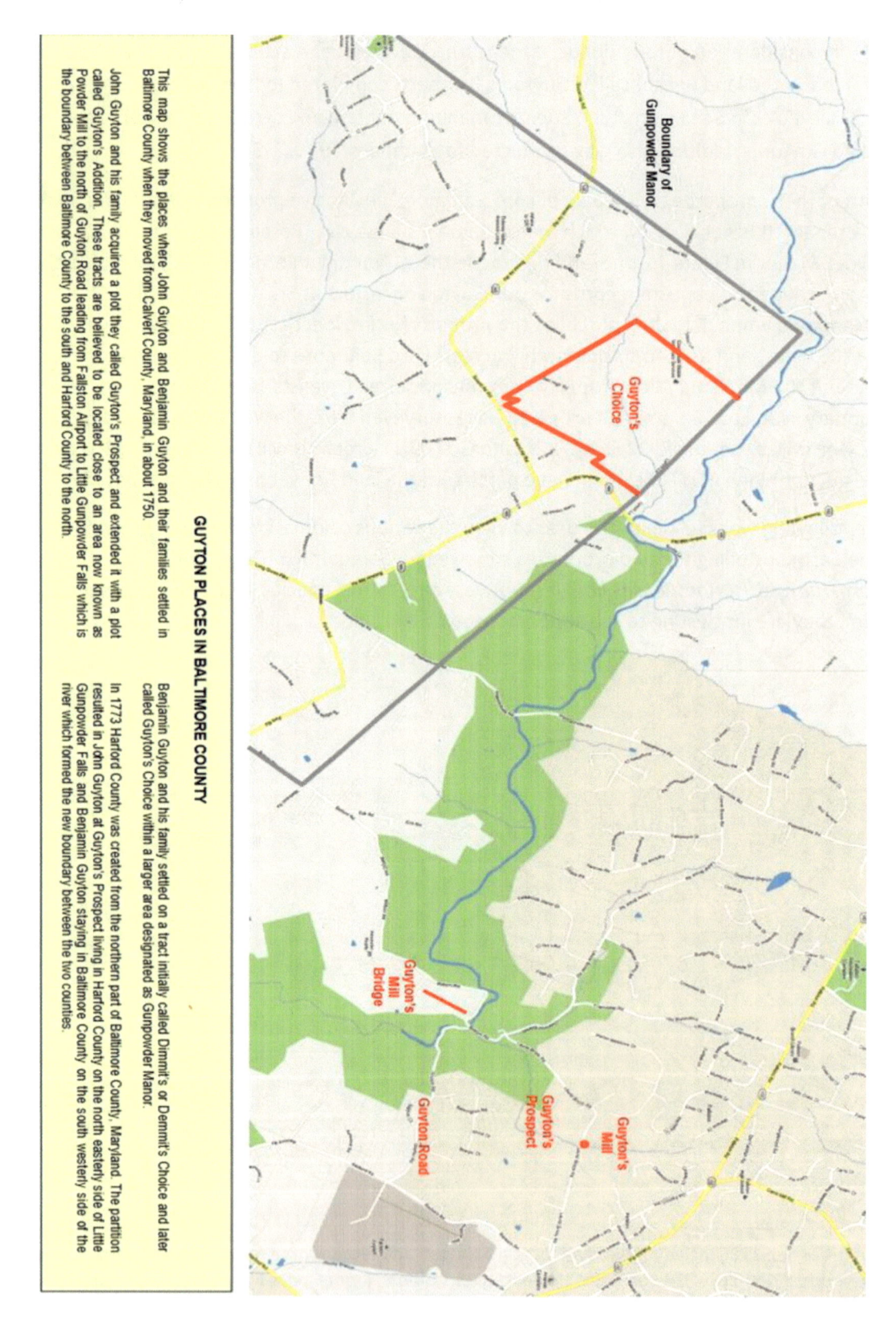

This map shows the places where John Guyton and Benjamin Guyton and their families settled in Baltimore County when they moved from Calvert County, Maryland, in about 1750.

John Guyton and his family acquired a plot they called Guyton's Prospect and extended it with a plot called Guyton's Addition. These tracts are believed to be located close to an area now known as Powder Mill to the north of Guyton Road leading from Fallston Airport to Little Gunpowder Falls which is the boundary between Baltimore County to the south and Harford County to the north.

Benjamin Guyton and his family settled on a tract initially called Dimmit's or Demmit's Choice and later called Guyton's Choice within a larger area designated as Gunpowder Manor.

In 1773 Harford County was created from the northern part of Baltimore County, Maryland. The partition resulted in John Guyton at Guyton's Prospect living in Harford County on the north easterly side of Little Gunpowder Falls and Benjamin Guyton staying in Baltimore County on the south westerly side of the river which formed the new boundary between the two counties.

Figure 11 Guyton Places in Baltimore County, David F. GUYTON

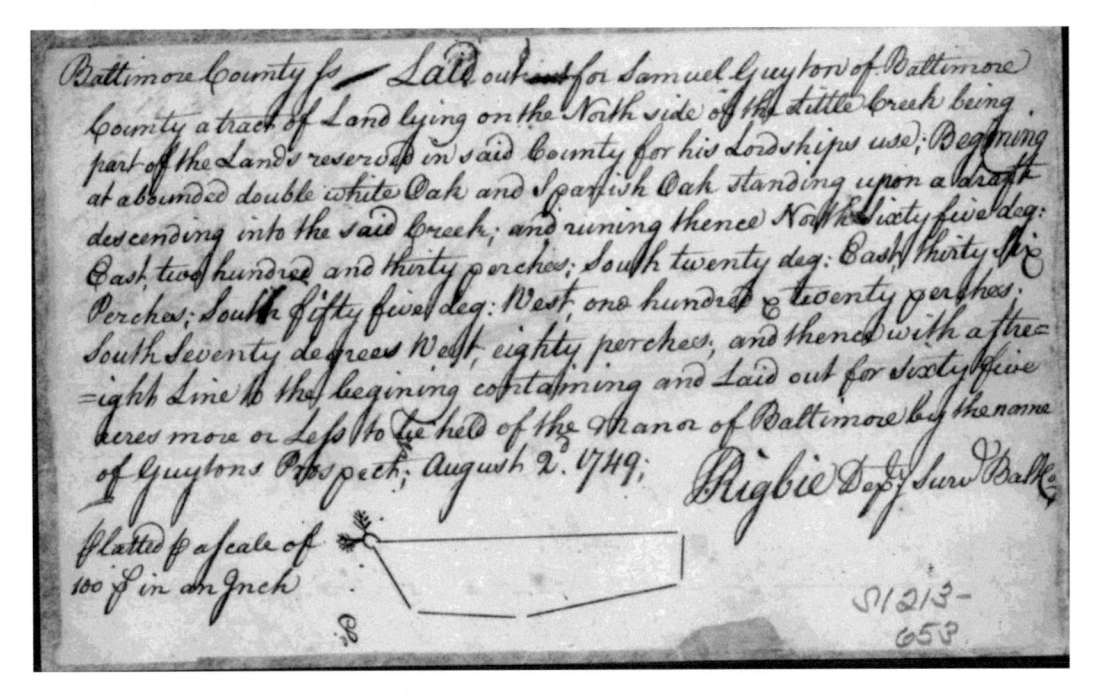

Figure 12 Survey of Guyton's Prospect for Samuel GUYTON on 2 Aug 1749

Guyton's Road still exists in the area. See Figure 13. It lies partially in Gunpowder Falls State Park. The hilly area in the park probably means at least part of the Guyton land was not good farmland. However, the steep grades on the rivers did make for large numbers of mills (primarily wheat grist mills) in the 1800s, including Dr. Benjamin A. Guyton's grist and saw mill on the falls on Bottom Road. The mill burned on 8 May 1883.[111] Note that Guyton's Road in Figure 13 ends at Bottom Road, where the bridge is visible.

When the Guytons moved to Baltimore County in the 1750s, Joppa was the county seat, a political and economic center. Joppa became the county seat in 1712. The plat of Joppa dates to 1725 and shows 41 divisions including one for the courthouse and one for St. John's Gunpowder Parish Church. Joppa imposed building restrictions requiring the owner to "build a dwelling house covering not less than four hundred square feet and to have a good brick or stone chimney. The town was soon to contain forty or fifty residences, two prisons, a courthouse, St. John's Gunpowder Parish Church, several large warehouses, wharves, inns, stores and shops."[112] Ships from Europe and the West Indies brought their cargoes of manufactured goods and received for the return trip tobacco and other products.

---

[111] "Baltimore City and County Mills," *Maryland State Archives,* n.d., accessed 24 Jun 2018, <http://msa.maryland.gov/...ricted/baltimore_county_mills.pdf>.

[112] Reynolds, J., "A Short History of Joppatowne," *Church of the Resurrection: Copley Parish, Gunpowder Hundred*, n.d., accessed 24 Jun 2018, <http://www.copleyparish.org/?page=history>. Herman, Benjamin, "At Joppa, It's Daffodils For Remembrance On the Now Empty Townsite, Flowers Still Spring Up to Recall the Once-Gay Gardens," *Baltimore Sunday Sun Magazine*, 16 Nov 1952, accessed 24 Jun 2018, <http://www.copleyparish.org/?page=history>.

Figure 13 Intersection of Guyton Road and Bottom Road in Fallston, Harford Co., MD

Baltimore Town became the new county seat in 1768, taking with it much of the political and economic vibrancy. Waterways were key to early Marylanders. Clear-cutting forests upstream along the Gunpowder River contributed to major silting of the harbor in Joppa. Joppa's town center seemed to move further and further inland as the shoreline moved outward. The loss of the harbor, outbreaks of malaria, and the loss of the county seat resulted in the town's desertion. By 1814 only four houses and the fading remains of the church were left.

Farming methods in colonial Maryland led to exhaustion of the soil. Farmers like the Guytons probably raised a single crop, tobacco, without rotating it with other crops to maintain soil fertility. By 1765 farmers turned to manure to condition the soil due to declining crop yields. Deforestation created problems with erosion resulting in sedimentation (as seen in Joppa). Farmers turned to larger farms to offset lower yields and started to abandon exhausted land in exchange for new land. Free white families began to move westward in the 1790s, particularly to the Carolinas. German farmers from Pennsylvania poured into Maryland bringing with them their knowledge of wheat farming.[113] In 1793 wheat mills sprang up as wheat replaced tobacco as the most important crop in Maryland. The elevation and the fall of the land in eastern Maryland meant there were many streams and rivers conducive to milling. Baltimore became known as a center for milling.[114]

Representatives of William and Mary (King and Queen of England) established the Church of England in Maryland. They divided the original Baltimore County into three parishes. In 1695 they had

---

[113] *Ibid.*

[114] *Foods and Food Production Encyclopedia.* Considine, Douglas M. and Considine, Glenn D., Eds. Berlin: Springer Science and Business Media, 2012, p. 2123.

built St. John's Gunpowder Parish Church in Gunpowder Hundred[115] from crude logs. After Joppa became a successful center of business, wealthy planters, merchants, and sea captains built a new St. John's Church out of brick in the center of Joppa. Joshua and Abraham GUYTON subscribed to financially support the building of the new church according to a church document dated 7 Aug 1750. John GUYTON I, who died in 1782, may be buried there. The church moved many gravestones (but not bodies) to the new St. John's Church in Kingsville, Maryland after Joppa declined.[116] And according to Helen GUYTON REES, John GUYTON I was a member of St. George's Parish Church, called Old Spesutia in Perryman, Maryland.[117]

Maryland instituted the Oath of Fidelity in 1777, requiring every free male 18 years and older to subscribe to an oath renouncing the King of England and pledging allegiance to the revolutionary government of Maryland. The government required men not taking the oath to pay triple the ordinary taxes on real and personal property for the rest of their lives. Moreover, they could not practice their commercial trades, practice the law or medicine, preach the gospel, teach in public or private schools, vote, or hold any office of profit or trust, civil or military, among other restrictions. Magistrates of each county administered the oaths before 1 Mar 1778. Exempted were men engaged in military action.[118] Needless to say, John GUYTON I (spelled GUYON in the records) is recorded in Harford County, Maryland as having taken the oath.[119]

John GUYTON I wrote his will on 17 Nov 1782, witnessed by John GRAY, John McDONALD, and William PATTERSON, and proven 25 March 1783. The will named his wife, Mary GUITTON; his sons, Samuel, Joseph I, Nathaniel, Abraham, Isaac, Jacob, John II and Joshua; his daughters, Sarah GUITON and Mary UNDERHILL; and his grandson, Thomas Mitchel GUYTON.[120] Helen GUYTON REES provided a copy of his original will.[121] My transcription, true to the spelling and grammar, is below:

In The Name of God Amen

I John Guyton of Harford County in the State of Maryland being weak of Body but of Perfect mind and Memory Thanks be to God for it Therfore but Calling unto Mind the uncertainty of This Transitory Life do for the Better Settling of my worldly Estate Make Constitute and Appoint This Present Wrighting to be my last will & Testament and Dispose of my Temporal Goods in Manner & form following

---

[115] A hundred is a measure of the amount of land necessary to sustain 100 men who could be called to action when needed.
[116] Hinkle, Daniel, W., "A History of St. John's Episcopal Church Kingsville, Maryland," July 2015 <https://images.yourfaithstory.org/wp-content/uploads/sites/37/2020/02/11194452/A-History-of-St-Johns-Kingsville-REVISED.docx.pdf> (28 May 2020).
[117] Guyton Rees, Helen. *Guytons Galore: From French Huguenots to Oregon Pioneers*. Portland, OR: Binford & Mort, 1986.
[118] "Oaths of Fidelity or Oaths of Allegiance, 1775-1778," MS 3088, *Maryland Historical Society*, n.d. <http://www.mdhs.org/findingaid/oaths-fidelity-or-oaths-allegiance-1775-1778-ms-3088> (28 Jun 2018).
[119] Brumbaugh, Gaius Marcus, *Maryland Records: Colonial, Revolutionary, County and Church from Original Sources, Vol 2*, Genealogical Publishing Co., Inc.: Baltimore, 1975, p. 242.
[120] Guyton, David F., "Wills and Administration: John Guyton in Harford Co., MD," *Guyton Ancestry*, <http://guyton.co.uk/wp-content/uploads/America/Wills/jg1697_Will.pdf> (28 May 2020).
[121] Guyton Rees, Helen. *Guytons Galore: From French Huguenots to Oregon Pioneers*. Portland, OR: Binford & Mort, 1986, p. 20.

Item to my grandson Thomas Mitchel Guyton I Give and Bequeath one Ewe and no more to him and his heirs for Ever

Item To my Daughter Sarah Guiton I Give and Bequeath Ten pounds to her and her heirs for Ever

Item I Give to my Seven Sons & one Daughter Mary Underhill That is to say Saml, Joseph, Nathaniel, Isaac, Jacob, John, Joshua one Shilling Sterling and no more to them and Their heirs for Ever

Item I also Give and Bequeath unto my well Beloved wife Mary Guiton my whole Estate Both Real & Personal During her Natural Life or Widowhood and to be at her own Disposal and I also Apoint my son Abr^{am} Guiton with her my whole and sole Executors of this my Last will and Testament In Witness Whereof I have hearunto Set my hand and Affixed my seal This 17th Day of November 1782.

Signed John Guyton (his hand)

Sign^d Seal^d & Acknowledged to be his Last will and Testament and by his Request we Asign^d and Evidences

John Gray
John McDonald
William Patterson

Benjamin GUYTON I (Samuel II, Samuel I, John)

Benjamin's parents were Samuel GUYTON II (bap. 10 Jan 1668, bur. 15 Jan 1728) and Margaret UNDERWOOD (b. Unknown, bur. 16 Jan 1730/31). Benjamin GUYTON I[122] was baptized on 4 Feb 1701 at St. Martin at Palace Church in Norwich, Norfolk County, England.[123] His first wife, by whom he had his children, is unknown. His second wife was Catherine ADAMS (married 26 Sep 1765 in Baltimore Co., MD).[124] In his will, Benjamin I named her as Katran.[125]

i   Margaret GUYTON (b. ABT 1730,[126] d. Unknown) m. Samuel FOSTER on 11 Feb 1750 in St. John's Parish, Joppa, Baltimore Co., MD.[127]

---

[122] Information about Benjamin GUYTON I is heavily drawn from: Barnes, Robert William. *Colonial Families of Maryland: Bound and Determined to Succeed*. Baltimore, Maryland: Clearfield, c2007 and from Guyton Rees, Helen. *Guytons Galore: From French Huguenots to Oregon Pioneers*. Portland, OR: Binford & Mort, 1986.
[123] "England, Select Births and Christenings, 1538-1975," digital image s.v. "Benjamin Gyton," (baptized 4 Feb 1701), *Ancestry.com*.
[124] "Maryland Marriages, 1655 to 1850," s.v. "Benjamin Guyton," (marriage 26 Sep 1765) *Ancestry.com*.
[125] Guyton, David F., "Wills and Administration: Benjamin Guyton in Baltimore Co., MD," written 14 April 1774; probated 7 July 1776, *Guyton Ancestry*, n.d., accessed 28 May 2020, <http://guyton.co.uk/wp-content/uploads/America/Wills/bg1702_Will.pdf>.
[126] "American Genealogical-Biographical Index" s.v. "Margaret Foster," (birth 1730), *Ancestry.com*.
[127] "Maryland, Compiled Marriage Index, 1634-1850," s.v. "Margaret Guiton," (marriage 11 Feb 1750), *Ancestry.com*.

ii	Benjamin GUYTON II (b. ABT 1732, d. 22 June 1801)[128] m. Amelia SCARFF (b. Unknown, d. AFT 1801 as she was named in Benjamin's will) on 13 Dec 1753.[129]
iii	Underwood GUYTON (b. ABT 1734, d. ABT 1824)[130] m. Prissilla JACKSON (b. Unknown, d. Unknown) on 12 Aug 1762 in Baltimore Co., MD.[131]
iv	Henry GUYTON (b. ABT 1737, Calvert Co., MD, d. Feb 1816, Baltimore Co., MD)[132] m. Sarah HOLT (b. Unknown, d. BEF 1816 as she is not named in Henry's will) on 17 Apr 1758 in St. John's Parish, Joppa, Baltimore Co., MD.[133]
v	Lydia GUYTON (b. Unknown, d. AFT 1774 as she is named in her father's will) m. James WATTERS on 13 Mar 1760 in Baltimore Co., MD.[134] We know she later married Unknown TOUT or FOUT because she is named thus in her father's will.[135]
vi	Elizabeth Eleander GUYTON (b. Unknown, d. Unknown) m. Alexander SMITH on 24 Jan 1758 in Baltimore Co., MD.[136]

Benjamin I came to the British Colonies as an indentured servant.[137] He is described as a 17 year-old man, a hot presser who signed a contract (versus making his mark) for five years at either Barbados or Maryland. He sailed from England on 17 Jul 1719. For more information about the life of Benjamin GUYTON I, see the section on his brother, John GUYTON I.

---

[128] Guyton, David F., "Wills and Administration: Benjamin Guyton in Baltimore Co., MD," written 22 Jun 1801; probated 22 Jul 1801, *Guyton Ancestry*, n.d., accessed 28 May 2020, <http://guyton.co.uk/wp-content/uploads/America/Wills/bg1732_Will.pdf>.

[129] "Maryland, Compiled Marriage Index, 1634-1777," s.v. "Benjamin Gayton," (marriage 13 Dec 1753), *Ancestry.com*.

[130] Guyton, David F., "Wills and Administration: Underwood Guyton in Baltimore Co., MD," written 30 Nov 1822; probated 25 Aug 1824, *Guyton Ancestry*, n.d., accessed 28 May 2020, <http://guyton.co.uk/wp-content/uploads/America/Wills/ug1734_Will.pdf>.

[131] "Maryland, Compiled Marriage Index, 1634-1777," s.v. "Underwood Guyton," (marriage 12 Aug 1762), *Ancestry.com*.

[132] Guyton, David F., "Wills and Administration: Henry Guyton in Baltimore Co., MD," written 14 Feb 1816; probated 24 Feb 1816, *Guyton Ancestry*, n.d., accessed 28 May 2020, <http://guyton.co.uk/wp-content/uploads/America/Wills/hg1737_Will.pdf>.

[133] "Maryland, Compiled Marriage Index, 1655-1850," s.v. "Henry Guyton," (marriage 17 Apr 1758), *Ancestry.com*.

[134] "Maryland, Compiled Marriage Index, 1634-1777," s.v. "Lydia Guyton," (marriage 13 Mar 1760), *Ancestry.com*.

[135] Guyton, David F., "Wills and Administration: Benjamin Guyton in Baltimore Co., MD," written 14 April 1774; probated 7 July 1776, *Guyton Ancestry*, n.d. 28 May 2020, <http://guyton.co.uk/wp-content/uploads/America/Wills/bg1702_Will.pdf>.

[136] "Maryland, Compiled Marriage Index, 1634-1777," s.v. "Eliz Guyton," (marriage 24 Jan 1758), *Ancestry.com*.

[137] "A List of Emigrants from England to America, 1682-1692, 1718-1759" transcribed digital image s.v. "Benjamin Guyton," (departure date 17 Jul 1719), *Ancestry.com*.

Generation #4

Joseph GUYTON I (John I, Samuel II, Samuel I, John)

Joseph GUYTON I was born 17 Sep 1732 in Baltimore County, Maryland[138] to John GUYTON I (b. 1696/7 d. 1782/3) and Mary UNKNOWN (b. Unknown, d. AFT 1785). He married Hannah Lyon WHITAKER (b. 26 Mar 1729, d. 30 May 1812)[139] at St. George's Parish Church, Perryman, Baltimore (now Harford) County, Maryland on 12 Dec 1754.[140] He died on 13 Jul 1818 in Union (now Cherokee) County, South Carolina and is buried in the Guyton Cemetery in Gaffney, Cherokee County, South Carolina.[141] In Guyton Cemetery Hannah's headstone inscription reads, "In memory of Hannah W. GUYTON who died May 30, 1812 in the 81st year of her life."[142]

Joseph I and Hannah had at least ten children:

i   Moses GUYTON I (b. 27 Oct 1758, Baltimore Co., MD, d. 21 Jun 1807, Spartanburg Co., SC).[143] His first wife was Tabitha SAXON (b. 10 Dec 1764, Spartanburg Co., SC, d. 10 Feb 1811, Charleston, SC).[144] Moses I married his second wife, Nancy COLE, (b. unknown, d. 1856[145]) in Dec 1814. Nancy applied for a widow's Revolutionary War pension based on Moses' service as a private and Lieutenant of Calvary in South Carolina.[146] Her request was denied because she died before the decision was made. Three of Moses' daughters were mentioned in Joseph GUYTON I's will (Hannah FONDRIN, Salley GUYTON, and Tabitha GUYTON).[147]

ii   Aaron Steele GUYTON (b. 21 Oct 1761, Baltimore Co., MD, d. 30 June 1841, Anderson District, SC).[148] He lived in Ninety-Six District (which later became Union District, South Carolina) at the time of his enlistment in the Revolutionary War in 1779. He later moved to York District, South Carolina for 4 or 5 years and married Margaret McCURDY (b. 1773, d. 1861) in 1789, Aaron applied for a pension on 1 Oct 1833.

iii   Mary GUYTON (b. Unknown, d. Unknown).

---

[138] "Family Data Collection - Individual Records," s.v. "Joseph Guyton," (birth 17 Sep 1732, death 13 Aug 1818), *Ancestry.com*.

[139] "Family Data Collection – Births," s.v. "Hannah Whitaker," (birth 26 Mar 1729), *Ancestry.com*. "FindaGrave 1600s to Current," s.v. "Hannah Guyton," (death 1812), *Ancestry.com*.

[140] "Maryland, Compiled Marriage Index, 1634-1777," s.v. "Jos Guyton," (marriage 12 Dec 1754), *Ancestry.com*.

[141] "FindaGrave 1600s to Current," s.v. "Joseph Guyton," (death 1812), *Ancestry.com*.

[142] McCall, Guyton Bobo, "Some Descendants of Joseph Guyton (Guiton) and Hannah Whitaker," a typescript at the Maryland Historical Society Library, 1987, accessed 2 Jun 2020, <http://www.bholliman.com/files/Descendants-of-Joseph-Guyton-and-Hannah-Whitaker-by-Guyton-Bobo-McCall-14pp.pdf>.

[143] "Georgia Bible Records," s.v. "Moses Guyton, Sr.," (27 Oct 1758-21 Jun 1807), *Ancestry.com*. "North America, Family Histories, 1500-2000," s.v. "Moses Guyton," (death 1807), *Ancestry.com*. Hart, Bertha Sheppard. *The Official History of Laurens Co., Georgia, 1807-1941*. Dublin, GA: John Laurens Chapter of the Daughters of the American Revolution, Georgia State Society, p. 382.

[144] *Ibid*.

[145] *Ibid*.

[146] "U.S., Revolutionary War Pension and Bounty-Land Warrant Application Files, 1800-1900" s.v. "Moses Guyton," *Ancestry.com*.

[147] "South Carolina, Wills and Probate Records, 1670-1980," digital image, s.v. "Joseph Guyton," (probated 26 May 1818), *Ancestry.com*.

[148] "Family Data Collection - Individual Records," s.v. "Aaron Steele Guyton," (birth 21 Oct 1761, death 30 Jun 1841), *Ancestry*.com.

iv		Sarah GUYTON (b. 29 Oct 1763, Baltimore Co. (later Harford Co.), MD, d. 1800, bur. John Smith Cemetery, Hickory Grove, York Co., SC)[149] m. John SMITH (b. Feb 1748, d. 31 Dec 1834, bur. John Smith Cemetery, Hickory Grove, York Co., SC)[150] John was named as a son-in-law in Joseph GUYTON I's will.[151]
v		Abraham GUYTON (b. 17 Mar 1765, d. 15 Feb 1816, Union District, SC)[152] m. Martha Patsy ELLIS (b. 1769, d. 19 Feb 1838, bur. Guyton Cemetery, Gaffney, Cherokee Co., SC).[153] Abraham's will was written on 14 Feb 1816 and probated on 4 Mar 1816.[154] His wife's name in his will is Patsy. Her will shows her name as Martha E. GUYTON.[155]
vi		Joseph GUYTON II (b. ABT 1776, d. Jun 1865, Union District, SC)[156] m. (1) Unknown and (2) Maria (Mariah) PRIDMORE (b. ABT 1799, d. 30 Oct 1878).[157]
vii		Hannah GUYTON (b. 18 Aug 1773, Union District, SC, d. Jan 1850, Ethelsville, Pickens Co., AL)[158] m. Alexander MARTIN (b. 26 Feb 1774, SC, d. 18 Jun 1846, Ethelsville, Pickens Co., AL).[159] Hannah and Alexander moved from South Carolina to Alabama after their son died and was interred near Gaffney, South Carolina. Hannah was the first of Joseph Guyton I's children to move further west. Hannah and Alexander were buried in the Martin Cemetery, located just south of Ethelsville, Alabama and west of Pickens CR 75. It is situated in a wooded area with the main cemetery enclosed by a chain link fence.[160]
xiii		Elizabeth (Betsey) GUYTON (b. ABT 1774, d. ABT 1818, SC, bur. Parker Cemetery, Gaffney, Cherokee Co., SC)[161] m. Isaiah PARKER (b. 1770, d. 1806, bur. Parker Cemetery, Cherokee Co., SC).[162] They had 7 children: Aaron, John, Isaac G., Hannah (wife of General James SMITH; moved first to Tennessee and then to Texas;[163] she is

---

[149] "U.S., FindaGrave Index, 1600s-Current," digital image s.v. "Sarah Smith," (birth 29 Oct 1763, death 17 Aug 1800), *Ancestry.com*.

[150] "U.S., FindaGrave Index, 1600s-Current," digital image s.v. "John Smith," (birth Feb 1748, death 31 Dec 1834), *Ancestry.com*.

[151] "South Carolina, Wills and Probate Records, 1670-1980," digital image, s.v. "Joseph Guyton," (probated 26 May 1818), *Ancestry.com*. Will Books, Vol A-B, 1792-1849; Author: South Carolina. Probate Court (Union County); Probate Place: Union, South Carolina.

[152] Guyton, David F., "Wills: Abraham Guyton in Union Co., SC," written 14 Feb 1816; probated 4 Mar 1816, n.d., accessed 30 May 2020, *Guyton Ancestry*, <http://guyton.co.uk/america-wills>.

[153] "U.S., FindaGrave Index, 1600s-Current," digital image s.v. "Martha Patsy GUYTON," (birth 1769, death 19 Feb 1838), *Ancestry.com*.

[154] Guyton, David F., "Wills and Administration: Abraham Guyton in Union Co., SC," written 14 Feb 1816; probated 4 Mar 1816, *Guyton Ancestry*, n.d., accessed 30 May 2020, <http://guyton.co.uk/wp-content/uploads/America/Wills/ag1765_Will.pdf>.

[155] "South Carolina, Wills and Probate Records, 1670-1980," digital image of transcribed will, s.v. "Martha E. Guyton," (probated 6 Mar 1838), *Ancestry.com*.

[156] Guyton, David F., "Wills: Joseph Guyton in Union Co., SC," (c. 17760-June 1865), *Guyton Ancestry*, n.d., accessed 31 May 2020, <http://guyton.co.uk/america-wills>.

[157] "South Carolina, Wills and Probate Records, 1670-1980," digital image, s.v. "Joseph Guyton," (probated 2 Aug 1865), *Ancestry.com*. Joseph named "Mariah" as his wife in his will. Maria's death notice: "Obituary for Maria Guyton," *Yorkville Enquirer*, 21 Nov 1878, p. 3; digital image, s.v. "Maria Guyton," *Newspapers.com* <https://www.newspapers.com/clip/21495236/yorkville-enquirer/?xid=637&_ga=2.62491183.2085232010.1590606594-1270059515.1576622426>.

[158] "U.S., FindaGrave Index, 1600s-Current," digital image s.v. "Hannah Martin," (18 Aug 1773-Jan 1850), *Ancestry.com*.

[159] "U.S., FindaGrave Index, 1600s-Current," digital image s.v. "Alexander Martin," (18 Aug 1773-Jan 1850), *Ancestry.com*.

[160] "Martin Cemetery," digital image s.v. "Martin Cemetery, Macedonia," *FindaGrave.com* <https://www.findagrave.com/cemetery/24219/martin-cemetery>.

[161] "U.S., Finda A Grave Index, 1600s-Current," digital image s.v. "Elizabeth Parker," (1774-1818), *Ancestry.com*.

[162] "U.S., FindaGrave Index, 1600s-Current," digital image s.v. "Isaiah Parker," (1770-1806), *Ancestry.com*.

[163] "Elizabeth (Betsy) Guyton Parker," *FindaGrave.com*, <https://www.findagrave.com/memorial/33146652>.

buried in Henderson, Rusk County, Texas), Rachel (married David MACOMSON), Joseph, and Sarah (married James C. CHILDRESS).[164]

ix   Margaret Catherine (Molly) GUYTON (b. Unknown, d. AFT 1818) m. Jonathan SMITH BEF 1787.[165] Both Molly and Jonathan SMITH were mentioned in Joseph GUYTON I's will.[166]

Joseph GUYTON I was born in either Calvert or Baltimore (later Harford) County, Maryland in 1732. In 1754, he and Hannah Lyon WHITAKER married at St. George's Spesutia Parish Church in Perryman, Baltimore (now Harford) County, Maryland.[167] See Figure 14 for the parish register showing their marriage. St. George is the oldest Episcopal (originally Church of England) parish in Maryland, having been founded in 1671. The original church, made of crude logs, stood at Michaelsville, Maryland on the current location of Aberdeen Proving Grounds.[168] The original structure burned and was replaced by two other St. George's Parish Churches before the existing 1851 building was constructed.[169] See Figure 15.

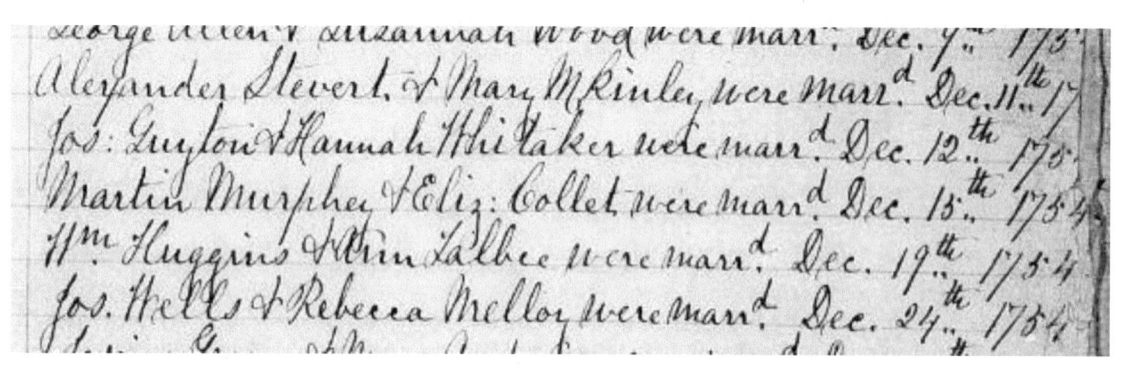

Figure 14 St. George's Parish Marriage of Joseph GUYTON and Hannah Lyon WHITAKER[170]

---

[164] "Martin Cemetery," digital image s.v. "Martin Cemetery, Macedonia," *FindaGrave.com* <https://www.findagrave.com/cemetery/24219/martin-cemetery>.

[165] "U.S., Sons of the American Revolution Membership Applications, 1889-1970," digital image s.v. "Jonathan Smith," *Ancestry.com*.

[166] "South Carolina, Wills and Probate Records, 1670-1980," digital image, s.v. "Joseph Guyton," (probated 26 May 1818), *Ancestry.com*.

[167] "U.S. and International Marriage Records, 1560-1900," s.v. "Jos Guyton," (marriage 12 Dec 1754), *Ancestry.com*.

[168] "The Migrations of Baltimore Town," *Maryland Historical Society*, n.d., accessed 30 Jun 2018, <http://www.mdhs.org/migrations-baltimore-town>.

[169] Vought, Allan, "St. George's Spesutia, Maryland's Oldest Episcopal parish, to End Worship Services," photo by Ted Hendricks (Aegis staff), *The Baltimore Sun*, 9 Nov 2012, accessed 30 Jun 2018, <http://www.baltimoresun.com/ph-ag-st-georges-closing-1109-20121108-story.html>.

[170] "Maryland, Church Records, 1668-1995," digital image s.v. "Hannah Whitaker," (marriage 12 Dec 1754), *FamilySearch*.

Figure 15 St. George's Parish Episcopal Church in Perryman, MD[171]

In 1761 a surveyor laid out property rented from the Lord of Baltimore for Joseph GUYTON I. The 26-acre property was called Hit or Miss. See Figure 16. He also had 73 acres in Baltimore County called Deniston.[172] The colony of South Carolina created the Ninety-Six District in 1769 and, according to the 1779 Ninety-Six census, Joseph I lived there.[173] The Ninety-Six District was a huge area lying east of Indian lands. Figure 17 shows the likely path (based on the early road system) that Joseph I and Hannah took on their move to Gaffney in Ninety-Six District, a distance of over 500 miles.[174] See Figure 18 for a graphic of the district.[175]

Joseph I and Hannah GUYTON's older children were born in Maryland (Calvert and/or Harford County). By the time of Hannah's birth in 1773, the Guyton family already lived around Gaffney, South Carolina in the District of Ninety-Six. South Carolina drew northern families to its more mountainous inland area (Upcountry) by the 1750s, a good twenty years before the Guyton family made the trip.[176]

---

[171] "Spesutia Church: St. George's Parish (Episcopal)," *The Historical Marker Database*, n.d., accessed 30 Jun 2018, <https://www.hmdb.org/marker.asp?marker=1263>.
[172] "Unpatented Certificates for Baltimore County: MSA S1213-433," 3 digital images, s.v. "Deniston," Unpatented Certificate Number 433, 23 Oct 1761, accessed 31 May 2020, <http://map-maker.org/Helper/land/UnpatentedCerts.html>.
[173] "South Carolina, Compiled Census and Census Substitutes Index, 1790-1890," s.v. "Joseph Guyton," (census 1779), *Ancestry.com*.
[174] "Maryland to South Carolina." Map. *Google Maps*. Google. 31 May 2020. Web. 31 May 2020.
[175] "South Carolina: Districts and Counties, 1785," *South Carolina Department of Archives and History*, accessed 1 Jul 2018, <http://www.archivesindex.sc.gov/guide/CountyRecords/1785.htm>. Sarrett, Jr., Paul R., "List of 2,154 Residents of the Ninety-Six District," 10 Nov 1996, accessed 31 May 2020, *USGenWeb Archives*.
[176] "History of South Carolina," *Wikipedia*, n.d.

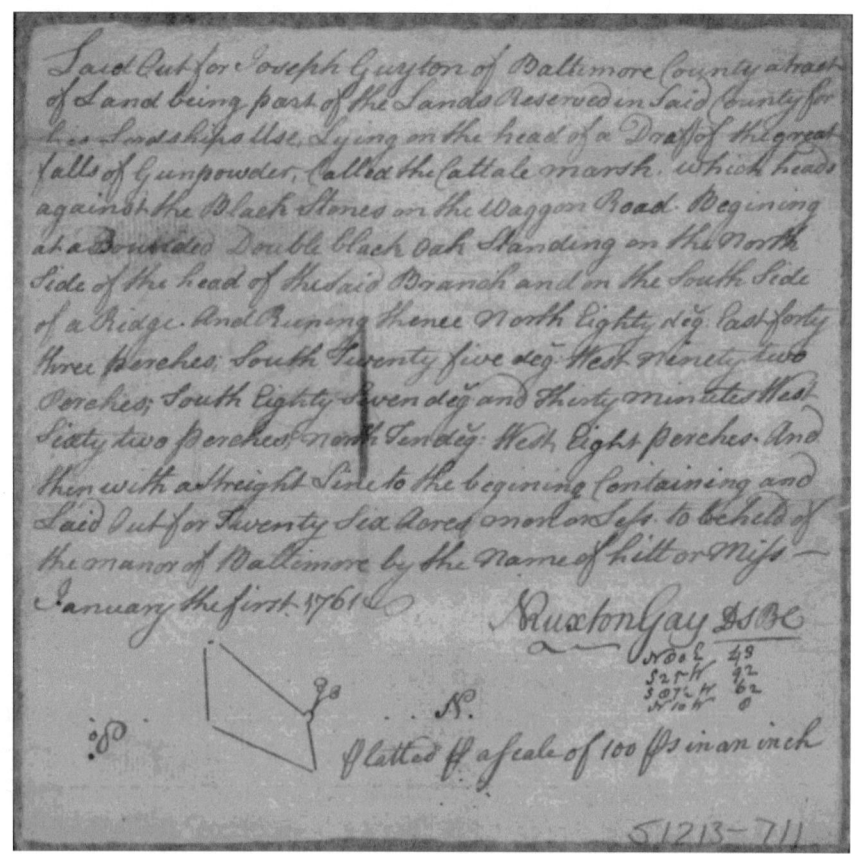

Figure 16 Joseph GUYTON I's Survey for Property Called Hit or Miss in Harford Co., MD[177]

---

[177] "Unpatented Certificates for Baltimore County: MSA S1213-725," 3 digital images, s.v. "MSA S1213-725," (Unpatented Certificate Number 711, 23 Oct 1761, accessed 31 May 2020, <http://guide.msa.maryland.gov/pages/item.aspx?ID=S1213-725>. Or "Unpatented Certificates for Baltimore County: MSA S1213-725," 3 digital images, s.v. "Hit or Miss," Unpatented Certificate Number 711, 23 Oct 1761, accessed 31 May 2020, <http://map-maker.org/Helper/land/UnpatentedCerts.html>.

Figure 17 Joseph GUYTON I's Move from Maryland to South Carolina[178]

---

[178] "Likely Route of Guytons from Maryland to Gaffney, South Carolina." Map. *Google Maps,* Google, 31 May 2020. Web. 31 May 2020.

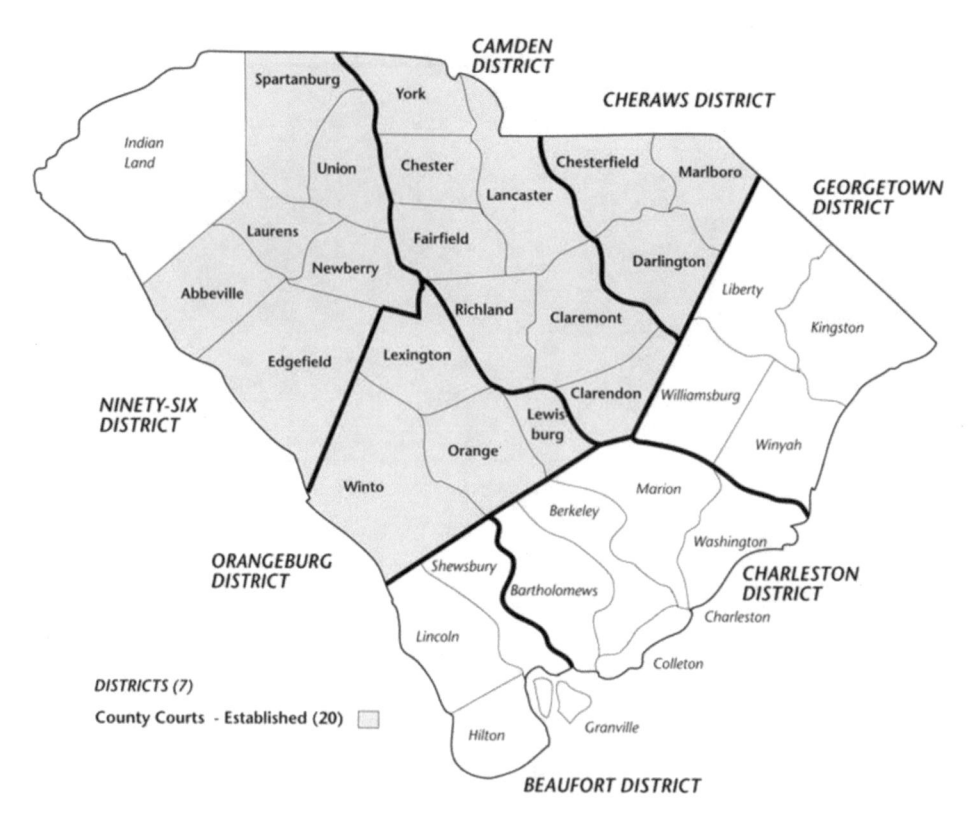

Figure 18 Map of Old Ninety-Six District, SC in 1785

South Carolina reflected cultural differences in its two main regions.[179] Slaveholding planters settled the coastal areas (the Low Country) beginning in the 1670s. These planters, relative to the later-arriving subsistence farmers of the Upcountry, were educated, wealthy, and retained the colony's political power. Dissenting Protestant worshipers dominated the Upcountry. That is, the Upcountry people subscribed to churches (like Presbyterians and Baptists) at odds with the Church of England (Anglican), popular with the Low Country worshipers. The cultural, wealth, and political differences between people in the two regions led to distrust and hostility. The Upcountry contained nearly half of the colony's white population (about 30,000 settlers) by the time of the Revolution. More Loyalists came from Upcountry settlers who believed they were better off with the British than being dominated by the rich planter class in the Low Country. The population of South Carolina split nearly evenly between Loyalists and Patriots.

The Revolutionary War would have impacted the Guyton family. More than two hundred Revolutionary battles were fought in South Carolina, more than in any other colony. Two important battles occurred within twenty miles of Gaffney, South Carolina. Patriot and Loyalist militias engaged at the Battle of Kings Mountain in 1780 in rural Cherokee County, South Carolina.[180] The Patriot win came after a string of defeats in the Southern campaign, thus raising troop morale. The battlefield is eighteen miles northeast of Gaffney. The American victory against the British at the Battle of Cowpens in January

---

[179] "History of South Carolina," *Wikipedia*, n.d.
[180] "Battle of Kings Mountain," *Wikipedia*, n.d.

1781 is often considered the turning-point in the War of Independence.[181] The battlefield is located twelve miles northwest of Gaffney. In 1776 when the colonies declared independence from Great Britain, Joseph GUYTON I was 44 years old. His older two sons, Moses I and Aaron Steele, were 18 and 15, respectively. Moses I entered the war in 1778, when he was 21. Aaron Steele joined him in 1779, when he was 18.

"A List of Petit-Jury Men and Jury Men in Civil Causes" in the Ninety-Six sub-district of Spartan included Joseph I in 1779/1780.[182] Ninety-Six was both a district and a town in 1770s. The British and Americans fought the first land battle south of New England there in 1775 and from May 22 to June 18, 1781, Major General Nathanael Greene and his troops laid an unsuccessful siege of the heavily British fortified town and fort of Ninety-Six. The British abandoned and burned Ninety-Six in the summer of 1781, but the town was reborn as Cambridge in 1787.[183]

Unequal trade between the American colonies and Great Britain resulted in a shortage of hard currency (money) in the colonies. If Americans did have hard currency, it likely originated in Spain or Portugal. The colonies produced commodities like cotton, tobacco, and lumber; Great Britain made manufactured goods, such as tools and furnishings. The colonies traded the commodities for the manufactured goods but the value of the manufactured goods always outweighed the value of the commodities. Therefore, Great Britain always ran a trade surplus with the colonies. Americans were given credit for their commodities in Britain that they used to buy their needed manufactured goods. Americans did not receive currency in the colonies that could circulate among people in trade. In the early days of the American colonies farmers often used commodities to pay their taxes and to trade for goods they needed. Governments usually offered a discount if taxpayers paid in silver or gold. Only the wealthy could take advantage of the opportunity. Joseph I and his family likely depended upon commodities to purchase what they could not grow or make themselves. If Joseph I did have any hard currency, it was likely a Spanish dollar, or real (ray all'), which could be divided into "pieces of eight." See Figure 19.

Figure 19 Silver Dollar of Charles III of Spain, 1776[184]

Commodity trading is not an efficient way to purchase what a buyer needs. The buyer has to find a seller of what he wants who also wants the commodity the buyer is offering. Money, a medium of

---

[181] "Battle of Cowpens," *Wikipedia*, n.d.
[182] *"U.S. Census Reconstructed Records, 1660-1820,"* s.v. "Joseph Guyton," (petit-jury 1780), *Ancestry.com*.
[183] Lewis, J. D., "History of Cambridge, South Carolina," *Carolana*, n.d., accessed 1 Jul 2018, <http://www.carolana.com/SC/Towns/Cambridge_SC.html>.
[184] "Spanish Dollar," *Wikipedia*, n.d.

exchange, allows a seller to exchange a product for cash. With cash the seller can then buy whatever he needs. The colonies were desperate for cash. Without British money, the colonies resorted to printing their own money that citizens could use to pay taxes and mortgages on their land and that the government could use to pay soldiers and war supplies. The Continental Congress started printing money in 1775. The problem with printing money is that the value of the paper becomes worth less and less (inflation). In the case of the Revolutionary War period, the colonies experienced hyper-inflation. Hyper-inflation certainly made financial survival more difficult for the family. Farm tools, sugar, tea, cloth (if not homemade), and other of life's luxuries could not be purchased without sacrifice that grew as inflation increased.

President Madison declared war against the British in 1812 that would end in 1815 before Joseph I's death. The Americans felt compelled to enter a war because the British supported Indian tribes who fought with settlers on the westward moving frontier and the impressment of American sailors into the British Navy. Although there were no battles in the state of South Carolina, the U.S. embargo on trade with Great Britain and British blockades of American ports likely affected South Carolina. The militia of South Carolina did see action but it transpired in the Indian wars in Georgia and Alabama.[185]

Figure 20 shows the general areas where Joseph GUYTON I (shown in orange and his adult children (shown in blue) lived in South Carolina. Notice that Hannah GUYTON and her husband, Alexander MARTIN, had already moved to Pickens County, Alabama.

Hannah Lyon WHITAKER died in 1812 followed by Joseph I in 1818. They died near Gaffney, South Carolina in what is now called Cherokee County, South Carolina and are both buried in the Guyton Cemetery. Photos of Joseph I and Hannah's headstones can be seen in Figure 21 and Figure 22, respectively. Joseph I's gravestone says, "In memory of Joseph Guiton who died July 13, 1818 in 86th year of his life."[186] The cemetery is on private property out in the woods near Gaffney, South Carolina. It has not been maintained. David F. GUYTON visited the graves. He said that he needed the property owner to help him find the graves and he almost didn't find his way back to his car.

---

[185] "The Creek War," *Wikipedia*, n.d.
[186] Luciejaynewilson, "Joseph GUYTON I Headstone Inscription," 14 Dec 2007, *Ancestry.com*.

Figure 20 Approximate Locations of Joseph GUYTON I and his Children in South Carolina[187]

---

[187] "South Carolina Locations of the Children of Joseph Guyton I," Map. *Google Maps*. Google. 1 Jun 2020. Web. 1 Jun 2020.

Figure 21 Joseph GUYTON I Gravestone in Guyton Cemetery, Cherokee Co., SC[188]

Figure 22 Hannah WHITAKER GUYTON Gravestone in Guyton Cemetery, Cherokee Co., SC[189]

South Carolina created Cherokee County from parts of Spartanburg, Union, and York Counties in 1897.[190] See Figure 23. The map in Figure 24 shows the specific location of Gaffney, the seat of Cherokee County. The reader can see Cowpens National Battlefield in green to the northeast of Gaffney.

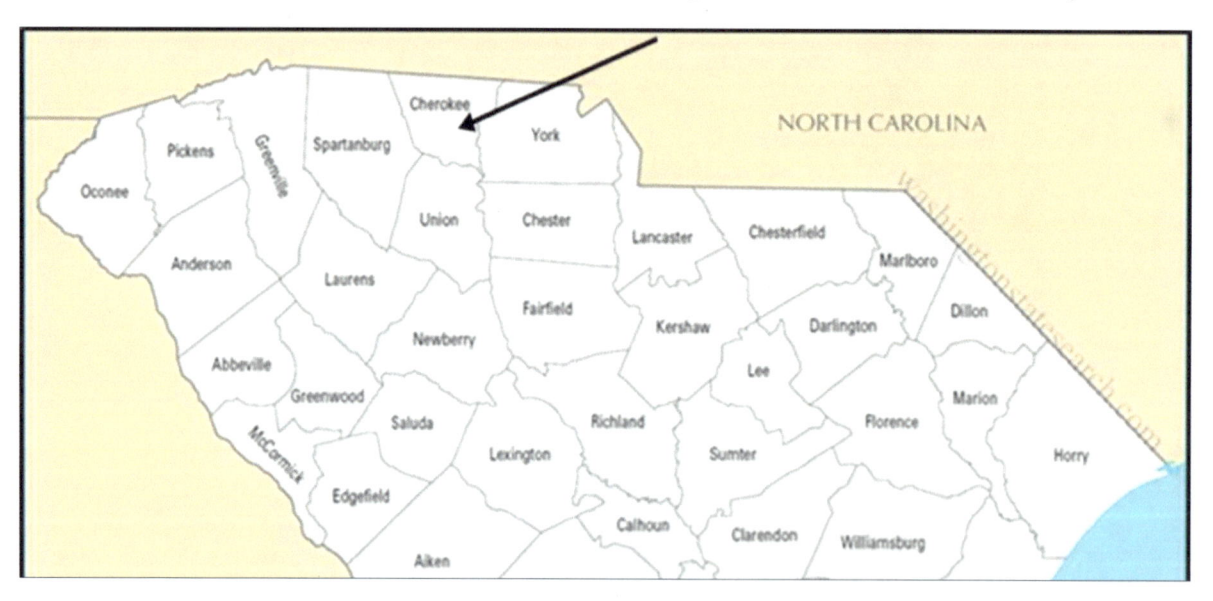

Figure 23 County Map of South Carolina

---

[188] Joseph Guiton, gravemarker, Guyton Cemetery, Gaffney, Cherokee County, South Carolina, digital image s.v. "Joseph Guyton," *FindaGrave.com*.

[189] Hannah Guiton, grave marker, Guyton Cemetery, Gaffney, Cherokee County, South Carolina, digital image s.v. "Hannah Guyton," *FindaGrave.com*.

[190] "South Carolina: Counties, 1878-1907," *South Carolina Department of Archives and History*, n.d., accessed 1 Jul 2018, <http://www.archivesindex.sc.gov/guide/CountyRecords/1878.htm>.

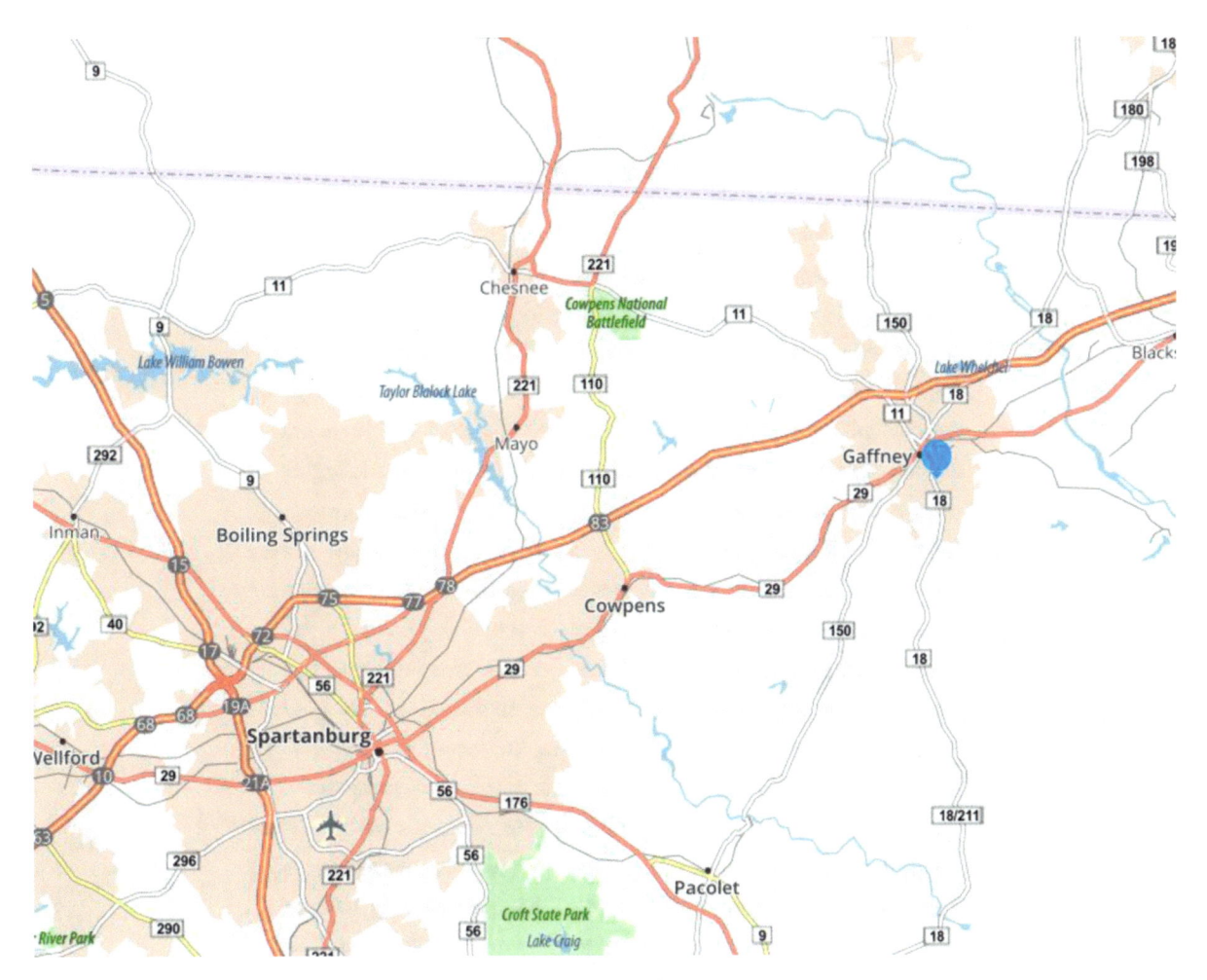

Figure 24 Map Showing Location of Gaffney, South Carolina[191]

Joseph GUYTON I's transcribed will (pages 1 and 2) in Union District, South Carolina is shown in Figure 25 and Figure 26.[192] He bequeathed land, furniture, a wagon, a feather bed, and enslaved people to his children and to his deceased children's children.

---

[191] "Spartanburg and Gaffney, South Carolina." Map. G*oogle Maps.* Google, 1 Jun 2020. Web. 1 Jun 2020.
[192] "South Carolina, Wills and Probate Records, 1670-1980," digital image, s.v. "Joseph Guyton," (probated 26 May 1818), *Ancestry.com*.

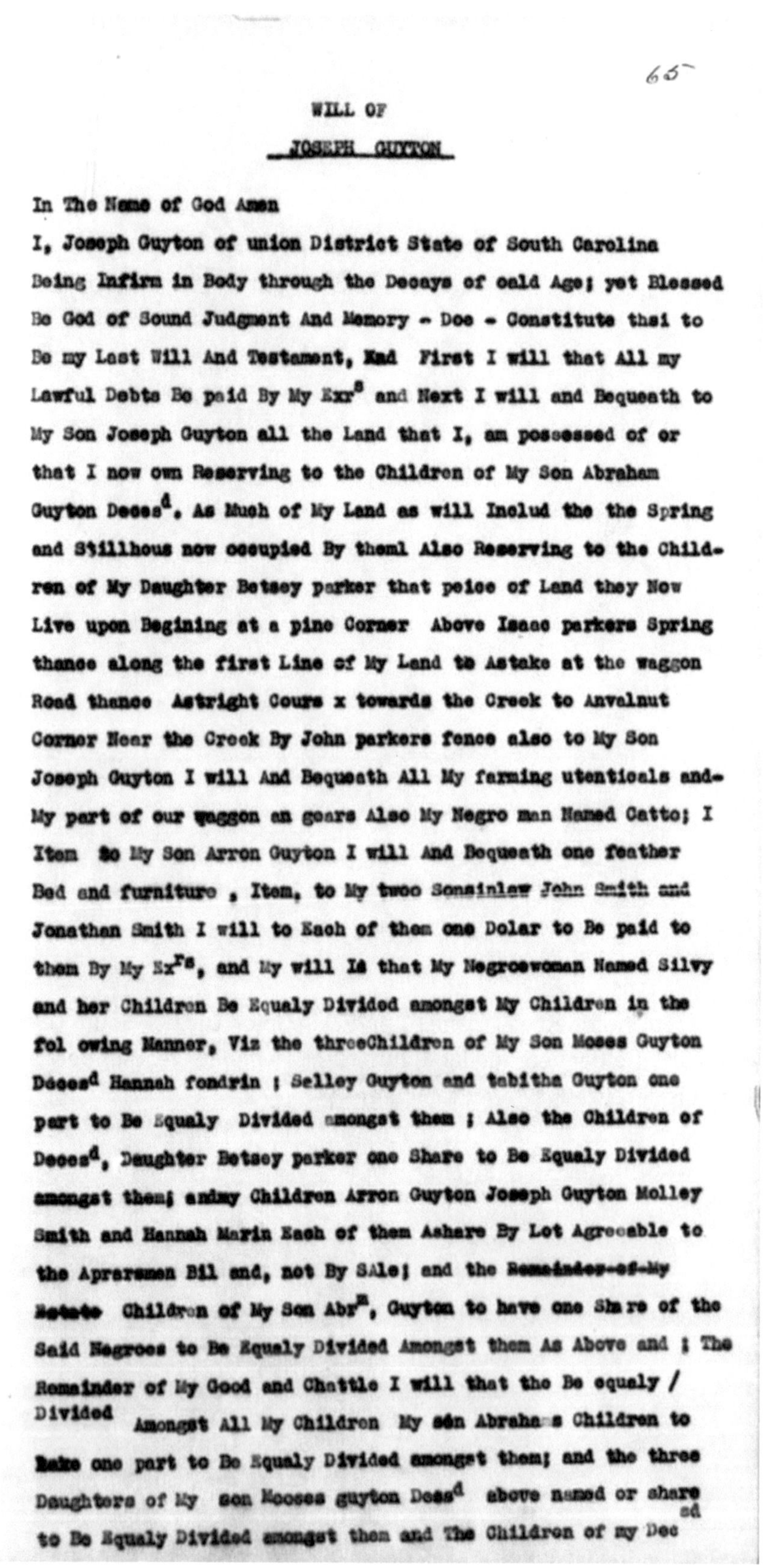

WILL OF
JOSEPH GUYTON

In The Name of God Amen

I, Joseph Guyton of union District State of South Carolina Being Infirm in Body through the Decays of oald Age; yet Blessed Be God of Sound Judgment And Memory - Doe - Constitute thsi to Be my Last Will And Testament, Xad First I will that All my Lawful Debts Be paid By My Exr^s and Next I will and Bequeath to My Son Joseph Guyton all the Land that I, am possessed of or that I now own Reserving to the Children of My Son Abraham Guyton Dcces^d. As Much of My Land as will Includ the the Spring and Stillhous now occupied By theml Also Reserving to the Children of My Daughter Betsey parker that peice of Land they Now Live upon Begining at a pine Corner Above Isaac parkers Spring thence along the first Line of My Land to Astake at the waggon Road thence Astright Cours x towards the Creek to Anvalnut Corner Near the Creek By John parkers fence also to My Son Joseph Guyton I will And Bequeath All My farming utenticals and My part of our waggon an gears Also My Negro man Named Catto; I Item to My Son Arron Guyton I will And Bequeath one feather Bed and furniture , Item, to My twoo Sonsinlaw John Smith and Jonathan Smith I will to Each of them one Dolar to Be paid to them By My Ex^{rs}, and My will Is that My Negroewoman Named Silvy and her Children Be Equaly Divided amongst My Children in the fol owing Manner, Viz the threeChildren of My Son Moses Guyton Dcces^d Hannah fondrin ; Selley Guyton and tabitha Guyton one part to Be Equaly Divided amongst them ; Also the Children of Dcces^d, Daughter Betsey parker one Share to Be Equaly Divided amongst them; and my Children Arron Guyton Joseph Guyton Molley Smith and Hannah Marin Each of them Ashare By Lot Agreeable to the Aprarsmen Bil and, not By SAle; and the Remainder of My Estate Children of My Son Abr^m, Guyton to have one Share of the Said Negroes to Be Equaly Divided Amongst them As Above and ; The Remainder of My Good and Chattle I will that the Be equaly / Divided Amongst All My Children My sen Abrahams Children to hake one part to Be Equaly Divided amongst them; and the three Daughters of My son Mooses guyton Dces^d above named or share sd to Be Equaly Divided amongst them and The Children of my Dec

Figure 25 Joseph GUYTON I Transcribed Will 1818 p. 1/2 Union District, SC

WILL OF JOSEPH GUYTON PAGE 2

Daughter Betsey parker one Share To Be Equaly Divided Amongst them and also to My Son Aaron Guyton and My Son Joseph Guyton one Share Equaly, Divided Among them also My twoo Daughters Molley Smith and Hannah Marin Each of them one Share as Above; Reserving My Saddle Which Which I will and Bequeath to My Grandson Abraham Guyton By My Son Joseph --------------------------- and Lastly Of all I Doe hereby Constitute and apoint My Sons Joseph Guyton and My Son Irlan Alexander Marin Executors of this My Last will and Testament Signed Seled Published and Declared this 26th of May Ano Dom 1816

In presence of us
Nicholas Corry
Gabriel Petty   Joseph (his mark) Guyton (L.S.)
Salley Batty

Recorded 5 of August 1818
RECORDED IN WILL BOOK PAGE 45
BOX 11 PACKAGE 1

Wm. RICE (OBY)

Figure 26 Joseph GUYTON I Transcribed Will 1818 p. 2/2 Union District, SC

Generation #5

Moses GUYTON I (Joseph I, John I, Samuel II, Samuel I, John)

Moses Guyton I (b. 27 Oct 1758, Baltimore Co., MD, d. 17 Feb 1816, Spartanburg Co., SC).[193] His parents were Joseph GUYTON I (b. 17 Sep 1732, d. 13 Jul 1818)[194] and Hannah Lyon WHITAKER (b. 26 Mar 1729, d. 1812).[195] Moses I was first married to Tabitha SAXON (b. 10 Dec 1764, SC, d. 10 Feb 1811, SC) in 1782/1784.[196] Moses I was married to his second wife, Nancy COLE (b. Unknown, d. 1855) at his death.[197] Among Moses I and Tabitha's children were the following:

i　John GUYTON (b. 4 Feb 1784, SC, d. Oct 1826, Macon or Dublin, GA, bur. Fort Hill Cemetery, Macon, Bibb Co., GA).[198]

ii　Judith Saxon GUYTON (b. 22 Mar 1786, d. Unknown).[199]

iii　Hannah GUYTON (b. 22 Jun 1788, d. ABT 1818, SC)[200] m. Matthew FONDREN (b. Unknown, d. ABT 1816, SC).[201]

iv　Mary GUYTON (b. 6 Apr 1790, d. 21 Mar 1863, SC)[202] m. Joseph WEBBER (b. 23 May 1785, VA, d. 10 Feb 1870, SC).[203]

---

[193] Bible records place Moses' death in 1807. But the Census of 1810, his remarriage to Nancy COLE, and the history of Laurens County, Georgia suggests the later date. I cannot explain such a wide discrepancy. "Georgia Bible Records," s.v. "Moses Guyton, Sr.," (27 Oct 1758-21 Jun 1807), *Ancestry.com*. "North America, Family Histories, 1500-2000," s.v. "Moses Guyton," (death 1807), *Ancestry.com*. Hart, Bertha Sheppard. *The Official History of Laurens Co., Georgia, 1807-1941*. Dublin, GA: John Laurens Chapter of the Daughters of the American Revolution, Georgia State Society, p. 382.

[194] "Family Data Collection - Individual Records," s.v. "Joseph Guyton," (17 Sep 1732-13 Aug 1818), *Ancestry*.com.

[195] "Family Data Collection – Births," s.v. "Hannah Whitaker," (26 Mar 1729), *Ancestry.com*. "FindaGrave 1600s to Current," s.v. "Hannah Guyton," (1812), *Ancestry.com*.

[196] As with Moses GUYTON I, dates for Tabitha SAXON vary significantly. "Georgia Bible Records," s.v. "Moses Guyton, Sr.," (10/27/1758-6/21/1807), *Ancestry.com*. "North America, Family Histories, 1500-2000," s.v. "Tabitha Saxon," (1764-1811, marriage 1782), *Ancestry.com*. Hart, Bertha Sheppard. *The Official History of Laurens Co., Georgia, 1807-1941*. Dublin, GA: John Laurens Chapter of the Daughters of the American Revolution, Georgia State Society, p. 382.

[197] "Revolutionary War Pension and Bounty-Land Warrant Application Files, 1800-1900," s.v. "Moses Guyton," (rejected pension application file), *Ancestry.com*.

[198] John Guyton, grave marker, Fort Hill Cemetery, Macon, Bibb County, Georgia, s.v. "John Guyton," *FindaGrave.com*.

[199] "Georgia Bible Records," s.v. "Moses Guyton, Sr.," (27 Oct 1758-21 Jun 1807), *Ancestry.com*.

[200] *Ibid.* Hannah FONDRIN is mentioned in her grandfather's will. "South Carolina, Wills and Probate Records, 1670-1980," digital image, s.v. "Joseph Guyton," (26 May 1818), *Ancestry.com*. Her will: "South Carolina, Wills and Probate Records, 1670-1980," digital image, s.v. "Hannah Fondren," (1818), *Ancestry.com*.

[201] "South Carolina, Wills and Probate Records, 1670-1980," digital image, s.v. "Matthew Fondren," (1816), *Ancestry.com*.

[202] Hannah Guyton, grave marker, Buffalo Baptist Church Cemetery, Blacksburg, Cherokee County, South Carolina, digital image s.v. "Hannah Webber," *FindaGrave.com*.

[203] Joseph Webber, grave marker, Buffalo Baptist Church Cemetery, Blacksburg, Cherokee County, South Carolina, digital image s.v. "Joseph Webber," *FindaGrave.com*.

v	Charles Saxon GUYTON (b. 16 Sep 1793, Spartanburg Co., SC, d. 3 Dec 1848, Laurens Co., GA)[204] m. Elmina Horn TUCKER (b. 1810, d. Unknown)[205] on 27 Jan 1836 in Laurens County, Georgia.[206]
vi	Joseph GUYTON (b. 12 Sep 1795, d. Unknown)[207] m. Catherine COLLIER on 21 Aug 1817 in Laurens County, Georgia.[208]
vii	Sarah GUYTON (b. 24 Aug 1797, d. AFT 1818).[209]
viii	Moses GUYTON II (b. 4 Sep 1799, d. 12 Dec 1870, Laurens Co., GA).
ix	Tabitha GUYTON (b. 11 Aug 1801, d. AFT 1818).[210]
x	Elizabeth GUYTON (b. 25 Nov 1803, d. ABT 1880, Spartanburg Co., SC).[211]

Nancy COLE GUYTON's request in 1854 for a Revolutionary War Pension was denied but it seems possible she died before the request was processed. In her request for the pension, Nancy claimed Moses I was a private and lieutenant of the cavalry. He entered service in 1778 in the company commanded by Captain James STEEN of the 2nd Spartan Regiment commanded by Colonel Thomas BRATTON. He also served under Captain Robert MONTGOMERY as Lieutenant of Cavalry in either the Camden District Regiment or the 2nd Spartanburg Regiment. He was in the latter service between 1779 until the close of the war. There is evidence that he was paid for duty in the war.[212] His brother, Aaron Steele GUYTON was a private under Moses I.[213] Captain MONTGOMERY (and presumably Moses I) participated in Purrysburg (1779) (the first headquarters of the Southern Continental Army within South Carolina); the Battle of Williamson's Plantation (1780); Wofford's Iron Works (1780); the Blackstocks (1780); Cowpens (1781); Siege of Ninety-Six (1781); and Eutaw Springs (1781), the last major battle in South Carolina that completely broke the British hold in the South.[214] Six weeks later Lord CORNWALLIS capitulated to General George WASHINGTON at Yorktown, and American independence was assured.

---

[204] Charles Saxon Guyton, grave marker, Charles Guyton Cemetery, East Dublin, Laurens County, Georgia, digital image s.v. "Charles Saxon Guyton," *FindaGrave.com*.

[205] Charles Saxon Guyton, grave marker, Charles Guyton Cemetery, East Dublin, Laurens County, Georgia, s.v. "Elmina Guyton Horn Mizell," *FindaGrave.com*.

[206] "Georgia Marriages to 1850," s.v. "Charles B. Guyton," (marriage 27 Jan 1836), *Ancestry.com*.

[207] "Georgia Bible Records," s.v. "Moses Guyton, Sr.," (27 Oct 1758-21 Jun 1807), *Ancestry.com*.

[208] "Georgia Marriages to 1850," s.v. "Joseph Guyton," (marriage 21 Aug 1817), *Ancestry.com*.

[209] "Georgia Bible Records," s.v. "Moses Guyton, Sr.," (27 Oct 1758-21 Jun 1807), *Ancestry.com*. Sarah GUYTON is mentioned in her grandfather's will. "South Carolina, Wills and Probate Records, 1670-1980," digital image, s.v. "Joseph Guyton," (probated 26 May 1818), *Ancestry.com*.

[210] "Georgia Bible Records," s.v. "Moses Guyton, Sr.," (27 Oct 1758-21 Jun 1807), *Ancestry.com*. Tabitha GUYTON is mentioned in her grandfather's will. "South Carolina, Wills and Probate Records, 1670-1980," digital image, s.v. "Joseph Guyton," (probated 26 May 1818), *Ancestry.com*.

[211] "Georgia Bible Records," s.v. "Moses Guyton, Sr.," (27 Oct 1758-21 Jun 1807), *Ancestry.com*.

[212] "Revolutionary War Pension and Bounty-Land Warrant Application Files, 1800-1900," s.v. "Moses Guyton," (rejected pension application file), *Ancestry.com*.

[213] Lewis, J. D., "The American Revolution in South Carolina," *Carolana*, accessed 1 Jul 2018, <https://www.carolana.com/SC/Revolution/patriots_sc_capt_robert_montgomery.html>.

[214] *Ibid.*

Aaron Steele GUYTON (Joseph I, John I, Samuel II, Samuel I, John)

Aaron Steele GUYTON (b. 26 Oct 1761, Baltimore Co, MD, d. 30 Jun 1841, Anderson Co., SC)[215] m. Margaret McCURDY[216] (b. 2 Dec 1773, d. 1861, Anderson Co., SC)[217] on 6 Oct 1789. His parents were Joseph GUYTON I (b. 17 Sep 1732, d. 13 Jul 1818)[218] and Hannah Lyon WHITAKER (b. 26 Mar 1729, d. 1812).[219] They had at least twelve children:

i   Mary McRee (Polly) GUYTON (b. Unknown, d. Unknown).
ii Hannah GUYTON (b. 18 Dec 1793, Anderson Co., SC, d. 22 Feb 1864, Anderson Co., SC)[220] m. Wyatt SMITH (21 Jan 1793, d. 15 Mar 1864, Anderson Co., SC).[221]
iii Elizabeth (Betsey) GUYTON (b. 7 Nov 1795, d. 1866, Anderson Co., SC)[222] m. William WEBB (b. 1789, VA, d. 1852, Anderson Co., SC).[223]
iv Patience GUYTON (b. 1798, d. 1798, Anderson Co., SC).[224]
v   Jane Malissa GUYTON (b. 31 Dec 1800, d. 30 Aug 1802, Anderson Co., SC).[225]
vi Robert McCurdy GUYTON (b. Unknown, d. ABT 1841, Anderson Co., SC)[226] m. Hester DUCKWORTH (b. 6 Aug 1814, Anderson Co., SC, d. 23 Jul 1889, Smith Co., MS). Hester married John Luke PAGETT and moved to Mississippi after Robert died.[227]

---

[215] Aaron Steele Guyton, grave marker, Old Hopewell Cemetery, Anderson, Anderson County, South Carolina, s.v. "Aaron Steele Guyton," *FindaGrave.com*. "Family Data Collection: Individual Records," s.v. "Aaron Steele Guyton," (birth 26 Oct 1761, marriage Oct 1789, death 30 June 1831), *Ancestry.com*.

[216] Helen GUYTON REES tells a very interesting story about Margaret McCURDY as a child of seven during the Revolutionary War. See her book *Guytons Galore: From French Huguenots to Oregon Pioneers*. Binford & Mort: Portland, OR, 1986, pp. 251-253. A hint: Lord Cornwallis was among her friends.

[217] Margaret McCurdy Guyton, grave marker, Old Hopewell Cemetery, Anderson, Anderson County, South Carolina, s.v. "Margaret "Peggy" McCurdy Guyton," *FindaGrave.com*.

[218] "Family Data Collection - Individual Records," s.v. "Joseph Guyton," (birth 17 Sep 1732, death 13 Aug 1818), *Ancestry*.com.

[219] "Family Data Collection – Births," s.v. "Hannah Whitaker," (birth 26 Mar 1729), *Ancestry.com*. "FindaGrave 1600s to Current," s.v. "Hannah Guyton," (death 1812), *Ancestry.com*.

[220] Hannah Guyton, grave marker, Old Hopewell Cemetery, Anderson, Anderson County, South Carolina, digital image s.v. "Hannah Guyton Smith," *FindaGrave.com*.

[221] Wyatt Smith, grave marker, Old Hopewell Cemetery, Anderson, Anderson County, South Carolina, digital image s.v. "Wyatt Smith," *FindaGrave.com*.

[222] Elizabeth Guyton, grave marker, Old Hopewell Cemetery, Anderson, Anderson County, South Carolina, s.v. "Elizabeth 'Betsey' Guyton Webb," *FindaGrave.com*.

[223] William Webb, grave marker, Old Hopewell Cemetery, Anderson, Anderson County, South Carolina, s.v. "William Webb," *FindaGrave.com*.

[224] Patience Guyton, grave marker, Old Hopewell Cemetery, Anderson, Anderson County, South Carolina, s.v. "Patience Guyton," *FindaGrave.com*.

[225] Jane Malissa Guyton, grave marker, Old Hopewell Cemetery, Anderson, Anderson County, South Carolina, s.v. "Jane Malissa Guyton," *FindaGrave.com*.

[226] "South Carolina: Wills and Probate Records 1670-1980," digital image s.v. "Robert Guyton," (schedule appraisal 1841), *Ancestry.com*.

[227] Hester O. Duckworth, grave marker, Fellowship Cemetery, Taylorsville, Smith County, Mississippi, s.v. "Hester O. Duckworth Pagett," *FindaGrave.com*.

vii   Joseph A. GUYTON (b. 14 Apr 1805, Anderson Co., SC, d. 7 Apr 1880, Sallis, Attala Co., MS)[228] m. Zemuely Coats McCLUSKY (10 Nov 1811, Hall Co., GA, d. 17 Mar 1872, Sallis, Attala Co., MS)[229] on 13 Mar 1828 in Hall County, Georgia.[230] He moved with his brother Aaron Whitaker GUYTON to Attala County, Mississippi.

viii   Margaret Watson GUYTON (b. 6 Jan 1807, Anderson Co., SC, d. 13 Dec 1876, Oconee Co., SC)[231] m. Capt. William Love STEELE (b. 12 Oct 1796, d. 17 May 1874, Oconee Co., SC).[232] Capt. STEELE was a midshipman on the frigate *Constitution* during the War of 1812 and served as a member of the South Carolina Legislature.[233]

ix   Aaron Whitaker (Whit) GUYTON (b. 22 Nov 1808, Anderson Co., SC, d. ABT 1881, Sallis, Attala Co., MS).[234] He moved with his brother Joseph A. GUYTON to Attala County, Mississippi.

x   Sarah Matilda (Sally) GUYTON (b. 9 Feb 1812, Anderson Co., SC, d. 16 Sep 1850, Anderson Co., SC)[235] m. Thomas DUCKWORTH (b. 17 Feb 1807, Anderson Co., SC, d. 29 Sep 1852, Anderson Co., SC).[236]

xi   John Washington GUYTON (b. 1 Jun 1814, d. 16 Sep 1871, Anderson Co., SC)[237] m. Sarah Ann WELBORN (b. 7 Oct 1822, Anderson Co., SC, d. 22 Nov 1905, Anderson Co., SC).[238] He served as Brigadier General of Cavalry prior to the Civil War.[239] John D. ASHMORE sued John and his brother, Guyton (or Gyte), and received a judgment for about $5,000 (or about $95,000 today). Gyte disappeared leaving John to be placed in custody while his creditors addressed the court. John sold land, tools, and personal property to settle the debt.[240]

xii   Guyton GUYTON (b. Unknown, d. AFT 1880).[241] John D. ASHMORE sued John and his brother, Guyton (or Gyte), and received a judgment for about $5,000 (or about $95,000 today). Gyte disappeared leaving John to be placed in custody while his creditors addressed the court. John sold land, tools, and personal property to settle the debt.[242]

---

[228] Joseph A. Guyton, grave marker, Ellington Cemetery, Attala County, Mississippi, digital image s.v. "Joseph Guyton," *FindaGrave.com*.

[229] Zemuely Coats McClusky, grave marker, Ellington Cemetery, Attala County, Mississippi, digital image s.v. "Zemuely Coats McClesky Guyton," *FindaGrave.com*.

[230] "Georgia Marriages to 1850," s.v. "Joseph Guyton," (marriage 13 Mar 1828), *Ancestry.com*.

[231] Margaret Watson Guyton, grave marker, Retreat Presbyterian Church Cemetery, Oconee County, South Carolina, digital image s.v. "Margaret Watson Guyton Steele," *FindaGrave.com*.

[232] William Love Steele, grave marker, Retreat Presbyterian Church Cemetery, Oconee County, South Carolina, digital image s.v. "William Steele," *FindaGrave.com*.

[233] "A Voice from Old Pickens: Three Prominent Families – Steeles, McElroys and Craigs," *Keowee Courier*, 14 Jan 1903, p. 1; digital image, s.v. "William Steele," *Newspapers.com*, <https://www.newspapers.com/clip/19133734/william_love_steele_this_article_lists/?xid=637>.

[234] Aaron Whitaker Guyton, grave marker, Ellington Cemetery, Attala County, Mississippi, s.v. "Aaron Whitaker Guyton," *FindaGrave.com*. The date of Aaron's death is not known with specificity. His will was probated in 1883.

[235] Sarah Matilda (Sally) Guyton, grave marker, unknown cemetery, s.v. "Sarah Matilda Guyton Duckworth," *FindaGrave.com*.

[236] Thomas Duckworth, grave marker, unknown cemetery, s.v. "Thomas Duckworth," *FindaGrave.com*.

[237] John Washington Guyton, grave marker, Hopewell Cemetery, Anderson, Anderson County, South Carolina, digital image s.v. "Gen John Washington Guyton," *FindaGrave.com*.

[238] Sarah Ann Wellborn, grave marker, Hopewell Cemetery, Anderson, Anderson County, South Carolina, digital image s.v. "Sarah Ann Wellborn Guyton," *FindaGrave.com*.

[239] "Death Notice for General John W. Guyton," *The Daily Phoenix*, 22 Sep 1871, p.2; digital image, s.v. "John W. Guyton," *Newspapers.com*, <https://www.newspapers.com/clip/48510699/the-daily-phoenix/>.

[240] "John W. Guyton in Custody," *Intelligencer*, Anderson, South Carolina, 7 Feb 1867, p. 3; digital image, s.v. "John W. Guyton," *Newspapers.com*, <https://www.newspapers.com/clip/48511229/the-intelligencer/>. "Judgment against John W. Guyton and Guyton Guyton," *Intelligencer*, Anderson, South Carolina, 9 Dec 1869, p. 3; digital image, s.v. "John W. Guyton," *Newspapers*.com, <https://www.newspapers.com/clip/28112640/judgement-against-john-w-guyton-and/>.

[241] 1880 U.S. Federal Census, Precinct 4, Red River County, Texas, digital image s.v. "G. G. Gyden," *Ancestry.com*. Guyton was a boarder.

[242] "John W. Guyton in Custody," *Intelligencer*, Anderson, South Carolina, 7 Feb 1867, p. 3; digital image, s.v. "John W. Guyton," *Newspapers.com*, <https://www.newspapers.com/clip/48511229/the-intelligencer>. "Judgment

The map in Figure 27 shows the migrations of Aaron Steele's children where I have been able to ascertain them and the migration of his sister, Hannah GUYTON MARTIN, and her husband, Alexander MARTIN, to Pickens County, Alabama. Joseph GUYTON I's children are in blue; Aaron's are in green).

Aaron Steele GUYTON lived in Ninety-Six District (which later became Union District), South Carolina at the time of his enlistment in the Revolutionary War in 1779. He served under Capt. Moses GUYTON I, his brother, in 1780 and throughout the war, participating in the Siege of 96 and the Battles of Cowpens and Eutaw Springs. He later moved to York District, South Carolina for 4 or 5 years where he married Margaret McCURDY. In 1796 they moved to Pendleton District (later became Anderson District), South Carolina.

Aaron applied for a pension on 1 Oct 1833 and died on 30 June 1841 in Anderson District, South Carolina. Margaret, his widow, applied for a pension (W21237) on 10 Feb 1845 in Anderson District, South Carolina and received Bounty Land Warrant #36605-160-55.[243] According to Helen GUYTON REES, Aaron GUYTON's two-times great-granddaughter, Margaret McCABE, heard stories that Aaron was too young to be in the war, having enlisted at 15. He was enlisted for one week and engaged in one battle before his brother, Moses GUYTON I, enlisted. When Moses I revealed Aaron's age, officers sent Aaron home to grow up. Aaron returned to the war when he was old enough to serve. Aaron's age of 15 seems to conflict with his reported birth dates.

---

against John W. Guyton and Guyton Guyton," *Intelligencer*, Anderson, South Carolina, 9 Dec 1869, p. 3; digital image, s.v. "John W. Guyton," *Newspapers*.com, <https://www.newspapers.com/clip/28112640/judgement-against-john-w-guyton-and/>.

[243] Peden, Jr. Henry C. *Marylanders to Carolina: Migration of Marylanders to North Carolina and South Carolina Prior to 1800*. Family Line Publications: Westminster, MD, 1994, p. 71.

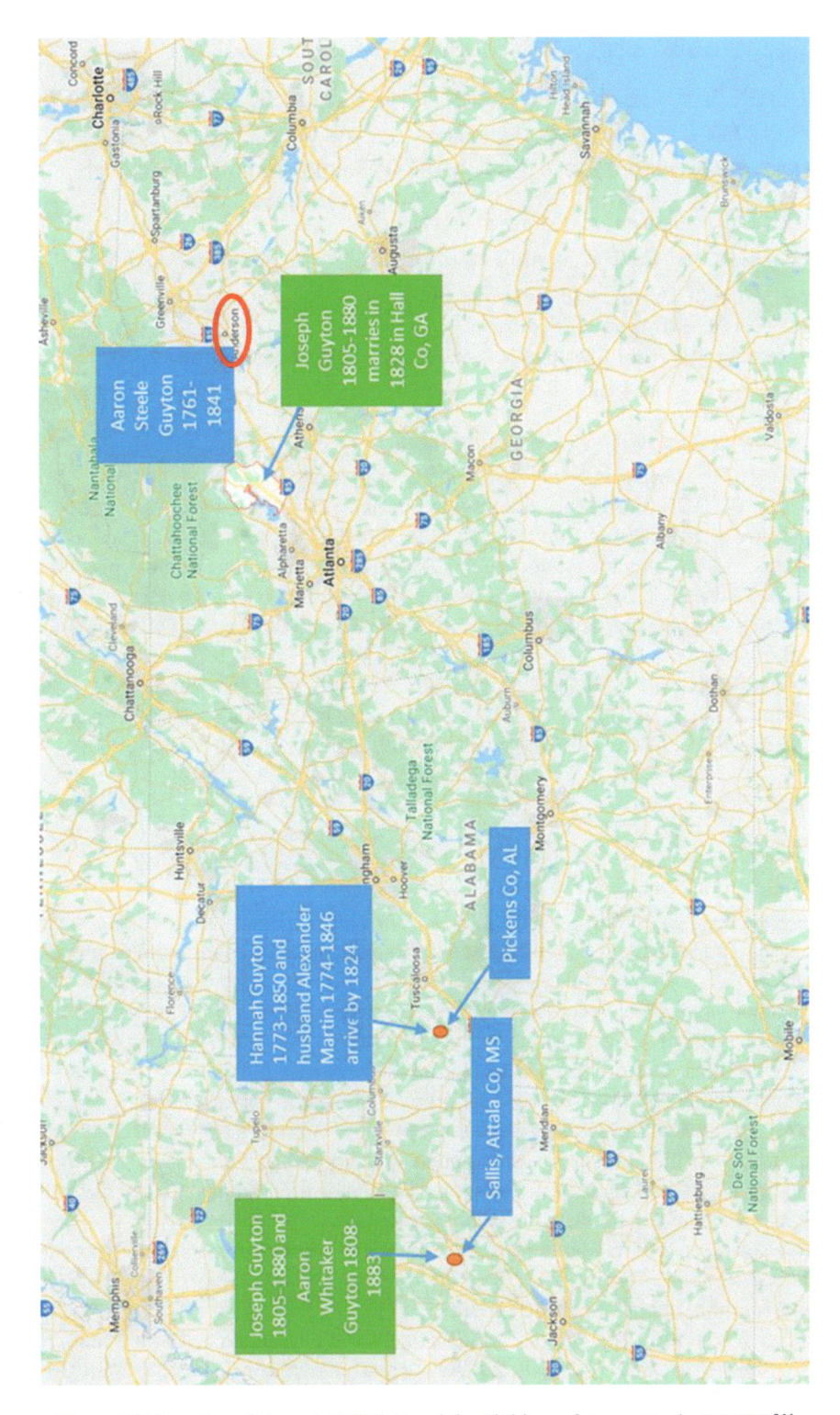

Figure 27 Migration of Hannah GUYTON and the Children of Aaron Steele GUYTON[244]

---

[244] "Mississippi, Alabama, Georgia, and South Carolina." *Google Maps*. Google. 1 Jun 2020. Web. 1 Jun 2020. Adapted by Dorla Coleman Evans.

Abraham GUYTON (Joseph I, John I, Samuel II, Samuel I, John)

Abraham GUYTON (b. Unknown, d. ABT 1816, Union District, SC).[245] His parents were Joseph GUYTON I (b. 17 Sep 1732, d. 13 Jul 1818)[246] and Hannah Lyon WHITAKER (b. 26 Mar 1729, d. 1812).[247] He married Martha Patsy ELLIS (b. 1769, d. 19 Feb 1838)[248] and they had at least eight children:

i   Luther C. GUYTON (b. Unknown, d. Unknown).
ii John Ellis GUYTON (b. ABT 1798, SC, d. AFT 1860, likely Tippah Co., MS)[249] m. Unknown.
iii Mary Nancy GUYTON (b. Unknown, d. Unknown).
iv Catherine GUYTON (b. Unknown, d. Unknown).
v   Martha Patsy (Passy) GUYTON (b. 9 Nov 1804, SC, d. 2 Oct 1869, Washington Co., TX)[250] m. cousin Isaac GUYTON (b. 25 July 1801, d. 21 Nov 1860, Washington Co., TX),[251] son of her uncle, Joseph GUYTON II (ABT 1777-ABT 1865).[252]
vi Joseph B. GUYTON (b. ABT 1803, SC, d. AFT 1860, likely in Washington Co., TX) moved to Pickens County, Alabama and on to Texas with his sister, Passy, and cousin, Isaac GUYTON.
vii Rev. Whitaker W. GUYTON (b. 29 May 1806, Union District, SC, d. 4 Feb 1860, Pickens Co., AL)[253] m. Luvena N. BANKHEAD (b. 30 Apr 1812, Rutherford Co., TN, d. 14 Sep 1887, Pickens Co., AL)[254] on 27 Nov 1834 in Marion County, Alabama.[255] According to *Findagrave.com*, there are two Guyton Family cemeteries listed in Pickens County. One is off Hwy 82, in the yard of P.F. LANGDON; the other, is listed in Pickens County as "Between McShan & McShan Lumber company, in the woods with two adult graves and possibly 2-3 small graves in this cemetery in the woods."[256]
viii Abraham Jenkins GUYTON (b. 2 Jul 1809, SC, d. 1 Feb 1881, MS) m. (1) Luvicia (Luvicy) WARLICK (b. 4 Feb 1817, Lincoln Co., NC, d. 6 Jan 1856, Tippah Co., MS) on 1 Jan 1838 in Lincoln Co., North Carolina and (2) Sarah J. McINTIRE (b. 3 Jun 1833, d. 30 May 1914) on 2 Jun 1856 in Alcorn Co., Mississippi.)

---

[245] "South Carolina, Wills and Probate Records, 1670-1980," digital image s.v. "Abraham Guyton," (probate 14 Feb 1816), *Ancestry.com*.

[246] "Family Data Collection - Individual Records," s.v. "Joseph Guyton," (17 Sep 1732-13 Aug 1818), *Ancestry*.com.

[247] "Family Data Collection – Births," s.v. "Hannah Whitaker," (birth 26 Mar 1729), *Ancestry.com*. "FindaGrave 1600s to Current," s.v. "Hannah Guyton," (death 1812), *Ancestry.com*.

[248] Martha Patsy Ellis, grave marker, Small Guyton Cemetery, Gaffney, Cherokee County, South Carolina, digital image s.v. "Martha Patsy Ellis Guyton," *FindaGrave.com*.

[249] 1860 United States Census, Tippah County, Mississippi, digital image s.v. "John E Guiton," *Ancestry.com*.

[250] Martha Patsy Guyton, grave marker, Roberts Cemetery #2, Washington County, Texas, digital image of false crypt s.v. "Passy "Patsy; Martha" Guyton Guyton," *FindaGrave.com*.

[251] Isaac Guyton, grave marker, Roberts Cemetery #2, Washington County, Texas, digital image of false crypt s.v. "Isaac Guyton," *FindaGrave.com*.

[252] See Generation #5 for more about Joseph GUYTON II.

[253] "Obituary: Whitaker W. Guyton," *The Pickens Republican*, Carrollton, Alabama, 15 Mar 1860, p. 2, digital image, s.v. "Whitaker W. Guyton," *Newspapers.com*, <https://www.newspapers.com/clip/48027036/the-pickens-republican/>.

[254] Luvina N. Bankhead, grave marker, Guyton Family Cemetery, Pickens County, AL, s.v. "Luvina N. Bankhead Guyton," *FindaGrave.com*.

[255] "Obituary: Whitaker W. Guyton," *The Pickens Republican*, Carrollton, Alabama, 15 Mar 1860, p. 2, digital image, s.v. "Whitaker W. Guyton," *Newspapers.com*, <https://www.newspapers.com/clip/48027036/the-pickens-republican/>.

[256] "Location of Guyton Family Cemetery in Pickens County, Alabama," *FindaGrave.com*, <https://www.findagrave.com/cemetery/2502896/guyton-family-cemetery>.

Joseph GUYTON II [(Joseph I, John I, Samuel II, Samuel I, John)]

Joseph GUYTON II (b. ABT 1776, d. Jun 1865, Union District, SC).[257] His parents were Joseph GUYTON I (b. 17 Sep 1732, d. 13 Jul 1818)[258] and Hannah Lyon WHITAKER (b. 26 Mar 1729, d. 1812).[259] He married (1) Unknown and (2) Maria (Mariah) PRIDMORE (b. ABT 1799, d. 30 Oct 1878).[260] Your author's (Dorla COLEMAN EVANS) lineage goes through Joseph II. Joseph II and his first wife had at least eight children:

i   Elizabeth GUYTON (b. 18 Mar 1800, SC, d. 24 Sep 1868, Pickens Co., AL)[261] m. Unknown KENNEDY (b. Unknown, d. BEF 1850). Elizabeth was a widow by the 1850 U.S. Census when she lived in Pickens County, Alabama.[262]

ii   Isaac GUYTON (b. 25 July 1801, d. 21 Nov 1860, Washington Co., TX)[263] m. his first cousin, Patsy Martha (Passy) GUYTON (b. 9 Nov 1804, SC, d. 2 Oct 1869, Washington Co., TX).[264] By 1883 Isaac and Passy lived in Pickens County, Alabama. The U.S. Census of 1850 showed Isaac GUYTON and his family living in Pickens County, Alabama but living in Washington County, Texas by 1860.[265] Passy was the daughter of Abraham GUYTON, Isaac's uncle.

iii   Abraham P. GUYTON (b. 1804, SC, d. 7 Oct 1851, Pickens Co., AL)[266] m. Nancy M. UNKNOWN) (b. 8 Nov 1827 d. 25 Dec 1873, AL or SC).[267] Nancy's children probated her will in Greene County, Alabama.[268] She had two children with Abraham: Drucilla (Gilly) L. H. GUYTON and Abraham J. (Bud) GUYTON. Nancy later married William Peyton SMARR (b. 18 Apr 1824, Cherokee Co., SC, d. 13 Apr 1872, Greene Co., AL)[269] by whom she had four children whom she left under the care of Drucilla during the time of their minority. Nancy's headstone is in South

---

[257] Guyton, David F., "Wills: Joseph Guyton in Union Co., SC," (ABT 1776-Jun 1865), *Guyton Ancestry*, n.d., accessed 31 May 2020, <http://guyton.co.uk/america-wills>.

[258] "Family Data Collection - Individual Records," s.v. "Joseph Guyton," (17 Sep 1732-13 Aug 1818), *Ancestry*.com.

[259] "Family Data Collection – Births," s.v. "Hannah Whitaker," (26 Mar 1729), *Ancestry.com*. "FindaGrave 1600s to Current," s.v. "Hannah Guyton," (death 1812), *Ancestry.com*.

[260] "South Carolina, Wills and Probate Records, 1670-1980," digital image, s.v. "Joseph Guyton," (probated 2 Aug 1865), *Ancestry.com*. Joseph named "Mariah" as his wife in his will. Maria's death notice. "Obituary for Maria Guyton," *Yorkville Enquirer*, 21 Nov 1878, p. 3; digital image, s.v. "Maria Guyton," *Newspapers.com*, <https://www.newspapers.com/clip/21495236/yorkville-enquirer/>.

[261] Elizabeth Guyton, grave marker, Martin Cemetery, Macedonia, Pickens County, AL, digital image s.v. "Elizabeth Kennedy," *FindaGrave.com*.

[262] 1850 U.S. Federal Census, Southern District, Pickens County, Alabama, digital image s.v. "Elizabeth Rineday," *Ancestry.com*.

[263] Isaac Guyton, grave marker, Roberts Cemetery #2, Washington County, Texas, digital image of false crypt s.v. "Isaac Guyton," *FindaGrave.com*.

[264] Martha Patsy Guyton, grave marker, Roberts Cemetery #2, Washington County, Texas, digital image of false crypt s.v. "Passy "Patsy; Martha" Guyton Guyton," *FindaGrave.com*.

[265] 1850 United States Census, Southern District, Pickens County, Alabama, digital image s.v. "Isaac Guyton," *Ancestry.com*. 1860 United States Census, Washington, Washington County, Texas, digital image s.v. "Isaac Guyton," *Ancestry.com*.

[266] Abraham P. Guyton, grave marker, Martin Cemetery, Macedonia, Pickens County, Alabama, digital image s.v. "Abraham P Guyton," *FindaGrave.com*.

[267] Nancy M. UNKNOWN, grave marker, Hopewell Baptist Church Cemetery, Blacksburg, Cherokee County, South Carolina, digital image s.v. "Nancy M Smarr," *FindaGrave.com*.

[268] "Alabama Wills and Probate Records, Greene County, Alabama," digital image s.v. "Nancy M Smarr," (probate 27 Jan 1874), *Ancestry.com*.

[269] William Peyton Smarr, grave marker, Pleasant Ridge Church Cemetery, Greene County, Alabama, digital image s.v. "William P Smarr," (1824-1872), *FindaGrave.com*.

	Carolina. In the 1860 U.S. Census Nancy and William owned assets valued at $31,000. Gilly and Bud, at the ages of 10 and 8, owned assets worth $8,000 each.[270]
iv	Joseph William (Whit) GUYTON (b. 2 Nov 1805, SC, d. 5 Mar 1885, Pickens Co., AL)[271] m. Sarah JOHNSON (b. 1 Apr 1809, NC, d. 17 Jun 1875, Pickens Co., AL).[272]
v	Violet GUYTON (b. 9 Oct 1807, SC, d. 17 Jul 1881, near Howell's Ferry on Broad River in Cherokee Co., SC)[273] m. William MITCHELL (b. 14 Oct 1794, d. 29 Sep 1869).[274]
vi	Isaiah P. GUYTON (b. 20 Aug 1809, SC, d. 6 Jun 1845, Pickens Co., AL)[275] m. Harriett N. JEFFERIES (b. 1819, d. 29 Apr 1855).[276]
vii	Mary GUYTON (b. 19 Sep 1813, SC, d. 15 Dec 1859, SC)[277] m. Joseph W. LEECH, Sr. (b. 1791, d. 6 Feb 1868, SC).[278]
viii	John Luther GUYTON (b. 3 Apr 1815, York Co., SC, d. 6 Oct 1882, Pickens Co., AL)[279] m. (1) Adaline WHISONANT (b. 1822, d. 8 Dec 1844, Pickens Co., AL)[280] and (2) Cintha Susan (Sue C.) WOODS (b. 12 Nov 1838, SC, d. 8 Aug 1911, Pickens Co., AL).[281]

Joseph II died in Union District or Anderson County, South Carolina. His four-page transcribed will is shown in Figure 28, Figure 29, Figure 30, and Figure 31.[282] He signed his will on 15 July 1861. It was proved 2 Aug 1865, a few months after the end of the Civil War. His will suggests he was well-to-do financially at the beginning of the war. Enslaved people and land would have been the biggest portion of his wealth. The 1860 U.S. Census does not indicate large wealth relative to his neighbors. The Census placed his land value at $1,600 and personal property at $3,000. His neighbor's property was valued at

---

[270] 1860 United States Census, Yorkville, Pickens County, Alabama, digital image s.v. "Nancy Smarr," (birth ABT 1837), *Ancestry.com*.

[271] Joseph William (Whit) Guyton, grave marker, J. W. Guyton Family Cemetery, Reform, Pickens County, Alabama, digital image s.v. "John William Guyton," *FindaGrave.com*.

[272] Sarah Johnson, grave marker, J. W. Guyton Family Cemetery, Reform, Pickens County, Alabama, digital image s.v. "Sarah Guyton," *FindaGrave.com*.

[273] Violet Guyton, grave marker, Salem Presbyterian Church Cemetery, Gaffney, Cherokee, South Carolina, digital image s.v. "Violet Mitchell," *FindaGrave.com*. "Obituary: Violet Mitchell," *Yorkville Enquirer*, York, South Carolina, 28 Jul 1881, p. 3, digital image, s.v. "Violet Mitchell," *Newspapers.com*, <https://www.newspapers.com/clip/21492448/yorkville-enquirer/>.

[274] William Mitchell, grave marker, Salem Presbyterian Church Cemetery, Gaffney, Cherokee, SC, digital image s.v. "William Mitchell," *FindaGrave.com*.

[275] Isaiah P. Guyton, grave marker, Martin Cemetery, Macedonia, Pickens, Alabama, digital image s.v. "Isaiah Guyton," *FindaGrave.com*.

[276] Harriet N. Jefferies, grave marker, Martin Cemetery, Macedonia, Pickens, Alabama, digital image s.v. "Harriet Jefferies Griffin," *FindaGrave.com*.

[277] Mary Guyton, grave marker, Salem Presbyterian Church Cemetery, Gaffney, Cherokee County, South Carolina, digital image s.v. "Mary Leech," *FindaGrave.com*.

[278] Joseph Leech, grave marker, Salem Presbyterian Church Cemetery, Gaffney, Cherokee County, South Carolina, digital image s.v. "Joseph Leech," *FindaGrave.com*.

[279] John Luther Guyton, grave marker, Martin Cemetery, Macedonia, Pickens County, Alabama, digital image s.v. "John L Guyton," *FindaGrave.com*.

[280] Adaline Whisonant, grave marker, Martin Cemetery, Macedonia, Pickens County, Alabama, digital image s.v. "Adaline Guyton," (1822-1844), *FindaGrave.com*.

[281] Cintha Susan Woods, grave marker, Mt. Moriah Church Cemetery, Ethelsville, Pickens County, Alabama, digital image s.v. "Cintha Susan Guyton," *FindaGrave.com*.

[282] "South Carolina: Wills and Probate Records, 1670-1980, Union County, South Carolina," digital image s.v. "Joseph Guyton," (probate 2 Aug 1865), *Ancestry.com*.

$15,000 and personal property at $42,500.[283] But all of Joseph's bequests of enslaved people to his family were moot by the end of the Civil War.

---

[283] 1860 United States Census, Gondiesville, Union County, South Carolina, digital image s.v. "Joseph Guiton," *Ancestry.com.*

WILL OF
JOSEPH GUYTON

So. Carolina)
)
U. District) In the name of God Amen.

I. Joseph Guyton of the State and District above named Being of Sound mind and memory do make and publish this my last will and testament in manner and form following . First I give and bequeath unto my beloved wife Moriah Guyton the following Property to wit. one negro Boy Sam three feather beds and furnature three cows and calves one note that I hoald on Tersha and Marthy Leech to be hers her heirs and assigns forever. Also I will and bequeath to my Wife Mariah Guyton the following property one negro man Pompy one boy Mager one girl Betsey one woman Adeline one Boy washington one girl Julia dulcena and their increase to be hers during her natural life and at her death to be Equally devided among my heirs with the exception of the increase which she shall have a childs part to dispose of as she sees fit. I will and bequeath to my Wife Mariah Guyton one tract of land commencing on cerreys line at Dr. Davis corner west side of the crek thense north east with correys line to Eleazer Parkers line to a Red oak corner thense with Parkers line south west to the Road from my house to E. Parkers. thense along said road to the big Road thense down the big road to the Rockey branch thense up the branch to my Red oak corner thense a streigt line to the begining to be hers during her natural life time or widowhood and at her death or marriage to be equally devided among my heirs. I also give and bequeath to my Wife Mariah Guyton my Carriage and Harness two choice horses Cuboards and furniture Clock kitchen furnature Shovle and tongs fire dogs half of the Jars one third of the barrels and pickling tubs one half of the crop after my debts are paid one third of my catle one third of my

Figure 28 Joseph GUYTON II'S 1861 Will p 1/4

WILL OF JOSEPH GUYTON   PAGE 2

hogs and sheep two small tables half dozen chairs all the chests and small bureau one side sadle and man sadle bridles and blankets two blind bridles two leather collars three pairs of drawing chains and haines three clevices and pair of double trees one log chain all my Bells Blacksmith tools two Iron wedges matcih and Sprauting hoe and all farming tools and cooper tools wash tubs my axes loom and operates wheels and Peel to be hers during her natural life and at her death to be equally devided among my heirs I will and bequeath unto my wife Mariah Guyton a childs part of all the money or notes I have on hand at my death I will and bequeath unto my Daughter Elizabeth Kennady one negro boy George one girl Betty Mariah. I will and bequeath unto my son Joseph W. Guyton two negro Boys Bill and Green one feather bed and furnature . I will and bequeath unto my son John L. Guyton one negro woman Fanney and her children Tom Josephene and Mary and their Increase one feather bed and furnature I will and bequeath unto my Daughter Vilet Mitchell one negro boy Mooss. I will and bequeath unto my Daughter Mary Leeches children one negro boy Calvin.

I will that my son Isaac Guyton children have one equal share with mine in money. I will that my son Abaraham Guyton children have one equel share in money with mine. I will that my son Isaiah Guyton children have one equel share with mine in money in case Abraham Guytons children should die before they are of age then the legacy left them shall go to my children .
I will that Joseph W. Guyton and John L. Guyton Receive the legacy left to Abraham Guytons children and Isaiah Guytons children and pay it over to them with the Interest as they become of age I will that the negroes willed to my children be valued by three

Figure 29 Joseph GUYTON II'S 1861 Will p 2/4

WILL OF JOSEPH GUYTON   PAGE 3

Disinterred persons so that when they throw in to Hatchpoch what they have Received here to- fore they may all share and share alike   I will that thee balance of my estate both Real and personal be scald by my Executors and equally devided among my heirs so that each one share and share alike after they have thrown into Hatchpotch wat they have Recd. here tofore. I hereby constitute and appoint Joseph W. Guyton John L. Guyton . William Mitchel and Joseph Leech my Executors to excute this my last Will and Testament . In Testimony whereoff I have hereunto set my hand and affixed my seal This 18th Janurary in the year of our Lord one Thousand Eight hundred and Sixty one

Signed Sealed and acknowledge in the presence of the Subscribing witnesses

John M McKown

Isaac L. Parker

Eleazer Parker

                        Joseph Guyton (LS)

Codicil

Codidil to the above will

I will and bequeath unto Vilet Mitchell and Mary Leeches Children one negro woamn Adeline and her children at the Death of my wife Mariah Guyton I will and bequeath unto Elizabeth Kennady J. W. Guyton and I.H. Guyton one negro woman Betsey and her increase at the death of my wife Mariah Guyton the above families of negroes to be put in lots and valied by three Disinterested men Viz; Vilet Mitchel one lot and Mary Leeches Children one lot of Adelines familey also Elizabeth Kennady. I . W. Guyton and J.L. Guyton each a lot of Betseys familey the above named Vilet Mitchel Mary Leeches children

Figure 30 Joseph GUYTON II'S 1861 Will p 3/4

WILL OF JOSEPH GUYTON   PAGE 4

E. Kennady Joseph W. Guyton and John L Guyton shall pay to Isaac Guytons children one ninth part of the Value of the above negroes also Abraham Guytons children one ninth part and Isaiah Guytons children one ninth part also my Wife Mariah Guyton has the disposel of one ninth part of the increase as she sees fit

Signed the 15th day of July Eighteen hundred and sixty one in presence of

                                        Joseph Guyton (. LS)

Test
John M McKown
John Weber
Eleazer Parker

Recorded in Will Book C
Pages 276 - 277- 278
Box 48   Pkg. 8
Recorded August 2nd 1865
C. Gage (ordy)

Figure 31 Joseph GUYTON II'S 1861 Will p 4/4

Hannah GUYTON (Joseph I, John I, Samuel II, Samuel I, John)

Hannah GUYTON (b. 18 Aug 1773, Union District, SC, d. Jan 1850, Ethelsville, Pickens Co., AL)[284] m. Alexander MARTIN (b. 26 Feb 1774, SC, d. 18 Jun 1846, Ethelsville, Pickens Co., AL).[285] Her parents were Joseph GUYTON I (b. 17 Sep 1732, d. 13 Jul 1818)[286] and Hannah Lyon WHITAKER (b. 26 Mar 1729, d. 1812).[287] She was the first of Joseph I's descendants to move out of South Carolina. Hannah and Alex are buried in Martin Cemetery, located just south of the Ethelsville, Alabama, and west of Pickens CR 75. It is situated in a wooded area with the main cemetery enclosed by a chain link fence.[288]

Hannah and Alexander had at least four children:

i   Joseph MARTIN (b. 1802, Union District, SC, d. 6 Aug 1838, Pickens Co., AL)[289] He was buried in a $20.00 black walnut coffin lined with flannel.[290] He represented Pickens County in the Alabama State Legislature between 1836 and 1838.[291]

ii   Mary Elizabeth MARTIN (b. 15 Sep 1805, Marion Co., SC, d. 8 Sep 1868, Pickens Co., AL, bur. Martin Cemetery, Pickens Co., AL)[292] m. James Tarrant BURDINE (b. 1 Mar 1799, SC, d. 6 Oct 1880, Pickens Co., AL, bur. Martin Cemetery, Pickens Co., AL).[293]

iii Frances Virginia MARTIN (b. 1805-1810, d. AFT 1860 and BEF 1870, likely in TX)[294] m. (1) Dr. BRUTON of Fayette County, Alabama (or perhaps BURTON or BARTON) (b. Unknown, d. ABT 1828),[295] (2) Rufus King

---

[284] "U.S., FindaGrave Index, 1600s-Current," digital image s.v. "Hannah Martin," (18 Aug 1773-Jan 1850), *Ancestry.com*.

[285] "U.S., FindaGrave Index, 1600s-Current," digital image s.v. "Alexander Martin," (26 Feb 1774-18 Jun 1846), *Ancestry.com*.

[286] "Family Data Collection - Individual Records," s.v. "Joseph Guyton," (17 Sep 1732-13 Aug 1818), *Ancestry*.com.

[287] "Family Data Collection – Births," s.v. "Hannah Whitaker," (26 Mar 1729), *Ancestry.com*. "FindaGrave 1600s to Current," s.v. "Hannah Guyton," (death 1812), *Ancestry.com*.

[288] "Martin Cemetery," digital image s.v. "Martin Cemetery, Macedonia," *FindaGrave.com* <https://www.findagrave.com/cemetery/24219/martin-cemetery>.

[289] Joseph Martin, grave marker, Martin Cemetery, Macedonia, Pickens County, Alabama, digital image s.v. "Col. Joseph Martin," *FindaGrave.com*.

[290] "Alabama Wills and Probate Records: 1753-1999, Lawrence County, Alabama," digital image s.v. "Joseph Martin," (probate 1838), *Ancestry.com*.

[291] Smith, Nelson F., *Annals of Northwest Alabama: History of Pickens County*," 1856, v. 1(1), p. 72, *Ancestry.com*.

[292] Mary Elizabeth Martin, grave marker, Martin Cemetery, Macedonia, Pickens County, Alabama, digital image s.v. "Mary Elizabeth Burdine," (1805-1868), *FindaGrave.com*.

[293] James Tarrant Burdine, grave marker, Martin Cemetery, Macedonia, Pickens County, Alabama+, digital image s.v. "James Tarrant Burdine" (1799-1880), *FindaGrave.com*.

[294] The 1850 and 1860 U. S. Census differ in her age by five years. 1850 United States Census, Harrison County, Texas, digital image s.v. "F Smith," (birth 1810), *Ancestry.com*. 1860 United States Census, Harrison County, Texas, digital image s.v. "F Smith," (birth 1805), *Ancestry.com*.

[295] Smith, Nelson F., *Annals of Northwest Alabama: History of Pickens County*," digital image, 1856, v. 1(1), p. 109, *Ancestry.com*. Several Barton families lived next to or close to the Alexander Martin family in the earliest township and range public land survey in Pickens Co., Alabama. "U.S., Indexed Early Land Ownership and Township Plats, 1785-1898 Earliest Township and Range Public Land Survey," digital image s.v. "Alex Martin," (S and W R1 T1 - S and W R17 T22) *Ancestry.com*.

ANDERSON (b. 19 Jun 1801, d. 29 May 1834, Pickens Co., AL)[296] and (3) Nathan Alexander SMITH (b. 1785-1790, Virginia, d. AFT 1860 and BEF 1870, Texas).[297]

iv   John MARTIN (b. 20 Dec 1808, SC, d. 21 Oct 1821, SC).

Hannah and Alexander moved from South Carolina to Alabama after their son, John's, death in 1821. They moved probably around 1824, five years after Alabama entered the Union as a state. At that point, Alex started purchasing lands, ultimately amassing around 960 acres. The table below shows the purchases I have identified.[298]

\multicolumn{4}{c}{Land Purchases by Alexander Martin in Pickens and Lamar Counties, AL}
Date	Certificate Number	County	Land Description
19 Apr 1824	2113	Pickens	E ½ SE ¼ HUNTSVILLE T19S 16W Section 31
19 Apr 1824	2116	Pickens	E ½ NE ¼ HUNTSVILLE T19S 16W Section 31
19 Apr 1824	2117	Pickens	W ½ NE ¼ HUNTSVILLE T19S 16W Section 29
19 Apr 1824	2126	Pickens	E ½ SE ¼ HUNTSVILLE T19S 16W Section 30
19 Apr 1824	2134	Pickens	W ½ NW ¼ HUNTSVILLE T19S 16W, Section 33
22 Apr 1824	2386	Pickens	W ½ SW ¼ HUNTSVILLE T19S 16W Section 29
4 May 1824	2787	Pickens	W ½ SE ¼ HUNTSVILLE T19S 16W Section 30
30 Mar 1837	13782	Pickens	W ½ NW ¼ HUNTSVILLE T19S R16W Section 29
30 Mar 1837	13876	Pickens	E ½ NW ¼ HUNTSVILLE T19S R16W Section 29
7 Nov 1837	16764	Lamar	W ½ NE ¼ HUNTSVILLE T15S R16W Section 12
10 Sep 1838	10036	Lamar	SW ¼ NW ¼ HUNTSVILLE T14S R15W Section 30
10 Sep 1838	10037	Lamar	NW ¼ SW ¼ HUNTSVILLE T14S R15W Section 32
10 Jul 1844	23836	Pickens	E ½ NE ¼ HUNTSVILLE T19S R16W Section 30

A map of Alex and Hannah's land is shown below in Figure 32. Highlighted is the location of Martin Cemetery where many Martins and Guytons are buried. Hannah and Alexander's headstones are in Figure 33 and Figure 34, respectively.

---

[296] Rufus K. Anderson, grave marker, Martin Cemetery, Macedonia, Pickens County, Alabama, digital image s.v. "Rufus K Anderson," *FindaGrave.com*. His headstone reads, "In memory of Rufus K Anderson, Esq., born June 19, A. D. 1801, died May 29, A. D. 1834. Warm and enthusiastic in his feelings and ardent in his attachments, he possessed many friends, and for several years represented Pickens County in the State Senate."

[297] The 1850 and 1860 U. S. Census differ in his age by five years. 1850 United States Census, Harrison County, Texas, digital image s.v. "N Smith," (birth 1790), *Ancestry.com*. 1850 United States Census, Harrison County, Texas, digital image s.v. "N Smith," (birth 1785), *Ancestry.com*. He was in the 1860 U.S. Census but did not show up in the 1870 U.S. Census.

[298] "U.S. General Land Office Records, 1796-1907," digital image s.v. "Alexander Martin," (land purchase various dates), *Ancestry.com*.

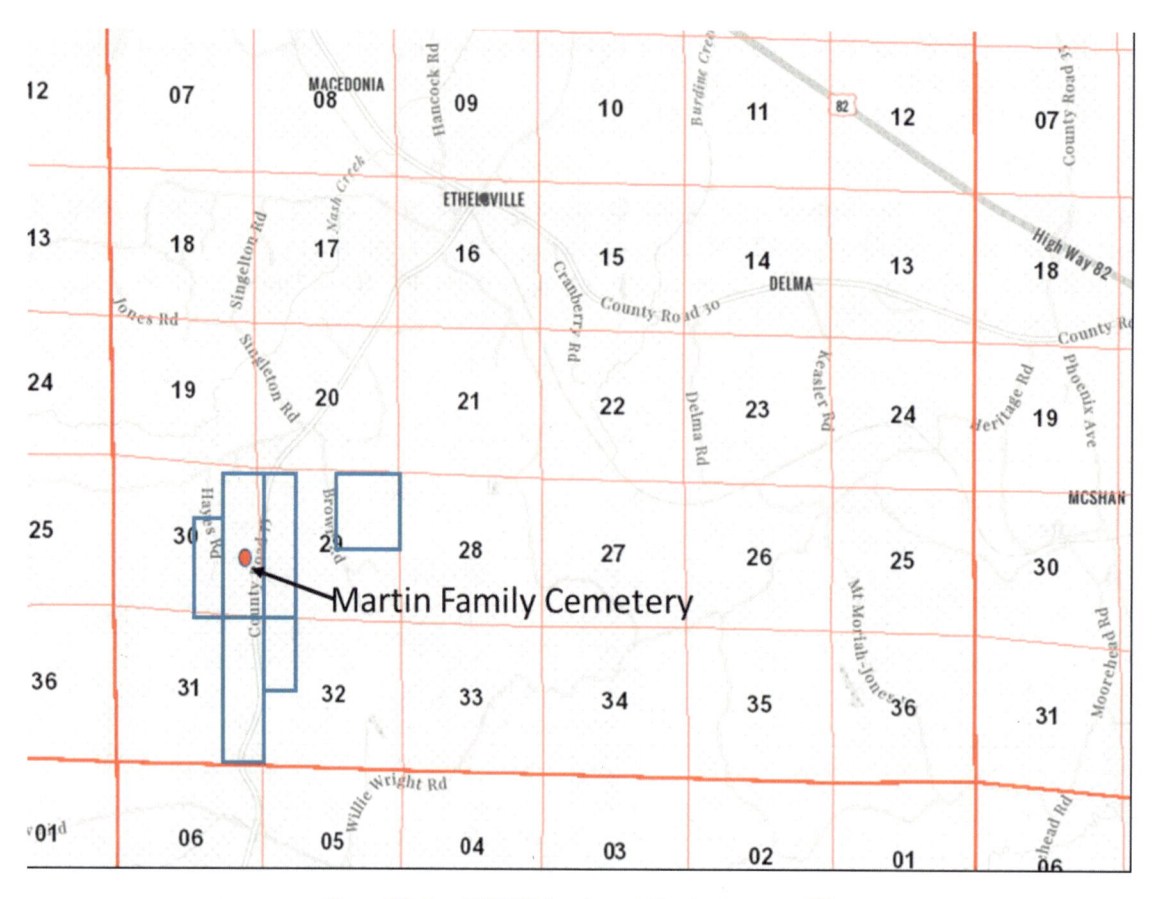

Figure 32 Alex MARTIN Lands and Martin Cemetery[299]

Figure 33 Hannah GUYTON MARTIN's Headstone

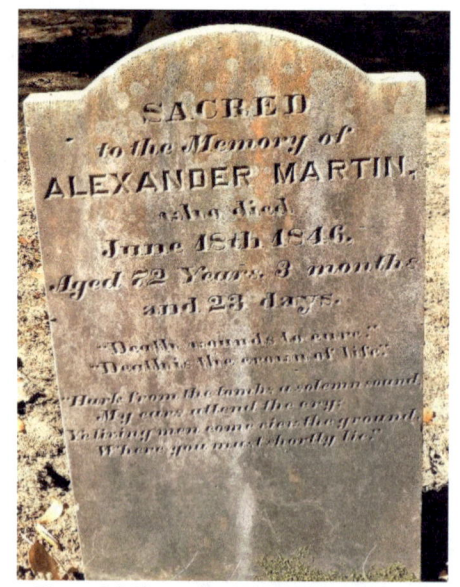

Figure 34 Alexander MARTIN's Headstone

---

[299] "Map of Township 19S, Ranges 14W, 15W, and 16W, Huntsville Meridian," Public Land Survey System, *Bureau of Land Management*, <https://www.arcgis.com/apps/View/index.html?appid=019dd6f39fda4d3b811abfab0878b63b>.

Frances Virginia MARTIN's marriage to Rufus King ANDERSON ended tragically. Rufus, a lawyer, migrated to Alabama from Tennessee around 1825. He served in the Alabama State Legislature from 1829 to 1833 but he was considered "an overbearing, reckless man, who insulted whom he pleased, and was generally regarded as a dangerous man."[300] Most men went out of their way to not antagonize him because he already had a history of violence. He was tried for murdering his brother-in-law, Thomas P. TAUL (or TOLL), in Kentucky. After a trial of eighteen days, the jury acquitted him. In Alabama the Grand Jury found a true bill for his murder of a slave from beating her to death. Again, the jury acquitted Rufus.

Another lawyer in town, Gideon FRIERSON, expressed his displeasure concerning Rufus' murder of his slave. When Rufus heard, he threatened Frierson's life. At some point, while working in his law office, Frierson learned Rufus called him out. Rufus carried two pistols. Knowing Rufus had threatened him, Frierson brought an early version of a double-barreled shotgun to the street. When shots both directions didn't stop the violence, Frierson clubbed Rufus over the head, killing him. Frierson turned himself into authorities but he was not prosecuted. Everyone knew the truth.

Frances and Rufus had three daughters, one born after his death. Based on the ages and sexes of the people living with Alexander MARTIN in the 1840 U.S. Census, I think Frances lived with her parents after Rufus' death. By 1842 she gave birth to her first child with Nathan SMITH in Alabama. Sometime after the birth of her second child in Alabama, they moved to Harrison County, Texas. In Texas they lived close to Sarah PARKER and her husband, James C. CHILDRESS. Frances and Sarah were first cousins. Their mothers, Hannah GUYTON MARTIN and Elizabeth (Betsey) GUYTON PARKER, respectively, were sisters. I hope she found a better man in Nathan SMITH and left her past behind in Alabama.

---

[300] Quoted from Colonel Garrett in his *History of the Public Men of Alabama.* Saunders, James Edmonds. *Early Settlers of Alabama.* Tuscaloosa, Alabama: Willo Publishing Company, 1961, pp. 94-95. Originally published in New Orleans by L. Graham in 1899.

Generation #6

Aaron Whitaker (Whit) GUYTON (Aaron Steele, Joseph I, John I, Samuel II, Samuel I, John)

Aaron Whitaker (Whit) GUYTON was born in 1808 in Anderson Co., SC and died between 1881 and 1883 in Sallis, Attala Co., MS.[301] He was the son of Aaron Steele GUYTON (1761-1841)[302] and Margaret McCURDY (1791-1853),[303] and was the grandson of Joseph GUYTON I (1732-1818)[304] and Hannah WHITAKER (1729-1812).[305] Many descendants believe he is buried in the Ellington Cemetery (see Figure 35) located off Attala County Road 4116 at GPS Coordinates: 32.9943000, -89.7463900 [306] although there is no grave marker. They believe that Whit is buried with his brother, Joseph A. GUYTON, and his sister-in-law, Zemuely McCLUSKY GUYTON, in the chain-linked fence area. See Figure 36 and Figure 37.

Figure 35 Ellington Cemetery

---

[301] Aaron Whitaker Guyton, grave marker, Ellington Cemetery, Attala County, Mississippi, s.v. "Aaron Whitaker Guyton," *FindaGrave.com*. "Mississippi, Wills and Probate Records, 1780-1982," digital image s.v. "A. W. Guyton," (will signed 5 Dec 1881), *Ancestry.com*. The date of Aaron's death is not clear. *FindaGrave.com* errs with a date of 1889 because Aaron's will was dated 1883. Aaron signed his will in 1881. His death occurred between the end of 1881 and mid-1883.

[302] Aaron Steele Guyton, grave marker, Old Hopewell Cemetery, Anderson, Anderson County, South Carolina, s.v. "Aaron Steele Guyton," *FindaGrave.com*. "Family Data Collection: Individual Records," s.v. "Aaron Steele Guyton," (birth 26 Oct 1761, marriage Oct 1789, death 30 June 1831), *Ancestry.com* (1 Jun 2020).

[303] Margaret McCurdy Guyton, grave marker, Old Hopewell Cemetery, Anderson, Anderson County, South Carolina, s.v. "Margaret "Peggy" McCurdy Guyton," *FindaGrave.com*.

[304] "Family Data Collection - Individual Records," s.v. "Joseph Guyton," (birth 17 Sep 1732, death 13 Aug 1818), *Ancestry*.com (16 Oct 2016).

[305] "Family Data Collection – Births," s.v. "Hannah Whitaker," (birth 26 Mar 1729), *Ancestry.com* (30 May 2020). "FindaGrave 1600s to Current," s.v. "Hannah Guyton," (death 1812), *Ancestry.com* (30 May 2020).

[306] Aaron Whitaker Guyton, grave marker, Ellington Cemetery, Attala County, Mississippi, s.v. "Aaron Whitaker Guyton," *FindaGrave.com*.

Figure 36 Joseph GUYTON and Zemuely MCCLUSKY GUYTON Headstones in Ellington Cemetery

Figure 37 Distant Photo of Joseph and Zemuely GUYTON Area in Ellington Cemetery

Aaron Whitaker (Whit) GUYTON is the beginning of the African American genealogy which is the focus on this book. David F. GUYTON identified the earliest recorded African Guytons as Amashire (Amershire) and Flora GUYTON, listed in the 1870 U.S. Census for Augusta, Richmond County, Georgia. They were born about 1798 and 1797, respectively. They were the only two Guytons reported as being born in Africa and must have been brought to America enslaved.[307]

The 1870 and 1880 U.S. Census showcased the many cases where African American and white Guyton households lived next to or close to one other.[308] After emancipation, the families still lived on the same land and in the same small rural communities. The most numerous references to African American Guytons in these censuses are in Pickens County, Alabama; St. Francis County, Arkansas; Bartow, Johnson, Laurens, and Thomas Counties, Georgia; Attala, Lowndes, and Tippah Counties, Mississippi; Anderson, Union, and York Counties, South Carolina; and Washington County, Texas.[309] These are all locations where the descendants of Joseph GUYTON I migrated.

According to David F. GUYTON, in 2000 there were an estimated 7,300 Guytons living in the United States. Of these, perhaps around a third (or about 2,500) were of African origin or of mixed race. The majority of these Guytons were likely descendants of enslaved people in the southern states where many emancipated enslaved people adopted the Guyton names of their farm or plantation slaveholders following the end of the Civil War in 1865. "The lives and livelihoods of these slaves and later free African Americans were thus closely entwined with members and locations of various branches of white Guyton families in the second half of the nineteenth century."[310]

---

[307] *Ibid.* "1870 United States Census," Augusta, Richmond County, Georgia, digital image s.v. "Amashire Guyton," (birth ABT 1798), *Ancestry.com*.
[308] David F. Guyton.
[309] Guyton, David F., "African Americans," *Guyton Ancestry*, n.d., accessed 31 May 2020. <http://guyton.co.uk/america-african>.
[310] Guyton, David F., "African Americans," *Guyton Ancestry*, accessed 31 May 2020. <http://guyton.co.uk/america-african>.

Whit GUYTON never married legally under the laws of his time.[311] In the early colonial period in America (1492-1763), miscegenation was accepted until the latter end of the seventeenth century, when it became less acceptable and was eventually forbidden in some colonies.[312] Evidence suggests Whit had three African American partners with whom he had children. After the Civil War, states in the South passed anti-mescengenation laws. In 1865, Mississippi passed a miscegenation statute. It "declared a felony for any freedman, free Negro, or mulatto to intermarry with any white person. The penalty was set as imprisonment in state penitentiary for life." Mississippi's 1868 constitution permitted common-law and interracial marriages following its ratification.[313] In 1890, Mississippi prohibited miscegenation through its new constitution. It "prohibited marriage of a white person with a Negro or mulatto or person who has one-eighth or more of Negro blood." The penalty could be a ten-year prison sentence.

Kathryn Schumaker provides insights into the legal aspects of interracial relationships in Mississippi in the early 1900s.[314] Although the time period she studied falls long after Whit GUYTON's death, her reporting on specific Mississippi cases allows us to sense how local rural communities may have viewed these relationships. Using court records from Adams County, MS, she examined eighteen cases of "unlawful cohabitation" during the early era of anti-miscengenation organizations. Eighteen cases were plainly an undercount of interracial relationships as some records have been lost. But cases also required an aggressive prosecutor who usually only addressed cases in which the relationship approximated a marriage. A marriage between couples of different races could result in a prison sentence for both parties. Cohabitation, a more casual and transitory relationship, was a misdemeanor if it were deemed unlawful. Few couples risked the prison sentence with a marriage but their relationships did assume other aspects of family life, "including cohabitation, child-rearing, and the transmission of property among kin."

Complicating prosecution, Mississippi recognized both traditional marriages and common law marriages, in which couples merely presented themselves to their communities as a married couple. Before bringing cohabitation cases to court, prosecutors had to assess whether their white male neighbors crossed the line between lawful and unlawful cohabitation. Jurors drawn from the local area had to be convinced with evidence about the nature of the intimate relationship between a white man and an African American woman including their sleeping arrangements and their private sexual

---

[311] "Handout: Mississippi Miscegenation Laws Founding Era Primary Source," *Facing History and Ourselves*, <https://www.facinghistory.org/sites/default/files/2023-03/Mississippi_Miscegenation_Laws.pdf>, accessed 24 Mar 2024.

[312] Nyla Provost, "Mixing: A History of Anti-Miscegenation Laws in the United States," Vol. 16, Article 7, 2023, <https://scholarworks.lib.csusb.edu/cgi/viewcontent.cgi?article=1284&context=history-in-the-making>, accessed 24 Mar 2024.

[313] McMillen, Neil R., *Dark Journey: Black Mississippians in the Age of Jim Crow*. Urbana: University of Illinois Press. 1989.

[314] Schumaker, Kathryn, "'Unlawful Intimacy': Mixed-Race Families, Miscegenation Law, and the Legal Culture of Progressive Era Mississippi," *Law and History Review*, Cambridge University Press, Volume 41, Issue 4, November 2023, pp. 773-794, <DOI: https://doi.org/10.1017/S0738248023000317>.

behavior.[315] Judges were usually not from the local area. Instead, they rotated among circuit courts with brief periods in residence. Witnesses called to testify about a relationship may have refused to testify or been reluctant to testify truthfully if they or someone close to them had similar relationships or the man held a position of high social or economic status. Because judges understood that their role likely conflicted with the desires of the local community, they focused on the legal process, case precedents, and tradition rather than standing for "racial purity" at the center of the anti-miscengenation laws.

Schumaker concludes, "The unintended consequence of the Progressive Era efforts to prosecute interracial couples was to reveal a widespread disinterest in punishing these kinds of legal and cultural infractions through the courts… At stake was a more fundamental question about the extent of the authority of white men to govern their private lives, including whether they could choose to form families with Black women. This history reveals the contradictions of Jim Crow law, which protected white men's prerogative to choose their partners as they saw fit even as some formed interracial families that made a mockery of the spirit of segregation."

We have a rare opportunity in Southern history to have at least limited documentation in our family on the relationships between a white Guyton man (Whit GUYTON), his African American partners (Sarah UNKNOWN later known as Sarah RUSSELL; Patsy GIBSON; and Artie RAINEY), and their children during a period that spans from the 1860s before the Civil War into the 1880s. At the crux of our judgment of Whit GUYTON is the nature of his relationships with his partners.[316] The resources in the footnote provide some guidance to our consideration. The dissertation by Evan ASHFORD specifically includes the relationship between Whit GUYTON and Artie RAINEY.

The very essense of an intimate relationship between a slaveholder and an enslaved woman is presumed to include one or more forms of coersion. Coersion could range from subtle threats, ruthless physical violence, and enticing opportunities. Rape of an enslaved woman was not considered a crime in most jurisdictions. Fear of separation from their children or the mistreatment of their children would be enough to secure most unwilling women to cooperate. In our case, Whit's partners and their children depended on Whit for their basic human needs – sustenance, clothing, housing, and protection. They lived under Whit's whims on how to employ their labor. Would he punish them with heavier work for failure to behave as he dictated? Would he entreat compliance through a promise of easier work? Would he offer to emancipate their children? The reader can imagine many subtle and blatantly coersive scenarios that would lead an enslaved woman to unwillingly enter an intimate relationship with a slaveholder.

But what if Whit GUYTON was not that type of man? Does unexpected consideration toward enslaved people by a slaveholder not suggest there may have been some mutual trust in his

---

[315] Because of the ubiquity of lynchings, cohabitation between African American men and white women were rare but were considered to be of a much more serious nature than white men and African American women.
[316] Kennedy, Randall, *Interracial Intimacies: Sex, Marriage, Identity, and Adoption*, excerpted in the *New York Times,* 26 Jan 2003, <https://www.nytimes.com/2003/01/26/books/chapters/interracial-intimacies.html>. Ashford, Evan, "The Privilege of Blackness: Black Empowerment and the Fight for Liberation in Attala County, Mississippi 1865-1915" (2018). Doctoral Dissertations.

relationships with his partners? Would legally recognizing his children at a time period in Mississippi when such recognition could potentially cause social ostracism indicate that his relationships may have been meaningful to Whit? Could such legal recognition be considered an act of tenderness or love?

Evan ASHFORD makes the argument that in cases like Whit GUYTON's, his African American women partners held some power in the relationships by giving heirs to an otherwise childless man. He argued that the benefits of such relationships fell primarily to the children (through paid education, land gifts, emancipation, etc.). The mothers could benefit indirectly by the well-being of their children and directly by economic assistance in later life provided by their children. I reviewed the 1900 and 1910 U.S. Censuses for Whit's children because the censuses indicate whether people owned real property and whether it was mortgaged or owned free and clear. All of Whit's children that I found on either census owned property free and clear at some point in their lives. In the individual sections for each child, I address this issue.

Did Whit's partners have a degree of autonomy in whether they had an intimate relationship with him and in the dynamics of the relationship? We are likely to never know the answers to those questions from any of his three partners. It is likely that Whit's interpretation of the relationships differed from the interpretations of the women. There is very little information from other women in similar circumstances to enlighten us on how they may have felt.

At least four of Whit's children with three sequential African American partners – Sarah UNKNOWN/RUSSELL, Patsy GIBSON, and Artie RAINEY – were born before the end of the Civil War. All three women were born in the slavery period, although Channie BROWN-CURRIE informs us that her family traditions hold that Artie was never enslaved. Sarah and Patsy were likely enslaved and listed on Whit GUYTON's 1850 and 1860 U.S. Census Slave Schedule. Six other children were born to Artie after the War.

Record-keeping for African Americans often varied from poor to non-existent. The 1840 Census showed that Whit lived alone in Hall Co., GA, with two enslaved people. The enslaved man was between 10- and 23-years-old;[317] the enslaved woman was of the same age. Aaron Whitaker GUYTON was first documented in Attala County, Mississippi in the 1850 U.S. Census. He was 42 years old (although the Census shows him as 38) and lived without a listed family. The 1850 U.S. Census Slave Schedules showed Whit enslaved six persons, ranging in age from 23 years to 6 months. See Figure 38. The enslaved persons were not named in the schedules, as was the norm, regrettably.

---

[317] The U.S. Federal Census before 1850 included age brackets within sex and racial categories, not specific ages.

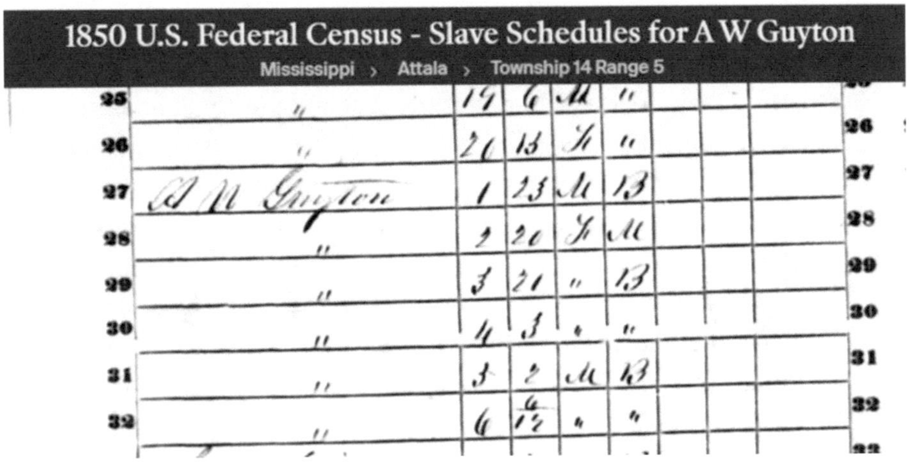

25	"	19	6	M	"
26	"	21	13	F	"
27	A W Guyton	1	23	M	B
28	"	2	20	F	M
29	"	3	21	"	B
30	"	4	3	"	"
31	"	5	2	M	B
32	"	6	6/12	"	"

Figure 38 1850 U.S. Census -- Slave Schedule for Aaron Whitaker Guyton

The three children, as described above, were likely Caroline (age 3), Pinkney (age 2), and Elijah (age 6 months). The two adult females (ages 21 and 20) could be Sarah UNKNOWN, Whit's first partner later known as Sarah RUSSELL, and Patsy GIBSON. There was also an adult male (age 23). Sarah was born about 1829 in South Carolina.[318] We find no evidence that Whit married but he lived down the road from his brother, Joseph A. GUYTON. According to Evan ASHFORD, Whit owned two enslaved women (Patsy GIBSON and Sarah UNKNOWN) and had four children with them, but David F. GUYTON believes they actually had three children.[319]

Aaron Whitaker GUYTON and Sarah UNKNOWN/RUSSELL had one child:

i Caroline GUYTON (b. Jan 1947, Attala Co., MS, d. 1915, Attala Co., MS)[320] m. Vincent (Vinson) TERRY (b. 1839, d. 8 Oct 1904, Attala Co., MS).[321]

The 1900 U.S. Census indicated that Green and Sarah RUSSELL were married 50 years.[322] If the years are accurate, then they married or partnered around 1850, three years after Caroline's birth. Their marriage took place (or relationship started) a decade before the Civil War, suggesting that Whit GUYTON approved of the relationship. According to Duane Helweg (duaneehe on *Ancestry.com*), in the 1900 and 1910 U.S. Censuses reporting on Sarah UNKNOWN and Green RUSSELL, Sarah is shown as having had one child with one still living. Also in the 1910 Census, under marital status, Sarah's marriage

---

318 "1900 United States Census," Attala Co., MS, digital image s.v. "Sarah Russell," (birth 1829), Ancestry.com.
319 Personal correspondence.
320 Caroline's birth year varies considerably from 1843 to 1851 across all the sources I have for her. Caroline Guyton, grave marker, Russell Cemetery, Attala Co., MS, digital image s.v. "Caroline J. Terry," (1843-1915), *FindaGrave.com*. "1900 United States Census," Kosciusko, Attala Co., MS, digital image s.v. "Clalline Terry," (birth Jan 1847), *Ancestry.com.*
321 Vincent (Vinson) Terry, grave marker, Russell Cemetery, Attala Co., MS, digital image s.v. "Venson Terry," (1839-1904), *FindaGrave.com.* His birth date varies from 1831 to 1841 across my sources.
322 "1900 United States Census," Attala County, Mississippi, digital image s.v. "Sarah Russell," (birth 1829), Ancestry.com.

status was shown as M2 (a second marriage) while Green's was M1 (a first marriage).[323] Did Sarah consider herself married to Whit GUYTON? In the 1870 U.S. Census, Green and Sarah RUSSELL lived with Aaron Whitaker GUYTON.[324] They lived together after the War and the abolition of slavery. It may have been a strictly financial arrangement at an age when Whit GUYTON may have needed assistance or he might have enjoyed the company. In the 1900 U.S. Census, Green and Sarah UNKNOWN/RUSSELL own their farm free and clear. Did Whit give them property or sell them land at an affordable price?

Trying to determine the birth dates of Whit's children is difficult. The 1850 U.S. Census Slave Schedule shows Whit GUYTON enslaved three children, aged 3, 2, and 6/12.[325] That implies Caroline was born in 1847; Pinkney in 1848; and Elijah in 1850. Depending on the nature of Whit's relationships with Sarah UNKNOWN/RUSSELL and Patsy GIBSON, Whit may have treated the children as slaves, or he may have treated them as his children. Whit's second partner was Patsy GIBSON, about whom little is known. David F. GUYTON believes she was born around 1832 and died around 1860. We know her name through their son, Pinkney GUYTON's, death certificate.[326] See Figure 94. Their two sons are listed below:

i   Pinkney GUYTON (b. Jan 1848, Attala Co., MS, d. AFT 1920)[327] m. Fannie SALLIS (b. Oct 1855, d. AFT 1940).[328]

ii   Elijah (Lige) GUYTON (b. 1850, Attala Co., MS, d. 1901)[329] m. (1) Sarah RUSSELL (b. ABT 1856, d. 1893)[330] and (2) Tennie FULLER (b. 16 Feb 1869, d. 21 Oct 1939, St. Louis, MO).[331]

Pinkney was born about a year after Caroline GUYTON's birth. The 1860 U.S. Census Slave Schedules likely listed the same adult male (age 30 – ages were not well-documented in the early census) and one of the same adult females (age 28).[332] See Figure 39. The other adult female was not in

---

[323] Duane Helweg (duaneehe), "Family Revelation(s) from a Will Written in 1905," originally shared on 27 Apr 2021, *Ancestry.com*.

[324] "1880 United States Census," Attala County, Mississippi, digital image s.v. "Sarah Russell," (birth 1835), Ancestry.com.

[325] "1850 United States Census: Slave Schedule," Township 14 Range 5, Attala County, Mississippi, digital image s.v. "A W Guyton," *Ancestry.com*.

[326] Mississippi, Death Certificates, "Pink Guyton," (1848-1929), personal copy.

[327] "1900 United States Census," Kosciusko, Attala County, Mississippi, digital image s.v. "Pink Guyton," (birth Jan 1848), *Ancestry.com*. His birth date ranges between 1845 and 1850. He last appears in the 1920 United States Census. "1920 United States Census," Kosciusko, Attala County, Mississippi, digital image s.v. "Pink Guyton," (birth ABT 1848), *Ancestry.com*.

[328] "1900 United States Census," Kosciusko, Attala County, Mississippi, digital image s.v. "Fannie Guyton," (birth Oct 1855), *Ancestry.com*. Her birth date ranges from 1853 to 1857. She last appears in the 1940 U.S. Census. "1940 United States Census," Kosciusko, Attala County, Mississippi, digital image s.v. "Fannie Guyton," (birth ABT 1855), *Ancestry.com*.

[329] Elijah Guyton, grave marker, Russell Cemetery, Attala County, Mississippi, digital image s.v. "Lige Guyton," (1853-1901), *FindaGrave.com*.

[330] Sarah Russell, grave marker, Russell Cemetery, Attala County, Mississippi, digital image s.v. "Sarah Guyton," (1856-1893), *FindaGrave.com*.

[331] "Missouri, Death Certificates, 1910-1962," digital image s.v. "Tennie Geyton," (1869-1939), *Ancestry.com*.

[332] "1860 United States Census: Slave Schedule," Township 13 Range 6, Attala County, Mississippi, digital image s.v. "A W Guyton," *Ancestry.com*.

the household. There were four children (again unnamed): probably Caroline (age 14), Pinkney (age 12), Elijah (age 10), and perhaps Adeline (age 6). David F. GUYTON believes Adeline may be Lawson GUYTON's daughter and the sister of Whit's third partner, Artie RAINEY. Artie's family does not believe Lawson is Artie RAINEY's father.

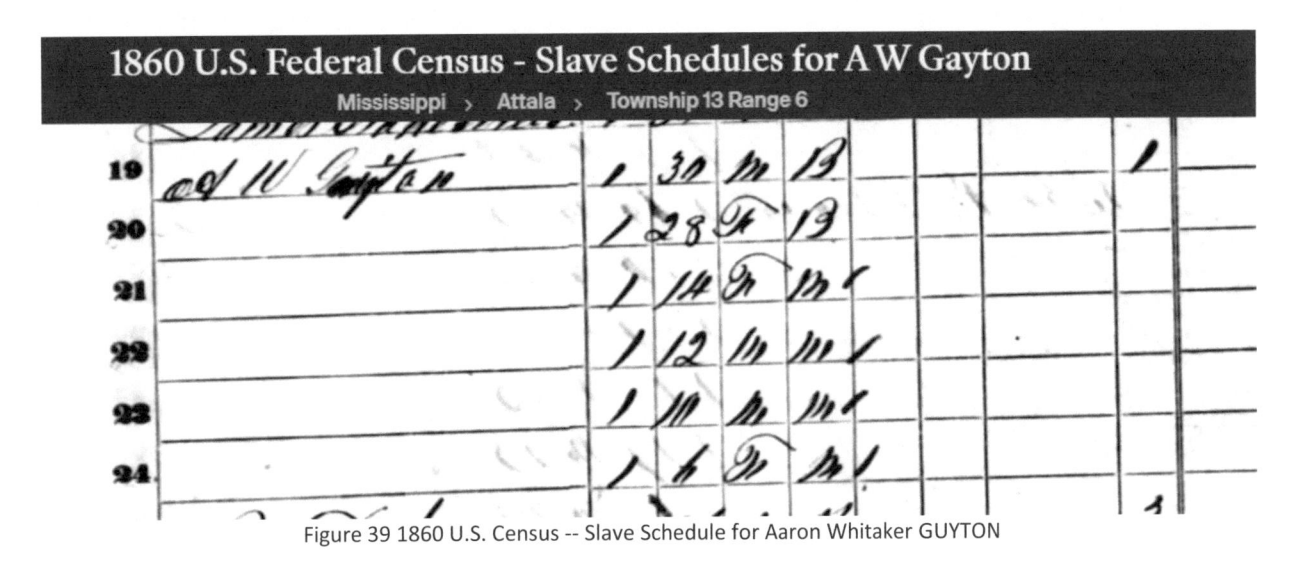

![1860 U.S. Federal Census - Slave Schedules for A W Gayton, Mississippi > Attala > Township 13 Range 6]

Figure 39 1860 U.S. Census -- Slave Schedule for Aaron Whitaker GUYTON

Pinkney and Lige lived with their father through at least 1870, per the 1850, 1860, and 1870 U.S. Censuses.[333] Pinkney (age 22) and Elijah (age 21) GUYTON lived in Whit's household under their own names in the 1870 U.S. Census, after slavery ended. Although the 1870 U.S. Census did not collect relationship information, it did collect race. The young men were shown as mulattoes, or of mixed race. Living with Whit was another young man, Allen BART, a 15-year-old mulatto, of unknown relationship with Whit. There are many Burt family members in this genealogy. Allen may have been a Burt rather than a Bart.

Per David F. GUYTON, several years prior to his death in about 1881, Whit conveyed part of his property to Pinkney GUYTON and Elijah GUYTON. Vincent (or Vinson) TERRY (1836-1904), husband of Caroline GUYTON, purchased land from his white father-in-law, Whit GUYTON. Such purchases by African Americans began shortly after the end of the Civil War.

According to Evan ASHFORD, Whit's third partner was Artie (perhaps short for Artemesia) RAINEY.[334] Evan ASHFORD wrote that "Aaron Whitaker GUYTON publicly acknowledged his illegitimate children and his mistress while legally incorporating them into his white family." Artie was born in

---

[333] "1850 United States Slave Census," Attala Co., MS, digital image s.v. "Male 2-years-old," (birth 1848), Ancestry.com. "1860 United States Slave Census," Attala Co., MS, digital image s.v. "Male 12-years old" (birth 1848), Ancestry.com. "1870 United States Census," Attala Co., MS, digital image s.v. "Penkney" (birth 1848), Ancestry.com. "1850 United States Slave Census," Attala Co., MS, digital image s.v. "Male 6/12-years-old," (birth 1850), Ancestry.com. "1860 United States Slave Census," Attala Co., MS, digital image s.v. "Male 10-years old" (birth 1848), Ancestry.com. "1870 United States Census," Attala Co., MS, digital image s.v. "Elizah Guyton" (birth 1849), Ancestry.com.

[334] Ashford, Evan, "The Privilege of Blackness: Black Empowerment and the Fight for Liberation in Attala County, Mississippi 1865-1915" (2018). Doctoral Dissertations.

January 1848 in Mississippi.[335] Both Evan ASHFORD and David F. GUYTON believe Artie was the daughter of Lawson GUYTON and Ellen RUSSELL. The descendants of Artie RAINEY also believe she is the daughter of Ellen RUSSELL but do not believe Lawson GUYTON is her father.[336] Evan believes Lawson was enslaved by Whit's brother, Joseph A. GUYTON.[337] Aaron Steele GUYTON's will, however, shows Whit GUYTON inherited Lawson from his father.[338] David F. Guyton's diagram below (Figure 40) shows his opinion of the relationships.

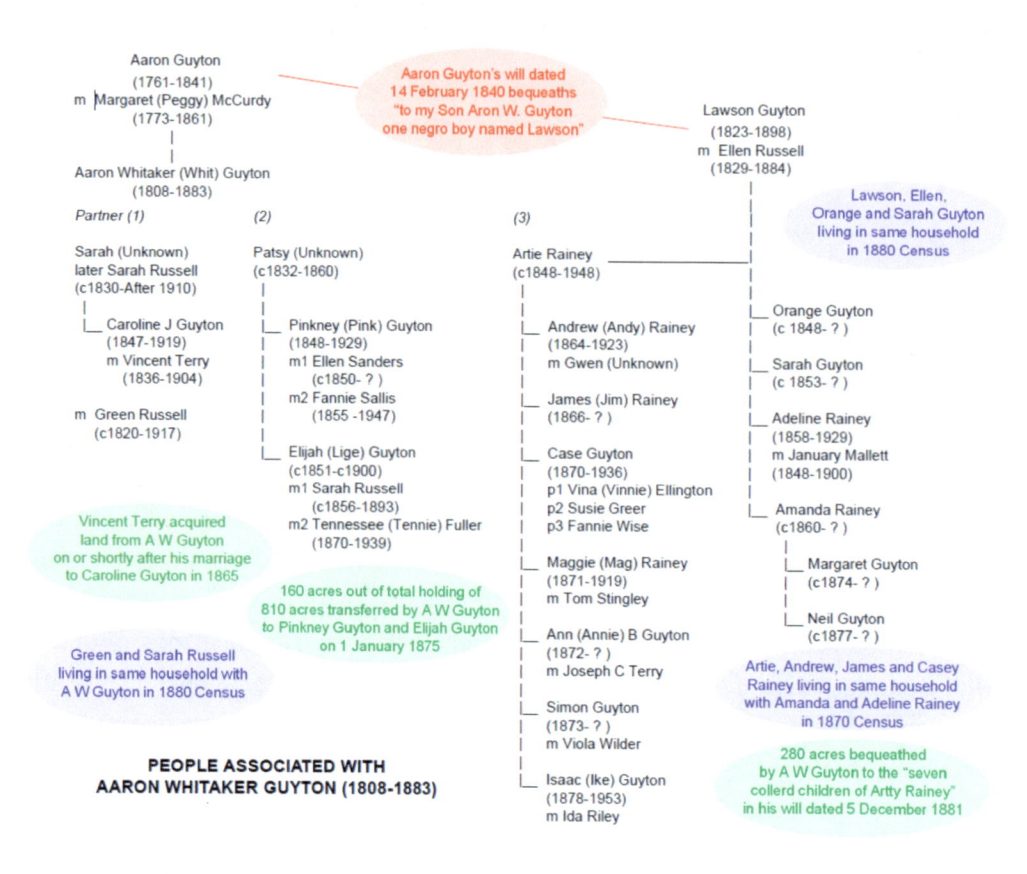

Figure 40 Aaron Whitaker GUYTON Family Schematic from David F. GUYTON[339]

---

[335] "1900 United States Census," Newport, Attala Co., MS, digital image s.v. "Arty Guyton," (birth Jan 1848), *Ancestry.com*.
[336] Channie Brown-Currie, Oreatha Guyton-Winston, Kenya Jenkins-Wright, et al., "2017 Guyton Family Reunion Genealogy," self-published and shared with the author.
[337] Ashford, Evan, "The Privilege of Blackness: Black Empowerment and the Fight for Liberation in Attala County, Mississippi 1865-1915" (2018). Doctoral Dissertations. Private communication with David F. Guyton in 2023.
[338] "South Carolina, Wills and Probate Records, 1670-1980," Anderson Co., SC, "Aaron Guyton," (probate 16 Nov 1841), *Ancestry.com*.
[339] From David F. Guyton.

See Figure 41 for an image of Artie RAINEY.

Figure 41 Artie RAINEY[340]

Together, Whit and Artie had at least eight children:

i   Andrew (A. J.) RAINEY GUYTON (b. 18 Jan 1866 Attala Co., MS, d. 18 Jan 1923 Attala Co., MS)[341] m. Gwen UNKNOWN (b. ABT 1867 Attala Co., MS, d. Unknown).[342]

ii   James (J. T.) GUYTON (b. ABT 1868 Attala Co., MS, d. AFT 1880).[343]

iii   Case GUYTON (b. Jan 1869 Attala Co., MS, d. 24 Apr 1936 St. Louis, MO)[344] m. Susie LUCKETT (b. 16 Feb 1880 Sallis, Attala Co., MS, d. 26 Dec 1962 Sallis, Attala Co., MS).[345]

iv   Amanda (Annie B.) GUYTON (b. Aug 1872, d. AFT 1930)[346] m. Joseph Thomas (Joe) TERRY (b. ABT 1870).[347]

v   Maggie GUYTON (b. ABT 1874, d. 4 May 1919)[348] m. Thomas (Tom) STINGLEY (b. ABT 1875, d. 1957).[349]

---

[340] Chancuuri. 6 May 2013. Posted on *Ancestry.com*.

[341] Andrew Rainey Guyton, grave marker, Russell Cemetery, Attala County, Mississippi, s.v. "Andrew Rainey," (1866-1923), *FindaGrave.com*.

[342] Based on information from Artie Rainey descendant, Channie Brown Currie.

[343] James Rainey Guyton, grave marker, Russell Cemetery, Attala County, Mississippi, s.v. "James Rainey," (1868-Unknown), *FindaGrave.com*. He appears in the *1880 United States Census*. "1870 United States Census," Newport, Attala County, Mississippi, digital image s.v. "J. T. Delpha," (birth ABT 1870), *Ancestry.com*.

[344] Case Rainey Guyton, grave marker, Russell Cemetery, Attala County, Mississippi, s.v. "Case Guyton," (1869-1936), *FindaGrave.com*.

[345] Susie Luckett, grave marker, Barlow United Methodist Church Cemetery, Attala County, Mississippi, digital image s.v. "Susie Luckett," (1880-1962), *FindaGrave.com*.

[346] Annie Black Rainey Guyton, grave marker, Russell Cemetery, Attala County, Mississippi, s.v. "Amanda Terry," (1872-Unknown), *FindaGrave.com*. "1930 United States Census," Beat 1, Attala County, Mississippi, digital image s.v. "Anne Terry," (birth ABT 1880), *Ancestry.com*. According to Channie Brown-Currie, Whit's daughter is known as Amanda to his descendants. Documents, however, refer to her as Annie or Annie B. I've tried to note this throughout the book.

[347] "1910 United States Census," Beat 1, Attala County, Mississippi, digital image s.v. "Joseph C Terry," (birth ABT 1870), *Ancestry.com*.

[348] Maggie Rainey Guyton, grave marker, Russell Cemetery, Attala County, Mississippi, digital image s.v. "Maggie Stingley," (1874-1919), *FindaGrave.com*.

[349] Thomas (Tom) Stingley, grave marker, Russell Cemetery, Attala County, Mississippi, s.v. "Tom Stingley," (1875-1957), *FindaGrave.com*.

vi Simon GUYTON, Sr.(b. 15 Jan 1876 Sallis, Attala Co., MS d. AFT 1940)[350] m. Viola UNKNOWN (b. ABT 1879 MS, d. AFT 1940).[351]
vii Ike GUYTON (b. 12 May 1878 d. 10 Feb 1953)[352] m. Ida RILEY (b. 1887 d. 18 May 1951).
viii James (Baby James) GUYTON (b. 1880 Kosciusko Beat 4, Attala Co., MS, d. 1882 Sallis, Attala Co., MS).

In the 1870 U. S. Census Artie RAINEY was identified as a 24-years old mulatto with five children living next door to Whit.[353] See Figure 42. Three of the five appear to be her children with Whit (Andrew 6, James 4, and Case 6/12), all mulattoes. According to David F. GUYTON, Amanda (age 10, black) and Adeline (age 17, mulatto) RAINEY are Artie's sisters.[354] According to Channie BROWN-CURRIE, Amanda is Artie's daughter but Adeline is Artie's sister. Artie RAINEY's family refers to Amanda as Amanda although almost all her records refer to her as Annie or Annie B.

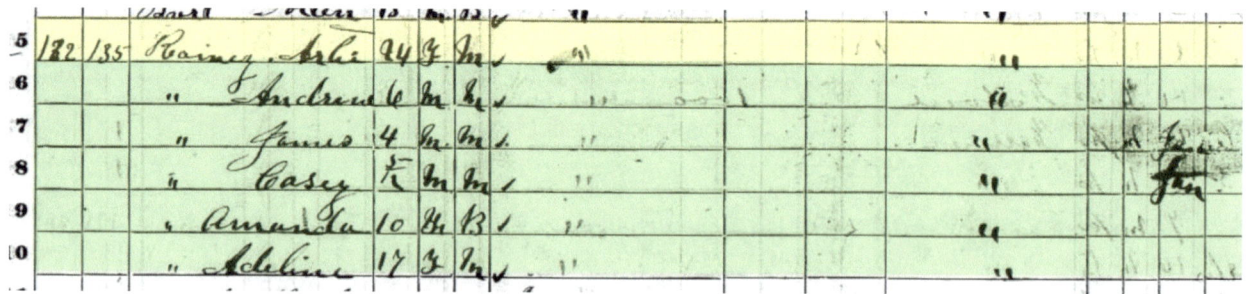

Figure 42 Artie RAINEY's Family in the 1870 U.S. Census

Whit lived with Green RUSSELL and Sarah UNKNOWN/RUSSELL in the 1880 U.S. Census.[355] Sarah was Whit's first partner. In 1880, Artie RAINEY had the seven children named in Whit's will: A. J. (Andrew, 13), J. T. (James, 10), Case (9), Maggy (7), A. B. (Annablack, Annie B, Amanda[356]) (6), Simon (4), and Ike (2).[357] Artie lived next door to James William Sunderland GUYTON, the executor of Whit's will, and close to Whit. He shows up in the 1880 U.S. Census on the page before Artie does. The 1880 Enumeration of Males and Females Under 21 indicated Artie was the guardian/parent of the children. They were attending Mallett School. See Figure 43.

---

[350] "U.S., Social Security Applications and Claims Index, 1936-2007," s.v. "Simon Guyton," (birth 15 Jan 1876), *Ancestry.com*. Simon is in the *1940 United States Census*, but I cannot date his death after that. "1940 United States Census," Newport, Attala County, Mississippi, digital image s.v. "Simon Guyton," (birth ABT 1873), *Ancestry.com*.

[351] "1900 United States Census," Newport, Attala County, Mississippi, digital image s.v. "Viola Guyton," (birth ABT 1879), *Ancestry.com*.

[352] Ike Rainey Guyton, grave marker, Russell Cemetery, Attala County, Mississippi, s.v. "Ike Guyton," (1878-1953), *FindaGrave.com*.

[353] "1870 United States Census," Beat 4, Attala County, Mississippi, digital image s.v. "Arlie Rainey," (birth ABT 1846), *Ancestry.com*.

[354] Personal conversation, 2023.

[355] "1880 United States Census," Newport, Attala County, Mississippi, digital image s.v. "Whit Guyton," (birth ABT 1808), *Ancestry.com*.

[356] Per Channie Brown-Currie.

[357] "1880 United States Census," Newport, Attala County, Mississippi, digital image s.v. "Arta Delpha," (birth ABT 1847), *Ancestry.com*.

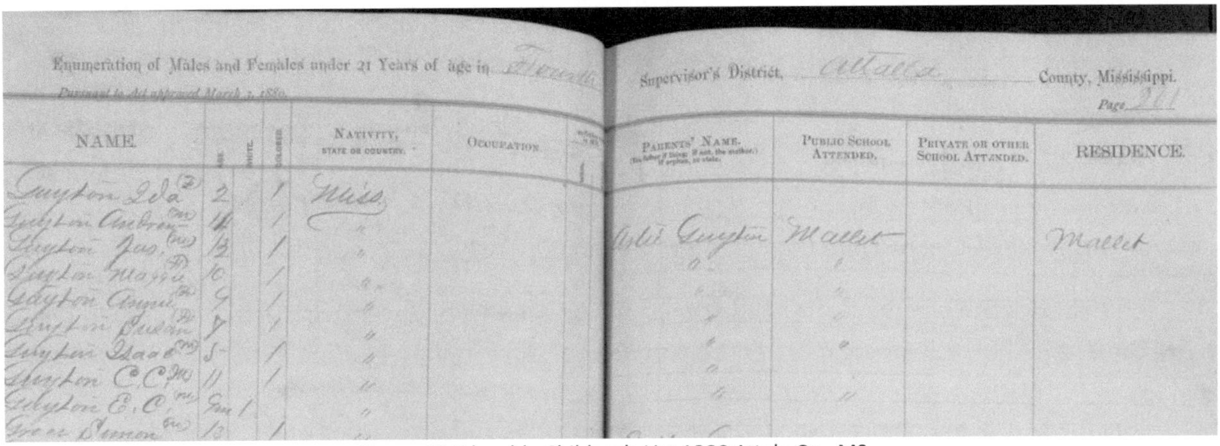
Enumeration of Males and Females under 21 Years of age in ______ Supervisor's District, Attala County, Mississippi.
Pursuant to Act approved March 1, 1880. Page 261

NAME	Age	White	Colored	Nativity, State or Country	Occupation		Parents' Name	Public School Attended	Private or Other School Attended	Residence
Guyton Ida (F)	2		1	Miss.						
Guyton Andrew (M)	14		1	"						
Guyton Jas. (M)	13		1	"			Whit Guyton	Mallet		Mallet
Guyton Maggie (F)	10		1	"			"	"		
Guyton Annie (F)	9		1	"			"	"		
Guyton Susan (F)	8		1	"			"	"		
Guyton Isaac (M)	5		1	"			"	"		
Guyton C.C. (M)	11		1	"			"	"		
Guyton E.C. (M)	9m	1		"			"	"		
Green Simon (M)	13		1	"						

Figure 43 Educable Children's List 1880 Attala Co., MS

On December 5, 1881, Whit signed his last will and testament; it was filed with the Attala County Chancery Court in 1883:[358]

> In the name of God Amen I A.W. Guyton of the County of Attala and State of Mississippi being of sound mind and memory and understanding do make publish and declare this my last will and testament in force following to wit. I give my body to dust my soul to God who gave it. My property or worldly estate I dispose of as follows first I give to the seven colored children of Artty Rainy named as follows Andrew Ike James Cassay Maggy Annablack [Amanda[359]], Simon all of the following tracts of land laying and being in the County of Attala and State of Mississippi known and designated as the NE ¼ & E ½ NW ¼ Section nineteen and the NW ¼ of the NW ¼ Section Twenty all in Township Thirteen. Range Six East also Two choice mules that may belong to me at my death and one good wagon, one years supply of corn meat and all other family supplies to do the seven above named children twelve months from said death and all of my house hold and kitchen furniture and farming tools for to carry on the said farm Second I appoint my nephew Joseph W. S. Guyton of said County Executor of this my last will and testament given under my hand and seal on this the fifth day of December a.D. 1881.
>
> A.W. Guyton

"Although Whit does not explicitly claim the children as his own in the will, the likelihood that a white man would legally provide for children whom he had no connection was not likely. Whit's will gave Artie's children legal recognition. Whit's final will and testament was upheld and administered by

---

[358] *Mississippi. Probate Court (Attala County)*; Probate Place: *Attala, Mississippi*. Accessed 12 Apr 2020.

[359] Per Channie Brown-Currie, the family genealogist of the Rainey descendants, reports that the woman listed as Annablack in Whit's will is known as Amanda to the family. Many of the documents related to her name her as Annie or Annie B. I have attempted to include both names for clarity.

his nephew, J.W.S. GUYTON."[360] Evan ASHFORD concludes that the Guyton family members held sufficient power to delegitimize Aaron's will and swindle Artie's children but they did not.

Descendants of Aaron W. GUYTON followed the path of many African Americans during the Great Migration. They left the poverty and oppression of the South to find better places to raise their families. Just as Whit and his brother, Joseph A. GUYTON, moved together so did these families. Frequent destinations for the Guytons were Chicago, Detroit, St. Louis, Milwaukee, and Waterloo, IA.

The following are comments from one of his African American descendants, Karl Glenn BOYD (aka Nykki Lamarr STARR) on learning more about his ancestor, Aaron Whitaker GUYTON:

> In the heart of Mississippi, amidst the sprawling fields and whispering pines, lived Aaron Whitaker GUYTON, a man shrouded in mystery and resilience. His story, a tapestry of love, defiance, and perseverance, was one that could never be fully told but resonated through the generations that followed. Aaron was a man ahead of his time, a white landowner who dared to defy the oppressive norms of his era by forming a forbidden relationship with Patsy GIBSON, a woman he was compelled to list as a slave along with their children due to the strict laws and prejudices of the time. Despite the harsh judgment and ostracism, he faced from his own family for his unconventional choices, Aaron stood unwavering, choosing to embrace his true family and the life he had built with them on his land.
>
> Through the ages, the whispers of Aaron's legacy endured, passed down through the generations until they reached my ears. As I learned more about his story, I became a proud descendant, who bore witness to the strength and love that defined my ancestor. It was my mother, Icy Viola BOYD, who instilled in me the importance of honoring and respecting Aaron's memory, sparking a journey of discovery and reconnection with his descendants scattered across time and distance.
>
> As the descendants of Aaron's children, who had long lost contact with him, gathered to learn of his untold story, a sense of unity and belonging began to bloom. Together, we celebrated the life and courage of a man who had faced adversity with grace and determination, paving the way for our existence and the opportunity to know our shared heritage.
>
> In the pages of this book [a book of tributes to Nykki's family], the testament to Aaron Whitaker GUYTON's resilience and love will be immortalized, a beacon of hope and reconciliation for his descendants and the family he had once lost. Through the act of reintroduction and remembrance, Aaron found his way back home, embraced and accepted by those who understood the depth of his sacrifices and the power of his legacy. And so, standing together as one family, united by blood and by the unwavering spirit of Aaron Whitaker GUYTON, we have found solace in the knowledge that his story, though

---

[360] Ashford, Evan, "The Privilege of Blackness: Black Empowerment and the Fight for Liberation in Attala County, Mississippi 1865-1915" (2018). Doctoral Dissertations. 1417, p. 109. <https://scholarworks.umass.edu/dissertations_2/1417>.

veiled in mystery, would forever be a source of strength and inspiration for generations to come. Family, bound by love and shared history, we honor the man who defied the odds and chose love above all else. 🙏

N.L. STARR, descended from Aaron Whitaker GUYTON's eldest son, Pinkney GUYTON

Figure 44 Karl Glenn BOYD (aka Nykki Lamarr STARR)[361]

---
[361] Photo from Karl Boyd.

Background Information of Relevant Towns in Attala County, MS[362]

This section provides background information of many of the towns where the descendants of Aaron Whitaker GUYTON lived. According to the Attala Historical Society's website, the source material for the history of the communities was *Kosciusko - Attala History*, by Joyce Williams Sanders, published by the Attala Historical Society in the late 1970s. Statistics included in the descriptions below were from the 1970s unless otherwise noted. The book is available from the Society. Note the names of many of the white settlers of the communities and leading citizens. Many of those names were adopted by their formerly enslaved African American descendants.

Attala County[363]

Attala County was established on December 23, 1833, as one of the sixteen counties carved from the territory of the Choctaw Nation ceded to the United States in 1830 by the Treaty of Dancing Rabbit Creek. The name Attala is said to be derived from Atala, the heroine of an Indian romance by Chateaubriand. It is located in the geographical center of Mississippi, bounded by Montgomery and Choctaw counties to the north, Choctaw and Winston counties to the east, Leake and Madison counties to the south, and the Big Black River forming its western boundary, dividing it from Holmes County.

The largest town and county seat was Kosciusko, a rapidly growing community of over 2,500 people. Kosciusko offered excellent public schools, numerous churches, and growing industries, including a large cotton mill with 12,500 spindles. The county's population was primarily agricultural, with other notable towns being McCool (400 people), Sallis (250 people), and Ethel (150 people).

Attala County is traversed by a branch of the Illinois Central Railroad, which played a significant role in harvesting the county's natural resources and enhancing its productivity. The county's soil was fertile, yielding agricultural products worth over $1,500,000 in 1900, including corn, cotton, oats, wheat, potatoes, peas, peanuts, sorghum, and various fruits and vegetables. The livestock industry, once neglected, grew rapidly owing to improved shipping facilities and excellent grasslands.

Timber was a significant contributor to the county's wealth, and while manufacturing was still in its infancy, a considerable number of saw and planing mills were in operation. Early settlers of Attala County came from the Carolinas, Tennessee, the Ohio Valley, Georgia, and Alabama. Among the oldest settlements in the county, now extinct, were Attalaville, Valena, Burkettsville, and Bluff Springs.

By 1837, Attala County had a population of 1,713 whites and 708 enslaved persons, with over 4,003 acres of land under cultivation. In its first census in 1840, Attala County reported 3,221 free people and 1,082 enslaved individuals. The economy was primarily agricultural, though a small manufacturing sector provided local employment at cotton gins, blacksmith shops, and lumber mills. By 1860, the county ranked twenty-ninth in the state in cotton production, twenty-fifth in livestock value, and nineteenth in corn production.

---

[362] "All About... Attala County: Brief History of Communities of Attala County," Attala Historical Society, Kosciusko, Mississippi, Everette Cox, webmaster, <https://sites.rootsweb.com/~msahs/allabout3.html>. The source material for this site is *Kosciusko - Attala History*, Chapter 18 by Joyce Williams Sanders, published by the Attala Historical Society in the late 1970s.
[363] "Encyclopedia of Mississippi History, Vol. 1," published in 1907 by Dunbar Rowland, LL.D., <https://archive.org/details/EncyclopediaOfMississippiHistoryVolume1>.

The county's population in 1900 was 26,248, comprising 13,875 whites and 12,373 African Americans. Farming dominated the workforce, with most being white farmers (63 percent) owning their land, while more than 75 percent of black farmers worked as sharecroppers. Attala was also home to numerous manufacturing establishments, although industrial development offered limited employment opportunities. By 1906 the total population exceeded 30,000. By 1930, the county's manufacturing labor force had exceeded eleven hundred.

In 1960, the county's primary agricultural products were corn, cotton, soybeans, and cattle, and the timber industry began to generate substantial economic benefits. However, a population decline during the 1960s and 1970s contributed to decreased agricultural production. Over 2,600 people were employed in farming, a number that dropped to only 200 by 1980. Between 1960 and 2010, Attala County's population declined slightly from 21,355 to 19,564. Like other central Mississippi counties in the early twenty-first century, Attala County was largely white (56 percent). Attala County featured 154 public schools, 100 for white students and 54 for African American students, with a school term length of six months.

Ethel

In 1882, the area now known as Ethel was referred to as "Davis' old field." Mr. LANE and Mr. Charles BELL then purchased the land. BELL built a residence and a steam mill on his portion, while LANE made some improvements to his section. This remained the extent of development until the arrival of the Illinois Central Railroad in 1883. A station was established and named Ethel, after the daughter of a railroad official. This sparked a boom period as town lots were laid out.

T.J. MIDDLEBROOK was among the first residents and was appointed Postmaster. J.A. and Ella BROWN opened the first drugstore, and Charles BELL operated the first storehouse in 1883. Around the same time, Charles RABERN started a mercantile business. In 1884, Doctor J. S. COLLINS began his medical practice, followed by other doctors including Dr. J. T. HEALD, Dr. W.R. POPE, Dr. W.S. CLAITOR, Dr. H.H. PURYEAR, and Dr. W.W. McBRIDE.

North of Ethel, residents had established the Presbyterian Church at Stonewall, and the Stonewall Cemetery was in use before Ethel was founded. Although it was a Presbyterian cemetery, it served as the final resting place for people of various denominations in the area. For some time, inquiries about the Ethel Cemetery would often be directed to the Stonewall Cemetery.

In 1887, a schoolhouse was built on the lot later occupied by the Masonic Hall Building, with Rev. W. P. McBRYDE as the first teacher. The Methodist Church was organized in 1894 with Rev. PARROTT as pastor, and the Baptist Church followed in 1896 with Rev. John RAY as its first pastor.

By 1897, Rev. John RAY, Burris RAY, J. R. RILEY, and A. E. GREGORY were the principal merchants in Ethel. Mr. CLAITOR had a millinery shop, R.J. BELL operated a steam mill and gin, and E.M. GREGORY ran an axe-handle factory and steam saw and planing machine, making these enterprises the leading manufacturers in the late 19th century. R. J. BELL also owned a pear orchard, which generated significant revenue.

Ethel was incorporated as a town in 1911. The first brick school building was constructed in 1916, with Mr. F.A. ELKIN as Principal, supported by four teachers.

By the late 1970s, Ethel, with a population of about six hundred, was the second largest town in Attala County.

McAdams

The McAdams community has a long history of settlement. According to land records, the following many individuals were granted land by the U.S. Government in 1834 with the last names of ABERNATHY, ALLEN, AYERS, BOYD, COOPWOOD, DODD, HARRIS, HENRY, JENKINS, LACOST, MALLETT, McBRIDE, McGEE, NASH, NICHOLS, PACE, PENDER, POPE, SIMMONS, STAPLETON, WEATHERBY, and WINSTON. Soon more people joined the community: BROWN, ELLIOTT, EUBANKS, GOWEN, MARTIN, McADORY McNEIL, MONTGOMERY, MUSSLEWHITE, PEARL, RAINEY, RECTOR, ROSS, SMITH, TERRY, THOMPSON, THORNTON, WARREN, WIGLEY, and VAUGHN. Not all land acquirers lived on their land; many were speculators who lived elsewhere or had agents to manage their interests.

Many descendants of early settlers still reside in McAdams today. In 1896, Samuel COLEMAN, Thomas P. TERRY, and Uriah THWEATT were notable residents. Tom TERRY served multiple terms as Justice of the Peace and Constable, while Uriah THWEATT, a Mexican War veteran, had lived in his home for nearly fifty years. "Uncle Sam" COLEMAN was the oldest inhabitant in 1896, a self-sufficient and diversified farmer. Another resident at that time was Jeptha McADAMS. The Coleman Cemetery in McAdams is the final resting place for many early settlers.

McAdams had a long-standing tradition of good schools. Early schools were in the outlying areas. Over time, additional areas, including parts of Thomastown and Sallis, joined the McAdams school system.

McVille

McVille, a community along the Yockanookany River, was settled soon after the removal of the Choctaws opened the county for settlement. The fertile river bottomland and location on the Natchez Trace attracted many wealthy slaveholders. Early white settlers included the DOBBS, GLASSES, IVEYS, and EASTS, but they left no lasting impact. It was named after the Baptist Church founded around 1842. On the northern edge of the community, at the site of C.A. BALLARD'S home in 1936, there once stood a Spanish Trading Post, evidenced by the discovery of many Spanish coins. A trader said that he was the only white man between the Tombigbee settlements and Mt. Salus, now Clinton, when he started his Trading Post. Additionally, there was an Indian arrowhead making site and a large burial ground located on MCMILLAN land, just half a mile east of the McVille store.

Early settlers, many of whom have descendants in McVille today, included ATKINSON, BEAUCHAMPS, BURT, COOKS, DAVIS, DEAR, FOREMAN, ISAAC, McKINNON, McMILLAN, RILEY, ROBY, SANDERS, and SEARIGHT. Dr. Frederick ZOLLICOFFER, a Swiss baron, planter, and slaveholder, introduced mule-raising to the area.

Religious activities were centered around the Baptist Church, one of the first organized by the Baptist denomination. Initially a log house with a fireplace, it was replaced by a one-room plank building and later by a larger church with a spacious sanctuary and several Sunday School rooms. McVille has several cemeteries: the church cemetery, the McMillan or Isaacs Graveyard, the Dear Cemetery, and another cemetery across from the SEVIER Home.

After the establishment of Planters' Academy, the community adopted that name for nearly fifty years. Before the Academy, children were taught in private homes. Planters' Academy, organized several years before the Civil War, required its superintendents to be graduates of the University of Virginia or leading New England colleges. It offered a course of study comparable to junior colleges in the 1930s. However, post-war hardships led to the Academy's closure, and the community relied on makeshift four-month schools. Today, McVille no longer has a school, but it maintains a church and a store.

New Port

The village of New Port is located a few miles west of Bolatusha Creek. In 1812, Mrs. RUTHERFORD and her son settled near the Indian Village of Bolatusha, becoming the first white settlers in this part of Mississippi. They crossed the Yockanookany River near where McVille would eventually be. After Mississippi was admitted to the Union in 1817, and particularly after Attala County was organized in 1833, the government opened Indian land to homesteaders. Early homesteaders included: CHENNAULT, ELLINGTON, FRASIER, McMILLAN, and WILSON.

By 1854, the village of New Port was located at the crossroads of the Kosciusko and Goodman Roads and the Thomastown and Sallis Road. That same year, land ownership began to change. People with the following last names began to arrive: BARWICK, BUSTER, DRENNAN, HARMON, HARRIS, HAZLETT, HEMINGWAY, KENDALL, LOVE, MADDOX, MARTIN, MEEK, PEARCE, REDMOND, ROBY, SIMMONS, STEBBIN, STINGLEY, and WAUGH.

By 1898, significant changes had occurred. The railroad had been destroyed and stopped by the outbreak of the Civil War. When rebuilt, the route was changed, and it went six miles north of New Port through Sallis. The once booming village of New Port began to disappear, and by 1898 only one store remained in operation. Today, there are two stores in the New Port community.

The Salem Methodist Church still stands after all these years. The New Port School burned in 1910, and the rest of the term was taught in the doctor's office. Before the next school term, a new building was erected on the west side of the HUTCHINSON place. This building also burned in the 1920s, and another was built. New Port was consolidated with McAdams in 1932.

Sallis

Twelve miles west of Kosciusko, in the western part of Attala County, lies the town of Sallis. Established with the building of the railroad in 1870, the community was first settled by Dr. J. G. SALLIS in 1848. Before Sallis became a town, several nearby communities existed, including Attalaville, Bluff Springs, and New Port.

In 1840, a Baptist Church was built in Bluff Springs, originally known as the Bluff Springs Baptist Church, later renamed the Long Creek Church. The pastor and the nine charter members carried the last names of ASHLEY, BROWN, NASH, SIMMONS, SMITH, TEAGUE, and TERRY. It which would eventually become the Sallis Baptist Church.

In the 1870s, Dr. SALLIS donated land for the construction of a depot, and using convict labor, the Mississippi Central Railroad was built. The arrival of the railroad brought significant changes. While the convenience of transportation was welcomed by some, the thriving communities of Attalaville, Bluff Springs, and New Port were bypassed by the rail line and soon dwindled. These small outlying communities migrated toward the railroad, consolidating into the town of Sallis, named after the Sallis family.

By 1872, Sallis had become a major shipping center for cotton, which had previously been transported overland. With the population increase, it became necessary to form a government, and Sallis was incorporated as a town. At that time, Sallis consisted of twelve or more general stores, a blacksmith shop, and a livery stable. However, with the decline of cotton and timber industries, Sallis, like its former neighboring communities, began to fade from its former glory.

Zemuly

Zemuly, located twelve miles southwest of Kosciusko, is named after Mrs. Zemuly MORGAN, wife of Charlie MORGAN. It is bordered by Leake County to the south, New Port District to the west, Joseph to the north, and the Palestine Negro community to the east.

Morgan School, established early on, was located one mile north of the Zemuly Store. The second school building was constructed in 1906, about two hundred yards east of Zemuly. South Union School operated opposite a store at the church from 1909 to 1939. Cedar Grove Negro Public School was situated three-fourths of a mile north of the store.

Early settlers included: DUBARD, FRAZIER, HINES, LEWIS, McATEE, McKAY, MEEK, MORGAN, and POPE. Today, Zemuly has one remaining store and a distinctive church. The church, situated at a crossroads, does not favor either side. Its front faces the point where the roads intersect, with a square tower overseeing all who pass by.

Relevant Cemeteries in Attala County[364]

Many of Aaron Whitaker GUYTON's descendants and their families were buried in the following cemeteries in Attala County:[365]

Cemetery	Coordinates	Coordinates	Town
Bullock Cemetery	33.00083	-89.62056	Kosciusko
Ellington Cemetery	32.99444	-89.74611	Joseph
Harmon Cemetery	32.97194	-89.74083	Joseph
Hill Springs Cemetery	32.99611	-89.71694	Joseph
Mallett Cemetery	32.9825	-89.66361	Joseph
Roby Cemetery	32.935	-89.82472	New Port
Russell Cemetery	32.97306	-89.70639	Joseph
Sallis Cemetery	33.02444	-89.76444	Durant
Shelley Cemetery 1	32.97139	-89.63306	Joseph96
Shelley Cemetery 2	32.97639	-89.63889	Joseph

Nash Cemetery:[366] Abandoned Cemetery - "Location: T14N-R8E-S6. Proceeding from Kosciusko, drive up the old Ethel Road to Mrs. Sudie LAMPKIN's and there turn right toward Ethel Road, just past the second house with a barn on a hill. To the left in a field is this marker. At one time there was evidence of other graves and a marker for a RASBERRY child which has disappeared. Copied Oct. 28, 1958, by Mrs. Ernest AKIN and Mrs. E.C. FENWICK. Note: The Nash Cemetery is so called for the Nash family. Eugenia ATKINSON was the daughter of Rev. W.W. NASH, first pastor of the Kosciusko Baptist Church and the earliest or one of the earliest Baptist preachers in Attala County."

---

[364] "Genealogy Trails History Group, "Cemeteries of Attala County," <https://genealogytrails.com/miss/attala/cemeteries.html>.
[365] <https://mississippiencyclopedia.org/entries/attala-county/>.
[366] Source: Attala County, MS, Cemeteries by Marymaganos McCool Fenwick, *FindAGrave.com*, <https://www.findagrave.com/cemetery/2743378/nash-cemetery>.

Range Maps of Attala County

To help identify where certain parcels of land are located, it is helpful to gain some knowledge of how land boundaries are legally described. Originally, surveyors in the American colonies used a system that depended upon local markers and bounds drawn, often based on topography. For example, a legal description of land could be: From the point on the east bank of Cypress Creek one-half mile above the joining of Cypress Creek and Clear Bottom Creek, north for 200 yards, then northwest to the large pile of rocks, west to the large split maple tree, south to Cypress Creek, then down the center of the creek to the starting point.[367]

The system of range, section, and township is part of the Public Land Survey System (PLSS), which was established in the United States by the Land Ordinance of 1785 to simplify this arbitrary system.[368] Trees die, piles of rocks fall, etc. The PLSS system is used to survey and divide land, primarily in the central and western United States. The reader is encouraged to review Figure 45 as he reads the background information. Here's an overview of each component:

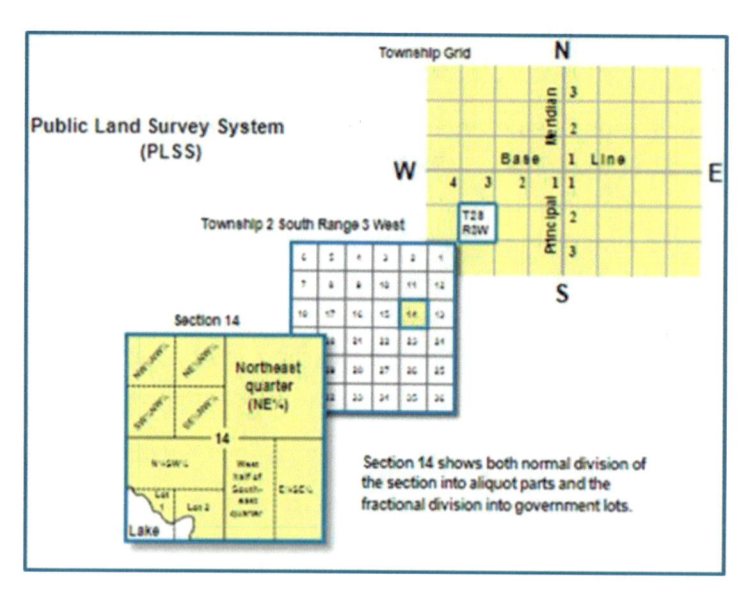

Figure 45 Diagram of Township, Range, and Sections[369]

A township is a square unit of land that is 6 miles on each side, containing 36 square miles or sections. The description of the location of a township depends on its position relative to a preset baseline that runs east-west, and to a principal meridian, a line that runs north-south. See the top right diagram in Figure 45. Townships are labeled as lying above or below the base line. For example, we may read "Township X North" or "Township X South," depending on whether the township lies north of the base line or south of the base line.

---

[367] "Public Land Survey System," *Wikipedia*, accessed 7 Aug 2024.
[368] Information generated by ChapGPT using the prompt, "Please provide basic information on the origin and workings of range, section, townships," 2024 Aug 7.
[369] By Scottycc - Own work, Public Domain, <https://commons.wikimedia.org/w/index.php?curid=132930745>.

The north/south information is insufficient information to locate the township. We also need its east/west location. Ranges are numbered east or west of the principal meridian. For example, "Range 3 West" would be the third column of townships west of the principal meridian. The specific meridian should always be specified in land descriptions.

In Figure 45, the reader can see the example of T2S R3W in the top right diagram. This is read as Township 2 South, Range 3 West. In other words, we are describing the location of a township (a 6-mile by 6-mile piece of land, 36 square miles, over 23,000 acres) that lies two townships south of the east-west baseline and 3 ranges west of the north-south meridian. Because not everyone wants to purchase or sell an entire township, the PLSS must have a system of further subdividing the land.

The middle diagram in the Figure shows that the land is subdivided into 36 smaller squares, called sections of approximately 1 square mile, or 640 acres. Sections are numbered starting from the northeast corner and ending at the southeast corner. The numbering follows a boustrophedonic pattern (a method where numbers snake back and forth across the grid).

Again, a section of 640 acres is a great deal of land. The PLSS must further subdivide each section. Each section is divided into four quarters of 160 acres, measuring 0.25 square miles on each side. See the bottom diagram in the Figure. A person could own an entire quarter of a section, as in the Northeast quarter, designated as NE¼. Or a quarter could be further divided into quarters as shown in the Northwest quarter. In this case, there are descriptions for each quarter of a section quarter. Going counterclockwise from the northeast, there are the northeast quarter of the northwest quarter (NE¼ NW¼), the northwest quarter of the northwest quarter (NW¼ NW¼); the southwest quarter of the northwest quarter (SW¼ NW¼), and the southeast quarter of the northwest quarter (SE¼ NW¼). The descriptions are read from left to right. That same diagram shows other ways a quarter of a section could be divided. In the southeast quarter, the quarter is divided into an eastern and a western section. The western section would be designated T2S R3W W½ SE¼, or the western one-half of the southeastern one-quarter of Township 2 South Range 3 West.

Whit GUYTON bought forty acres of land from the U.S. (receipt # 37046) through the General Land Office on 1 Apr 1856 in Columbus, Mississippi. He purchased the NE ¼ NW ¼ of Section 20 T13N R6E in Attala County. Channie BROWN-CURRIE tells me that Whit GUYTON was a large landholder of over 600 acres. Figure 46 is a map indicating the location of the section with an arrow indicating the northwest quarter. Whit's land would be in the northeast quarter of that northwest quarter. It is very likely that Whit purchased more than than this one transaction indicates. Note that Whit lived closer to Sallis than to Kosciusko. Also note the two circled communities of Joseph and Zemuly, supposedly named for Joseph A. GUYTON and his wife, Zemuely McCLUSKY GUYTON. The naming conflicts with information given previously on background information on towns of Attala County.

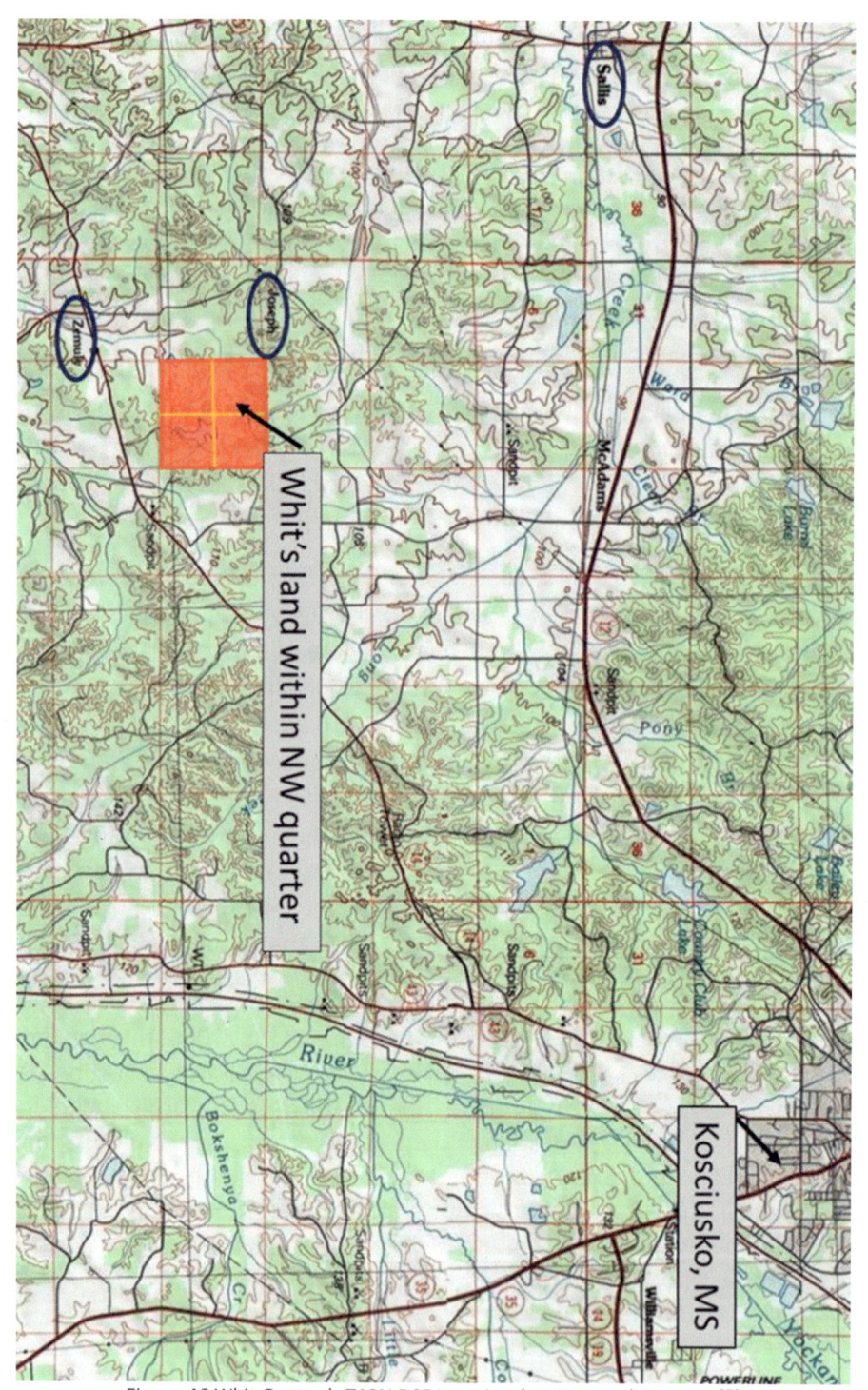

Figure 46 Whit Guyton's T13N R6E Location (NE ¼ NW ¼) 40 Acres[370]

---

[370] "Historic Resources Inventory Map," *Mississippi Department of Archives and History*, input in Tools under Township/Range/Section Finder T13N R6E, Attala County, accessed 2024 Aug 7, <https://www.apps.mdah.ms.gov/mapping_pub/index.html?pk=home&wid=MDAH%20Search&caller=public/search.aspx&realm=archist&scope=home&aspect=public&route=in>.

Figure 47 is a satellite image of Section 20. Whit's portion would be the upper-right quadrant of the image, above what may be a water filled old sandpit. A sandpit is noted southeast of Section 20. The heavy horizontal lines from left to right in the image are a pipeline per the Historical Resources Inventory Map. His property is just south of Russell Cemetery.

Figure 47 Section 20 T13N R6E, Whit Owned NE ¼, Upper Right Quadrant[371]

---

[371] "Historic Resources Inventory Map," *Mississippi Department of Archives and History*, input in Tools under Township/Range/Section Finder T13N R6E, Attala County, accessed 2024 Aug 7, <https://www.apps.mdah.ms.gov/mapping_pub/index.html?pk=home&wid=MDAH%20Search&caller=public/search.aspx&realm=archist&scope=home&aspect=public&route=in>.

Churches and Cemeteries in Attala County

The Attala Historical Society produced a map in 1976 of cemeteries and churches in the county. They labeled them for "white" versus "Negro" membership. See Figure 48.

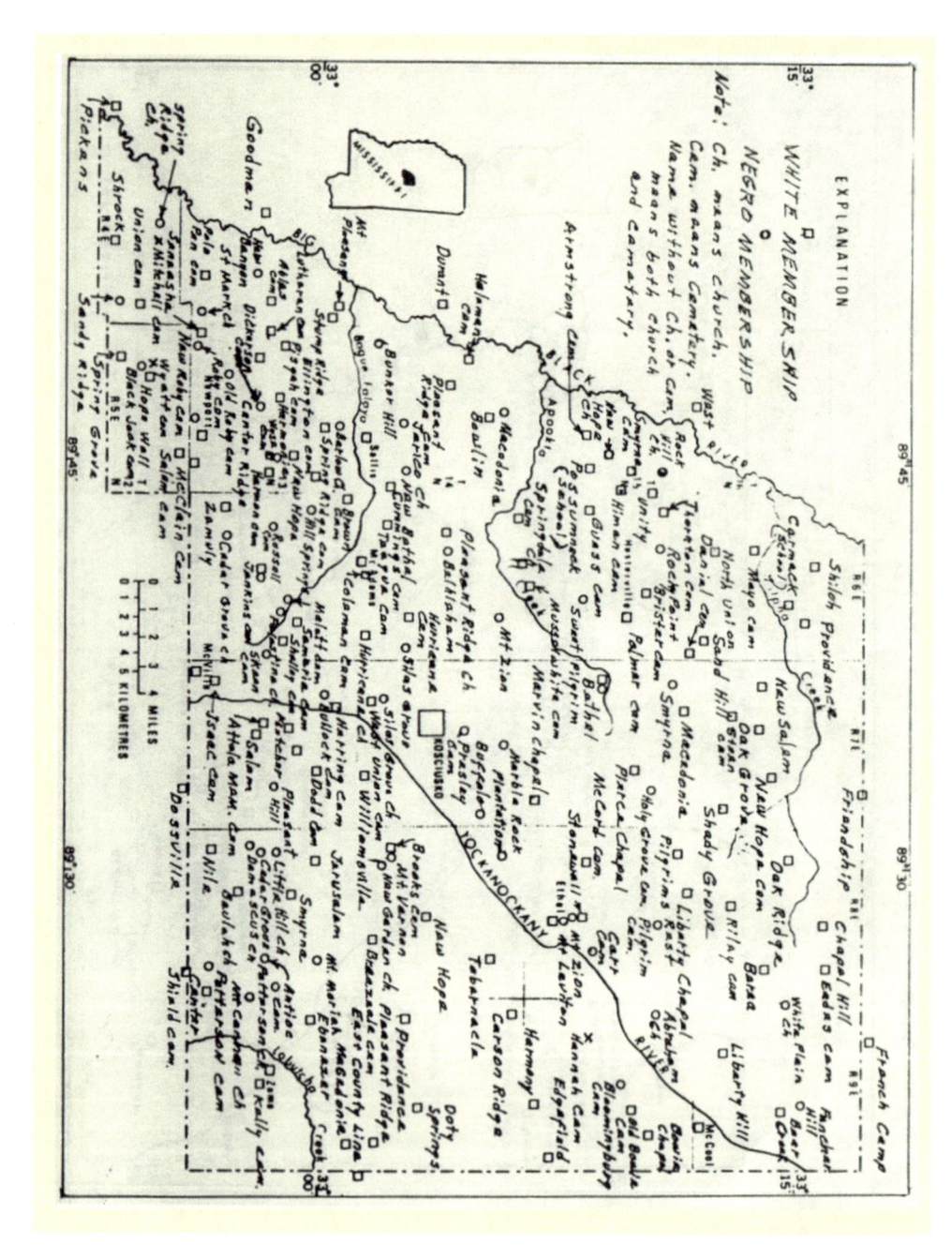

Figure 48 Map of Cemeteries and Churches in Attla County, MS in 1976[372]

---

[372] Attala Historical Society, Attala County, Mississippi, <https://sites.rootsweb.com/~msahs/allabout52.html>.

The Great Migration of African Americans to the Industrial North[373]

Beginning with this generation, many African Americans started to migrate to the industrial cities of the north. The Great Migration stands as one of the most significant demographic shifts in American history, marking the movement of over six million African Americans from the rural South to the urban North between 1916 and 1970.

To fully understand the Great Migration, it's essential to delve deeper into the pre-migration context in the South. By the early 20th century, the promise of emancipation had given way to a harsh reality of systemic racism and economic exploitation. Despite the legal end of slavery, African Americans in the South faced severe limitations on their freedom and opportunities. The threat of lynching and other forms of racial violence created an atmosphere of terror. Organizations like the Ku Klux Klan and other white supremacist groups used terror and violence to enforce racial hierarchies, resulting in thousands of brutal lynchings from the late 19th to the mid-20th century.

Segregation and disenfranchisement under Jim Crow laws severely restricted the rights and freedoms of African Americans. Through literacy tests, poll taxes, and outright intimidation, Southern states disenfranchised African American voters. The 1890 Mississippi Plan and similar tactics in other states effectively nullified the 15th Amendment for African Americans, excluding them from political participation and leaving them vulnerable to racial injustices. Political disenfranchisement incentivized African Americans to migrate.

Sharecropping, the dominant agricultural system post-Civil War, essentially trapped African American farmers in a cycle of debt and poverty. Landowners provided land, seeds, and tools in exchange for a portion of the crop yield, but high interest rates and dishonest bookkeeping often left sharecroppers with little or no profit. See the family story of the Conways in this book. Limited access to quality education in the South also pushed families to seek better prospects for their children.

The Great Migration occurred in two main waves. The first wave, from 1916 to 1940, was driven by World War I and the economic opportunities it created in the North. The second wave, from 1941 to 1970, coincided with World War II and the subsequent economic boom. The nearby table highlights the major destinations and the number of African Americans who migrated to these cities.

The industrial boom in the North created a demand for labor, which was a significant pull factor for African American Southerners. These industries offered higher wages compared to the agricultural jobs in the South. African Americans became integral to the industrial workforce, filling roles that were vital to the economic expansion of the United States during the 20th century. The booming industrial sector provided jobs in manufacturing plants, steel mills, automobile factories, shipyards, and meatpacking plants. These jobs, while often dangerous and low-paying compared to those held by white workers,

---

[373] ChatGPT, accessed 6 June 2024, with prompt: Please write a 2000-word essay on the great migration of black Americans from the south to the industrial cities of the north. When were the peak periods? What cities were the most frequent destinations. Provide a table with those destinations and the numbers of blacks who migrated there. What jobs did these people take? What social issues started the migration? what issues faced the people in their new locations. Material was then edited.

represented a marked improvement over agricultural work in the South. Northern cities needed construction workers to support their growing needs for extensive infrastructure development.

City	Number of Migrants (Approx.)
Chicago	500,000
New York City	450,000
Detroit	400,000
Philadelphia	300,000
Los Angeles	200,000
Cleveland	200,000
Baltimore	150,000
Pittsburgh	150,000
St. Louis	120,000
Milwaukee	100,000

Many African American men worked as porters in the railroads, while women often found employment as domestic workers in white households. Service industry jobs, such as in restaurants, hotels, and other service-oriented businesses also became common.

These roles, while not without their own challenges and limitations, provided steady income and opportunities for community building. Some African American migrants capitalized on the growing African American population in northern cities by starting their own businesses. Barbershops, beauty salons, grocery stores, and restaurants became central hubs in African American neighborhoods, fostering economic independence and community cohesion.

The decision to migrate was often fraught with uncertainty and peril. Migrants left behind family, friends, and the familiarity of the South, embarking on journeys that were both physically and emotionally taxing. Transportation ranged from crowded trains to automobiles, with many families pooling resources to afford the trip. The migration was facilitated by networks of family and friends who had previously moved north. Letters detailing life in northern cities served both as a source of information and inspiration. These personal accounts often portrayed the North as a land of opportunity, free from the most brutal forms of Southern racism.

Upon arrival, migrants faced the immediate challenge of finding housing and employment. Many found themselves in ethnically segregated neighborhoods, often in the poorest sections of cities. The adjustment to urban life, with its fast pace and different social norms, was a significant shift for those accustomed to the rural South.

The Great Migration not only transformed the economic landscape but also had profound social and cultural implications. The influx of African Americans to northern cities like New York, Chicago, and Detroit catalyzed cultural renaissances. The Harlem Renaissance in New York City is perhaps the most famous, featuring luminaries like Langston Hughes, Zora Neale Hurston, and Duke Ellington. This cultural flowering celebrated African American life and culture, influencing American art, music, and literature. Jazz and blues, musical genres with roots in the South, flourished in northern cities. Chicago became a hub for blues music, while jazz thrived in cities like New York and Detroit. These musical movements not only provided entertainment but also became powerful expressions of African American identity and resistance.

As African American communities grew in northern cities, so did their political power. The presence of a more significant number of African Americans led to increased political representation and the formation of powerful civil rights organizations. The National Association for the Advancement of Colored People (NAACP) gained momentum during this period, advocating for the rights of African Americans on a national scale. Churches, schools, and social clubs played crucial roles in the lives of African American migrants. These institutions provided social support, education, and a sense of community. They also became centers for political and social activism, helping to organize efforts to combat racial discrimination and improve living conditions.

Despite the opportunities the North presented, African American migrants faced significant challenges that required resilience and adaptability. Housing discrimination was one such challenge. Redlining and restrictive covenants were widespread practices that confined African American residents to overcrowded and poorly maintained neighborhoods. These policies not only limited housing options but also had long-term economic impacts, as property values in African American neighborhoods were artificially depressed.

Racial discrimination in the workplace meant that African American workers were often relegated to the lowest-paying jobs with fewer benefits and the least security compared to their white counterparts. Labor unions, while instrumental in improving workers' rights, were often segregated or outright exclusionary, leaving African American workers to form their own unions and advocacy groups.

Schools in African American neighborhoods were typically underfunded and overcrowded, reflecting broader inequalities in public services. Despite these challenges, African American communities placed a high value on education as a pathway to advancement, resulting in efforts to improve educational opportunities through community initiatives.

The rapid demographic changes in northern cities sometimes led to racial tensions and violence. The Chicago Race Riot of 1919 and the Detroit Riot of 1943 are examples of the violent backlash against African American migrants, fueled by competition for jobs and housing, as well as deeply ingrained racial prejudices. The transition from rural to urban life required significant cultural adjustments, with migrants often facing isolation and cultural dislocation.

The Great Migration was a transformative period in American history, driven by the pursuit of freedom and opportunity. While it presented significant challenges, it also offered new possibilities and laid the foundation for substantial social and cultural changes. The legacy of the Great Migration is a testament to the resilience and determination of African Americans in the face of systemic oppression, and it continues to shape the nation's journey toward equality and justice.

Many of Aaron Whitaker GUYTON's descendants took advantage of the opportunity to improve their lives by moving north. The reader will find many of his descendants moved to St. Louis, Detroit, Chicago, Milwaukee, and Waterloo, IA.

Sharecropping in the South: A Deep Dive into Its Impact on African Americans[374]

Sharecropping emerged in the Southern United States after the Civil War, as a system of agriculture that significantly shaped the socio-economic landscape for decades. It became a predominant way of life for many African Americans, who had recently been emancipated from slavery but found themselves trapped in a new form of economic bondage.

After the Civil War, the South's economy was in disarray. Plantation owners, deprived of slave labor, needed a way to maintain their lands without the capital to pay wages. Simultaneously, freedmen, who had little to no access to land or capital, needed work. Sharecropping was a compromise. Landowners provided land, seeds, tools, and sometimes housing. In return, sharecroppers – who were typically responsible for providing their own labor – would give a share of their crop (usually half) to the landowner as rent. This system allowed landowners to maintain control over their land and labor while giving freedmen a way to work the land without the need for initial capital.

Sharecropping contracts were often highly exploitative. Terms were dictated by landowners, and illiteracy among many freedmen meant they could not understand or contest the agreements. These contracts typically ensured that sharecroppers remained in debt, as they had to buy supplies on credit at high-interest rates from stores owned by landowners. Sharecropping created a cycle of debt and poverty. Sharecroppers rarely made enough profit to cover their debts, let alone to save money or buy their own land. The economic exploitation inherent in the system kept African American families in a state of semi-slavery, bound to the land and the whims of the landowners. See the section on Nealie Eugene TERRY CONWAY for an interesting story on how sharecropping affected the family.

The living conditions of sharecroppers were often dire. Housing provided by landowners was typically rudimentary, lacking basic amenities. Malnutrition and poor health were common, as the meager earnings could scarcely cover necessities. Sharecropping limited educational opportunities. Children often had to work in the fields alongside their parents, which impeded their ability to attend school. The lack of education further entrenched the cycle of poverty and limited social mobility.

Economically dependent on white landowners, African American sharecroppers were vulnerable to political manipulation. They were often coerced into voting according to the landowners' preferences or prevented from voting altogether, undermining the political gains made during Reconstruction.

The harsh realities of sharecropping and the systemic racism prevalent in the South were significant push factors for migration. The promise of better economic opportunities and a chance to escape the oppressive social order motivated many African Americans to move northward during the Great Migration. Between 1916 and 1970, more than six million African Americans migrated from the rural South to the urban North. While not all were sharecroppers, a significant portion of migrants came from agricultural backgrounds seeking better prospects in industrial cities.

According to the U.S. Department of Agriculture (USDA), in 1920, about one in seven Black farmers owned their land. This meant approximately 14% of African American farmers were landowners, while

---

[374] ChatGPT, accessed 6 June 2024, with prompt: Please write a 2000-word essay on share cropping in the south. How did it affect Black Americans? Were they more likely to migrate to the north? How many black farmers sharecropped versus owning their own farms?

the vast majority, around 86%, were either sharecroppers or tenant farmers. African American landowners faced significant challenges. Racist policies and practices, such as discriminatory lending by banks, made it difficult for African American farmers to acquire and maintain land. Violence and intimidation were also common, with white supremacists often targeting successful African American farmers.

African American landowners typically owned smaller plots and less fertile land compared to their white counterparts. Despite these challenges, land ownership represented a critical form of economic autonomy and was a goal for many African American families. Land ownership allowed for the development of independent African American communities, which became centers of resistance against racial oppression. These communities fostered a sense of pride and solidarity and were instrumental in the early civil rights movement.

The economic impact of sharecropping persisted long after the system itself declined. The cycle of debt and poverty left many African American families without the financial resources to invest in education, health, or business opportunities. The lack of educational opportunities for sharecroppers had long-term effects on literacy and economic mobility. Generations of African American families were hindered by the inability to access quality education, which is a crucial determinant of economic success. Sharecropping entrenched social hierarchies and racial segregation. The legacy of this system contributed to ongoing racial inequalities in wealth, health, and education.

The advent of agricultural mechanization in the mid-20th century reduced the need for labor-intensive farming. Tractors and other machinery made it possible for landowners to manage their farms with fewer workers, leading to a decline in the sharecropping system. As cities grew and industrial jobs became more prevalent, the rural workforce dwindled. The Great Migration significantly contributed to this urbanization, as millions of African Americans left the countryside in search of better opportunities. New Deal policies in the 1930s and subsequent agricultural reforms aimed to improve the conditions for farmers. While these policies were not always equitable, they did contribute to the decline of traditional sharecropping arrangements.

It appears that Aaron Whitaker GUYTON ensured his children owned farms. David F. GUYTON, an English Guyton genealogist, reports that Vinson TERRY acquired land from Caroline's father, Whit GUYTON, shortly after their marriage.[375] On 1 Jan 1875, shortly before Pinkney's marriage, Whit GUYTON conveyed 160 acres to Pink GUYTON and Elijah GUYTON in Land Deed Book O, p. 639.[376] I could not find Andrew GUYTON's family in the 1900, 1910, or 1920 U.S. Censuses. Therefore, I cannot determine whether he owned land free and clear. James died too young to determine if he ever owned any land free and clear. In 1910, Case and his younger brother, Ike, lived with their mother in Beat 4, Attala Co., MS. They were engaged in farming the land owned without a mortgage by Artie and/or by her sons. In 1910, Maggie and Tom were married and lived in Beat 4, Attala Co., MS. The family owned its farm without a mortgage. In 1910, Amanda (Annie B.) GUYTON lived with her husband, Joe TERRY, in

---

[375] Personal communication with David Guyton, about 2022.
[376] Source on *Ancestry.com* is given as: David F Guyton Springfield, 22 Lache Lane, Chester CH4 7LR, England E-mail: DFGuyton@compuserve.com Courtesy of Ann Breedlove genealogy librarian Attala County, Mississippi. In the posted document, the ultimate source of the information was a letter from John D. Guyton, written on 22 Jul 2002.

Beat 1, Attala Co., MS.[377] The family lived on its farm which they owned free and clear. In the 1900 U.S. Census, Simon GUYTON and his wife, Viola, lived in New Port, Attala Co., MS on a farm that Simon owned free and clear.[378] Baby James GUYTON died as an infant. Whit GUYTON's children were clearly provided resources for their futures.

---

[377] "1910 United States Census," Beat 1, Attala Co., MS, digital image s.v. "Annie B. Terry," (birth ABT 1874), *Ancestry.com*.

[378] "1900 United States Census," Newport, Attala Co., MS, digital image s.v. "Simon Guyton," (birth Feb 1876), *Ancestry.com*.

CHILD OF AARON WHITAKER GUYTON AND SARAH UNKNOWN: CAROLINE'S LINE
Generation #7

Caroline GUYTON (Aaron Whitaker, Aaron Steele, Joseph I, John I, Samuel II, Samuel I, John)

Caroline, born in January 1947 in Attala Co., MS, and passing away in 1915 in the same locale, was the daughter of Aaron Whitaker GUYTON and Sarah UNKNOWN/RUSSELL. The familial ties between Sarah and Caroline were documented in the will of Green RUSSELL, Sarah's husband, penned on October 2, 1905.[379]

> "I devise and bequeath all of my property both real and personal that I now own or may own at my death to William W. Terry of said Attala County Mississippi who is the grandson of my wife, Sarah, and the son of Caroline Terry."

Caroline married Vincent (Vinson) TERRY (b. ABT 1833 Alabama, d. 8 Oct 1904 Attala Co., MS). According to the 1900 U.S. Census, Caroline and Vincent married about 1865. Various U.S. Censuses recorded Vinson as a farmer throughout his life while Caroline kept house. Neither could read or write. See Figure 49 and Figure 50 for their headstones.

Figure 49 Caroline GUYTON TERRY's Headstone in Russell Cemetery[380]

Figure 50 Vinson TERRY's Headstone in Russell Cemetery[381]

---

[379] Mississippi, U.S., Wills and Probate Records, 1780-1982, digital image s.v. "Green Russell," (will date 2 Oct 1905, Case Number 3559, Vol E-G, 1904-1921), *Ancestry.com*.

[380] Caroline J. Terry, grave marker, Russell Cemetery, Attala Co, MS, digital image s.v. "Carolyn J. Terry," Memorial ID 119606854, *FindaGrave.com*.

[381] Vincent (Vinson) Terry, grave marker, Russell Cemetery, Attala Co, MS, digital image s.v. "Venson Terry," Memorial ID 119616415, *FindaGrave.com*.

According to the 1900 Federal Census, Caroline and Vinson TERRY were married for 35 years, implying they married in 1865. Vinson worked as a farmer. David F. GUYTON, an English Guyton genealogist, indicates that Vinson TERRY acquired land from Caroline's father, Whit GUYTON, shortly after their marriage.[382]

In the 1870 Federal Census, Caroline (age 21) and Vinson (age 39) lived in Kosciusko Township in Attala County, MS in Supervisor's Beat No. 4. They had three children by this time. The couple owned personal property worth $40 and $100 worth of real estate. See Figure 51.

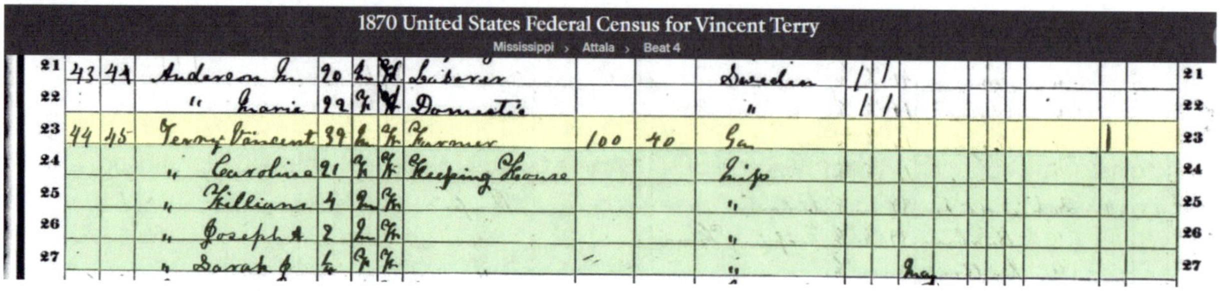

Figure 51 1870 Federal Census for Caroline and Vinson TERRY

According to the 1880 Federal Census, neither Caroline nor Vinson could read or write. They lived next door to Adeline RAINEY MALLETT's family[383] and very close to Pickney GUYTON and Elijah GUYTON, who had their own families. Their location was Supervisor's District 2, Township 13 Range 6 Section 2, Beat 1 in Attala County. This land description is not complete enough to locate them on a township map. Is it Section 20 (not 2) T13N R6E, the land where Whit GUYTON lived? In 1880, Whit lived with Green and Sarah RUSSELL in a different Enumeration District than the Terrys.

The 1890 U.S. Census has been destroyed. In the 1900 U.S. Census, people were asked about their ownership of real property and whether it was mortgaged. Caroline and Vinson owned their farm free of a mortgage.[384] I could not find Caroline in the 1910 U.S. Census.

The children of Caroline GUYTON and Vinson TERRY were:

i   William M. TERRY, Sr. (b. 8 Aug 1868 Attala Co., MS, d. 13 Jul 1956 Memphis, Shelby Co., TN)[385] m. Mary BURT (b. 15 Mar 1864 Attala Co., MS, d. 27 Feb 1937 buried Russell Cemetery, Attala Co., MS).

ii   Joseph Thomas (Joe) TERRY (b. Aug 1869 Attala Co., MS, d. AFT 1940) m. Amanda (Annie B.) GUYTON (b. Aug 1872 Sallis, Attala Co., MS, d. 1933 Sallis, Attala Co., MS).[386] Amanda is the name known by her descendants although most records note her as Annie B.

---

[382] Personal communication with David Guyton, about 2022.
[383] She is likely Artie RAINEY's sister.
[384] "1900 United States Census," Beat 1, Attala Co., MS, digital image s.v. "Vinson Terry," (birth Sep 1836), Ancestry.com.
[385] William Terry, Sr., grave marker, Russell Cemetery, Attala Co., MS, s.v. "William Terry, Sr." (birth 15 Mar 1864; death 27 Feb 1937), FindaGrave.com. Mary Burt, grave marker, Russell Cemetery, Attala Co., MS, s.v. "Mary Terry," (birth 15 Mar 1864; death 27 Feb 1937), FindaGrave.com.
[386] "1900 United States Census," Kosciusko, Attala Co., MS, digital image s.v. "Joseph Terry," (birth 1869), Ancestry.com. The last Census I find Joseph Terry in is the 1940 Census. "1900 United States Census," Kosciusko, Attala Co., MS, digital image s.v. "Ann Terry," (birth 1872), Ancestry.com. The last Census I find Amanda Guyton Terry in is the 1940 Census.

iii		Sarah J. (Sallie) TERRY (b. ABT 1870, MS, d. Unknown).[387]
iv		Mary TERRY (b. ABT 1872, d. Unknown).[388]
v		John TERRY (b. Mar 1875 MS, d. Unknown)[389] m. Eula BOYETT (b. Sep 1876 MS, d. Unknown)[390] around 1897.
vi		Patsy TERRY (b. ABT 1876, d. Unknown).[391]
viii		Green TERRY (b. ABT 1887 MS, d. Unknown)[392] m. Magnolia (Maggie) UNKNOWN (b. ABT 1884, d. Unknown).[393]
ix		Walter G. TERRY, Sr. (b. 1 Jan 1880 MS, d. Sep 1928 Attala Co., MS)[394] m. Dora GRIFFIN (ABT 1892 MS, d. May 1929 Attala Co., MS).[395]
x		Jacob G. (Jake) TERRY (b. 9 May 1891 Kosciusko, Attala Co., MS).[396]

---

[387] "1870 United States Census," Kosciusko, Attala Co., MS, digital image s.v. "Sallie Terry," (birth ABT 1870), *Ancestry.com*.

[388] "1880 United States Census," Kosciusko, Attala Co., MS, digital image s.v. "Mary Terry," (birth ABT 1872), *Ancestry.com*.

[389] "1900 United States Census," Kosciusko, Attala Co., MS, digital image s.v. "John A. Terry," (birth ABT Mar 1875; married ABT 1897), *Ancestry.com*.

[390] "1900 United States Census," Kosciusko, Attala Co., MS, digital image s.v. "Eula Terry," (birth ABT Sep 1876), *Ancestry.com*.

[391] "1880 United States Census," Kosciusko, Attala Co., MS, digital image s.v. "Patsy Terry," (birth ABT 1872), *Ancestry.com*.

[392] "1880 United States Census," Kosciusko, Attala Co., MS, digital image s.v. "Green Terry," (birth ABT 1887), *Ancestry.com*.

[393] "1910 United States Census," Kosciusko, Attala Co., MS, digital image s.v. "Maggie Terry," (birth ABT 1887), *Ancestry.com*.

[394] "U.S., World War I Draft Registration Cards, 1917-1918," digital image s.v. "Walter Terry," (birth 1 Jan 1880), *Ancestry.com*. "Mississippi, U.S., Index to Deaths, 1912-1943," digital image s.v. "Walter Terry," (death Sep 1928), *Ancestry.com*.

[395] "1910 United States Census," Attala Co., MS, digital image s.v. "Dover Terry," (birth ABT 1887), *Ancestry.com*. "Mississippi, U.S., Index to Deaths, 1912-1943," digital image s.v. "Dora Terry," (death May 1929), *Ancestry.com*.

[396] "U.S., World War I Draft Registration Cards, 1917-1918," digital image s.v. "Jake Terry," (birth 9 May 1891), *Ancestry.com*.

Generation #8

William M. TERRY, Sr. (Caroline, Aaron Whitaker, Aaron Steele, Joseph I, John I, Samuel II, Samuel I, John)

William M. TERRY, Sr. was the son of Caroline GUYTON (b. Jan 1847 Attala Co., MS, d. 1915 Attala Co., MS)[397] and Vincent (Vinson) TERRY (b. ABT 1833 AL, d. 8 Oct 1904 Attala Co., MS).[398] According to the 1900 U.S. Census, Caroline and Vinson married about 1865.[399]

William was born on 8 Aug 1868 in Attala Co., MS and died on 13 Jul 1956 in Memphis, Shelby Co., TN).[400] He married Mary BURT, who was born on 15 Mar 1864 in Attala Co., MS and died on 27 Feb 1937. They married around 1885 based on the birth of their first child. They are both buried in Russell Cemetery, located in Attala Co., MS. See Figure 52 for a photo of William TERRY, Sr.

Figure 52 William M. TERRY, Sr.[401]

In the 1900 U.S. Census, William was labeled a farmer on rented property in Kosciusko, Attala Co., MS. He and Mary had five children: Mary Emma TERRY (14), Nealie TERRY (12), Ethel TERRY (11), Walter

---

[397] Caroline's birth year varies considerably from 1843 to 1851 across all the sources I have for her. Caroline Guyton, grave marker, Russell Cemetery, Attala County, Mississippi, digital image s.v. "Caroline J. Terry," (1843-1915), *FindaGrave.com*. "1900 United States Census," Kosciusko, Attala County, Mississippi, digital image s.v. "Clalline Terry," (birth Jan 1847), *Ancestry.com*.

[398] Vincent (Vinson) Terry, grave marker, Russell Cemetery, Attala County, Mississippi, digital image s.v. "Venson Terry," (1839-1904), *FindaGrave.com*. His birth date varies from 1831 to 1841 across my sources. "1900 United States Census," Kosciusko, Attala County, Mississippi, digital image s.v. "Vinson Terry," (birth Sep 1836), *Ancestry.com*.

[399] "1900 United States Census," Kosciusko, Attala Co., MS, digital image s.v. "Vinson Terry," (marriage ABT 1865), *Ancestry.com*.

[400] William Terry, Sr., grave marker, Russell Cemetery, Attala County, Mississippi, s.v. "William Terry, Sr." (birth 15 Mar 1864; death 27 Feb 1937), *FindaGrave.com*. Mary Burt, grave marker, Russell Cemetery, Attala County, Mississippi, s.v. "Mary Terry," (birth 15 Mar 1864; death 27 Feb 1937), *FindaGrave.com*.

[401] Christopher Conway, photo, Ancestry.com, 19 Mar 2016.

TERRY (10) and Sarah V. TERRY (4).[402] Both William and Mary TERRY could read and write. In the 1910 Census, William and Mary lived in Beat 1, Attala Co., MS. where they lived on a farm owned free of a mortgage. They lived with their five younger children: Ethel (18), Walter G. TERRY (17), Sarah TERRY (14), Lula TERRY (5), and William Vinson TERRY, Jr. (3).[403]

By the 1930 Census, William and Mary likely lived on the same farm he owned in 1910. It was in Beat 1, Attala Co., MS, on Goodman Road.[404] Their son, William Vinson TERRY, Jr. (23), and his wife Beatrice Z. ISLAND TERRY (22), lived with them. In 1950, William was an 82-year-old widower.[405] He lived with his daughter, Ethel TERRY HARMON (age 60) and two of her children: Johnnie M. (12) and Queen T. HARMON, Jr. (8). They lived on a farm located on an unnamed road toward the town of McAdams. William was unable to work and Ethel was not searching for work.

William and Mary had seven children:

i   Mary Emma TERRY (b. 19 Jan 1886 Kosciusko, Attala Co., MS, d. 15 Nov 1982 Detroit, Wayne Co., MI)[406] m. James R. (Jim) EDWARDS (b. Nov 1874 MS, d. Unknown).[407]

ii   Ethel TERRY (b. 18 Dec 1888 Attala Co., MS, d. 15 May 1969)[408] m. John HARMON (b. 15 Jun 1895, d. 8 Dec 1971).[409]

iii   Nealie Eugene TERRY (b. 2 Jul 1890 Bolivar Co., MS, d. 17 Jun 1990 Dundee, Tunica Co., MS)[410] m. William Major CONWAY, Jr. (b. 14 Mar 1879 MS, d. 2 Jun 1951 Dundee, Tunica Co., MS).[411]

iv   Walter G. TERRY (b. 16 Feb 1893 Sallis, Attala Co., MS, d. 27 Nov 1945 Memphis, Shelby Co., TN)[412] m. Lula HEWETT (b. 26 Aug 1881 MS, d. 23 Nov 1960 Memphis, Shelby Co., TN).[413]

---

[402] "1900 United States Census," Kosciusko, Attala Co., MS, digital image s.v. "William M. Terry," (birth Aug 1867), *Ancestry.com*.

[403] "1910 United States Census," Beat 1, Attala Co., MS, digital image s.v. "William W. Terry," (birth ABT 1868), *Ancestry.com*.

[404] "1930 United States Census," Beat 1, Attala Co., MS, digital image s.v. "William Terry," (birth ABT 1865), *Ancestry.com*.

[405] "1950 United States Census," Kosciusko, Attala Co., MS, digital image s.v. "W. W. Terry," (birth ABT 1868), *Ancestry.com*.

[406] "Michigan, U.S., Death Index, 1971-1996," s.v. "Emma Edwards," (birth 19 Jan 1886, death 9 Nov 1982), *Ancestry.com*

[407] "1900 United States Census," Kosciusko, Attala Co., MS, digital image s.v. "James R. Edward," (birth ABT Nov 1874), *Ancestry.com*.

[408] Ethel Terry, grave marker, Russell Cemetery, Attala Co., MS, digital image s.v. "Ethel Harmon," (birth 18 Dec 1888, death 15 May 1969), *FindaGrave.com*.

[409] John Harmon, grave marker, Russell Cemetery, Attala Co., MS, digital image s.v. "John Harmon," (birth 15 Jun 1895, death 8 Dec 1971), *FindaGrave.com*.

[410] Nealie Eugene Terry, grave marker, Bethlehem Cemetery, Lula, Coahoma Co., MS, digital image s.v. "Nealie Eugene Conway," (birth 2 Jul 1890, death 17 Jun 1990), *FindaGrave.com*.

[411] William Major Conway, Jr., grave marker, Bethlehem Cemetery, Lula, Coahoma Co., MS, digital image s.v. "Major Conway, Sr.," (birth 14 Mar 1879, death 2 Jun 1951), *FindaGrave.com*.

[412] Walter G. Terry., grave marker, Memphis National Cemetery, Memphis, Shelby County, TN, digital image s.v. "Walter Terry," (birth 16 Feb 1893, death 27 Nov 1943), *FindaGrave.com*.

[413] Lula Hewett, grave marker, Memphis National Cemetery, Memphis, Shelby County, TN, digital image s.v. "Lula Terry," (birth 16 Feb 1893, death 27 Nov 1943), *FindaGrave.com*.

v	Sarah V. TERRY (b. 15 May 1897 Sallis, Attala Co., MS, d. 14 Feb 1979 Detroit, Wayne Co., MI)[414] m. Walter HARMON (b. 22 Jun 1895 McAdams, MS, d. 6 Apr 1969).[415]
vi	Alexander TERRY (b. ABT 1905 Attala Co., MS, d. Unknown).[416]
vi	Lula TERRY (b. 1905 MS, d. Unknown).[417]
vii	William Vinson TERRY, Jr. (b. 19 Jun 1907 Attala Co., MS, d. 30 Sep 1981)[418] m. Beatrice ISLAND (b. 7 Feb 1902 MS, d. 16 Dec 1987 Indianapolis, Marion Co., IN).[419]

Joseph Thomas (Joe) TERRY (Caroline, Aaron Whitaker, Aaron Steele, Joseph I, John I, Samuel II, Samuel I, John)

Joseph Thomas (Joe) TERRY was the son of Caroline GUYTON (b. Jan 1847 Attala Co., MS, d. 1915 Attala Co., MS)[420] and Vincent (Vinson) TERRY (b. ABT 1833 AL, d. 8 Oct 1904 Attala Co., MS).[421] Caroline was the daughter of Aaron Whitaker GUYTON and Sarah UNKNOWN/RUSSELL. Joe was born in Aug 1869 in Attala Co., MS, and died sometime after 1940. I don't find a date of death for Joe but he was included in the 1940 U.S. Census and he is buried in Russell Cemetery, Attala Co., MS.[422]

Joe married Amanda (also known in records as Annie B.) GUYTON (b. Aug 1872 Sallis, Attala Co., MS, d. 1933 Sallis, Attala Co., MS). Amanda GUYTON was the daughter of Aaron Whitaker GUYTON and Artemesia (Artie) RAINEY. If my analysis is correct, then it was a marriage between half-aunt and half-nephew.

In the 1900 U.S. Census, Amanda was married and using the last name Terry, but she lived with her brother, Case, and her oldest child, Lela TERRY in New Port, Attala Co., MS.[423] Amanda could read and write. In 1910, Amanda lived with Joe TERRY in Beat 1, Attala Co., MS.[424] The family lived on their farm

---

[414] "Michigan, U.S., Death Index, 1971-1996," s.v. "Sarah Harmon," (birth 15 May 1897, death 14 Feb 1979), *Ancestry.com*.

[415] "U.S., World War I Civilian Draft Registrations, 1917-1918," s.v. "Walter Harmon," (22 Jun 1895), *Ancestry.com*.

[416] "1920 United States Census," Kosciusko, Attala Co., MS, digital image s.v. "Alexander Terry," (birth ABT 1905), *Ancestry.com*.

[417] "1910 United States Census," Beat 1, Attala Co., MS, digital image s.v. "Lula Terry," (birth ABT 1905), *Ancestry.com*.

[418] William Vinson Terry, grave marker, Russell Cemetery, Attala Co., MS, digital image s.v. "William V. Terry," (birth 19 Jun 1907, death 30 Sep 1981), *FindaGrave.com*.

[419] "U.S., Social Security Death Index, 1935-2014," s.v. "Beatrice Terry," (birth 7 Feb 1902, death Dec 1987), *Ancestry.com*.

[420] Caroline's birth year varies considerably from 1843 to 1851 across all the sources I have for her. Caroline Guyton, grave marker, Russell Cemetery, Attala County, Mississippi, digital image s.v. "Caroline J. Terry," (1843-1915), *FindaGrave.com*. "1900 United States Census," Kosciusko, Attala County, Mississippi, digital image s.v. "Clalline Terry," (birth Jan 1847), *Ancestry.com*.

[421] Vincent (Vinson) Terry, grave marker, Russell Cemetery, Attala County, Mississippi, digital image s.v. "Venson Terry," (1839-1904), *FindaGrave.com*. His birth date varies from 1831 to 1841 across my sources. "1900 United States Census," Kosciusko, Attala County, Mississippi, digital image s.v. "Vinson Terry," (birth Sep 1836), *Ancestry.com*.

[422] Annie B. Guyton and Joseph Thomas (Joe) Terry, grave marker, Russell Cemetery, Attala Co., MS, digital image s.v. "Annie Guyton Terry," and "Joseph Terry," (Memorial ID 107273730 and 201392258, *FindaGrave.com*.

[423] "1900 United States Census," Newport, Attala Co., MS, digital image s.v. "Ann Terry," (birth Aug 1872), *Ancestry.com*.

[424] "1910 United States Census," Beat 1, Attala Co., MS, digital image s.v. "Annie B. Terry," (birth ABT 1874), *Ancestry.com*.

which they owned free and clear. The Census indicates they had been married for eighteen years and had three children: Lela TERRY (11), Quesada TERRY (9), and Carnes TERRY (2). Joe could read and write.

In 1920, the family lived on New Port Road, Kosciusko, Attala Co., MS.[425] Living with Amanda and Joe on the farm were Carnes Fred TERRY (10) and Stella Mae TERRY (8). The 1930 U.S. Census show Amanda and Joe living on their owned farm with Lela (a 38-year-old married woman but with no children living with her) and her younger brother, Carnes Fred (22).[426] Carnes helped Joe to farm the property. In 1940, Joe and Amanda lived on the farm with their son, Carnes, his wife Beatrice, and the younger couple's two children, Yvonne and Bernice Marie.[427]

Joe and Amanda GUYTON TERRY had at least four children:

i   Lela TERRY (b. Apr 1892 MS, d. Unknown).[428]
ii   Quesada TERRY (b. ABT 1901 MS, d. Unknown).[429]
iii Carnes Fred TERRY (b. 7 Oct 1907 Sallis, Attala Co., MS, d. Jun 1973 Jackson, Hinds Co., MS)[430] m. Callie Beatrice McMICHAEL (b. 20 Sep 1915 Attala Co., MS, d. 19 May 1979 Memphis, Shelby Co., TN).[431]
iv Stella Mae TERRY (b. 17 Aug 1912 Sallis, Attala Co., MS, d. 1 Jan 1993 Lexington, Holmes Co., MS)[432] m. Joe Dale (Joe D.) GUYTON (b. 24 Dec 1901 MS, d. Dec 1967 Sallis, Attala Co., MS).[433] Joe D. was the son of Simon and Viola GUYTON. He is a cousin to Stella Mae.

John TERRY (Caroline, Aaron Whitaker, Aaron Steele, Joseph I, John I, Samuel II, Samuel I, John)

John TERRY was the son of Caroline GUYTON (b. Jan 1947 Attala Co., MS, d. 1915 Attala Co., MS)[434] and Vincent (Vinson) TERRY (b. ABT 1833 AL, d. 8 Oct 1904 Attala Co., MS).[435] He was born in March

---

[425] "1920 United States Census," Kosciusko, Attala Co., MS, digital image s.v. "Annie Terry," (birth ABT 1880), *Ancestry.com*.
[426] "1930 United States Census," Natchez Trace Road, Beat 1, Attala Co., MS, digital image s.v. "Anne Terry," (birth ABT 1880), *Ancestry.com*.
[427] "1940 United States Census," Goodman Road, Kosciusko, Attala Co., MS, digital image s.v. "Annie Grory," (birth ABT 1880), *Ancestry.com*.
[428] "1900 United States Census," Newport, Attala Co., MS, digital image s.v. "Lela Terry," (birth Apr 1892), *Ancestry.com*.
[429] "1910 United States Census," Beat 1, Attala Co., MS, digital image s.v. "Quesada Terry," (birth ABT 1901), *Ancestry.com*.
[430] "Social Security Death Index," s.v. "Fred Terry," (birth 7 Oct 1907, death Jun 1973), *Ancestry.com*.
[431] Callie Beatrice McMichael, grave marker, Hollywood Cemetery, Memphis, Shelby Co., TN, digital image s.v. "Callie Beatrice Terry Anthony," (birth 20 Sep 1915, death 19 May 1979), *FindaGrave.com*.
[432] Stella Mae Terry, grave marker, Mallett Cemetery, Attala Co., MS, digital image s.v. "Stella Mae Guyton," (birth 17 Aug 1912, death 1 Jan 1993), *FindaGrave.com*.
[433] "Social Security Death Index," s.v. "Joe Guyton," (birth 24 Dec 1901, death Dec 1967), *Ancestry.com*.
[434] Caroline's birth year varies considerably from 1843 to 1851 across all the sources I have for her. Caroline Guyton, grave marker, Russell Cemetery, Attala County, Mississippi, digital image s.v. "Caroline J. Terry," (1843-1915), *FindaGrave.com*. "1900 United States Census," Kosciusko, Attala County, Mississippi, digital image s.v. "Clalline Terry," (birth Jan 1847), *Ancestry.com*.
[435] Vincent (Vinson) Terry, grave marker, Russell Cemetery, Attala County, Mississippi, digital image s.v. "Venson Terry," (1839-1904), *FindaGrave.com*. His birth date varies from 1831 to 1841 across my sources. "1900 United States Census," Kosciusko, Attala County, Mississippi, digital image s.v. "Vinson Terry," (birth Sep 1836), *Ancestry.com*.

1875 in MS, and died at an unknown date.[436] He married Eula BOYETT (b. Sep 1876, MS, d. Unknown)[437] around 1897.

They were married 3 years at the time of the 1900 census. John (25) was married to Eula BOYETT (23) and lived in Kosciusko, Attala Co., MS, living with their son Isaac H. TERRY (1) and Eula's sister Eva BOYETT. John was a farmer, who could read and write, and lived on a rented farm. Eula worked as a farm laborer and could read and write. They lived next door to Vinson TERRY and Doss GUYTON.

In 1910 John TERRY was 34 and Eula was 28. They lived with five children: Isaac TERRY (10), Lula Cladis TERRY (9), Edna F. TERRY (7), Blanche TERRY (4), and Retha TERRY (2). They worked on their own farm, held without a mortgage, in Beat 1, Attala Co., MS.

In 1920 John (45) was reported to be a widower. He lived on his own farm on New Port Rd. in Kosciusko, Attala Co., Mississippi. He lived with Lula (18), Frank (16), Blanche (14), and Retha (12), and Grover (7). Not surprisingly, I did not find Eula in the Census. Edna was included in the 1910 Census but Frank was not. Frank showed up in the 1920 Census, but Edna did not.

Lula Cladis TERRY died at the age of 24 (b. 30 Dec 1900, d. 26 Jul 1925). She was buried in Russell Cemetery, Attala Co., MS. The marker was broken and may have had the married name of Stingley.

In 1930 U.S. Census, Eula (51) lived at Natchez Trace Road in Beat 1, Attala Co., MS. She was divorced and the head of the household. She owned the farm without a mortgage. She lived with Grover TERRY (17) and two granddaughters: Gladys TERRY (10) and Locile RILEY (5). Grover farmed with Eula. The granddaughters are too old to be Grover's children. Eula donated to Wesley M.E. Church for a hospital.[438]

In the 1940 Census, Eula TERRY was 65 years old. She was widowed. Did John die since the 1930 Census? She had a 4th grade education. She owned her home on Goodman Road in Kosciusko, Attala Co., MS. She stilled lived with her granddaughters: Gladys HARMAN (20 with a 6th grade education) and Locile RILEY (14 with an 8th grade education). Their home value was $300. It is not clear whether they were living on the farm.

Eula and John TERRY had at least six children:

i   Isaac H. TERRY (b. 11 Jan 1898 Attala Co., MS, d. 4 Jan 1913 Attala Co., MS).[439]

ii   Lula Cladis TERRY (b. 30 Dec 1900 Attala Co., MS, d. 26 Jul 1925 Attala Co., MS. She was buried in Russell Cemetery. Noted on *FindaGrave*: Marker broken - but possibly married name of STINGLEY).[440]

---

[436] "1900 United States Census," Kosciusko, Attala Co., MS, digital image s.v. "John A. Terry," (birth ABT Mar 1875; married ABT 1897), *Ancestry.com*.

[437] "1900 United States Census," Kosciusko, Attala Co., MS, digital image s.v. "Eula Terry," (birth ABT Sep 1876), *Ancestry.com*.

[438] "Negroes Urged to Rally in Hospital Drive," *The Star-Herald*, 7 Oct 1937, p. 1; digital image, s.v. "Eula Terry," *Newspapers.com*, <https://www.newspapers.com/image/305535540/?xid=5506&clipping_id=145308165>.

[439] Isaac H. Terry, grave marker, Russell Cemetery, Attala Co., MS, digital image s.v. "Isaac Terry," (birth 11 Jan 1898, death 4 Jan 1913, Russell Cemetery, Attala Co., MS), *FindaGrave*.

[440] Lula Cladis Terry, grave marker, Russell Cemetery, Attala Co., MS, digital image s.v. "Lula Cladis Terry," (birth 30 Dec 1900, death 26 Jul 1925), *FindaGrave.com*.

iii		Edna F. TERRY (b. 7 Feb 1903 Attala Co., MS, d. 12 Dec 1929 Chicago, Cook Co., IL)[441] m. Andrew HARMON (b. Unknown, d. Unknown).
iv		Blanche TERRY (b. ABT 1906 Sallis, Attala Co., MS, d. Unknown).[442]
v		Retha TERRY (b. 25 Nov 1908, Sallis, Attala Co., MS, d. 14 Jul 1999).[443]
vi		Grover TERRY (b. ABT 1920, Attala Co., MS, d. Unknown).[444]

Green TERRY (Caroline, Aaron Whitaker, Aaron Steele, Joseph I, John I, Samuel II, Samuel I, John)

Green TERRY was the son of Caroline GUYTON (b. Jan 1847 Attala Co., MS, d. 1915 Attala Co., MS)[445] and Vincent (Vinson) Terry (b. ABT 1833 AL, d. 8 Oct 1904 Attala Co., MS).[446] Green was born on 16 Aug 1876 in Holmes Co. and he died sometime after the 1940 U.S. Census).[447] He married Magnolia (Maggie) UNKNOWN (b. ABT 1884, d. Unknown).[448]

In the 1910 Census, Green (age 30) and Maggie (age 26) had been married for nine years and lived in Beat 3, Holmes Co., MS. Green and Maggie lived on a rented farm and both could read and write. They lived with their children: Ruth TERRY (8), Lockett TERRY (6), Lillian TERRY (4), Howard TERRY (3), and Andrew TERRY (1). By 1920, Green (41) and Maggie TERRY (37) lived on a rented farm at Richland, Holmes Co., MS.[449] Living with them were Rufey (Ruth) TERRY (17), Lockett TERRY (15), Lillian TERRY (14), Howard TERRY (12), Andrew TERRY (11), Johnnie TERRY (9), Rommie TERRY (8), Tommie TERRY (6), Joseph TERRY (4), and Wyley TERRY (2).

In the 1930 Census, Green (age 48) and Magnolia (age 42) lived at Beat 3, Holmes Co., MS. The family was farming cotton on a rented farm.[450] They lived with their children John TERRY (18), Ramas (likely Romie) TERRY (16), Tommie TERRY (14), Joe TERRY (12), Wiley F. TERRY (8), and Tertis TERRY (6).

---

[441] "Illinois, Deaths and Stillbirths Index, 1916-1947," s.v. "Edna Harmon," (birth 7 Feb 1903, death 12 Dec 1929), *Ancestry.com*.

[442] "1900 United States Census," Beat 1, Attala Co., MS, digital image s.v. "Blanche Terry," (birth ABT 1906), *Ancestry.com*.

[443] Retha Terry, grave marker, Garden Memorial Park, Jackson, Hinds Co., MS, digital image s.v. "Retha Terry," (birth 25 Nov 1908, death 14 Jul 1999), *FindaGrave*.

[444] "1900 United States Census," Kosciusko, Attala Co., MS, digital image s.v. "Grover Terry," (birth ABT 1913), *Ancestry.com*.

[445] Caroline's birth year varies considerably from 1843 to 1851 across all the sources I have for her. Caroline Guyton, grave marker, Russell Cemetery, Attala County, Mississippi, digital image s.v. "Caroline J. Terry," (1843-1915), *FindaGrave.com*. "1900 United States Census," Kosciusko, Attala County, Mississippi, digital image s.v. "Clalline Terry," (birth Jan 1847), *Ancestry.com*.

[446] Vincent (Vinson) Terry, grave marker, Russell Cemetery, Attala County, Mississippi, digital image s.v. "Venson Terry," (1839-1904), *FindaGrave.com*. His birth date varies from 1831 to 1841 across my sources. "1900 United States Census," Kosciusko, Attala County, Mississippi, digital image s.v. "Vinson Terry," (birth Sep 1836), *Ancestry.com*.

[447] "U.S., World War I Civilian Draft Registrations, 1917-1918," Kosciusko, Attala Co., MS, digital image s.v. "Green Terry," (birth 16 Aug 1876), *Ancestry.com*.

[448] "1910 United States Census," Kosciusko, Attala Co., MS, digital image s.v. "Maggie Terry," (birth ABT 1884), *Ancestry.com*.

[449] "1920 United States Census," Richland, Holmes Co., MS, digital image s.v. "Green Terry," (birth ABT 1879), *Ancestry.com*.

[450] "1930 United States Census," Beat 3, Holmes Co., MS, digital image s.v. "Green Terry," (birth ABT 1882), *Ancestry.com*.

Green TERRY (60) was shown as divorced in the 1940 U.S. Census.[451] He lived with his son Romie TERRY (27), Romie's wife, Elizabeth (22), and their children, L.I. or L.J. TERRY (a boy, aged 4), and Ruby L. TERRY (3). In 1940 Maggie TERRY's U.S. Census entry also indicated that she was divorced. She lived in Holmes Co., MS with sons Joe TERRY (24) and Peat TERRY (22), and grandson Leroy COLEMAN.

i   Ruth G. TERRY (b. 5 Jan 1904 Kosciusko, Attala Co., MS, d. 8 Mar 1942 Memphis, Shelby Co., TN)[452] m. Julius D. COOK (b. ABT 1891 Arkansas, d. Unknown).[453]

ii   Lockett Joseph TERRY, Sr. (b. 20 Aug 1904 MS, d. Nov 1980 St. Louis, St. Louis Co., MO)[454] m. (1) Gertrude CRANE (b. ABT 1908 AR, d. Unknown)[455] and (2) Mary Elizabeth MITCHELL (b. 14 Jul 1914 Edwardsville, Madison Co., IL, d. Aug 1986 St Louis Co., MO).[456]

iii   Lillian TERRY (b. 1906 MS, d. Unknown).[457]

iv   Howard TERRY (b. 1907 MS, d. Unknown).[458]

v   Andrew TERRY (b. 15 Mar 1909 MS, d. 25 Jan 1979 Detroit, Wayne Co., MI)[459] m. Eva LEVY (b. 20 May 1911 MS, d. 1 Feb 1999).[460]

vi   Johnnie TERRY (b. ABT 1912 MS, d. Unknown).[461]

vii   Romie TERRY, Sr. (b. 19 Sep 1913 Holmes Co., MS, d. 9 May 2008 Unknown)[462] m. Elizabeth UNKNOWN (b. ABT 1917 Pickens, Holmes Co., MS, d. 17 Dec 1998 Pickens, Holmes Co., MS).[463]

viii   Tommie TERRY (b. ABT 1916 MS, d. Unknown).[464]

ix   Peat TERRY (b. 1 Mar 1918 Pickens, Holmes Co., MS., d. Aug 1979).[465]

x   Joseph TERRY (b. 8 Sep 1918 Pickens, Holmes Co., MS, d. Unknown).[466]

---

[451] "1940 United States Census," Holmes Co., MS, digital image s.v. "Gwen Terry," (birth ABT 1880), *Ancestry.com*.

[452] "Tennessee, U.S., Death Records, 1908-1965," digital image s.v. "Ruth Terry Cook," (birth 5 Jan 1904, death 8 Mar 1942), *Ancestry.com*.

[453] "1930 United States Federal Census," AR, digital image s.v. "JH Cook," (birth ABT 1891), *Ancestry.com*.

[454] Lockett Joseph Terry, Sr., grave marker, St. Peter's Cemetery, Normandy, St. Louis Co., MO, digital image s.v. "Lockett Joseph Terry, Sr.," (birth 20 Aug 1904, death Nov 1980), *FindaGrave.com*.

[455] "1930 United States Federal Census," Jackson, Hinds Co., MS, digital image s.v. "Gertrude Terry," (birth ABT 1908), *Ancestry.com*.

[456] "Social Security Death Index," s.v. "Mary Terry," (birth 14 Jul 1914, death Aug 1986), *Ancestry.com*.

[457] "1920 United States Census," Richard, Holmes Co., MS, digital image s.v. "Lillian Terry," (birth ABT 1906), Ancestry.com.

[458] "1920 United States Census," Richard, Holmes Co., MS, digital image s.v. "Howard Terry," (birth ABT 1908), Ancestry.com.

[459] "Michigan, U.S., Death Index, 1971-1996," s.v. "Andrew Terry," (birth 15 Mar 1909, death 25 Jan 1979), *Ancestry.com*.

[460] "U.S., Social Security Death Index, 1935-2014," s.v. "Eva Terry," (birth 20 May 1911, death 1 Feb 1999), *Ancestry.com*.

[461] "1930 United States Census," Beat 3, Holmes Co., MS, digital image s.v. "John Terry," (birth ABT 1912), *Ancestry.com*.

[462] "U.S., Social Security Death Index, 1935-2014," s.v. "Romie Terry," (birth 3 Sep 1911, death 9 May 2008), *Ancestry.com*.

[463] "Elizabeth Terry: Homemaker," Clarion-Ledger, 20 Dec 1998, p. 24; digital image, s.v. "Elizabeth Terry," Newspapers.com, <https://www.newspapers.com/image/185454175/?article=10147629-3539-4427-9b0d-444cdc909d98&focus=0.5414884,0.5798436,0.6971703,0.6901017&xid=3355>.

[464] "1930 United States Census," Beat 3, Holmes Co., MS, digital image s.v. "Tommie Terry," (birth ABT 1916), Ancestry.com.

[465] "U.S., Social Security Applications and Claims Index, 1936-2007," s.v. "Peat Terry," (birth 1 Mar 1918, death Aug 1979), *Ancestry.com*.

[466] "U.S., World War II Draft Cards Young Men, 1940-1947," digital image s.v. "Joe Terry," (birth 8 Sep 1918), Ancestry.com.

xi   Wiley F. TERRY (b. ABT 1922 MS, d. Unknown).[467]

xii   Tertis or Gert TERRY (b. ABT 1924 MS, d. Unknown).[468]

Walter G. TERRY, Sr. (Caroline, Aaron Whitaker, Aaron Steele, Joseph I, John I, Samuel II, Samuel I, John)

Walter G. TERRY, Sr. was born 1 Jan 1880 in MS and died in Sep 1928 in Attala Co., MS.[469] He married Dora GRIFFIN (b. ABT 1892 MS, d. May 1929 Attala Co., MS).[470] He was the son of Caroline GUYTON (b. Jan 1947 Attala Co., MS, d. 1915 Attala Co., MS)[471] and Vincent (Vinson) TERRY (b. ABT 1833 AL, d. 8 Oct 1904 Attala Co., MS).[472] In 1900 Walter was single, living with his parents Vinson (63) and Caroline (52) and his siblings Joseph (30) and Jacob (11) in Kosciusko.[473] By 1910, Walter was married to Dora and had their first child, Minnie TERRY (0).[474] They lived on a farm that they owned free and clear in Beat 1, Attala Co., MS. They lived next door to Walter's brother, Joseph TERRY. Both Walter and Dora could read and write.

In 1920, the Walter G. TERRY, Sr. family lived in Kosciusko, Attala Co., MS on New Port Road.[475] The family consisted of Walter TERRY (38), Dora TERRY (28), Minnie TERRY (10), Hattie TERRY (8), Leon TERRY (6), and Walter TERRY (2). They still lived on their own mortgage-free farm. Dora and Walter died one year apart, leaving at least four orphans. I'm not sure what happened to the children.

---

[467] "1930 United States Census," Beat 3, Holmes Co., MS, digital image s.v. "Wylie F Terry," (birth ABT 1922), Ancestry.com.

[468] "1930 United States Census," Beat 3, Holmes Co., MS, digital image s.v. "Tertis Terry," (birth ABT 1924), Ancestry.com.

[469] "U.S., World War I Draft Registration Cards, 1917-1918," digital image s.v. "Walter Terry," (birth 1 Jan 1880), *Ancestry.com*. "Mississippi, U.S., Index to Deaths, 1912-1943," digital image s.v. "Walter Terry," (death Sep 1928), *Ancestry.com*.

[470] "1910 United States Census," Attala Co., MS, digital image s.v. "Dover Terry," (birth ABT 1887), *Ancestry.com*. "Mississippi, U.S., Index to Deaths, 1912-1943," digital image s.v. "Dora Terry," (death May 1929), *Ancestry.com*.

[471] Caroline's birth year varies considerably from 1843 to 1851 across all the sources I have for her. Caroline Guyton, grave marker, Russell Cemetery, Attala County, Mississippi, digital image s.v. "Caroline J. Terry," (1843-1915), *FindaGrave.com*. "1900 United States Census," Kosciusko, Attala County, Mississippi, digital image s.v. "Clalline Terry," (birth Jan 1847), *Ancestry.com*.

[472] Vincent (Vinson) Terry, grave marker, Russell Cemetery, Attala County, Mississippi, digital image s.v. "Venson Terry," (1839-1904), *FindaGrave.com*. His birth date varies from 1831 to 1841 across my sources. "1900 United States Census," Kosciusko, Attala County, Mississippi, digital image s.v. "Vinson Terry," (birth Sep 1836), *Ancestry.com*.

[473] "1900 United States Census," Kosciusko, Attala Co., MS, digital image s.v. "Walter G. Terry," (birth Jan 1885), Ancestry.com.

[474] "1910 United States Census," Beat 1, Attala Co., MS, digital image s.v. "Walter Terry," (birth 1885), Ancestry.com.

[475] "1920 United States Census," Kosciusko, Attala Co., MS, digital image s.v. "Walter Terry," (birth 1882), Ancestry.com.

Jacob G. (Jake) TERRY [Caroline, Aaron Whitaker, Aaron Steele, Joseph I, John I, Samuel II, Samuel I, John]

Jacob G. (Jake) TERRY was the son of Vincent (Vinson) TERRY (b. ABT 1833 AL, d. 8 Oct 1904 Attala Co., MS) and Caroline Guyton (b. Jan 1947 Attala Co., MS, d. 1915 Attala Co., MS).[476] He was born on 9 May 1891 in Kosciusko, Attala Co., MS.[477]

---

[476] Caroline's birth year varies considerably from 1843 to 1851 across all the sources I have for her. Caroline Guyton, grave marker, Russell Cemetery, Attala County, Mississippi, digital image s.v. "Caroline J. Terry," (1843-1915), *FindaGrave.com*. "1900 United States Census," Kosciusko, Attala County, Mississippi, digital image s.v. "Clalline Terry," (birth Jan 1847), *Ancestry.com*.
[477] "U.S., World War I Draft Registration Cards, 1917-1918," digital image s.v. "Jake Terry," (birth 9 May 1891), *Ancestry.com*.

Generation #9

Mary Emma TERRY (William TERRY, Caroline, Aaron Whitaker, Aaron Steele, Joseph I, John I, Samuel II, Samuel I, John)

Mary Emma TERRY was the daughter of William M. TERRY, Sr. (b. 8 Aug 1868 Attala Co., MS, d. 13 Jul 1956 Memphis, Shelby Co., TN) and Mary BURT (b. 15 Mar 1864 Attala Co., MS, died on 27 Feb 1937).[478] Emma was born on 19 Jan 1886 in Kosciusko, Attala Co., MS and she died 15 Nov 1982 in Detroit, Wayne Co., MI).[479] She was the second wife of James R. (Jim) EDWARDS (b. Nov 1874 MS, d. Unknown).[480] See Figure 53, Figure 54, Figure 55, and Figure 56.

Jim had six children with his first wife, Fannie GLASS: John H. EDWARDS, James Thomas (Tommie) EDWARDS, Pearlie EDWARDS, Ivery L. (Ive) EDWARDS, Estella (Stella) EDWARDS, and Rosa (Rosie) EDWARDS. Jim and Emma married three months before the 1910 U.S. Census was recorded.[481] Emma (22) was raising five of Jim's (36) children: Tommie (13), Pearl (11), Ive (8), Estella (7), and Rosa (5). They worked at a rented farm in Beat 5, Attala Co., MS.

The family lived on a rented farm in Center, Attala Co., MS when the 1920 Census was recorded.[482] The house was full of family: James R. EDWARDS (44), Emma (32), Ive EDWARDS (18), Estelle EDWARDS (17), Rosa EDWARDS (15), Willie H. EDWARDS (10), Ulysses (Julious) EDWARDS (8), Estela [Della] EDWARDS (5), Effie EDWARDS (4), and Luria EDWARDS (1). In 1930, they lived in Beat 5, Attala Co., MS near where the Kosciusko and Louisville Roads intersect.[483] Jim and Emma owned the farm. Ulysses (Julious) EDWARDS (16), Stella EDWARDS (14), and Effie EDWARDS (13) worked as farm labor. The other children were Loni EDWARDS (7), Ernest EDWARDS (6), Walter EDWARDS (4), Malina EDWARDS (3), Minnie L. EDWARDS (2), and Willie EDWARDS (0). The 1950 Census provided a better location for the farm: Center, Attala Co., MS, on the road turning right off Kosciusko and Louisville Road at the old Toplin School House.[484] Only two grandsons lived with Jim and Emma – Ardice (11) and Charles JAMISON (9).

---

[478] William Terry, Sr., grave marker, Russell Cemetery, Attala County, Mississippi, s.v. "William Terry, Sr." (birth 15 Mar 1864; death 27 Feb 1937), *FindaGrave.com*. Mary Burt, grave marker, Russell Cemetery, Attala County, Mississippi, s.v. "Mary Terry," (birth 15 Mar 1864; death 27 Feb 1937), *FindaGrave.com*.

[479] "Michigan, U.S., Death Index, 1971-1996," s.v. "Emma Edwards," (birth 19 Jan 1886, death 9 Nov 1982), *Ancestry.com*

[480] "1900 United States Census," Kosciusko, Attala Co., MS, digital image s.v. "James R. Edward," (birth abt Nov 1874), *Ancestry.com*.

[481] "1910 United States Census," Beat 5, Attala Co., MS, digital image s.v. "Emma Edwards," (birth abt 1888), *Ancestry.com*.

[482] "1920 United States Census," Center, Attala Co., MS, digital image s.v. "Emma Edwards," (birth abt 1888), *Ancestry.com*.

[483] "1930 United States Census," Beat 5, Attala Co., MS, digital image s.v. "Emma A Edwards," (birth abt 1885), *Ancestry.com*.

[484] "1950 United States Census," Center, Attala Co., MS, digital image s.v. "Emma Edwards," (birth abt 1886), *Ancestry.com*.

Figure 53 Mary Emma TERRY[485]

Figure 54 Young James R. (Jim) EDWARDS[486]

Figure 55 Older James R. (Jim) EDWARDS[487]

They had at least twelve children:

i   Willie H. EDWARDS (b. 22 Dec 1911 Kosciusko, Attala Co., MS, d. 21 Jun 1983 Detroit, Wayne Co., MI)[488] m. Grace Ora HARRISON (b. 16 Jan 1914 Good Pine, La Salle Parish, LA, d. 14 Dec 1993 Detroit, Wayne Co., MI)[489] on 30 Mar 1934 in Detroit, Wayne Co., MI.[490]

ii   Della EDWARDS (b. ABT 1915 MS, d. Unknown).[491]

iii   Effie EDWARDS (b. 16 Jul 1916 Attala Co., MS, d. 7 Oct 2014 Milwaukee, Milwaukee Co., WI)[492] m. (1) Unknown JAMISON (Unknown)[493] and (2) Dan HUTCHINS, Sr. (b. 20 May 1914 Conway, Leake Co., MS, d. 19 Dec 1994 Milwaukee, Milwaukee Co., WI)[494] on 23 Nov 1942 in Dubuque, IA.[495]

iv   Luria EDWARDS (b. 23 Apr 1918 MS, d. AFT the 1950 Census)[496] m. Willie D. BARTON (b. 15 May 1914 MS, d. 26 May 1990 Detroit, Wayne Co., MI).[497]

v   Ulysses (Julious) EDWARDS (b. 8 Dec 1919 Attala Co., MS, d. 15 Jun 1993 Detroit, Wayne Co., MI)[498] m. Luegene UNKNOWN (b. 5 Sep 1906 MS, d. 27 Dec 1982 Detroit, Wayne Co., MI).[499]

---

[485] Posted by Avis James on 21 Jun 2023 to *Ancestry.com*.

[486] Posted by sonja flippin on 25 Nov 2023 to *Ancestry.com*.

[487] sonja flippin originally shared this on 26 Nov 2023 to *Ancestry.com*.

[488] "Michigan, U.S., Death Index, 1971-1996," s.v. "Willie H Edwards," (birth 22 Dec 1910, death 21 Jun 1983), *Ancestry.com*.

[489] "Michigan, U.S., Death Index, 1971-1996," s.v. "Grace O. Edwards," (birth 16 Jan 1914, death 14 Dec 1993), *Ancestry.com*.

[490] "Michigan, U.S., Marriage Records, 1867-1952," digital image s.v. "Mr. Willie Edwards," (marriage 30 Mar 1934 to Grace Harrison), *Ancestry.com*.

[491] "1920 United States Census," Center, Attala Co., MS, digital image s.v. "Estela [Della] Edwards," (birth abt 1915), *Ancestry.com*.

[492] "Obituary Daily Times Index, 1995-2016," s.v. "Effie Hutchins," (birth abt 1916, death abt 2014), *Ancestry.com*. Specific dates were from the *Ancestry.com* tree of sonja flippin.

[493] See Effie's marriage certificate to Dan Hutchins.

[494] "U.S., Social Security Death Index, 1935-2014," s.v. "Dan Hutchins," (birth 20 May 1914, death 19 Dec 1994), *Ancestry.com*.

[495] "U.S., Marriage Records, 1880-1947," digital image s.v. "Effie Jannison," (marriage 23 Nov 1942 to Dan Hutchins), *Ancestry.com*.

[496] "U.S., Public Records Index, 1950-1993, Volume 1," s.v. "Luria Barton," (birth 23 Apr 1918), *Ancestry.com*.

[497] "Michigan, Death Index, 1971-1996," s.v. "Willie D Barton," (birth 15 May 1914, death 26 May 1990), *Ancestry.com*.

[498] "Michigan, Death Index, 1971-1996," s.v. "Ulysses Edwards," (birth 8 Dec 1919, death 15 Jun 1993), *Ancestry.com*.

[499] "Michigan, Death Index, 1971-1996," s.v. "Luegin Edwards," (birth 5 Sep 1906, death 27 Dec 1982), *Ancestry.com*.

vi		Ernest EDWARDS (b. 14 Oct 1920 Attala Co., MS, d. 11 Feb 1989 Carthage, Leake Co., MS)[500] m. (1) Ira Mae CROSS (b. 8 Jul 1922 Attala Co., MS, d. 28 Feb 1963 Attala Co., MS)[501] and (2) Ruth Griffin VEASLEY (b. Unknown, d. Unknown).[502]
vii		Walter EDWARDS (b. 23 Jan 1922 Attala Co., MS, d. Unknown).[503]
viii		Loni EDWARDS (b. ABT 1923 MS, d. Unknown).[504]
ix		Minda Lou (Malina) EDWARDS (b. ABT 1927 MS, d. Unknown).[505]
x		Minnie L. EDWARDS (b. ABT 1928 MS, d. Unknown).[506]
xi		Betty Mae EDWARDS (b. ABT 1930 MS, d. Unknown).[507]
xii		Kile King EDWARDS (b. ABT 1938 MS, d. Unknown).[508]

Figure 56 John EDWARDS' Sons Johnnie, Tommie, Bill, Ulysses, Ernest, and Walter[509]

---

[500] Ernest Edwards, grave marker, Mount Moriah Cemetery, Attala Co., MS, digital image s.v. "Ernie Edwards," (birth 14 Oct 1920, death 11 Feb 1989), *FindaGrave.com*.
[501] Ira Mae Edwards, grave marker, Mount Moriah Cemetery, Attala Co., MS, digital image s.v. "Ernie Edwards," (birth 8 Jul 1922, death 28 Feb 1963), FindaGrave.com.
[502] See Earnest Edwards obituary on *FindaGrave.com*.
[503] "U.S., World War II Draft Cards Young Men, 1940-1947," digital image s.v. "Walter Edwards," (birth 23 Jan 1922), *Ancestry.com*.
[504] "1930 United States Census," Beat 5, Attala Co., MS, digital image s.v. "Loni Edwards," (birth abt 1923), *Ancestry.com*.
[505] "1930 United States Census," Beat 5, Attala Co., MS, digital image s.v. "Malina Edwards," (birth abt 1927), *Ancestry.com*.
[506] "1930 United States Census," Beat 5, Attala Co., MS, digital image s.v. "Minnie L Edwards," (birth abt 1928), *Ancestry.com*.
[507] "1940 United States Census," Center, Attala Co., MS, digital image s.v. "Betty Mae Edwards," (birth abt 1930), *Ancestry.com*.
[508] "1940 United States Census," Center, Attala Co., MS, digital image s.v. "Kile King Edwards," (birth abt 1938), *Ancestry.com*.
[509] sonja flippin originally shared this on 26 Nov 2023 on *Ancestry.com*.

Ethel TERRY (William TERRY, Caroline, Aaron Whitaker, Aaron Steele, Joseph I, John I, Samuel II, Samuel I, John)

Ethel TERRY was the daughter of William M. TERRY, Sr. (b. 8 Aug 1868 Attala Co., MS, d. 13 Jul 1956 Memphis, Shelby Co., TN) and Mary BURT (b. 15 Mar 1864 Attala Co., MS, died on 27 Feb 1937).[510] Ethel was born on 18 Dec 1888 Attala Co., MS, and died on 15 May 1969).[511] She married John HARMON (b. 15 Jun 1895, d. 8 Dec 1971).[512] They had the following children:

i. Johnnie M. HARMON (b. 7 May 1921 Attala Co., MS, d. 15 Aug 2006 Kosciusko, Attala Co., MS)[513] m. (1) Unknown TRUSS about 1938,[514] (2) Henry NEWELL (b. abt 1908),[515] and (3) UNKNOWN.[516]
ii. Jim Roger HARMON (b. 3 Dec 1922 Sallis, Attala Co., MS, d. 11 Jun 1998 Jackson, Hinds Co., MS)[517] m. Bonnie Jean SANDIFER (b. 28 May 1926 MS, d. 17 May 2011 Jackson, Hinds Co., MS).[518]
iii. Bessie Mae HARMON (b. 6 Sep 1924 Kosciusko, Attala Co., MS, d. 30 Oct 2006)[519] m. (1) Unknown PATTERSON; (2) Unknown EVANS; (3) Unknown WILLIAMS; (4) Unknown WILLIAMS; (5) Unknown WILSON.
iv. Esre HARMON (b. ABT 1926 MS).[520]
v. Roy Willie HARMON (b. 7 MAR 1929 Attala Co., MS, d. Unknown)[521] m. Eula M. UNKNOWN (b. abt 1929 MS).[522]

---

[510] William Terry, Sr., grave marker, Russell Cemetery, Attala County, Mississippi, s.v. "William Terry, Sr." (birth 15 Mar 1864; death 27 Feb 1937), *FindaGrave.com*. Mary Burt, grave marker, Russell Cemetery, Attala County, Mississippi, s.v. "Mary Terry," (birth 15 Mar 1864; death 27 Feb 1937), *FindaGrave.com*.

[511] Ethel Terry, grave marker, Russell Cemetery, Attala Co., MS, digital image s.v. "Ethel Harmon," (birth 18 Dec 1888, death 15 May 1969), *FindaGrave.com*.

[512] John Harmon, grave marker, Russell Cemetery, Attala Co., MS, digital image s.v. "John Harmon," (birth 15 Jun 1895, death 8 Dec 1971), *FindaGrave.com*.

[513] Johnnie M. Harmon, grave marker, Kosciusko City Cemetery, Kosciusko, Attala Co., MS, digital image s.v. "Mrs Johnnie M Newell," (birth 7 May 1921, death 15 Aug 2006), *FindaGrave.com*.

[514] "1940 United States Census," Newport, Attala Co., MS, digital image s.v. "Johnnie Mae Truer [Truss]," (birth abt 1939), *Ancestry.com*.

[515] "1950 United States Federal Census," Kosciusko, Attala Co., MS, digital image s.v. "Henry Newell," (birth abt 1908), *Ancestry.com*.

[516] "1950 United States Federal Census," Kosciusko, Attala Co., MS, digital image s.v. "Queen T. Harmon," (birth abt 1942), *Ancestry.com*. Daughter of Johnnie M. Harmon.

[517] Jim Roger Harmon, grave marker, Parkway Cemetery, Kosciusko, Attala Co., MS, digital image s.v. "Jim Roger Harmon," (birth 3 Dec 1922, death 11 Jun 1998), *FindaGrave.com*.

[518] "U.S., Social Security Death Index, 1935-2014," s.v. "Bonnie J. Harmon," (birth 28 May 1926, death 17 May 2011), *Ancestry.com*.

[519] "U.S., Social Security Applications and Claims Index, 1936-2007," s.v. "Bessie Harmon," (birth 6 Sep 1924, death 30 Oct 2006, other last names used HARMON, PATTERSON, EVANS, WILLIAMS, WILSON), *Ancestry.com*.

[520] "1950 United States Census," Newport, Attala Co., MS, digital image s.v. "Esra Harmon," (birth abt 1926), *Ancestry.com*.

[521] "U.S., World War II Draft Cards Young Men, 1940-1947," digital image s.v. "Roy Willie Harmon," (born 7 Mar 1929), *Ancestry.com*.

[522] "1950 United States Census," Newport, Attala Co., MS, digital image s.v. "Eula M. Harmon," (birth abt 1929), *Ancestry.com*.

Nealie Eugene TERRY (William TERRY, Caroline, Aaron Whitaker, Aaron Steele, Joseph I, John I, Samuel II, Samuel I, John)

Nealie Eugene TERRY was the daughter of William M. TERRY, Sr. (b. 8 Aug 1868 Attala Co., MS, d. 13 Jul 1956 Memphis, Shelby Co., TN) and Mary BURT (b. 15 Mar 1864, Attala Co., MS, died on 27 Feb 1937).[523] She was born on 2 Jul 1890 Bolivar Co., MS and died 17 Jun 1990 in Dundee, Tunica Co., MS.[524] She married William Major CONWAY, Jr. (b. 14 Mar 1879 MS, d. 2 Jun 1951 Dundee, Tunica Co., MS).[525] See Figure 57, Figure 58, and Figure 59. Note to the reader: William Major CONWAY, Jr., in this book, is often called William Major CONWAY, Sr. by others. His father was also Major CONWAY. I will refer to William Major CONWAY, Jr.'s father as William Major CONWAY, Sr. William Major CONWAY, Jr. has a son named William Alvin CONWAY, but is often called by others, William Major CONWAY, Jr. I will refer to this son as William Alvin CONWAY..

Figure 57 Nealie TERRY CONWAY[526]

Figure 58 Young Nealie TERRY CONWAY[527]

Figure 59 William Major CONWAY[528]

An interesting sharecropping family history about William Major CONWAY, Jr.'s family, was uploaded to *Ancestry.com*.[529] I have changed the nam1es in the story to match my nomenclature listed above.

Major CONWAY, Sr. [b. abt 1822 TN, d. abt 1889 Attala Co., MS] and wife, Melinda [Melinda ZOLLICOFFER CONWAY b. Jun 1829 TN, d. abt 1912 Attala Co., MS], lived at

---

[523] William Terry, Sr., grave marker, Russell Cemetery, Attala County, Mississippi, s.v. "William Terry, Sr." (birth 15 Mar 1864; death 27 Feb 1937), *FindaGrave.com*. Mary Burt, grave marker, Russell Cemetery, Attala County, Mississippi, s.v. "Mary Terry," (birth 15 Mar 1864; death 27 Feb 1937), *FindaGrave.com*.
[524] Nealie Eugene Terry, grave marker, Bethlehem Cemetery, Lula, Coahoma Co., MS, digital image s.v. "Nealie Eugene Conway," (birth 2 Jul 1890, death 17 Jun 1990), *FindaGrave.com*.
[525] Major Conway, Jr., grave marker, Bethlehem Cemetery, Lula, Coahoma Co., MS, digital image s.v. "Major Conway, Sr.," (birth 14 Mar 1879, death 2 Jun 1951), *FindaGrave.com*.
[526] Christopher Conway originally shared this on 18 Mar 2016, *Ancestry.com*.
[527] Christopher Conway originally shared this on 18 Mar 2016, *Ancestry.com*.
[528] Yolee60 originally shared this on 15 Aug 2020, *Ancestry.com*.
[529] "Conway Family History as told by Nealie (Terry) Conway (b. 2 Jul 1887, d. 17 Jun 1990) to James Conway (b. 17 Dec 1927)," *Ancestry.com*.

Kosciusko, Attala County, Mississippi where he owned farmland. After his death around 1867, the oldest son, Lenard CONWAY [b. abt 1859] took over to care for his mother, a sister named Alice, and 11-year-old Major Jr.[William Major CONWAY, Jr.] Richard moved away and was last known to be living in Birmingham, Alabama when contact ceased. Porter and his family moved to Monticello, Arkansas. Porter and his wife, Sally, had a big family; he kept in contact by letter until 1937. Efforts have been made to contact members of his family on several occasions without success. After Alice grew up and married, Lenard continued caring for his mother and William Major CONWAY, Jr. until his [Lenard's] death, after which William Major [CONWAY, Jr.] continued to care for his mother and farm the land. William Major [Jr.] married Willie M. LANGSTON: they had one child, a boy named Willie. When he (Willie) was about six months old, his mother went to visit relatives a short distance from the house and was returning home when a heavy rain came up and she got wet and came down with pneumonia and died. A year later Major [William Major CONWAY, Jr.] met and married Nealie TERRY on 23 Feb 1910 and she cared for Willie and his grandmother, Melinda, who died in 1912.

William Major [Jr.] and Nealie had a daughter, [Ethel] Lavelle, three boys, Lenard, Earl (who died of acute indigestion at age 3- or 4-years-old), and Major Jr. [Major Alvin CONWAY].

Some of William Major's sisters wanted to be paid for their part of the home place causing confusion and problems for him. In disgust, he moved the family to the vicinity of Shelby, Bolivar County, Mississippi in 1917. He came to Shelby because his sister, Lucy, and her husband, Henry FULLER, lived there. The Conway family of two adults and four children lived in the house with the Fullers until a house could be prepared for them.

At this particular time, there was a large community of Blacks who owned land around Shelby. A Reverend Winters owned the land where the Fullers lived as well as the Conway family from 1917 to 1919. The family moved just a short distance to the land owned by a Mr. Bob LOWE, also a Black man. The Conways lived there from 1919 to 1922. Farmland owned by Blacks was not referred to as plantations possibly because of the size, 120 to 200 acres. During the period 1919 to 1927, five additional children were born to William Major [Jr.] and Nealie: Mary Eugenia (1919), Ruth (1921), Vernice (1923), Ollie (a little boy who lived only a few days), and James (1927).

In the fall of 1922, the family moved to what was known as the Fleming Place. It was located 3 miles east of the town of Hushpuckena, Mississippi.[530] In the fall of 1928, the family moved again to Thompson's plantation, not very far from the Bob LOWE's place. By now, William Major CONWAY [Jr.] had been able to acquire two mules, a wagon, and

---

[530] Hushpuckena is an unincorporated community located in Bolivar County, Mississippi, United States along U.S. Route 61. Hushpuckena is located approximately 3 miles south of Duncan and approximately 4 miles north of Shelby. "Hushpuckena, Mississippi," *Wikipedia*, n. d. A post office operated under the name Hushpuckena from 1885 to 1968.

necessary plow tools for farming. The plantation owner allowed William Major [Jr.] to use his mules to plow and plant cotton and corn. The plantation owner was to give William Major [Jr.] credit for the use of his mules and plows even though he was still considered to be a "sharecropper." The term means that you were allowed farm the land and the owner takes ½ of the crop, cotton and corn and then, from the remaining half, he collects for the cost of the seed and any money or food purchased on credit or money borrowed for any other necessities including doctor bills. The standard cost for all the above credit was 0.25 percent on the dollar, however, the plantation owner was the keeper of the books, and generally speaking, what he said was the final accounting.

William Major [Jr.] realized in the fall of 1931 that when the crop was gathered and sold, he was to come out in debt (leaving a balance owed) to be carried over to the next year. He informed the owner that he was not going to complete gathering the cotton and would be moving his family. The owner's response was that he would take the mules and plowing equipment, but later he said that if the family would rather stay in the house until all of the cotton was gathered, or if he promised to come back and gather the cotton, he would not take the mules and plowing equipment. The family moved to a plantation owned by a Mr. A.D. Murphy, again east of Hushpuckena, Mississippi.

James [Velmer] CONWAY, [Sr.], youngest son of William Major CONWAY, Jr., wrote: I can clearly remember walking with my brother Major [Major Alvin CONWAY] and my little puppy ahead of the wagon piled high with all of our furniture and cook stove, bedding covers and clothes. My mother's milk cow was tied to the rear of the wagon. A second and third trip had to be made to bring the hogs and chickens. True to his word, William Major [Jr.] and the family traveled back to Thompson's plantation daily until all of the cotton was gathered, after which, the debt was forgiven.

Life was not immediately much better, but my mother always raised chickens and a garden from which she would can in glass jars all kinds of vegetables and we raised potatoes, onions, collard greens, turnips, rutabaga and peanuts which was stored for long winter months. Many good foods grew wild in the woods like wild pears, hickory nuts, wild grapes, muscadines, persimmons, blackberries, dewberries and elder berries.

Hogs were raised and butchered during late November to mid-December when the weather was cold enough to prevent spoilage. The meat was packed in salt for a period of time after which it would be taken up and the excess salt would be brushed off before the meat would be hung by wire to a pole that was placed across the smoke house high enough to be protected from rodents and other animals that sometimes found a means of entering into the smoke house. Sometimes later smoke salt was available; this gave a wonderful smoke flavor to the meat. Also available was a liquid smoke which could be applied to the meat with a brush or a mop made from strips of cloth tied to the end of a stick. On cold winter days when the ham meat was being prepared for breakfast, the aroma would fill the house and the call to the table couldn't come fast enough.

The day after the hogs had been butchered was a very busy day for the women. They would eat some of the meat, wrap it, and send the children to deliver it to the neighbors, which was then a custom. All of the trimmings cut from the hams, shoulders and sides was cut into small pieces, the lean was put aside to be grinded into sausage and the fat was placed into a large cast iron pot under which wood was placed for the fire that would cook out the fat/lard that would later be used for cooking. After the fat was skimmed off and placed in tin cans, the leavings was cooled and put away for later use. It was known as cracklins that was later used for cornbread (crackling bread), it made good eating. Children have been known to raid the crackling box to get the skins, sprinkle them with salt and make an impromptu meal out of them.

The making of sausage was a lot of work for the children because someone had to turn the handle of the meat grinder when preparing the sausage. When the meat had been grounded, the women would seasoning it with salt, red and black peppers, and parched sage. Some of the sausage would be pushed into the small intestines after they had been cleaned. An attachment to the grinder was used for this purpose. The filed caseins would be tied off in 5- or 6-inch sections. It could be dried over a smoke fire or cooked and placed into fruit jars where it would keep for months or longer until eaten. Almost nothing was wasted; the head, ears and feet was boiled until the meat could be pulled from the bones, it was then seasoned with red and black pepper, sage, and vinegar placed into a galvanized pan that had been lined with heavy brown paper, a piece of board cut to fit inside of the pan was placed on top of heavy brown paper and on top of heavy brown paper and on top of the board was placed a heavy object like an iron or brick. This was done to press out the excess fat which was absolved [absorbed?] by the brown paper. When the meat had congealed, the weight and board was removed, the brown paper and the souse was dumped out onto a plate or table, cut into slices or squares to be eaten with bread. It made a great winter-time snack.

Our experience on the A. D. Murphy plantation was better, but far from perfect. In 1932 there was seven able bodied family members, we worked 20 acres of cotton and 10 acres of corn in additional to one acre for potatoes, peanuts, a garden, a barn and stable for the mules and hogs. Our house was less than a quarter of mile from Woodbine school, but that did not really matter until all of the crops was gathered, which was a rule, meant that the school did not open until late October. One year, the school did not start until after Thanksgiving. Mr. MURPHY maintained a small store or commissary for tenants which was opened in early spring where the bare essentials was stocked: flour, corn meal, salt pork, soda, baking powder, canned sausage, dry beans, tobacco, snuff, chewing tobacco, lamp wicks, globes and kerosene. Tenants could shop here on credit with payment being due at the end of the year. Mr. MURPHY kept the books and the debt was subtracted from the one half of the amount that the family was said to have earned. Cost of credit was believed to be $0.25 on the dollar. Mr. MURPHY'S practice was to settle with his tenants around mid-

December, but one year he settled on Christmas Eve. That year after all was said and done, we cleared $278.00.

The life saver came when President Roosevelt began the Public Works Authority. This program provided an opportunity for men to work at clearing roadways, drainage ditches, and removal of undergrowth on ditch and road banks. The rule was that only one man of the family was allowed to work and the pay was $1.50 per day. Work groups were assigned work projects and one member was designated as supervisor for each group. The main supervisor had authority to hire and assign work. This man happened to know William Major [Jr.] and he hired my brothers Willie [Major Alvin CONWAY?] and Lenard and assigned them to different work locations. They had to walk each day to the assigned location leaving before daylight and returning well after dark. Mama would make lunch for each and it was carried in a bucket with a lid on it to keep out ants and other insects. The work continued through the month of February and the extra money was a big help to the family.

There was also a program known as the Commodity Program. Families could receive some basic food items with the amount being based on the number of family members. The items consisted of dried fruit, beans, flour, salt pork, and lard.

The family remained on the A. D. MURPHY plantation until November 1940 when we moved about 50 miles north to Lula, Mississippi onto a plantation owned by a Mr. HAMLETT. We remained there until 1943 when Papa met a wealthy black man, T. J. HUDDELSTON from Yazoo, Mississippi.[531] Mr. HUDDELSTON owned several funeral homes, and he was the organizer of an organization known as the Knights and Daughter of Tabor [The organization was the Afro-American Sons and Daughters. See footnote.] Dues-paying members was afforded a monetary burial allowance. He came to Lula, Mississippi for an organization meeting and Papa was introduced to him. Some months later Papa learned of the pending sale of 202.5 acres of land located a short distance from where we lived. With the aid of a mutual friend, a meeting was arranged with Mr. HUDDELSTON to propose that he purchase the land and in turn sell 67.5 acres to Papa, 67.5 acres to Mr. BRAZELL and 67.5 acres to Rev. Sanders.

---

[531] Thomas Jefferson Huddleston Sr. (June 1, 1876 – October 1959) was a distinguished Black entrepreneur and community leader in Yazoo City, Mississippi. Known for his remarkable oratory skills and salesmanship, he built a legacy as the owner of numerous funeral homes across the state. His gift for captivating audiences led him to establish a chain of funeral homes, making him a prominent figure in Mississippi's business landscape. In addition to his entrepreneurial endeavors, T.J. Huddleston Sr. was a visionary leader who founded the Afro-American Sons and Daughters in 1924. This fraternal organization quickly became one of the leading Black voluntary associations in Mississippi, boasting a membership of 35,000 by the 1930s. His commitment to community building and empowerment left a lasting impact on Mississippi's Black community during a pivotal period in history. "T. J. Huddleston Sr.," *Wikipedia*, n. d.

Mr. HUDDELSTON offered to buy and sell the entire 202.5 acres to Papa, but Papa thought that the land would be more than he could handle. With the purchase of the 67.5 acres, plantation life came to an end for the Conway Family.

According to the 1940 U.S. Census, William Major CONWAY, Jr. (58) lived in Beat 3, Bolivar Co., MS on a rented farm. He lived with his wife, Nealie (46), and children Lavelle CONWAY (24, single, and worked as a teacher in a primary school), Major Alvin CONWAY, Jr. (21), Mary CONWAY (20), Ruth CONWAY (18), Vernice CONWAY (16), and James (13). Lenard CONWAY lived next door with his wife, Ocelee BLACKMAN. William Major CONWAY, Jr., Lenard, and Major Alvin CONWAY all worked as cotton farmers.[532]

In the 1950 U.S. Census, Major CONWAY Jr. (72) was unable to work. He lived in Beat 4, Tunica Co., MS on the Coahoma County Line Road. He lived with Nealie (61); his daughter, Lavelle CONWAY WARD (39 and separated from her husband), Lavelle's three children, Oscela WARD (7), Willie James WARD (5), and Felton WARD (3); his daughter, Ruth Elizabeth CONWAY; and two grandsons, Charles CONWAY (9) and Leon CONWAY (5).[533]

William Major CONWAY, Jr. and Nealie Eugene TERRY's children include:

i   Ethel Lavelle (b. 15 Jan 1911 Kosciusko, Attala Co., MS, d. Mar 1984 Dundee, Tunica Co., MS)[534] m. Johnny Howard WARD (b. 5 Feb 1900 Claiborne, MS).[535] They were separated in the U.S. 1950 Census.
ii   Lenard CONWAY (b. 22 Jul 1913 Kosciusko, Attala Co., MS, d. 19 Dec 2004 Clarksdale, Coahoma Co., MS)[536] m. Ocelee BLACKMAN (b. 12 Oct 1915 Shelby, Bolivar Co., MS, death 7 Feb 2000 Dundee, Tunica Co., MS).[537]
iii   Earl CONWAY (b. 21 Oct 1914 Kosciusko, Attala Co., MS, d. 9 Feb 1917).[538]
iv   Major Alvin CONWAY (b. 30 Oct 1917 Attala Co., MS, d. 14 Oct 1994 Lula, Coahoma Co., MS)[539] m. Katie Mae HARRIS (b. 23 Apr 1926 Bolivar Co., MS, d. Jul 1983 Dundee, Tunica Co., MS).[540]
v   Mary Eugenia CONWAY (b. 6 Dec 1919 AR, d. 7 May 1956).[541]

---

[532] "1940 United States Census," Beat 3, Bolivar Co., MS, digital image s.v. "Major Conway," (birth abt 1882), *Ancestry.com*.

[533] "1950 United States Census," Beat 4, Tunica Co., MS, digital image s.v. "Major Conway," (birth abt 1878), *Ancestry.com*.

[534] "U.S., Social Security Death Index, 1935-2014," s.v. "Lavelle Ward," (birth 15 Jan 1911, death Mar 1984), *Ancestry.com*.

[535] "U.S., Social Security Death Index, 1935-2014," s.v. "John Ward," (birth 5 May 1899, death Jan 1977), *Ancestry.com*.

[536] "U.S., Social Security Applications and Claims Index, 1936-2007," s.v. "Lenard Conway,"(birth 22 Jul 1913, death 19 Dec 2004), *Ancestry.com*.

[537] "U.S., Social Security Applications and Claims Index, 1936-2007," s.v. "O C Conway," (birth 12 Oct 1915, death 7 Feb 2000), *Ancestry.com*.

[538] No hard data but Earl is discussed in the Conway Family History, *Ancestry.com*.

[539] "Major Alvin Conway," grave marker, Bethlehem Cemetery, Lula, Coahoma Co., MS, digital image s.v. "Major Conway Jr.," (birth 30 Oct 1917, death 14 Oct 1994), *FindaGrave.com*.

[540] "U.S., Social Security Death Index, 1935-2014," s.v. "Katie Conway," (birth 23 Apr 1926, death Jul 1983), *Ancestry.com*.

[541] See Conway Family History, *Ancestry.com*.

vi	Ruth Elizabeth CONWAY (b. 5 Apr 1921 Kosciusko, Attala Co., MS, d. 20 Nov 2011).[542]
vii	Vernice CONWAY (b. 21 Jul 1924 MS, d. Unknown)[543] m. James AGEE (b. ABT 1920, d. Unknown).[544] Vernice lived in Chicago when her brother, Willie, died.
viii	Ollie CONWAY (b. 21 Nov 1925, d. 26 Nov 1925).[545]
ix	James Welmer CONWAY, Sr. (b. 17 Dec 1927 Bolivar Co., MS, d. 26 Dec 2012 Montgomery, Montgomery Co., AL)[546] m. Frenetter WHITTINGTON (b. 9 Dec 1924 MS, d. 13 Aug 2019 Montgomery, Montgomery Co., AL).[547]

Sarah V. TERRY (William TERRY, Caroline, Aaron Whitaker, Aaron Steele, Joseph I, John I, Samuel II, Samuel I, John)

Sarah V. TERRY was the daughter of William M. TERRY, Sr. (b. 8 Aug 1868 Attala Co., MS, d. 13 Jul 1956, Memphis, Shelby Co., TN) and Mary BURT (b. 15 Mar 1864, Attala Co., MS, died on 27 Feb 1937).[548] She was born on 15 May 1897 in Sallis, Attala Co., MS, and died on 14 Feb 1979 in Detroit, Wayne Co., MI).[549] She married Walter HARMON (b. 22 Jun 1895 McAdams, MS, d. 6 Apr 1969).[550]

Sarah V. and Walter had at least eleven children:

i	Leila HARMON (b. 9 Jun 1918 Sallis, Attala Co., MS, d. 5 May 2010 Detroit, Wayne Co., MI)[551] m. Otis KERN (b. 10 Jan 1918 Center, Attala Co., MS, d. 3 Mar 1961 Chicago, Cook Co., IL).[552]
ii	Fannie Mae HARMON (b. 1 Nov 1919 Kosciusko, Attala Co., MS, d. 6 Apr 1992 Detroit, Wayne Co., MI)[553] m. Leport ESTERS (b. 17 Oct 1919 Attala Co., MS, d. 20 Jul 1948 Northville, Wayne Co., MI).[554]
iii	Walter Alvin HARMON (b. 15 Jul 1922 McAdams, Attala Co., MS, d. 9 Jun 1974)[555] m. Dolores SUMMERS (b. 29 Sep 1929 St Louis, MO, d. 24 Jun 1999.)[556]

---

[542] "U.S., Social Security Death Index, 1935-2014," s.v. "Ruth Conway," (birth 5 Apr 1921, death 20 Nov 2011), *Ancestry.com*.

[543] See Conway Family History, *Ancestry.com*.

[544] "Obituary for Mr. Willie Conway," *The Memphis Press-Scimitar*, Memphis, TN, Sat, 30 Jun 1973, p. 15.

[545] Carol Canada's tree, Conway Family Tree, *Ancestry.com*, accessed 19 Apr 2024.

[546] "James Welmer CONWAY, Sr.," grave marker, Alabama National Cemetery, Montevallo, Shelby Co., AL, digital image s.v. "James Welmer Conway Sr.," (birth 17 Dec 1927, death 26 Dec 2012), *FindaGrave.com*.

[547] "Frenetter WHITTINGTON," grave marker, Alabama National Cemetery, Montevallo, Shelby Co., AL, digital image s.v. "Frenetter W. Conway (birth 9 Dec 1924, death 13 Aug 2019), *FindaGrave.com*.

[548] William Terry, Sr., grave marker, Russell Cemetery, Attala County, Mississippi, s.v. "William Terry, Sr." (birth 15 Mar 1864; death 27 Feb 1937), *FindaGrave.com*. Mary Burt, grave marker, Russell Cemetery, Attala County, Mississippi, s.v. "Mary Terry," (birth 15 Mar 1864; death 27 Feb 1937), *FindaGrave.com*.

[549] "Michigan, U.S., Death Index, 1971-1996," s.v. "Sarah Harmon," (birth 15 May 1897, death 14 Feb 1979), *Ancestry.com*.

[550] "U.S., World War I Civilian Draft Registrations, 1917-1918," s.v. "Walter Harmon," (22 Jun 1895), *Ancestry.com*.

[551] Per Kelli Kern's Family Tree, *Ancestry.com*, accessed 11 May 2024. "1930 United States Federal Census," Beat 4, Attala Co., MS, digital image s.v. "Leila Harmon," (birth abt 1918), *Ancestry.com*. I found no documents for the place or date of her death. Leila may have remarried after Otis' death, making tracking her more difficult.

[552] "Otis Kern," grave marker, Antioch Cemetery, Center, Attala Co., MS, digital image s.v. "Otis Kern," (birth 10 Jan 1918, death 3 Mar 1961), *FindaGrave.com*.

[553] "Michigan, Death Index, 1971-1996," s.v. "Fannie M Esters (birth 1 Nov 1919, death 6 Apr 1992), *Ancestry.com*.

[554] "Michigan, Death Index, 1867-1952," s.v. "Leport Esterz," (birth 17 Oct 1918, death 20 Jul 1948), *Ancestry.com*.

[555] "U.S., Headstone Applications for Military Veterans, 1861-1985," digital image s.v. "Walter Alvin Harmon," (birth 15 Jul 1922, death 10 Feb 1943), *Ancestry.com*.

[556] "U.S., Social Security Death Index, 1935-2014," s.v. "Dolores A. Boswell," (birth 30 Sep 1929, death 24 Jun 1999), *Ancestry.com*.

iv	Kattie M. HARMON (b. ABT 1925 MS, d. Unknown).[557]	
v	Edward HARMON (b. ABT 1928 MS, d. Unknown).[558]	
vi	Arvin Howard HARMON (b. ABT 1930 MS, d. Unknown).[559]	
vii	Louis HARMON (b. ABT 1932 MS, d. Unknown).[560]	
viii	Murie (Murray) HARMON (b. 22 Oct 1933 Kosciusko, Attala Co., MS, d. 13 Aug 2002 Detroit, Wayne Co., MI)[561] m. Lelia Mae STEVENSON (b. 13 Jul 1935 Norfolk, VA, d. Unknown).[562]	
ix	Sarah Mae HARMON (b. ABT 1934 MS, d. 6 Apr 1992 Detroit, Wayne Co., MI).[563]	
x	Willie Ray HARMON (b. ABT 1936 MS, d. Unknown).[564]	
xi	Youngs HARMON (b. ABT 1939 MS, d. Unknown).[565]	

William Vinson TERRY (William TERRY, Caroline, Aaron Whitaker, Aaron Steele, Joseph I, John I, Samuel II, Samuel I, John)

William Vinson TERRY was the son of William M. TERRY, Sr. (b. 8 Aug 1868 Attala Co., MS, d. 13 Jul 1956 Memphis, Shelby Co., TN)[566] and Mary BURT (b. 15 Mar 1864 Attala Co., MS, d. 27 Feb 1937). They married around 1885 based on the birth of their first child. They are both buried in Russell Cemetery, located in Attala Co., MS.

William was born on 19 Jun 1907 in Attala Co., MS, and died on 30 Sep 1981.[567] See Figure 60. He married Beatrice ISLAND, who was born on 7 Feb 1902 in MS, and died on 16 Dec 1987 in Indianapolis, Marion Co., IN).[568] They had at least two daughters:

---

[557] "1930 United States Federal Census," Beat 4, Attala Co., MS, digital image s.v. "Kattie M Harmon," (birth abt 1925), *Ancestry.com*.

[558] "1930 United States Federal Census," Beat 4, Attala Co., MS, digital image s.v. "Edward Harmon," (birth abt 1928), *Ancestry.com*.

[559] "1930 United States Federal Census," Beat 4, Attala Co., MS, digital image s.v. "Arvin Howard Harmon," (birth abt 1930), *Ancestry.com*.

[560] "1950 United States Federal Census," Beat 4, Attala Co., MS, digital image s.v. "Louis Harmon," (birth abt 1932), *Ancestry.com*.

[561] "U.S., Social Security Death Index, 1935-2014," s.v. "Murie Harmon," (birth 28 Oct 1933, death 13 Aug 2002), *Ancestry.com*.

[562] "Virginia, U.S., Birth Records, 1912-2015, Delayed Birth Records, 1721-1920," s.v. "Leila May Stevenson," (birth 13 Jul 1935), *Ancestry.com*.

[563] "1950 United States Federal Census," Kosciusko, Attala Co., MS, digital image s.v. "Sarah Mae Harmon," (birth abt 1934), *Ancestry.com*.

[564] "1950 United States Federal Census," Kosciusko, Attala Co., MS, digital image s.v. "Willie Ray Harmon," (birth abt 1936), *Ancestry.com*.

[565] "1950 United States Federal Census," Kosciusko, Attala Co., MS, digital image s.v. "Norras Harmon," (birth abt 1939), *Ancestry.com*. The Census shows his name was Youngs but it is transcribed as Norras. These words don't look anywhere alike. His age was given in the Census as 11 but was transcribed as Nev (for never married).

[566] William Terry, Sr., grave marker, Russell Cemetery, Attala County, Mississippi, s.v. "William Terry, Sr." (birth 15 Mar 1864; death 27 Feb 1937), *FindaGrave.com*. Mary Burt, grave marker, Russell Cemetery, Attala County, Mississippi, s.v. "Mary Terry," (birth 15 Mar 1864; death 27 Feb 1937), *FindaGrave.com*.

[567] William Vinson Terry, grave marker, Russell Cemetery, Attala County, Mississippi, s.v. "William V. Terry" (birth 19 Jun 1907, death 30 Sep 1981), *FindaGrave.com*.

[568] "U.S., Social Security Applications and Claims Index, 1936-2007," s.v. "Beatrice Terry," (birth 7 Feb 1902 death Dec 1987), *Ancestry.com*.

i   Irma Jean TERRY (b. ABT 1941 Attala Co., MS, d. Unknown) [569] m. (1) Unknown BURT (Unknown) and (2) Eugene NAYLOR (ABT 1905 MS, d. 15 Apr 1991 Kosciusko, Attala Co., MS).[570]

ii   Annie Z. TERRY (b. ABT 1946 Indianapolis, Marion Co., IN, d. Unknown).[571]

Figure 60 William Vinson TERRY[572]

Carnes Fred TERRY (Joseph Thomas TERRY, Caroline, Aaron Whitaker, Aaron Steele, Joseph I, John I, Samuel II, Samuel I, John)

Carnes Fred TERRY was the son of Joseph Thomas (Joe) TERRY (b. Aug 1869, Attala Co., MS, d. AFT 1940) and Amanda (Annie B. in most documents) GUYTON (b. Aug 1872, Sallis, Attala Co., MS, d. AFT 1940, Sallis, Attala Co., MS). I don't find dates of death for Joe and Amanda, but they were included in the 1940 U.S. Federal Census, and they are buried in Russell Cemetery, Attala Co., MS.[573] See Figure 61.

Carnes Fred TERRY was born on 7 Oct 1907 in Sallis, Attala Co., MS. He died in Jun 1973 Jackson, Hinds Co., MS).[574] He married Callie Beatrice McMICHAEL (b. 20 Sep 1915 Attala Co., MS, d. 19 May 1979 Memphis, Shelby Co., TN).[575]

---

[569] "Beatrice Terry," *The Star-Herald*, Kosciusko, Attala Co., MS, Thu, Dec 24, 1987, p. 9, *Newspapers.com.* Irma Jean Terry Naylor was listed as a surviving daughter.

[570] "Obituary of Eugene Naylor," digital image s.v. "Eugene Naylor," *The Star-Herald*, Kosciusko, Attala Co., MS, Thu, 25 Apr 1991, p. 13, *Newspapers.com,* < https://www.newspapers.com/article/the-star-herald-obituary-for-eugene-nayl/150210509/>.

[571] "1950 United States Federal Census," Kosciusko, Attala Co., MS, digital image s.v. "Annie Z. Terry," (birth abt 1946), *Ancestry.com*. William Vinson is listed as Annie's stepfather, yet she carries the Terry name.

[572] Christopher Conway originally shared this on 19 Mar 2016 on IAncestry.com.

[573] Amanda (Annie B.) Guyton and Joseph Thomas (Joe) Terry, grave marker, Russell Cemetery, Attala Co., MS, digital image s.v. "Annie Guyton Terry," and "Joseph Terry," (Memorial ID 107273730 and 201392258, *FindaGrave.com*.

[574] "Social Security Death Index," s.v. "Fred Terry," (birth 7 Oct 1907, death Jun 1973), *Ancestry.com*.

[575] Callie Beatrice McMichael, grave marker, Hollywood Cemetery, Memphis, Shelby Co., TN, digital image s.v. "Callie Beatrice Terry Anthony," (birth 20 Sep 1915, death 19 May 1979), *FindaGrave.com*.

In the 1940 Census, Carnes was 30.[576] He lived with his parents, Joe (65) and Amanda (60) on Goodman Road, Kosciusko, Attala Co., MS on a farm. He also lived with his wife, Beatrice (22), and daughters 3 and 9 months. The spelling of the girls' names is not possible to decipher without hints from later sources. Carnes and Callie had three daughters together. Callie had another marriage that resulted in a fourth daughter, Henrietta ANTHONY MAXWELL (born in 1945) so Anetha TERRY PERKINS (Carnes' third daughter with Callie) was possibly born around 1942. The two oldest girls were Yvonne Jacquiline TERRY JONES and Beatrice Marie TERRY BURNSIDE. I could not find Carnes and his daughters in the 1950 U.S. Census. Anetha did not live with Callie and her husband in 1950.

i   Yvonne Jacquline TERRY (b. 11 Jun 1936 Center, Attala Co., MS, d. 9 Jun 2009 Center, Attala Co., MS)[577] m. Leavernard JONES, Sr. (b. 12 Jan 1923 Unknown, d. 13 Apr 2008 likely Jackson, Hinds Co., MS).[578]

ii   Bernice Marie TERRY (b. 19 Jun 1940 Kosciusko, Attala Co., MS, d. 19 Oct 2004 Memphis, Shelby Co., TN)[579] m. (1) Vernon JOHNSON, Sr. (Unknown) and (2) Curtis Lee BURNSIDE (b. 7 Aug 1930 Stallo, MS, d. 19 Oct 1998, Unknown).[580]

iii   Anetha TERRY (b. AFT 1940 Unknown, d. 15 Jul 1922 McAdams, Attala Co., MS, d. 9 Jun 1974)[581] m. Unknown PERKINS (Unknown).[582]

---

[576] "1940 United States Federal Census," Kosciusko, Attala Co., MS, digital image s.v. "Cauns Grory," (birth abt 1910), *Ancestry.com*.

[577] "Yvonne Jacquline Terry," grave marker, Antioch Cemetery, Center, Attala Co., MS, digital image s.v. "Yvonne Jacquline Jones," (birth 11 Jun 1936, death 9 Jun 2009), *FindaGrave.com*.

[578] "Leavenard Jones, Sr.," grave marker, Natchez National Cemetery, Natchez, Adams Co., MS, digital image s.v. "Leavernard Jones, Sr.," (birth 11 Jun 1936, death 9 Jun 2009), *FindaGrave.com*.

[579] "Bernice Marie Terry," grave marker, New Park Cemetery, Memphis, Shelby Co., TN, digital image s.v. "Beatrice Marie Burnside," (birth 19 Jun 1940, death 19 Oct 2004), *FindaGrave.com*.

[580] "Curtis Lee Burnside," grave marker, San Joaquin Valley National Cemetery, Santa Nella, Merced Co., CA, digital image s.v. "Curtis Lee Burnside," (birth 7 Aug 1930, death 19 Oct 1998), *FindaGrave.com*.

[581] "Obituary for Bernice Burnside," *The Commercial Appeal,* Memphis, TN, 20 Oct 2004, p. 18; digital image, s.v. "Anitha Perkins," *Newspapers.com*.

[582] "Obituary for Bernice Burnside," *The Commercial Appeal,* Memphis, TN, 20 Oct 2004, p. 18; digital image, s.v. "Anitha Perkins," *Newspapers.com*.

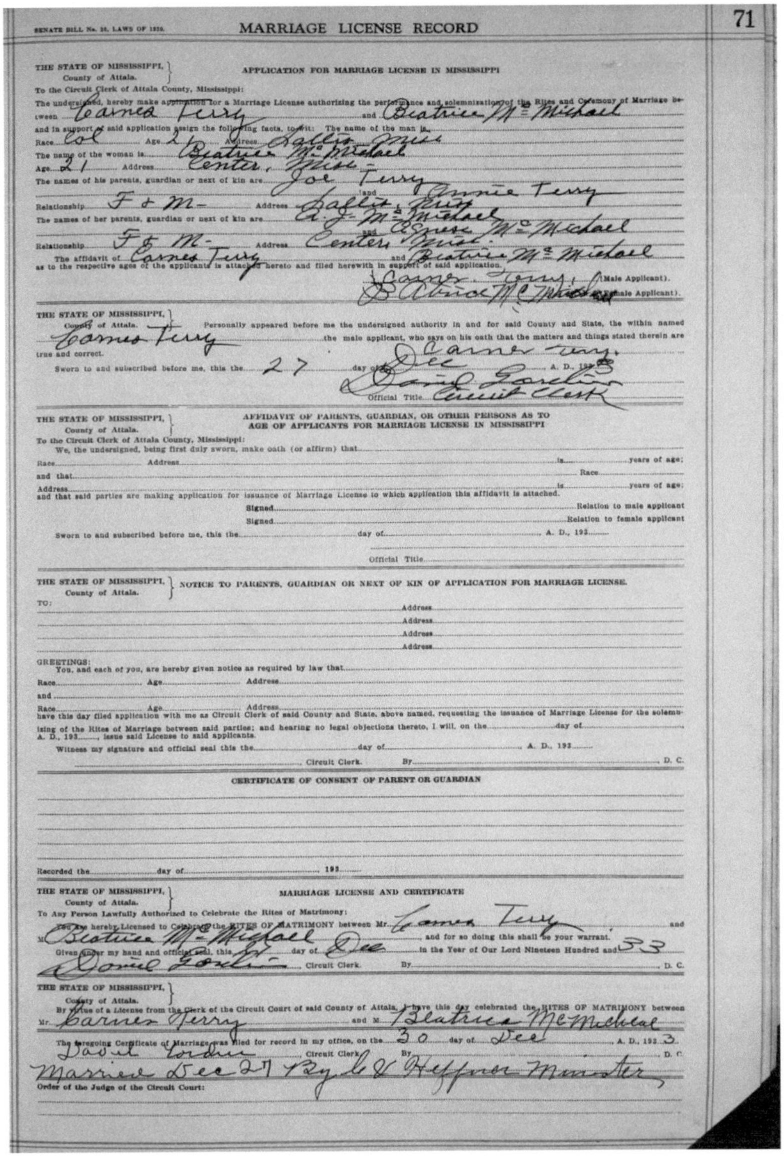

Figure 61 Marriage Record of Carnes TERRY and Callie McMICHAEL[583]

Stella Mae TERRY (Joseph Thomas TERRY, Caroline, Aaron Whitaker, Aaron Steele, Joseph I, John I, Samuel II, Samuel I, John)

Stella Mae TERRY was the daughter of Joseph Thomas (Joe) TERRY (b. Aug 1869, Attala Co., MS, d. sometime after 1940)[584] and Amanda (Annie B. in most documents) GUYTON (b. Aug 1872, Sallis, Attala Co., MS, d. 1933, Sallis, Attala Co., MS). Stella Mae TERRY was born on 17 Aug 1912 Sallis, Attala Co., MS,

---

[583] duaneehe originally shared this on 22 Apr 2021 on *Ancestry.com*.

[584] Amanda Guyton and Joseph Thomas (Joe) Terry, grave marker, Russell Cemetery, Attala Co., MS, digital image s.v. "Annie Guyton Terry," and "Joseph Terry," (Memorial ID 107273730 and 201392258, *FindaGrave.com*. I don't find a date of death for Joseph but he was included in the 1940 U.S. Census and he is buried in Russell Cemetery, Attala Co., MS.

and died on 1 Jan 1993 in Lexington, Holmes Co., MS.[585] She married Joe Dale (Joe D.) GUYTON (b. 24 Dec 1901 MS, d. Dec 1967 Sallis, Attala Co., MS).[586] Joe D. was the son of Simon and Viola GUYTON. He is first cousin once-removed to Stella Mae. See Figure 62, Figure 63, and Figure 64.

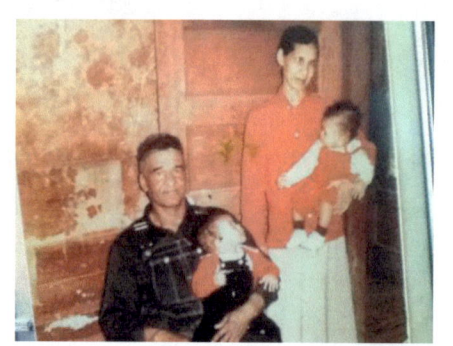

Figure 62 Joe D. and Stella Mae TERRY GUYTON with Babies[587]

Figure 63 Obituary of Stella Mae TERRY GUYTON[588]

Figure 64 Joe D. GUYTON[589]

---

[585] Stella Mae Terry, grave marker, Mallett Cemetery, Attala Co., MS, digital image s.v. "Stella Mae Guyton," (birth 17 Aug 1912, death 1 Jan 1993), *FindaGrave.com*.
[586] "Social Security Death Index," s.v. "Joe Guyton," (birth 24 Dec 1901, death Dec 1967), *Ancestry.com*.
[587] chancurri originally shared this on 16 Nov 2015 on *Ancestry.com*.
[588] "Mrs. Stella T. Guyton, Obituary," *The Star-Herald*, Kosciusko, MS, 14 Jan 1993, Page 9, *Newspapers.com*.
[589] Twanda Gary originally shared this on 30 Nov 2021 on *Ancestry.com*.

They had at least nine children:

i   Velma Ruth GUYTON (b. 27 Nov 1929 MS, d. Unknown)[590] m. Unknown CROSS.

ii   Joe Frank GUYTON, Sr. (b. 20 Aug 1930 Attala Co., MS, d. 10 Sep 1994 Kosciusko, Attala Co., MS)[591] m. Allene HUTCHINS (b. 6 Jan 1937 Kosciusko, Attala Co., MS, d. 11 Dec 2019 Jackson, Hinds Co., MS).[592] Allene HUTCHINS is the twin sister of Irene HUTCHINS, who married Joe Frank's brother, Ike Young GUYTON.

iii   Ike Young GUYTON (b. 19 Jun 1933 MS, d. 20 May 1984 Sallis, Attala Co., MS)[593] m. Irene HUTCHINS (b. 6 Jan 1937 Kosciusko, Attala Co., MS., d 6 Jan 2021 Jackson, Hinds Co., MS).[594]

iv   Jimmie Dell GUYTON (b. 4 Feb 1937 MS, d. AFT 1993 when his mother died).[595] Twin of his sister Johnnie Lavelle GUYTON.

v   Johnnie Lavelle GUYTON (b. 4 Feb 1937 MS, d. Unknown) m. (1) Unknown DOTSON (Unknown) and (2) Unknown RUBENS (Unknown).[596] Twin of her brother Jimmie Dell GUYTON. She had two children: Tina DOTSON and Jerome DOTSON.

vi   Stellie Rose GUYTON (b. Mar 1940 MS, d. Unknown)[597] m. Evell DOTSON (b. 1 Sep 1936 Attala Co., MS, d. 1 Jan 1991 Lincoln Park, Wayne Co., MI).[598]

vii   David GUYTON (b. ABT 1943, d. Unknown).[599] He had two sons: Jeremiah GUYTON and Melvin GUYTON.[600] Jeremiah GUYTON married Clarice UNKNOWN (Unknown).

viii   Hubert GUYTON (b. 25 Aug 1945 Attala Co., MS, d. 14 Feb 1988 Jackson, Hinds Co., MS)[601] m. Judy Kate ALLEN (Unknown).[602]

ix   Sadie GUYTON (b. Aug 1949, d. Unknown)[603] m. Unknown LITTLE.

---

[590] "1930 United States Federal Census," Beat 4, Attala Co., MS, digital image s.v. "Vilma Ruth Gytor," (birth abt 1928), *Ancestry.com*. "U.S., Public Records Index, 1950-1993, Volume 1," s.v. "Velma Ruth Cross," (birth 27 Nov 1929), *Ancestry.com*.

[591] Joe Frank Guyton, Sr., grave marker, Mallett Cemetery, Attala Co., MS, digital image s.v. "Joe Frank Guyton Sr," (birth 20 Aug 1930, death 10 Sep 1994), *FindaGrave.com*.

[592] Allene Hutchins., grave marker, Mallett Cemetery, Attala Co., MS, digital image s.v. "Allene Guyton," (birth 6 Jan 1937, death 11 Dec 2019), *FindaGrave.com*.

[593] Ike Young Guyton, grave marker, Mallett Cemetery, Attala Co., MS, digital image s.v. "Ike Young Guyton," (birth 9 Jun 1933, death 20 May 1984), *FindaGrave.com*.

[594] Irene Hutchins, grave marker, Mallett Cemetery, Attala Co., MS, digital image s.v. "Irene Guyton," (birth 6 Jan 1937, death 6 Jan 2021), *FindaGrave.com*.

[595] "U.S. Public Records Index, 1950-1993, Volume 2," s.v. "Jimmie D Guyton," (birth 4 Feb 1937), *Ancestry.com*.

[596] "1950 United States Federal Census," Kosciusko, Attala Co., MS, digital image s.v. "Johnny L Guyton," (birth must be 4 Feb 1937 as she is same age as her brother Jimmie), *Ancestry.com*. Note that the Census erroneously transcribed Johnnie's age as 20, instead of 10. Her last name was Rubens in her mother's obituary. Channie Brown-Currie reports that Johnnie was married to a Dotson and had two children.

[597] "U.S., Index to Public Records, 1994-2019," s.v. "Stellie Rose Dotson," (birth Mar 1940), *Ancestry.com*.

[598] "U.S., Department of Veterans Affairs BIRLS Death File, 1850-2010," s.v. "E Dotson," (birth 1 Sep 1936, death 1 Jan 1991), *Ancestry.com*.

[599] "1950 United States Federal Census," Kosciusko, Attala Co., MS, digital image s.v. "David Guyton," (birth abt 1943), *Ancestry.com*.

[600] Per Channie Brown-Currie.

[601] Hubert Guyton, grave marker, Mallett Cemetery, Attala Co., MS, digital image s.v. "Hubert Guyton," (birth 25 Aug 1945, death 14 Feb 1988), *FindaGrave.com*.

[602] See Hubert Guyton's FindaGrave record.

[603] "1950 United States Federal Census," Kosciusko, Attala Co., MS, digital image s.v. "Sadie Guyton," (birth abt 1950), *Ancestry.com*. Her married last name can be found on her mother's obituary.

Ruth G. TERRY (Green TERRY, Caroline, Aaron Whitaker, Aaron Steele, Joseph I, John I, Samuel II, Samuel I, John)

Ruth G. TERRY was the daughter of Green TERRY (b. 16 Aug 1876 Holmes Co., MS d. sometime after the 1940 U.S. Census).[604] Green married Magnolia (Maggie) UNKNOWN (b. abt 1884, d. Unknown).[605] Ruth was born on 5 Jan 1904 in Kosciusko, Attala Co., MS. She died on 8 Mar 1942 in Memphis, Shelby Co., TN.[606] Ruthie married Julius D. COOK, who was born about 1891 in Arkansas.[607] Information about his death is unknown.

i   Ruth G. COOK (b. 1 Aug 1925 Memphis, TN, d. 11 Nov 1970 Upland, Delaware Co., PA).[608]
ii   Julius COOK (b. ABT 1928 TN, d. Unknown).[609]
iii   Gertrude COOK (b. ABT 1934 TN, d. Unknown).[610]

Lockett Joseph TERRY, Sr. (Green TERRY, Caroline, Aaron Whitaker, Aaron Steele, Joseph I, John I, Samuel II, Samuel I, John)

Lockett Joseph TERRY, Sr. was the son of Green TERRY (b. 16 Aug 1876 Holmes Co., MS, d. sometime after the 1940 U.S. Census).[611] Green married Magnolia (Maggie) UNKNOWN (b. ABT 1884, d. Unknown).[612] Lockett Joseph TERRY, Sr. was born on 20 Aug 1904 MS, d. Nov 1980 St. Louis, St. Louis Co., MO.[613] He married (1) Gertrude CRANE (b. ABT 1917 AR, d. Unknown)[614] and divorced around 1943; and (2) Mary Elizabeth MITCHELL (b. 14 Jul 1914 Edwardsville, Madison Co., IL, d. Aug 1986 St Louis, MO).[615] See Figure 65.

---

[604] "U.S., World War I Civilian Draft Registrations, 1917-1918," Kosciusko, Attala Co., MS, digital image s.v. "Green Terry," (birth 16 Aug 1876), *Ancestry.com*.

[605] "1910 United States Census," Kosciusko, Attala Co., MS, digital image s.v. "Maggie Terry," (birth abt 1884), *Ancestry.com*.

[606] "Tennessee, U.S., Death Records, 1908-1965," digital image s.v. "Ruth Terry Cook," (birth 5 Jan 1904, death 8 Mar 1942), *Ancestry.com*.

[607] "1930 United States Federal Census," Memphis, Shelby Co., TN, digital image s.v. "J H Cook," (birth abt 1891), *Ancestry.com*.

[608] "Pennsylvania, U.S., Death Certificates, 1906-1970," s.v. "Ruth Cook," (birth 1 Aug 1925, death 11 Nov 1970), *Ancestry.com*.

[609] "1930 United States Federal Census," Memphis, Shelby Co., TN, digital image s.v. "Julius Cook, Jr.," (birth abt 1928), *Ancestry.com*.

[610] "1940 United States Federal Census," Memphis, Shelby Co., TN, digital image s.v. "Gertrude Cook," (birth abt 1934), *Ancestry.com*.

[611] "U.S., World War I Civilian Draft Registrations, 1917-1918," Kosciusko, Attala Co., MS, digital image s.v. "Green Terry," (birth 16 Aug 1876), *Ancestry.com*.

[612] "1910 United States Census," Kosciusko, Attala Co., MS, digital image s.v. "Maggie Terry," (birth abt 1884), *Ancestry.com*.

[613] Lockett Joseph Terry, Sr., grave marker, St. Peter's Cemetery, Normandy, St. Louis Co., MO, digital image s.v. "Lockett Joseph Terry, Sr.," (birth 20 Aug 1904, death Nov 1980), *FindaGrave.com*.

[614] "1930 United States Census," Jackson, Hinds Co., MS, digital image s.v. "Gertrude Terry," (birth abt 1908), *Ancestry.com*.

[615] "Social Security Death Index," s.v. "Mary Terry," (birth 14 Jul 1914, death Aug 1986), *Ancestry.com*. "Missouri, U.S., Death Records, 1968-2015," s.v. "Mary E. Terry," (death 1 Aug 1986), *Ancestry.com*.

Figure 65 Lockett Joseph TERRY, Sr.[616]

I do not have documentation to clearly identify the mothers of Lockett's children:

i   Lockett Joseph TERRY, Jr. (b. 10 Oct 1926 Memphis, Shelby Co., TN, d. 17 Apr 1997).[617]
ii   Shirley A. TERRY (b. ABT 1932 MO, d. Unknown).[618]
iii   Vincent Green TERRY (b. 15 Oct 1934 MO, d. Unknown)[619] m. Loretha Vernetia SMART (b. 8 Feb 1937 Camp Co., TX, d. Unknown) on 13 Jun 1959 in St. Louis, MO.[620]
iv   Margaret TERRY (b. ABT 1937 MO, d. Unknown.[621]
v   Michael Joseph TERRY, Sr. (b. 8 Feb 1939 St. Louis, MO, d. 17 Jan 2022 Hinesville, GA).[622]
vi   Magnolia TERRY (b. ABT 1944 MO, d. 2023). [623]
vii   Lillian P. TERRY (b. ABT 1946 MO, d. Unknown).[624]

---

[616] tlockhart283 originally shared this on 29 Jun 2016 on *Ancestry.com*.
[617] "Lockett Joseph Terry, Jr.," grave marker, Elmwood Cemetery, Detroit, Wayne Co., MI, digital image s.v. "Lockett Joseph Terry, Jr.," (birth 10 Oct 1926, death 17 Apr 1997), *FindaGrave.com*.
[618] "1950 United States Census," St. Louis, MO, digital image s.v. "Shirley A Terry," (birth abt 1932), *Ancestry.com*.
[619] "Missouri, U.S., Birth Registers, 1847-2002," s.v. "Vincent Green Terry," (birth 15 Oct 1934), *Ancestry.com*.
[620] "Missouri, U.S., Marriage Records, 1805-2002," s.v. "Vincent Green Terry," (marriage 13 Jun 1959 to Loretha Vernita Smart), *Ancestry.com*.
[621] "1940 United States Census," St. Louis, MO, digital image s.v. "Margaret Terry," (birth abt 1937), *Ancestry.com*.
[622] Michael Joseph Terry Sr, grave marker, Georgia Veterans Memorial Cemetery, Glennville, Tattnall Co., GA, digital image s.v. "Michael Joseph Terry Sr," (birth 8 Feb 1939, death 17 Jan 2022), *FindaGrave.com*.
[623] "1950 United States Census," St. Louis, MO, digital image s.v. "Magnolia Terry," (birth abt 1944), *Ancestry.com*.
[624] "1950 United States Census," St. Louis, MO, digital image s.v. "Lillian P Terry," (birth abt 1946), *Ancestry.com*.

Andrew TERRY (Green TERRY, Caroline, Aaron Whitaker, Aaron Steele, Joseph I, John I, Samuel II, Samuel I, John)

Andrew TERRY was the son of Green TERRY (b. 16 Aug 1876 Holmes Co., MS d. sometime after the 1940 U.S. Census[625] and Magnolia (Maggie) UNKNOWN (b. ABT 1884, d. Unknown).[626] Andrew was born on 15 Mar 1909 in Mississippi and died on 25 Jan 1979 in Detroit, Wayne Co., MI.[627] He married Eva LEVY (b. 20 May 1911 MS, d. 1 Feb 1999 Unknown.)[628] They had at least one child:

i   Bernice TERRY (b. 19 Apr 1929 Pickens, Holmes Co., MS, d. 31 Jul 1997 Detroit, Wayne Co., MI)[629] m. (1) Benjamin Harrison HALL (b. 25 Jan 1929 Ofahoma, Leake Co., MS, d. 31 Jan 1983 Detroit, Wayne Co., MI) on 17 Sep 1949),[630] and (2) Calvin Vernon LONGS (b. 29 Dec 1927 Cruger, Holmes Co., MS, d. 2 Nov 2009 Detroit, Wayne Co., MI).[631]

Romie TERRY, Sr. (Green TERRY, Caroline, Aaron Whitaker, Aaron Steele, Joseph I, John I, Samuel II, Samuel I, John)

Romie TERRY, Sr. was the son of Green TERRY (b. 16 Aug 1876 Holmes Co., d. sometime after the 1940 U.S. Census)[632] and Magnolia (Maggie) UNKNOWN (b. abt 1884, d. Unknown).[633]

Romie was born on 13 Sep 1913 in Holmes Co., MS, and he died on 9 May 2008 in Macomb Co., MI.[634] He married Elizabeth UNKNOWN (b. ABT 1917 Pickens, Holmes Co., MS, d. 17 Dec 1998 Pickens, Holmes Co., MS).[635] Elizabeth's obituary was the key to locate where her surviving children lived in 1998.

---

[625] "U.S., World War I Civilian Draft Registrations, 1917-1918," Kosciusko, Attala Co., MS, digital image s.v. "Green Terry," (birth 16 Aug 1876), *Ancestry.com*.

[626] "1910 United States Census," Kosciusko, Attala Co., MS, digital image s.v. "Maggie Terry," (birth abt 1884), *Ancestry.com*.

[627] "Michigan, U.S., Death Index, 1971-1996," s.v. "Andrew Terry," (birth 15 Mar 1909, death 5 Jan 1979), *Ancestry.com*.

[628] "U.S., Social Security Death Index, 1935-2014," s.v. "Eva Terry," (birth 20 May 1911, death 1 Feb 1999), *Ancestry.com*.

[629] "U.S., Social Security Death Index, 1935-2014," s.v. "Bernice Longs," (birth 19 Apr 1929, death 31 Jul 1997), *Ancestry.com*.

[630] "Michigan, U.S., Marriage Records, 1867-1952," s.v. "Bernice Terry," (marriage 17 Sep 1949 to Benjamin Harrison Hall), *Ancestry.com*. "Michigan, U.S., Death Index, 1971-1996," s.v. "Benjamin H Hall," (birth 25 Jan 1929, death 31 Jan 1983), *Ancestry.com*.

[631] Calvin Vernon Longs, grave marker, Chapel of Memorial Gardens, Belleville, Wayne Co., MI, digital image s.v. "Calvin Vernon Longs," (birth 29 Dec 1927, death 2 Nov 2009), *FindaGrave.com*.

[632] "U.S., World War I Civilian Draft Registrations, 1917-1918," Kosciusko, Attala Co., MS, digital image s.v. "Green Terry," (birth 16 Aug 1876), *Ancestry.com*.

[633] "1910 United States Census," Kosciusko, Attala Co., MS, digital image s.v. "Maggie Terry," (birth abt 1884), *Ancestry.com*.

[634] "U.S., Social Security Death Index, 1935-2014," s.v. "Romie Terry," (birth 13 Sep 1911, death 9 May 2008), *Ancestry.com*.

[635] "1940 United States Federal Census," Holmes Co., MS, digital image s.v. "Elizabeth Terry," (birth abt 1917), *Ancestry.com*. Elizabeth Unknown Terry, grave marker, Union Cemetery, Acona, Holmes Co., MS, digital image s.v. "Elizabeth Terry," (death 17 Dec 1998), *FindaGrave.com*. "Elizabeth Terry: Homemaker," *Clarion-Ledger*, 20 Dec 1998, p. 24; digital image, s.v. "Elizabeth Terry," *Newspapers.com*,

Their children included:

i Ernest TERRY (b. ABT 1933 MS, d. bef. Dec 1998).[636]
ii Lockett J. TERRY (b. Jan 1936 MS, d. Unknown).[637]
iii Ruby Lee TERRY (b. Apr 1937 MS, d. Unknown) m. Unknown GASTON (Unknown).[638]
iv Howard Lee TERRY (b. 19 Jan 1944 MS, d. 15 Apr 2016 Detroit, Wayne Co., MI).[639]
v Gertie Mae TERRY (b. 29 May 1945 MS, d. Unknown) m. Unknown GRIFFIN.[640]
vi Sarah Ann TERRY (b. ABT 1947 MS, d. Unknown).[641]
vii Romie TERRY, Jr. (b. ABT 1949 MS, d. Unknown).[642]

<https://www.newspapers.com/image/185454175/?article=10147629-3539-4427-9b0d-444cdc909d98&focus=0.5414884,0.5798436,0.6971703,0.6901017&xid=3355>.

[636] "1950 United States Federal Census," Holmes Co., MS, digital image s.v. "Ernest Terry," (birth abt 1933, death before his mother's Dec 1998 death), *Ancestry.com*.

[637] "U.S., Index to Public Records, 1994-2019," s.v. "Terry M. Lockett," corrected to "Lockett Terry," (birth Jan 1936, lived in Detroit, MI at the time of his mother's death in 1998), *Ancestry.com*.

[638] "U.S., Index to Public Records, 1994-2019," s.v. "Ruby Lee Gatson," (birth Apr 1937, lived in East Point, MI at the time of her mother's death in 1998), *Ancestry.com*.

[639] Howard Lee Terry, grave marker, Great Lakes National Cemetery, Oakland Co., MI, digital image s.v. "Howard Lee Terry," (birth 19 Jan 1944, death 15 Apr 2016), *FindaGrave.com*.

[640] "U.S. Public Records Index, 1950-1993, Volume 1," s.v. "Gertie M Griffin," (birth 29 May 1945, lived in Detroit, MI at the time of her mother's death in 1998), *Ancestry.com*.

[641] "1950 United States Federal Census," Holmes Co., MS, digital image s.v. "Sarah Ann Terry," (birth abt 1947, lived in East Pointe, MI at the time of her mother's Dec 1998 death), *Ancestry.com*.

[642] "1950 United States Federal Census," Holmes Co., MS, digital image s.v. "Remie Terry, Jr.," (birth abt 1949, lived in Jackson, MS at the time of his mother's Dec 1998 death), *Ancestry.com*.

Generation #10

Willie H. EDWARDS (Mary Emma TERRY EDWARD, William TERRY, Caroline, Aaron Whitaker, Aaron Steele, Joseph I, John I, Samuel II, Samuel I, John)

Willie H. EDWARDS was the son of Mary Emma TERRY (b. 19 Jan 1886 Kosciusko, Attala Co., MS, d. 15 Nov 1982 Detroit, Wayne Co., MI)[643] and James R. (Jim) EDWARDS (b. Nov 1874 MS, d. Unknown).[644] Willie was born on 22 Dec 1911 in Kosciusko, Attala Co., MS. He died on 21 Jun 1983 in Detroit, Wayne Co., MI.[645] He married Grace Ora HARRISON. (b. 16 Jan 1914 Good Pine, La Salle Parish, LA, d. 14 Dec 1993 Detroit, Wayne Co., MI).[646] See Figure 66.

Figure 66 Grace HARRISON and Willie H. EDWARDS[647]

---

[643] "Michigan, U.S., Death Index, 1971-1996," s.v. "Emma Edwards," (birth 19 Jan 1886, death 9 Nov 1982), *Ancestry.com*
[644] "1900 United States Census," Kosciusko, Attala Co., MS, digital image s.v. "James R. Edward," (birth abt Nov 1874), *Ancestry.com*.
[645] "Michigan, U.S., Death Index, 1971-1996," s.v. "Willie H Edwards," (birth 22 Dec 1910, death 21 Jun 1983), *Ancestry.com*.
[646] "Michigan, U.S., Death Index, 1971-1996," s.v. "Grace O Edwards," (birth 16 Jan 1914, death 14 Dec 1993), *Ancestry.com*.
[647] Avis James originally shared this on 23 Apr 2023, *Ancestry.com*

Effie EDWARDS (Mary Emma TERRY EDWARD, William TERRY, Caroline, Aaron Whitaker, Aaron Steele, Joseph I, John I, Samuel II, Samuel I, John)

Effie EDWARDS was the daughter of Mary Emma TERRY (b. 19 Jan 1886 Kosciusko, Attala Co., MS, d. 15 Nov 1982 Detroit, Wayne Co., MI)[648] and James R. (Jim) EDWARDS (b. Nov 1874 MS, d. Unknown).[649] Effie was born on 16 Jul 1916 in Attala Co., MS, and died on 7 Oct 2014 in Milwaukee, Milwaukee Co., WI.[650] She married or partnered with Unknown JAMISON (Unknown) with whom she had two boys.[651]

iArdess (Dutch) JAMISON (b. 9 Mar 1938 Attala Co., MS, d. likely in Milwaukee, Milwaukee Co., WI).[652]
iiCharles JAMISON (b. ABT 1941 Attala Co., MS, d. 21 Feb 1986 Detroit, Wayne Co., MI).[653]

Effie married Dan HUTCHINS, Sr. (b. 20 May 1914 Conway, Leake Co., MS, d. 19 Dec 1994 Milwaukee, Milwaukee Co., WI)[654] on 23 Nov 1942.[655] I cannot find their children.

Luria EDWARDS (Mary Emma TERRY EDWARD, William TERRY, Caroline, Aaron Whitaker, Aaron Steele, Joseph I, John I, Samuel II, Samuel I, John)

Luria EDWARDS was the daughter of Mary Emma TERRY (b. 19 Jan 1886 Kosciusko, Attala Co., MS, d. 15 Nov 1982 Detroit, Wayne Co., MI)[656] and James R. (Jim) EDWARDS (b. Nov 1874 MS, d.

---

[648] "Michigan, U.S., Death Index, 1971-1996," s.v. "Emma Edwards," (birth 19 Jan 1886, death 9 Nov 1982), *Ancestry.com*
[649] "1900 United States Census," Kosciusko, Attala Co., MS, digital image s.v. "James R. Edward," (birth abt Nov 1874), *Ancestry.com*.
[650] "Web: Obituary Daily Times Index, 1995-2016," s.v. "Effie Hutchins," (birth abt 1916, death abt 2014), *Ancestry.com*. Sonja Flippin, Phoenix, Maricopa Co., AZ, "Sonja Gaffney Flippin Family Tree," (birth 16 Jul 1916, death 7 Oct 2014), *Ancestry.com*, accessed 1 Jun 2024.
[651] "1950 United States Federal Census," digital image s.v. "Ardice JAMISON," (birth abt 1939), "Charles JAMISON," (birth abt 1941), *Ancestry.com*. The two boys are living with their maternal grandparents.
[652] "1950 United States Federal Census," Center, Attala Co., MS, digital image s.v. "Ardice Jamison," (birth abt 1939), *Ancestry.com*. Sonja Flippin, Phoenix, Maricopa Co., AZ, "Sonja Gaffney Flippin Family Tree," (birth 16 Jul 1916, death 7 Oct 2014), *Ancestry.com*, accessed 1 Jun 2024.
[653] "1950 United States Federal Census," Center, Attala Co., MS, digital image s.v. "Charles Jamison," (birth abt 1941), *Ancestry.com*.
[654] "U.S., Social Security Applications and Claims Index, 1936-2007," s.v. "Dan Hutchins," (birth 11 May 1914, death 19 Dec 1994," *Ancestry.com*.
[655] "Iowa, U.S., Marriage Records, 1880-1947," s.v. "Effie Jannison," (marriage 23 Nov 1942), *Ancestry.com*.
[656] "Michigan, U.S., Death Index, 1971-1996," s.v. "Emma Edwards," (birth 19 Jan 1886, death 9 Nov 1982), *Ancestry.com*

Unknown).[657] Luria EDWARDS was born about 1918 in MS and died abt 2002.[658] She married Willie D. BARTON (b. abt 1917, d. Unknown).[659] See Figure 67.

Figure 67 Luria EDWARDS BARTON[660]

Ulysses (Julious) EDWARDS (Mary Emma TERRY EDWARD, William TERRY, Caroline, Aaron Whitaker, Aaron Steele, Joseph I, John I, Samuel II, Samuel I, John)

Ulysses (Julious) EDWARDS was the son of Mary Emma TERRY (b. 19 Jan 1886 Kosciusko, Attala Co., MS, d. 15 Nov 1982 Detroit, Wayne Co., MI)[661] and James R. (Jim) EDWARDS (b. Nov 1874 MS, d. Unknown).[662] Ulysses was born on 8 Dec 1919 in Attala Co., MS, and died on 15 Jun 1993 in Detroit, Wayne Co., MI.[663] m. Luegene UNKNOWN (b. 5 Sep 1906 MS, d. 27 Dec 1982 Detroit, Wayne Co., MI).[664] See Figure 68 and Figure 69.

The couple had at least eight children:

i   Mary Lou EDWARDS (b. ABT 1934 Attala Co., MS, d. Unknown).[665]
ii   Willie Ray EDWARDS (b. ABT 1936 MS, d. Unknown).[666]

---

[657] "1900 United States Census," Kosciusko, Attala Co., MS, digital image s.v. "James R. Edward," (birth abt Nov 1874), *Ancestry.com*.
[658] "Web: Obituary Daily Times Index, 1995-2016," s.v. "Luria Barton," (birth abt 1918, death abt 2002), *Ancestry.com*.
[659] "1950 United States Federal Census," digital image s.v. "Willie D. Barton," (birth abt 1917), *Ancestry.com*.
[660] sonja flippin originally shared this on 26 Nov 2023 on *Ancestry.com*.
[661] "Michigan, U.S., Death Index, 1971-1996," s.v. "Emma Edwards," (birth 19 Jan 1886, death 9 Nov 1982), *Ancestry.com*
[662] "1900 United States Census," Kosciusko, Attala Co., MS, digital image s.v. "James R. Edward," (birth abt Nov 1874), *Ancestry.com*.
[663] "Michigan, Death Index, 1971-1996," s.v. "Ulysses Edwards," (birth 8 Dec 1919, death 15 Jun 1993), *Ancestry.com*.
[664] "Michigan, Death Index, 1971-1996," s.v. "Luegin Edwards," (birth 5 Sep 1906, death 27 Dec 1982), *Ancestry.com*.
[665] "1940 United States Federal Census," Kosciusko, Attala Co., MS, digital image s.v. "Mary Lou Edwards," (birth abt 1934), *Ancestry.com*.
[666] "1940 United States Federal Census," Kosciusko, Attala Co., MS, digital image s.v. "Willie Ray Edwards," (birth abt 1936), *Ancestry.com*.

- iii   Geneva EDWARDS (b. ABT 1937 MS, d. Unknown).[667]
- iv   Frances M. (Fannie) EDWARDS (b. ABT 1939 MS, d. Unknown).[668]
- v   Pearlie M. EDWARDS (b. ABT 1939 MS, d. Unknown).[669]
- vi   Johnnie C. EDWARDS (male) (b. ABT 1942 MS, d. Unknown).[670]
- vii   Willie D. EDWARDS (b. ABT 1944 MS, d. Unknown).[671]
- viii   Wiley W. EDWARDS (b. ABT 1949 MS, d. Unknown).[672]

Figure 68 Ulysses EDWARDS[673]

Figure 69 Luegene UNKNOWN EDWARDS[674]136

Ernest EDWARDS (Mary Emma TERRY EDWARD, William TERRY, Caroline, Aaron Whitaker, Aaron Steele, Joseph I, John I, Samuel II, Samuel I, John)

Ernest EDWARD was the son of Mary Emma TERRY (b. 19 Jan 1886 Kosciusko, Attala Co., MS, d. 15 Nov 1982 Detroit, Wayne Co., MI)[675] and James R. (Jim) EDWARD (b. Nov 1874 MS, d. Unknown).[676] Ernest was born on 14 Oct 1920 in Attala Co., MS, and died on 11 Feb 1989 in Carthage, Leake Co.,

---

[667] "1940 United States Federal Census," Kosciusko, Attala Co., MS, digital image s.v. "Geneva Edwards," (birth abt 1937), *Ancestry.com*.

[668] "1940 United States Federal Census," Kosciusko, Attala Co., MS, digital image s.v. "Fanny M Edwards," (birth abt 1939), *Ancestry.com*.

[669] "1940 United States Federal Census," Kosciusko, Attala Co., MS, digital image s.v. "Pearlie M Edwards," (birth abt 1939), *Ancestry.com*.

[670] "1950 United States Federal Census," Center, Attala Co., MS, digital image s.v. "Johnnie C Edward," (birth abt 1942), *Ancestry.com*.

[671] "1950 United States Federal Census," Center, Attala Co., MS, digital image s.v. "Willie D Edward," (birth abt 1944), *Ancestry.com*.

[672] "1950 United States Federal Census," Center, Attala Co., MS, digital image s.v. "Wiley W Edward," (birth abt 1949), *Ancestry.com*.

[673] sonja flippin originally shared this on 26 Nov 2023 on *Ancestry.com*.

[674] sonja flippin originally shared this on 27 Nov 2023 ON *Ancestry.com*.

[675] "Michigan, U.S., Death Index, 1971-1996," s.v. "Emma Edwards," (birth 19 Jan 1886, death 9 Nov 1982), *Ancestry.com*

[676] "1900 United States Census," Kosciusko, Attala Co., MS, digital image s.v. "James R. Edward," (birth abt Nov 1874), *Ancestry.com*.

MS).[677] He married (1) Ira Mae CROSS (b. 8 Jul 1922 Attala Co., MS, d. 28 Feb 1963 Attala Co., MS)[678] and (2) Ruth Griffin VEASLEY (Unknown).[679]

Ernest and Ira Mae had six children together. Ernest and Ruth had four children together.[680] The obituary is vague enough that it is difficult to know which children belong to which mother.

Ernest and Ira Mae had the following children:

i   Lucious James (L.J.) EDWARDS (b. 5 Oct 1940 Kosciusko, Attala Co., MS, d. 30 Apr 1985 Gulfport, Harrison Co., MS).[681]
ii   E. J. EDWARDS (b. ABT 1941 MS, d. Unknown).[682]
iii   Ernest EDWARDS, Jr. (b. 21 Jan 1943 MS, d. 16 Oct 2007 Milwaukee, Milwaukee Co., WI)[683] m. Fannie UNKNOWN.
iv   Jimmie Kyles EDWARDS, Sr. (b. 11 Sep 1946 Kosciusko, Attala Co., MS, d. 13 Mar 2004 Milwaukee, Milwaukee Co., WI)[684] m. Emma Jane NASH (b. 28 Mar 1950 Kosciusko, Attala Co., MS, d. 15 Jan 1995 Milwaukee, Milwaukee Co., WI).[685]
v   Will E. EDWARDS (b. ABT 1948 MS, d. Unknown)[686] m. Carol UNKNOWN.
vi   Ira G. EDWARDS (b. ABT 1950 MS, d. Unknown)[687] m. Frederick AIKENS (Unknown).

Ernest and Ruth had four children together:

i   Linda J. EDWARDS (b. AFT 1950 MS, d. Unknown).[688]
ii   Mark EDWARDS (b. AFT 1950 MS, d. Unknown).[689]

---

[677] Ernest Edwards, grave marker, Mount Moriah Cemetery, Attala Co., Mississippi, s.v. "Ernest Edwards," (birth 4 Oct 1920, death 11 Feb 1989), *FindaGrave.com*.

[678] Ira Mae Cross, grave marker, Mount Moriah Cemetery, Attala Co., Mississippi, s.v. "Ira Mae Edwards," (birth 8 Jul 1922, death 28 Feb 1963), *FindaGrave.com*.

[679] Obituary for Ernest Edwards," *The Star-Herald, Kosciusko*, Attala Co., MS, 16 Feb 1989, p. 12; digital image, s.v. "Ernest Edwards," <https://www.newspapers.com/image/271421755/?article=6986ee83-9cc9-4e17-bdc1-7717dac7f963&focus=0.5079891,0.24858123,0.6647883,0.4486187&xid=3355>, *Newspapers.com*.

[680] Obituary for Ernest Edwards," *The Star-Herald, Kosciusko*, Attala Co., MS, 16 Feb 1989, p. 12; digital image, s.v. "Ernest Edwards," <https://www.newspapers.com/image/271421755/?article=6986ee83-9cc9-4e17-bdc1-7717dac7f963&focus=0.5079891,0.24858123,0.6647883,0.4486187&xid=3355>, *Newspapers.com*.

[681] Lucious James (LJ) Edwards, grave marker, Mount Moriah Cemetery, Attala Co., Mississippi, s.v. "Lucious James Edwards," (birth 5 Oct 1940, death 30 Apr 1985), *FindaGrave.com*.

[682] "1950 United States Federal Census," Center, Attala Co., MS, digital image s.v. "E J Edwards," (birth abt 1941), *Ancestry.com*.

[683] "U.S., Social Security Death Index, 1935-2014," s.v. "Ernest Edwards," (birth 21 Jan 1943, death 16 Oct 2007), *Ancestry.com*.

[684] "U.S., Social Security Applications and Claims Index, 1936-2007," s.v. "Jimmie Kyle Edwards, Sr.," (birth 11 Sep 1946, d. 13 Mar 2004), *Ancestry.com*.

[685] "U.S., Social Security Applications and Claims Index, 1936-2007," s.v. "Emma Jane Edwards," (birth 28 Mar 1950, death 15 Jan 1995), *Ancestry.com*.

[686] "1950 United States Federal Census," Center, Attala Co., MS, digital image s.v. "Will E Edwards," (birth abt 1948), *Ancestry.com*.

[687] "1950 United States Federal Census," Center, Attala Co., MS, digital image s.v. "Ira G Edward," (birth abt 1950), *Ancestry.com*.

[688] I assume Ruth's children were born after Ira's children.

[689] I assume Ruth's children were born after Ira's children.

iii   Ernestine EDWARDS (b. AFT 1950 MS, d. bef 1989).[690]
iv   James EDWARDS (b. AFT 1950 MS, bef 1989).[691]

Figure 70 Ernest EDWARDS[692]

Johnnie M. HARMON (Ethel TERRY HARMON, William TERRY, Caroline, Aaron Whitaker, Aaron Steele, Joseph I, John I, Samuel II, Samuel I, John)

Johnnie M. HARMON was the first child, a daughter, of Ethel TERRY (b. 18 Dec 1888 Attala Co., MS, d. 15 May 1969)[693] and John HARMON (b. 15 Jun 1895, d. 8 Dec 1971).[694] Johnnie was born on 7 May 1921 in Attala Co., MS, and died on 15 Aug 2006 Kosciusko, Attala Co., MS.[695] She married (1) Unknown TRUSS about 1938,[696] (2) Henry NEWELL (b. abt 1908),[697] and (3) UNKNOWN.[698]

She had two children, one with Unknown TRUSS and one with UNKNOWN.

i   Johnnie Mae TRUSS (b. ABT 1939 Attala Co., MS, d. Unknown).[699]
ii   Queen T. HARMON (b. ABT 1942 MS., d. Unknown).[700]

---

[690] I assume Ruth's children were born after Ira's children. She died before her father' death, per his obituary.
[691] I assume Ruth's children were born after Ira's children. He died before her father' death, per his obituary.
[692] sonja flippin originally shared this on 26 Nov 2023 on *Ancestry.com*.
[693] Ethel Terry, grave marker, Russell Cemetery, Attala Co., MS, digital image s.v. "Ethel Harmon," (birth 18 Dec 1888, death 15 May 1969), *FindaGrave.com*.
[694] John Harmon, grave marker, Russell Cemetery, Attala Co., MS, digital image s.v. "John Harmon," (birth 15 Jun 1895, death 8 Dec 1971), *FindaGrave.com*.
[695] Johnnie M. Harmon, grave marker, Kosciusko City Cemetery, Kosciusko, Attala Co., MS, digital image s.v. "Mrs Johnnie M Newell," (birth 7 May 1921, death 15 Aug 2006), *FindaGrave.com*.
[696] "1940 United States Census," Newport, Attala Co., MS, digital image s.v. "Johnnie Mae Truer [Truss]," (birth abt 1939), *Ancestry.com*.
[697] "1950 United States Federal Census," Kosciusko, Attala Co., MS, digital image s.v. "Henry Newell," (birth abt 1908), *Ancestry.com*.
[698] "1950 United States Federal Census," Kosciusko, Attala Co., MS, digital image s.v. "Queen T. Harmon," (birth abt 1942), *Ancestry.com*. Daughter of Johnnie M. Harmon.
[699] "1940 United States Federal Census," Newport, Attala Co., MS, digital image s.v. "Johnnie Mae Truer," (birth abt 1939), *Ancestry.com*.
[700] "1950 United States Federal Census," Kosciusko, Attala Co., MS, digital image s.v. "Oueen T Harmon Jr," (birth abt 1942), *Ancestry.com*.

Jim Roger HARMON (Ethel TERRY HARMON, William TERRY, Caroline, Aaron Whitaker, Aaron Steele, Joseph I, John I, Samuel II, Samuel I, John)

Jim Roger HARMON was the son of Ethel TERRY (b. 18 Dec 1888 Attala Co., MS, d. 15 May 1969)[701] and John HARMON (b. 15 Jun 1895, d. 8 Dec 1971).[702] Jim was born on 3 Dec 1922 in Sallis, Attala Co., MS, and died on 11 Jun 1998 in Jackson, Hinds Co., MS).[703] He married Bonnie Jean SANDIFER (b. 28 May 1926 MS, d. 17 May 2011 Jackson, Hinds Co., MS).[704]

Bonnie SANDIFER's obituary, posted on her *FindaGrave* site, is shown below:

Mother Bonnie Jean SANDIFER HARMON was born on May 14, 1926, to the Late Chapel and Mattie Graham SANDIFER. Mother HARMON was united in marriage to Mr. Jim HARMON on March 7, 1946. At an early age, she joined St. John M. B. Church in McAdams, MS. She received her formal education in the public schools of Kosciusko, MS; and Jacob Chapel School. She furthered her education by taking courses at Saint Jr. College, Tougaloo College, Rust College, and Mississippi State University. Mother HARMON was a member of the NAACP. She was an active community leader and participated in the boycotting of Fred's Dollar Store in Kosciusko and Durant, MS. She worked the polling booths in McAdams, MS; and strongly supported and advocated the need for registering to vote. Her commitment to civil rights led her to spearhead and successfully procure water rights for her rural areas of the county. Mother HARMON taught Head Start School for Central MS. Inc at Christian Liberty and Barlow Head Start centers for 30 years. Mother HARMON always put God first and strongly believed that education was the key to success, whether it was formal or informal. One of her favorite mottos was "Be the job great or small, do it well or not at all." She always taught the golden rule: "Do unto others as you would have them to do unto you, and always put God first in whatever you do." Mother HARMON served faithfully on the Hospitality Committee, Mother's Board, Missionary Board, Choir, and taught Sunday School. In 2010, she was chosen "Mother of the Year." Mother HARMON was preceded in death by her husband, Mr. Jim R. HARMON. To this union twelve children were conceived; one daughter, Mildred HARMON, preceded her in death, and one son.

---

[701] Ethel Terry, grave marker, Russell Cemetery, Attala Co., MS, digital image s.v. "Ethel Harmon," (birth 18 Dec 1888, death 15 May 1969), *FindaGrave.com*.
[702] John Harmon, grave marker, Russell Cemetery, Attala Co., MS, digital image s.v. "John Harmon," (birth 15 Jun 1895, death 8 Dec 1971), *FindaGrave.com*.
[703] Jim Roger Harmon, grave marker, Parkway Cemetery, Kosciusko, Attala Co., MS, digital image s.v. "Jim Roger Harmon," (birth 3 Dec 1922, death 11 Jun 1998), *FindaGrave.com*.
[704] "U.S., Social Security Death Index, 1935-2014," s.v. "Bonnie J. Harmon," (birth 28 May 1926, death 17 May 2011), *Ancestry.com*. Bonnie Jean Sandifer, grave marker, Parkway Cemetery, Kosciusko, Attala Co., MS, digital image s.v. "Bonnie Jean Harmon," (birth 14 May 1926, death 17 May 2011), *FindaGrave.com*.

Jim and Bonnie's obituaries contain a list of their children. See Jim's obituary in Figure 71.[705]

Jim Roger Harmon

Funeral services for Jim Roger Harmon, 75, of Sallis were held Sunday at 10 a.m. at St. John Baptist Church with burial in Parkway Cemetery.

Harmon, retired from hospital housekeeping, died June 11, 1998 at St. Dominic Hospital in Jackson. He was a native of Attala County and a member of St. John Baptist Church.

He leaves his wife, Mrs. Bonnie J. Harmon of Sallis; seven daughters, Ms. Janie Harmon, Mrs. Brenda Teague, Mrs. Sharon Woods, Mrs. Daisy Harmon of Bellwood, Ill., Mrs. Vickie Edwards of Meridian, Mrs. Clara Smith and Mrs. Mary Burnside of Chicago, Ill.,

Also sons, Larry Harmon of Bellwood, Ill., Charles Harmon of Sallis, Jimmie Harmon of Kosciusko and Willie D. Ellis of Milwaukee, Wis.; two sisters, Mrs. Johnnie Newell of Kosciusko and Mrs. Ezra Ferguson of Sallis; a brother, Roy Harmon of Milwaukee; 20 grandchildren, seven great-grandchildren.

Deacon Larry Harmon officiated and Winters Funeral Home was in charge of arrangements.

Pallbearers were Roy Harmon, Paul Harmon, Charles Harmon, King Harmon, James Harmon and Jimmie Harmon.

Figure 71 Jim Roger HARMON's Obituary[706]

They had at least twelve children:

i   Jimmie HARMON (male) (b. 14 Dec 1946 Sallis, Attala Co., MS, d. 2017 Kosciusko, Attala Co., MS).[707]
ii Daisy J. HARMON (b. 8 Sep 1948 MS, d. Unknown)[708] m. Johnnie ALLEN.
iii Ollie Clara HARMON (b. AFT 1950 Census Sallis, Attala Co., MS, d. Unknown) m. Thomas SMITH (Unknown).
iv Mary HARMON (b. 2 Nov 1953 Sallis, Attala Co., MS, d. Unknown)[709] m. Curtis Lee BURNSIDE (b. 7 Aug 1930 Stallo, Neshoba Co., MS, d. 19 Oct 1998).[710]
v   Larry Wade HARMON, Sr. (b. Jun 1959, d. Unknown)[711] m. Jackie UNKNOWN.
vi Brenda HARMON (b. Unknown, MS, d. Unknown) m. Unknown TEAGUE (Unknown).

---

[705] Obituary for Jim Roger Harmon," *The Star-Herald*, Kosciusko, Attala Co., MS, 18 Jun 1998, p. 6; digital image, s.v. "Jim Roger Harmon," <https://www.newspapers.com/article/the-star-herald-obituary-for-jim-roger-h/128856190/>, *Newspapers.com*.

[706] "Jim Roger Harmon Obituary," *The Star-Herald*, Kosciusko, Attala Co., MS, Thu, 18 Jun 1998, p. 6, digital image s.v. "Jim Roger Harmon," *Newspapers.com*.

[707] Jimmie Harmon, grave marker, Parkway Cemetery, Attala Co., MS, digital image s.v. "Jimmie Harmon," (birth 14 Dec 1946, death 4 Jul 2017), *FindaGrave.com*.

[708] "1950 United States Federal Census," Newport, Attala Co., MS, digital image s.v. "Daisy Harmon," (birth abt 1949), *Ancestry.com*.

[709] "U.S. Public Records Index, 1950-1993, Volume 1," s.v. "Mary E. Burnside," (birth 2 Nov 1953, d. Unknown), *Ancestry.com*.

[710] Curtis Lee Burnside, grave marker, San Joaquin Valley National Cemetery, Santa Nella, Merced Co., CA, digital image s.v. "Curtis Lee Burnside," (birth 7 Aug 1930, death 19 Oct 1998), *FindaGrave.com*.

[711] "U.S., Index to Public Records, 1994-2019," s.v. "Larry Wade Harmon Sr," (birth Jun 1959), *Ancestry.com*.

vii	Charles HARMON (b. 1 Sep 1961 Sallis, Attala Co., MS, d. Unknown).[712]
viii	Vickie Lynn HARMON (b. abt 1963 Sallis, Attala Co., MS, d. Unknown) m. (1) Michael Octavius HOPSON (b. abt 1961, d. Unknown) on 18 Jun 1983 in McAdams, Attala Co., MS;[713] (2) Unknown EDWARDS (Unknown).
ix	Sharon HARMON (b. 18 Nov 1963 Sallis, Attala Co., MS, d. Unknown) m. Unknown WOODS (Unknown).
x	Janice (or Janie) HARMON (b. ABT 1965 Sallis, Attala Co., MS, d. Unknown) m. Henry HOWARD (Unknown).
xi	Mildred HARMON (b. Unknown, d. BEF 2011 when her mother died).
xii	Unknown son who predeceased his mother.

Ethel Lavelle CONWAY (Nealie TERRY CONWAY, William TERRY, Caroline, Aaron Whitaker, Aaron Steele, Joseph I, John I, Samuel II, Samuel I, John)

Ethel Lavelle CONWAY was the daughter of Nealie Eugene TERRY (b. 2 Jul 1890 Bolivar Co., MS, d. 17 Jun 1990 Dundee, Tunica Co., MS)[714] and William Major CONWAY, Jr. (b. 14 Mar 1879 MS, d. 2 Jun 1951 Dundee, Tunica Co., MS).[715] Note to the reader: William Major CONWAY, Jr., in this book, is often called William Major CONWAY, Sr. by others. His father was also Major CONWAY. I will refer to William Major CONWAY, Jr.'s father as William Major CONWAY, Sr. William Major CONWAY, Jr. has a son named William Alvin CONWAY, but is often called by others, William Major CONWAY, Jr. I will refer to this son as William Alvin CONWAY..

Ethel Lavelle CONWAY was born on 15 Jan 1911 in Kosciusko, Attala Co., MS, and died on Mar 1984 in Dundee, Tunica Co., MS.[716] She married Johnny Howard WARD (b. 5 Feb 1900 Claiborne, MS, d. Jan 1977).[717] They were separated in the U.S. 1950 Census and Ethel lived with her parents.[718] See Figure 72.

---

[712] "U.S. Public Records Index, 1950-1993, Volume 1," s.v. "Charles Harmon," (birth 1 Sep 1961), *Ancestry.com*.

[713] "Newspapers.com Marriage Index, 1800s-1999," s.v. "Pvt Vickie Lynn Harmon," (marriage 18 Jun 1983 to Michael Hopson), *Ancestry.com*.

[714] Nealie Eugene Terry, grave marker, Bethlehem Cemetery, Lula, Coahoma Co., MS, digital image s.v. "Nealie Eugene Conway," (birth 2 Jul 1890, death 17 Jun 1990), *FindaGrave.com*.

[715] Major Conway, Jr., grave marker, Bethlehem Cemetery, Lula, Coahoma Co., MS, digital image s.v. "Major Conway, Sr.," (birth 14 Mar 1879, death 2 Jun 1951), *FindaGrave.com*.

[716] "U.S., Social Security Death Index, 1935-2014," s.v. "Lavelle Ward," (birth 15 Jan 1911, death Mar 1984), *Ancestry.com*.

[717] "U.S., Social Security Death Index, 1935-2014," s.v. "John Ward," (birth 5 May 1899, death Jan 1977), *Ancestry.com*.

[718] "1950 United States Federal Census," Tunica Co., MS, digital image s.v. "Lavelle Ward," (birth abt 1911), *Ancestry.com*.

Figure 72 Ethel Lavelle CONWAY WARD[719]

They had at least three children:

i   Osceola WARD (b. 4 Dec 1942 MS, d. 4 Jun 2016 Kansas City, MO)[720] m. James E. THOMAS (Unknown) on 21 Dec 1968 in Kansas City, MO.[721]

ii   Willie James WARD (b. ABT 1945 MS, d. 8 Sep 1969 Cook Co., IL, bur. Lula, Coahoma Co., MS).[722]

iii   Felton WARD (b. ABT 1947 MS, d. Unknown).[723]

Lenard CONWAY (Nealie TERRY CONWAY, William TERRY, Caroline, Aaron Whitaker, Aaron Steele, Joseph I, John I, Samuel II, Samuel I, John)

Lenard CONWAY was the son of Nealie Eugene TERRY (b. 2 Jul 1890 Bolivar Co., MS, d. 17 Jun 1990 Dundee, Tunica Co., MS)[724] and William Major CONWAY, Jr. (b. 14 Mar 1879 MS, d. 2 Jun 1951 Dundee, Tunica Co., MS).[725] Note to the reader: William Major CONWAY, Jr., in this book, is often called William Major CONWAY, Sr. by others. His father was also Major CONWAY. I will refer to William Major CONWAY, Jr.'s father as William Major CONWAY, Sr. William Major CONWAY, Jr. has a son named William Alvin CONWAY, but is often called by others, William Major CONWAY, Jr. I will refer to this son as William Alvin CONWAY.

---

[719] Yolee60 originally shared this on 3 Dec 2009, *Ancestry.com*.

[720] Osceola Ward Thomas, grave marker, Mount Moriah Cemetery, Kansas City, Jackson Co., MO, digital image s.v. "Osceola Thomas," (birth 1942, death 2016), *FindaGrave.com*.

[721] "Missouri, U.S., Jackson County Marriage Records, 1840-1985," digital image s.v. "Oscela Ward," (marriage to James E. Thomas on 21 Dec 1968), *Ancestry.com*.

[722] "U.S., Headstone Applications for Military Veterans, 1861-1985," digital image s.v. "Willie James Ward," (birth 1945, death 1969), *Ancestry.com*.

[723] "1950 United States Federal Census," Tunica Co., MS, digital image s.v. "Felton Ward," (birth abt 1947), *Ancestry.com*.

[724] Nealie Eugene Terry, grave marker, Bethlehem Cemetery, Lula, Coahoma Co., MS, digital image s.v. "Nealie Eugene Conway," (birth 2 Jul 1890, death 17 Jun 1990), *FindaGrave.com*.

[725] Major Conway, Jr., grave marker, Bethlehem Cemetery, Lula, Coahoma Co., MS, digital image s.v. "Major Conway, Sr.," (birth 14 Mar 1879, death 2 Jun 1951), *FindaGrave.com*.

Lenard was born on 22 Jul 1913 in Kosciusko, Attala Co., MS, and died on 19 Dec 2004 in Clarksdale, Coahoma Co., MS).[726] He married Ocelee BLACKMAN (b. 12 Oct 1915 Shelby, Bolivar Co., MS, death 7 Feb 2000 Dundee, Tunica Co., MS).[727] See Figure 73.

Figure 73 Lenard CONWAY[728]

The couple had at least one child:

i   Alvin CONWAY (b. 6 Mar 1945 Dundee, Tunica Co., MS, d. 18 Aug 2007).[729]

Major Alvin CONWAY (Nealie TERRY CONWAY, William TERRY, Caroline, Aaron Whitaker, Aaron Steele, Joseph I, John I, Samuel II, Samuel I, John)

Major Alvin CONWAY, Sr. was the son of Nealie Eugene TERRY (b. 2 Jul 1890 Bolivar Co., MS, d. 17 Jun 1990 Dundee, Tunica Co., MS)[730] and William Major CONWAY, Jr. (b. 14 Mar 1879 MS, d. 2 Jun 1951 Dundee, Tunica Co., MS). [731] Note to the reader: William Major CONWAY, Jr., in this book, is often called William Major CONWAY, Sr. by others. His father was also Major CONWAY. I will refer to William Major CONWAY, Jr.'s father as William Major CONWAY, Sr. William Major CONWAY, Jr. has a son named William

---

[726] "U.S., Social Security Applications and Claims Index, 1936-2007," s.v. "Lenard Conway,"(birth 22 Jul 1913, death 19 Dec 2004), *Ancestry.com*.
[727] "U.S., Social Security Applications and Claims Index, 1936-2007," s.v. "O C Conway," (birth 12 Oct 1915, death 7 Feb 2000), *Ancestry.com*.
[728] Carolyn Canada originally shared this on 12 Aug 2019, *Ancestry.com*.
[729] "U.S., Social Security Applications and Claims Index, 1936-2007," s.v. "Alvin Conway," (birth 6 Mar 1945, death 18 Aug 2007), *Ancestry.com*.
[730] Nealie Eugene Terry, grave marker, Bethlehem Cemetery, Lula, Coahoma Co., MS, digital image s.v. "Nealie Eugene Conway," (birth 2 Jul 1890, death 17 Jun 1990), *FindaGrave.com*.
[731] Major Conway, Jr., grave marker, Bethlehem Cemetery, Lula, Coahoma Co., MS, digital image s.v. "Major Conway, Sr.," (birth 14 Mar 1879, death 2 Jun 1951), *FindaGrave.com*.

Alvin CONWAY, but is often called by others, William Major CONWAY, Jr. I will refer to this son as William Alvin CONWAY.

Major Alvin was born on 30 Oct 1917 in Attala Co., MS, and died on 14 Oct 1994 in Lula, Coahoma Co. MS.[734] He married Katie Mae HARRIS (b. 23 Apr 1926 Bolivar Co., MS, d. Jul 1983 Dundee, Tunica Co., MS).[735] See Figure 74 and Figure 75.

Figure 74 Major Alvin CONWAY[732]

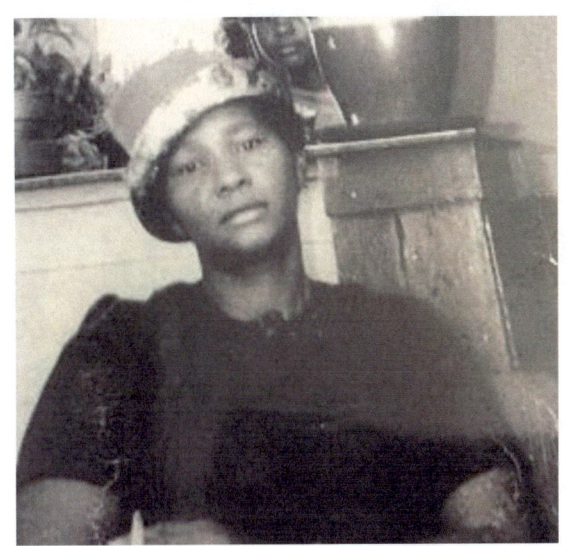

Figure 75 Katie Mae HARRIS CONWAY[733]

James Welmer CONWAY, Sr. (Nealie TERRY CONWAY, William TERRY, Caroline, Aaron Whitaker, Aaron Steele, Joseph I, John I, Samuel II, Samuel I, John)

James Welmer CONWAY, Sr. was the son of Nealie Eugene TERRY (b. 2 Jul 1890 Bolivar Co., MS, d. 17 Jun 1990 Dundee, Tunica Co., MS)[736] and William Major CONWAY, Jr. (b. 14 Mar 1879 MS, d. 2 Jun 1951 Dundee, Tunica Co., MS).[737] Note to the reader: William Major CONWAY, Jr., in this book, is often called William Major CONWAY, Sr. by others. His father was also Major CONWAY. I will refer to William Major CONWAY, Jr.'s father as William Major CONWAY, Sr. William Major CONWAY, Jr. has a son named William

---

[732] Yolee60 originally shared this on 15 Aug 2020, *Ancestry.com*.
[733] Carolyn Canada originally shared this on 13 Aug 2019, *Ancestry.com*.
[734] "Major Alvin Conway," grave marker, Bethlehem Cemetery, Lula, Coahoma Co., MS, digital image s.v. "Major Conway Jr.," (birth 30 Oct 1917, death 14 Oct 1994), *FindaGrave.com*.
[735] "U.S., Social Security Death Index, 1935-2014," s.v. "Katie Conway," (birth 23 Apr 1926, death Jul 1983), *Ancestry.com*.
[736] Nealie Eugene Terry, grave marker, Bethlehem Cemetery, Lula, Coahoma Co., MS, digital image s.v. "Nealie Eugene Conway," (birth 2 Jul 1890, death 17 Jun 1990), *FindaGrave.com*.
[737] Major Conway, Jr., grave marker, Bethlehem Cemetery, Lula, Coahoma Co., MS, digital image s.v. "Major Conway, Sr.," (birth 14 Mar 1879, death 2 Jun 1951), FindaGrave.com.

Alvin CONWAY, but is often called by others, William Major CONWAY, Jr. I will refer to this son as William Alvin CONWAY.

James was born on 17 Dec 1927 in Bolivar Co., MS, and died on 26 Dec 2012 in Montgomery, Montgomery Co., AL.[738] He married Frenetter WHITTINGTON (b. 9 Dec 1924 MS, d. 13 Aug 2019 Montgomery, Montgomery Co., AL).[739] See Figure 76, Figure 77, and Figure 78.

Figure 76 James Welmer CONWAY and Frenetter WHITTINGTON CONWAY[740]

Figure 77 Frenetter WHITTINGTON CONWAY[741]

Figure 78 James Welmer CONWAY[742]

The couple had at least three children:

i   James Welmer CONWAY, Jr. (b. 19 MAR 1949 San Francisco Co., CA, d. Unknown).[743]
ii Daniel CONWAY (Unknown).
iii Jerry Leon CONWAY (b. 20 Sep 1960 TX, d. Unknown).[744]

Leila HARMON (Sarah TERRY HARMON, William TERRY, Caroline, Aaron Whitaker, Aaron Steele, Joseph I, John I, Samuel II, Samuel I, John)

Leila HARMON was the daughter of Sarah TERRY (b. 15 May 1897 Sallis, Attala Co., MS, d. 14 Feb 1979 in Detroit, Wayne Co., MI)[745] and Walter HARMON (b. 22 Jun 1895 McAdams, MS, d. 6 Apr 1969).[746] Leila was born on 9 Jun 1918 in Sallis, Attala Co., MS, and died on 5 May 2010 in Detroit, Wayne Co.,

---

[738] "James Welmer CONWAY, Sr.," grave marker, Alabama National Cemetery, Montevallo, Shelby Co., AL, digital image s.v. "James Welmer Conway Sr.," (birth 17 Dec 1927, death 26 Dec 2012), *FindaGrave.com*.
[739] "Frenetter WHITTINGTON," grave marker, Alabama National Cemetery, Montevallo, Shelby Co., AL, digital image s.v. "Frenetter W. Conway (birth 9 Dec 1924, death 13 Aug 2019), *FindaGrave.com*.
[740] Yolee60 originally shared this on 31 Mar 2022, *Ancestry.com*.
[741] Christopher Conway originally shared this on 19 Mar 2016, *Ancestry.com*
[742] BillPtrston1900 originally shared this on 24 Jan 2013 on *Ancestry.com*.
[743] "California Birth Index, 1905-1995," s.v. "James Welmer Conway, Jr.," (birth 19 Mar 1949), *Ancestry.com*.
[744] "Texas, U.S., Birth Index, 1903-1997," digital image s.v. "Jerry Leon Conway," (birth 20 Sep 1960), *Ancestry.com*.
[745] "Michigan, U.S., Death Index, 1971-1996," s.v. "Sarah Harmon," (birth 15 May 1897, death 14 Feb 1979), *Ancestry.com*.
[746] "U.S., World War I Civilian Draft Registrations, 1917-1918," s.v. "Walter Harmon," (22 Jun 1895), *Ancestry.com*.

MI.[747] She married Otis KERN (b. 10 Jan 1918 Center, Attala Co., MS, d. 3 Mar 1961 Chicago, Cook Co., IL).[748] See Figure 79 and Figure 80.

Figure 79 Leila HARMON and Otis KERN[749]

Figure 80 Leila HARMON and Otis KERN Enjoying LIfe[750]

The couple had at least four children:

i   Olton Ray KERN (b. 28 Mar 1944 MS, d. Unknown).[751]
ii   Alice KERN (b. ABT 1950), d. Unknown).[752]
iii   Alton Ralph KERN (b. 4 Jun 1951 Chicago, Cook Co., IL, d. 16 Jul 2011 Detroit, Wayne Co., MI).[753]
iv   Owen Reed KERN (b. 13 Feb 1954 Chicago, Cook Co., IL, 4 Aug 2010 likely in Detroit, Wayne Co., MI).[754]

---

[747] Per Kelli Kern's Family Tree, *Ancestry.com,* accessed 11 May 2024. "1930 United States Federal Census," Beat 4, Attala Co., MS, digital image s.v. "Leila Harmon," (birth abt 1918), *Ancestry.com*. I found no documents the place or date of her death. Leila may have remarried after Otis' death, making tracking her more difficult.
[748] "Otis Kern," grave marker, Antioch Cemetery, Center, Attala Co., MS, digital image s.v. "Otis Kern," (birth 10 Jan 1918, death 3 Mar 1961), *FindaGrave.com*.
[749] Kelli Kern originally shared this on 10 Oct 2020 on *Ancestry.com*.
[750] Kelli Kern originally shared this on 10 Oct 2020 on *Ancestry.com*.
[751] "U.S., Public Records Index, 1950-1993, Volume 1," s.v. "Olton Ray Kern," (birth 28 Mar 1944), *Ancestry.com*.
[752] "1950 United States Federal Census," digital image s.v. "Alice Kern," (birth abt 1950), *Ancestry.com*.
[753] "U.S., Social Security Death Index, 1935-2014," s.v. "Alton R. Kern," (birth 4 Jun 1951, death 16 Jul 2011), *Ancestry.com*.
[754] "Social Security Death Index," s.v. "Owen R. Kern," (birth 13 Feb 1954, death 4 Aug 2010), *Ancestry.com*.

Fannie Mae HARMON (Sarah TERRY HARMON, William TERRY, Caroline, Aaron Whitaker, Aaron Steele, Joseph I, John I, Samuel II, Samuel I, John)

Fannie Mae HARMON was the daughter of Sarah TERRY (b. 15 May 1897 Sallis, Attala Co., MS, d. 14 Feb 1979 in Detroit, Wayne Co., MI)[755] and Walter HARMON (b. 22 Jun 1895 McAdams, MS, d. 6 Apr 1969).[756] Fannie was born on 1 Nov 1919 Kosciusko, Attala Co., MS, and died on 6 Apr 1992 in Detroit, Wayne Co., MI).[757] She married Leport ESTERS (b. 17 Oct 1919 Attala Co., MS, d. 20 Jul 1948 Northville, Wayne Co., MI).[758] The couple had at least two children:

i   Lamar ESTERS (b. 16 Jun 1939 Kosciusko, Attala Co., MS, d. 23 Oct 1982 Detroit, Wayne Co., MI).[759]
ii   Sarah L. ESTERS (b. ABT 1944 MS), d. Unknown).[760]

Walter Alvin HARMON (Sarah TERRY HARMON, William TERRY, Caroline, Aaron Whitaker, Aaron Steele, Joseph I, John I, Samuel II, Samuel I, John)

Walter Alvin HARMON was the son of Sarah TERRY (b. 15 May 1897 Sallis, Attala Co., MS, d. 14 Feb 1979 in Detroit, Wayne Co., MI)[761] and Walter HARMON (b. 22 Jun 1895 McAdams, MS, d. 6 Apr 1969).[762] Walter Alvin HARMON was born on 15 Jul 1922 in McAdams, Attala Co., MS, and died on 9 Jun 1974, likely in Detroit, Wayne Co., MI.[763] He married Dolores Augusta SUMMERS (b. 29 Sep 1929 St Louis MO, d. 24 Jun 1999.)[764] Walter Alvin served as Private 1st Class in the Army. He is buried in Woodlawn Cemetery in Detroit, Wayne Co., MI.[765] His Service Number was 34 620 884. He enlisted on 10 Feb 1943 and was discharged on 20 Mar 1946.

---

[755] "Michigan, U.S., Death Index, 1971-1996," s.v. "Sarah Harmon," (birth 15 May 1897, death 14 Feb 1979), *Ancestry.com*.
[756] "U.S., World War I Civilian Draft Registrations, 1917-1918," s.v. "Walter Harmon," (22 Jun 1895), *Ancestry.com*.
[757] "Michigan, Death Index, 1971-1996," s.v. "Fannie M Esters (birth 1 Nov 1919, death 6 Apr 1992), *Ancestry.com*.
[758] "Michigan, Death Index, 1867-1952," s.v. "Leport Esterz," (birth 17 Oct 1918, death 20 Jul 1948), *Ancestry.com*.
[759] "Michigan, U.S., Death Index, 1971-1996," s.v. Lamar Esters," (birth 16 Jun 1939, death 23 Oct 1982), *Ancestry.com*.
[760] "1950 United States Federal Census," Detroit, Wayne Co., MI, digital image s.v. "Sarah Esters," (birth abt 1943), *Ancestry.com*.
[761] "Michigan, U.S., Death Index, 1971-1996," s.v. "Sarah Harmon," (birth 15 May 1897, death 14 Feb 1979), *Ancestry.com*.
[762] "U.S., World War I Civilian Draft Registrations, 1917-1918," s.v. "Walter Harmon," (22 Jun 1895), *Ancestry.com*.
[763] "U.S., Headstone Applications for Military Veterans, 1861-1985," digital image s.v. "Walter Alvin Harmon," (birth 15 Jul 1922, death 10 Feb 1943), *Ancestry.com*.
[764] "U.S., Social Security Death Index, 1935-2014," s.v. "Dolores A. Boswell," (birth 30 Sep 1929, death 24 Jun 1999), *Ancestry.com*.
[765] "U.S., Headstone Applications for Military Veterans, 1861-1985," digital image s.v. "Walter Alving Harmon," *Ancestry.com*.

Murie (Murray) HARMON [Sarah TERRY HARMON, William TERRY, Caroline, Aaron Whitaker, Aaron Steele, Joseph I, John I, Samuel II, Samuel I, John]

Murie (Murray) HARMON was the son of Sarah TERRY (b. 15 May 1897 Sallis, Attala Co., MS, d. 14 Feb 1979 Detroit, Wayne Co., MI)[766] and Walter HARMON (b. 22 Jun 1895 McAdams, MS, d. 6 Apr 1969).[767] Murie HARMON was born on 22 Oct 1933 in Kosciusko, Attala Co., MS, and died on 13 Aug 2002 in Detroit, Wayne Co., MI.[768] He married Lelia Mae STEVENSON (b. 13 Jul 1935 Norfolk, VA, d. Unknown).[769]

Irma Jean TERRY [William Vinson TERRY, William TERRY, Caroline, Aaron Whitaker, Aaron Steele, Joseph I, John I, Samuel II, Samuel I, John]

Irma Jean TERRY was the daughter of William Vinson TERRY (b. 19 Jun 1907 Attala Co., MS, d. 30 Sep 1981 and Beatrice ISLAND (b. 7 Feb 1902 MS, d. 16 Dec 1987 Indianapolis, Marion Co., IN).[770] Irma's birth and death dates are unknown. She married (1) Unknown BURT (Unknown) and (2) Eugene NAYLOR (ABT 1905 MS, d. 15 Apr 1991 Kosciusko, Attala Co., MS).[771]

Based on the obituary of Eugene NAYLOR, Irma had the following children with Mr. BURT:

i   Douglas BURT (Unknown).
ii   Terrance BURT (Unknown).
iii Richard BURT (Unknown).
iv   George Allen BURT (b. ABT 1972, d. 26 Jun 1986). George died at the age of 14. He was living with his mother and stepfather, Eugene NAYLOR.[772]

She had the following children with Eugene NAYLOR:

i   Beatrice F. NAYLOR (Unknown).
ii   Francis NAYLOR (Unknown).
iii Priscilla NAYLOR (Unknown).

---

[766] "Michigan, U.S., Death Index, 1971-1996," s.v. "Sarah Harmon," (birth 15 May 1897, death 14 Feb 1979), *Ancestry.com*.

[767] "U.S., World War I Civilian Draft Registrations, 1917-1918," s.v. "Walter Harmon," (22 Jun 1895), *Ancestry.com*.

[768] "U.S., Social Security Death Index, 1935-2014," s.v. "Murie Harmon," (birth 28 Oct 1933, death 13 Aug 2002), *Ancestry.com*.

[769] "Virginia, U.S., Birth Records, 1912-2015, Delayed Birth Records, 1721-1920," s.v. "Leila May Stevenson," (birth 13 Jul 1935), *Ancestry.com*.

[770] William Vinson Terry, grave marker, Russell Cemetery, Attala County, Mississippi, s.v. "William V. Terry" (birth 19 Jun 1907, death 30 Sep 1981), *FindaGrave.com*. "U.S., Social Security Applications and Claims Index, 1936-2007," s.v. "Beatrice Terry," (birth 7 Feb 1902, death Dec 1987), *Ancestry.com*. "Beatrice Terry," *The Star-Herald*, Kosciusko, Attala Co., MS, Thu, Dec 24, 1987, p. 9, *Newspapers.com*. Irma Jean Terry Naylor was listed as a surviving daughter.

[771] "Obituary of Eugene Naylor," digital image s.v. "Eugene Naylor," *The Star-Herald*, Kosciusko, Attala Co., MS, Thu, 25 Apr 1991, p. 13, *Newspapers.com*, < https://www.newspapers.com/article/the-star-herald-obituary-for-eugene-nayl/150210509/>.

[772] "George Allen Burt," *The Star-Herald*, Kosciusko, Attala Co., MS, Thu, Jul 10, 1986, p. 11, *Newspapers.com*. Irma Jean Naylor and her husband, Eugene Naylor, were listed as survivors.

Yvonne Jacquline TERRY (Carnes TERRY, Joseph TERRY, Caroline, Aaron Whitaker, Aaron Steele, Joseph I, John I, Samuel II, Samuel I, John)

Yvonne Jacquline TERRY was the daughter of Fred Carnes TERRY (b. 7 Oct 1907 Sallis, Attala Co., MS, d. Jun 1973 Jackson, Hinds Co., MS)[773] and Callie Beatrice McMICHAEL (b. 20 Sep 1915 Attala Co., MS, d. 19 May 1979 Memphis, Shelby Co., TN).[774] Yvonne was born on 11 Jun 1936 in Center, Attala Co., MS. She died on 9 Jun 2009 in Center, Attala Co., MS.[775] She married Leavernard JONES, Sr. (b. 12 Jan 1923 Unknown, d. 13 Apr 2008 likely Jackson, Hinds Co., MS).[776]

In 1959, the couple lived in Jackson, Hinds Co., MS. Leavernard worked as an assistant shipping clerk at Capitol Barber & Beauty Supplies. They lived at 3634 Bishop Street.[777]

Bernice Marie TERRY (Carnes TERRY, Joseph TERRY, Caroline, Aaron Whitaker, Aaron Steele, Joseph I, John I, Samuel II, Samuel I, John)

Bernice Marie TERRY was the daughter of Fred Carnes TERRY (b. 7 Oct 1907 Sallis, Attala Co., MS, d. Jun 1973 Jackson, Hinds Co., MS)[778] and Callie Beatrice McMICHAEL (b. 20 Sep 1915 Attala Co., MS, d. 19 May 1979 Memphis, Shelby Co., TN).[779] Bernice was born on 19 Jun 1940 in Kosciusko, Attala Co., MS, and died 19 Oct 2004 in Memphis, Shelby Co., TN.[780] She had two husbands: (1) Vernon JOHNSON, Sr. (Unknown) and (2) Curtis Lee BURNSIDE (b. 7 Aug 1930 Stallo, MS, d. 19 Oct 1998, Unknown).[781] See Figure 81.

---

[773] "Social Security Death Index," s.v. "Fred Terry," (birth 7 Oct 1907, death Jun 1973), *Ancestry.com*.
[774] Callie Beatrice McMichael, grave marker, Hollywood Cemetery, Memphis, Shelby Co., TN, digital image s.v. "Callie Beatrice Terry Anthony," (birth 20 Sep 1915, death 19 May 1979), *FindaGrave.com*.
[775] "Yvonne Jacquline Terry," grave marker, Antioch Cemetery, Center, Attala Co., MS, digital image s.v. "Yvonne Jacquline Jones," (birth 11 Jun 1936, death 9 Jun 2009), *FindaGrave.com*.
[776] "Leavernard Jones, Sr.," grave marker, Natchez National Cemetery, Natchez, Adams Co., MS, digital image s.v. "Leavernard Jones, Sr.," (birth 11 Jun 1936, death 9 Jun 2009), *FindaGrave.com*.
[777] "1959 Polk's Jackson (Hinds County) City Directory," digital image s.v. "Leavernard Jones," p. 298, *Ancestry.com*.
[778] "Social Security Death Index," s.v. "Fred Terry," (birth 7 Oct 1907, death Jun 1973), *Ancestry.com*.
[779] Callie Beatrice McMichael, grave marker, Hollywood Cemetery, Memphis, Shelby Co., TN, digital image s.v. "Callie Beatrice Terry Anthony," (birth 20 Sep 1915, death 19 May 1979), *FindaGrave.com*.
[780] "Bernice Marie Terry," grave marker, New Park Cemetery, Memphis, Shelby Co., TN, digital image s.v. "Beatrice Marie Burnside," (birth 19 Jun 1940, death 19 Oct 2004), *FindaGrave.com*.
[781] "Curtis Lee Burnside," grave marker, San Joaquin Valley National Cemetery, Santa Nella, Merced Co., CA, digital image s.v. "Curtis Lee Burnside," (birth 7 Aug 1930, death 19 Oct 1998), *FindaGrave.com*.

Figure 81 Curtis Lee BURNSIDE[782]

BERNICE BURNSIDE, 59, of Memphis, homemaker, died Monday at Methodist North Hospital. Services will be at 11 a.m. Monday at M.J. Edwards & Sons Funeral Home Whitehaven Chapel with burial in New Park Cemetery. She was a member of Mississippi Boulevard Christian Church. Mrs. Burnside, the widow of Curtis Lee Burnside, leaves four sons, Charles Burnside, Willie Burnside, Vernon Johnson Jr. and Anthony Burnside, all of Memphis; two sisters, Anitha Perkins of Memphis and Evon Terry of Jackson, Miss., 12 grandchildren and a great-grandchild.

Figure 82 Bernice Marie TERRY BURNSIDE's Obituary

I didn't find any information about Vernon JOHNSON, Sr. but Bernice's: obituary indicated that four sons survived her.[783] See Figure 81. One was Vernon JOHNSON, Jr., implying there was a Vernon JOHNSON, Sr. She had three sons with Curtis Lee BURNSIDE:

i   Anthony BURNSIDE (b. Unknown, d. AFT 2004 when his mother died).
Ii   Willie BURNSIDE (b. Unknown, d. AFT 2004 when his mother died).
iii   Charles BURNSIDE (b. Unknown, d. AFT 2004 when his mother died).

---

[782] Dana Burnside originally shared this on 22 Aug 2021 on *Ancestry.com*.
[783] "Obituary for Bernice Burnside," *The Commercial Appeal,* Memphis, TN, 20 Oct 2004, p. 18; digital image, s.v. "Anitha Perkins," <https://www.newspapers.com/image/775551073/?article=5d30f047-4087-4788-b84d-0e8f2355474b&focus=0.061804228,0.4818563,0.22532617,0.57242304&xid=3355>, *Newspapers.com*.

Anetha TERRY (Carnes TERRY, Joseph TERRY, Caroline, Aaron Whitaker, Aaron Steele, Joseph I, John I, Samuel II, Samuel I, John)

Anetha TERRY was the daughter of Fred Carnes TERRY (b. 7 Oct 1907 Sallis, Attala Co., MS, d. Jun 1973 Jackson, Hinds Co., MS)[784] and Callie Beatrice McMICHAEL (b. 20 Sep 1915 MS, d. 19 May 1979 Memphis, Shelby Co., TN).[785] Anetha was born after 1940 and died 15 Jul 1922 in McAdams, Attala Co., MS).[786] She married Unknown PERKINS (Unknown).[787]

Velma Ruth GUYTON (Stella Mae TERRY GUYTON, Joseph TERRY, Caroline, Aaron Whitaker, Aaron Steele, Joseph I, John I, Samuel II, Samuel I, John)

Velma Ruth GUYTON was the daughter of Stella Mae TERRY (b. 17 Aug 1912 Sallis, Attala Co., MS, d. 1 Jan 1993 Lexington, Holmes Co., MS)[788] and Joe Dale (Joe D.) GUYTON (b. 24 Dec 1901 MS, d. Dec 1967 Sallis, Attala Co., MS).[789]

Velma Ruth GUYTON was born on 27 Nov 1929 in Mississippi, but her death is unknown.[790] She married Unknown CROSS. Information from Channie BROWN-CURRIE suggests they had three children. Velma had two other children.

i   Judy GUYTON m. Tony PERNELL (Unknown).
ii   Leo GUYTON (Unknown).
iii   Marie CROSS (Unknown) m. Robert GILMORE (Unknown).
iv   Faye CROSS (Unknown).
v   June CROSS (Unknown) m. Lee TUBBS (Unknown).

---

[784] "Social Security Death Index," s.v. "Fred Terry," (birth 7 Oct 1907, death Jun 1973), *Ancestry.com*.
[785] Callie Beatrice McMichael, grave marker, Hollywood Cemetery, Memphis, Shelby Co., TN, digital image s.v. "Callie Beatrice Terry Anthony," (birth 20 Sep 1915, death 19 May 1979), *FindaGrave.com*.
[786] "Obituary for Bernice Burnside," *The Commercial Appeal,* Memphis, TN, 20 Oct 2004, p. 18; digital image, s.v. "Anitha Perkins," <https://www.newspapers.com/image/775551073/?article=5d30f047-4087-4788-b84d-0e8f2355474b&focus=0.061804228,0.4818563,0.22532617,0.57242304&xid=3355>, *Newspapers.com*. "Obituary for Bernice Burnside," *The Commercial Appeal,* Memphis, TN, 20 Oct 2004, p. 18; digital image, s.v. "Anitha Perkins," *Newspapers.com*.
[787] "Obituary for Bernice Burnside," *The Commercial Appeal,* Memphis, TN, 20 Oct 2004, p. 18; digital image, s.v. "Anitha Perkins," <https://www.newspapers.com/image/775551073/?article=5d30f047-4087-4788-b84d-0e8f2355474b&focus=0.061804228,0.4818563,0.22532617,0.57242304&xid=3355>, *Newspapers.com*.
[788] Stella Mae Terry, grave marker, Mallett Cemetery, Attala Co., MS, digital image s.v. "Stella Mae Guyton," (birth 17 Aug 1912, death 1 Jan 1993), *FindaGrave.com*.
[789] "Social Security Death Index," s.v. "Joe Guyton," (birth 24 Dec 1901, death Dec 1967), *Ancestry.com*.
[790] "1930 United States Federal Census," Beat 4, Attala Co., MS, digital image s.v. "Vilma Ruth Gytor," (birth abt 1928), *Ancestry.com*. "U.S., Public Records Index, 1950-1993, Volume 1," s.v. "Velma Ruth Cross," (birth 27 Nov 1929), *Ancestry.com*.

Joe Frank GUYTON, Sr. (Stella Mae TERRY GUYTON, Joseph TERRY, Caroline, Aaron Whitaker, Aaron Steele, Joseph I, John I, Samuel II, Samuel I, John)

Joe Frank GUYTON, Sr. was the son of Stella Mae TERRY (b. 17 Aug 1912 Sallis, Attala Co., MS, d. 1 Jan 1993 Lexington, Holmes Co., MS)[791] and Joe Dale (Joe D.) GUYTON (b. 24 Dec 1901 MS, d. Dec 1967 Sallis, Attala Co., MS).[792]

Joe Frank GUYTON, Sr. was born on 20 Aug 1930 Attala Co., MS, d. 10 Sep 1994 Kosciusko, Attala Co., MS.[793] He married Allene HUTCHINS (b. 6 Jan 1937 Kosciusko, Attala Co.,, MS, d. 11 Dec 2019 Jackson, Hinds Co., MS).[794] Allene HUTCHINS was the twin sister of Irene HUTCHINS, who married Joe Frank's brother, Ike Young GUYTON.

The couple had at least three children, per Joe Frank GUYTON, Sr.'s obituary. See Figure 83.

> **Joe Frank Guyton**
>
> Services for Joe Frank Guyton, 64, of Sallis, were held Sept. 15 at 11 a.m. at Winters Funeral Home Chapel with burial in Mallett Cemetery.
>
> Guyton, a retired factory worker, died Sept. 10, 1994 at his residence. He was a native of Attala County and a member of Palestine Baptist Church.
>
> He is survived by his wife, Mrs. Allean H. Guyton; a daughter, Mrs. Sylvia G. Hunt of Sallis; two sons, Joe F. Guyton of Kosciusko, Terrance Guyton of Sallis;
>
> Also four sisters, Mrs. Sadie Little of Sallis, Mrs. Johnnie L. Dotson, Mrs. Stellerole Dotson of Ecorse, Mi. and Mrs. Velma R. Cross of Chicago, Ill.; two brothers, Jimmy D. Guyton of Sallis, David Guyton of Milwaukee, Wis.; four grandchildren and one great-grandchild.
>
> The Rev. William Hawthorne officiated.

Figure 83 Joe Frank GUYTON, Sr.'s Obituary[795]

---

[791] Stella Mae Terry, grave marker, Mallett Cemetery, Attala Co., MS, digital image s.v. "Stella Mae Guyton," (birth 17 Aug 1912, death 1 Jan 1993), *FindaGrave.com*.
[792] "Social Security Death Index," s.v. "Joe Guyton," (birth 24 Dec 1901, death Dec 1967), *Ancestry.com*.
[793] Joe Frank Guyton, Sr., grave marker, Mallett Cemetery, Attala Co., MS, digital image s.v. "Joe Frank Guyton Sr," (birth 20 Aug 1930, death 10 Sep 1994), *FindaGrave.com*.
[794] Allene Hutchins, grave marker, Mallett Cemetery, Attala Co., MS, digital image s.v. "Allene Guyton," (birth 6 Jan 1937, death 11 Dec 2019), *FindaGrave.com*.
[795] "Obituary for Joe Frank Guyton, Sr.," *The Star-Herald,* Kosciusko, Attala Co., MS, 22 Sep 1994, p. 6; digital image, s.v. "Joe Frank Guyton," <https://www.newspapers.com/article/the-star-herald-joe-frank-guyton-obituar/131560656/>, *Newspapers.com.*

Allene HUTCHINS GUYTON's obituary from her *FindaGrave* entry is given below:

"I have fought the good fight, I have finished the race, I have kept the faith. II Timothy 4:7-8. Allene Hutchins GUYTON was born on January 6, 1937, to the late Mr. Jesse & Mrs. Adline Hutchins. She received her education in the Attala County School District. As a young child, she confessed her life to Christ and became a member of Palestine M.B. Church in Sallis, MS. On January 2, 1954, she was joined in Holy Matrimony to Joe Frank GUYTON. To this union, they were Blessed with three children- Joe (Clara) of Winona, MS, Terrance (Lena) of Sallis, MS and Sylvia (Tyrone) of Kosciusko, MS. On December 11, 2019, at University of Mississippi Medical Center, her Heavenly Father reached down and touched her calling her home to eternal rest and peace. She leaves to cherish the warmth of her presence and smile: four sisters, Christine NASH, Lorene HAYWOOD, Twin sister Irene GUYTON (all of Sallis, MS) and Viola McCALL of Milwaukee, WI; six grandchildren and a host of nieces, nephews, relatives and friends. Her father, mother, two sisters and four brothers preceded her in death.

Ike Young GUYTON (Stella Mae TERRY GUYTON, Joseph TERRY, Caroline, Aaron Whitaker, Aaron Steele, Joseph I, John I, Samuel II, Samuel I, John)

Ike Young GUYTON was the son of Stella Mae TERRY (b. 17 Aug 1912 Sallis, Attala Co., MS, d. 1 Jan 1993 Lexington, Holmes Co., MS)[796] and Joe Dale (Joe D.) GUYTON (b. 24 Dec 1901 MS, d. Dec 1967 Sallis, Attala Co., MS).[797] Ike Young GUYTON was born on 19 Jun 1933 in Mississippi, and died on 20 May 1984 in Sallis, Attala Co., MS.[798] He married Irene HUTCHINS (b. 6 Jan 1937 Kosciusko, Attala Co., MS., d 6 Jan 2021 Jackson, Hinds Co., MS).[799] Irene was the twin sister of Allene HUTCHINS. She married Ike's brother, Joe Frank GUYTON, Sr.

They had at least two children:[800]

i   Kennedy (or Kent) GUYTON (b. Sallis, Attala Co., MS, d. Unknown).
ii   Ellene Sue GUYTON (b. Sallis, Attala Co., MS, d. Unknown) m. Roy HARMAN (Unknown).

---

[796] Stella Mae Terry, grave marker, Mallett Cemetery, Attala Co., MS, digital image s.v. "Stella Mae Guyton," (birth 17 Aug 1912, death 1 Jan 1993), *FindaGrave.com*.
[797] "Social Security Death Index," s.v. "Joe Guyton," (birth 24 Dec 1901, death Dec 1967), *Ancestry.com*.
[798] Ike Young Guyton, grave marker, Mallett Cemetery, Attala Co., MS, digital image s.v. "Ike Young Guyton," (birth 9 Jun 1933, death 20 May 1984), *FindaGrave.com*.
[799] Irene Hutchins, grave marker, Mallett Cemetery, Attala Co., MS, digital image s.v. "Irene Guyton," (birth 6 Jan 1937, death 6 Jan 2021), *FindaGrave.com*.
[800] Per Channie Brown-Currie.

Stellie Rose GUYTON (Stella Mae TERRY GUYTON, Joseph TERRY, Caroline, Aaron Whitaker, Aaron Steele, Joseph I, John I, Samuel II, Samuel I, John)

Stellie Rose GUYTON was the daughter of Stella Mae TERRY (b. 17 Aug 1912 Sallis, Attala Co., MS, d. 1 Jan 1993 Lexington, Holmes Co., MS)[801] and Joe Dale (Joe D.) GUYTON (b. 24 Dec 1901 MS, d. Dec 1967 Sallis, Attala Co., MS).[802] Joe D. was the son of Simon and Viola GUYTON. He is first cousin once-removed to Stella Mae.

Stellie Rose GUYTON was born in Mar 1940 in MS, and I do not know her death).[803] She married Evell DOTSON (b. 1 Sep 1936 Attala Co., MS, d. 1 Jan 1991 Lincoln Park, Wayne Co., MI).[804]

In 1960, the couple lived in Memphis, Shelby Co., MS.[805] Evell worked as a driver for Midsouth Aggregates, Inc. They lived at 1612 ½ Rice Street. They shared the house which Ernest DOTSON, who might be Evell's brother. The house is shown below in Figure 84 from *Google Earth*. In 1993, they lived in Ecourse, MI at 3902 17th St. *Google Earth* is not clear whether this is the exact house but the homes on the street are similar. See Figure 85.

Figure 84 Evell and Stellie GUYTON DOTSON's House in Memphis, TN in 1960

Figure 85 The Dotson Home in Ecorse, Michigan

---

[801] Stella Mae Terry, grave marker, Mallett Cemetery, Attala Co., MS, digital image s.v. "Stella Mae Guyton," (birth 17 Aug 1912, death 1 Jan 1993), *FindaGrave.com*.
[802] "Social Security Death Index," s.v. "Joe Guyton," (birth 24 Dec 1901, death Dec 1967), *Ancestry.com*.
[803] "U.S., Index to Public Records, 1994-2019," s.v. "Stellie Rose Dotson," (birth Mar 1940), *Ancestry.com*.
[804] "U.S., Department of Veterans Affairs BIRLS Death File, 1850-2010," s.v. "E Dotson," (birth 1 Sep 1936, death 1 Jan 1991), *Ancestry.com*.
[805] "U.S., City Directories, 1822-1995," digital image s.v. "Evell Dotson," (lived in Memphis, TN in 1960), *Ancestry.com*.

The couple had at least four children:[806]

i   Ernie Vedel DOTSON (b. 6 Feb 1963 Ecorse, Wayne Co., MI, d. 18 Mar 2015 Dearborn, Wayne Co., MI)[807] m. Esther MILES (Unknown).
ii   Diane DOTSON (Unknown) m. Unknown FERGUSON (Unknown).
iii   Ruby DOTSON (Unknown).
iv   Danny DOTSON (Unknown).

Hubert GUYTON (Stella Mae TERRY GUYTON, Joseph TERRY, Caroline, Aaron Whitaker, Aaron Steele, Joseph I, John I, Samuel II, Samuel I, John)

Hubert GUYTON was the son of Stella Mae TERRY (b. 17 Aug 1912 Sallis, Attala Co., MS, d. 1 Jan 1993 Lexington, Holmes Co., MS)[808] and Joe Dale (Joe D.) GUYTON (b. 24 Dec 1901 MS, d. Dec 1967 Sallis, Attala Co., MS).[809] Joe D. was the son of Simon and Viola GUYTON. He is first cousin once-removed to Stella Mae. Hubert GUYTON was born on 25 Aug 1945 in Attala Co., MS, and died on 14 Feb 1988 in Jackson, Hinds Co., MS.[810] He married Judy Kate ALLEN (Unknown).[811]

Hubert's obituary was uploaded to his *FindaGrave entry:*[812]

Services for Hubert Guyton of Sallis, MS; were held Saturday at noon at Palestine M. B. Church. Guyton, 42, died Feb. 14, 1988, at the University Medical Center in Jackson, MS. He was a native of Attala County, MS; and a member of Palestine M. B. Church. He is survived by his wife, Mrs. Judy Kate ALLEN GUYTON; two daughters, Theresa GUYTON of Sallis, MS; and Angelia STEWART of TX; a son, Johnny GUYTON of CA; also our sisters, Mrs. Sadie LITTLE of Sallis, MS; Mrs. Johnnie Lavel DOTSON, Mrs. Stellerole [Stellie Rose] DOTSON of Detroit, MI; and Mrs. Velma Ruth CROSS of Chicago, IL; three brothers, Joe Frank GUYTON, Jimmy Dell GUYTON of Sallis, MS; and David GUYTON of Milwaukee, WI; one grandchild. Burial in Mallett Cemetery. Rev. F. Y. Clark officiated. Winters Funeral Home handled arrangements.

---

[806] Per Channie Brown-Currie.
[807] "U.S., Obituary Collection, 1930-Current," s.v. (Ernie V. Dotson), (birth 6 Feb 1963, death 4 Apr 2015), *Ancestry.com*. His wife, Esther, is mentioned.
[808] Stella Mae Terry, grave marker, Mallett Cemetery, Attala Co., MS, digital image s.v. "Stella Mae Guyton," (birth 17 Aug 1912, death 1 Jan 1993), *FindaGrave.com*.
[809] "Social Security Death Index," s.v. "Joe Guyton," (birth 24 Dec 1901, death Dec 1967), *Ancestry.com*.
[810] Hubert Guyton, grave marker, Mallett Cemetery, Attala Co., MS, digital image s.v. "Hubert Guyton," (birth 25 Aug 1945, death 14 Feb 1988), *FindaGrave.com*.
[811] See Hubert Guyton's *FindaGrave* record.
[812] "Obituary for Hubert Guyton," *The Star-Herald*, Kosciusko, Attala Co., MS, 25 Feb 1988, Thu, p. 6; digital image, s.v. "Hubert Guyton," <https://www.newspapers.com/image/305204771/?article=74d46647-cf1b-483b-bd36-26051996b0d7&focus=0.49923432,0.63991016,0.65022403,0.70669734&xid=3355>, *Newspapers.com*.

Hubert and Judy had at least three children, per Hubert GUYTON's obituary:

i   Johnny GUYTON (Unknown) lived in California at his father's death.
ii Theresa GUYTON (Unknown) lived in Sallis at his father's death.
iii Angelia GUYTON (Unknown) m. Unknown STEWART (Unknown). She lived in Texas when her father died.

Michael Joseph TERRY, Sr. (Lockett Joseph TERRY, Sr., Green TERRY, Caroline, Aaron Whitaker, Aaron Steele, Joseph I, John I, Samuel II, Samuel I, John)

Michael Joseph TERRY, Sr. was the son of Lockett Joseph TERRY, Sr. (b. 20 Aug 1904 MS, d. Nov 1980 St. Louis, St. Louis Co., MO),[813] who was married to (1) Gertrude CRANE (b. ABT 1917 AR, d. Unknown)[814] and divorced around 1943; and (2) Mary Elizabeth MITCHELL (b. 14 Jul 1914 Edwardsville, Madison Co., IL, d. Aug 1986 St Louis, MO).[815] I believe he was the son of Mary MITCHELL, but I cannot be sure. If he was her son, then he was born when his father was still married to Gertrude CRANE.

Michael Joseph TERRY, Sr. was born on 8 Feb 1939 in St. Louis, MO, and died on 17 Jan 2022 in Hinesville, Georgia.[816] He served in the U.S. Army as a Sergeant First Class, which explains why he lived in numerous places. He served during the Vietnam War period. He is buried at Section B Row 19 Site 911 at Georgia Veterans Memorial Cemetery in Glennville, GA. The address is: 8819 US Highway Glennville, GA 30427. See Figure 86.

Figure 86 Headstone of Michael Joseph TERRY, Sr.

---

[813] Lockett Joseph Terry, Sr., grave marker, St. Peter's Cemetery, Normandy, St. Louis Co., MO, digital image s.v. "Lockett Joseph Terry, Sr.," (birth 20 Aug 1904, death Nov 1980), *FindaGrave.com*.
[814] "1930 United States Census," Jackson, Hinds Co., MS, digital image s.v. "Gertrude Terry," (birth abt 1908), *Ancestry.com*.
[815] "Social Security Death Index," s.v. "Mary Terry," (birth 14 Jul 1914, death Aug 1986), *Ancestry.com*. "Missouri, U.S., Death Records, 1968-2015," s.v. "Mary E. Terry," (death 1 Aug 1986), *Ancestry.com*.
[816] Michael Joseph Terry, Sr., grave marker, Georgia Veterans Memorial Cemetery, Glennville, Tattnall Co., GA, digital image s.v. "Michael Joseph Terry Sr," (birth 8 Feb 1939, death 17 Jan 2022), *FindaGrave.com*.

While I do not know his spouse(s), his children are as follows:[817]

i	Michael Joseph TERRY, Jr. (Unknown).
ii	Sarah Elizabeth TERRY (Unknown).
iii	Delgardo TERRY (Unknown).
iv	Taffanye Michel TERRY (Unknown).
v	Bryford Andre TERRY (Unknown).
vi	Michael TERRY (why are there two Michaels?) (Unknown).

---

[817] "U.S., Obituary Collection, 1930-Current," s.v. "Michael Joseph Terry," (birth 8 Feb 1939, death 17 Jan 2022), *Ancestry.com*.

CHILD OF AARON WHITAKER GUYTON AND PATSY GIBSON: PINKNEY'S LINE
Generation #7

Pinkney (Pink) GUYTON (Aaron Whitaker, Aaron Steele, Joseph I, John I, Samuel II, Samuel I, John)

Pinkney GUYTON was born about 1848 in Attala Co., MS.[818] His father was likely Aaron Whitaker GUYTON (born in 1808 in Anderson Co., SC, d. between 1881 and 1883, Sallis, Attala Co., MS. Patsy GIBSON has been attributed his mother.[819] As discussed in the earlier section on Aaron Whitaker GUYTON, Pinkney was likely the 2-year-old boy in Aaron's household in the 1850 U.S. Census Slave Schedule. In the 1860 Census, Pinkney was likely the 12-year-old boy in Aaron's household.

Pinkney (age 22) and Elijah (age 21) GUYTON lived in Aaron's household in Beat 4, Attala Co., MS under their own names in the 1870 U.S. Census.[820] Although the 1870 U.S. Census did not collect relationship information, it did collect race. The young men were shown as mulattoes, or of mixed race. Living with Whit was another young man, Allen BART, a 15-year-old mulatto of unknown relationship with Aaron. His last name may be Burt, rather than Bart.

It appears that Pinkney married Ellen SANDERS in 1868 in Tippah Co., MS.[821] It is not a certainty that this is the Pinkney GUYTON we are looking for. I cannot find any other information about Ellen. According to Pinkney's descendant, Nic STARR, "I cannot find any other information about Ellen. I am certain that Grandpa Pink did not have another wife. I saw this record, too, and could not find any more info about her. However, I did put a call in to Odell, Pink's last remaining grandchild, and she said that the record had to be a mistake. She cared for Pink and Fannie herself in their final days. The only Ellen that Odell ever knew was Ellen RUSSELL, Lawson GUYTON's wife.

Pink GUYTON and Fannie SALLIS (b. Oct 1855, d. AFT 1940)[822] were logged as married in the 1880 U.S. Census and they lived in Kosciusko, Attala Co., MS.[823] They married in 1874 per the 1900 U.S. Census.[824] See Figure 87. They reported three children in the 1880 U.S. Census, the oldest being Emma

---

[818] "1860 U.S. Federal Census - Slave Schedules," digital image s.v. "Pinkney Guyton," (birth ABT 1848), *Ancestry.com*.
[819] Guyton, David F., "African Americans," Guyton Ancestry, accessed 31 May 2020. <http://guyton.co.uk/america-african>. Ashford, Evan, "The Privilege of Blackness: Black Empowerment and the Fight for Liberation in Attala County, Mississippi 1865-1915" (2018). Doctoral Dissertations. 1417. <https://scholarworks.umass.edu/dissertations_2/1417>.
[820] "1870 United States Census," Attala Co., MS, digital image s.v. "Penkey Guyton," (birth ABT 1848), *Ancestry.com*.
[821] "Mississippi Marriages, 1776-1935," Tippah Co., MS, s.v. "Pinkney Guyton," (marriage 1868), *Ancestry.com*.
[822] "1900 United States Census," Kosciusko, Attala County, Mississippi, digital image s.v. "Fannie Guyton," (birth Oct 1855), *Ancestry.com*. Her birth date ranges from 1853 to 1857. She last appears in the 1940 U.S. Census. "1940 United States Census," Kosciusko, Attala County, Mississippi, digital image s.v. "Fannie Guyton," (birth ABT 1855), *Ancestry.com*.
[823] "1880 United States Census," Attala Co., MS, digital image s.v. "Pinckney Guyton," (birth ABT 1845), *Ancestry.com*.
[824] "1900 United States Census," Attala Co., MS, digital image s.v. "Pink Guyton," (marriage 1874), *Ancestry.com*.

GUYTON, 5-years-old. They also had Patsy GUYTON (2-years-old) and Isolome (Icy) GUYTON (8 months old).

Figure 87 Fannie SALLIS and Pinkney GUYTON

On 1 Jan 1875, shortly before Pinkney's marriage, Whit GUYTON conveyed 160 acres to Pink GUYTON and Elijah GUYTON in Land Deed Book O, p. 639.[825]

The 1880 Alabama State Census for Attala Co., MS, shows both Pinkney and Elijah GUYTON. They were farmers and each produced 6 bales of cotton in 1879.[826] See Figure 88. Pinkney was a farmer and Fannie was a homemaker. Pinkney could not read or write, but Fannie could. In the 1900 U.S. Census, Pinkney reportedly owned his farm but it was mortgaged.[827] Per the 1910 U.S. Census, Pink and Fannie owned their farm free and clear.[828] The land must have been subsequently mortgaged because in 1916, the family lost the land due to missing payments. See discussion below. In 1920 U.S. Census, their son Amzy was the head of the household.[829]

---

[825] Source on *Ancestry.com* is given as: David F Guyton Springfield, 22 Lache Lane, Chester CH4 7LR, England E-mail: DFGuyton@compuserve.com Courtesy of Ann Breedlove genealogy librarian Attala County, Mississippi. In the posted document, the ultimate source of the information was a letter from John D. Guyton, written on 22 Jul 2002.
[826] "State Census Returns 1880, Box 2614," *Mississippi, U.S., State Archives, Various Records, 1820-1951*, digital image s.v. "Pinkney Guyton," *Ancestry.com*.
[827] "1900 United States Census," Kosciusko, Attala Co., MS, digital image s.v. "Pink Guyton," (birth Jan 1848, owned mortgaged farm), *Ancestry.com*.
[828] "1910 United States Census," Beat 1, Attala Co., MS, digital image s.v. "Pinckney Guyton," (birth ABT 1850, owned non-mortgaged farm), *Ancestry.com*.
[829] "1920 United States Census," Kosciusko, Attala Co., MS, digital image s.v. "Pink Guyton," (birth ABT 1848), *Ancestry.com*.

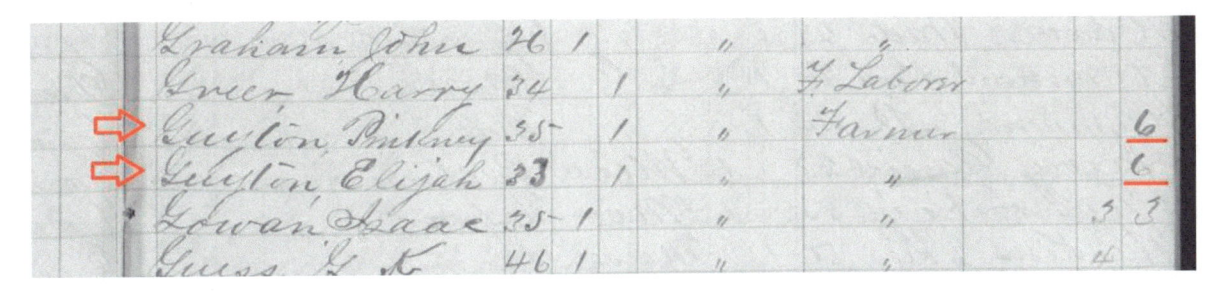

Figure 88 1880 Alabama Census of Males Over 21

Pinkney GUYTON and Fannie SALLIS had at least the following children:

i Emma GUYTON (b. Jun 1874 MS, d. BEF 1920 Attala Co., MS)[830] m. Addison D. ALLEN (b. Dec 1872 Attala Co., MS, d. 1963 Chicago, Cook Co., IL).[831]
ii Patsy J. GUYTON (b. Aug 1877 Sallis, Attala Co., MS, d. Jun 1938 Sallis, Attala Co., MS)[832] m. William (Willie) ROBY (b. Mar 1876 MS, d. May 1969 Sallis, Attala Co., MS).[833] They divorced before 1930.[834]
iii Agnes Isolome (Icy) GUYTON (b. Sep 1879 Kosciusko, South Beat 1, Attala Co., MS, d. 1963 Kosciusko, Attala Co., MS)[835] m. Albert GAMBLE (b. 15 Dec 1875 Shuqualak Township 13, Noxubee Co., MS, d. 1948 Kosciusko, Attala Co., MS).[836]
iv William Amzy GUYTON, Sr. (b. 24 Feb 1885 Attala Co., MS, d. 6 Jun 1949 Attala Co., MS)[837] m. Limmie Mae Douglas NASH (b. 8 Feb 1910 MS, d. 28 Sep 1944, MS).[838]
v Suegene GUYTON (b. 21 Dec 1887 MS, d. May 1976 Kosciusko, Attala Co., MS)[839] m. Dock WRIGHT (b. 31 Mar 1882 MS, d. 22 Jun 1969, bur. Wright Cemetery).[840]

The Star-Herald in Kosciusko, MS, published on Friday, 10 Nov 1916, a "Trustee's Sale" of Pink, Fannie, and son, Amzy's, Attala Co., MS property.[841] See Figure 89. This is the digitized copy of the original microfilmed published article announcing the trustee's sale of property of a deed made on 16 Jul

---

[830] "1900 United States Census," Attala Co., MS, digital image s.v. "Emma A. Allen," (birth Jun 1874), Ancestry.com. I assume she died before 1920 because I could not find her in the 1920 U.S. Census.
[831] "1900 United States Census," Attala Co., MS, digital image s.v. "Addison D Allen," (birth Dec 1872), Ancestry.com.
[832] "1900 United States Census," Attala Co., MS, digital image s.v. "Patsy J. Roby," (birth Aug 1877), Ancestry.com. I assume she died after 1950 because she was in the 1950 U.S. Census. "1950 United States Census," Newport, Attala Co., MS, digital image s.v. "Patsy Robey," (birth ABT 1877), Ancestry.com.
[833] "1900 United States Census," Attala Co., MS, digital image s.v. "Will Roby," (birth Mar 1876), Ancestry.com.
[834] "1930 United States Census," Attala Co., MS, digital image s.v. "Will Roby," (marital status divorced), Ancestry.com.
[835] Agnes Isolome Guyton, grave marker, Nash Cemetery, Leake County, MS, digital image s.v. "Agnes Icy Gamble," (birth Sep 1879, death 1963), FindaGrave.com.
[836] Albert Gamble, grave marker, Nash Cemetery, Leake County, MS, digital image s.v. "Albert Gamble," (birth 15 Dec 1875, death 1948), FindaGrave.com.
[837] Amzy William Guyton, grave marker, Mallett Cemetery, Attala County, MS, digital image s.v. "Amzy William Guyton," (birth 28 Feb 1885, death 6 Jun 1949), FindaGrave.com.
[838] Limmie Mae Douglas Nash, grave marker, Mallett Cemetery, Attala Co., MS, digital image s.v. "Limmie Guyton," (birth 8 Feb 1910, death 28 Sep 1944), FindaGrave.com.
[839] Suegene Guyton, grave marker, Wright Cemetery, Attala Co., MS, digital image s.v. "Sugena Wright," (birth 29 Dec 1888, death 1 May 1976), FindaGrave.com.
[840] Dock Wright, grave marker, Wright Cemetery, Attala Co., MS, digital image s.v. "Dock Wright," (birth 31 Mar 1882, death 22 Jun 1969), FindaGrave.com.
[841] "Trustee's Sale," *The Star-Herald*, Kosciusko, Attala Co., MS, Friday, 10 Nov 1916, Newspapers.com.

1913, to Mrs. M. SIMON and G. Loewenburg & Co.in Attala Co., MS. According to *Investopedia*, "deed of trust is a document sometimes used in financed real estate transactions, generally instead of a mortgage. Deeds of trust transfer the legal title of a property to a third party—such as a bank, escrow company, or title company—to hold until the borrower repays their debt to the lender." Deeds of trust are less common than they once were, but Mississippi is one of about twenty states that still mandate the use of one when financing is involved in the purchase of real estate.[842]

The article below describes the property owned by Pinkney, Fannie, and their son, Amzy, which had to be sold to satisfy a loan based on the value of the property. Go to Figure 90, Figure 91, and Figure 92 to see the land referenced in the newspaper article. According to Karl Glenn BOYD (aka Nykki Lamarr STARR), this land was given to Pinkney by his father, Aaron Whitaker GUYTON. If so, then we know Whit GUYTON owned more property than the one documented sale suggests. The Section 23 property would be approximately 120 acres. The Section 26 property would account for another 80 acres.

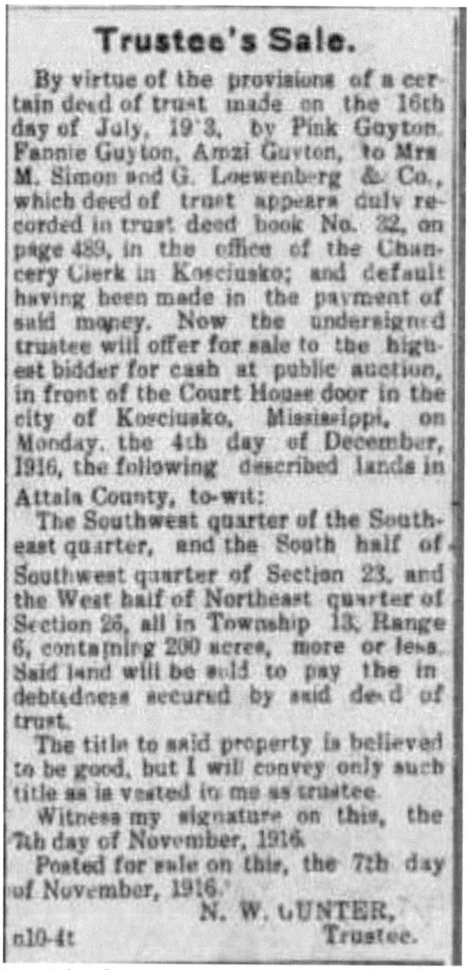

Trustee's Sale.

By virtue of the provisions of a certain deed of trust made on the 16th day of July, 19'3, by Pink Guyton, Fannie Guyton, Amzi Guyton, to Mrs M. Simon and G. Loewenberg & Co., which deed of trust appears duly recorded in trust deed book No. 32, on page 489, in the office of the Chancery Clerk in Kosciusko; and default having been made in the payment of said money. Now the undersigned trustee will offer for sale to the highest bidder for cash at public auction, in front of the Court House door in the city of Kosciusko, Mississippi, on Monday, the 4th day of December, 1916, the following described lands in Attala County, to-wit:

The Southwest quarter of the Southeast quarter, and the South half of Southwest quarter of Section 23, and the West half of Northeast quarter of Section 26, all in Township 13, Range 6, containing 200 acres, more or less. Said land will be sold to pay the indebtedness secured by said deed of trust.

The title to said property is believed to be good, but I will convey only such title as is vested in me as trustee.

Witness my signature on this, the 7th day of November, 1916.

Posted for sale on this, the 7th day of November, 1916.

N. W. GUNTER,
Trustee.

n10-4t

Figure 89 Deed of Trust Sale of Property Mortgaged by Pink, Fannie, and Amzy GUYTON

[842] "Deed of Trust," *Investopedia*, <https://www.investopedia.com/deed-of-trust-definition>.

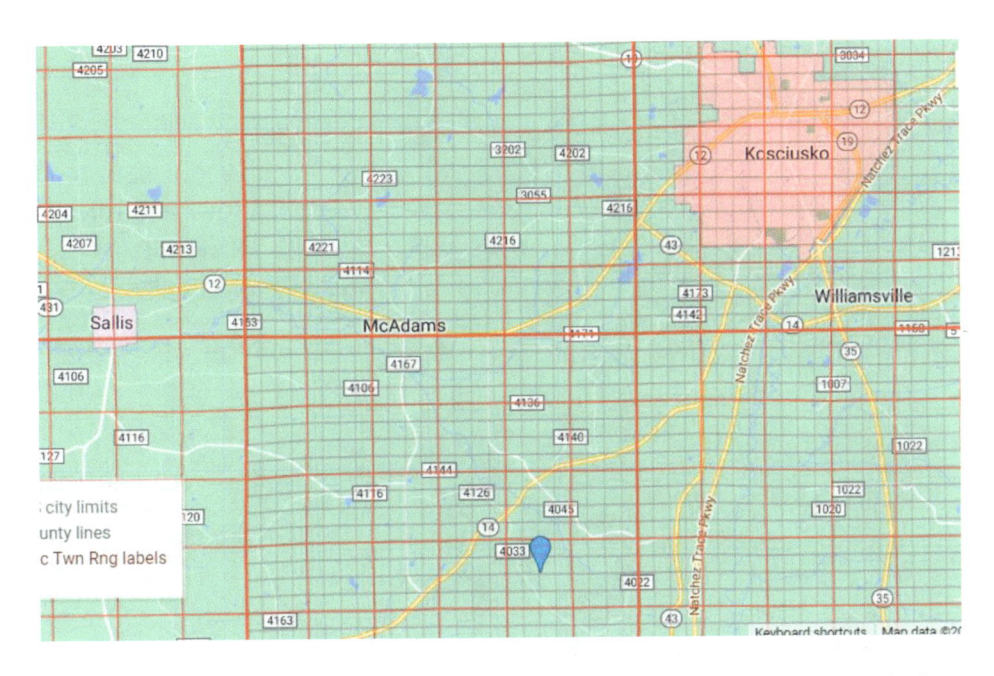

Figure 90 Blue Pin in Center of Section 23, Township 13N, Range 6E; Section 26 is Immediately South of Section 23[843]

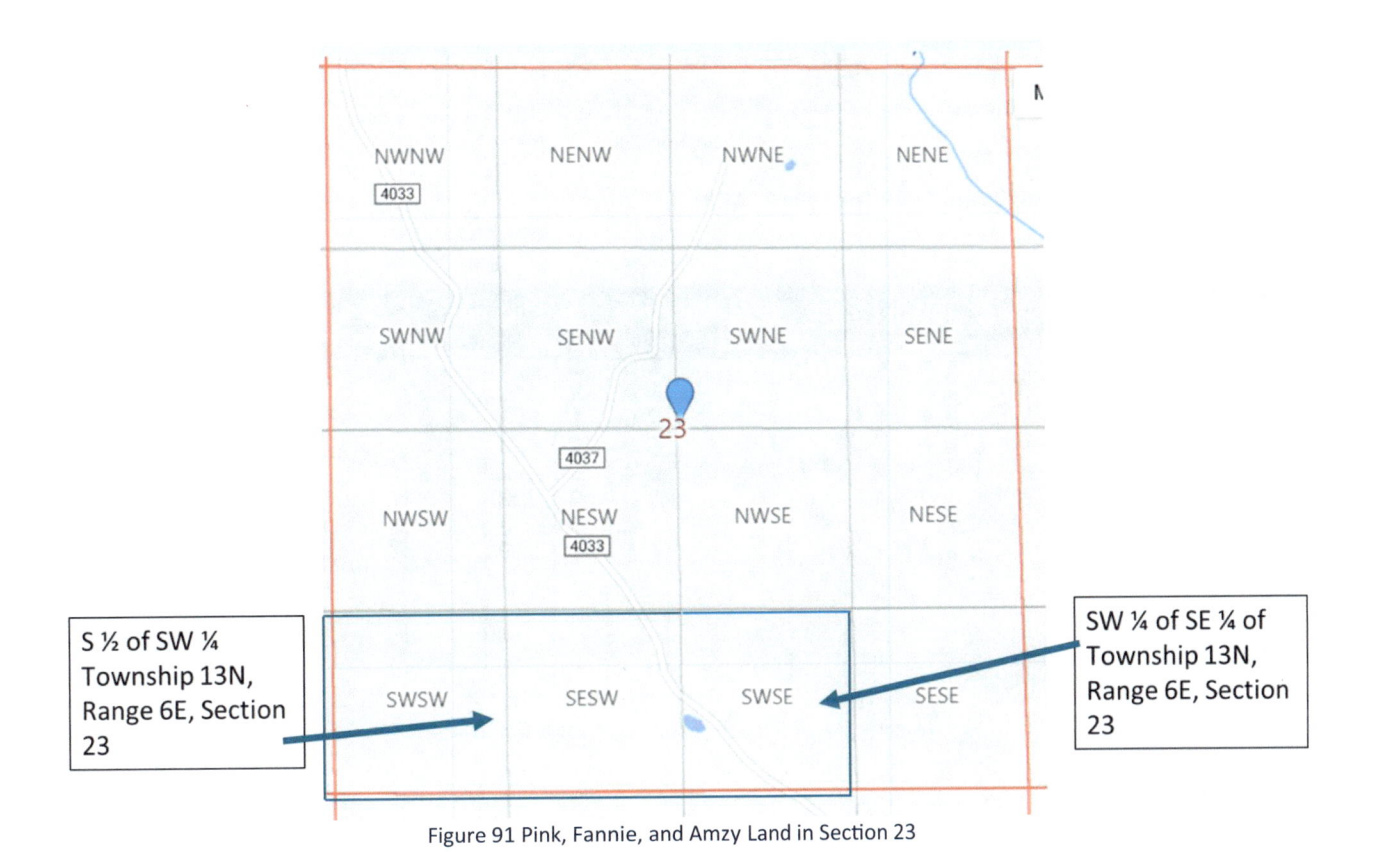

Figure 91 Pink, Fannie, and Amzy Land in Section 23

---

[843] Used <https://www.randymajors.org> to create the maps in the two figures.

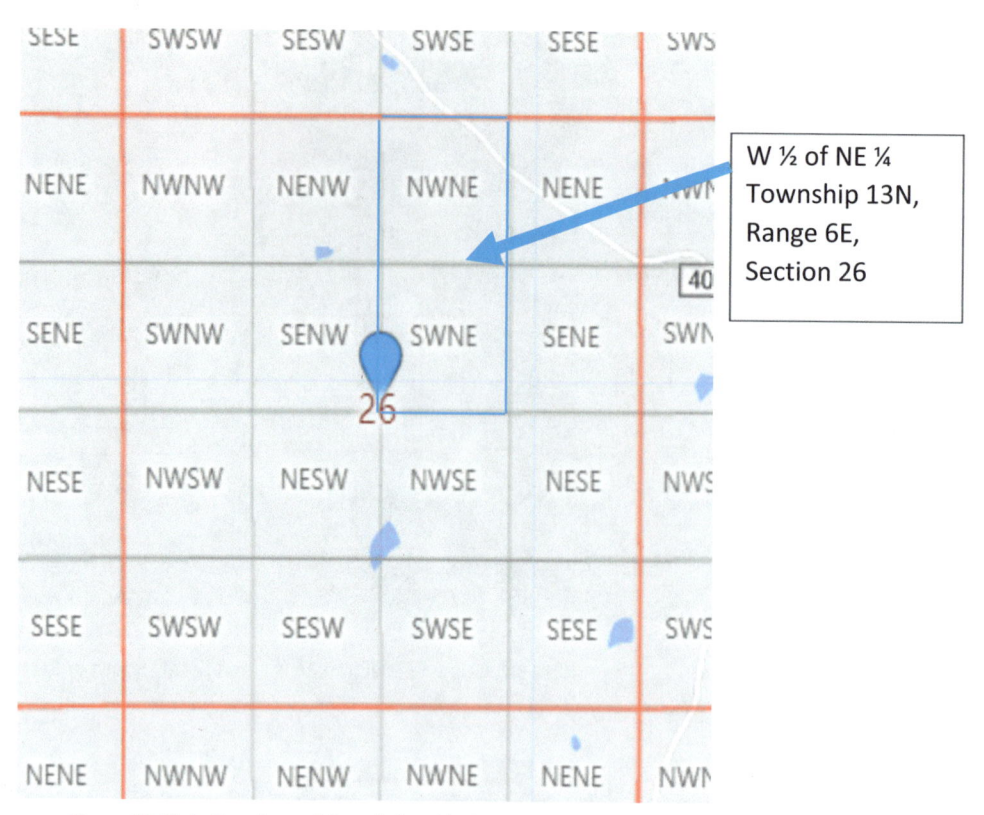

Figure 92 Pink, Fannie, and Amzy's Land in Section 26; Section 26 is Immediately South of Section 23

Pinkney died on 27 Aug 1929 (per Nic STARR) or 2 Aug 1929 in Kosciusko, Attala Co., MS.[844] See Figure 93[845] and Figure 94.[846]

Figure 93 Pinkney GUYTON in Mississippi Death Index

---

[844] "Mississippi, U.S., Index to Deaths, 1912-1943," digital image s.v. "Pink Guyton," (death Aug 1929), Ancestry.com.
[845] "Mississippi, U.S., Index to Deaths, 1912-1943," digital image s.v. "Pink Guyton," (death Sep 1929).
[846] Mississippi, Death Certificates, "Pink Guyton," (1848-1929), personal copy.

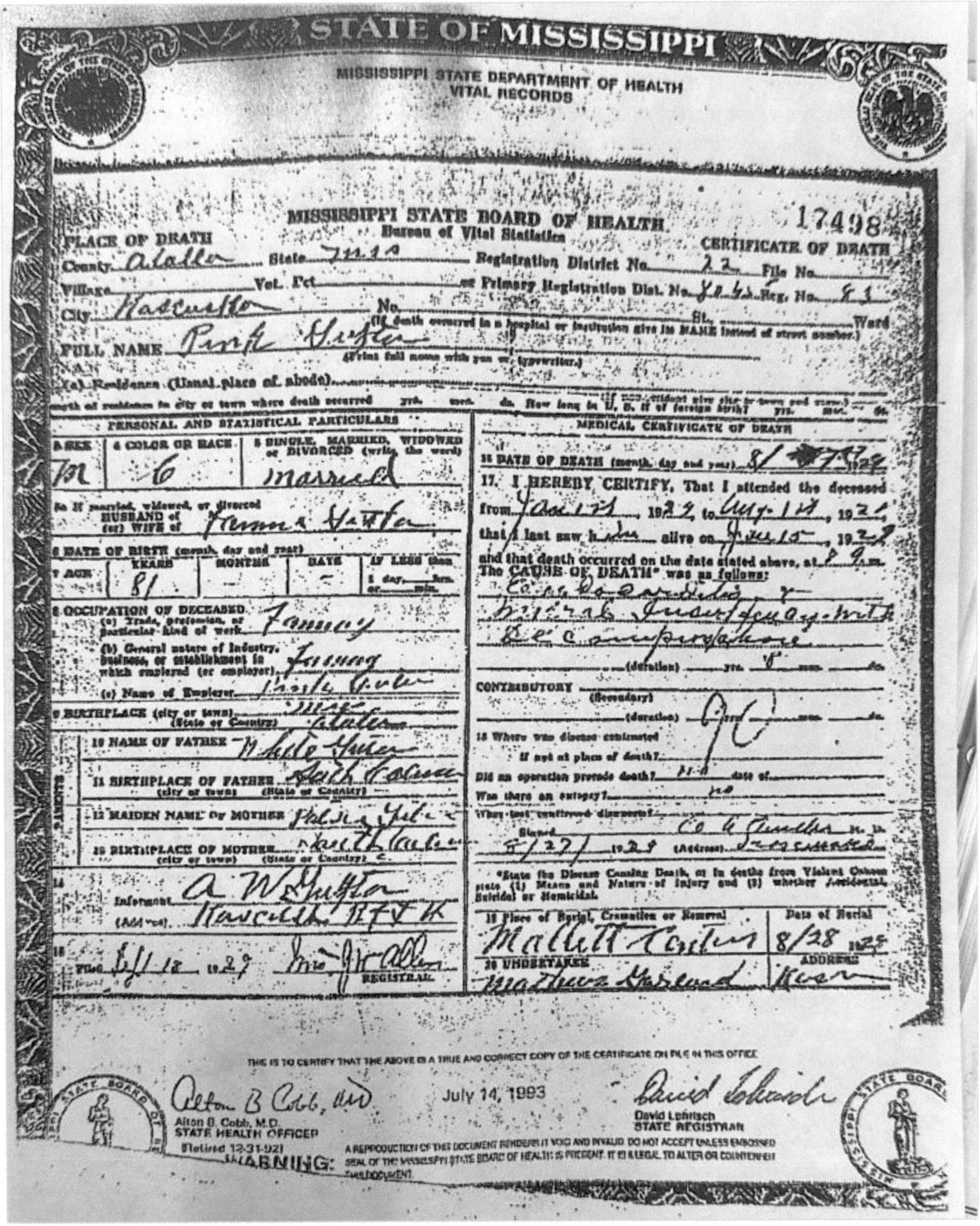

STATE OF MISSISSIPPI

MISSISSIPPI STATE DEPARTMENT OF HEALTH
VITAL RECORDS

MISSISSIPPI STATE BOARD OF HEALTH
Bureau of Vital Statistics

17498

CERTIFICATE OF DEATH

PLACE OF DEATH
County Atalla State Miss Registration District No. 22 File No.
Village Vot. Pct. or Primary Registration Dist. No. 8043 Reg. No. 83
City No. St. Ward
(If death occurred in a hospital or institution give its NAME instead of street number.)
FULL NAME Pink Guyton
(Print full name with pen or typewriter.)
(a) Residence (Usual place of abode)

PERSONAL AND STATISTICAL PARTICULARS
SEX M
COLOR OR RACE C
SINGLE, MARRIED, WIDOWED OR DIVORCED married
If married, widowed, or divorced HUSBAND of (or) WIFE of Fannie Guyton
DATE OF BIRTH (month, day and year)
AGE Years 81 Months – Days –
OCCUPATION OF DECEASED (a) Trade, profession, or particular kind of work Farmer
(b) General nature of industry, business, or establishment in which employed (or employer) farming
BIRTHPLACE (city or town) (State or Country) Miss
NAME OF FATHER White Guyton
BIRTHPLACE OF FATHER (city or town) (State or Country) South Carolina
MAIDEN NAME OF MOTHER
BIRTHPLACE OF MOTHER (city or town) (State or Country) South Carolina
Informant A W Guyton
(Address) Kosciusko R F D
Filed 8/18 1929 Mrs J W Allen Registrar

MEDICAL CERTIFICATE OF DEATH
DATE OF DEATH (month, day and year) 8/17 1929
I HEREBY CERTIFY, That I attended the deceased from Jan 1st, 1929 to Aug 1st, 1929, that I last saw him alive on June 15, 1929 and that death occurred on the date stated above, at 8 P.m.
The CAUSE OF DEATH was as follows:
(duration) yrs.
CONTRIBUTORY (Secondary) (duration)
Where was disease contracted if not at place of death?
Did an operation precede death? no Date of
Was there an autopsy? no
What test confirmed diagnosis?
Signed M.D.
8/27 1929 (Address)
*State the Disease Causing Death, or in deaths from Violent Causes state (1) Means and Nature of Injury and (2) whether Accidental, Suicidal or Homicidal.
Place of Burial, Cremation or Removal Mallett Cemetery Date of Burial 8/28 1929
UNDERTAKER ADDRESS

THIS IS TO CERTIFY THAT THE ABOVE IS A TRUE AND CORRECT COPY OF THE CERTIFICATE ON FILE IN THIS OFFICE

Alton B. Cobb, M.D.
STATE HEALTH OFFICER
(Retired 12-31-92)

July 14, 1993

David Lohrisch
STATE REGISTRAR

WARNING: A REPRODUCTION OF THIS DOCUMENT RENDERS IT VOID AND INVALID. DO NOT ACCEPT UNLESS EMBOSSED SEAL OF THE MISSISSIPPI STATE BOARD OF HEALTH IS PRESENT. IT IS ILLEGAL TO ALTER OR COUNTERFEIT THIS DOCUMENT.

Figure 94 Mississippi Death Certificate for Pinkney GUYTON

Nic STARR's Story about Honoring Pinkney GUYTON and Fannie SALLIS

My name is Nic STARR, though on *Ancestry.com* I am listed as Karl BOYD, my birth name. Originally from Chicago, Illinois, I am currently based in Atlanta, Georgia. My genealogy journey began 25 years ago, inspired by my mother, Icy Viola NASH BOYD (see Figure 95). She set me on a mission to find Grandpa Whit (Aaron Whitaker GUYTON) and Grandpa Pink GUYTON. While she knew of them, Grandpa Whit was more of a myth.

She had little information about them or their burial places. During a family reunion in Kosciusko, Mississippi, in 2005 she could have found answers, but the one person with the information, Cousin Odell DURHAM (see Figure 96), was only present on the first day. They didn't get the opportunity to talk, as Odell left the reunion due to a family emergency in Texas. My mom didn't know Odell had this information, and they never discussed it. My mom went home to glory a few years later, in 2009.

I was eager to learn more about Grandpa Whit and Grandpa Pink. Twenty-five years ago, I met Ann BREEDLOVE, Genealogy Librarian at the Attala County Library in the John D. Sanders and Zemuly Weeks Sanders Historical & Genealogical Room. See Ann and I in Figure 97. She went to the family genealogy files to show we are related through the Guyton family originating in Kosciusko, MS. Through *Ancestry.com*, I learned that Pink was the first identified male slave in my lineage. My Mom's search was over.

Fast forward to April 27, 2022. Cousin Rickey SIMMONS and I talked to Mama Odell (that's what family calls her, though she's our cousin) on a day when she was clear in thought and mind. While on the phone, she walked us to the two rocks in Mallet Cemetery under which my Grandpa Pink and Grandma Fannie were buried. Their resting places had been marked with these two rocks for 93 years, making them difficult to locate (see Figure 99, Figure 100, Figure 101, Figure 102, Figure 102 Mallett Cemetery and Figure 103). The family simply didn't have the funds to bury them properly. The family was cheated out of their land and couldn't afford it. I had finally located the resting places of my great-great-grandparents, Pink and Fannie.

Rickey and I decided to buy a headstone and organize a dedication ceremony so our family members can know who Pinkney was, where he is, and where he's been. Acknowledgement that he was here, and that through us, he is still here. On August 27, 2022, Pink and Fannie's descendants held a special ceremony to honor them, and they finally received proper headstones. The GPS coordinates for Mallett Cemetery are Latitude: 32.9826° (32° 58' 57") and Longitude: -89.6637° (-89° 39' 49").[847] See the footnote for directions from Kosciusko, Mississippi, to Mallett Cemetery.[848]

My Mom and Odell (Pink) are in the reunion picture (Figure 98). Mom is on the far bottom left and Odell is on the far upper right of the photo.

---

[847] The grassy photos of Mallett Cemetery were posted to FindAGrave by Lisa Goss OWENS (*FindAGrave* ID 47455611).

[848] Take MS-14 west out of Kosciusko, MS past Sudduth Road. Turn right on County Road 4126. Take the road about .2 of a mile. The cemetery is hidden in the woods on the right. *Google Earth* shows a trailer and house in a clearing a very short way beyond the cemetery on County Road 4126. If you reach them, you have gone too far. The cemetery appears cleared in the satellite image.

Figure 95 Icy Viola NASH BOYD

Figure 96 Odell GUYTON DURHAM

Figure 97 Nic STARR and Ann BREEDLOVE

Figure 98 2005 Guyton Reunion in Kosciusko, MS

Figure 99 Google Map Showing Mallett Cemetery's Location (Blue Dot)

Figure 100 Mallett Cemetery 1

Figure 101 Mallett Cemetery 2

Figure 102 Mallett Cemetery 3

Figure 103 Rocks Indicating Pinkney and Fannie's Graves

On the day of revealing the headstone, I wrote:

Hello Family...

As I sit in my room, preparing for this evening's presentation, I must share with you that my heart is full of this overflowing stream of love received from my newly found family! As I sit here, Elisa GUYTON ROTH [descendant of Joseph GUYTON, Aaron Whitaker GUYTON's brother] is downstairs in deep conversation with my little sisters as if they are long lost friends, just catching up. It does my heart good to see the bridge continue to grow. Elisa and her husband, William ROTH, drove from St. Louis to Kosciusko to not only witness, but also to participate in our family's Headstone Dedication! Our family is "Absolutely" AMAZING! My heart is full... would also like to thank Sam GUYTON and Jean Guyton for your generous contribution in support of this event. Proof positive that "Guytons are good Folks!"

Continued Blessings,
N.L. STARR

What brings this full circle is the fact that during my search for my Grandpa Pink, I discovered the descendants of Pink's who did not know or did not accept him, or his father Aaron Whitaker GUYTON, because of the type of world they lived in at the time before and after the end of slavery. Some would say that the world hasn't changed, and, at one time, I might have agreed. I still remember clearly, the feeling of returning from overseas in defense of my country, only to be called a nigger within the first hour back on American soil. However, on June 3, 2022, I took a step to reach out to my white family. I was met with open arms and love from my long-lost family, Grandpa Pink's family. Something has shifted, and we are proof that change is possible, and it begins within us. This is the whole premise of Grace for Guytons – through God's grace we've been given this opportunity. It's up to us individually to decide what we will do with it. A few of you have already stepped out on faith, and love. Sam GUYTON, Jean GUYTON, Linda GUYTON RINGWOOD, Tom RINGWOOD, and Dorla COLEMAN EVANS, you've all opened your homes to me, and we've had heart-warming, and deep discussions regarding this new family dynamic. Sam and Jean, your unsolicited contribution spoke volumes, and Ann BREEDLOVE, Elisa GUYTON ROTH, and William ROTH, your presence at the headstone dedication shows that we are well on our way. There is so much more to share, but suffice it to say that I am overjoyed with what we're building here, and I know that somewhere "OUR" Ancestors are smiling...

Much Love,

N.L. STARR

Link regarding Grandpa Pink and Grandma Fannie GUYTON's Dedication Ceremony (copy and paste into your browser):

https://youtu.be/6gPELRcyZTw?si=5JUXD49mAD-m1kGS

Link regarding Guyton Reunion June 22, 2022, in Kosciusko, Mississippi:

https://www.youtube.com/watch?v=T3g-y0az9Jg

Link for Grace for Guytons, a short story of Karl Glenn BOYD (aka Nykki Lamarr STARR) meeting his white family for the first time in Kosciusko, MS:

https://youtu.be/WvCcf55g4BQ?si=xRqZwe_nG1UlO7b7

See Figure 104, Figure 105, Figure 106, Figure 107, Figure 108, Figure 109, Figure 111, Figure 112, and Figure 113 from Karl Boyd (AKA Nykki Lamarr STARR).

Figure 104 Princess STARR and Elisa GUYTON ROTH

Figure 105 Ann BREEDLOVE in Red and Rickey SIMMONS in Blue

Figure 106 Family Breaking Bread Together after the Dedication... Long overdue!

Figure 107 Long Lost Cousins Happy to be Found - Elisa ROTH, Rhonda BALL, Princess STARR, Felicia BOYD

Figure 108 Nic and Princess STARR Visit Cousins Sam and Jean GUYTON in Denver, CO

Figure 109 Nic STARR and 5th Cousin Dorla COLEMAN EVANS

Figure 110 Nic STARR, Ann BREEDLOVE, Princess STARR, William ROTH, Elisa GUYTON ROTH, and Rickey SIMMONS

Figure 111 Brothers Nic and Rico STARR'S Visit to St. Louis, MO with our Cousins Elisa GUYTON ROTH and her sister, Annie GUYTON SEAL, and husband, Bob SEAL

During the June 2022 reunion and the various visits and communications that followed, discoveries were made, good and bad. However, one positive thing that happened is the inclusion of Aaron Whitaker GUYTON, AND HIS FAMILY in a publication about the Guytons.[849] Being welcomed, being included, being acknowledged is everything… and it all starts with Family. **Truly, Grace for Guytons**

---

[849] Evans, Dorla A., *Joseph Guyton Genealogy: From England to Maryland and across the American South,* Amazon, 2022.

Figure 112 Guyton Reunion June 2022 in Kosciusko, MS

Figure 113 Guyton Reunion in August 2022

Generation #8

Emma GUYTON (Pinkney, Aaron Whitaker, Aaron Steele, Joseph I, John I, Samuel II, Samuel I, John)

Emma GUYTON was the daughter of Pinkney GUYTON (b. Jan 1848 Attala Co., MS, d. Aug 1929)[850] and Fannie SALLIS (b. Oct 1855, d. AFT 1940).[851] Emma was born in Jun 1874 in MS.[852] She died sometime after 1915 but before the 1920 Census as her husband, Addison D. ALLEN (b. Dec 1872 Attala Co., MS, d. 1963 Chicago, Cook Co., IL) was shown as a widower.[853] See Figure 114. Emma's last child, Buster Brown Clinton ALLEN, was born in 1915.

In the 1900 U.S. Census, Emma (25) and Addison (27) lived in Kosciusko, Attala Co., MS. They had been married for five years and had three children: Edna Alma ALLEN (4), Nola J. ALLEN (3), and Unnamed (later named Iola) ALLEN (1). In 1920, Addison (37) and Emma (34) had seven children: Alma Edna ALLEN (14), Nola J. ALLEN (13), Iola E. ALLEN(11), Ethel S. ALLEN(7), Willie W. ALLEN(5), Clara F. ALLEN(3), and Otha B. ALLEN (0). They lived in Beat 4, Attala Co., MS.

Addison was a widower in the 1920 Census. He lived on a mortgaged farm in New Port, Attala Co., MS located west of Rock Port Road. Edna Alma ALLEN was a 24-year-old widow, living with her father. Other children still living with Addison were Ethel S. ALLEN (17), Willie Walter ALLEN (15), Clara F. ALLEN (13), Otha B. ALLEN (9), a new daughter, Johnnie ALLEN (7), new son, Buster Brown Clinton ALLEN (5), and a granddaughter, Stella ALLEN (7). Stella may have been Edna's daughter.

By 1930, Addison was remarried to a much younger woman, Martha (23). They had been married two years at the time of the Census. Living with them were Buster ALLEN (15) and Martha's sister. Willie ALLEN and his family lived nearby, and Otha ALLEN lived next door with a cousin.

Emma GUYTON and Addison D. ALLEN had at least ten children:

i   Edna Alma ALLEN (b. 14 Nov 1894 MS, d. Feb 1987 Sallis, Attala Co., MS)[854] m. Unknown POINTER (Unknown) and (2) Anthony TEAGUE (b. 17 Dec 1886 MS, d. Feb 1977).[855] See Figure 115. They had at

---

[850] "1870 United States Census," Attala Co., MS, digital image s.v. "Penkey Guyton," (birth ABT 1848), Ancestry.com. "Mississippi, Death Certificates," digitmal image s.v. "Pink Guyton," (1848-1929), personal copy.
[851] "1900 United States Census," Kosciusko, Attala County, Mississippi, digital image s.v. "Fannie Guyton," (birth Oct 1855), Ancestry.com. Her birth date ranges from 1853 to 1857. She last appears in the 1940 U.S. Census. "1940 United States Census," Kosciusko, Attala County, Mississippi, digital image s.v. "Fannie Guyton," (birth ABT 1855), Ancestry.com.
[852] "1900 United States Federal Census," Kosciusko, Attala Co., MS, digital image s.v. "Emma M. Allen," (birth ABT Jun 1874), Ancestry.com.
[853] "1920 United States Federal Census," Newport, Attala Co., MS, digital image s.v. "Addison Allen," (birth 1873, widowed), Ancestry.com.
[854] "1920 United States Federal Census," New Port, Attala Co., MS, digital image s.v. "Edna Allen," (birth 1896), Ancestry.com.
[855] "U.S., Social Security Death Index, 1935-2014," s.v. "Anthony Teague," (birth 17 Dec 1886, death Feb 1977), Ancestry.com.

least one child: Stella E. ALLEN POINTER (b. ABT 1913, d. Unknown).[856] Edna and Anthony adopted her sister, Johnnie Amzy ALLEN's, son, Allen JORDAN (b. 13 Aug 1929 MS, d. 24 Jun 1998).[857]

ii Nola J. ALLEN (b. Feb 1897 MS, d. 23 Jan 1997 Sallis, Attala Co., MS)[858] m. Sherman FORD (b. 30 Dec 1882 Durant, Holmes Co., MS, d. Nov 1967 Bolton, Hinds Co., MS).[859] See Figure 116.

iii Iola E. ALLEN (b. Apr 1899 MS, d. 23 Jan 1997 Sallis, Attala Co., MS).[860]

iv Ethel S. ALLEN (b. 1 Apr 1905 MS, d. 28 May 1992 Rockford, Winnebago Co., IL)[861] m. Leroy ARNOLD, Sr. (b. 20 Feb 1898 MS, d. 10 May 1978 Rockford, Winnebago Co., IL).[862]

v Willie Walter ALLEN (b. 18 Dec 1905 Sallis, Attala Co., MS, d. 1 Oct 1995 Chicago, Cook Co., IL)[863] m. Willie Mae LITTLE (b. 9 Jan 1910 MS, d. 19 Mar 1983 Kosciusko, Attala Co., MS).[864] See Figure 117.

vi Clara F. ALLEN (b. 12 Feb 1908 MS, d. 22 Jan 2001 St. Louis, Saint Louis Co., MO)[865] m. Unknown GOODWIN (Unknown).

vii Johnnie Amzy ALLEN (female) (b. 13 Jun 1909 MS, d. Mar 1982 Chicago, Cook Co., IL)[866] m. (1) John JORDAN (Unknown) with whom she had one son, Allen JORDAN (who was adopted by Johnnie's sister, Edna Alma ALLEN TEAGUE) (see above) and (2) Sixto Cruz SANCHEZ (Unknown) on 1 Oct 1960 in Cook Co., IL.[867]

viii Otha B. ALLEN (b. 23 Jun 1910 Sallis, Attala Co., MS, d. 14 Oct 1998 St. Louis, St. Louis City, MO).[868]

ix Asher ALLEN (b. ABT 1911 MS, d. Unknown).[869]

x Buster Brown Clinton ALLEN (b. 10 Jun 1915 Sallis, Attala Co., MS, d. Jun 1983 Jackson, Hinds Co., MS).[870]

---

[856] "1920 United States Federal Census," Newport, Attala Co., MS, digital image s.v. "Stella Allen," (birth ABT 1913), *Ancestry.com*. "1930 United States Federal Census," Beat 4, Attala Co., MS, digital image s.v. "Stella E. Pointer," (birth 1913), *Ancestry.com*.

[857] "U.S., Social Security Applications and Claims Index, 1936-2007," s.v. "Allen Jordan," (birth 13 Aug 1929, death 24 Jun 1998), *Ancestry.com*. "1940 United States Federal Census," Newport, Attala Co., MS, digital image s.v. "Allen Jerdon," (birth ABT 1930, adopted son), *Ancestry.com*.

[858] "1900 United States Federal Census," Kosciusko, Attala Co., MS, digital image s.v. "Nola J Allen," (birth ABT 1897), *Ancestry.com*.

[859] "U.S., Social Security Death Index, 1935-2014," s.v. "Sherman Ford," (birth 30 Dec 1882, death Nov 1967), *Ancestry.com*.

[860] "1910 United States Federal Census," Beat 4, Attala Co., MS, s.v. "Iala E Allen," (birth ABT 1899, death Unknown), *Ancestry.com*.

[861] "U.S., Social Security Death Index, 1935-2014," s.v. "Ethel I. Arnold," (birth 1 Apr 1905, death 28 May 1992), *Ancestry.com*.

[862] "Winnebago County, Illinois, U.S., Deaths, 1844-1992," digital image s.v. "Leroy Arnold," (death 10 May 1978), *Ancestry.com*. "U.S., Social Security Death Index, 1935-2014," s.v. "Leroy Arnold," (birth 20 Feb 1898), *Ancestry.com*.

[863] "U.S., Social Security Applications and Claims Index, 1936-2007," s.v. "Willie Walter Allen," (birth 18 Dec 1905, death 1 Oct 1995), *Ancestry.com*.

[864] Willie Mae Little, grave marker, Barlow United Methodist Church Cemetery, Sallis, Attala County, MS, digital image s.v. "Willie Mae Allen," (birth 9 Jan 1910, death 19 Mar 1983), *FindaGrave.com*.

[865] "U.S., Social Security Death Index, 1935-2014," s.v. "Clara Goodwin," (birth 12 Feb 1908, death 22 Jan 2001), *Ancestry.com*.

[866] "U.S., Social Security Death Index, 1935-2014," s.v. "Johnnie Allen," (birth 13 Jun 1909, death Mar 1982), *Ancestry.com*.

[867] "Cook County, Illinois Marriage Index, 1930-1960," s.v. "Sixto Cruz Sanchez," (marriage 1 Oct 1960 to Johnnie Amzy Allen), *Ancestry.com*.

[868] "U.S., Social Security Applications and Claims Index, 1936-2007," s.v. "Otha Allen," (birth 23 Jun 1910, death 14 Oct 1998), *FindaGrave.com*.

[869] "1920 United States Federal Census," Newport, Attala Co., MS, s.v. "Asher Allen," (birth ABT 1911, death Unknown), *Ancestry.com*.

[870] "U.S., Social Security Applications and Claims Index, 1936-2007," s.v. "Clinton Allen," (birth 28 Oct 1915, death 29 Apr 1972), *Ancestry.com*.

Figure 114 Addison D. ALLEN, Husband of Emma GUYTON

At some point, Addison moved to Chicago, where he died in 1963.

Figure 115 Edna Alma GUYTON[871]

Figure 116 Nola J. ALLEN FORD[872]

Figure 117 Willie Walter and Willie Mae ALLEN[873]

Patsy J. GUYTON (Pinkney, Aaron Whitaker, Aaron Steele, Joseph I, John I, Samuel II, Samuel I, John)

Patsy J. GUYTON was the daughter of Pinkney GUYTON (b. Jan 1848 Attala Co., MS, d. Aug 1929) and Fannie SALLIS (b. Oct 1855, d. AFT 1940).[874] She was born in Aug 1877 in Sallis, Attala Co., MS. She died sometime after 1950, likely in Sallis, Attala Co., MS).[875] Patsy J. married William (Willie) ROBY (b.

---

[871] Karl Boyd originally shared this on 21 Feb 2023 on *Ancestry.com*.
[872] Karl Boyd originally shared this on 16 Feb 2023 on *Ancestry.com*.
[873] Lotus781 originally shared this on 27 Dec 2021 on *Ancestry.com*.
[874] "1870 United States Census," Attala Co., MS, digital image s.v. "Penkey Guyton," (birth ABT 1848), *Ancestry.com*. "Mississippi, Death Certificates," digitmal image s.v. "Pink Guyton," (1848-1929), personal copy. "1900 United States Census," Kosciusko, Attala County, Mississippi, digital image s.v. "Fannie Guyton," (birth Oct 1855), *Ancestry.com*. Her birth date ranges from 1853 to 1857. She last appears in the 1940 U.S. Census. "1940 United States Census," Kosciusko, Attala County, Mississippi, digital image s.v. "Fannie Guyton," (birth ABT 1855), *Ancestry.com*.
[875] "1900 United States Federal Census," Attala Co., MS, digital image s.v. "Patsy J. Roby," (birth Aug 1877), *Ancestry.com*. I assume she died after 1950 because she was in the 1950 U.S. Census. "1950 United States Federal Census," Newport, Attala Co., MS, digital image s.v. "Patsy Robey," (birth ABT 1877), *Ancestry.com*.

Mar 1876 MS, d. May 1969 Sallis, Attala Co., MS)[876] in 1898, per the 1900 U.S. Census, and divorced before 1930.[877]

In the 1900 U.S. Census, Patsy and Willie were newly married with a baby boy, Pleas W. ROBY, only 5 months old.[878] Willie was a farmer. In 1910, the couple lived in Beat 4, Attala Co., MS. on Goodman New Port Kosciusko Road. They lived with their children: Pleas W. ROBY (10), Earnest Mitchell ROBY (8), Homer ROBY (6), Lillie Wardean ROBY (2), and Edna ROBY (0).[879] In 1920, the couple farmed at Kosciusko, Attala Co., MS on Beechaven Road. They lived with their children: Earnest ROBY (17), Homer ROBY (14), Wardean ROBY (11), Louella ROBY (8), Elmer ROBY (6), Ruthie ROBY (5), and Vamis ROBY (2).[880]

In the 1930 U.S. Census, Patsy (49) lived with a few of her children on a rented farm in Beat 4, Attala Co., MS on Goodman Highway. Willie did not live with them.[881] She lived with her children Homer ROBY (22), Elmer ROBY (17), Ruth ROBY (14), Vamis ROBY (12), and Odell (Pink) ROBY (8). In 1940, Patsy J. lived on a rented farm in New Port, Attala Co., MS with Homer ROBY, Ernest ROBY, and Odell (Pink) ROBY.[882] The 1950 Census reported that Patsy was widowed.[883] The earlier Census indicated she was married although she and Willie were clearly separated. At 73 years old, Patsy J. had given up farming to her sons, Homer ROBY and Elmer ROBY.

Patsy J. and Willie had at least the following children:

i   Pleas W. ROBY (b. Dec 1899 MS, d. 1924 Hinds Co., MS).[884]
ii   Earnest Mitchell ROBY (b. 29 Mar 1902 MS, d. Unknown)[885] m. Velma Lizzie STINGLEY (b. 1 Jan 1904 Attala Co., MS, d. 23 Sep 1992 Kosciusko, Attala Co., MS).[886]
iii   Homer ROBY (b. 4 Mar 1904 MS, d. May 1978 Sallis, Attala Co., MS).[887]

---

[876] "1900 United States Federal Census," Attala Co., MS, digital image s.v. "Will Roby," (birth Mar 1876), *Ancestry.com*.

[877] "1930 United States Federal Census," Attala Co., MS, digital image s.v. "Will Roby," (marital status divorced), *Ancestry.com*.

[878] "1900 United States Federal Census," Kosciusko, Attala Co., MS, digital image s.v. "Patsy J. Roby," (birth Aug 1877), *Ancestry.com*.

[879] "1910 United States Federal Census," Beat 4, Attala Co., MS, digital image s.v. "Patsey Roby," (birth 1878), *Ancestry.com*.

[880] "1920 United States Federal Census," Kosciusko, Attala Co., MS, digital image s.v. "Patsey Roley," (birth ABT 1881), *Ancestry.com*.

[881] "1930 United States Federal Census," Beat 4, Attala Co., MS, digital image s.v. "Patsy Roby," (birth ABT 1881), *Ancestry.com*.

[882] "1930 United States Federal Census," Newport, Attala Co., MS, digital image s.v. "Patsey Raby," (birth ABT 1877), *Ancestry.com*.

[883] "1950 United States Federal Census," Newport, Attala Co., MS, digital image s.v. "Patsy Robey," (birth ABT 1877), *Ancestry.com*.

[884] "1900 United States Federal Census," Kosciusko, Attala Co., MS, digital image s.v. "Pleas W Roby," (birth Dec 1899), *Ancestry.com*. "Mississippi, U.S., Index to Deaths, 1912-1943," Hinds Co., MS, s.v. "Pleas Roby," (death 1924), *Ancestry.com*.

[885] "U.S. WWII Draft Cards Young Men, 1940-1947," digital image s.v. "Earnest Mitchell Roby," (birth 29 Mar 1902), *Ancestry.com*.

[886] Velma Lizzie Stingley, grave marker, Barlow United Methodist Church Cemetery, Sallis, Attala County, MS, digital image s.v. "Velma Lizzie Roby," (birth 1 Jan 1904, death 23 Sep 1992915), *FindaGrave.com*. "U.S., Social Security Death Index," s.v. "Velma L. Roby," (birth 1 Jan 1904, death Sep 1992), *Ancestry.com*.

[887] "Social Security Death," s.v. "Homer Roby," (birth 4 Mar 1904, death May 1978), *Ancestry.com*.

iv		Lillie Wardean ROBY (b. 17 Nov 1909 Sallis, Attala Co., MS, d. 27 Oct 2003 Chicago, Cook Co., IL)[888] m. James (Jim) GUYTON (b. 2 Sep 1905 Sallis, Attala Co., MS, d. 1956 Sallis, Attala Co., MS).[889] Jim GUYTON was the son of Case GUYTON (son of Aaron Whitaker GUYTON and Artie RAINEY) and Susie STINGLEY. Lillie was the granddaughter of Pinkney GUYTON, Case GUYTON's half-brother.
v		Edna ROBY (b. ABT 1910 MS, d. Unknown).[890]
vi		Louella ROBY (b. 19 Jan 1911 Attala Co., MS, d. 3 Jun 2003 McAdams, Attala Co., MS)[891] m. Othar ROUNDTREE (b. 25 Aug 1909 Attala Co., MS, d. Unknown).[892]
vii		Elmer ROBY (b. 5 Mar 1913 Sallis, Attala Co., MS, d. 9 Jul 1992 Sallis, Attala Co., MS)[893] m. Unknown.
viii		Ruth Lee (Ruthie) ROBY (b. 7 May 1916 Sallis, Attala Co., MS., d. 13 Jan 1996 Wauwatosa, Milwaukee Co., WI)[894] m. Gus Davis GUYTON (b. 3 Mar 1909 Sallis, Attala Co., MS., d. 8 Jul 1990 Cook Co., IL).[895] Gus Davis GUYTON was the son of Ike GUYTON (son of Aaron Whitaker GUYTON and Artie RAINEY) and Ida RILEY.
ix		Vamis (Vammie) ROBY (b. ABT 1919 Sallis, Attala Co., MS, d. BEF 1950 Sallis, Attala Co., MS)[896] m. Shelton N. GUYTON (b. 12 Mar 1909 Sallis, Attala Co., MS., d. 30 May 1984 Sallis, Attala Co., MS).[897] Shelton N. GUYTON was the son of Case GUYTON and Susie STINGLEY. Case GUYTON was the son of Aaron Whitaker GUYTON and Artie RAINEY.
x		Odell (Pink) ROBY (b. 10 May 1924 MS, d. 29 Jan 2013)[898] m. Unknown DURHAM.

---

[888] Lillie Wardean Roby, grave marker, Burr Oak Cemetery, Alsip, Cook Co., MI, digital image s.v. "Mrs Lillie Wardean Guyton," (birth 17 Nov 1910, death 27 Oct 2003), *FindaGrave.com*.

[889] "U.S. WWII Draft Cards Young Men, 1940-1947," digital image s.v. "Jim Guyton," (birth 2 Sep 1905), *Ancestry.com*.

[890] "1910 United States Federal Census," Beat 4, Attala Co., MS, digital image s.v. "Edna Roby," (birth ABT 1910), *Ancestry.com*.

[891] "U.S., Social Security Death Index, 1935-2014," s.v. "Luella Roundtree," (birth 19 Jan 1911, death 3 Jun 2003), *Ancestry.com*.

[892] "U.S. WWII Draft Cards Young Men, 1940-1947," digital image s.v. "Othar Roundtree," (birth 25 Aug 1909), *Ancestry.com*.

[893] Elmer Roby, grave marker, Pleasant Hill Cemetery, Williamsville, Attala County, MS, digital image s.v. "Elmer Roby," (birth 5 Mar 1913, death 9 Jul 1992), *FindaGrave.com*.

[894] Ruth Lee Roby, grave marker, Russell Cemetery, Attala County, MS, digital image s.v. "Ruthie Guyton," (birth 7 May 1916, death 13 Jan 1996), *FindaGrave.com*.

[895] Gus Davis Guyton, grave marker, Russell Cemetery, Attala County, MS, digital image s.v. "Gus Davis Guyton," (birth 3 Mar 1909, death 8 Jul 1990), *FindaGrave.com*.

[896] "1940 United States Federal Census," Newport, Attala Co., MS, digital image s.v. "Vammie Guyton," (birth ABT 1919), *Ancestry.com*.

[897] "U.S., Social Security Applications and Claims Index, 1935-2014," s.v. "Shelton Guyton," (birth 12 Mar 1909), *Ancestry.com*. Shelton N Guyton, grave marker, Russell Cemetery, Attala County, MS, digital image s.v. "Shelton N. Guyton," (death 30 May 1984), *FindaGrave.com*.

[898] "Social Security Death Index," s.v. "Odell Roby," (birth 20 Dec 1922, death 29 Jan 2013), *Ancestry.com*. Odell's WWII draft card indicated his birth date was 10 May 1924, quite different from the Social Security date.

Agnes Isolome (Icy) GUYTON (Pinkney, Aaron Whitaker, Aaron Steele, Joseph I, John I, Samuel II, Samuel I, John)

Icy GUYTON was the daughter of Pinkney GUYTON (b. Jan 1848 Attala Co., MS, d. Aug 1929)[899] and Fannie SALLIS (b. Oct 1855, d. AFT 1940).[900] Icy GUYTON was born in Sep 1879 in Kosciusko, South Beat 1, Attala Co., MS. She died in 1963 in Kosciusko, Attala, Co., MS.[901] She married Albert GAMBLE (b. 15 Dec 1875 Shuqualak Township 13, Noxubee Co., MS, d. 1948 Kosciusko, Attala Co., MS).[902] See Figure 118 and Figure 119.

In 1910, the couple lived in Beat 1, Attala Co., MS.[903] Albert was 31; Icy was 30. They lived with their children: Betty GAMBLE (8), Fannie GAMBLE (7), Callie Pairee GAMBLE (5), Nathan Eugene GAMBLE (4), Fred GAMBLE (1) and Nola GAMBLE (6/12). Albert farmed his own land, owned without a mortgage. By 1920, they added to their family: Betty GAMBLE (17), Fannie B. GAMBLE (15) Pairee GAMBLE (14), Eugene GAMBLE (12), Nola GAMBLE (9), Fred GAMBLE (11), K D GAMBLE (7), Lovie GAMBLE (5), and Mable GAMBLE (3).[904] The 1920 Census noted the family's farm was located on Beechaven Road in Kosciusko, Attala Co., MS. The family may have hit upon hard times or was trying to expand because the farm was then mortgaged.

I could not find the couple in the 1930 U.S. Census but in 1940 all Albert (63) and Icy's (61) children were out of the house, and they lived with Icy's mother, Fannie SALLIS (85). They lived on Goodman Road in Kosciusko, Attala Co., MS. Albert GAMBLE worked as a farm laborer on rented property.[905] He died in 1948.

In 1950, Icy GUYTON lived with her son Fred GAMBLE and his family on the Kosciusko New Port Road.[906]

---

[899] "1860 U.S. Federal Census - Slave Schedules," digital image s.v. "Pinkney Guyton," (birth ABT 1848), *Ancestry.com*. "Mississippi, U.S., Index to Deaths, 1912-1943," digital image s.v. "Pink Guyton," (death Aug 1929), Ancestry.com.
[900] "1900 United States Census," Kosciusko, Attala County, Mississippi, digital image s.v. "Fannie Guyton," (birth Oct 1855), *Ancestry.com*. Her birth date ranges across documents from 1853 to 1857. She last appears in the 1940 U.S. Census. "1940 United States Census," Kosciusko, Attala County, Mississippi, digital image s.v. "Fannie Guyton," (birth ABT 1855), *Ancestry.com*.
[901] Agnes Isolome (Icy) Guyton, grave marker, Nash Cemetery, Attala County, MS, digital image s.v. "Agnes Icy Gamble," (birth Sep 1879, death 1963), *FindaGrave.com*.
[902] Albert Gamble, grave marker, Nash Cemetery, Attala County, MS, digital image s.v. "Agnes Icy Gamble," (birth 15 Dec 1875, death 1948), *FindaGrave.com*.
[903] "1910 United States Federal Census," Beat 1, Attala County, Mississippi, digital image s.v. "Agnes Gambrel," (birth abt 1880), *Ancestry.com*.
[904] "1920 United States Federal Census," Kosciusko, Attala County, Mississippi, digital image s.v. "Agnes Gamble," (birth 1882), *Ancestry.com*.
[905] "1940 United States Federal Census," Kosciusko, Attala Co., MS, digital image s.v. "Icey Gamble," (birth ABT 1879), *Ancestry.com*.
[906] "1950 United States Federal Census," Kosciusko, Attala Co., MS, digital image s.v. "Icey L Gambol," (birth ABT 1879), *Ancestry.com*.

Figure 118 Agnes Isolome (Icy) GUYTON[907]

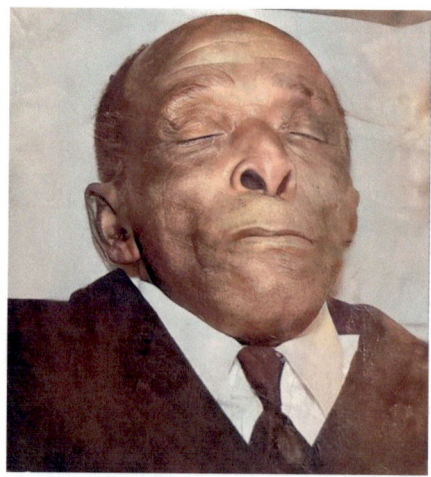

Figure 119 Death Photo of Albert GAMBLE[908]

Albert and Icy had at least nine children:

i   Bettie GAMBLE (b. ABT 1903 MS, d. Unknown.)[909]

ii   Fannie B. GAMBLE (b. 5 Aug 1903 MS, d. 24 Jul 1998 Kosciusko, Attala Co., MS)[910] m. Dock M. MALLETT (b. 4 Jan 1897 Kosciusko, Attala Co., MS, d. 21 Aug 1980 Kosciusko, Attala Co., MS).[911]

iii   Callie Pairee GAMBLE (b. 9 Jan 1905 Attala Co., MS, d. 19 Jun 1995 Maywood, Cook Co., IL)[912] m. Henry Porterwood SIMMONS (b. 11 Feb 1904 Attala Co., MS, d. Oct 1977 Kosciusko, Attala Co., MS).[913]

iv   Nathan Eugene GAMBLE (b. 9 Apr 1906 Attala Co., MS, d. Dec 1993 Kosciusko, Attala Co., MS).[914]

v   Fred (Big Baby) GAMBLE (b. 27 Feb 1909 Kosciusko Beat 1, Attala Co., MS, d. 31 Jul 1980 Kosciusko, Attala Co., MS)[915] m. Ella Mae MITCHELL (b. 29 Jun 1919 Kosciusko, Attala Co., MS, d. 3 Jul 2007 Kosciusko, Attala Co., MS).[916]

---

[907] Karl Boyd originally shared this on 19 Jun 2023 on *Ancestry.com*.

[908] Karl Boyd originally shared this on 31 Jul 2023 on *Ancestry.com*.

[909] "1920 United States Federal Census," Kosciusko, Attala Co., MS, digital image s.v. "Bettie Gamble," (birth ABT 1903), *Ancestry.com*.

[910] Fannie B. Gamble, grave marker, Wright Cemetery, Kosciusko, Attala Co., MS, digital image s.v. "Fannie Mallett," (birth 5 Aug 1903, death 24 Jul 1998), *FindaGrave.com*.

[911] Dock M. Mallett, grave marker, Wright Cemetery, Kosciusko, Attala Co., MS, digital image s.v. "Dock Mallett," (birth 4 Jan 1897, death 21 Aug 1980), *FindaGrave.com*.

[912] Callie Pairee Gamble, grave marker, Nash Cemetery, Leake Co., MS, digital image s.v. "Callie Pairee Simmons," (birth 9 Jan 1905, death 19 Jun 1995), *FindaGrave.com*.

[913] "U.S., Social Security Death Index, 1935-2014," s.v. "Henry Simmons," (birth 11 Feb 1904, death Oct 1977), *Ancestry.com*.

[914] Nathan Eugene Gamble, grave marker, Nash Cemetery, Leake Co., MS, digital image s.v. "Nathan Eugene Gamble," (birth 9 Apr 1906, death Dec 1993), *FindaGrave.com*.

[915] Fred "Big Baby" Gamble, grave marker, Nash Cemetery, Leake Co., MS, digital image s.v. "Fred Gamble," (birth 27 Feb 1909, death Jul 1980), *FindaGrave.com*.

[916] Ella Mae Mitchell, grave marker, Marble Rock Cemetery, Kosciusko, Attala Co., MS, digital image s.v. "Ella Mae Gamble," (birth 29 Jun 1919, death 3 Jul 2007), *FindaGrave.com*.

vi   Nola Mae GAMBLE (b. 19 Oct 1910 Attala Co., MS, d. 4 Feb 1994 Gulfport, Harrison Co., MS)[917] m. Damon RILEY (b. 10 Nov 1909 Leake Co., MS, d. 3 Feb 2005).[918]

vii   Katie D. (KD) GAMBLE (b. 17 Sep 1912 Kosciusko Beat 1, Attala Co., MS, d. 19 Jun 2007 Sallis, Attala Co., MS)[919] m. Claude (Pretty Boy) JOINER, Sr. (b. 3 Aug 1911 Attala Co., MS, d. 1 Sep 1986 Jackson, Hinds Co., MS).[920]

viii   Lovie GAMBLE (b. 29 Aug 1915 Kosciusko, Attala Co., MS, d. 16 Oct 2002 Chicago, Cook Co., IL)[921] m. (1) Woodrow Wilson NASH (b. 28 Aug 1916 Leake Co., MS, d. 11 Dec 1999 Chicago, Cook Co., IL)[922] perhaps div. and (2) Ilander N. PARKER, Sr. (b. 21 Oct 1910 Cruger, Holmes Co., MS, d. May 1959 Kosciusko, Attala Co., MS).[923]

ix   Mable Ethel GAMBLE (b. 27 Jun 1916 MS, d. 11 Jun 2012 Memphis, Shelby Co., TN)[924] m. Thomas Eugene (Uncle Bud) CLARK, Sr. (b. 17 Mar 1905 Unknown, d. 21 Aug 1978 Sallis, Attala Co., MS).[925]

---

[917] "U.S., Newspapers.com™ Obituary Index, 1800s-current," s.v. "Nola Mae Gamble Riley," (birth 19 Oct 1910, death 4 Feb 1994), *Ancestry.com*.

[918] "U.S., World War II Draft Cards Young Men, 1940-1947," s.v. "Damon Riley," (birth 8 Sep 1915), *Ancestry.com*. "U.S., Social Security Death Index, 1935-2014," s.v. "Daymon Riley," (birth 10 Nov 1909, death 3 Feb 2005), *Ancestry.com*. Note there is a significant difference in the birth date. It is possible these are different men. The birth location of Leake Co., MS was the same in both documents.

[919] "Katie D. (KD) Gamble, grave marker, Bullock Cemetery, Attala Co., MS, digital image s.v. "Katie D Joiner," (birth 7 Sep 1912, death 19 Jun 2007), *FindaGrave.com*.

[920] "Claude Joiner," grave marker, Bullock Cemetery, Attala Co., MS, digital image s.v. "Claude Joiner," (birth 8 Aug 1909, death 1 Sep 1986), *FindaGrave.com*.

[921] "U.S., Social Security Death Index, 1935-2014," s.v. "Lovie Parker," (birth 29 Aug 1915, death 16 Oct 2002), *Ancestry.com*.

[922] "Woodrow Wilson Nash," grave marker, Mount Hope Cemetery, Chicago, Cook Co., IL, digital image s.v. "Claude Joiner," (birth 28 Apr 1916, death 11 Dec 1999), *FindaGrave.com*. No two documents have the same birth date, but the dates are close together.

[923] "Social Security Death Index," s.v. "Ilander Parker," (birth 21 Sep 1909, death May 1959), *Ancestry.com*.

[924] "Mabel Ethel Gamble," grave marker, Wright Cemetery, Kosciusko, Attala Co., MS, digital image s.v. "Mable Ethel Clark," (birth 27 Jun 1916, d. 11 Jun 2012), *FindaGrave.com*.

[925] "Thomas Eugene Clark," grave marker, Wright Cemetery, Kosciusko, Attala Co., MS, digital image s.v. "Thomas Clark," (birth 17 Mar 1905, death 21 Aug 1978), *FindaGrave.com*.

William Amzy GUYTON, Sr. (Pinkney, Aaron Whitaker, Aaron Steele, Joseph I, John I, Samuel II, Samuel I, John)

William Amzy (or Amzie) GUYTON, Sr. was the son of Pinkney GUYTON (b. Jan 1848 Attala Co., MS, d. Aug 1929) and Fannie SALLIS (b. Oct 1855, d. AFT 1940).[926] William Amzy GUYTON, Sr. was born on 24 Feb 1885 in Attala Co., MS. He died on 6 Jun 1949 in the same county.[927] He married Limmie Mae Douglas NASH (b. 8 Feb 1910 MS, d. 28 Sep 1944 MS).[928] Amzy and Limmie Mae died young, leaving Lacey, their eldest child, to care for the younger children. See the section on Lacey GUYTON.

i   Lacey GUYTON (b. 15 Jul 1927 Kosciusko, Attala Co., MS, d. 24 Sep 1981 Detroit, Wayne Co., MI).[929]
ii   Emma Evester GUYTON (b. 4 Apr 1929 Kosciusko, Attala Co., MS, d. 12 Apr 2007 Kosciusko, Attala Co., MS)[930] m. John Wesley CLAYTON (b. 18 Jan 1921 Indianola, Sunflower Co., MS, d. 22 Sep 1995 Detroit, Wayne Co., MI).[931]
iii   Adel GUYTON (b. ABT 1931 MS, d. Unknown).[932]
iv   Cherry Mae GUYTON (b. 10 Aug 1932 Kosciusko, Attala Co., MS, d. 29 Aug 1998 Detroit, Wayne Co., MI)[933] m. Andrew PERKINS (b. 23 Sep 1927 Tallahatchie Co., MS, d. Unknown).[934]
v   William Amzy GUYTON, Jr. (b. 27 Mar 1934 Kosciusko, Attala Co., MS, d. 11 Nov 2000 Detroit, Wayne Co., MI)[935] m. Betty Janell CLAYTON (b. 12 Feb 1930 Kosciusko, Attala Co., MS, d. Apr 1992 Unknown).[936] I believe she is the sister of John Wesley CLAYTON, who married Emma Evester GUYTON.[937]
vi   Pink West (PW) GUYTON (b. 20 Jul 1938 Kosciusko, Attala Co., MS, d. 23 Aug 1991 Detroit, Wayne Co., MI).[938]

---

[926] "1870 United States Census," Attala Co., MS, digital image s.v. "Penkey Guyton," (birth ABT 1848), Ancestry.com. "Mississippi, Death Certificates," digitmal image s.v. "Pink Guyton," (1848-1929), personal copy. "1900 United States Census," Kosciusko, Attala County, Mississippi, digital image s.v. "Fannie Guyton," (birth Oct 1855), Ancestry.com. Her birth date ranges from 1853 to 1857. She last appears in the 1940 U.S. Census. "1940 United States Census," Kosciusko, Attala County, Mississippi, digital image s.v. "Fannie Guyton," (birth ABT 1855), Ancestry.com.

[927] Amzy William Guyton, grave marker, Mallett Cemetery, Attala County, MS, digital image s.v. "Amzy William Guyton," (birth 28 Feb 1885, death 6 Jun 1949), *FindaGrave.com*.

[928] Limmie Mae Douglas Nash, grave marker, Mallett Cemetery, Attala Co., MS, digital image s.v. "Limmie Guyton," (birth 8 Feb 1910, death 28 Sep 1944), *FindaGrave.com*.

[929] "Michigan, U.S., Death Index, 1971-1996," s.v. "Lacey Guyton," (birth 15 Jul 1927, death 25 Sep 1981), *Ancestry.com*.

[930] Emma Evester Guyton, grave marker, Mallett Cemetery, Attala County, MS, digital image s.v. "Emma Evester Guyton," (birth 4 Apr 1929, death 12 Apr 2007), *FindaGrave.com*.

[931] "U.S., Social Security Applications and Claims Index, 1936-2007," s.v. "John Wesley Clayton," (birth 18 Jan 1921, death Jul 1941), *Ancestry.com*. "Michigan, U.S., Death Index, 1971-1996," s.v. "John W. Clayton," (birth 19 Jan 1921, death 22 Sep 1995), *Ancestry.com*.

[932] "1940 United States Federal Census," Kosciusko, Attala Co., MS, digital image s.v. "Adel Guyton," (birth ABT 1931), Ancestry.com.

[933] "Social Security Death Index," s.v. "Cherry M. Perkins," (birth 10 Aug 1932, death 28 Aug 1998), *Ancestry.com*.

[934] "U.S., World War II Draft Cards Young Men, 1940-1947," digital image s.v. "Andrew Perkins," (birth 23 Sep 1927), *Ancestry.com*.

[935] "U.S., Social Security Death Index, 1935-2014," s.v. "William Guyton," (birth 27 Mar 1934, death 11 Nov 2000), *Ancestry.com*.

[936] "U.S., Social Security Death Index, 1936-2007," s.v. "Betty Janell Clark," (birth 12 Feb 1930, death Apr 1992), *Ancestry.com*.

[937] "1940 United States Federal Census," Leake Co., MS, digital image s.v. "Betty Clayton," (birth ABT 1930), *Ancestry.com*.

[938] "U.S., Social Security Death Index, 1936-2007," s.v. "Pink W Guyton," (birth 19 Jul 1938, death Aug 1991), *Ancestry.com*.

vii   Fannie Douglas GUYTON (b. 18 Jan 1942 Kosciusko, Attala Co., MS, d. 24 Oct 1988 Detroit, Wayne Co., MI).[939]

viii   Elizabeth GUYTON (b. 6 Aug 1943 Kosciusko, Attala Co., MS, d. 13 Nov 1982 Detroit, Wayne Co., MI)[940] m. (1) Willie James THOMAS (b. 28 Feb 1929 George Co., MS, d. 13 Mar 1979 Detroit, Wayne Co., MI) and (2) Ernest SMITH, Jr.(b. 10 Aug 1920 Macon Co., GA, d. Apr 2000 Detroit, Wayne Co., MI) on 13 Nov 1964 in Toledo, Lucas Co., OH).[941]

Suegene GUYTON (Pinkney, Aaron Whitaker, Aaron Steele, Joseph I, John I, Samuel II, Samuel I, John)

Suegene GUYTON was the daughter of Pinkney GUYTON (b. Jan 1848 Attala Co., MS, d. Aug 1929) and Fannie SALLIS (b. Oct 1855, d. AFT 1940).[942] Suegene was born on 21 Dec 1887 in MS.[943] She died on 1 May 1976 in Kosciusko, Attala Co., MS). She married Dock WRIGHT (b. 31 Mar 1882, MS, d. 22 Jun 1969, who is buried in Wright Cemetery).[944] See Figure 120 and Figure 121.

Figure 120 Suegene GUYTON WRIGHT Younger[945]

Figure 121 Suegene GUYTON WRIGHT Older[946]

Together they had at least twelve children:

i   Essie WRIGHT (b. ABT 1905 MS, d. Unknown).[947]

---

[939] "U.S., Social Security Death Index, 1936-2007," s.v. "Fannie Guyton," (birth 18 Jul 1942, death Nov 1988), Ancestry.com.

[940] "Michigan, Death Index, 1971-1996," s.v. "Elizabeth G Smith," (birth 6 Aug 1943, death 13 Nov 1982), Ancestry.com.

[941] "Cassandra Smith Family Tree," Sann098, Ancestry.com, accessed 13 May 2024.

[942] "1870 United States Census," Attala Co., MS, digital image s.v. "Penkey Guyton," (birth ABT 1848), Ancestry.com. "Mississippi, Death Certificates," digitmal image s.v. "Pink Guyton," (1848-1929), personal copy. "1900 United States Census," Kosciusko, Attala County, Mississippi, digital image s.v. "Fannie Guyton," (birth Oct 1855), Ancestry.com. Her birth date ranges from 1853 to 1857. She last appears in the 1940 U.S. Census. "1940 United States Census," Kosciusko, Attala County, Mississippi, digital image s.v. "Fannie Guyton," (birth ABT 1855), Ancestry.com.

[943] "Sugene Wright," grave marker, Wright Cemetery, Kosciusko, Attala Co., MS, digital image s.v. "Sugena Wright," (birth 29 Dec 1888, death 1 May 1976), FindaGrave.com.

[944] "Dock Wright," grave marker, Wright Cemetery, Kosciusko, Attala Co., MS, digital image s.v. "Dock Wright," (birth 31 Mar 1882, death 22 Jun 1969), FindaGrave.com.

[945] Karl Boyd originally shared this on 21 Feb 2023 on Ancestry.com.

[946] cpack1218 originally shared this on 1 Dec 2013 on Ancestry.com.

[947] "1920 United States Federal Census," Kosciusko, Attala Co., MS, digital image s.v. "Essie Right," (birth ABT 1905), Ancestry.com.

ii   Rose WRIGHT (b. ABT 1907 MS, d. Unknown).[948]
iii   Adeline WRIGHT (b. ABT 1910 MS, d. Unknown).[949]
iv   Gertrude WRIGHT (b. ABT 1911 MS, d. Unknown).[950]
v   Fannie WRIGHT (b. ABT 1913 MS, d. Unknown).[951]
vi   Viola WRIGHT (b. ABT 1915 MS, d. Unknown).[952]
vii   Silas D. WRIGHT (b. ABT 1916 MS, d. Unknown).[953]
viii Mitchell WRIGHT (b. 28 May 1920 Attala Co., MS, d. June 1978 Tallulah, Madison Parish, LA).[954] According to his obituary, he had one son survive him, Billie J. WRIGHT.
ix   Amzie WRIGHT (b. 11 Sep 1921 Tallulah, Madison Parish, LA, d. 22 Jul 1996 bur. in CA)[955] m. Inet FLOOD (b. 30 Dec 1937 Tallulah, Madison Parish, LA, d. 29 Nov 2020 Richmond, Contra Costa Co., CA)[956] on 2 Jul 1952 in Tallulah, Madison Parish, LA.[957]
x   Freddie WRIGHT (b. ABT 1923 MS, d. Unknown) m. Carrie PATTON on 31 Mar 1951 in Tallulah, Madison Parish, LA. [958]
xi   Christian WRIGHT (b. ABT 1925 MS, d. Unknown).[959]
xii   Jessie WRIGHT (female) (b. ABT 1927 MS, d. Unknown).[960]

---

[948] "1920 United States Federal Census," Kosciusko, Attala Co., MS, digital image s.v. "Rosie Right," (birth ABT 1907), *Ancestry.com.*

[949] "1920 United States Federal Census," Kosciusko, Attala Co., MS, digital image s.v. "Adline Right," (birth ABT 1910), *Ancestry.com.*

[950] "1920 United States Federal Census," Kosciusko, Attala Co., MS, digital image s.v. "Gertrue Right," (birth ABT 1911), *Ancestry.com.*

[951] "1920 United States Federal Census," Kosciusko, Attala Co., MS, digital image s.v. "Fannie Right," (birth ABT 1913), *Ancestry.com.*

[952] "1920 United States Federal Census," Kosciusko, Attala Co., MS, digital image s.v. "Viola Right," (birth ABT 1915), *Ancestry.com.*

[953] "1920 United States Federal Census," Kosciusko, Attala Co., MS, digital image s.v. "Silas Right," (birth ABT 1916), *Ancestry.com.*

[954] "1920 United States Federal Census," Kosciusko, Attala Co., MS, digital image s.v. "Mitchell Right," (birth ABT 1920), *Ancestry.com.* "U.S., World War II Draft Cards Young Men, 1940-1947," digital image s.v. "Mitchell Wright," (birth 28 May 1920), *Ancestry.com.* "Mr. Mitchell Wright," *The Madison Journal*, 15 Jun 1978, p. 3; digital image, s.v. "Mr. Mitchell Wright," *Newspapers.com* <https://www.newspapers.com/image/856159672/?article=8bde18d7-b856-407c-829d-b202d9ffae80&focus=0.011797058,0.87971395,0.33235678,0.9612616&xid=3355>. "U.S., Social Security Death Index, 1935-2014," s.v. "Mitchell Wright," (birth 24 Sep 1919, death Jun 1978), *Ancestry.com.*

[955] "U.S., Social Security Applications and Claims Index, 1936-2007," s.v. "Amzie Wright," (birth 11 Sep 1921, death 22 Jul 1996), *Ancestry.com.* "Amzie Wright," grave marker, San Joaquin Valley National Cemetery, Santa Nella, Merced Co., CA, digital image s.v. "Amzie O Wright," (birth 24 Sep 1924 [error], d. 22 Jul 1996), *FindaGrave.com.*

[956] "Inet Flood," grave marker, Memory Gardens Cemetery, Concord, Contra Costa Co., CA, digital image s.v. "Inet Williams," (birth 30 Dec 1937, d. 29 Nov 2020), *FindaGrave.com.*

[957] "Louisiana, U.S., Compiled Marriage Index, 1718-1925," digital image s.v. "Amzie Wright," (marriage 2 Jul 1952 to Inet Flood), *Ancestry.com.*

[958] "1950 United States Federal Census," Tallulah, Madison Parish, LA, digital image s.v. "Freddie Wright," (birth ABT 1923), *Ancestry.com.* "Louisiana, U.S., Compiled Marriage Index, 1718-1925," digital image s.v. "Freddy Wright," (marriage to Carrie Patton 31 Mar 1951), *Ancestry.com.*

[959] "1940 United States Federal Census," Kosciusko, Attala Co., MS, digital image s.v. "Christin Wright," (birth ABT 1925), *Ancestry.com.*

[960] "1940 United States Federal Census," Kosciusko, Attala Co., MS, digital image s.v. "Jessie Wright," (birth ABT 1927), *Ancestry.com.*

Generation #9

Nola J. ALLEN (Emma GUYTON ALLEN, Pinkney, Aaron Whitaker, Aaron Steele, Joseph I, John I, Samuel II, Samuel I, John)

Nola J. ALLEN was the daughter of Emma GUYTON (b. Jun 1874 MS, d. sometime after 1915 but before the 1920 Census) as her husband, Addison D. ALLEN (b. Dec 1872, Attala Co., MS, d. 1963 Chicago, Cook Co., IL) was shown as a widower.[961] Nola J. ALLEN was born in Feb 1897 MS, and died on 23 Jan 1997 Sallis, Attala Co., MS.[962] She married Sherman FORD (b. 30 Dec 1882 Durant, Holmes Co., MS, d. Nov 1967 Bolton, Hinds Co., MS)[963] around 1915 based on the birth of their first child. Sherman had been married before to Luvenia UNKNOWN.

In the 1920 U.S. Census, Nola J. ALLEN (23) and Sherman FORD (37) were married.[964] They lived in New Port, Attala Co., MS on a rented farm that Sherman worked. Living with them were Sherman's mother, Tena UNKNOWN. (82); children from Luvenia: Matthew FORD (17), Susan FORD (15), Grace FORD (14), and Nelson FORD (10) and Nola's children: Ruthie FORD (5), Emmett FORD (3) and Cicero FORD (0).

In the 1930 U.S. Census, Nola J. ALLEN (30) and Sherman FORD (50) lived in Beat 2, Hinds Co., MS on a rented farm. Luvenia's children had left home.[965] Living with them were Emmett FORD (13), David Cicero FORD (10), Joseph FORD (6), and Samuel Alonzo FORD (3). Ruthie FORD should be 15 but either died before the 1930 Census or married young and moved out of the house.

In the 1940 U.S. Census, Sherman (53) and Nola FORD (43) lived in rural Hinds Co., MS on a rented farm.[966] The children living with them were Joseph FORD (16), Samuel Alonzo FORD (12), Douglas FORD (8), Fannie Lee FORD (6) and Alberta FORD (3). In the 1950 U.S. Census, Sherman FORD (66) and Nola ALLEN FORD (52) lived with the following children: Joseph FORD (24) Fannie Lee FORD (17), Alberta FORD (13), and Nola Ann FORD (7).

---

[961] "1900 United States Federal Census," Kosciusko, Attala Co., MS, digital image s.v. "Emma M. Allen," (birth ABT Jun 1874), *Ancestry.com*. "1920 United States Federal Census," Newport, Attala Co., MS, digital image s.v. "Addison Allen," (birth 1873, widowed), *Ancestry.com*.
[962] "1900 United States Federal Census," Kosciusko, Attala Co., MS, digital image s.v. "Nola J. Allen," (birth Feb 1897), *Ancestry.com*.
[963] "U.S., Social Security Death Index, 1935-2014," s.v. "Sherman Ford," (birth 30 Dec 1882, death Nov 1967), *Ancestry.com*.
[964] "1920 United States Federal Census," New Port, Attala Co., MS, digital image s.v. "Nola Ford," (birth abt 1897), *Ancestry.com*.
[965] "1930 United States Federal Census," Beat 2, Hinds Co., MS, digital image s.v. "Nola Ford," (birth abt 1900), *Ancestry*.
[966] "1940 United States Federal Census," Hinds Co., MS, digital image s.v. "Nola Ford," (birth abt 1897), *Ancestry*.

Based on the U.S. Census schedules, Nola J. ALLEN and Sherman FORD's children were:

i   Ruthie FORD (b. ABT 1915, d. Unknown).

ii   Emmett FORD (b. 10 Oct 1916 Attala Co., MS, d. AUG 1970 Bolton, Hinds Co., MS)[967] m. Mary UNKNOWN (b. ABT 1914 MS, d. Unknown).[968]

iii   David Cicero FORD (b. 14 Feb 1918 Attala Co., MS, d. Unknown)[969] m. Bertha Marie DAVIS (b. 2 Apr 1933 MS, d. 15 Oct 1990).[970] I found one child in the 1950 Census: Agnes Louise FORD (b. Jan 1950 Hinds Co., MS, d. Unknown).[971] They may have had more children, but the public Federal Census ends in 1950.

iv   Joseph FORD (b. 30 May 1923 Durant, Holmes Co., MS, d. Unknown).[972]

v   Samuel Alonzo FORD, Sr. (b. 4 Jan 1927 Hinds Co., MS, d. 14 Nov 2000 Chicago, Cook Co., IL)[973] m. Estelle BROWN (b. 30 Jan 1928 MS, d. Jun 1972 Chicago, Cook Co., IL).[974]

vi   Douglas FORD (b. 24 May 1930 MS, d. 19 Jun 1953 Korea)[975] m. Ruth Mae BUTLER (b. 7 Mar 1926 MS, d. 12 Apr 2011 Clinton, Hinds Co., MS).[976] Douglas died in a hostile action in Korea of wounds. His service number was 53139158, Unit A/S Inf, Co F, 7 Inf Regt, Company F. 7th Inf. Opa 468.[977]

vii   Fannie Lee FORD (b. abt 1934 MS, d. Unknown).[978]

viii   Alberta FORD (b. abt 1937 MS, d. Unknown).[979]

ix   Nola Ann FORD (b. 18 Jul 1942 MS, d. 9 Jan 2023 CA)[980] m. Unknown JONES.

---

[967] "U.S., Social Security Death Index, 1935-2014," s.v. Emmitt Ford, (birth 10 Oct 1916, death Aug 1970), *Ancestry.com.*

[968] "1940 United States Federal Census," Hinds Co., MS, digital image s.v. "Mary Ford," (birth abt 1914), *Ancestry.com.*

[969] "U.S., World War II Draft Cards Young Men, 1940-1947," digital image s.v. "David Cicero Ford," (birth 14 Feb 1918), *Ancestry.com.*

[970] Bertha Marie Davis, grave marker, Mount Elizabeth Missionary Baptist Church Cemetery, Bolton, Hinds Co., MS, digital image s.v. "Bertha Marie Davis," (birth 2 Apr 1933, death 15 Oct 1990), *FindaGrave.com.*

[971] "1950 United States Federal Census," Hinds Co., MS, digital image s.v. "Agnes Louis Ford," (birth Jan 1950), *Ancestry.com.*

[972] "U.S., World War II Draft Cards Young Men, 1940-1947," digital image s.v. "Joe Ford," (birth 30 May 1923), *Ancestry.com.*

[973] "U.S., Social Security Death Index, 1935-2014," s.v. "Samuel A. Ford," (birth 4 Jan 1927, death 13 Nov 2000), *Ancestry.com.*

[974] "Social Security Death Index, 1935-2014," s.v. "Estella Ford," (birth 30 Jan 1928, death Jun 1972), *Ancestry.com.*

[975] "Douglas Ford, grave marker, Zion Chapel Cemetery, Bolton, Hinds Co., MS, digital image s.v. "Douglas Ford," (birth 24 May 1930, death 19 Jun 1953), *FindaGrave.com.*

[976] "U.S., Social Security Death Index, 1935-2014," s.v. "Ruthie M. Ford," (birth 7 Mar 1926, death 12 Apr 2011), *Ancestry.com.*

[977] "U.S., Headstone Applications for Military Veterans, 1861-1985," digital image s.v. "Douglas Ford," (enlistment date 13 Oct 1952, death 19 Jun 1953), *Ancestry.com.*

[978] "1940 United States Federal Census," Hinds Co., MS, digital image s.v. "Fanny Lee Ford," (birth abt 1934), *Ancestry.com.*

[979] "1940 United States Federal Census," Hinds Co., MS, digital image s.v. "Alberta Ford," (birth abt 1937), Ancestry.com.

[980] "Nola Ann Ford, grave marker, Rose Hills Memorial Park, Whittier, Los Angeles Co., CA, digital image s.v. "Nola Ann Jones," (birth 18 Jul 1942, death 9 Jan 2023), *FindaGrave.com.*

Ethel S. ALLEN (Emma GUYTON ALLEN, Pinkney, Aaron Whitaker, Aaron Steele, Joseph I, John I, Samuel II, Samuel I, John)

Ethel S. ALLEN was the daughter of Emma GUYTON (b. Jun 1874 MS, d. sometime after 1915 but before the 1920 Census) and her husband, Addison D. ALLEN (b. Dec 1872, Attala Co., MS, d. 1963 Chicago, Cook Co., IL) was shown as a widower.[981] Ethel was born on 1 Apr 1905 MS, d. 28 May 1992 Rockford, Winnebago Co., IL.[982] She married Leroy ARNOLD, Sr. (b. 20 Feb 1898 MS, d. 10 May 1978 Rockford, Winnebago Co., IL).[983]

In the 1930 U.S. Federal Census, Leroy (32) and Ethel (27) were married, living in Beat 4, Attala Co., MS on 311 Durant Possum Neck Road, where the family farmed. They lived with their children Mabel ARNOLD (8), Leroy ARNOLD, Jr. (7), Otho James ARNOLD (4), and Willis C. ARNOLD (1).[984] In the 1940 Census Leroy (42) and Ethel (36) lived in New Port, Attala Co., MS.[985] Leroy and Ethel were laborers on a farm, perhaps a farm they rented. Leroy worked 60 hours in the week before the Census taking; Ethel worked 38 hours. Leroy had a 7th grade education and Ethel's education was 6th grade. They lived with their children Mabel ARNOLD (18), Leroy J. ARNOLD (16), Otho James ARNOLD (13), Myrtis ARNOLD (11), Willis C. ARNOLD (7), and Robert L. ARNOLD (2).

In the 1950 U.S. Federal Census, Leroy (52) and Ethel ALLEN ARNOLD (45) lived on 279 US Highway, Holmes Co., MS.[986] Leroy was a carpenter's helper in construction. Ethel operated a café, and her daughter Myrtis was a waitress at the café. The children living at home were Myrtis ARNOLD (17), Robert L. ARNOLD (12), and Jimmy Dale ARNOLD (9).

---

[981] "1900 United States Federal Census," Kosciusko, Attala Co., MS, digital image s.v. "Emma M. Allen," (birth ABT Jun 1874), *Ancestry.com*. "1920 United States Federal Census," Newport, Attala Co., MS, digital image s.v. "Addison Allen," (birth 1873, widowed), *Ancestry.com*.
[982] "U.S., Social Security Death Index, 1935-2014," s.v. "Ethel I. Arnold," (birth 1 Apr 1905, death 28 May 1992), *Ancestry.com*.
[983] "Leroy Arnold, Sr., grave marker, Cedar Bluff Cemetery, Rockford, Winnebago Co., Il, digital image s.v. "LeRoy Arnold," (birth 21 Feb 1898, death 10 May 1978), *FindaGrave.com*.
[984] "1930 United States Federal Census," Beat 4, Attala Co., MS, digital image s.v. "Leroy Arnold," (birth 1898), *Ancestry.com*.
[985] "1940 United States Federal Census," Newport, Attala Co., MS, digital image s.v. "Leroy Arnold," (birth 1898), *Ancestry.com*.
[986] "1950 United States Federal Census," Holmes Co, Attala Co., MS, digital image s.v. "Ethel Arnold," (birth 1905), *Ancestry.com*.

Based on the Census schedules, Leroy and Ethel had the following children:

i   Mabel (Maybell) ARNOLD (b. 14 Aug 1921 MS, d. 15 Dec 2016 St. Louis, St. Louis Co., MO)[987] m. William Samuel BUSH (b. 2 Sep 1920 MS, d. 25 Apr 2000 St. Louis, St Louis Co., MO).[988]

ii   Leroy ARNOLD, Jr. (b. 28 JUN 1923 Attala Co., MS, d. Unknown).[989]

iii   Otho James ARNOLD (b. 8 Mar 1926 Attala Co., MS, d. 20 Nov 1971 IL).[990] Otho had at least one son killed in Vietnam and had a grandchild through him.

iv   Willis C. ARNOLD (b. ABT 1929 Attala Co., MS, d. Unknown).[991]

v   Myrtis ARNOLD (b. ABT 1933 MS, d. Unknown).[992]

vi   Robert L. ARNOLD (b. ABT 1938 MS).[993]

vii   Jimmy Dale ARNOLD (b. 21 Mar 1940 Sallis Attala Co., MS, d. 26 May 2001 Rockford, Winnebago Co., IL).[994]

---

[987] "U.S., Veterans' Gravesites, ca.1775-2019," Jefferson Barracks National Cemetery, St. Louis, MO, s.v. "Mabel L Bush," (birth 14 Aug 1921, death 15 Dec 2016), *Ancestry.com*.

[988] "U.S., Veterans' Gravesites, ca.1775-2019," Jefferson Barracks National Cemetery, St. Louis, MO, s.v. "William S Bush," (birth 2 Sep 1920, service start date 19 Dec 1942, service end date 21 Oct 1945, death 25 Apr 2000), *Ancestry.com*.

[989] "U.S., World War II Draft Cards Young Men, 1940-1947," digital image s.v. Leroy Arnold, (birth 28 Jun 1923), *Ancestry.com*.

[990] "U.S., Headstone Applications for Military Veterans, 1861-1985," Cedar Bluff Cemetery, Rockford, IL, digital image s.v. "Otho J. Arnold," (birth 8 Mar 1926, service number 34 929 709, service branch US Army, enlistment 28 Jul 1944, discharge 23 Jul 1946, death 20 Nov 1971), *Ancestry.com*.

[991] "1930 United States Federal Census," Beat 4, Attala Co., MS, digital image s.v. "Willis C Arnold," (birth 1929), *Ancestry.com*.

[992] "1950 United States Federal Census," Holmes Co., MS, digital image s.v. "Myrtis Arnold," (birth 1933), *Ancestry.com*.

[993] "1950 United States Federal Census," Holmes Co., MS, digital image s.v. "Robert L Arnold," (birth 1938), *Ancestry.com*.

[994] "U.S., Social Security Applications and Claims Index, 1936-2007," s.v. "Jimmy Dale Arnold," (birth 21 Mar 1940, death 26 May 2001), *Ancestry.com*.

Willie Walter ALLEN (Emma GUYTON ALLEN, Pinkney, Aaron Whitaker, Aaron Steele, Joseph I, John I, Samuel II, Samuel I, John)

Willie Walter ALLEN was the son of Emma GUYTON (b. Jun 1874 MS, d. sometime after 1915 but before the 1920 Census) and her husband, Addison D. ALLEN (b. Dec 1872, Attala Co., MS, d. 1963 Chicago, Cook Co., IL) was shown as a widower.[995] Willie was born on 18 Dec 1905 Sallis, Attala Co., MS, and died on 1 Oct 1995 Chicago, Cook Co., IL).[996] He married Willie Mae LITTLE (b. 9 Jan 1910 MS, d. 19 Mar 1983 Kosciusko, Attala Co., MS).[997]

In the 1930 U.S. Federal Census, Willie Walter (24) and Willie Mae (20) were married. They lived in Beat 1, Holmes Co., MS working on a rented farm. They lived with their two children Annie Louise ALLEN (4) and Dorothy May ALLEN (0).[998] In 1940 the U.S. Census reported that the couple lived in New Port, Attala Co., MS on a rented farm. Willie Walter (34) had a sixth-grade education; Willie Mae (30) had a fifth-grade education. They both labored on the farm. Willie Walter put in 55 hours of work the week before the Census was taken and Willie May worked 30 hours. They lived with their children Annie Louise ALLEN (14), Dorothy May ALLEN (10), and Fred ALLEN (8).[999]

The 1950 U.S. Federal Census reported that Willie Walter (43) and Willie Mae (40) lived in New Port, Attala Co., MS on Old Highway 12 west of Sallis Rd. They were still farming. Living with them was their youngest child, Fred ALLEN (18).[1000]

The children of Willie Walter ALLEN and Willie May LITTLE, according to the U.S. Census schedules, were as follows:

i   Anna Louise ALLEN (b. ABT 1926 MS, d. Unknown).
ii Dorothy May ALLEN (b. ABT 1930 MS, d. Unknown).
iii Fred ALLEN (b. 26 Nov 1931 Lexington, Holmes Co., MS, d. 23 Jan 1997 Sallis, Attala Co., MS).[1001]

---

[995] "1900 United States Federal Census," Kosciusko, Attala Co., MS, digital image s.v. "Emma M. Allen," (birth ABT Jun 1874), *Ancestry.com*. "1920 United States Federal Census," Newport, Attala Co., MS, digital image s.v. "Addison Allen," (birth 1873, widowed), *Ancestry.com*.

[996] "U.S., Social Security Applications and Claims Index, 1936-2007," s.v. "Willie Walter Allen," (birth 18 Dec 1905, death 1 Oct 1995), *Ancestry.com*.

[997] Willie Mae Little, grave marker, Barlow United Methodist Church Cemetery, Sallis, Attala County, MS, digital image s.v. "Willie Mae Allen," (birth 9 Jan 1910, death 19 Mar 1983), *FindaGrave.com*.

[998] "1930 United States Federal Census," Beat 1, Holmes Co., MS, s.v. "Willie Allen," (birth abt 1908), *Ancestry.com*.

[999] "1940 United States Federal Census," Newport, Holmes Co., MS, s.v. "Willie W Allen," (birth abt 1906), *Ancestry.com*.

[1000] "1950 United States Federal Census," Newport, Holmes Co., MS, s.v. "Willie Walter Allen," (birth abt 1907), *Ancestry.com*.

[1001] "U.S., Social Security Applications and Claims Index, 1936-2007, s.v. "Freddie Allen," (birth 26 Nov 1931, death 23 Jan 1997), *Ancestry.com*.

Earnest Mitchell ROBY (Patsy J., Pinkney, Aaron Whitaker, Aaron Steele, Joseph I, John I, Samuel II, Samuel I, John)

Earnest Mitchell ROBY was the son of Patsy J. GUYTON (b. Aug 1877 Sallis, Attala Co., MS, d. after 1950, likely in Sallis, Attala Co., MS)[1002] and William (Willie) ROBY (b. Mar 1876, MS, d. Unknown).[1003] She married William (Willie) ROBY in 1898, per the 1900 U.S. Census and divorced before 1930.[1004]

Earnest Mitchell ROBY was born 29 Mar 1902 MS, but his death is unknown.[1005] He married Velma Lizzie STINGLEY (b. 1 Jan 1904 Attala Co., MS, d. 23 Sep 1992 Kosciusko, Attala Co., MS). See Figure 122.

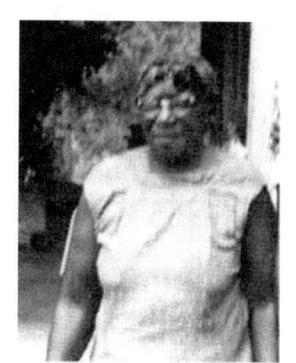

Figure 122 Velma Lizzie STINGLEY

Earnest ROBY and Velma STINGLEY's children were:

i Katie ROBY (b. 14 Jan 1927 Attala Co., MS, d. 29 Mar 2017 Hinds Co., MS)[1006] m. Oscar SNOW (b. 18 Oct 1925 Attala Co., MS, d. Unknown).[1007] Oscar SNOW was the brother of Ernest Jim SNOW, the husband of Katie's sister, Linnie B.

ii Mitchell ROBY (b. 10 Jun 1930 MS, d. 9 July 1987 Sallis, Attala Co., MS).[1008] His obituary indicated he had one child, Linda G. MALLETT. I don't know if Mallett is a maiden name or a married name. No wife was mentioned.

[1002] "1900 United States Federal Census," Attala Co., MS, digital image s.v. "Patsy J. Roby," (birth Aug 1877), *Ancestry.com*. I assume she died after 1950 because she was in the 1950 U.S. Census. "1950 United States Federal Census," Newport, Attala Co., MS, digital image s.v. "Patsy Robey," (birth abt 1877), *Ancestry.com*.

[1003] "1900 United States Federal Census," Attala Co., MS, digital image s.v. "Will Roby," (birth Mar 1876), *Ancestry.com*.

[1004] "1930 United States Federal Census," Attala Co., MS, digital image s.v. "Will Roby," (marital status divorced), *Ancestry.com*.

[1005] "U.S. WWII Draft Cards Young Men, 1940-1947," digital image s.v. "Earnest Mitchell Roby," (birth 29 Mar 1902), *Ancestry.com*.

[1006] Katie Roby, grave marker, Barlow United Methodist Church Cemetery, Sallis, Attala Co., MS, digital image s.v. "Katie Snow," (birth 14 Jan 1927, death 29 Mar 2017), *FindaGrave.com*.

[1007] "U.S., World War II Draft Cards Young Men, 1940-1947," digital image s.v. "Oscar Snow," (birth 18 Oct 1925 in Attala Co., MS), *Ancestry.com*. "1950 United States Federal Census," Newport, Attala Co., MS, digital image s.v. "Oscar Snow," (birth abt 1920), *Ancestry.com*.

[1008] Mitchell Roby, grave marker, Barlow United Methodist Church Cemetery, Sallis, Attala Co., MS, digital image s.v. "Mitchell Roby," (birth 10 Jun 1930, death 9 Jul 1987), *FindaGrave.com*. "Mitchell Roby," *The Star-Herald*, 17 Jul 1987, p. 7; digital image, s.v. "Mitchell Roby," *Newspapers.com*, <https://www.newspapers.com/image/305176054/?article=f82f3546-55ce-44fa-b7e1-d8b8235af47f&focus=0.021087984,0.16623946,0.19452462,0.33489597&xid=3355>.

iii	Linnie B. ROBY (b. 29 Jun 1934 MS, d. 29 Jun 2018 Sallis, Attala Co., MS)[1009] m. Earnest Jim SNOW (b. 12 Jan 1928 MS, d. Dec 1984).[1010] Ernest Jim SNOW was the brother of Oscar SNOW, the husband of Linnie's sister, Katie.
iv	Velma Mae ROBY (b. 7 Mar 1938 Sallis, Attala Co., MS, d. 16 Dec 2014 Sallis, Attala Co., MS)[1011] m. Archie (Bud) LEVY (b. 28 Jan 1931 MS, d. 31 Mar 2012 Sallis, Attala Co., MS).[1012]
v	Vernon L. (Booger) ROBY (b. 17 Jan 1950 MS, d. 24 Feb 2014 WI).[1013] According to his obituary on his *FindaGrave* site, "He was the proud father of two sons, James Lamar of Sallis, MS; and Willie Charles of Milwaukee, WI; and one daughter, Joyrosea of Milwaukee, WI."

Lillie Wardean ROBY (Patsy J., Pinkney, Aaron Whitaker, Aaron Steele, Joseph I, John I, Samuel II, Samuel I, John)

Lillie Wardean ROBY was the daughter of Patsy J. GUYTON (b. Aug 1877 Sallis, Attala Co., MS, d. after 1950, likely in Sallis, Attala Co., MS)[1014] and William (Willie) ROBY (b. Mar 1876, MS, d. Unknown).[1015] Lillie was born on 17 Nov 1909 Sallis, Attala Co., MS, and she died 27 Oct 2003 Chicago, Cook Co., IL.[1016] She married James (Jim) GUYTON (b. 2 Sep 1905 Sallis, Attala Co., MS, d. Unknown).[1017] Jim GUYTON is related to Lillie as he is the son of Case GUYTON (son of Aaron Whitaker GUYTON and Artie RAINEY) and Susie STINGLEY. Patsy J. GUYTON was the granddaughter of Aaron Whitaker GUYTON and Patsy GIBSON.

More information on the family can be seen in the section on James (Jim). Together they had at least twelve children:

[1009] Linnie B. Roby, grave marker, Barlow United Methodist Church Cemetery, Sallis, Attala Co., MS, digital image s.v. "Linnie Snow," (birth 29 Jun 1934, death 29 Jun 2018), *FindaGrave.com*.

[1010] "U.S., Social Security Death Index, 1935-2014," s.v. "Earnest Snow," (birth 12 Jan 1928, death Dec 1984), *Ancestry.com*.

[1011] Velma Mae Roby, grave marker, Barlow United Methodist Church Cemetery, Sallis, Attala Co., MS, digital image s.v. "Velma Levy," (birth 7 Mar 1938, death 16 Dec 2014), *FindaGrave.com*.

[1012] Archie (Bud) Levy, grave marker, Barlow United Methodist Church Cemetery, Sallis, Attala Co., MS, digital image s.v. "Archie Levy," (birth 28 Jan 1931, death 31 Mar 2012), *FindaGrave.com*.

[1013] Vernon L. Roby, grave marker, Barlow United Methodist Church Cemetery, Sallis, Attala Co., MS, digital image s.v. "Vernon L Roby," (birth 17 Jan 1950, death 24 Feb 2014), *FindaGrave.com*.

[1014] "1900 United States Federal Census," Attala Co., MS, digital image s.v. "Patsy J. Roby," (birth Aug 1877), *Ancestry.com*. I assume she died after 1950 because she was in the 1950 U.S. Census. "1950 United States Federal Census," Newport, Attala Co., MS, digital image s.v. "Patsy Robey," (birth abt 1877), *Ancestry.com*.

[1015] "1900 United States Federal Census," Attala Co., MS, digital image s.v. "Will Roby," (birth Mar 1876), *Ancestry.com*.

[1016] Lillie Wardean Roby, grave marker, Burr Oak Cemetery, Alsip, Cook Co., IL, digital image s.v. "Mrs Lillie Wardean Guyton," (birth 17 Nov 1909, death 27 Oct 2003), *FindaGrave.com*.

[1017] "U.S. WWII Draft Cards Young Men, 1940-1947," digital image s.v. "Jim Guyton," (birth 2 Sep 1905), *Ancestry.com*.

i   Casey Glenn GUYTON, Sr. (b. 13 Jan 1926 Sallis, Attala Co., MS, d. Unknown)[1018] m. Mildred TATE (b. 1 Mar 1928 Kosciusko, Attala Co., MS d. Unknown)[1019] on 8 Aug 1952 in Cook Co., IL.[1020]

ii   Rozell J. GUYTON (b. 1 Mar 1928 Kosciusko Attala Co., MS, d. 7 May 2008 Milwaukee, Milwaukee Co., WI)[1021] m. Ollie D. Riley, Sr. (b. 17 Sep 1921 Sallis, Attala Co., MS, d. 31 Dec 1993, Milwaukee, Milwaukee Co., WI).[1022]

iii   Genova GUYTON (b. 20 May 1930, Sallis, Attala Co., MS, d. 17 Jun 2023 Chicago, Cook Co., IL)[1023] m. (1) Ben GUYTON (b. 2 Apr 1920 Sallis, Attala Co., MS, d. 8 Nov 1996 Sallis, Attala Co., MS)[1024] and (2) Daniel WALKER (b. 23 Jul 1934 Port Gibson, Claiborne Co., MS, d. 2 Dec 2002, Chicago, Cook Co., IL).[1025] Genova was first cousin to Ben GUYTON, who was Ike GUYTON's son.

iv   Lovell GUYTON (b. 16 Oct 1933 Sallis, Attala Co., MS, d. 22 May 2009 Milwaukee, Milwaukee Co., WI)[1026] m. Albert BEAMON (b. 22 Dec 1928, d. 22 Sep 1978).[1027]

v   Maebell GUYTON (b. ABT 1934 MS, d. Unknown)[1028] m. Lee EVANS (Unknown).[1029]

vi   Lucy GUYTON (b. ABT 1936 MS, d. Unknown)[1030] m. John Lee THURMAN (Unknown).

vii   Susie Jean GUYTON (b. ABT 1937 MS, d. Unknown)[1031] m. Terry LAFLORE (b. Sallis, Attala Co., MS, d. Unknown).[1032]

viii   Jimmie Ruth GUYTON (b. ABT 1938 MS, Unknown)[1033] m. Wardell HILL (b. Unknown, d. Chicago, Cook Co., IL).[1034]

ix   Joe Troy GUYTON (b. Nov 1945, d. Unknown).[1035]

x   Ray GUYTON (b. ABT 1946 MS, d. Unknown).[1036]

[1018] "World War II Draft Cards Young Men, 1940-1947," digital image s.v. "Casey Glenn Guyton," (birth 13 Jan 1926, residence, Chicago, IL), *Ancestry.com*.

[1019] "U.S., Public Records Index, 1950-1993, Volume 1," s.v. "Mildred Guyton," (birth 3 Jun 1930), *Ancestry.com*.

[1020] "Cook County, Illinois Marriage Index, 1930-1960," s.v. "Mildred Tate," (marriage 8 Aug 1952 to Kasey Guyton), *Ancestry.com*.

[1021] Rozell J. Roby, grave marker, Parkway Cemetery, Kosciusko, Attala Co., MS, digital image s.v. "Rozell J. Riley," (birth 1 Mar 1928, death 7 May 2008), *FindaGrave.com*.

[1022] Ollie D. Riley, grave marker, Parkway Cemetery, Kosciusko, Attala Co., MS, digital image s.v. "Ollie D Riley," (birth 17 Sep 1921, death 31 Dec 1993), *FindaGrave.com*.

[1023] Per Channie Brown-Currie.

[1024] Per Channie Brown-Currie.

[1025] Per Channie Brown-Currie.

[1026] Lovell GUYTON, grave marker, Lincoln Memorial Cemetery, Milwaukee, Milwaukee Co., WI, digital image s.v. "Mrs. Lovell Beamon," (birth 16 Oct 1933, death 22 May 2009), *FindaGrave.com*.

[1027] Albert Beamon, grave marker, Lincoln Memorial Cemetery, Milwaukee, Milwaukee Co., WI, digital image s.v. "Albert Beamon," (birth 22 Dec 1928, death 22 Sep 1978), *FindaGrave.com*.

[1028] "1950 United States Federal Census," Newport, Attala Co., MS, digital image s.v. "May Guyton," (birth ABT 1934), *Ancestry.com*.

[1029] Per Channie Brown-Currie.

[1030] "1950 United States Federal Census," Newport, Attala Co., MS, digital image s.v. "Lucy Guyton," (birth ABT 1936), *Ancestry.com*.

[1031] "1950 United States Federal Census," Newport, Attala Co., MS, digital image s.v. "Jean Guyton," (birth ABT 1937), *Ancestry.com*.

[1032] Per Channie Brown-Currie.

[1033] "1950 United States Federal Census," Newport, Attala Co., MS, digital image s.v. "Ruth Guyton," (birth ABT 1937), *Ancestry.com*.

[1034] Wardell Hill information from Channie Brown-Currie.

[1035] "U.S., Index to Public Records, 1994-2019" s.v. "Joe Troy Guyton," (birth Nov 1945), *Ancestry.com*.

[1036] "1950 United States Federal Census," Newport, Attala Co., MS, digital image s.v. "Ray Guyton," (birth ABT 1946), *Ancestry.com*.

xi   Lanell GUYTON (female) (b. ABT 1949 MS, d. Unknown).[1037]

xii   Caaye GUYTON (male) (b. ABT 1949 MS, d. Unknown).[1038]

Channie BROWN-CURRIE's records do not show the last three children I show above. I find the three in the 1950 U.S. Census. She wrote in her book a different set of three children: Shirley GUYTON, Ike Roby GUYTON, and Hubert GUYTON. I cannot explain the difference. I will include future generations of the three children reported by Channie.

Louella ROBY (Patsy J., Pinkney, Aaron Whitaker, Aaron Steele, Joseph I, John I, Samuel II, Samuel I, John)

Louella ROBY was the daughter of Patsy J. GUYTON (b. Aug 1877 Sallis, Attala Co., MS, d. after 1950, likely in Sallis, Attala Co., MS)[1039] and William (Willie) ROBY (b. Mar 1876, MS, d. Unknown).[1040] Louella was born on 19 Jan 1911 Attala Co., MS. She died on 3 Jun 2003 McAdams, Attala Co., MS.[1041] She married Othar ROUNDTREE (b. 15 Sep 1909 Attala Co., MS, d. 7 Aug 1975).[1042] See Figure 123, Figure 124, and Figure 125.

Figure 123 Louella Roby ROUNDTREE Headstone[1043]

Figure 124 Othar ROUNDTREE'S Headstone[1044]

Figure 125 Othar ROUNDTREE[1045]

[1037] "1950 United States Federal Census," Newport, Attala Co., MS, digital image s.v. "Lanell Guyton," (birth ABT 1949), Ancestry.com.
[1038] "1950 United States Federal Census," Newport, Attala Co., MS, digital image s.v. "Caaye Guyton," (birth ABT 1949), Ancestry.com.
[1039] "1900 United States Federal Census," Attala Co., MS, digital image s.v. "Patsy J. Roby," (birth Aug 1877), Ancestry.com. I assume she died after 1950 because she was in the 1950 U.S. Census. "1950 United States Federal Census," Newport, Attala Co., MS, digital image s.v. "Patsy Robey," (birth abt 1877), Ancestry.com.
[1040] "1900 United States Federal Census," Attala Co., MS, digital image s.v. "Will Roby," (birth Mar 1876), Ancestry.com.
[1041] "U.S., Social Security Death Index, 1935-2014," s.v. "Luella Roundtree," (birth 19 Jan 1911, death 3 Jun 2003), Ancestry.com.
[1042] "U.S. WWII Draft Cards Young Men, 1940-1947," digital image s.v. "Othar Roundtree," (birth 25 Aug 1909), Ancestry.com.
[1043] Memorial ID 104611959, Barlow United Methodist Church Cemetery, FindaGrave.
[1044] Memorial ID 104611763, Barlow United Methodist Church Cemetery, FindaGrave.
[1045] KsAllanEvans originally shared this on 28 Jul 2014 on Ancestry.com.

Together they had eleven children:

i	Andrew ROUNDTREE (b. 7 Dec 1927 Attala Co., MS, d. 24 Oct 2011 Milwaukee, Milwaukee Co., WI).[1046]
ii	Ulla Mae ROUNDTREE (b. ABT 1929 MS, d. Unknown).[1047]
iii	Vellar ROUNDTREE (b. ABT 1931 MS, d. Unknown).[1048]
iv	Mary Lee ROUNDTREE (b. ABT 1934 MS, d. Unknown).[1049]
v	Patsey ROUNDTREE (b. 27 Jul 1935 Kosciusko, Attala Co., MS, d. 7 Mar 1999 Milwaukee, Milwaukee Co., WI)[1050] m. Unknown MARTIN.
vi	Cleotha ROUNDTREE (b. 15 Jul 1937 Sallis, Attala Co., MS, d. 25 May 2000 Unknown).[1051]
vii	Annie Christine ROUNDTREE (b. ABT 1939 MS, d. Feb 1942 MS).[1052]
viii	Jessie D. ROUNDTREE (b. ABT 1942 MS, d. Unknown).[1053]
ix	July Jean ROUNDTREE (b. ABT 1945 MS, d. Unknown).[1054]
x	Bobbie Jean ROUNDTREE (b. ABT 1947 MS, d. Unknown).[1055]
xi	Clyde Wade ROUNDTREE (b. 5 Jul 1948 MS., d. Unknown).[1056]

[1046] "U.S., Social Security Death Index, 1935-2014," s.v. "Andrew Roundtree," (birth 7 Dec 1927, death 24 Oct 2011), *Ancestry.com*.

[1047] "1930 United States Federal Census," Beat 4, Attala Co., MS, digital image s.v. "Ullar Mae Roundtree," (birth abt 1929), *Ancestry.com*.

[1048] "1940 United States Federal Census," Newport, Attala Co., MS, digital image s.v. "Vellar Roundtree," (birth abt 1931), *Ancestry.com*.

[1049] "1940 United States Federal Census," Newport, Attala Co., MS, digital image s.v. "Mary Lee Roundtree," (birth abt 1934), *Ancestry.com*.

[1050] "U.S., Social Security Applications and Claims Index, 1936-2007," s.v. "Potsey Ann Martin," (birth 27 Jul 1935, death 7 Mar 1999), *Ancestry.com*.

[1051] "U.S., Social Security Applications and Claims Index, 1936-2007," s.v. "Cleotha Roundtree," (birth 15 Jul 1937, death 25 May 2000), *Ancestry.com*.

[1052] "1940 United States Federal Census," Newport, Attala Co., MS, digital image s.v. "Annie Christine Roundtree," (birth abt 1939), *Ancestry.com*. "Mississippi, U.S., Index to Deaths, 1912-1943," digital image s.v. "Annie C Roundtree," (death Feb 1942, Attala, MS), *Ancestry.com*.

[1053] "1950 United States Federal Census," Newport, Attala Co., MS, digital image s.v. "Jessie D. Roundtree," (birth abt 1942), *Ancestry.com*.

[1054] "1950 United States Federal Census," Newport, Attala Co., MS, digital image s.v. "July Jean Roundtree," (birth abt 1945), *Ancestry.com*.

[1055] "1950 United States Federal Census," Newport, Attala Co., MS, digital image s.v. "Bobbie Jean Roundtree," (birth abt 1947), *Ancestry.com*.

[1056] "U.S., Public Records Index, 1950-1993, Volume 1," s.v. "Clyde W Roundtree," (birth 5 Jul 1948), Milwaukee, WI, *Ancestry.com*.

Elmer ROBY (Patsy J., Pinkney, Aaron Whitaker, Aaron Steele, Joseph I, John I, Samuel II, Samuel I, John)

Elmer Gene ROBY was the son of Patsy J. GUYTON (b. Aug 1877 Sallis, Attala Co., MS, d. after 1950, likely in Sallis, Attala Co., MS)[1057] and William (Willie) ROBY (b. Mar 1876, MS, d. Unknown).[1058] Elmer Gene ROBY was born on 5 Mar 1913 in Sallis, Attala Co., MS, and died on 9 Jul 1992 in the same town.[1059] I could not locate his wife's name.

The couple had at least four children:

i   Wilmer Dean ROBY (b. Jan 1943, d. Unknown).[1060]
ii   Elmer Gene ROBY (b. Jan 1943, d. Unknown).[1061]
iii   Lillian ROBY (b. Unknown, d. Unknown)[1062] m. Unknown HUGHES.
iv   Velma ROBY (b. Unknown, d. Unknown).[1063]

[1057] "1900 United States Federal Census," Attala Co., MS, digital image s.v. "Patsy J. Roby," (birth Aug 1877), Ancestry.com. I assume she died after 1950 because she was in the 1950 U.S. Census. "1950 United States Federal Census," Newport, Attala Co., MS, digital image s.v. "Patsy Robey," (birth abt 1877), Ancestry.com.

[1058] "1900 United States Federal Census," Attala Co., MS, digital image s.v. "Will Roby," (birth Mar 1876), Ancestry.com.

[1059] Elmer Roby, grave marker, Pleasant Hill Cemetery, Williamsville, Attala Co., MS, digital image s.v. "Elmer Roby," (birth 5 Mar 1913, death 9 Jul 1992), FindaGrave.com.

[1060] "U.S., Index to Public Records, 1994-2019," s.v. "Wilmer Roby," (birth Jan 1943), California, Ancestry.com.

[1061] "U.S., Public Records Index, 1950-1993, Volume 1," s.v. "Elmer G Roby," (birth 3 Jan 1943), California, Ancestry.com.

[1062] "Elmer Roby," *The Star-Herald*, 16 Jul 1992, p. 7; digital image, s.v. "Elmer Roby," *Newspapers.com*, <https://www.newspapers.com/image/268369307/?article=f103b92e-e370-431c-865c-5b6207b2d334&focus=0.8045782,0.16571607,0.96600544,0.3296459&xid=3355>. Mrs. Lillian Hughes of Kosciusko is listed as one of Elmer's surviving daughters.

[1063] "Elmer Roby," *The Star-Herald*, 16 Jul 1992, p. 7; digital image, s.v. "Elmer Roby," *Newspapers.com*, <https://www.newspapers.com/image/268369307/?article=f103b92e-e370-431c-865c-5b6207b2d334&focus=0.8045782,0.16571607,0.96600544,0.3296459&xid=3355>. Miss Velma Roby of Rockford, IL is listed as one of Elmer's surviving daughters.

Ruth Lee (Ruthie) ROBY (Patsy J., Pinkney, Aaron Whitaker, Aaron Steele, Joseph I, John I, Samuel II, Samuel I, John)

Ruthie Lee ROBY was the daughter of Patsy J. GUYTON (b. Aug 1877 Sallis, Attala Co., MS, d. after 1950, likely in Sallis, Attala Co., MS)[1064] and William (Willie) ROBY (b. Mar 1876, MS, d. Unknown).[1065] Ruthie was born on 7 May 1916 in Sallis, Attala Co., MS. She died on 13 Jan 1996 in Wauwatosa, Milwaukee Co., WI.[1066] Her husband was Gus Davis GUYTON (b. 3 Mar 1909 Sallis, Attala Co., MS., d. 8 Jul 1990 Cook Co., IL).[1067] Ruthie and Gus were cousins. Aaron Whitaker GUYTON was Ruthie's great-grandfather; he was Gus Davis GUYTON's grandfather. See Figure 126 and Figure 127.

Figure 126 Ruth Lee (Ruthie) ROBY GUYTON[1068]

Figure 127 Gus Davis GUYTON[1069]

Gus and Ruthie had at least nine children:

i   Earlene GUYTON (b. 19 Aug 1933 Sallis, Attala Co., MS d. 22 May 1965 Unknown)[1070] m. Otha LANDINGHAM (b. 31 Oct 1922 Marked Tree, Poinsett Co., AR, d. 19 May 1981 Chicago, Cook Co., IL).[1071]

ii   Bernice GUYTON (b. 17 Jun 1935 Attala Co., MS, d. 14 Dec 2002 McAdams, Attala Co., MS)[1072] m. Joseph Lee PHILLIPS, Sr. (b. ABT 1935, d. Unknown).[1073]

[1064] "1900 United States Federal Census," Attala Co., MS, digital image s.v. "Patsy J. Roby," (birth Aug 1877), *Ancestry.com*. I assume she died after 1950 because she was in the 1950 U.S. Census. "1950 United States Federal Census," Newport, Attala Co., MS, digital image s.v. "Patsy Robey," (birth abt 1877), *Ancestry.com*.

[1065] "1900 United States Federal Census," Attala Co., MS, digital image s.v. "Will Roby," (birth Mar 1876), *Ancestry.com*.

[1066] Ruth Lee (Ruthie) Roby, grave marker, Russell Cemetery, Attala Co., MS, digital image s.v. "Ruthie Guyton," (birth 7 May 1916, death 13 Jan 1996), *FindaGrave.com*.

[1067] Gus Davis Guyton, grave marker, Russell Cemetery, Attala Co., MS, digital image s.v. "Gus Davis Guyton," (birth 3 Mar 1909, death 8 Jul 1990), *FindaGrave.com*.

[1068] chancurri originally shared this on 27 May 2013 on *Ancestry.com*.

[1069] Nathaniel Guyton originally shared this on 25 May 2014 on *Ancestry.com*.

[1070] Earlene Guyton, grave marker, Restvale Cemetery, Alsip, Cook Co., IL, digital image s.v. "Otha Landingham," (birth 31 Oct 1922, death 19 May 1981), *FindaGrave.com*.

[1071] Otha Landingham, grave marker, Russell Cemetery, Attala Co., MS, digital image s.v. "Gus Davis Guyton," (birth 3 Mar 1909, death 8 Jul 1990), *FindaGrave.com*.

[1072] Bernice Guyton, grave marker, Russell Cemetery, Attala Co., MS, digital image s.v. "Bernice Phillips," (birth 17 Jun 1935, death 14 Dec 2002), *FindaGrave.com*.

[1073] "Bernice Guyton-Phillips," *The Star-Herald*, 25 Dec 2002, p. 6; digital image, s.v. "Bernice Guyton-Phillips," *Newspapers.com*, <https://www.newspapers.com/image/305104740/?focus=0.356137%2C0.18697402%2C0.5030061%2C0.3336987&xid=3355&clipping_id=147233545>.

iii   Irene (Polly) GUYTON (b. ABT 1936 Sallis, Attala Co., MS, d. Unknown).[1074]

iv   Curtis GUYTON (b. 29 Jul 1937 MS, d. Unknown).[1075]

v   Joan GUYTON (b. 2 Jul 1939 MS, d. Unknown)[1076] m. Fred CULPEPPER (Unknown).

vi   Arthur David (Buddy) GUYTON (b. 30 Mar 1942 Sallis, Attala Co., MS, d. 19 Apr 2014 Maywood, Cook Co., IL).[1077] He had at least one child: Marketta GUYTON per his obituary.

vii   Billie Ruth GUYTON (b. 20 Sep 1945, d. Unknown)[1078] m. Clinton Lee MALLET (b. 17 Feb 1944 MS, d. Unknown).[1079]

viii   Barbara GUYTON (b. Unknown, d. Unknown)[1080] m. Unknown LELAND.

ix   Patricia GUYTON (b. Unknown, d. Unknown).[1081]

[1074] "1940 United States Federal Census," Newport, Attala Co., MS, digital image s.v. "Irene Guyton," (birth abt 1936), Ancestry.com.

[1075] "U.S., Public Records Index, 1950-1993, Volume 2," s.v. "Curtis Guyton," (birth 29 Jul 1937), Maywood, IL, *Ancestry.com*.

[1076] "U.S., Public Records Index, 1950-1993, Volume 1," s.v. "Joan Culpepper," (birth 2 Jul 1939), Markham, IL, *Ancestry.com*. "Cook County, Illinois Marriage Index, 1930-1960," s.v. "Joan Guyton," (marriage 17 May 1958 to Fred Culpepper), *Ancestry.com*.

[1077] Arthur David Guyton, grave marker, Oakridge-Glen Oak Cemetery, Hillside, Cook Co., IL, digital image s.v. "Arthur David Guyton," (birth 30 Mar 1942, death 19 Apr 2014), FindaGrave.com.

[1078] "U.S., Public Records Index, 1950-1993, Volume 1," s.v. "Billie R Mallett," (birth 20 Sep 1944), Milwaukee, WI, *Ancestry.com*. "Wisconsin, U.S., Marriage Records, 1820-2004," s.v. "Billie Ruth Guyton," (marriage 28 Dec 1968 to Clinton L. Mallett), *Ancestry.com*.

[1079] "U.S., Public Records Index, 1950-1993, Volume 2," s.v. "Clinton Mallett," (birth 17 Feb 1944), Milwaukee, WI, *Ancestry.com*.

[1080] "Bernice Guyton-Phillips," *The Star-Herald*, 25 Dec 2002, p. 6; digital image, s.v. "Bernice Guyton-Phillips," *Newspapers.com*, <https://www.newspapers.com/image/305104740/?focus=0.356137%2C0.18697402%2C0.5030061%2C0.3336987&xid=3355&clipping_id=147233545>. Barbara Leland of Milwaukee is listed as one of Bernice's surviving daughters.

[1081] "Bernice Guyton-Phillips," *The Star-Herald*, 25 Dec 2002, p. 6; digital image, s.v. "Bernice Guyton-Phillips," *Newspapers.com*, <https://www.newspapers.com/image/305104740/?focus=0.356137%2C0.18697402%2C0.5030061%2C0.3336987&xid=3355&clipping_id=147233545>. Patricia Guyton of Milwaukee is listed as one of Bernice's surviving daughters.

Vamis (Vammie) ROBY (Patsy J., Pinkney, Aaron Whitaker, Aaron Steele, Joseph I, John I, Samuel II, Samuel I, John)

Vamis (Vammie) ROBY was the daughter of Patsy J. GUYTON (b. Aug 1877 Sallis, Attala Co., MS, d. after 1950, likely in Sallis, Attala Co., MS)[1082] and William (Willie) ROBY (b. Mar 1876, MS, d. Unknown).[1083] Vammie was born about 1919 in Sallis, Attala Co., MS. She died sometime after 1940 in Sallis, Attala Co., MS.[1084] She married Shelton N. GUYTON (b. 12 Mar 1909 Sallis, Attala Co., MS., d. 30 May 1984 Sallis, Attala Co., MS).[1085] Shelton and Vammie are cousins. Shelton's grandparents were Aaron Whitaker GUYTON and Artie RAINEY. Vammie is the great-granddaughter of Aaron Whitaker GUYTON and Patsy GIBSON.

It is not clear what children are his. The couple had at least four children:[1086]

i   Dorothy Jean GUYTON (b. ABT 1936 MS, d. Unknown)[1087] m. Willie BUTLER (Unknown).
ii   Pauline GUYTON (b. ABT 1939 Sallis, Attala Co., MS, d. Unknown).[1088]
iii   Betty GUYTON (b. ABT 1942 MS, d. Unknown).[1089]
iv   Clarence (Buddy) GUYTON (b. ABT 1944 MS, d. Unknown)[1090] m. Rose GUYTON (Unknown).

[1082] "1900 United States Federal Census," Attala Co., MS, digital image s.v. "Patsy J. Roby," (birth Aug 1877), *Ancestry.com*. I assume she died after 1950 because she was in the 1950 U.S. Census. "1950 United States Federal Census," Newport, Attala Co., MS, digital image s.v. "Patsy Robey," (birth abt 1877), *Ancestry.com*.
[1083] "1900 United States Federal Census," Attala Co., MS, digital image s.v. "Will Roby," (birth Mar 1876), *Ancestry.com*.
[1084] "1920 United States Federal Census," Kosciusko, Attala Co., MS, digital image s.v. "Varna Roley," (birth 1918), *Ancestry.com*. She died sometime after 1944 when her child Buddy Guyton was born and before the 1950 U.S. Census.
[1085] "U.S., Social Security Death Index, 1935-2014," s.v. "Shelton Guyton," (birth 12 Mar 1909, death May 1984), *Ancestry.com*. Shelton N. Guyton, grave marker, Russell Cemetery, Attala Co., MS, digital image s.v. "Shelton N. Guyton," (death 30 May 1984), *FindaGrave.com*.
[1086] "1950 United States Federal Census," Newport, Attala Co., MS, digital image s.v. "Shelton Guyton," (birth abt 1913), *Ancestry.com*.
[1087] "1940 United States Federal Census," Newport, Attala Co., MS, digital image s.v. "Dorothy Gene Guyton," (birth abt 1936), *Ancestry.com*.
[1088] "1940 United States Federal Census," Newport, Attala Co., MS, digital image s.v. "Pauline Guyton," (birth abt 1939), *Ancestry.com*.
[1089] "1950 United States Federal Census," Newport, Attala Co., MS, digital image s.v. "Betty Guyton," (birth abt 1942), *Ancestry.com*.
[1090] "1950 United States Federal Census," Newport, Attala Co., MS, digital image s.v. "Buddy Guston," (birth abt 1944), *Ancestry.com*.

Fannie B. GAMBLE (Agnes Icy GUYTON GAMBLE, Pinkney, Aaron Whitaker, Aaron Steele, Joseph I, John I, Samuel II, Samuel I, John)

Fannie B. GAMBLE was the daughter of Agnes Isolome (Icy) GUYTON (b. Sep 1879, Kosciusko, South Beat 1, Attala Co., MS, d. 1963 Kosciusko, Attala, Co., MS)[1091] and Albert GAMBLE (b. 15 Dec 1875, Shuqualak Township 13, Noxubee Co., MS, d. 1948, Kosciusko, Attala Co., MS).[1092] Fannie was born on 5 Aug 1903 in MS, and died on 24 Jul 1998 in Kosciusko, Attala Co., MS.[1093] She married Dock M. MALLETT, who was born on 4 Jan 1897 in Kosciusko, Attala Co., MS. He died on 21 Aug 1980 in Kosciusko, Attala Co., MS.[1094] See Figure 128.

Figure 128 Fannie GUYTON and Dock MALLETT[1095]

In 1930, the couple lived on the Natchez Trace Parkway in Thomastown, Leake Co., MS on a farm they owned. Dock was 33 and Fannie was 28. They lived with five children: J C MALLETT (8), Rubell (Ruby) Bonita MALLETT (6), Katie MALLETT (5), Fred MALLETT (3), and Dock MALLETT (1). In the 1940 U.S. Census, the family lived in Leake Co., MS on Goodman Road. Their inferred residence in 1935 was Thomastown, Leake Co., MS. Dock MALLETT was farming his own property. In 1950, the family appeared to be living in the same place.[1096]

[1091] Agnes Isolome (Icy) Guyton, grave marker, Nash Cemetery, Attala County, MS, digital image s.v. "Agnes Icy Gamble," (birth Sep 1879, death 1963), *FindaGrave.com*.
[1092] Albert Gamble, grave marker, Nash Cemetery, Attala County, MS, digital image s.v. "Agnes Icy Gamble," (birth 15 Dec 1875, death 1948), *FindaGrave.com*.
[1093] Fannie B. Gamble, grave marker, Wright Cemetery, Kosciusko, Attala Co., MS, digital image s.v. "Fannie Mallett," (birth 5 Aug 1903, death 24 Jul 1998), *FindaGrave.com*.
[1094] Dock M. Mallett, grave marker, Wright Cemetery, Kosciusko, Attala Co., MS, digital image s.v. "Dock Mallett," (birth 4 Jan 1897, death 21 Aug 1980), *FindaGrave.com*.
[1095] Karl Boyd originally shared this on 11 Nov 2021 on *Ancestry.com*.
[1096] "1930 United States Federal Census," Thomastown, Leake Co., MS, digital image s.v. "Annie Mallett," (birth abt 1902), *Ancestry.com*. "1940 United States Federal Census," Leake Co., MS, digital image s.v. "Fannie G Mallett," (birth abt 1904), *Ancestry.com*. "1950 United States Federal Census," Leake Co., MS, digital image s.v. "Fannie Mallitt," (birth abt 1905), *Ancestry.com*.

The couple had thirteen children:

i J.C. MALLETT (b. 28 Feb 1922 Kosciusko, Attala Co., MS, d. 30 Oct 1981 Milwaukee, Milwaukee Co., WI)[1097] m. Clara ZOLICOFFER (b. 1926 MS, d. Unknown)[1098] on 9 Mar 1948 in Detroit, Wayne Co., MI.[1099]

ii Rubell Bonita (Ruby) MALLET (b. 20 Jul 1924 Leake Co., MS, d. 22 Jan 1998 Waterloo, Black Hawk Co., IA)[1100] m. George Louis CULPEPPER (b. 10 Jan 1927 Durant, Holmes Co., MS, d. 4 Aug 2000 Waterloo, Black Hawk Co., IA).[1101]

iii Katie K. MALLETT (b. 15 Jan 1925 Kosciusko, Attala Co., MS, d. 29 Aug 2009 Waterloo, Black Hawk Co., IA)[1102] m. (1) Thomas JOHNSON (b. abt 1925 MS, d. Unknown)[1103] and (2) William (Sleepy) FAGAN, Sr. (b. 19 Nov 1919 Adams Co., MS, d. 31 Jul 1989 Waterloo, Black Hawk Co., IA).[1104]

iv Fred MALLETT (b. 6 Oct 1927 Kosciusko, Attala Co., MS, d. 6 Mar 1999 Waterloo, Black Hawk Co., IA)[1105] m. Vergie Lee NASH (b. 10 Apr 1931 Kosciusko, Attala Co., MS, d. 6 Jul 1998 Waterloo, Black Hawk Co., IA).[1106]

v Dock Jeremiah MALLETT, Jr. (b. 9 Apr 1929 MS, d. Unknown).[1107]

vi Alphonzo L. (A.L.) MALLETT (9 Jan 1931 Thomastown, Leake Co., MS, d. 7 May 1989 Kosciusko, Attala Co., MS)[1108] m. Bobbie UNKNOWN. They had two daughters: Shirley MALLETT COFFEE and Brenda MALLETT RILEY, per his obituary on his *FindaGrave* site.

vii Katherine MALLETT (separate person from Katie) (b. ABT 1935 MS, d. Unknown).[1109]

viii R.D. MALLETT (b. 14 Nov 1937 Thomastown, Leake Co., MS, d. 12 Jan 1995 Jackson, Hinds Co., MS).[1110]

ix Christine MALLETT (b. ABT 1942 MS, d. Unknown).[1111]

x Louise MALLETT (b. ABT 1943 MS, d. Unknown).[1112]

[1097] J C Mallett, grave marker, Wood National Cemetery, Milwaukee, Milwaukee Co., MI, digital image s.v. "J C Mallett," (birth 28 Feb 1922, death 30 Oct 1981), *FindaGrave.com*.

[1098] "1940 United States Federal Census," Kosciusko, Attala Co., MS, digital image s.v. "Clara Zolicoffer," (birth abt 1926), *Ancestry.com*.

[1099] "Michigan, U.S., Marriage Records, 1867-1952," s.v. "J C Mallet," (marriage to Clara Zolicoffer on 9 Mar 1948), *Ancestry.com*.

[1100] Rubell Bonita Mallett, grave marker, Fairview Cemetery, Waterloo, Black Hawk Co., IA, digital image s.v. "Rubell Bonita Culpepper," (birth 20 Jul 1924, death 22 Jan 1998), *FindaGrave.com*.

[1101] George Louis Culpepper, grave marker, Fairview Cemetery, Waterloo, Black Hawk Co., IA, digital image s.v. "Rev George Louis Culpepper," (birth 10 Jan 1927, death 4 Aug 2000), *FindaGrave.com*.

[1102] "U.S., Social Security Death Index, 1935-2014," s.v. "Katie Fagan," (birth 15 Jan 1925, death 29 Aug 2009), *Ancestry.com*.

[1103] "U.S., Obituary Collection, 1930-Current," s.v. "Thomas Johnson," (spouse Katie Fagan), *Ancestry.com*.

[1104] "William (Sleepy) Fagan, Sr., grave marker, Garden of Memories, Waterloo, Black Hawk Co., IA, digital image s.v. "Fred Mallett," (birth 19 Nov 1919, death 31 Jul 1989), *FindaGrave.com*.

[1105] "Fred Mallett, grave marker, Garden of Memories, Waterloo, Black Hawk Co., IA, digital image s.v. "Fred Mallett," (birth 6 Oct 1927, death 6 Mar 1999), *FindaGrave.com*.

[1106] "Vergie Lee Nash, grave marker, Garden of Memories, Waterloo, Black Hawk Co., IA, digital image s.v. "Fred Mallett," (birth 10 Apr 1931, death 6 Jul 1998), *FindaGrave.com*.

[1107] "U.S. Public Records Index, 1950-1993, Volume 1," s.v. "Jeremiah M Mallett," (birth 9 Apr 1929), *Ancestry.com*.

[1108] "Alphonzo L. Mallett, grave marker, Wright Cemetery, Kosciusko, Attala Co., MS, digital image s.v. "Alphonzo Mallett," (birth 9 Jan 1931, death 7 May 1989), *FindaGrave.com*.

[1109] "1940 United States Federal Census," Kosciusko, Attala Co., MS, digital image s.v. "Katherine Mallett," (birth abt 1935), *Ancestry.com*.

[1110] "R.D. Mallett, grave marker, Wright Cemetery, Kosciusko, Attala Co., MS, digital image s.v. "R.D. Mallett," (birth 14 Nov 1937, death 12 Jan 1995), *FindaGrave.com*.

[1111] "1950 United States Federal Census," Leake Co., MS, digital image s.v. "Christian Mallitt," (birth abt 1942), *Ancestry.com*.

[1112] "1950 United States Federal Census," Leake Co., MS, digital image s.v. "Louis Mallitt," (birth abt 1943), *Ancestry.com*.

xi   Fannie MALLETT (b. ABT 1946 MS, d. Unknown).[1113]

xii   Ollie MALLETT (b. ABT 1947 MS, d. Unknown).[1114]

xiii   Jessie MALLETT (male) (b. Unknown, d. Unknown).[1115]

Callie Pairee GAMBLE (Agnes Icy GUYTON GAMBLE, Pinkney, Aaron Whitaker, Aaron Steele, Joseph I, John I, Samuel II, Samuel I, John)

Callie Pairee GAMBLE was the daughter of Agnes Isolome (Icy) GUYTON (b. Sep 1879 Kosciusko, South Beat 1, Attala Co., MS, d. 1963 Kosciusko, Attala Co., MS)[1116] and Albert GAMBLE (b. 15 Dec 1875 Shuqualak Township 13, Noxubee Co., MS, d. 1948 Kosciusko, Attala Co., MS).[1117] Callie was born on 9 Jan 1905 in Attala Co., MS. She died on 19 Jun 1995 in Maywood, Cook Co., IL.[1118] She married Henry Porterwood SIMMONS (b. 11 Feb 1904 Attala Co., MS, d. Oct 1977 Kosciusko, Attala Co., MS).[1119] See Figure 129 and Figure 130.

In the 1930 U.S. Federal Census, Callie and Henry lived on Goodman Highway in Beat 4, Attala Co., MS. The Census recorded that Henry and Callie married at 17 and 16 years old, respectively. Henry was a farmer. In 1930 Henry was 25 and Callie was 24. They had five children: Henry (L. C.) (5), Everlean (4), Zenolia (3), Lois (1), and Iola (1). In the 1940 Census, the family lived on Beauchamp Road in Kosciusko, Attala Co., MS on a farm it owned. I could not find a road named Beauchamp in the area today. The family consisted of nine children. By 1950, the family lived in Kosciusko, Attala Co., MS on an unnamed road. Henry was no longer farming. He worked as a timber cutter at a sawmill. At age 46, Henry had six children living at home.[1120]

An article in a 1955 issue of *The Star-Herald* contained this passage about Henry L.C. SIMMONS that occurred when Henry was 32 and his father was 51:[1121]

[1113] "1950 United States Federal Census," Leake Co., MS, digital image s.v. "Fannie Mallitt," (birth abt 1946), *Ancestry.com*.

[1114] "1950 United States Federal Census," Leake Co., MS, digital image s.v. "Ollie Mallitt," (birth abt 1947), *Ancestry.com*.

[1115] Jessie Mallett, grave marker, Wright Cemetery, Kosciusko, Attala Co., MS, digital image s.v. "Jessie Mallett," (no dates given, perhaps he was an infant), *FindaGrave.com*.

[1116] Agnes Isolome (Icy) Guyton, grave marker, Nash Cemetery, Attala Co., MS, digital image s.v. "Agnes Icy Gamble," (birth Sep 1879, death 1963), *FindaGrave.com*.

[1117] Albert Gamble, grave marker, Nash Cemetery, Attala County, MS, digital image s.v. "Agnes Icy Gamble," (birth 15 Dec 1875, death 1948), *FindaGrave.com*.

[1118] Callie Pairee Gamble, grave marker, Nash Cemetery, Leake Co., MS, digital image s.v. "Callie Pairee Simmons," (birth 9 Jan 1905, death 19 Jun 1995), *FindaGrave.com*.

[1119] "U.S., Social Security Death Index, 1935-2014," s.v. "Henry Simmons," (birth 11 Feb 1904, death Oct 1977), *Ancestry.com*.

[1120] "1930 United States Federal Census," Beat 4, Attala Co., MS, digital image s.v. "Henry Simmons," (birth abt 1905), *Ancestry.com*. "1940 United States Federal Census," Kosciusko, Attala Co., MS, digital image s.v. "Henry P Simmons," (birth abt 1909), *Ancestry.com*. "1950 United States Federal Census," Kosciusko, Attala Co., MS, digital image s.v. "Henry Simmons," (birth abt 1904), *Ancestry.com*.

[1121] "Events Move Fast in Monday's Court, Rapist and Three Others Sentenced," *The Star-Herald*, 29 Sep 1955, p. 1; digital image, s.v. "Henry L. C. Simmons," *Newspapers.com*, <https://www.newspapers.com/image/272997854/?xid=5506&clipping_id=148204434>.

Henry L. C. SIMMONS, Negro from the south end of Attala County, was charged with assault and battery upon the person of his father. He plead [sic] guilty, was given a one year sentence to the County Farm, suspended by Judge Henry Rodgers.

Figure 129 Callie Pairee GAMBLE SIMMONS[1122]

Figure 130 Henry Porterwood SIMMONS[1123]

See Figure 131 for a view of the family tree.

The couple had fifteen children with many of them listed in Callie GAMBLE SIMMONS' obituary:[1124] RITA McLEAN contributed significantly to the information contained in the book for Callie and Henry's descendants.

i Henry (L. C.) SIMMONS (b. 15 Aug 1923 Attala Co., MS, d. 13 Jun 2009 Sallis, Attala Co., MS)[1125] m. (1) Lue Bertha WINDOMS. (b. 22 May 1937, d. Unknown)[1126] and perhaps (2) Unknown.
ii Everlean SIMMONS (b. 28 Dec 1924 MS, d. Unknown)[1127] m. (1) Unknown LONG[1128] and (2) George Van HILL, Jr. (Unknown) on 8 Dec 1952 in Cook Co., IL.[1129] See Figure 132.
iii Zenolia SIMMONS (9 Dec 1926 Kosciusko, Attala Co., MS, d. 19 Jan 2018 Eau Claire, Berrien Co., MI)[1130] m. Ellon MURPHY (b. 20 Oct 1922 Kosciusko, Attala Co., MS, d. 20 Jul 1993 Berrien, Berrien Co., MI).[1131]

[1122] Rickey Simmons originally shared this on 31 Oct 2021 on *Ancestry.com*.

[1123] Karl Boyd originally shared this on 31 Jul 2023 on Ancestry.com.

[1124] "Mrs. Callie Simmons," *The Star-Herald*, 29 Jun 1995, p. 6; digital image, s.v. "Mrs. Callie Simmons," *Newspapers.com*, <https://www.newspapers.com/image/278328371/?focus=0.67398393%2C0.07939047%2C0.8261525%2C0.25768572&xid=3355&clipping_id=148211399>.

[1125] "U.S., Social Security Death Index, 1935-2014," s.v. "Henry L. Simmons," (birth 5 Aug 1922, death 13 Jun 2009), *Ancestry.com*.

[1126] Personal conversation with their grandson, Ricky SIMMONS (b. abt 1958).

[1127] "U.S., Cemetery and Funeral Home Collection, 1847-Current," s.v. "Everlean E Long," (birth 28 Dec 1924), *Ancestry.com*.

[1128] Per the obituary of Callie GAMBLE SIMMONS.

[1129] "Cook County, Illinois Marriage Index, 1930-1960," s.v. "Everlean Long," (marriage 8 Dec 1952 to George Van Hill Jr.), *Ancestry.com*.

[1130] "U.S., Cemetery and Funeral Home Collection, 1847-Current," digital image s.v. "Zenolia Murphy Murphy," (birth 9 Dec 1926, death 19 Jan 2018), *Ancestry.com*.

[1131] "U.S., Social Security Applications and Claims Index, 1936-2007," s.v. "Ellon Murphy," (birth 20 Oct 1922, death 20 Jul 1993," *Ancestry.com*.

iv		Lois SIMMONS (b. ABT 1929 Attala Co., MS, d. Unknown)[1132] m. Unknown CARTER).[1133] See Figure 133.
v		Iola SIMMONS (b. ABT 1929 MS, d. Unknown).[1134] Had no children.
vi		Rebecca SIMMONS (b. ABT 1932 MS, d. Unknown) m. Unknown MERKSON [1135]
vii		Clara SIMMONS (b. abt 1933 MS, d. Unknown).[1136]
viii		S. Thomas (S.T.) SIMMONS (b. 6 Jun 1933 Mcville, Leake Co., MS, d. 14 Oct 2006 Chicago, Cook Co., IL).[1137] See Figure 135.
ix		Lester (Tot) SIMMONS (b. 16 Jan 1935 MS, d. 3 Oct 2008).[1138]
x		Lona Mae SIMMONS (b. ABT 1940 MS, d. Unknown).[1139]
xii		Callie Jean SIMMONS (b. ABT 1947 MS, d. Unknown)[1140] m. James DELANEY (Unknown) on 21 Sep 1960 in Cook Co., IL.[1141] See Figure 134.
xiii		Robert SIMMONS (b. Unknown, d. Unknown).[1142]
xiv		Lovie (Mae) SIMMONS (b. Unknown, d. Unknown) m. Unknown WALTON.[1143]

[1132] "1930 United States Federal Census," Beat 4, Attala Co., MS, digital image s.v. "Baby Simmons," (birth abt 1929), *Ancestry.com*.

[1133] Per the obituary of Callie Gamble Simmons.

[1134] "1930 United States Federal Census," Beat 4, Attala Co., MS, digital image s.v. "Iola Simmons," (birth abt 1929), *Ancestry.com*.

[1135] "1940 United States Federal Census," Kosciusko, Attala Co., MS, digital image s.v. "Rebeka Simmons," (birth abt 1932), *Ancestry.com*. Per the obituary of Callie GAMBLE SIMMONS.

[1136] "1940 United States Federal Census," Kosciusko, Attala Co., MS, digital image s.v. "Clara Simmons," (birth abt 1933), *Ancestry.com*.

[1137] "U.S., Social Security Applications and Claims Index, 1936-2007," s.v. "S T Simmons," (birth 6 Jun 1933, death 14 Oct 2006), *Ancestry.com*.

[1138] "1940 United States Federal Census," Kosciusko, Attala Co., MS, digital image s.v. "Lester Simmons," (birth abt 1935), *Ancestry.com*.

[1139] "1940 United States Federal Census," Kosciusko, Attala Co., MS, digital image s.v. "Lone Mae Simmons," (birth abt 1940), *Ancestry.com*.

[1140] "1950 United States Federal Census," MS, digital image s.v. "Callie J. Simmons," (birth abt 1944), *Ancestry.com*.

[1141] "Cook County, Illinois Marriage Index, 1930-1960," s.v. "Callie J. Simmons," (marriage on 21 Sep 1960 in Cook Co., MS).

[1142] Per the obituary of Callie GAMBLE SIMMONS.

[1143] Per the obituary of Callie GAMBLE SIMMONS.

Figure 131 Henry and Callie SIMMONS Tree[1144]

Below are photos of some of their children who, due to lack of information, will not have a separate section on them in the next generation.

[1144] Tree from the Simmons Family Reunion, July 2024. Courtesy of Rita McLean.

Figure 132 Everlean SIMMONS LONG[1145]

Figure 133 Lois SIMMONS[1146]

Figure 134 Callie Jean SIMMONS[1147]

Figure 135 S. Thomas (S.T.) SIMMONS[1148]

[1145] Karl Boyd originally shared this on 23 Nov 2021 on *Ancestry.com*.
[1146] Karl Boyd originally shared this on 23 Nov 2021 on *Ancestry.com*.
[1147] Karl Boyd originally shared this on 23 Nov 2021 on *Ancestry.com*.
[1148] gmantires originally shared this on 7 Apr 2024 on *Ancestry.com*.

Nathan Eugene GAMBLE (Agnes Icy GUYTON GAMBLE, Pinkney, Aaron Whitaker, Aaron Steele, Joseph I, John I, Samuel II, Samuel I, John)

Nathan Eugene GAMBLE was the son of Agnes Isolome (Icy) GUYTON (b. Sep 1879 Kosciusko, South Beat 1, Attala Co., MS, d. 1963 Kosciusko, Attala, Co., MS)[1149] and Albert GAMBLE (b. 15 Dec 1875 Shuqualak Township 13, Noxubee Co., MS, d. 1948, Kosciusko, Attala Co., MS).[1150] Nathan was born on 9 Apr 1906 on Attala Co., MS, and died on Dec 1993 in Kosciusko, Attala Co., MS).[1151] He married Estelle UNKNOWN by 1930. See Figure 136.

Figure 136 Nathan Eugene GAMBLE[1152]

In the 1930 U.S. Federal Census, Nathan (25) and Estelle (23) lived on Goodman Highway in Beat 1, Attala Co., MS. The Census recorded that Nathan and Estelle married at 23 and 21 years old, respectively. Nathan worked as a laborer on a farm as an unpaid worker, but he was not living with his family. In the 1940 Census, the family lived in New Port, Attala Co., MS on a farm he rented. By 1950, the family lived on Burch Road in Kosciusko, Attala Co., MS. Nathan was still farming. They had no children.[1153]

[1149] Agnes Isolome (Icy) Guyton, grave marker, Nash Cemetery, Attala Co., MS, digital image s.v. "Agnes Icy Gamble," (birth Sep 1879, death 1963), *FindaGrave.com*.

[1150] Albert Gamble, grave marker, Nash Cemetery, Attala County, MS, digital image s.v. "Agnes Icy Gamble," (birth 15 Dec 1875, death 1948), *FindaGrave.com*.

[1151] Nathan Eugene Gamble, grave marker, Nash Cemetery, Leake Co., MS, digital image s.v. "Nathan Eugene Gamble," (birth 9 Apr 1906, death Dec 1993), *FindaGrave.com*.

[1152] Karl Boyd originally shared this on 30 Aug 2023 on *Ancestry.com*.

[1153] "1930 United States Federal Census," Beat 1, Attala Co., MS, digital image s.v. "Eugene Gambol," (birth abt 1905), *Ancestry.com*. "1940 United States Federal Census," Newport, Attala Co., MS, digital image s.v. "Eugene Gamber," (birth abt 1908), *Ancestry.com*. "1950 United States Federal Census," Kosciusko, Attala Co., MS, digital image s.v. "Eugene Gamble," (birth abt 1904), *Ancestry.com*.

Fred (Big Baby) GAMBLE (Agnes Icy GUYTON GAMBLE, Pinkney, Aaron Whitaker, Aaron Steele, Joseph I, John I, Samuel II, Samuel I, John)

Fred (Big Baby) GAMBLE was the son of Agnes Icy GUYTON (b. Sep 1879 Kosciusko, South Beat 1, Attala Co., MS, d. 1963 Kosciusko, Attala, Co., MS)[1154] and Albert GAMBLE (b. 15 Dec 1875 Shuqualak Township 13, Noxubee Co., MS, d. 1948 Kosciusko, Attala Co., MS).[1155] Fred was born on 27 Feb 1909 in Kosciusko Beat 1, Attala Co., MS. Fred died on 31 Jul 1980 in Kosciusko, Attala Co., MS).[1156] He married (1) Lula M. CLARK (Unknown),[1157] (2) Josephine UNKNOWN (b. ABT 1921, d. Unknown),[1158] and (3) Ella Mae MITCHELL (b. 29 Jun 1919 Kosciusko, Attala Co., MS, d. 3 Jul 2007 Kosciusko, Attala Co., MS).[1159]

Fred and Lula had one child I could find. I don't believe Eva May is Josephine's child because in the 1940 U.S. Census, Eva May was six years old, and Josephine was 19. If Josephine were Eva's mother, Josephine would have given birth at thirteen, well out of the norm. Also, Social Security for Eva May GAMBLE indicates her mother was Lula M. CLARK.

i   Eva May GAMBLE (b. 10 Mar 1934 MS, d. 15 Jun 2000) m. Unknown NEAL.[1160]

Fred and Ella Mae MITCHELL had one child that I could find:

i   Mitchell GAMBLE (b. ABT 1948, d. Unknown).[1161]

[1154] Agnes Isolome (Icy) Guyton, grave marker, Nash Cemetery, Attala County, MS, digital image s.v. "Agnes Icy Gamble," (birth Sep 1879, death 1963), *FindaGrave.com*.
[1155] Albert Gamble, grave marker, Nash Cemetery, Attala County, MS, digital image s.v. "Agnes Icy Gamble," (birth 15 Dec 1875, death 1948), *FindaGrave.com*.
[1156] Fred "Big Baby" Gamble, grave marker, Nash Cemetery, Leake Co., MS, digital image s.v. "Fred Gamble," (birth 27 Feb 1909, death Jul 1980), *FindaGrave.com*.
[1157] "U.S., Social Security Applications and Claims Index, 1936-2007," s.v. "Eva May Gamble," (birth 10 Mar 1934, death 15 Jun 2000, parents Fred Gamble and Lula M. Clark), *Ancestry.com*. The index refers to her mother Lula M. Clark.
[1158] "1940 United States Federal Census," Leflore Co., MS, digital image s.v. "Josephine Gamble," (birth abt 1921), *Ancestry.com*.
[1159] Ella Mae Mitchell, grave marker, Marble Rock Cemetery, Kosciusko, Attala Co., MS, digital image s.v. "Ella Mae Gamble," (birth 29 Jun 1919, death 3 Jul 2007), *FindaGrave.com*.
[1160] "U.S., Social Security Applications and Claims Index, 1936-2007," s.v. "Eva May Gamble," (birth 10 Mar 1934, death 15 Jun 2000," *Ancestry.com*.
[1161] "1950 United States Federal Census," Kosciusko, Attala Co., MS, digital image s.v. "Mitchell Gambol," (birth abt 1948), *Ancestry.com*.

Nola Mae GAMBLE (Agnes Icy GUYTON GAMBLE, Pinkney, Aaron Whitaker, Aaron Steele, Joseph I, John I, Samuel II, Samuel I, John)

Nola Mae GAMBLE was the daughter of Agnes Icy GUYTON (b. Sep 1879 Kosciusko, South Beat 1, Attala Co., MS, d. 1963 Kosciusko, Attala, Co., MS)[1162] and Albert GAMBLE (b. 15 Dec 1875, Shuqualak Township 13, Noxubee Co., MS, d. 1948, Kosciusko, Attala Co., MS).[1163] Nola Mae was born on 19 Oct 1910 in Attala Co., MS, and died on 4 Feb 1994 in Gulfport, Harrison Co., MS).[1164] She married Damon RILEY (b. 10 Nov 1909 Leake Co., MS, d. 3 Feb 2005).[1165] See Figure 137.

Figure 137 Nola Mae GAMBLE RILEY[1166]

Nola Mae and Damon married between the 1930 and 1940 U.S. Census. In the 1940 U.S. Census, Damon (23) and Nola Mae (24) had a 9-month-old baby, Mae D. (Mary or Mardell) RILEY. They likely married around 1938 or 1939. By 1950, they lived on Beauchamp Road in Kosciusko, Attala Co., MS. Damon farmed on a rented farm.[1167] By this time, Damon (39) and Nola (38) had the following children living with them: Mardell (10), Susie (8), Emma (6) James (4), Charlie (0).

Their children, based on census records and Nola Mae's obituary, included:[1168]

[1162] Agnes Isolome (Icy) Guyton, grave marker, Nash Cemetery, Attala County, MS, digital image s.v. "Agnes Icy Gamble," (birth Sep 1879, death 1963), *FindaGrave.com*.
[1163] Albert Gamble, grave marker, Nash Cemetery, Attala County, MS, digital image s.v. "Agnes Icy Gamble," (birth 15 Dec 1875, death 1948), *FindaGrave.com*.
[1164] "U.S., Newspapers.com™ Obituary Index, 1800s-current," s.v. "Nola Mae Gamble Riley," (birth 19 Oct 1910, death 4 Feb 1994), *Ancestry.com*.
[1165] "U.S., World War II Draft Cards Young Men, 1940-1947," s.v. "Damon Riley," (birth 8 Sep 1915), *Ancestry.com*. "U.S., Social Security Death Index, 1935-2014," s.v. "Daymon Riley," (birth 10 Nov 1909, death 3 Feb 2005), *Ancestry.com*. Note there is a significant difference in the birth date. It is possible these are different men. The birth location of Leake Co., MS was the same in both documents.
[1166] Karl Boyd originally shared this on 11 Nov 2021 on *Ancestry.com*.
[1167] "1940 United States Federal Census," Kosciusko, Attala Co., MS, digital image s.v. "Damon Riley," (birth abt 1917), *Ancestry.com*. "1950 United States Federal Census," Kosciusko, Attala Co., MS, digital image s.v. "Damon Riley," (birth abt 1911), *Ancestry.com*.
[1168] "Nola Mae Gamble," *The Sun*, Biloxi, MS, 10 Feb 1994, p. 2; digital image, s.v. "Mrs. Nola Mae Gamble Riley," *Newspapers.com*, <https://www.newspapers.com/image/744225616/?article=f866ca73-c1db-404c-9454-48efa60bbd1e&focus=0.8154281,0.41309255,0.97455966,0.6110824&xid=3355>.

i	Mary D. (Mae or Mardell) RILEY (b. ABT 1939 MS, d. Unknown) m. Unknown BOATMAN.[1169]	
ii	Susie I. (Sue) RILEY (b. ABT 1942 MS, d. Unknown) m. Unknown LINDSAY.[1170]	
iii	Emma A. RILEY (b. ABT 1944 MS) m. Unknown TAYLOR.[1171]	
iv	James E. RILEY (b. ABT 1946 MS).[1172]	
v	Charlie E. RILEY (b. ABT 1950, d. Unknown).[1173]	
vi	Donnie RILEY (Unknown).[1174]	
vii	Ronnie RILEY (Unknown).[1175]	

Katie D. (KD) GAMBLE (Agnes Icy GUYTON GAMBLE, Pinkney, Aaron Whitaker, Aaron Steele, Joseph I, John I, Samuel II, Samuel I, John)

Katie D. (KD) GAMBLE was the daughter of Agnes Icy GUYTON (b. Sep 1879 Kosciusko, South Beat 1, Attala Co., MS, d. 1963 Kosciusko, Attala, Co., MS)[1176] and Albert GAMBLE (b. 15 Dec 1875 Shuqualak Township 13, Noxubee Co., MS, d. 1948 Kosciusko, Attala Co., MS).[1177] KD was born on 17 Sep 1912 in Kosciusko Beat 1, Attala Co., MS, and died on 19 Jun 2007 Sallis, Attala Co., MS.[1178] She married Claude (Pretty Boy) JOINER, Sr. (b. 3 Aug 1911 Attala Co., MS, d. 1 Sep 1986 Jackson, Hinds Co., MS).[1179] See Figure 138 and Figure 139.

[1169] "1940 United States Federal Census," Kosciusko, Attala Co., MS, digital image s.v. "Mae D Riley," (birth abt 1939), *Ancestry.com*.

[1170] "1950 United States Federal Census," Kosciusko, Attala Co., MS, digital image s.v. "Susie I Riley," (birth abt 1942), *Ancestry.com*.

[1171] "1950 United States Federal Census," Kosciusko, Attala Co., MS, digital image s.v. "Emma A Riley," (birth abt 1944), *Ancestry.com*.

[1172] "1950 United States Federal Census," Kosciusko, Attala Co., MS, digital image s.v. "James E Riley," (birth abt 1946), *Ancestry.com*.

[1173] "1950 United States Federal Census," Kosciusko, Attala Co., MS, digital image s.v. "Charlie Riley," (birth abt 1950), *Ancestry.com*.

[1174] See Nola Mae Gamble Riley's obituary.

[1175] See Nola Mae Gamble Riley's obituary.

[1176] Agnes Isolome (Icy) Guyton, grave marker, Nash Cemetery, Attala County, MS, digital image s.v. "Agnes Icy Gamble," (birth Sep 1879, death 1963), *FindaGrave.com*.

[1177] Albert Gamble, grave marker, Nash Cemetery, Attala County, MS, digital image s.v. "Agnes Icy Gamble," (birth 15 Dec 1875, death 1948), *FindaGrave.com*.

[1178] "Katie D. (KD) Gamble, grave marker, Bullock Cemetery, Attala Co., MS, digital image s.v. "Katie D Joiner," (birth 7 Sep 1912, death 19 Jun 2007), *FindaGrave.com*.

[1179] "Claude Joiner," grave marker, Bullock Cemetery, Attala Co., MS, digital image s.v. "Claude Joiner," (birth 8 Aug 1909, death 1 Sep 1986), *FindaGrave.com*.

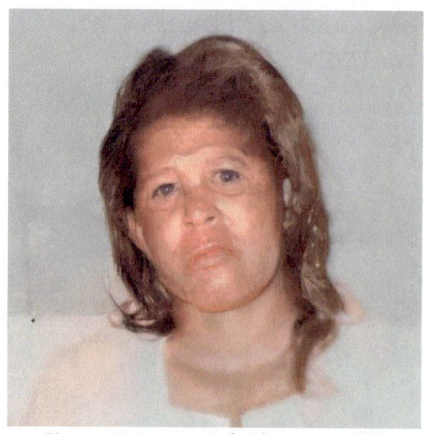

Figure 138 Katie D. (KD) GAMBLE[1180]

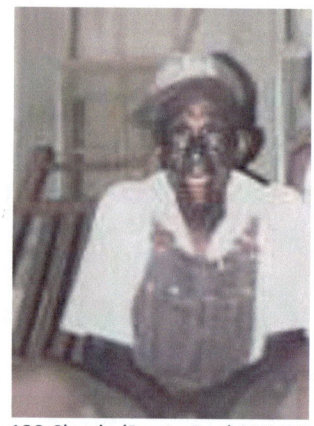

Figure 139 Claude (Pretty Boy) JOINER, Sr.[1181]

KD and Claude's children are known from census data and the obituaries of Claude JOINER.[1182]

i   Claude JOINER, Jr. (b. 3 Sep 1935 Mcville, Attala Co. , MS, d. 22 Mar 2005 Chicago, Cook Co., IL).[1183]
ii   Vernestine (Susie) JOINER (b. 27 Aug 1936 Attala Co., MS, d. 5 Oct 2018 Jackson, Hinds Co., MS)[1184] m. Luther D. (Rabbit) WINGARD (b. 24 Apr 1936 Kosciusko, Attala Co., MS, d. 1 Mar 2022 Kosciusko, Attala Co., MS).[1185]
iii   Dorothy Jean JOINER (b. abt 1939 MS, d. Unknown).[1186]
iv   Percy Lee (Sunny) JOINER (b. 4 Apr 1945 Kosciusko, Attala Co., MS, d. 20 Oct 1983 Milwaukee, Milwaukee Co., WI).[1187]
v   Icy Dean JOINER (b. Nov 1952, MS, d. Unknown) m. Unknown PERTEET.[1188]

[1180] Karl Boyd originally shared this on 31 Jul 2023 on *Ancestry.com*.
[1181] Redd Face originally shared this on 16 Nov 2023 on *Ancestry.com*.
[1182] "Claude (Pretty Boy" Joiner, Sr.," *The Star-Herald*, Kosciusko, Attala Co., MS, 11 Sep 1986, p. 11; digital image, s.v. "Claude Joiner," *Newspapers.com*, <https://www.newspapers.com/article/the-star-herald-obituary-for-claude-join/146262588/>.
[1183] "U.S., Social Security Death Index, 1935-2014," s.v. "Claude Joiner," (birth 3 Sep 1935, death 22 Mar 2005), *Ancestry.com*.
[1184] "Vernestine 'Susie' Joiner," grave marker, Jenkins Cemetery, Attala Co., MS, digital image s.v. "Vernestine Wingard," (birth 27 Aug 1936, death 5 Oct 2018), *FindaGrave.com*.
[1185] "Luther D. 'Rabbit' Wingard," grave marker, Jenkins Cemetery, Attala Co., MS, digital image s.v. "Luther D Wingard," (birth 24 Apr 1936, death 1 Mar 2022), *FindaGrave.com*.
[1186] "1940 United States Federal Census," Kosciusko, Attala Co., MS, digital image s.v. "Dorothy D Joiner," (birth abt 1939), *Ancestry.com*.
[1187] "Percy Lee 'Sunny' Joiner," grave marker, Bullock Cemetery, Attala Co., MS, digital image s.v. "Percy Joiner," (birth 4 Apr 1945, death 20 Oct 1983), *FindaGrave.com*.
[1188] "U.S., Index to Public Records, 1994-2019," s.v. "Icy Dean Perteet," (birth Nov 1952), *Ancestry.com*.

Lovie GAMBLE (Agnes Icy GUYTON GAMBLE, Pinkney, Aaron Whitaker, Aaron Steele, Joseph I, John I, Samuel II, Samuel I, John)

Lovie GAMBLE was the daughter of Agnes Icy GUYTON (b. Sep 1879 Kosciusko, South Beat 1, Attala Co., MS, d. 1963 Kosciusko, Attala, Co., MS)[1189] and Albert GAMBLE (b. 15 Dec 1875 Shuqualak Township 13, Noxubee Co., MS, d. 1948 Kosciusko, Attala Co., MS).[1190] Lovie was born on 29 Aug 1915 in Kosciusko, Attala Co., MS, and died on 16 Oct 2002 in Chicago, Cook Co., IL).[1191] She married (1) Woodrow Wilson NASH (b. 28 Aug 1916 in Leake Co., MS, d. 11 Dec 1999 in Chicago, Cook Co., IL)[1192] perhaps div. and (2) Ilander N. PARKER, Sr. (b. 21 Oct 1910 Cruger, Holmes Co., MS, d. May 1959 Kosciusko, Attala Co., MS).[1193] See Figure 140, Figure 141, and Figure 142.

Grandson Karl BOYD (also known as Nykki STARR) provided the material below in 2024:

This Is my Life

"On a farm near Kosciusko, Mississippi on August 29, 1914, I was born to the proud parents of Icy and Albert Gamble. I am the eighth child of nine children. I grew up a happy and very inquisitive child. At the age of five, I was off to Jack and Jill School carrying my lunch in a jelly bucket. As children growing up, we didn't have store-bought toys to play with. We made our dolls from pieces of fabric and stuffed them with cotton and rags. These dolls have become known as rag dolls. I can remember my sisters and me racing to gather flowers to see who could gather the prettiest flowers. Whoever had the prettiest flowers would be the winner. Another one of our past time favorites was a game called jack rocks. Some of the younger folks call this game JAXS. Well, we didn't have JAXS... And as most of you know, the rocks worked just as well, and didn't cost a thing. Growing up was not always fun and games. We had many chores, and we worked many hours. Farming was our means of supporting the family. We raised all our food except coffee, sugar, rice, and flour."

Lovie Parker

[1189] Agnes Isolome (Icy) Guyton, grave marker, Nash Cemetery, Attala County, MS, digital image s.v. "Agnes Icy Gamble," (birth Sep 1879, death 1963), *FindaGrave.com*.
[1190] Albert Gamble, grave marker, Nash Cemetery, Attala County, MS, digital image s.v. "Agnes Icy Gamble," (birth 15 Dec 1875, death 1948), *FindaGrave.com*.
[1191] "U.S., Social Security Death Index, 1935-2014," s.v. "Lovie Parker," (birth 29 Aug 1915, death 16 Oct 2002), *Ancestry.com*.
[1192] "Woodrow Wilson Nash," grave marker, Mount Hope Cemetery, Chicago, Cook Co., IL, digital image s.v. "Claude Joiner," (birth 28 Apr 1916, death 11 Dec 1999), *FindaGrave.com*. No two documents have the same birth date, but the dates are close together.
[1193] "Social Security Death Index," s.v. "Ilander Parker," (birth 21 Sep 1909, death May 1959), *Ancestry.com*.

Figure 140 Icy GAMBLE PARKER and Natasha PARKER OLGUIN[1194]

Figure 141 Woodrow Wilson NASH[1195]

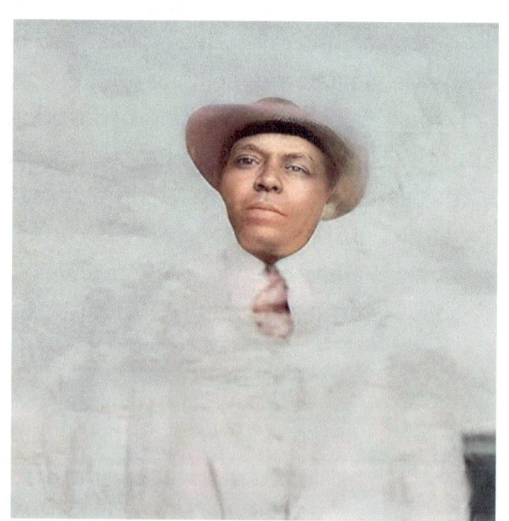

Figure 142 Ilander N. PARKER, Sr.[1196]

[1194] Natasha Parker Olguin originally shared this on 8 Jun 2023 on *Ancestry.com*.
[1195] Karl Boyd originally shared this on 12 Oct 2021 on *Ancestry.com*.
[1196] Karl Boyd originally shared this on 29 Jul 2023 on *Ancestry.com*.

Karl BOYD (also known as Nykki STARR) contributed his memories of his grandmother:[1197]

> ***My Memories of Grandma Lovie.*** There are a plethora of stories that are told about Grandma Lovie throughout my family, in EVERY generation! That was her magic. Grandma Lovie found a way to have a personal relationship with all of us! It didn't matter if you saw her every day, or once a year, she made you feel loved, and made you feel like she was "YOUR" very own personal Grandmother! Grandma Lovie was a Rock! My favorite stories about Grandma were from her days in Mississippi. I remember hearing my mom, and my aunts and uncles talk about whippings they got from her when they were kids. They painted pictures of this absolute demon! Like when she put Uncle George in the smokehouse because she was tired of whipping him! Evidently my mom and Uncle George were Lil' Devils, so it made sense that this woman, raising nine children on her own, had to be tough! When her husband Ilander PARKER died, three white men (Mama always referred to one them as Mr. Charlie) came to Grandma's shack thinking he was going to take a truck that Mr. PARKER had been paying on for ten years! When they came to the house, Grandma came out on the porch with her shotgun and told them, "You can reach out and touch my truck if you want to, you'll draw back a nub!" They threatened to come up on the porch, and she told them, "You can come up here. Somebody will have to carry you off!" Now imagine this happening in Mississippi... in 1959!!! Grandma Lovie was always my Super Hero! Mama told me that after her husband died, she'd dress like a man and walk those roads to town carrying a big stick while wearing a big floppy hat, and when cars came, she'd jump in the bushes and hide. My Grandma was everything. She left Kosciusko, and went to Cruger, Mississippi, where she raised her family. I'm told she left for Cruger so that she wouldn't end up married to her own family!

Lovie GAMBLE had at least two children with Woodrow Wilson NASH:

i   Icy Viola NASH (b. 16 OCT 1935 Kosciusko, Attala Co., MS, d. 14 Oct 2009 Naperville, DuPage Co., IL)[1198] m. Thornton BOYD, Sr. (b. 5 Oct 1935, d. 1 Feb 2008) on 4 Mar 1960 in Cook Co., IL.[1199]

ii   George W. NASH (b. 11 Oct 1937 Holmes Co., MS, d. 17 Feb 2019 Chicago, Cook Co., IL)[1200] m. (1) Annie Ruth SHARP (b. 25 Dec 1938 Birmingham, Jefferson Co., AL, d. 26 Oct 2017 Chicago, Cook Co., IL)[1201] and (2) Unknown.

[1197] Personal correspondence, May 2024.
[1198] "Icy Viola Nash," grave marker, Forest Home Cemetery, Forest Park, Cook Co., IL, digital image s.v. "Icy V Boyd," (birth 16 Oct 1935, death 14 Oct 2009), *FindaGrave.com*.
[1199] "U.S., Social Security Death Index, 1935-2014," s.v. "Thornton Boyd," (birth 5 Oct 1935, death 1 Feb 2008), *Ancestry.com*. "Cook County, Illinois Marriage Index, 1930-1960," s.v. "Icy Nash," (marriage to Thorton Boyd on 4 Mar 1960).
[1200] "Vernestine 'Susie' Joiner," grave marker, Jenkins Cemetery, Attala Co., MS, digital image s.v. "Vernestine Wingard," (birth 27 Aug 1936, death 5 Oct 2018), *FindaGrave.com*.
[1201] "Luther D. 'Rabbit' Wingard," grave marker, Jenkins Cemetery, Attala Co., MS, digital image s.v. "Luther D Wingard," (birth 24 Apr 1936, death 1 Mar 2022), *FindaGrave.com*.

Lovie GAMBLE and Ilander N. PARKER, Sr. had at least six children:

i   Lena Mae PARKER (b. ABT 1939 MS, d. Unknown)[1202] m. Herbert MOORE (b. 22 Jan 1932 Chicago, Cook Co., IL, d. 28 Oct 2001 Bellwood, Cook Co., IL).[1203]

ii   Ilander "Junior Boy" PARKER, Jr. (b. 24 Aug 1941 Cruger, Holmes Co., MS, d. 24 Oct 2005 Chicago, Cook Co., IL).[1204]

iii   Betty Jean PARKER (b. 8 Oct 1943 MS, d. Unknown)[1205] m. Ben REDMOND (b. 22 Jul 1946 MS, 11 Oct 2015 Chicago, Cook Co., IL).[1206]

iv   Willie A. PARKER (b. ABT 1946 MS, d. Unknown).[1207]

v   Arthur Lee PARKER (b. Oct 1947 MS, d. Unknown).[1208]

vi   Charlene PARKER (b. 10 Oct 1952, d. Living)[1209] m. Buvern FRANCISCO, Jr. (b. 19 Aug 1952 Chicago, Cook Co., IL, d. Living).

vii   Shirley PARKER (b. 20 Oct 1954 Kosciusko, Attala Co., MS, d. 5 Jun 1992 Chicago, Cook Co., IL).[1210]

Mable Ethel GAMBLE (Agnes Icy GUYTON GAMBLE, Pinkney, Aaron Whitaker, Aaron Steele, Joseph I, John I, Samuel II, Samuel I, John)

Mable Ethel GAMBLE was the daughter of Agnes Icy GUYTON (b. Sep 1879 Kosciusko, South Beat 1, Attala Co., MS, d. 1963 Kosciusko, Attala, Co., MS)[1211] and Albert GAMBLE (b. 15 Dec 1875 Shuqualak Township 13, Noxubee Co., MS, d. 1948 Kosciusko, Attala Co. MS).[1212] Mable was born on 27 Jun 1916 in MS and died on 11 Jun 2012 in Memphis, Shelby Co., TN.[1213] She married Thomas Eugene (Uncle Bud) CLARK, Sr. (b. 17 Mar 1905 Unknown, d. 21 Aug 1978 Sallis, Attala Co., MS).[1214] See Figure 143, Figure 144, and Figure 145.

[1202] "1940 United States Federal Census," Holmes Co., MS, digital image s.v. "Lena M Parker," (birth abt 1939), *Ancestry.com*.

[1203] Per Karl Glenn Boyd (AKA Nykki Lamarr Starr).

[1204] "U.S., Social Security Death Index, 1935-2014," s.v. "Ilander Parker," (birth 24 Aug 1941, death 24 Oct 2005), *FindaGrave.com*.

[1205] "1950 United States Federal Census," Holmes Co., MS, digital image s.v. "Lena M Parker," (birth abt 1944), *Ancestry.com*. Information from Karl Boyd.

[1206] Per Karl Glenn Boyd (AKA Nykki Lamarr Starr).

[1207] "1950 United States Federal Census," Holmes Co., MS, digital image s.v. "Willie A Parker," (birth abt 1946), *Ancestry.com*.

[1208] "1950 United States Federal Census," Holmes Co., MS, digital image s.v. "Albert Lee Parker," (birth abt 1948), *Ancestry.com*.

[1209] Per her nephew Karl Boyd.

[1210] Per Karl Boyd (also known as Nykki Starr), nephew, from his tree on 12 Oct 2021 on Ancestry.com.

[1211] Agnes Isolome (Icy) Guyton, grave marker, Nash Cemetery, Attala County, MS, digital image s.v. "Agnes Icy Gamble," (birth Sep 1879, death 1963), *FindaGrave.com*.

[1212] Albert Gamble, grave marker, Nash Cemetery, Attala County, MS, digital image s.v. "Agnes Icy Gamble," (birth 15 Dec 1875, death 1948), *FindaGrave.com*.

[1213] "Mabel Ethel Gamble," grave marker, Wright Cemetery, Kosciusko, Attala Co., MS, digital image s.v. "Mable Ethel Clark," (birth 27 Jun 1916, d. 11 Jun 2012), *FindaGrave.com*.

[1214] "Thomas Eugene Clark," grave marker, Wright Cemetery, Kosciusko, Attala Co., MS, digital image s.v. "Thomas Clark," (birth 17 Mar 1905, death 21 Aug 1978), *FindaGrave.com*.

Figure 143 Mable Ethel GAMBLE CLARK[1215]

Figure 144 Thomas Eugene (Uncle Bud) CLARK, Sr.[1216]

MABLE ETHEL CLARK, 95, transitioned from this life to her heavenly home on Monday, June 11, 2012, at Baptist Memorial Hospital in Memphis, TN. She was born June 27, 1916 in Attala County, MS to Albert and Icy Gamble. She was preceded in death by her husband, Thomas Clark, Sr. She is survived by son Thomas Clark, Jr. of Milwaukee, WI; daughter Emma Hughes of Brown Deer, WI; daughter Rena Lewis of Milwaukee, WI; and daughter Linda Patterson of Germantown, TN. She leaves 11 grandchildren, 16 great-grandchildren; and a host of nieces, nephews, cousins, and friends. Funeral Services will be held at 12 noon on Saturday, June 16, 2012, at Galilee Missionary Baptist Church, 3817 Beamon Road, Kosciusko, MS.

Figure 145 Obituary of Mabel Ethel GAMBLE CLARK[1217]

[1215] Karl Boyd originally shared this on 11 Nov 2021 on *Ancestry.com*.
[1216] Karl Boyd originally shared this on 23 Nov 2021 on *Ancestry.com*.
[1217] "Mabel Ethel Clark.," *The Commercial Appeal*, Memphis, Shelby Co., TN, 13 Jun 2012, p. 12; digital image, s.v. "Mabel Ethel Clark," *Newspapers.com*, <https://www.newspapers.com/article/the-commercial-appeal-obituary-for-mable/146263584/>.

The couple had at least four children. See Mabel's obituary above.

i   Thomas CLARK, Jr. (b. ABT 1947 Kosciusko, Attala Co., MS, d. Unknown).[1218]
ii   Emma Jean CLARK (b. ABT 1949 Kosciusko, Attala Co., MS, d. Unknown)[1219] m. Unknown HUGHES (Unknown).
iii   Rena CLARK (b. ABT 1950 MS, d. Unknown) m. Unknown LEWIS (Unknown).[1220]
iv   Brenda CLARK (Unknown) m. Unknown PATTERSON (Unknown).

Lacey GUYTON (William Amzy, Pinkney, Aaron Whitaker, Aaron Steele, Joseph I, John I, Samuel II, Samuel I, John)

Lacey GUYTON was the son of William Amzy GUYTON, Sr. (b. 24 Feb 1885 Attala Co., MS, d. 6 Jun 1949 Attala Co., MS)[1221] and Limmie Mae Douglas NASH (b. 8 Feb 1910 MS, d. 28 Sep 1944 MS).[1222] Lacey was born on 15 Jul 1927 in Kosciusko, Attala Co., MS, and died on 24 Sep 1981 Detroit, Wayne Co., MI.[1223] See Figure 146 and Figure 147.

Figure 146 Young Lacey GUYTON[1224]

Figure 147 Lacey GUYTON in Uniform[1225]

When the 1950 U.S. Census was recorded, Lacey was the head of household at 22 living with several of his siblings – Cherry (17), Pink West (11), Fannie (8), and Elizabeth (6) in Detroit at 944 Fort Street. Both of his parents had died by 1950.[1226] In fact, his mother had died when Elizabeth was about 1

[1218] "1940 United States Federal Census," Kosciusko, Attala Co., MS, digital image s.v. "Thomas Clark Jr," (birth abt 1947), *Ancestry.com*.

[1219] "1940 United States Federal Census," Kosciusko, Attala Co., MS, digital image s.v. "Emma Jean Clark," (birth abt 1949), *Ancestry.com*.

[1220] "1950 United States Federal Census," Kosciusko, Attala Co., MS, digital image s.v. "Rena Clark," (birth abt 1950), *Ancestry.com*.

[1221] Amzy William Guyton, grave marker, Mallett Cemetery, Attala County, MS, digital image s.v. "Amzy William Guyton," (birth 28 Feb 1885, death 6 Jun 1949), *FindaGrave.com*.

[1222] Limmie Mae Douglas Nash, grave marker, Mallett Cemetery, Attala Co., MS, digital image s.v. "Limmie Guyton," (birth 8 Feb 1910, death 28 Sep 1944), *FindaGrave.com*.

[1223] "Michigan, U.S., Death Index, 1971-1996," s.v. "Lacey Guyton," (birth 15 Jul 1927, death 25 Sep 1981), *Ancestry.com*.

[1224] cpack1218 originally shared this on 1 Dec 2013 on *Ancestry.com*.

[1225] Karl Boyd originally shared this on 26 Jan 2022 on *Ancestry.com*.

[1226] "1950 United States Federal Census," Detroit, Wayne Co., MI, digital image s.v. "Lacey Guyton," (birth abt 1928), *Ancestry.com*.

years old. Today, Fort Street appears to be a major highway and there are no buildings at 944 Fort Street. There is a nearby neighborhood, however.

Lacey died in Detroit in 1981, but I was not able to find him in the public records. Perhaps he went by a different name. Perhaps he had a career in the military and lived in different places.

Emma Evester GUYTON (William Amzy, Pinkney, Aaron Whitaker, Aaron Steele, Joseph I, John I, Samuel II, Samuel I, John)

Emma Evester GUYTON was the daughter of William Amzy GUYTON, Sr. (b. 24 Feb 1885 Attala Co., MS, d. 6 Jun 1949 Attala Co., MS)[1227] and Limmie Mae Douglas NASH (b. 8 Feb 1910 MS, d. 28 Sep 1944 MS).[1228] She was born on 4 Apr 1929 in Kosciusko, Attala Co., MS, and died on 12 Apr 2007 Kosciusko, Attala Co., MS.[1229] Emma married John Wesley CLAYTON (b. 18 Jan 1921 Indianola, Sunflower Co., MS, d. 22 Sep 1995 Detroit, Wayne Co., MI).[1230] See Figure 148 and Figure 149.

Figure 148 Emma Evester GUYTON CLAYTON[1231]

Figure 149 John Wesley CLAYTON[1232]

[1227] Amzy William Guyton, grave marker, Mallett Cemetery, Attala County, MS, digital image s.v. "Amzy William Guyton," (birth 28 Feb 1885, death 6 Jun 1949), *FindaGrave.com*.
[1228] Limmie Mae Douglas Nash, grave marker, Mallett Cemetery, Attala Co., MS, digital image s.v. "Limmie Guyton," (birth 8 Feb 1910, death 28 Sep 1944), *FindaGrave.com*.
[1229] Emma Evester Guyton, grave marker, Mallett Cemetery, Attala County, MS, digital image s.v. "Emma Evester Guyton," (birth 4 Apr 1929, death 12 Apr 2007), *FindaGrave.com*.
[1230] "U.S., Social Security Applications and Claims Index, 1936-2007," s.v. "John Wesley Clayton," (birth 18 Jan 1921, death Jul 1941), *Ancestry.com*. "Michigan, U.S., Death Index, 1971-1996," s.v. "John W. Clayton," (birth 19 Jan 1921, death 22 Sep 1995), *Ancestry.com*.
[1231] cpack1218 (Carol Pack) originally shared this on 24 Feb 2014 on *Ancestry.com*.
[1232] cpack1218 (Carol Pack) originally shared this on 1 Dec 2013 on *Ancestry.com*.

In the 1950 U.S. Census, Emma and her husband, John W. CLAYTON, lived in Leake Co., MS. He was a farmer. They lived next door to Dock MALLETT and Lewis MALLETT. John W.'s mother, Beulah, was a Mallett. The census taker noted that these families lived one mile off Thomastown Road on Mcville Road. I believe the Thomastown Road is the road to Thomastown, which would be MS Highway 43, which runs parallel to the Natchez Trace Parkway. See the map in Figure 150.

It is not clear when the couple moved to Michigan, likely 1951. They lived in Mississippi in 1950 but Emma was issued her Social Security card in Michigan in 1951.[1233] John W. lived in Detroit when his mother, Beulah MALLET, died in 1989.[1234] It is not clear whether the couple separated during their time in Detroit, with Emma returning to Mississippi. Emma may have returned to Mississippi during an illness.

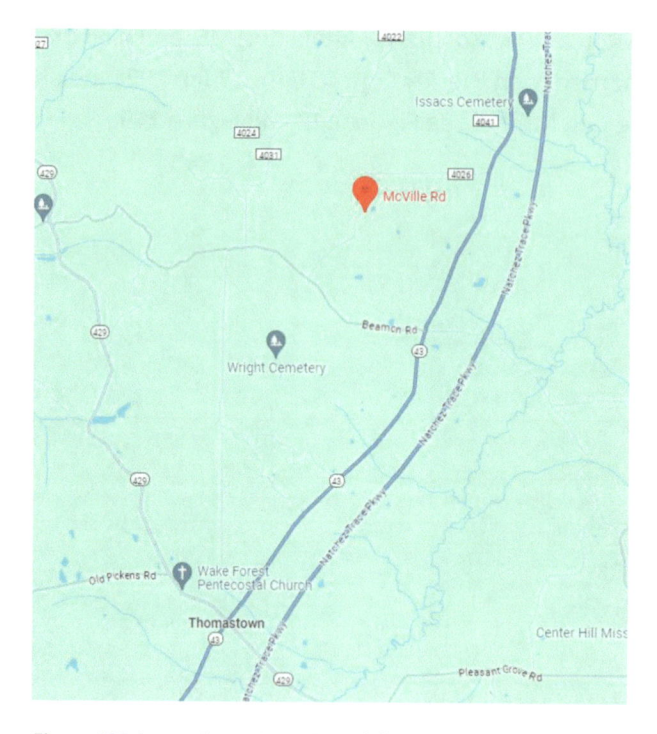

Figure 150 Approximate Location of the Clayton Family in 1950

[1233] "U.S., Social Security Death Index, 1935-2014," s.v. "Emma Clayton," (residence Michigan in 1951, birth 4 Apr 1929, death 12 Apr 2007), *Ancestry.com*.

[1234] "Mrs. Beulah Mallett," *The Star-Herald*, 1 Jun 1989, p. 14; digital image, s.v. "Mrs. Beulah Mallett," *Newspapers.com*, <https://www.newspapers.com/image/268386945/?article=f4420ef1-39aa-48c1-83d5-4ca436815c6f&focus=0.506573,0.2983581,0.6636632,0.47908175&xid=3355>.

Cherry Mae GUYTON (William Amzy, Pinkney, Aaron Whitaker, Aaron Steele, Joseph I, John I, Samuel II, Samuel I, John)

Cherry Mae GUYTON was the daughter of William Amzy GUYTON, Sr. (b. 24 Feb 1885 Attala Co., MS, d. 6 Jun 1949 Attala Co., MS)[1235] and Limmie Mae Douglas NASH (b. 8 Feb 1910 MS, d. 28 Sep 1944 MS).[1236] She was born on 10 Aug 1932 in Kosciusko, Attala Co., MS, and died on 29 Aug 1998 Detroit, Wayne Co., MI.[1237] Cherry was twelve years old when her mother died and seventeen when her father died. Her oldest brother, Lacey, cared for her and some of her siblings in Detroit.[1238] She married Andrew PERKINS (b. 23 Sep 1927 Tallahatchie, MS, d. Unknown)[1239] on 27 Jan 1951 in Wayne Co., MI[1240] when she was eighteen and Andrew was twenty-three. See Figure 151, Figure 152, and Figure 153.

Figure 151 Cherry Mae GUYTON PERKINS[1241]

Figure 152 Andrew PERKINS[1242]

In 1995-1996, the couple lived at 14888 Mayfield St. in Detroit. Today, the home is boarded up, but it was likely a lovely home in 1995. See a *Google Street* view map in Figure 153.

[1235] Amzy William Guyton, grave marker, Mallett Cemetery, Attala County, MS, digital image s.v. "Amzy William Guyton," (birth 28 Feb 1885, death 6 Jun 1949), *FindaGrave.com*.

[1236] Limmie Mae Douglas Nash, grave marker, Mallett Cemetery, Attala Co., MS, digital image s.v. "Limmie Guyton," (birth 8 Feb 1910, death 28 Sep 1944), *FindaGrave.com*.

[1237] "Social Security Death Index," s.v. "Cherry M. Perkins," (birth 10 Aug 1932, death 28 Aug 1998), *Ancestry.com*.

[1238] "1950 United States Federal Census," Detroit, Wayne Co., MI, digital image s.v. "Lacey Guyton," (birth abt 1928), *Ancestry.com*.

[1239] "U.S., World War II Draft Cards Young Men, 1940-1947," digital image s.v. "Andrew Perkins," (birth 23 Sep 1927), *Ancestry.com*.

[1240] "Michigan, Marriage Records, 1867-1952," s.v. "Cherry Mae Guyton," (birth abt 1933, parents Amzy Guyton and Timmie Nash), *Ancestry.com*.

[1241] cpack1218 (Carol Pack) originally shared this on 24 Feb 2014 on *Ancestry.com*.

[1242] cpack1218 (Carol Pack) originally shared this on 1 Dec 2013 on *Ancestry.com*.

Figure 153 Cherry GUYTON PERKINS Home in 1995 Detroit

The couple had at least two children. *Ancestry.com* will not permit viewers to see information on living people to protect their privacy.

i   Lamar Andrew PERKINS (b. 12 Mar 1951 Detroit, Wayne Co., MI, d. 20 May 2010 Norfolk, Norfolk Co., VA).[1243] See Figure 154.

ii   William Henry PERKINS (b. 1 Feb 1954 Detroit, Wayne Co., MI, d. 21 Feb 1986 Detroit, Wayne Co., MI).[1244] See Figure 155.

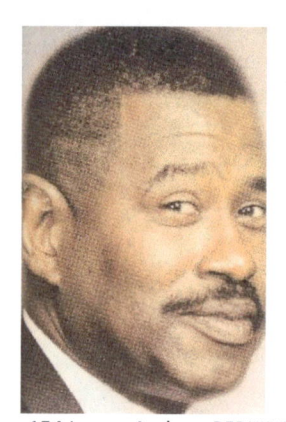

Figure 154 Lamar Andrew PERKINS[1245]

Figure 155 William Henry PERKINS[1246]

[1243] "U.S., Social Security Death Index, 1935-2014," s.v. "Lamar A. Perkins," (birth 12 Mar 1951, death 20 May 2010), *Ancestry.com*.

[1244] "Michigan, U.S., Death Index, 1971-1996," s.v. "William H Perkins," (birth 1 Feb 1954, death 21 Feb 1986), *Ancestry.com*.

[1245] cpack1218 (Carol Pack) originally shared this on 24 Feb 2014 on *Ancestry.com*.

[1246] cpack1218 (Carol Pack) originally shared this on 1 Dec 2013 on *Ancestry.com*.

William Amzy GUYTON, Jr. (William Amzy, Pinkney, Aaron Whitaker, Aaron Steele, Joseph I, John I, Samuel II, Samuel I, John)

William Amzy GUYTON, Jr. was the son of William Amzy GUYTON, Sr. (b. 24 Feb 1885 Attala Co., MS, d. 6 Jun 1949 Attala Co., MS)[1247] and Limmie Mae Douglas NASH (b. 8 Feb 1910 MS, d. 28 Sep 1944 MS).[1248] He was born on 27 Mar 1934 in Kosciusko, Attala Co., MS, and died on 11 Nov 2000 in Detroit, Wayne Co., MI.[1249] He married Betty Janell CLAYTON (b. 12 Feb 1930 Kosciusko, Attala Co., MS, d. Apr 1992 Unknown).[1250] I believe she is the sister of John Wesley CLAYTON, who married Emma Evester GUYTON.[1251] See Figure 156 and Figure 157.

Figure 156 Cherry GUYTON PERKINS, Betty CLARK PERKINS, and William Amzy GUYTON[1252]

Figure 157 William Amzy GUYTON, Jr.[1253]

At points in their lives in Detroit, William and Betty lived at 15342 Ardmore Street and 19308 Hartwell Street.[1254]

[1247] Amzy William Guyton, grave marker, Mallett Cemetery, Attala County, MS, digital image s.v. "Amzy William Guyton," (birth 28 Feb 1885, death 6 Jun 1949), *FindaGrave.com*.
[1248] Limmie Mae Douglas Nash, grave marker, Mallett Cemetery, Attala Co., MS, digital image s.v. "Limmie Guyton," (birth 8 Feb 1910, death 28 Sep 1944), *FindaGrave.com*.
[1249] "U.S., Social Security Death Index, 1935-2014," s.v. "William Guyton," (birth 27 Mar 1934, death 11 Nov 2000), *Ancestry.com*.
[1250] "U.S., Social Security Death Index, 1936-2007," s.v. "Betty Janell Clark," (birth 12 Feb 1930, death Apr 1992), *Ancestry.com*.
[1251] "1940 United States Federal Census," Leake Co., MS, digital image s.v. "Betty Clayton," (birth abt 1930), *Ancestry.com*.
[1252] cpack1218 (Carol Pack) originally shared this on 7 Dec 2013 on *Ancestry.com*.
[1253] Karl Boyd originally shared this on 5 Apr 2022 on *Ancestry.com*.
[1254] "U.S., Public Records Index, 1950-1993, Volume 1," s.v. "William A Guyton Jr," (address 15342 Ardmore St., 48227-3223 and 19308 Hartwell St 48235-1271), *Ancestry.com*.

Pink West (PW) GUYTON (William Amzy, Pinkney, Aaron Whitaker, Aaron Steele, Joseph I, John I, Samuel II, Samuel I, John)

Pink West GUYTON was the son of William Amzy GUYTON, Sr. (b. 24 Feb 1885 Attala Co., MS, d. 6 Jun 1949 Attala Co., MS)[1255] and Limmie Mae Douglas NASH (b. 8 Feb 1910 MS, d. 28 Sep 1944 MS).[1256] Pink was born on 20 Jul 1938 in Kosciusko, Attala Co., MS, and died on 23 Aug 1991 in Detroit, Wayne Co., MI).[1257] He was five years old when his mother died and ten when her father died. His oldest brother, Lacey, cared for him and some of his siblings in Detroit.[1258] See Figure 158.

Figure 158 Pink West GUYTON[1259]

[1255] Amzy William Guyton, grave marker, Mallett Cemetery, Attala County, MS, digital image s.v. "Amzy William Guyton," (birth 28 Feb 1885, death 6 Jun 1949), *FindaGrave.com*.
[1256] Limmie Mae Douglas Nash, grave marker, Mallett Cemetery, Attala Co., MS, digital image s.v. "Limmie Guyton," (birth 8 Feb 1910, death 28 Sep 1944), *FindaGrave.com*.
[1257] "U.S., Social Security Death Index, 1936-2007," s.v. "Pink W Guyton," (birth 19 Jul 1938, death Aug 1991), *Ancestry.com*.
[1258] "1950 United States Federal Census," Detroit, Wayne Co., MI, digital image s.v. "Lacey Guyton," (birth abt 1928), *Ancestry.com*.
[1259] cpack1218 (Carol Pack) originally shared this on 7 Dec 2013 on *Ancestry.com*.

Fannie Douglas GUYTON (William Amzy, Pinkney, Aaron Whitaker, Aaron Steele, Joseph I, John I, Samuel II, Samuel I, John)

Fannie Douglas GUYTON was the daughter of William Amzy GUYTON, Sr. (b. 24 Feb 1885 Attala Co., MS, d. 6 Jun 1949 Attala Co., MS)[1260] and Limmie Mae Douglas NASH (b. 8 Feb 1910 MS, d. 28 Sep 1944 MS).[1261] She was born on 18 Jan 1942 in Kosciusko, Attala Co., MS, and died on Nov 1988 in Detroit, Wayne Co., MI.[1262] She was not yet two years old when her mother died and about seven when her father died. Her oldest brother, Lacey, cared for her and some of his siblings in Detroit.[1263] See Figure 159.

Figure 159 Fannie Douglas GUYTON[1264]

[1260] Amzy William Guyton, grave marker, Mallett Cemetery, Attala County, MS, digital image s.v. "Amzy William Guyton," (birth 28 Feb 1885, death 6 Jun 1949), *FindaGrave.com*.

[1261] Limmie Mae Douglas Nash, grave marker, Mallett Cemetery, Attala Co., MS, digital image s.v. "Limmie Guyton," (birth 8 Feb 1910, death 28 Sep 1944), *FindaGrave.com*.

[1262] "U.S., Social Security Death Index, 1936-2007," s.v. "Fannie Guyton," (birth 18 Jul 1942, death Nov 1988), *Ancestry.com*.

[1263] "1950 United States Federal Census," Detroit, Wayne Co., MI, digital image s.v. "Lacey Guyton," (birth abt 1928), *Ancestry.com*.

[1264] cpack1218 (Carol Pack) originally shared this on 2 Dec 2013 on *Ancestry.com*.

Elizabeth GUYTON (William Amzy, Pinkney, Aaron Whitaker, Aaron Steele, Joseph I, John I, Samuel II, Samuel I, John)

Elizabeth GUYTON was the daughter of William Amzy GUYTON, Sr. (b. 24 Feb 1885 Attala Co., MS, d. 6 Jun 1949 Attala Co., MS)[1265] and Limmie Mae Douglas NASH (b. 8 Feb 1910 MS, d. 28 Sep 1944 MS).[1266] She was born on 18 Jan 1942 in Kosciusko, Attala Co., MS, and died on Nov 1988 in Detroit, Wayne Co., MI).[1267] See Figure 160 and Figure 161. She was about one-year-old when her mother died and about six when her father died. Her oldest brother, Lacey, cared for her and some of his siblings in Detroit.[1268]

She married (1) Willie James THOMAS (b. 28 Feb 1929 George Co., MS, d. 13 Mar 1979 Detroit, Wayne Co., MI)[1269] and (2) Ernest SMITH, Jr. (b. 10 Aug 1920 Macon Co., GA, d. Apr 2000 Detroit, Wayne Co., MI) on 13 Nov 1964 in Toledo, OH).[1270] With Ernest SMITH, Jr., Elizabeth gave birth to Chandra Valencia SMITH (b. 29 Aug 1967 Detroit, Wayne Co., MI, d. 27 Feb 2020 Detroit, Wayne Co., MI).[1271] See Figure 162.

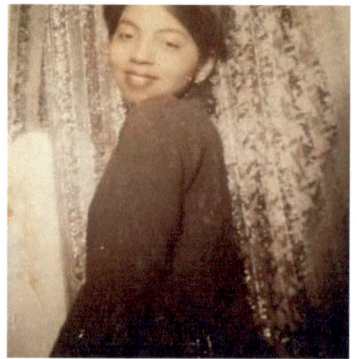

Figure 160 Young Elizabeth GUYTON SMITH[1272]

Figure 161 Mature Elizabeth GUYTON SMITH[1273]

Figure 162 Chandra Valencia SMITH, Daughter of Elizabeth GUYTON[1274]

[1265] Amzy William Guyton, grave marker, Mallett Cemetery, Attala County, MS, digital image s.v. "Amzy William Guyton," (birth 28 Feb 1885, death 6 Jun 1949), *FindaGrave.com*.
[1266] Limmie Mae Douglas Nash, grave marker, Mallett Cemetery, Attala Co., MS, digital image s.v. "Limmie Guyton," (birth 8 Feb 1910, death 28 Sep 1944), *FindaGrave.com*.
[1267] "Michigan, Death Index, 1971-1996," s.v. "Elizabeth G Smith," (birth 6 Aug 1943, death 13 Nov 1982), *Ancestry.com*.
[1268] "1950 United States Federal Census," Detroit, Wayne Co., MI, digital image s.v. "Lacey Guyton," (birth abt 1928), *Ancestry.com*.
[1269] Per Karl Glenn Boyd (AKA Nykki Lamarr Starr).
[1270] "Cassandra Smith Family Tree," Sann098, *Ancestry.com*, accessed 13 May 2024.
[1271] "Cassandra Smith Family Tree," Sann098, *Ancestry.com*, accessed 13 May 2024.
[1272] Sann098 (Cassandra Smith) originally shared this on 12 Sep 2022 on *Ancestry.com*.
[1273] cpack1218 (Carol Pack) originally shared this on 2 Dec 2013 on *Ancestry.com*.
[1274] Sann098 (Cassandra Smith) originally shared this on 5 Mar 2024 on *Ancestry.com*.

Generation #10

Samuel Alonzo FORD, Sr. (Nola ALLEN FORD, Emma GUYTON ALLEN, Pinkney, Aaron Whitaker, Aaron Steele, Joseph I, John I, Samuel II, Samuel I, John)

Samuel Alonzo FORD, Sr. was the son of Nola J. ALLEN (b. Feb 1897 MS, d. 23 Jan 1997 Sallis, Attala Co., MS)[1275] and Sherman FORD (b. 30 Dec 1882 Durant, Holmes Co., MS, d. Nov 1967 Bolton, Hinds Co., MS).[1276] Samuel was born on 4 Jan 1927 in Hinds Co., MS, and died on 14 Nov 2000 in Chicago, Cook Co., IL).[1277] He married Estelle BROWN (b. 30 Jan 1928 MS, d. Jun 1972 Chicago, Cook Co., IL).[1278]

According to the 1950 U.S. Federal Census, Samuel (23) and Estelle (22) lived in Hinds Co., MS. They were farming. They lived with Estelle's brother, Jessie BROWN (25), and their children: Maggie Jean FORD (4), Ernestine FORD (2), Mary Ann FORD (1) and Verian Louise FORD (Feb). Samuel's obituary (see Figure 163) identified twos additional sons, Frank FORD and Samuel A. [Alonzo] FORD, Jr.

Their children included:

i   Maggie Jean FORD (b. ABT 1946 MS, d. Unknown).
ii   Earnestine FORD (b. ABT 1948 MS, d. Unknown).
iii   Mary Ann FORD (b. ABT 1949 MS, d. Unknown).
iv   Verian Louise FORD (b. ABT 1950 MS, d. Unknown).
v   Samuel Alonzo FORD, Jr. (b. Jan 1952, d. Unknown).
vi   Frank FORD (Unknown).

[1275] "1900 United States Federal Census," Kosciusko, Attala Co., MS, digital image s.v. "Nola J Allen," (birth abt 1897), *Ancestry.com*.
[1276] "U.S., Social Security Death Index, 1935-2014," s.v. "Sherman Ford," (birth 30 Dec 1882, death Nov 1967), *Ancestry.com*.
[1277] "U.S., Social Security Death Index, 1935-2014," s.v. "Samuel A. Ford," (birth 4 Jan 1927, death 13 Nov 2000), *Ancestry.com*.
[1278] "Social Security Death Index, 1935-2014," s.v. "Estella Ford," (birth 30 Jan 1928, death Jun 1972), *Ancestry.com*.

FORD

MR. SAMUEL A. FORD SR. — June 5, 1979 at 2:25 p.m. in Baptist Memorial Hospital. Late residence 1005 No. Avalon. Beloved husband of Mrs. Mary Ella Ford, father of Messers Frank and Samuel A Ford Jr. of Fort Lauderdale, Florida, brother of Mrs. Ernestine Ford of Memphis, father-in-law of Geraldine and Jerutha, brother-in-law of Rev. & Mrs. Albert Lee of East St Louis, Ill., a host of grandchildren, a host of nieces, nephews, other relatives and friends surviving. Remains will lie in state Friday, June 8, 1979 at St Paul Baptist Church, 1543 Brookins St. from 4:30 p.m. to 9:00 p.m. and Saturday, June 9, 1979 (same church) from 9:30 a.m. to 11:00 a.m. Funeral commencing at 11:00 a.m. Rev. J. E. Ferguson, pastor, officiating. Remains will not be viewed following eulogy. Interment in Calvary Cemetery Saturday. **J. O. PATTERSON FUNERAL HOME, INC. SERVICES,** 2204 Chelsea, 274-8623.

Figure 163 Obituary for Samuel Alonzo FORD, Sr.[1279]

[1279] Samuel Alonza Ford, Sr.," *Memphis Press-Scimitar*, Memphis, Shelby Co., TN, Fri, 8 Jun 1979, p. 22; digital obituary, s.v. "Mr. Samuel A. Ford, Sr.," <https://www.newspapers.com/article/the-memphis-press-scimitar-obituary-samu/131919775/>, Newspapers.com.

Casey Glenn GUYTON, Sr. (Lillie Wardean ROBY GUYTON, Patsy J., Pinkney, Aaron Whitaker, Aaron Steele, Joseph I, John I, Samuel II, Samuel I, John)

Casey Glenn GUYTON, Sr. was the son of Lillie Wardean ROBY (b. 17 Nov 1909 Sallis, Attala Co., MS, d. 27 Oct 2003 Chicago, Cook Co., IL)[1280] and James (Jim) GUYTON (b. 2 Sep 1905 Sallis, Attala Co., MS, d. Unknown).[1281] Jim GUYTON was related to Lillie ROBY as he was the son of Case GUYTON (son of Aaron Whitaker GUYTON and Artie RAINEY) and Susie STINGLEY. Patsy J. GUYTON was the granddaughter of Aaron Whitaker GUYTON and Patsy GIBSON. Casey Glenn GUYTON, Sr. was born on 13 Jan 1926 in Sallis, Attala Co., MS, and died on 7 Jul 2018 in Chicago, Cook Co., IL.[1282] He married Mildred TATE (b. Jun 1930 TN, d. 12 Jan 2019 Chicago, Cook Co., IL) on 8 Aug 1952 in Cook Co., IL.[1283] They had at least six children:

i   Ernest GUYTON (b. ABT 1945 IL, d. Unknown).[1284]
ii Gloria GUYTON (b. ABT 1949 IL, d. Unknown).[1285]
iii Dorothy Ann GUYTON (b. 23 Jul 1950 Chicago, Cook Co., IL, d. 10 Sep 1980 Cook Co., IL).[1286]
iv Kasey Glen GUYTON, Jr. (b. 18 May 1955 Chicago, Cook Co., IL, d. 15 Mar 1996 Chicago, Cook Co., IL).[1287]
v   Diane GUYTON (Unknown).[1288]
vi Patricia GUYTON (Unknown).[1289]

[1280] Lillie Wardean Roby, grave marker, Burr Oak Cemetery, Alsip, Cook Co., IL, digital image s.v. "Mrs Lillie Wardean Guyton," (birth 17 Nov 1909, death 27 Oct 2003), *FindaGrave.com*.
[1281] "U.S. WWII Draft Cards Young Men, 1940-1947," digital image s.v. "Jim Guyton," (birth 2 Sep 1905), *Ancestry.com*.
[1282] "U.S., Public Records Index, 1950-1993, Volume 1," s.v. "Kasey G. Guyton Jr.," (birth 13 Jan 1926), *Ancestry.com*. His death is given by Audrey Guyton on *Ancestry.com* as 7 Jul 2018. Audrey is Casey and Mildred Guyton's granddaughter.
[1283] "U.S., Public Records Index, 1950-1993, Volume 1," s.v. "Mildred Guyton," (birth 3 Jun 1930), *Ancestry.com*. Her death is given by Audrey Guyton on *Ancestry.com* as 12 Jan 2019. Audrey is Casey and Mildred Guyton's granddaughter. "Cook County, Illinois Marriage Index, 1930-1960," s.v. "Kasey Guyton," (marriage 8 Aug 1952 to Mildred Tate), *Ancestry.com*.
[1284] "1950 United States Census," Chicago, Cook Co., IL, digital image s.v. "Ernest Guyton," (birth abt 1945), *Ancestry.com*.
[1285] "1950 United States Census," Chicago, Cook Co., IL, digital image s.v. "Gloria Guyton," (birth abt 1949), *Ancestry.com*.
[1286] "Cook County, Illinois Death Index, 1908-1988," s.v. "Dorothy Guyton," (death 10 Sep 1980), *Ancestry.com*. "U.S., Social Security Applications and Claims Index, 1936-2007," s.v. Dorothy Ann Guyton," (birth 23 Jul 1950, death Sep 1980), *Ancestry.com*.
[1287] "U.S., Social Security Applications and Claims Index, 1936-2007," s.v. "Kasey Guyton," (birth 18 May 1954, death 15 Mar 1996), *Ancestry.com*.
[1288] Per Channie Brown-Currie.
[1289] Per Channie Brown-Currie.

Rozell J. GUYTON (Lillie Wardean ROBY GUYTON, Patsy J., Pinkney, Aaron Whitaker, Aaron Steele, Joseph I, John I, Samuel II, Samuel I, John)

Rozell J. GUYTON was the daughter of Lillie Wardean ROBY (b. 17 Nov 1909 Sallis, Attala Co., MS, d. 27 Oct 2003 Chicago, Cook Co., IL)[1290] and James (Jim) GUYTON (b. 2 Sep 1905 Sallis, Attala Co., MS, d. Unknown).[1291] Jim GUYTON was related to Lillie ROBY as he was the son of Case GUYTON (son of Aaron Whitaker GUYTON and Artie RAINEY) and Susie STINGLEY. Patsy J. GUYTON was the granddaughter of Aaron Whitaker GUYTON and Patsy GIBSON.

Rozell J. GUYTON was born on 1 Mar 1928 in Kosciusko, Attala Co., MS, and died on 7 May 2008 in Milwaukee, Milwaukee Co., WI).[1292] She married Ollie D. RILEY, Sr. (b. 17 Sep 1921 Sallis, Attala Co., MS, d. 31 Dec 1993 Milwaukee, Milwaukee Co., WI).[1293]

They had at least four children, per Ollie's obituary. See Figure 164.

i   Rosie Jean RILEY (b. ABT 1944 MS, d. Unknown)[1294] m. Unknown RILEY.
ii   Ollie D. RILEY, Jr. (b. ABT 1947 MS, d. Unknown)[1295] m. Donna Louella BODDEN (b. ABT 1948, d. Unknown) on 9 Oct 1974 in Meade, SD.[1296]
iii   Willie Claude RILEY (b. 8 MAR 1949 MS, d. Unknown).[1297]
iv   Genet RILEY (b. Sep 1955, d. Unknown)[1298] m. Paul Wilton ALFRED (Unknown) on 22 Sep 1984 in Harris Co., TX) and divorced on 13 Apr 2011 in Walker, TX.[1299] They had at least one child: Alexander Paul ALFRED (b. 5 Aug 1985 Harris Co., TX).[1300]

[1290] Lillie Wardean Roby, grave marker, Burr Oak Cemetery, Alsip, Cook Co., IL, digital image s.v. "Mrs Lillie Wardean Guyton," (birth 17 Nov 1909, death 27 Oct 2003), *FindaGrave.com*.
[1291] "U.S. WWII Draft Cards Young Men, 1940-1947," digital image s.v. "Jim Guyton," (birth 2 Sep 1905), *Ancestry.com*.
[1292] Rozell J. Guyton, grave marker, Parkway Cemetery, Kosciusko, Attala Co., IL, digital image s.v. "Rozell J Riley," (birth 1 Mar 1928, death 7 May 2008), *FindaGrave.com*.
[1293] Ollie D. Riley, Sr., grave marker, Parkway Cemetery, Kosciusko, Attala Co., IL, digital image s.v. "Ollie D. Riley," (birth 17 Sep 1921, death 31 Dec 1993), *FindaGrave.com*.
[1294] "1950 United States Census," Leake Co., MS, digital image s.v. "Rose Jean Riley," (birth abt 1944), *Ancestry.com*.
[1295] "1950 United States Census," Leake Co., MS, digital image s.v. "Ollie Riley Jr," (birth abt 1947), *Ancestry.com*.
[1296] "South Dakota, Marriages, 1905-2017," s.v. "Ollie Riley," (marriage 9 Oct 1974 to Donna Bodden), *Ancestry.com*. "Marriage Licenses," *Rapid City Journal*, Rapid City, SD, 17 Oct 1974, Thu, p. 3; digital obituary, s.v. "Ollie Riley Jr.," <https://www.newspapers.com/image/351481146/?article=1f23cafd-fe36-402d-a7fb-1dc21dc6bb90/37ab3014-8378-423e-8cc0-87054b18663a&focus=0.33140522,0.5328587,0.48897287,0.6445842&xid=3398/>, *Newspapers.com*.
[1297] "1950 United States Census," Leake Co., MS, digital image s.v. "Willie C Riley," (birth abt 1949), *Ancestry.com*. "U.S. Public Records Index, 1950-1993, Volume 1," s.v. "Willie C Riley," (birth 8 Mar 1949), *Ancestry.com*.
[1298] "U.S., Index to Public Records, 1994-2019," s.v. "Genet Riley," (birth Sep 1955), *Ancestry.com*.
[1299] "Texas, U.S., Divorce Index, 1968-2015," s.v. "Genet Riley," (marriage 20 Sep 1984, divorce 13 Apr 2011), *Ancestry.com*.
[1300] "Texas Birth Index, 1903-1997," s.v. "Alexander Paul Alfred," (birth 5 Aug 1985), *Ancestry.com*.

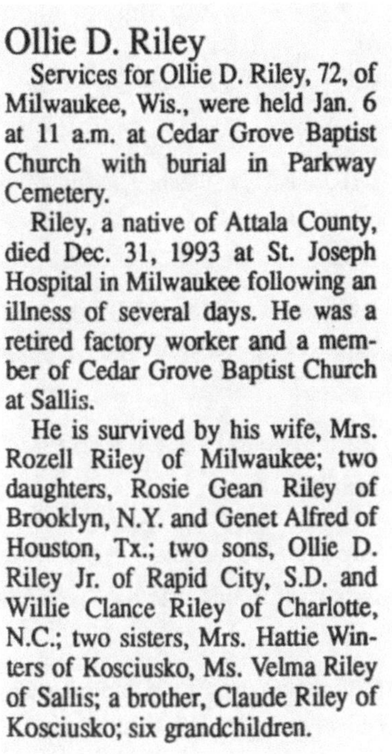

> **Ollie D. Riley**
>
> Services for Ollie D. Riley, 72, of Milwaukee, Wis., were held Jan. 6 at 11 a.m. at Cedar Grove Baptist Church with burial in Parkway Cemetery.
>
> Riley, a native of Attala County, died Dec. 31, 1993 at St. Joseph Hospital in Milwaukee following an illness of several days. He was a retired factory worker and a member of Cedar Grove Baptist Church at Sallis.
>
> He is survived by his wife, Mrs. Rozell Riley of Milwaukee; two daughters, Rosie Gean Riley of Brooklyn, N.Y. and Genet Alfred of Houston, Tx.; two sons, Ollie D. Riley Jr. of Rapid City, S.D. and Willie Clance Riley of Charlotte, N.C.; two sisters, Mrs. Hattie Winters of Kosciusko, Ms. Velma Riley of Sallis; a brother, Claude Riley of Kosciusko; six grandchildren.

Figure 164 Obituary of Ollie D. RILEY, Sr.[1301]

Jimmie Ruth GUYTON (Lillie Wardean ROBY GUYTON, Patsy J., Pinkney, Aaron Whitaker, Aaron Steele, Joseph I, John I, Samuel II, Samuel I, John)

Jimmie Ruth GUYTON was the daughter of Lillie Wardean ROBY (b. 17 Nov 1909 Sallis, Attala Co., MS, d. 27 Oct 2003 Chicago, Cook Co., IL)[1302] and James (Jim) GUYTON (b. 2 Sep 1905 Sallis, Attala Co., MS, d. Unknown).[1303] Jim GUYTON was related to Lillie ROBY as he was the son of Case GUYTON (son of Aaron Whitaker GUYTON and Artie RAINEY) and Susie STINGLEY. Patsy J. GUYTON was the granddaughter of Aaron Whitaker GUYTON and Patsy GIBSON.

Jimmie Ruth GUYTON was born about 1938 in MS and her death is unknown).[1304] She married Wardell HILL (b. Unknown, d. Chicago, Cook Co., IL).[1305] They had two children:[1306]

[1301] "Obituary for Ollie D. Riley, Sr.," *The Star-Herald,* Kosciusko, Attala Co., MS, 13 Jan 1994, Thu, p. 18; digital image, s.v. "Ollie D. Riley," <https://www.newspapers.com/article/the-star-herald-ollie-d-riley-obituary/132200674/>, *Newspapers.com*.
[1302] Lillie Wardean Roby, grave marker, Burr Oak Cemetery, Alsip, Cook Co., IL, digital image s.v. "Mrs Lillie Wardean Guyton," (birth 17 Nov 1909, death 27 Oct 2003), *FindaGrave.com*.
[1303] "U.S. WWII Draft Cards Young Men, 1940-1947," digital image s.v. "Jim Guyton," (birth 2 Sep 1905), *Ancestry.com*.
[1304] "1950 United States Federal Census," Newport, Attala Co., MS, digital image s.v. "Ruth Guyton," (birth ABT 1937), *Ancestry.com*.
[1305] Wardell Hill information from Channie Brown-Currie.
[1306] Per Channie Brown-Currie.

i	Michael HILL (b. 1 Dec 1964 Chicago, Cook Co., IL, d. Unknown) m. Shannon BROOKS (b. Chicago, Cook Co., IL, d. Unknown).
ii	Keshia HILL (b. 18 Nov 1965 Chicago, Cook Co., IL, d. Unknown).

Lucy GUYTON (Lillie Wardean ROBY GUYTON, Patsy J., Pinkney, Aaron Whitaker, Aaron Steele, Joseph I, John I, Samuel II, Samuel I, John)

Lucy GUYTON was the daughter of Lillie Wardean ROBY (b. 17 Nov 1909 Sallis, Attala Co., MS, d. 27 Oct 2003 Chicago, Cook Co., IL)[1307] and James (Jim) GUYTON (b. 2 Sep 1905 Sallis, Attala Co., MS, d. Unknown).[1308] Jim GUYTON was related to Lillie ROBY as he was the son of Case GUYTON (son of Aaron Whitaker GUYTON and Artie RAINEY) and Susie STINGLEY. Patsy J. GUYTON was the granddaughter of Aaron Whitaker GUYTON and Patsy GIBSON.

Lucy GUYTON was born about 1936 in Sallis, Attala Co., MS and her death is unknown.[1309] She married John Lee THURMAN, who was born in Sallis, Attala Co., MS.[1310] They had three children:[1311]

i	Linda THURMAN (b. Milwaukee, Milwaukee Co., WI, d. Unknown).
ii	Anita THURMAN (b. Milwaukee, Milwaukee Co., WI, d. Unknown).
iii	Mary THURMAN (b. Milwaukee, Milwaukee Co., WI, d. Unknown).

Maebell GUYTON (Lillie Wardean ROBY GUYTON, Patsy J., Pinkney, Aaron Whitaker, Aaron Steele, Joseph I, John I, Samuel II, Samuel I, John)

Maebell GUYTON was the daughter of Lillie Wardean ROBY (b. 17 Nov 1909 Sallis, Attala Co., MS, d. 27 Oct 2003 Chicago, Cook Co., IL)[1312] and James (Jim) GUYTON (b. 2 Sep 1905 Sallis, Attala Co., MS, d. Unknown).[1313] Jim GUYTON was related to Lillie ROBY as he was the son of Case GUYTON (son of Aaron Whitaker GUYTON and Artie RAINEY) and Susie STINGLEY. Patsy J. GUYTON was the granddaughter of Aaron Whitaker GUYTON and Patsy GIBSON.

Maebell married Lee EVANS and they had three children:[1314]

[1307] Lillie Wardean Roby, grave marker, Burr Oak Cemetery, Alsip, Cook Co., IL, digital image s.v. "Mrs Lillie Wardean Guyton," (birth 17 Nov 1909, death 27 Oct 2003), *FindaGrave.com*.
[1308] "U.S. WWII Draft Cards Young Men, 1940-1947," digital image s.v. "Jim Guyton," (birth 2 Sep 1905), *Ancestry.com*.
[1309] "1950 United States Federal Census," Newport, Attala Co., MS, digital image s.v. "Lucy Guyton," (birth ABT 1936), *Ancestry.com*.
[1310] Per Channie Brown-Currie.
[1311] Per Channie Brown-Currie.
[1312] Lillie Wardean Roby, grave marker, Burr Oak Cemetery, Alsip, Cook Co., IL, digital image s.v. "Mrs Lillie Wardean Guyton," (birth 17 Nov 1909, death 27 Oct 2003), *FindaGrave.com*.
[1313] "U.S. WWII Draft Cards Young Men, 1940-1947," digital image s.v. "Jim Guyton," (birth 2 Sep 1905), *Ancestry.com*.
[1314] Per Karl Glenn Boyd (AKA Nykki Lamarr Starr).

i	Tony EVANS (b. Chicago, Cook Co., MI, d. Unknown).
ii	Brenda EVANS (b. Chicago, Cook Co., MI, d. Unknown).
iii	Sheila EVANS (b. Chicago, Cook Co., MI, d. Unknown).

Earlene GUYTON (Ruth Lee (Ruthie) ROBY GUYTON, Patsy J., Pinkney, Aaron Whitaker, Aaron Steele, Joseph I, John I, Samuel II, Samuel I, John)

Earlene GUYTON was the daughter of Ruthie Lee ROBY (b. 7 May 1916 in Sallis, Attala Co., MS, d. 13 Jan 1996 in Wauwatosa, Milwaukee Co., WI[1315] and Gus Davis GUYTON (b. 3 Mar 1909 Sallis, Attala Co., MS., d. 8 Jul 1990 Cook Co., IL).[1316] Ruthie and Gus were cousins. Aaron Whitaker GUYTON was Ruthie's great-grandfather; he was Gus Davis GUYTON's grandfather.

Earlene was born on 19 Aug 1933 in Sallis, Attala Co., MS, and died on 22 May 1965).[1317] She married Otha LANDINGHAM (b. 31 Oct 1922 Marked Tree, Poinsett Co., AR, d. 19 May 1981 Chicago, Cook Co., IL).[1318] See Figure 165Figure 166. They had two children:[1319]

i	Susie GUYTON-LANDINGHAM (b. Sallis, Attala Co., WI, d. Unknown) m. Unknown CALVIN (Unknown).
ii	Linda Faye GUYTON-LANDINGHAM (b. Chicago, Cook Co., IL, d. Unknown) m. Unknown O'HARA (Unknown).

Figure 165 Earlene GUYTON LANDINGHAM[1320]

[1315] Ruth Lee (Ruthie) Roby, grave marker, Russell Cemetery, Attala Co., MS, digital image s.v. "Ruthie Guyton," (birth 7 May 1916, death 13 Jan 1996), *FindaGrave.com*.
[1316] Gus Davis Guyton, grave marker, Russell Cemetery, Attala Co., MS, digital image s.v. "Gus Davis Guyton," (birth 3 Mar 1909, death 8 Jul 1990), *FindaGrave.com*.
[1317] Earlene Guyton, grave marker, Russell Cemetery, Attala Co., MS, digital image s.v. "Earlene Landingham," (birth 19 Aug 1933, death 22 May 1965), *FindaGrave.com*.
[1318] Otha Landingham, grave marker, Russell Cemetery, Attala Co., MS, digital image s.v. "Otha Landingham," (birth 31 Oct 1922, death 19 May 1981), *FindaGrave.com*.
[1319] Per Karl Glenn Boyd (AKA Nykki Lamarr Starr).
[1320] chancurri originally shared this on 16 May 2013 on *Ancestry.com*.

Bernice GUYTON (Ruth Lee (Ruthie) ROBY GUYTON, Patsy J., Pinkney, Aaron Whitaker, Aaron Steele, Joseph I, John I, Samuel II, Samuel I, John)

Bernice GUYTON was the daughter of Ruthie Lee ROBY (b. 7 May 1916 in Sallis, Attala Co., MS, d. 13 Jan 1996 in Wauwatosa, Milwaukee Co., WI[1321] and Gus Davis GUYTON (b. 3 Mar 1909 Sallis, Attala Co., MS., d. 8 Jul 1990 Cook Co., IL).[1322] Ruthie and Gus were cousins. Aaron Whitaker GUYTON was Ruthie's great-grandfather; he was Gus Davis GUYTON's grandfather.

Bernice was born on 17 Jun 1935 in Attala Co., MS, and died on 14 Dec 2002 in McAdams, Attala Co., MS).[1323] She married Joseph Lee PHILLIPS, Sr. (b. abt 1935, d. Unknown).[1324] See Figure 166. Bernice GUYTON and Joseph PHILLIPS, Sr. had at least five children, per her obituary. See Figure 167.

Figure 166 Bernice GUYTON PHILLIPS[1325]

i	Darren PHILLIPS (Unknown).	
ii	Patrick PHILLIPS (Unknown).	
iii	Joseph Lee PHILLIPS, Jr. (Unknown).	
iv	Yolanda PHILLIPS (Unknown).	
v	Jacqueline PHILLIPS (Unknown).	

[1321] Ruth Lee (Ruthie) Roby, grave marker, Russell Cemetery, Attala Co., MS, digital image s.v. "Ruthie Guyton," (birth 7 May 1916, death 13 Jan 1996), *FindaGrave.com*.
[1322] Gus Davis Guyton, grave marker, Russell Cemetery, Attala Co., MS, digital image s.v. "Gus Davis Guyton," (birth 3 Mar 1909, death 8 Jul 1990), *FindaGrave.com*.
[1323] Bernice Guyton, grave marker, Russell Cemetery, Attala Co., MS, digital image s.v. "Bernice Phillips," (birth 17 Jun 1935, death 14 Dec 2002), *FindaGrave.com*.
[1324] "Bernice Guyton-Phillips," *The Star-Herald*, 25 Dec 2002, p. 6; digital image, s.v. "Bernice Guyton-Phillips," *Newspapers.com*, <https://www.newspapers.com/image/305104740/?focus=0.356137%2C0.18697402%2C0.5030061%2C0.3336987&xid=3355&clipping_id=147233545>.
[1325] chancurri originally shared this on 23 May 2013 on *Ancestry.com*.

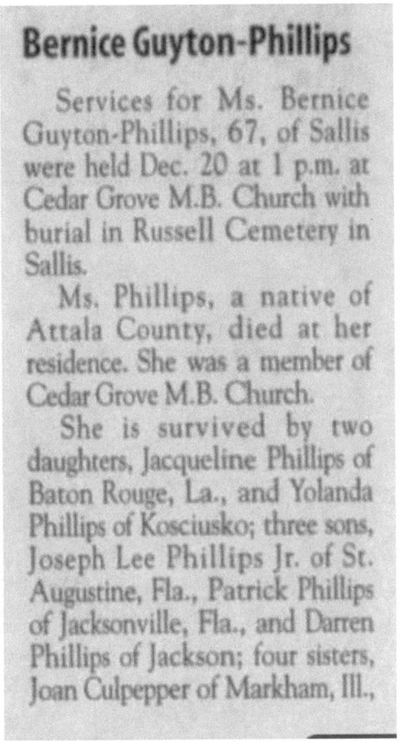

Bernice Guyton-Phillips

Services for Ms. Bernice Guyton-Phillips, 67, of Sallis were held Dec. 20 at 1 p.m. at Cedar Grove M.B. Church with burial in Russell Cemetery in Sallis.

Ms. Phillips, a native of Attala County, died at her residence. She was a member of Cedar Grove M.B. Church.

She is survived by two daughters, Jacqueline Phillips of Baton Rouge, La., and Yolanda Phillips of Kosciusko; three sons, Joseph Lee Phillips Jr. of St. Augustine, Fla., Patrick Phillips of Jacksonville, Fla., and Darren Phillips of Jackson; four sisters, Joan Culpepper of Markham, Ill., Billie Mallet, Barbara Leland, and Patricia Guyton of Milwaukee; two brothers, Curtis Guyton of Broadview, Ill., Arthur Guyton of Maywood, Ill.; 11 grandchildren.

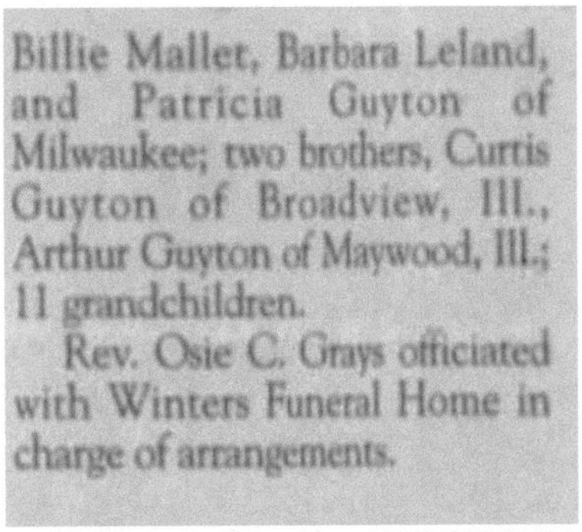

Rev. Osie C. Grays officiated with Winters Funeral Home in charge of arrangements.

Figure 167 Obituary of Bernice GUYTON-PHILLIPS[1326]

[1326] "Bernice Guyton-Phillips," *The Star-Herald*, 25 Dec 2002, p. 6; digital image, s.v. "Bernice Guyton-Phillips," *Newspapers.com*, <https://www.newspapers.com/image/305104740/?focus=0.356137%2C0.18697402%2C0.5030061%2C0.3336987&xid=3355&clipping_id=147233545>.

J.C. MALLETT (Fannie GAMBLE, Agnes Icy GUYTON GAMBLE, Pinkney, Aaron Whitaker, Aaron Steele, Joseph I, John I, Samuel II, Samuel I, John)

J.C. MALLETT was the son of Fannie B. GAMBLE (b. 5 Aug 1903 in MS, d. 24 Jul 1998 Kosciusko, Attala Co., MS)[1327] and Dock M. MALLETT (b. 4 Jan 1897 in Kosciusko, Attala Co., MS, d. 21 Aug 1980 Kosciusko, Attala Co., MS).[1328] J.C. was born on 28 Feb 1922 in Kosciusko, Attala Co., MS, and died on 30 Oct 1981 in Milwaukee, Milwaukee Co., WI.[1329] He married Clara ZOLICOFFER (b. 1926 MS, d. Unknown)[1330] on 9 Mar 1948 in Detroit, Wayne Co., MI.[1331] See Figure 168 and Figure 169.

Figure 168 J.C. MALLETT[1332]

Figure 169 J.C. MALLETT's Headstone[1333]

J.C. served in World War II. He enlisted on 5 Dec 1942 at Camp Shelby, MS as a Private. His records indicate he had a grammar school education and had worked unskilled sawmill jobs. His service number was 4486176. He stood 70" high and weighed 159 pounds.[1334] At his death, he was buried in Wood National Cemetery, located at 5000 West National Ave. Bldg. 1301 in Milwaukee, WI 53295. He is buried in Plot Section 7 Site 3n.

[1327] Fannie B. Gamble, grave marker, Wright Cemetery, Kosciusko, Attala Co., MS, digital image s.v. "Fannie Mallett," (birth 5 Aug 1903, death 24 Jul 1998), *FindaGrave.com*.
[1328] Dock M. Mallett, grave marker, Wright Cemetery, Kosciusko, Attala Co., MS, digital image s.v. "Dock Mallett," (birth 4 Jan 1897, death 21 Aug 1980), *FindaGrave.com*.
[1329] J C Mallett, grave marker, Wood National Cemetery, Milwaukee, Milwaukee Co., MI, digital image s.v. "J C Mallett," (birth 28 Feb 1922, death 30 Oct 1981), *FindaGrave.com*.
[1330] "1940 United States Federal Census," Kosciusko, Attala Co., MS, digital image s.v. "Clara Zolicoffer," (birth abt 1926), *Ancestry.com*.
[1331] "Michigan, U.S., Marriage Records, 1867-1952," s.v. "J C Mallet," (marriage to Clara Zolicoffer on 9 Mar 1948), *Ancestry.com*.
[1332] Karl Boyd originally shared this on 11 Nov 2021 on *Ancestry.com*.
[1333] See J.C. Mallet's *FindaGrave entry above*.
[1334] "U.S., World War II Army Enlistment Records, 1938-1946," s.v. "J C Mallett," (enlistment date 5 Dec 1942), *Ancestry.com*.

In the 1950 U.S. Census, J.C. MALLET (28), Clara (23), and daughter, Georgia (less than one-year-old) lived as lodgers with the King family who lived in Detroit, Wayne Co., IL.[1335] J.C. worked as a laborer in a steel factory. Georgia was born in Michigan.

Rubell (Ruby) Bonita MALLETT (Fannie GAMBLE, Agnes Icy GUYTON GAMBLE, Pinkney, Aaron Whitaker, Aaron Steele, Joseph I, John I, Samuel II, Samuel I, John)

Rubell Bonita MALLETT was the daughter of Fannie B. GAMBLE (b. 5 Aug 1903 in MS, d. 24 Jul 1998 Kosciusko, Attala Co., MS[1336] and Dock M. MALLETT (b. 4 Jan 1897 in Kosciusko, Attala Co., MS, d. 21 Aug 1980 in Kosciusko, Attala Co., MS).[1337] Rubell was born on 20 Jul 1924 in Leake Co., MS, and died on 22 Jan 1998 in Waterloo, Black Hawk Co., IA.[1338] She married the Reverend George Louis CULPEPPER (b. 10 Jan 1927 Durant, Holmes Co., MS, d. 4 Aug 2000 Waterloo, Black Hawk Co., IA).[1339] See Figure 170 and Figure 171.

Figure 170 Rubell Bonita MALLETT CULPEPPER[1340]

Figure 171 George Louis CULPEPPER[1341]

In the 1950 U.S. Census, Rubell (25) and George (22) lived in Waterloo, Black Hawk Co., IA with three children: Earl CULPEPPER (4), Willy J. CULPEPPER (2), and Martin L. CULPEPPER (less than one-year-

---

[1335] "1950 United States Federal Census," Detroit, Wayne Co., MI, digital image s.v. "J C. Mallett," (birth abt 1922), *Ancestry.com*.
[1336] Fannie B. Gamble, grave marker, Wright Cemetery, Kosciusko, Attala Co., MS, digital image s.v. "Fannie Mallett," (birth 5 Aug 1903, death 24 Jul 1998), *FindaGrave.com*.
[1337] Dock M. Mallett, grave marker, Wright Cemetery, Kosciusko, Attala Co., MS, digital image s.v. "Dock Mallett," (birth 4 Jan 1897, death 21 Aug 1980), *FindaGrave.com*.
[1338] Rubell Bonita Mallett, grave marker, Fairview Cemetery, Waterloo, Black Hawk Co., IA, digital image s.v. "Rubell Bonita Culpepper," (birth 20 Jul 1924, death 22 Jan 1998), *FindaGrave.com*.
[1339] George Louis Culpepper, grave marker, Fairview Cemetery, Waterloo, Black Hawk Co., IA, digital image s.v. "Rev George Louis Culpepper," (birth 10 Jan 1927, death 4 Aug 2000), *FindaGrave.com*.
[1340] purlinerobinson originally shared this on 5 Oct 2019 on *Ancestry.com*.
[1341] purlinerobinson originally shared this on 5 Oct 2019 on Ancestry.com.

old). They lived on 134 Webster St. George worked as a hog sticker in the meat packing business.[1342] They lived next door to Ruby's brother, Fred MALLETT, and his family.

Ruby's obituary lists the couple's children. See Figure 172.

> WATERLOO — **Rubell Culpepper,** 74, of Waterloo, died Thursday, Jan. 22, at Allen Memorial Hospital of natural causes.
> She was born July 20, 1924, in Leake County, Miss., daughter of Dock and Fannie Mallett. She married the Rev. George L. Culpepper Sr. on March 2, 1945, in Attala County, Miss.
> Mrs. Culpepper taught school after graduation.
> **Survived by:** five sons, Edward L., Willie J., Martin L., and Jerry L., all of Waterloo, and George L. of Rockford, Ill.; six daughters, Ruby E. Culpepper of Denver, Colo., Darlene Culpepper of Freeport, Ill., Mary J. McCoy of Maxton, N.C., Linda M. Harris of Waterloo, Betsy L. Culpepper of Minneapolis and Annette Culpepper of Orange County, Calif.; 29 grandchildren; 15 great-grandchildren; her mother of Kosciusko, Miss.; four sisters, Katie Fagan of Waterloo, Fannie I. Black of Muskegon, Mich., Christine Mallett of Kosciusko, and Katherine Young of Milwaukee, Wis.; and four brothers, Fred Mallett of Waterloo, Jeremiah Mallett of Detroit and Lovie and Ollie Mallett, both of Kosciusko.
> **Preceded in death by:** five brothers, Jessie, A.L., James, J.C. and R.D. Mallett; and a grandson.
> **Services:** 1 p.m. Tuesday at Payne Memorial AME Church, 1044 Mobile St., with burial in Fairview Cemetery. Friends may call from 4 to 7 p.m. Monday at Greer Funeral Home, 710 Logan Ave.
> **Memorials:** may be directed to the family at 1119 Cottage Grove Ave.

Figure 172 Rubell Bonita (Ruby) MALLETT CULPEPPER's Obituary[1343]

i   Edward L. (Eddie) CULPEPPER (b. 3 Apr 1946 Sallis, Attala Co., MS, d. 19 Jan 2015 Waterloo, Black Hawk Co., IA)[1344] m. Barbara Ruth SAFFOLD (b. 4 Jun 1948, d. Unknown)[1345] on 11 Jul 1964 Fillmore Co., MN,[1346] div.).

ii   Willy J. CULPEPPER (b. ABT 1948 MS, d. Unknown) m. Alice UNKNOWN (Unknown).

iii   Martin L. CULPEPPER (b. ABT 1950 MS, d. Unknown) m. Terry UNKNOWN (Unknown).

[1342] "1950 United States Federal Census," Waterloo, Black Hawk Co., IA, digital image s.v. "Ruby Culpepper," (birth abt 1925), *Ancestry.com*.

[1343] "Rubel Bonita Mallett," *The Courier*, Waterloo, Black Hawk Co., IA, 25 Jan 1998, Sun, p. 17; digital image, s.v. "Rubel Culpepper," *Newspapers.com*, <https://www.newspapers.com/image/358268723/?article=b9d37f10-8e37-4e00-acd6-0e1edffbe7c3&focus=0,0.6746023,0.31753126,0.8544291&xid=3355>.

[1344] Edward L. (Eddie) Culpepper, grave marker, Fairview Cemetery, Waterloo, Black Hawk Co., IA, digital image s.v. "Edward L. Culpepper," (birth 3 Apr 1946, death 19 Jan 2015), *FindaGrave.com*.

[1345] "U.S., Public Records Index, 1950-1993, Volume 2," s.v. "Barbara R Culpepper-Schee," (birth 4 Jun 1948), *Ancestry.com*.

[1346] "Minnesota, U.S., Marriages from the Minnesota Official Marriage System, 1850-2022," s.v. "Barbara Ruth Saffold," (marriage 11 Jul 1964 to Edward Culpepper), *Ancestry.com*.

iv   Darlene CULPEPPER (b. 10 Dec 1952 Waterloo, Black Hawk Co., IA, d. 28 Aug 1999 Monroe, Adams Co., WI)[1347] m. Lynn D. MORGAN (Unknown) ABT 1973) and divorced, per her obituary. They had at least one child: Sarah Lynn MORGAN (Unknown). See Figure 173.

v   Mary Jean CULPEPPER (b. 22 Jul 1954 Waterloo, Black Hawk Co., IA, d. 18 Jul 1999 Burnsville, Iowa Co., IA, but lived and worked in Maxton, Robeson Co., NC at the time of her death)[1348] m. (1) Unknown DUNSON (Unknown) abt 1976 and (2) John McCOY (Unknown) on 28 Nov 1992 Marietta, Cobb Co., GA (per her obituary). They had one child: Amaris Vania McCOY (b. Sep 1993, NC). See Figure 174.

vi   Annette CULPEPPER (Unknown).

vii   Betsy L. CULPEPPER (Unknown) m. Rory LUCAS (Unknown).

viii   Linda M. CULPEPPER (Unknown) m. Laverne UNKNOWN (Unknown).

ix   Ruby (middle name perhaps Elaine) CULPEPPER (Unknown).

x   George Lewis CULPEPPER, Jr., (b. 3 Jan 1962 IA, d. Unknown).

xi   Jerry L. CULPEPPER (Unknown).

Figure 173 Daughter Darlene CULPEPPER MORGAN[1349]

Figure 174 Daughter Mary Jean CULPEPPER McCOY[1350]

[1347] Darlene Culpepper, grave marker, Fairview Cemetery, Waterloo, Black Hawk County, IA, digital image s.v. "Darlene Morgan," (birth 10 Dec 1952, death 28 Aug 1999), *FindaGrave.com*.

[1348] Mary Jean Culpepper, grave marker, Fairview Cemetery, Waterloo, Black Hawk County, IA, digital image s.v. "Mary Jean McCoy," (birth 22 Jul 1954, death 18 Jul 1999), *FindaGrave.com*.

[1349] "School Yearbooks, 1900-2016," digital image s.v. "Darlene Culpepper," (birth 1953, East High School, Waterloo, IA), *Ancestry.com*.

[1350] purlinerobinson originally shared this on 10 Jan 2021 on *Ancestry.com*.

Katie K. MALLETT (Fannie GAMBLE, Agnes Icy GUYTON GAMBLE, Pinkney, Aaron Whitaker, Aaron Steele, Joseph I, John I, Samuel II, Samuel I, John)

Katie K. MALLETT was the daughter of Fannie B. GAMBLE (b. 5 Aug 1903 MS, d. 24 Jul 1998 Kosciusko, Attala Co., MS)[1351] and Dock M. MALLETT (b. 4 Jan 1897 in Kosciusko, Attala Co., MS, d. 21 Aug 1980 Kosciusko, Attala Co., MS).[1352] Katie was born on 15 Jan 1925 in Kosciusko, Attala Co., MS, and died on 29 Aug 2009 in Waterloo, Black Hawk Co., IA.[1353] She married (1) Thomas JOHNSON (b. abt 1925 MS, d. Unknown),[1354] divorced before 1950[1355] and (2) William (Sleepy) FAGAN, Sr. (b. 19 Nov 1919 Adams Co., MS, d. 31 Jul 1989 Waterloo, Black Hawk Co., IA) on 13 Feb 1953 in Waterloo.[1356] See their obituaries in Figure 175 and Figure 176.

Katie and Thomas J. JOHNSON had at least three children:

i   Thomas J. JOHNSON, Jr. (b. ABT 1947 MS).[1357]
ii   Leroy JOHNSON (b. ABT 1948 MS).[1358]
iii Kate Emma JOHNSON (b. ABT 1949 MS)[1359] m. Richard V. CROSS (Unknown).[1360]

Katie and William (Sleepy) FAGAN, Sr. had at least four children, per her obituary:

i   Leonard FAGAN (Unknown).
ii   Mary Gordon FAGAN (Unknown).
iii William FAGAN, Jr. (Unknown).
iv   Patricia FAGAN (Unknown).

[1351] Fannie B. Gamble, grave marker, Wright Cemetery, Kosciusko, Attala Co., MS, digital image s.v. "Fannie Mallett," (birth 5 Aug 1903, death 24 Jul 1998), *FindaGrave.com*.

[1352] Dock M. Mallett, grave marker, Wright Cemetery, Kosciusko, Attala Co., MS, digital image s.v. "Dock Mallett," (birth 4 Jan 1897, death 21 Aug 1980), *FindaGrave.com*.

[1353] "U.S., Social Security Death Index, 1935-2014," s.v. "Katie Fagan," (birth 15 Jan 1925, death 29 Aug 2009), *Ancestry.com*.

[1354] "U.S., Obituary Collection, 1930-Current," s.v. "Thomas Johnson," (married to Katie FAGAN), *Ancestry.com*.

[1355] "1950 United States Federal Census," Leake Co., MS, digital image s.v. "Kattie Mallitt," (birth abt 1926), *Ancestry.com*.

[1356] William Fagan, grave marker, Garden of Memories, Waterloo, Black Hawk County, IA, digital image s.v. "William Fagan," (birth 19 Nov 1919, death 31 Jul 1989), *FindaGrave.com*. The marriage date to Katie is given in his obituary.

[1357] "1950 United States Federal Census," Leake Co., MS, digital image s.v. "Thomas J Mallitt," (birth abt 1947), *Ancestry.com*.

[1358] "1950 United States Federal Census," Leake Co., MS, digital image s.v. "Roy Mallitt," (birth abt 1948), *Ancestry.com*.

[1359] "1950 United States Federal Census," Leake Co., MS, digital image s.v. "Kate Emma Mallitt," (birth abt 1949), *Ancestry.com*.

[1360] "Newspapers.com Marriage Index, 1800s-1999," s.v. "Katie Emma Johnson," (marriage abt 1969 to Richard V. Cross), *Ancestry.com*.

Katie Fagan (1925-2009)

WATERLOO — Katie Fagan, 84, of Waterloo, died Saturday, Aug. 29, at Windsor Care Center, Cedar Falls, of congestive heart failure.

She was born Jan. 15, 1925, in Kosciusko, Miss., daughter of Fannie Gamble Mallett and Dock Mallett. She married Thomas Johnson in 1945, in Kosciusko, and they later divorced. She married William Fagan on Feb. 13, 1953, in Waterloo. He preceded her in death July 31, 1989.

Survived by: three daughters, Katie Emma Cross of Freeport, Ill., Mary Gordon Fagan of Mesa, Ariz., and Patricia (Bob) Jackson of Altamonte Springs, Fla.; four sons, Thomas Johnson Jr. of Kosciusko, Leroy (Ida Mae) Johnson of Freeport, and William (Maralyn) Fagan and Leonard (Betty) Fagan, both of St. Louis; 21 grandchildren; 41 great-grandchildren; three sisters, Catherine Young of Milwaukee, Fannie Black of Muskegon, Mich., and Christine Mallet of Kosciusko; and three brothers, Jeremiah Mallett of Detroit, and Lovie Mallet and Ollie Mallet, both of Kosciusko.

Preceded in death by: six brothers, Jessee, Al, James, JC, RD and Fred Mallett; and a sister, Rubell Culpepper.

Services: 2 p.m. Thursday at New Hope Missionary Baptist Church, with burial in Garden of Memories Cemetery. Public visitation from 6 to 8 p.m. today at Sanders Funeral Service and for an hour before services Thursday at the church.

Memorials: may be directed to the family at 1146 Ackermant St., where they will receive friends.

Figure 175 Katie K. MALLETT FAGAN's Obituary[1361]

William 'Sleepy' Fagan

Services for William "Sleepy" Fagan Sr., 69, of 406 Almond St., will be 1 p.m. Friday at Antioch Baptist Church, with graveside services at Garden of Memories Cemetery.

Full military rites will be conducted by American Legion Post No. 138 and VFW Post No. 1623.

He died Monday (July 31) at Covenant Medical Center at Kimball Avenue of cancer.

He was born Nov. 19, 1919, in Adams County, Miss., son of Allen and Mary Galmore Fagan. He married Katie Mallett Feb. 13, 1953 in Waterloo.

He retired from Chamberlain Manufacturing Corp. May 1, 1985 after 38 years of service. He served in the U.S. Army during World War II.

Survivors include his wife; two daughters, Mary L. Fagan of Waterloo and Mrs. Patricia Jackson of Memphis, Tenn.; a stepdaughter, Mrs. Katie E. Cross of Freeport, Ill.; two sons, William H. Fagan Jr. of Waterloo and Leonard A. Fagan of St. Louis; two stepsons, Leroy Johnson and Thomas Johnson, both of Freeport; a sister, Cressie Washington of Natchez, Miss.; three brothers, West Haynerd of Mallard, La., Charles Turner and Jeff Turner Jr., both of Natchez; four grandchildren; nine step-grandchildren and two step-great-grandchildren.

Friends may call at Sanders Funeral Chapel until 9 p.m. today and on Friday from 9 a.m. until 11 a.m. and one hour before service time at the church. Memorials may be directed to the family at 406 Almond St., where they are receiving friends.

Figure 176 William FAGAN's Obituary[1362]

[1361] "Obituary of Katie Fagan (1925-2009)," *The Courier*, Waterloo, Black Hawk Co., IA, 2 Sep 2009, Wed, p. 15, digital image, s.v. "Katie Fagan," *Newspapers.com*, <https://www.newspapers.com/article/the-courier-obituary-for-katie-fagan-ag/107109319/>.

[1362] "Obituary of William Sleepy Fagan," *The Courier*, Waterloo, Black Hawk Co., IA, 3 Aug 1989, Thu, p. 6, digital image, s.v. "William Sleepy Fagan)," *Newspapers.com*, <https://www.newspapers.com/image/359283741/?article=58a1d839-8f01-4dab-8ea2-5bad1cc611a0&xid=5499&terms=William__Sleepy__Fagan_Sr.>.

Fred MALLETT (Fannie GAMBLE, Agnes Icy GUYTON GAMBLE, Pinkney, Aaron Whitaker, Aaron Steele, Joseph I, John I, Samuel II, Samuel I, John)

Fred MALLETT was the son of Fannie B. GAMBLE (b. 5 Aug 1903 MS, d. 24 Jul 1998 Kosciusko, Attala Co., MS)[1363] and Dock M. MALLETT (b. 4 Jan 1897 in Kosciusko, Attala Co., MS, d. 21 Aug 1980 in Kosciusko, Attala Co., MS.[1364] Fred was born on 6 Oct 1927 in Kosciusko, Attala Co., MS, and died on 6 Mar 1999 Waterloo, Black Hawk Co., IA.[1365] He married Vergie Lee NASH (b. 10 Apr 1931 Kosciusko, Attala Co., MS, d. 6 Jul 1998 Waterloo, Black Hawk Co., IA).[1366] See their obituaries in Figure 177 and Figure 178.

Figure 177 Obituary of Fred MALLETT[1367]

Figure 178 Obituary of Vergie Lee NASH MALLETT[1368]

Google Earth shows their home at 321 Rickers St. in Waterloo. See Figure 179.

[1363] Fannie B. Gamble, grave marker, Wright Cemetery, Kosciusko, Attala Co., MS, digital image s.v. "Fannie Mallett," (birth 5 Aug 1903, death 24 Jul 1998), *FindaGrave.com*.
[1364] Dock M. Mallett, grave marker, Wright Cemetery, Kosciusko, Attala Co., MS, digital image s.v. "Dock Mallett," (birth 4 Jan 1897, death 21 Aug 1980), *FindaGrave.com*.
[1365] "Fred Mallett, grave marker, Garden of Memories, Waterloo, Black Hawk Co., IA, digital image s.v. "Fred Mallett," (birth 6 Oct 1927, death 6 Mar 1999), *FindaGrave.com*.
[1366] "Vergie Lee Nash, grave marker, Garden of Memories, Waterloo, Black Hawk Co., IA, digital image s.v. "Fred Mallett," (birth 10 Apr 1931, death 6 Jul 1998), *FindaGrave.com*.
[1367] "Obituary of Fred Mallett," *The Courier*, Waterloo, Black Hawk Co., IA, 10 Mar 1999, Wed, p. 10, digital image, s.v. "Fred Mallett)," *Newspapers.com*, <https://www.newspapers.com/article/the-courier-obituary-for-fred-mallett/148192376/>.
[1368] "Obituary of Vergie Lee Mallett," *The Courier*, Waterloo, Black Hawk Co., IA, 8 Jul 1998, Wed, p. 18, digital image, s.v. "Vergie Lee Mallett)," *Newspapers.com*, <https://www.newspapers.com/article/the-courier-obituary-for-vergie-lee-mall/148193545/>.

Figure 179 Fred and Vergie NASH MALLETT Home in Waterloo, IA

Fred and Vergie had at least six children, per their obituaries:

i   Dorothy J. MALLETT (b. Mar 1949, d. Unknown)[1369] m. Unknown ANTHONY (Unknown).
ii   Gloria MALLETT (b. perhaps around 1950, d. Unknown) m. Unknown RILEY (Unknown).
iii   Judy A. MALLETT (b. 18 Jul 1952 Waterloo, Black Hawk Co., IA, d. 14 Sep 2008 Waterloo, Black Hawk Co., IA)[1370] m. (1) Lincoln LEFLORE (and divorced) and (2) Willie N. WISE, Jr. (and divorced).
iv   Vergie MALLETT (b. ABT 1954 (guess), d. Unknown) m. Unknown HECHAVARRIA (Unknown).
v   Frederick J. MALLETT Jr. (b. 17 Feb 1956 Waterloo, Black Hawk Co., IA, d. Unknown).[1371]
vi   Wendell MALLETT (b. 14 Jul 1959 Waterloo, Black Hawk Co., IA, d. Unknown).[1372]

[1369] "1950 United States Federal Census," Waterloo, Black Hawk Co., IA, digital image s.v. "Dorothy J. Mallett," (birth abt 1949), Ancestry.com. "U.S., Index to Public Records, 1994-2019," s.v. "Dorothy J. Anthony," (birth Mar 1949), Ancestry.com.

[1370] "Obituary of Judy A. Wise," *The Courier*, Waterloo, Black Hawk Co., IA, 17 Sep 2008, Wed, p. 6, digital image, s.v. "Judy A. Wise)," *Newspapers.com*, <https://www.newspapers.com/article/the-courier-obituary-for-l-judy-a-wise/148999587/>.

[1371] "U.S. Public Records Index, 1950-1993, Volume 2," s.v. "Frederick J. Mallett," (birth 17 Feb 1956), *Ancestry.com*.

[1372] "U.S. Public Records Index, 1950-1993, Volume 2," s.v. "Wendell Mallett," (birth 14 Jul 1959), *Ancestry.com*.

Alphonzo L. (A.L.) MALLETT (Fannie GAMBLE, Agnes Icy GUYTON GAMBLE, Pinkney, Aaron Whitaker, Aaron Steele, Joseph I, John I, Samuel II, Samuel I, John)

Alphonzo L. MALLETT was the son of Fannie B. GAMBLE (b. 5 Aug 1903 MS, d. 24 Jul 1998 Kosciusko, Attala Co., MS)[1373] and Dock M. MALLETT (b. 4 Jan 1897 in Kosciusko, Attala Co., MS, d. 21 Aug 1980 in Kosciusko, Attala Co., MS).[1374] Alphonzo was born on 9 Jan 1931 in Thomastown, Leake Co., MS, and died on 7 May 1989 in Kosciusko, Attala Co., MS.[1375] He married Bobbie G. EVANS. They had two daughters: Shirley MALLETT COFFEE and Brenda MALLETT RILEY, per his obituary on his *FindaGrave* site.

He served as a Corporal in the U.S. Army in Korea. He is buried in Wright Cemetery next to his wife. See Figure 180 and Figure 181.

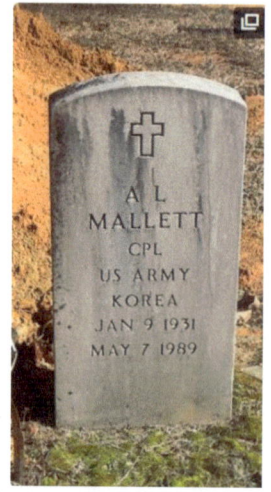

Figure 180 A.L. MALLET's Headstone in Wright Cemetery[1376]

Figure 181 Bobbie EVANS MALLET's Headstone at Wright Cemetery[1377]

The couple had two daughters, per their parents' obituaries:

i Shirley MALLETT m. Unknown COFFEE (Unknown).
ii Brenda MALLETT m. Unknown RILEY (Unknown).

[1373] Fannie B. Gamble, grave marker, Wright Cemetery, Kosciusko, Attala Co., MS, digital image s.v. "Fannie Mallett," (birth 5 Aug 1903, death 24 Jul 1998), *FindaGrave.com*.
[1374] Dock M. Mallett, grave marker, Wright Cemetery, Kosciusko, Attala Co., MS, digital image s.v. "Dock Mallett," (birth 4 Jan 1897, death 21 Aug 1980), *FindaGrave.com*.
[1375] "Alphonzo L. Mallett, grave marker, Wright Cemetery, Kosciusko, Attala Co., MS, digital image s.v. "Alphonzo Mallett," (birth 9 Jan 1931, death 7 May 1989), *FindaGrave.com*.
[1376] Photo by Chris Hunt on A.L.'s *FindaGrave* site.
[1377] Photo by Beth Austin on Bobbie's *FindaGrave* site.

Henry (L.C.) SIMMONS (Callie Pairee GAMBLE, Agnes Icy GUYTON GAMBLE, Pinkney, Aaron Whitaker, Aaron Steele, Joseph I, John I, Samuel II, Samuel I, John)

Henry (L.C.) SIMMONS was the son of Callie Pairee GAMBLE (b. 9 Jan 1905 in Attala Co., MS, d. 19 Jun 1995 Maywood, Cook Co., IL)[1378] and Henry Porterwood SIMMONS (b. 11 Feb 1904 Attala Co., MS, d. Oct 1977 Kosciusko, Attala Co., MS).[1379] L.C. was born on 15 Aug 1923 in Attala Co., MS, and died on 13 Jun 2009 Sallis, Attala Co., MS.[1380] He married (1) Lue Bertha WINDOMS (b. 22 May 1937, d. Unknown)[1381] and perhaps (2) Unknown. See Figure 182 and Figure 183. Rita McLean was very helpful with L.C.'s line.

Figure 182 Henry (L.C.) SIMMONS[1382]

Figure 183 Lue Bertha WINDOMS[1383]

L.C. and Lue had the following children together, per a personal conversation with Rickey SIMMONS, their oldest son.[1384]

[1378] Callie Pairee Gamble, grave marker, Nash Cemetery, Leake Co., MS, digital image s.v. "Callie Pairee Simmons," (birth 9 Jan 1905, death 19 Jun 1995), *FindaGrave.com*.
[1379] "U.S., Social Security Death Index, 1935-2014," s.v. "Henry Simmons," (birth 11 Feb 1904, death Oct 1977), *Ancestry.com*.
[1380] "U.S., Social Security Death Index, 1935-2014," s.v. "Henry L. Simmons," (birth 5 Aug 1922, death 13 Jun 2009), *Ancestry.com*.
[1381] Personal conversation with their grandson, Ricky Simmons (b. abt 1958).
[1382] Karl Boyd originally shared this on 26 Nov 2021 on Ancestry.com.
[1383] Karl Boyd originally shared this on 26 Nov 2021 on Ancestry.com.
[1384] Personal conversation with Rickey Simmons.

i   Rickey SIMMONS (b. 4 Aug 1958 Attala Co., MS, d. Living) (see Figure 184) m. (1) partner Carrie ROCKETT (Unknown), (2) partner UNKNOWN, (3) partner UNKNOWN.
ii Vertrishe SIMMONS (b. 29 Dec 1960 Kosciusko, Attala Co., MS, d. Living) (see Figure 185). She has two children: Shaneka Latrisha SIMMONS PATTERSON and Jeremy Juawon WILLIAMS. Shaneka is a family nurse practitioner in Jackson, Hinds Co., MS. See Figure 186.
iii Wakeco SIMMONS (b. 23 Oct 1963 Kosciusko, Attala Co., MS, d. Living) (see Figure 187) m. partner UNKNOWN. Wakeco has a son, Rodney MOORE.
iv Jeannie Mae SIMMONS (b. 1 Feb 1964 Attala Co., MS, d. Living) (see Figure 188 m. Unknown STRAUSS. She has two children: Tiffany Simmons STRAUSS and Travis SIMMONS.
v   Diana SIMMONS (Living) (see Figure 189) m. Unknown COTTON. She has a son, Justin Simmons COTTON.
vi Jeanette SIMMONS (Living) (see Figure 190) m. Unknown McKELLAR. She has two children: Decekka Diante LITTLE and Marcus Simmons McKELLAR.
vii Tracey SIMMONS (Living) (see Figure 191) had multiple partners. His children are Courtney Malone REDMOND, Dremetris HOOKER, Trayvon SIMMONS, Tracey Lebron SIMMONS, and Tracvon SIMMONS.
viii Larry Lamar SIMMONS (Living) (see Figure 192) m. Unknown. He has two daughters: Felicia SIMMONS and Ishida SIMMONS.

L.C. and UNKNOWN had three children:

i   Joyce SIMMONS (Living).
ii Bobo SIMMONS (Living).
iii Katie SIMMONS (Living).

Photos are courtesy of Rickey SIMMONS.

Figure 184 Rickey SIMMONS

Figure 185 Vertrishe SIMMONS WILLIAMS

Figure 186 Shaneka Latrisha SIMMONS PATTERSON

Figure 187 Wakeco SIMMONS

Figure 188 Jeannie Mae SIMMONS STRAUSS

Figure 189 Diana SIMMONS COTTON

Figure 190 Jeanette SIMMONS McKELLAR

Figure 191 Tracy SIMMONS

Figure 192 Larry Lamar SIMMONS

Zenolia SIMMONS (Callie Pairee GAMBLE, Agnes Icy GUYTON GAMBLE, Pinkney, Aaron Whitaker, Aaron Steele, Joseph I, John I, Samuel II, Samuel I, John)

Zenolia SIMMONS was the daughter of Callie Pairee GAMBLE (b. 9 Jan 1905 in Attala Co., MS, d. 19 Jun 1995 Maywood, Cook Co., IL)[1385] and Henry Porterwood SIMMONS (b. 11 Feb 1904 Attala Co. MS, d. Oct 1977 Kosciusko, Attala Co., MS).[1386] Zenolia SIMMONS was born on 9 Dec 1926 in Kosciusko, Attala Co., MS, and died on 19 Jan 2018 Eau Claire, Berrien Co., MI.[1387] She married Ellon MURPHY (b. 20 Oct 1922 Kosciusko, Attala Co., MS, d. 20 Jul 1993 Berrien, Berrien Co., MI).[1388] See Figure 193 and Figure 194.

Figure 193 Zenolia SIMMONS MURPHY[1389]

Figure 194 Ellon MURPHY[1390]

The couple had fourteen children, per Ellon MURPHY's obituary. See Figure 195.

i   Darlene MURPHY (b. 19 Jul 1945 New York, NY, d. 28 Dec 2010 Benton Harbor, Berrien Co., MI)[1391] m. (1) James Edward DELANEY, Sr. and (2) Matthew Ashley SHARPE, Sr. (Unknown).[1392]
ii Melvin MURPHY, Jr. (b. 9 Apr 1947 IL, d. Unknown).[1393]
iii Linda Carol MURPHY (b. ABT 1948 IL, d. Living)[1394] m. (1) Curtis PINDER and (2) Neal YOUNG.
iv Zenobia MURPHY (b. 25 May 1949 IL, d. Unknown)[1395] m. Harry BROWN (deceased).

[1385] Callie Pairee Gamble, grave marker, Nash Cemetery, Leake Co., MS, digital image s.v. "Callie Pairee Simmons," (birth 9 Jan 1905, death 19 Jun 1995), *FindaGrave.com*.
[1386] "U.S., Social Security Death Index, 1935-2014," s.v. "Henry Simmons," (birth 11 Feb 1904, death Oct 1977), *Ancestry.com*.
[1387] "U.S., Cemetery and Funeral Home Collection, 1847-Current," digital image s.v. "Zenolia Murphy Murphy," (birth 9 Dec 1926, death 19 Jan 2018), *Ancestry.com*.
[1388] "U.S., Social Security Applications and Claims Index, 1936-2007," s.v. "Ellon Murphy," (birth 20 Oct 1922, death 20 Jul 1993," *Ancestry.com*.
[1389] Ahmad Murphy originally shared this on 4 Dec 2022 on *Ancestry.com*.
[1390] Arlington Jones originally shared this on 4 Sep 2018 on *Ancestry.com*.
[1391] "U.S., Social Security Death Index, 1935-2014," s.v. "Darlene Sharpe," (birth 19 Jul 1945, death 28 Dec 2010), *Ancestry.com*.
[1392] Darlene Murphy had two sons who were juniors. I assumed the fathers carried the same names as seniors.
[1393] "U.S., Public Records Index, 1950-1993, Volume 2," s.v. "Melvin Murphy," (birth 9 Apr 1947), *Ancestry.com*.
[1394] "1950 United States Federal Census," Chicago, Cook Co., IL, digital image s.v. "Caroline Murphy," (birth abt 1948), *Ancestry.com*.
[1395] "U.S. Public Records Index, 1950-1993, Volume 1," s.v. "Zenbioa Brown," (birth 25 May 1949), *Ancestry.com*.

v	Murriel Delores MURPHY (b. 1 Oct 1952, d. Unknown).[1396] 2 kids, unmarried.	
vi	Patricia MURPHY (b. 1961, d. Unknown) m. Kenneth HARPER.	
vii	Tony MURPHY, Sr. (Unknown).	
viii	Sheila MURPHY (b. AFT 1950, d. Unknown) m. Unknown BROWN.	
ix	Rita MURPHY (b. AFT 1950, d. Unknown) m. L.C. McLEAN.	
x	Felicia MURPHY (b. AFT 1950, d. Unknown) m. Unknown DAVIS.	
xi	Larry MURPHY (b. AFT 1950, d. Unknown).	
xii	Vincent MURPHY (b. AFT 1950, d. Unknown).	
xiii	Curtis MURPHY (b. AFT 1950, d. Unknown). Lives in Ghana, Africa.	
xiv	Marvin MURPHY (b. AFT 1950, d. Unknown).	

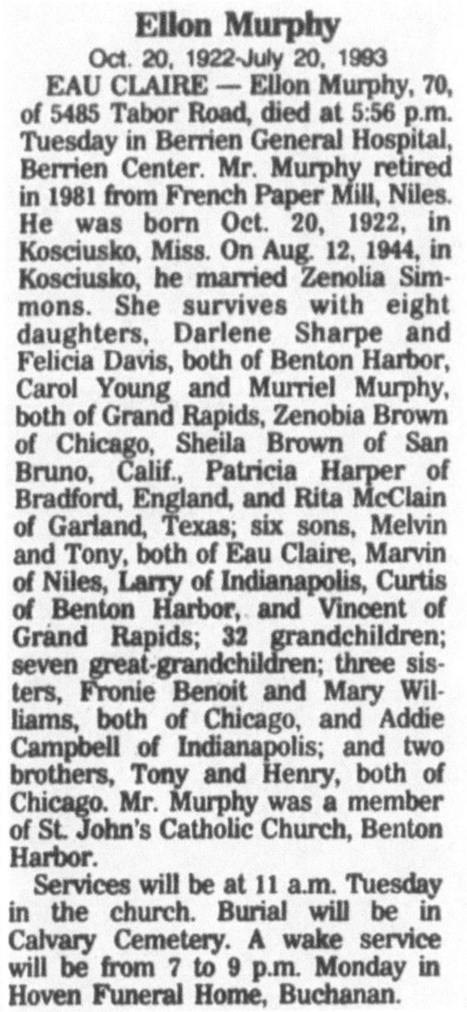

Ellon Murphy
Oct. 20, 1922-July 20, 1993

EAU CLAIRE — Ellon Murphy, 70, of 5485 Tabor Road, died at 5:56 p.m. Tuesday in Berrien General Hospital, Berrien Center. Mr. Murphy retired in 1981 from French Paper Mill, Niles. He was born Oct. 20, 1922, in Kosciusko, Miss. On Aug. 12, 1944, in Kosciusko, he married Zenolia Simmons. She survives with eight daughters, Darlene Sharpe and Felicia Davis, both of Benton Harbor, Carol Young and Murriel Murphy, both of Grand Rapids, Zenobia Brown of Chicago, Sheila Brown of San Bruno, Calif., Patricia Harper of Bradford, England, and Rita McClain of Garland, Texas; six sons, Melvin and Tony, both of Eau Claire, Marvin of Niles, Larry of Indianapolis, Curtis of Benton Harbor, and Vincent of Grand Rapids; 32 grandchildren; seven great-grandchildren; three sisters, Fronie Benoit and Mary Williams, both of Chicago, and Addie Campbell of Indianapolis; and two brothers, Tony and Henry, both of Chicago. Mr. Murphy was a member of St. John's Catholic Church, Benton Harbor.

Services will be at 11 a.m. Tuesday in the church. Burial will be in Calvary Cemetery. A wake service will be from 7 to 9 p.m. Monday in Hoven Funeral Home, Buchanan.

Figure 195 Ellon MURPHY's Obituary[1397]

[1396] "U.S., Public Records Index, 1950-1993, Volume 2," s.v. "Muriel Murphy," (birth 1 Oct 1952), *Ancestry.com*.
[1397] "Obituary of Ellon Murphy," *The South Bend Tribune*, South Bend, St. Joseph Co., IN, 22 Jul 1993, Thu, p. 20, digital image, s.v. "Ellon Murphy)," *Newspapers.com*, <https://www.newspapers.com/article/the-south-bend-tribune-obituary-for-ello/148214593/>.

Vernestine (Susie) JOINER (Katie GAMBLE, Agnes Icy GUYTON GAMBLE, Pinkney, Aaron Whitaker, Aaron Steele, Joseph I, John I, Samuel II, Samuel I, John)

Vernestine (Susie) JOINER was the daughter of Katie (KD) GAMBLE (b. 17 Sep 1912 Kosciusko Beat 1, Attala Co., MS, d. 19 Jun 2007 Sallis, Attala Co., MS)[1398] and Claude (Pretty Boy) JOINER, Sr. (b. 3 Aug 1911 Attala Co., MS, d. 1 Sep 1986 Jackson, Hinds Co., MS).[1399] Vernestine was born on 27 Aug 1936 in Attala Co., MS, and died on 5 Oct 2018 in Jackson, Hinds Co., MS).[1400] She married Luther D. (Rabbit) WINGARD (b. 24 Apr 1936 Kosciusko, Attala Co., MS, d. 1 Mar 2022 Kosciusko, Attala Co., MS).[1401]

Vernestine and Luther had at least eight children per the obituaries posted on each of their *FindaGrave sites*:

i	Tracy WINGARD (b. Unknown).
ii	Tremesha WINGARD (b. Unknown).
iii	Debra WINGARD (b. Unknown).
iv	Theresa WINGARD (b. Unknown) m. Glenn James CARTER (Unknown).
v	Stacy WINGARD (b. Unknown).
vi	Timothy WINGARD (b. Unknown).
vii	Tony WINGARD (b. Unknown).
viii	Sonji F. (Lisa) WINGARD (b. ABT 1968, d. 27 Nov 1994) m. Unknown HALL. Lisa had one child: Jalisa HALL.[1402]

[1398] "Katie D. (KD) Gamble, grave marker, Bullock Cemetery, Attala Co., MS, digital image s.v. "Katie D Joiner," (birth 7 Sep 1912, death 19 Jun 2007), *FindaGrave.com*.

[1399] "Claude Joiner," grave marker, Bullock Cemetery, Attala Co., MS, digital image s.v. "Claude Joiner," (birth 8 Aug 1909, death 1 Sep 1986), *FindaGrave.com*.

[1400] "Vernestine 'Susie' Joiner," grave marker, Jenkins Cemetery, Attala Co., MS, digital image s.v. "Vernestine Wingard," (birth 27 Aug 1936, death 5 Oct 2018), *FindaGrave.com*.

[1401] "Luther D. 'Rabbit' Wingard," grave marker, Jenkins Cemetery, Attala Co., MS, digital image s.v. "Luther D Wingard," (birth 24 Apr 1936, death 1 Mar 2022), *FindaGrave.com*.

[1402] "Obituary of Mrs. Sonji W. Hall," *The Star-Herald*, Kosciusko, Attala Co., MS, 8 Dec 1994, Thu, p. 6, digital image, s.v. "Mrs. Sonji W. Hall," *Newspapers.com*, <https://www.newspapers.com/article/the-star-herald-obituary-for-sonji-w-ha/149038806/>.

Icy Viola NASH (Lovie GAMBLE NASH PARKER, Agnes Icy GUYTON GAMBLE, Pinkney, Aaron Whitaker, Aaron Steele, Joseph I, John I, Samuel II, Samuel I, John)

Icy Viola NASH was the daughter of Lovie GAMBLE (b. 29 Aug 1915 Kosciusko, Attala Co., MS, d. 16 Oct 2002 Chicago, Cook Co., IL)[1403] and (1) Woodrow Wilson NASH (b. 28 Aug 1916 in Leake Co., MS, d. 11 Dec 1999 in Chicago, Cook Co., IL)[1404] and divorced. Icy was born on 16 Oct 1935 in Kosciusko, Attala Co., MS, and died on 14 Oct 2009 in Naperville, DuPage Co., IL.[1405] She married Thornton BOYD, Sr. (b. 5 Oct 1935, d. 1 Feb 2008) on 4 Mar 1960 in Cook Co., IL.[1406] See Figure 196 and Figure 197.

Figure 196 Icy Viola NASH BOYD[1407]

Figure 197 Thornton BOYD, Sr.[1408]

Icy and Thornton had five children per information from their first son, Karl Glenn BOYD (aka Nykki Lamarr STARR):

[1403] "U.S., Social Security Death Index, 1935-2014," s.v. "Lovie Parker," (birth 29 Aug 1915, death 16 Oct 2002), *Ancestry.com*.

[1404] "Woodrow Wilson Nash," grave marker, Mount Hope Cemetery, Chicago, Cook Co., IL, digital image s.v. "Claude Joiner," (birth 28 Apr 1916, death 11 Dec 1999), *FindaGrave.com*. No two documents have the same birth date, but the dates are close together.

[1405] "Icy Viola Nash," grave marker, Forest Home Cemetery, Forest Park, Cook Co., IL, digital image s.v. "Icy V Boyd," (birth 16 Oct 1935, death 14 Oct 2009), *FindaGrave.com*.

[1406] "U.S., Social Security Death Index, 1935-2014," s.v. "Thornton Boyd," (birth 5 Oct 1935, death 1 Feb 2008), *Ancestry.com*. "Cook County, Illinois Marriage Index, 1930-1960," s.v. "Icy Nash," (marriage to Thorton Boyd on 4 Mar 1960).

[1407] Karl Boyd originally shared this on 25 Mar 2021 on *Ancestry.com*.

[1408] Karl Boyd originally shared this on 25 Mar 2021 on *Ancestry.com*.

i   Karl Glenn BOYD aka Nykki Lamarr STARR (b. 18 May 1959 Chicago, Cook Co., IL, d. Living) m. (1) Cherry HILL (b. ABT 1958 Chicago, Cook Co., IL, d. Living) div., (2) Rosalind Lavon NORVELL (b. 6 Jan 1965 Temple, Bell Co., TX, d. Living) div., (3) partner Cynthia WILEY (b. Augusta, Richmond Co., GA, d. Living), (4) friend Dora Luzetta YOUNG (b. 17 Dec 1968 Philadelphia, Neshoba Co., MS, d. 11 Jun 2019 Philadelphia, Neshoba Co., MS, and (5) spouse Princess Monica WRIGHT (b. ABT 1959 Salisbury, MD, d. Living).

ii   Felicia Cabrini BOYD (b. 22 Aug 1960 Chicago, Cook Co., IL, d. Living).

iii   Carmelita Sabrina BOYD (b. 16 Oct 1935 Chicago, Cook Co., IL, d. Living) m. (1) Craig OUSLEY (Unknown), (2) Kevin (Kippie) CAMPBELL (Unknown), (3) LeCurtis JOHNSON (Unknown).

iv   Rhonda Larita BOYD (b. 28 Aug 1963 Chicago, Cook Co., IL, d. Living) m. (1) Richard BALL (b. ABT 1965 Chicago, Cook Co., IL, d. Living), (2) Jeffrey Wayne BUCHANAN (b. ABT 1953 Chicago, Cook Co., IL, d. Living), (3) Ronald SHAW (b. ABT 1962, d. Living), (4) Michael TURNER (b. ABT 1960 Chicago, Cook Co., IL, d. Living).

v   Thornton BOYD, Jr. aka Rikki STARR (b. ABT 1968 Chicago, Cook Co., IL, d. Living) m. (1) spouse Tabatha PETERSON (b. 18 Feb 1967 Chicago, Cook Co., IL, d. 21 Mar 2017 Allen, Collin Co., TX), (2) friend Oneko WHITE (b. ABT Mar 1971, d. Living), (3) spouse Cherylease M. PRATT (b. 20 Jul 1973, d. Living), (4) spouse Marcy L. RHONE (b. ABT 1973, d. Living), (5) spouse LaTonya Cheri SANDERS (b. 11 Feb 1972, d. Living), (6) spouse Tonya GREENE (Living), (7) partner Sarah CHOI (Living), (8) spouse Tracy GLOVER (Living), and (9) spouse Khankham (Candy) PHOMMAVONG (Living). He was adopted by his older brother, Karl Glenn BOYD (aka Nykki Lamarr STARR).

Icy's daughter, Carmelita Sabrina BOYD, contributed the following about her mother:

What can be said about my mama? If you knew her, you loved her… and if she loved you, you were truly LOVED! There are a lot of stories I can tell about my first Super Hero, and to me, the greatest inspiration I've ever had, but there are five us whom she loved and treasured, and there's not enough pages to speak on what she meant to us, and I know we all will want to share our stories. As I said, there are many stories, like the time she was in the kitchen cooking, and I was in the backyard shooting marbles and she heard me cursing. I still don't know how she heard me, but she called me into the house, that was the longest walk I ever had, cause I knew she was waiting for me on the back porch, but she didn't whip me (which scared me even more). She gave me a bar of soap and told me to take it to the bathroom, once there she told me to look in the mirror and start eating the soap to wash my mouth out. You have to understand me and Mama's relationship, the only person that I know is more stubborn than my mom, is me. The bar wasn't big, so I took big bites and swallowed… that made Mama mad, because she didn't like my attitude. So she went to the kitchen and got her biggest onion and gave it to me, and had Felecia [Carmelita's sister] bring her a chair from the kitchen. She sat there and watched me eat that whole onion. Till this day, I still can't stand the taste or smell of ONIONS. But I won't share that story, instead I'll share the one that capsulizes the very essence of my mother's love.

Her son, Karl Glenn BOYD (aka Nykki Lamarr STARR), contributed the following about his mother, Icy Viola NASH:

We always had what we needed, but there were times when we did "want" things that just weren't in the budget. This was a hard pill to swallow when you are 11 or 12 years old, and you go outside and all of the other kids had toys and candy, and you and your little sisters didn't have anything. Even harder when your dad comes home and puts a couple of wads of money on the dresser every night. This was a story I'd planned to take to the grave, however, at a recent 70's party that my crazy Baby sis, Rhonda, had at her place, I found out that they still remembered it, though they didn't know the intimate details. You see, sometimes Mama would wait until Daddy went to sleep to ease ten or twenty dollars from Daddy's wad of money. She'd give it to me and then send me to Jimmy's to get liverwurst, and crackers or any number of things she needed to run the house. It was a sunny day and kids were out playing, running through the opened fire hydrants, playing "It," that would eventually turn into "catch a girl, kiss a girl." In the distance, we heard the sound of the ice cream truck, as usual all of the kids lost their minds, running home to get money, or lining up to wait for the truck, we took our normal spot on the stairs in front of the house to watch the other kids enjoy their ice cream. However, this time I went into the house and crept into Mom and Dad's room and peeled off a twenty-dollar bill from Daddy's wad of money. I went back out and treated my sisters to ice cream, then I went to Jimmy's and bought Footsie's, Jacks, a bag full of penny candy, and whatever else we always wanted. It was literally Christmas in July. It was a good day... until it was time to go to bed. From the back room, we heard Mom and Dad fighting. That wasn't nothing new. Once we were sent to the room, we'd hear either an argument, some Sam Cook, or some Wes Montgomery. This night it was a bad fight. As I listened at the door, I heard Daddy accuse Mama of taking some of his money off the dresser. I was terrified! I was baffled at how he could possibly know? The more Mama denied it, the more upset Daddy got! Once I got older, I figured out why Dad was so sure. He always had two Rolls of money, one was $500 cash in twenties and fifties, this was his "Show" Roll. The other roll was the money he'd play with... I made the mistake of taking money from his "Show" Roll. I came out of the room and headed to the front room to tell Daddy that I'd taken the money. His back was to me, but Mama was looking me in my eyes. She could see that I was terrified, and I think she knew that it was me, I did it. She pushed by Daddy, and told me to be quiet. She sent me back to the room, before I could confess. She took my dad's abuse, and never said anything to me. She didn't chastise or ridicule me. We got up the next day, and I sat in my room, waiting for my whipping. My sisters ate, watched TV, and went outside to play with their new toys. My Mom came to the room and tossed my new ball to me and sent me outside to play. As I walked by the kitchen table, I left the change from the twenty dollars. I went outside, but I didn't play, everything was different. I knew my Mama loved me already, but for her to take that abuse because of something I'd done, showed me the kind of mother she was. She knew and understood me better than I knew myself. That was the first time I truly understood that my mom had my back, and loved me unconditionally, faults and all. We never talked about it, and it was from that point forward she treated me as if I was a lot older. She gave me more responsibility, and that made me feel better about myself, and that gave me a healthier self-esteem. Nic

George W. NASH (Lovie GAMBLE NASH PARKER, Agnes Icy GUYTON GAMBLE, Pinkney, Aaron Whitaker, Aaron Steele, Joseph I, John I, Samuel II, Samuel I, John)

George NASH was the son of Lovie GAMBLE (b. 29 Aug 1915 Kosciusko, Attala Co., MS, d. 16 Oct 2002 Chicago, Cook Co., IL)[1409] and Woodrow Wilson NASH (b. 28 Aug 1916 in Leake Co., MS, d. 11 Dec 1999 in Chicago, Cook Co., IL)[1410] and divorced. George was born on 11 Oct 1937 in Holmes Co., MS, d. 17 Feb 2019 Chicago, Cook Co., IL.[1411] He married (1) Annie Ruth SHARP (b. 25 Dec 1938 Birmingham, Jefferson Co., AL, d. 26 Oct 2017 Chicago, Cook Co., IL)[1412] and (2) spouse or partner Karlena L. MOORE (b. 19 Dec 1939, d. Unknown).[1413] The relationship between George and the two women appears to have been simultaneous because the children's ages overlap. See George NASH in Figure 198 and Figure 199. See Karlena MOORE in Figure 200.

I could not find obituaries for George or Annie to be clear who their children are. Most of the information below comes from the *Ancestry.com* tree of his cousin, Karl BOYD (Nykki Lamarr STARR) together with some guessing. George's children with Annie may be the following:

i   George NASH, Jr. (b. 14 Oct 1960 Chicago, Cook Co., IL, d. Living).[1414] See Figure 201.
ii Gregory NASH (b. 17 Jul 1962 Chicago, Cook Co., IL, d. Living).[1415] See Figure 202.
iii Jeffrey NASH (b. 11 Sep 1963 Chicago, Cook Co., IL, d. 3 May 2023 Chicago, Cook Co., IL).[1416] See Figure 203.
iv Margo NASH (b. 7 Nov 1964 Chicago, Cook Co., IL, d. Living).[1417] See Figure 204.

George's children with Karlena MOORE, again requiring some guessing, are shown below:[1418]

i   Sheila NASH (b. 17 JAN 1962 Chicago, Cook Co., IL, d. Living).
ii Sherron V. MOORE (b. 9 Jan 1963 Chicago, Cook Co., IL, d. 29 Oct 2012 Buffalo, Erie Co., NY). See Figure 205.
iii Gerald L. NASH (b. 1 Sep 1969 Chicago, Cook Co., IL, d. Living). See Figure 206.
iv Sheree Shante NASH (b. 5 Mar 1971 Chicago, Cook Co., IL, d. Living). See Figure 207.

[1409] "U.S., Social Security Death Index, 1935-2014," s.v. "Lovie Parker," (birth 29 Aug 1915, death 16 Oct 2002), *Ancestry.com*.
[1410] "Woodrow Wilson Nash," grave marker, Mount Hope Cemetery, Chicago, Cook Co., IL, digital image s.v. "Claude Joiner," (birth 28 Apr 1916, death 11 Dec 1999), *FindaGrave.com*. No two documents have the same birth date, but the dates are close together.
[1411] "Vernestine 'Susie' Joiner," grave marker, Jenkins Cemetery, Attala Co., MS, digital image s.v. "Vernestine Wingard," (birth 27 Aug 1936, death 5 Oct 2018), *FindaGrave.com*.
[1412] "Luther D. 'Rabbit' Wingard," grave marker, Jenkins Cemetery, Attala Co., MS, digital image s.v. "Luther D Wingard," (birth 24 Apr 1936, death 1 Mar 2022), *FindaGrave.com*.
[1413] "U.S., Public Records Index, 1950-1993, Volume 2," s.v. "Karlena Nash," (birth 19 Dec 1939), *Ancestry.com*.
[1414] "U.S. Public Records Index, 1950-1993, Volume 2," s.v. "George Nash," (birth 14 Oct 1960), *Ancestry.com*.
[1415] Per Karl Boyd. I could not find a Gregory Nash in Chicago with that birth date in the published records.
[1416] Per the cover of Jeffrey Nash's funeral program from Karl Boyd.
[1417] "U.S., Public Records Index, 1950-1993, Volume 1," s.v. "Margo E Nash," *Ancestry.com*.
[1418] Per Karl Glenn Boyd (AKA Nykkie Lamarr Starr).

Figure 198 George W. NASH Worked with Bands[1419]

Figure 199 George W. NASH in U.S. Army[1420]

Figure 200 Karlena L. MOORE[1421]

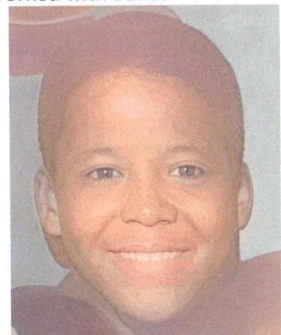

Figure 201 George NASH, Jr.[1422]

Figure 202 Gregory NASH[1423]

Figure 203 Jeffrey NASH[1424]

Figure 204 Margo NASH[1425]

Figure 205 Sherron V. MOORE[1426]

Figure 206 Gerald L. NASH[1427]

[1419] Karl Boyd originally shared this on 27 Nov 2021 on *Ancestry.com*.
[1420] Karl Boyd originally shared this on 11 Oct 2021 on *Ancestry.com*.
[1421] Karl Boyd originally shared this on 11 Oct 2021 on *Ancestry.com*.
[1422] Karl Boyd originally shared this on 31 Jul 2023 on *Ancestry.com*.
[1423] Karl Boyd originally shared this on 29 Jul 2023 on *Ancestry.com*.
[1424] Karl Boyd originally shared this on 8 Jul 2023 on *Ancestry.com*.
[1425] Karl Boyd originally shared this on 6 Aug 2023 on *Ancestry.com*.
[1426] Karl Boyd originally shared this on 29 Jul 2023 on *Ancestry.com*.
[1427] Karl Boyd originally shared this on 8 Jul 2023 on *Ancestry.com*.

Figure 207 Sheree Shante NASH[1428]

According to Karl BOYD (Nykki Lamarr STARR), George worked with bands and worked at a Aronson Furniture. Morris and Etta Aronson founded Aronson Furniture, a mid-price furniture retailer. When it closed in November 2006, it had nine locations. It had been in business for 65 years. The company announced it was a sad day for the family and its employees.[1429]

[1428] Karl Boyd originally shared this on 8 Jul 2023 on *Ancestry.com*.
[1429] Clint Engel, "Aronson Furniture Closing All Stores," *Furniture Today,* 13 Nov 2006, accessed 11 Jun 2024, <https://www.furnituretoday.com/business-news/aronson-furniture-closing-all-stores/>.

Lena Mae PARKER (Lovie GAMBLE NASH PARKER, Agnes Icy GUYTON GAMBLE, Pinkney, Aaron Whitaker, Aaron Steele, Joseph I, John I, Samuel II, Samuel I, John)

Lena Mae PARKER was the daughter of Lovie GAMBLE (b. 29 Aug 1915 Kosciusko, Attala Co., MS, d. 16 Oct 2002 Chicago, Cook Co., IL)[1430] and Ilander N. PARKER, Sr. (b. 21 Oct 1910 Cruger, Holmes Co., MS, d. May 1959 Kosciusko, Attala Co., MS).[1431] Lena Mae PARKER was born about 1939 in Mississippi and her death, if it occurred, is unknown).[1432] She married Herbert MOORE (b. 22 Jan 1932 Chicago, Cook Co., IL, d. 28 Oct 2001 Bellwood, Cook Co., IL).[1433]

According to her nephew, Karl Glenn BOYD (Nykki Lamarr STARR), she and Herbert had four children:

i   Herbert F. MOORE, Jr (b. 16 Jan 1955 Greenwood, Leflore Co., MS, d. 26 Aug 2016 Chicago, Cook Co., IL).[1434] See Figure 208.
ii Michael Anthony MOORE (b. 7 May 1958 Chicago, Cook Co., IL, d. 29 May 2022 MN).[1435] See Figure 209.
iii Belynda MOORE (b. 2 May 1959 Chicago, Cook Co., IL, d. Living)[1436] m. Jethro Alexander HEAD (b. 10 Dec 1953, d. Living)[1437] on 31 Dec 1983 in Clark Co., NV.[1438]
iv Timothy (Tim Man) MOORE (b. 27 Aug 1963 Chicago, Cook Co., IL, d. Unknown Attala Co., MS).[1439] See Figure 210.

Figure 208 Herbert F. MOORE[1440]

Figure 209 Michael Anthony MOORE[1441]

Figure 210 Timothy (Tim Man) MOORE[1442]

[1430] "1940 United States Federal Census," digital image s.v. "Lena M Parker," (birth abt 1939), *Ancestry.com*.
[1431] "Social Security Death Index," s.v. "Ilander Parker," (birth 21 Sep 1909, death May 1959), *Ancestry.com*.
[1432] "1940 United States Federal Census," Holmes Co., MS, digital image s.v. "Lena M Parker," (birth abt 1939), *Ancestry.com*.
[1433] Per Karl Boyd, nephew to Lena Mae Parker, on his *Ancestry.com* tree.
[1434] "Herbert F. Moore, Jr.," grave marker, Oakridge-Glen Oak Cemetery, Hillside, Cook Co., IL, digital image s.v. "Herbert F. Moore Jr," (birth 16 Jan 1955, death 26 Aug 2016), FindaGrave.com.
[1435] Per Karl Boyd and the cover of Michael Moore's funeral program.
[1436] "U.S., Public Records Index, 1950-1993, Volume 1," s.v. "Belynda Nmi Head," (birth 2 May 1959), *Ancestry.com*.
[1437] "U.S., Public Records Index, 1950-1993, Volume 1," s.v. "Jethro A Head," (birth 10 Dec 1953), *Ancestry.com*.
[1438] "Nevada, Marriage Index, 1956-2005," s.v. "Jethro A Head," (marriage 31 Dec 1983, recorded 5 Jan 1984 to Belynda Moore), *Ancestry.com*.
[1439] "U.S., Public Records Index, 1950-1993, Volume 1," s.v. "Sheree S Nash," (birth 5 Mar 1971), *Ancestry.com*.
[1440] Karl Boyd originally shared this on 21 Nov 2021 on *Ancestry.com*.
[1441] Karl Boyd originally shared this on 15 Aug 2023 on *Ancestry.com*.
[1442] Karl Boyd originally shared this on 21 Nov 2021 on *Ancestry.com*.

Ilander PARKER, Jr. (Lovie GAMBLE NASH PARKER, Agnes Icy GUYTON GAMBLE, Pinkney, Aaron Whitaker, Aaron Steele, Joseph I, John I, Samuel II, Samuel I, John)

Ilander PARKER, Jr. was the son of Lovie GAMBLE (b. 29 Aug 1915 Kosciusko, Attala Co., MS, d. 16 Oct 2002 Chicago, Cook Co., IL)[1443] and Ilander N. PARKER, Sr. (b. 21 Oct 1910 Cruger, Holmes Co., MS, d. May 1959 Kosciusko, Attala Co., MS).[1444] Ilander, Jr. was born on 24 Aug 1941 in Cruger, Holmes Co., MS, and died in 24 Oct 2005 Chicago, Cook Co., IL).[1445] He married Katherine UNKNOWN (b. Jul 1942).[1446] See Figure 211 and Figure 212.

Figure 211 Ilander PARKER, Jr.[1447]

Figure 212 Katherine UNKNOWN PARKER[1448]

Ilander and Katherine had at least eight children. Karl Glenn BOYD (Nykki Lamarr STARR) provided the list and most of the birth dates.

i	Cheryl Penny PARKER (b. 13 Aug 1963, d. Living) (see Figure 260) m. (1) Jerry BOONE (Unknown) and (2) Eric PARKER (b. 10 May Unknown).
ii	Chris PARKER (b. Jul 1964) m. Yvette UNKNOWN.
iii	Sandy D. PARKER (b. 11 Mar 1966, d. Living) m. Isaac L. DUNSON (b. 23 Aug 1960, d. Living).
iv	Tera M. PARKER (b. 23 Apr 1967, d. Living) m. Steven S. MORRIS, Sr. (b. 11 Aug 1967, d. Living).
v	Ollander (Odie) PARKER (b. 19 Jan 1971, d. Living) m. Lishon SEALS (b. Feb 1971, d. Living).
vi	LaTarshe (Toddy) PARKER (b. 23 Oct 1972, d. Living) m. David L. JENKINS, Sr. (b. 20 Aug 1974 Chicago, Cook Co., IL, d. Living).
vii	Bernard PARKER (b. 28 Aug 1975, d. Living) m. Latisha GRANT (b. Jan 1977, d. Living).
viii	Seconda PARKER (b. May 1979, d. Living) m. Rogelio WILLIAMS (b. Unknown, d. Living).

[1443] "U.S., Social Security Death Index, 1935-2014," s.v. "Lovie Parker," (birth 29 Aug 1915, death 16 Oct 2002), *Ancestry.com*.
[1444] "Social Security Death Index," s.v. "Ilander Parker," (birth 21 Sep 1909, death May 1959), *Ancestry.com*.
[1445] "U.S., Social Security Death Index, 1935-2014," s.v. "Ilander Parker," (birth 24 Aug 1941, death 24 Oct 2005), *FindaGrave.com*.
[1446] Per Karl Boyd's tree on *Ancestry.com*. He was nephew of Ilander Parker, Jr.
[1447] Karl Boyd originally shared this on 31 Aug 2023 on *Ancestry.com*.
[1448] Karl Boyd originally shared this on 31 Aug 2023 on *Ancestry.com*.

Arthur Lee PARKER (Lovie GAMBLE NASH PARKER, Agnes Icy GUYTON GAMBLE, Pinkney, Aaron Whitaker, Aaron Steele, Joseph I, John I, Samuel II, Samuel I, John)

Arthur Lee PARKER was the son of Lovie GAMBLE (b. 29 Aug 1915 Kosciusko, Attala Co., MS, d. 16 Oct 2002 Chicago, Cook Co., IL)[1449] and Ilander N. PARKER, Sr. (b. 21 Oct 1910 Cruger, Holmes Co., MS, d. May 1959 Kosciusko, Attala Co., MS).[1450] Arthur Lee was born on 1 Oct 1947 in MS, d. Unknown).[1451] See Figure 213. Arthur married (1) Rosemary PINK (B. 21 Jul 1947 Chicago, Cook Co., IL, d. 30 Dec 2007 Chicago, Cook Co., IL)[1452] (see Figure 214) and (2) Barbra Ann NORMAN (Unknown) (see Figure 215).

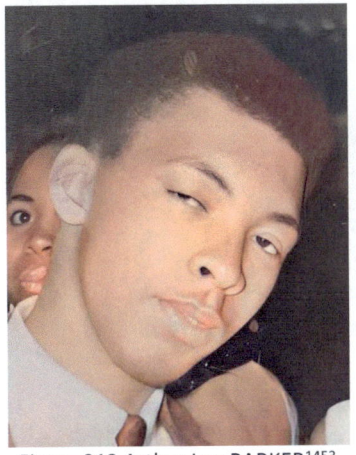

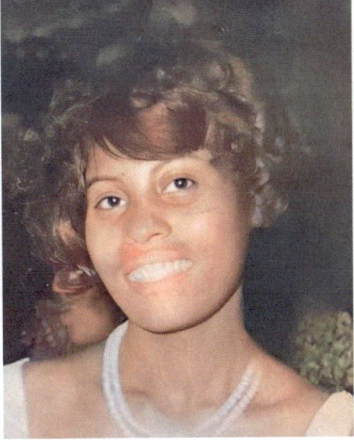

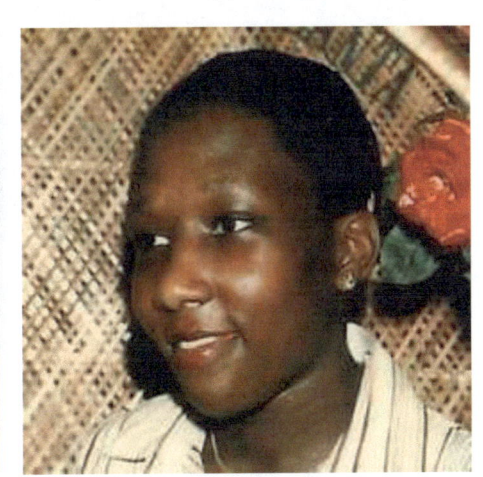

Figure 213 Arthur Lee PARKER[1453]

Figure 214 Rosemary PINK[1454]

Figure 215 Barbra Ann NORMAN[1455]

With Rosemary PINK, Arthur Lee had two children:[1456]

i   Keith Anthony PINK (b. 15 May 1968 Chicago, Cook Co., IL, d. 14 Nov 2013 Chicago, Cook Co., IL).[1457] See Figure 216. He had a daughter Brittany Danielle WALKER.
ii Toya PINK (b. 2 Mar 1974 Chicago, Cook Co., IL, d. Living)[1458] (see Figure 217) m. Larry Jason LLOYD (b. 18 Jan 1974, d. Living). They have three children: Jason Deon LLOYD, Tyler Christopher LLOYD, and Jailyn Breshae LLOYD.

[1449] "U.S., Social Security Death Index, 1935-2014," s.v. "Lovie Parker," (birth 29 Aug 1915, death 16 Oct 2002), *Ancestry.com*.
[1450] "Social Security Death Index," s.v. "Ilander Parker," (birth 21 Sep 1909, death May 1959), *Ancestry.com*.
[1451] "1950 United States Federal Census," Holmes Co., MS, digital image s.v. "Albert Lee Parker," (birth abt 1948), *Ancestry.com*. Date per Karl Glenn Boyd (aka Nykki Lamarr Starr).
[1452] "U.S., Social Security Death Index, 1935-2014," s.v. "Rosemary Pink," (birth 21 Jul 1948, death 30 Dec 2007), *Ancestry.com*.
[1453] Karl Boyd originally shared this on 31 Aug 2023 on *Ancestry.com*.
[1454] Karl Boyd originally shared this on 31 Aug 2023 on *Ancestry.com*.
[1455] Karl Boyd originally shared this on 10 Aug 2023 on *Ancestry.com*.
[1456] This information originates with Karl Boyd.
[1457] "Herbert F. Moore, Jr.," grave marker, Oakridge-Glen Oak Cemetery, Hillside, Cook Co., IL, digital image s.v. "Herbert F. Moore Jr," (birth 16 Jan 1955, death 26 Aug 2016), FindaGrave.com.
[1458] "U.S., Public Records Index, 1950-1993, Volume 1," s.v. "Toya N Pink," (birth 2 Mar 1974). The family information comes from Karl Boyd.

Arthur Lee PARKER and Barbra Ann NORMAN have three children:

i   Cecelia (Cece) Artrece NORMAN (b. 7 Mar 1980, d. Living) (see Figure 218) m. Michael Dre CARRINGTON (Unknown), div.[1459] They have a son: Zion Amir Malik CARRINGTON.

ii   Tyecheia Lynae NORMAN-LOPEZ (b. 23 Dec 1982 Chicago, Cook Co., IL, d. Living)[1460] (see Figure 219) m. Olga Lidia LOPEZ COTA (b. 2 Oct 1983 Sinaloa, Primera Sección, Cárdenas, Tabasco, Mexico, d. Living).

iii   Christopher Ezriel NORMAN, Sr. (b. 10 May 1985 Chicago, Cook Co., IL, d. Living).[1461] He has a son, Christopher Ezriel NORMAN, Jr. See Figure 220.

Figure 216 Keith Anthony PINK[1462]

Figure 217 Toya N. PINK[1463]

Figure 218 Cece NORMAN[1464]

Figure 219 Tyecheia Lynae NORMAN-LOPEZ[1465]

Figure 220 Christopher Ezriel NORMAN, Sr.[1466]

[1459] "U.S., Public Records Index, 1950-1993, Volume 2," s.v. "Cecelia A Norman," (birth 7 Mar 1980), *Ancestry.com*.
[1460] Per Karl Boyd.
[1461] Per Karl Boyd.
[1462] Karl Boyd originally shared this on 2 Dec 2021 on *Ancestry.com*.
[1463] Karl Boyd originally shared this on 21 Nov 2021 on *Ancestry.com*.
[1464] Karl Boyd originally shared this on 11 Aug 2023 on *Ancestry.com*.
[1465] Karl Boyd originally shared this on 11 Aug 2023 on Ancestry.com.
[1466] Karl Boyd originally shared this on 11 Aug 2023 on *Ancestry.com*.

Karl Glenn BOYD (aka Nykki Lamarr STARR) writes the following about his maternal uncle:

My Childhood memories of my Uncle Arthur Lee are memories that I treasure. Early on, and into my adulthood, my Uncle Arthur Lee was for me, the measurement of a Man. As a kid, it was his encouragement that made me feel like I could do anything... I remember begging and pleading with Mama that I wanted a bike. Seemed like all the other boys my age had one, I wanted one too. One afternoon, Arthur Lee pulls up, I can't remember if it was a truck, or old station wagon that he used to haul his fruits and vegetables around in, but he pulled this old Swinn, Stingray Bicycle out, and rolled it up to the porch and gave it to me. He asked me where was my Mama, (sounding like Lurch from the Adams Family) and went upstairs to talk to her. When he came back down, I was still sitting on the porch looking at the bike, and he just looked at me, and without me saying a word, he knew what was wrong! He said, "Boy, you made all that noise about getting a bicycle, and you don't even know how to ride??? I shook my head, and he said, "Shiiid, a closed mouth can't be fed." Three things confused me about that statement. One, what in the hell did that mean? Two, what did it have to do with the bike, and three, what happened to the "T" that went on the end of Shit? He always pronounced it shiiiid. Anyway, he said open you mouth and say something instead of shaking your head like a billy goat (still don't know what a billy goat is???), then he pointed to the kids riding their bikes up and down the sidewalk, and told me, "You see them doing it don't you?" I nodded my head again, and got that patented UNCLE ARTHUR LEE LOOK (*that, fool what did I just say look*) and I quickly said, "Yes sir!" he responded with words I live by till this day, "Then that should tell you, you can do it too." I got on the bike, and he held the back and walked with me halfway down the block... I guess, cause when I stopped and looked back, he was already in his car driving away... That was Uncle Arthur Lee, I always thought of him as the family enforcer. Mama called - he was there... you didn't want to do anything wrong, or anything to get reprimanded by him. He never put a hand on me, but he could look at you in such a way, that you know you were wrong, and you didn't want to disappoint him again. Whether he was escorting me to my Father and Son banquet or searching our house to rid it of hanks, my Uncle had my Mama's back, and I'll always love him for that! *Nic*

Tyecheia (Ty) Lynae NORMAN-LOPEZ wrote the following about her father, Arthur Lee PARKER:[1467]

Memories of Dad: I have some of the funniest and most amazing memories of my dad. Dad taught me how to fish and ride a bike, and would take my sister, brother, and me fishing and bike riding often. One funny memory that I have of Dad is when he took all three of us bike riding. We decided to go down a grassy hill because we thought it would be fast and fun. Dad followed behind us, and when I turned around to look behind me, I saw Dad rolling down the hill with his bike. I was yelling "let go" (of the bike), but Dad held on until he came to a stop. It took everything in me not to laugh while he was getting up. Dad

---

[1467] Originated with Karl Boyd.

showed up to support many milestones in my life, even when I didn't think he would make it because he was working, which always put the biggest smile on my face. Dad, by example, showed me the meaning of hard work, while giving tips and advice about life. As a child, I didn't quite understand it, but now well into my adulthood, I cherish every word he said. I am grateful and thankful for all that he has done for us, and proud to call him my Dad!

Charlene PARKER (Lovie GAMBLE NASH PARKER, Agnes Icy GUYTON GAMBLE, Pinkney, Aaron Whitaker, Aaron Steele, Joseph I, John I, Samuel II, Samuel I, John)

Charlene PARKER is the daughter of Lovie GAMBLE (b. 29 Aug 1915 Kosciusko, Attala Co., MS, d. 16 Oct 2002 Chicago, Cook Co., IL)[1468] and Ilander N. PARKER, Sr. (b. 21 Oct 1910 Cruger, Holmes Co., MS, d. May 1959 Kosciusko, Attala Co., MS).[1469] Charlene was born on 10 Oct 1952, d. Living).[1470] See Figure 221. She married Buvern FRANCISCO, Jr. (b. 19 Aug 1952 Chicago, Cook Co., IL, d. Living). See Figure 222. She and Buvern have two children, per Karl BOYD, her nephew:

i   Tonya Lashun FRANCISCO (b. 14 Apr 1970, d. Living) (see Figure 223) m. Jarrette WALLS (Unknown). They have two children: Alexis WALLS and Kennedy WALLS (female).
ii   Buvern J. FRANCISCO, III (b. 30 Sep 1978 Chicago, Cook Co., IL, d. 23 May 2012 Chicago, Cook Co., IL).[1471] See Figure 224.

Figure 221 Charlene PARKER[1472]

Figure 222 Buvern FRANCISCO, Jr.[1473]

Figure 223 Tonya Lashun FRANCISCO[1474]

Figure 224 Buvern FRANCISCO, III[1475]

[1468] "U.S., Social Security Death Index, 1935-2014," s.v. "Lovie Parker," (birth 29 Aug 1915, death 16 Oct 2002), *Ancestry.com*.
[1469] "Social Security Death Index," s.v. "Ilander Parker," (birth 21 Sep 1909, death May 1959), *Ancestry.com*.
[1470] Per her nephew Karl Boyd.
[1471] Per Karl Boyd.
[1472] Karl Boyd originally shared this on 31 Aug 2023 on *Ancestry.com*.
[1473] Karl Boyd originally shared this on 21 Nov 2021 on *Ancestry.com*.
[1474] Karl Boyd originally shared this on 11 Nov 2021 on *Ancestry.com*.
[1475] Karl Boyd originally shared this on 11 Nov 2021 on *Ancestry.com*.

Karl Glenn BOYD (aka Nykki Lamarr STARR) wrote the following about his maternal aunt:

Charlene FRANCISCO was born on the 10th of October in 1952. The business minded, and practical Auntie, who is proof positive that a woman can be stunningly beautiful and STILL be the smartest one in the room! She was the Auntie that I'd always tried to talk to before I made any big decisions. Thinking back, I probably would not have retired from the military almost thirty years ago had it not been for my Aunt Charlene's sound advise, desire to see, "Family WIN!" Thanks for always being there ready to share your sage advice and wisdom, and doing it in such a way that never made you feel dumb or stupid. I truly love you for that. Thank you for all you do! I love you Auntie... Nic

Shirley PARKER (Lovie GAMBLE NASH PARKER, Agnes Icy GUYTON GAMBLE, Pinkney, Aaron Whitaker, Aaron Steele, Joseph I, John I, Samuel II, Samuel I, John)

Shirley PARKER was the daughter of Lovie GAMBLE (b. 29 Aug 1915 Kosciusko, Attala Co., MS, d. 16 Oct 2002 Chicago, Cook Co., IL)[1476] and Ilander N. PARKER, Sr. (b. 21 Oct 1910 Cruger, Holmes Co., MS, d. May 1959 Kosciusko, Attala Co., MS).[1477] Shirley was born on 20 Oct 1954 in Kosciusko, Attala Co., MS, and died on 5 Jun 1992 Chicago, Cook Co., IL.[1478] See Figure 225. She married Hubert EVANS (Unknown). See Figure 226. They had at least one child per Karl Glenn BOYD (Nykki Lamarr STARR):

i   Natasha PARKER (b. 31 Oct 1974, d. Living) m. (1) Shannon R. SIMMONS (b. 4 May 1975, d. Living) and (2) De'Avlin V. OLGUIN (b. 18 Oct 1974, d. Living).

Karl Glenn BOYD (aka Nykki Lamarr STARR) wrote the following about his maternal aunt:

Shirley Ann Parker was the Babygirl of Ilander and Lovie PARKER. She was born in Cruger, Holmes County, Mississippi on October 20, 1954; she went home to Glory on June 5, 1992. Known as a spark that was willing and able to ignite and control any flame. The rebel of the family, but if you want straight truth, no chaser... talk to Auntie Shirley! Come in the house talking about what Santa Claus didn't bring, and she'd tell you, "There ain't no damned Santa Claus, you better be thankful for what you got!" Then she'd go on to the next topic without explaining anything. But she didn't have to, if you heard it from Shirley, there was some truth in it, and since she was the realist of the REAL. Her word was Bond. You didn't need any explanation, you just believed. Truly a force to be reckoned with, and never taken lightly. Rest Power, Auntie...

[1476] "U.S., Social Security Death Index, 1935-2014," s.v. "Lovie Parker," (birth 29 Aug 1915, death 16 Oct 2002), *Ancestry.com*.
[1477] "Social Security Death Index," s.v. "Ilander Parker," (birth 21 Sep 1909, death May 1959), *Ancestry.com*.
[1478] Per Karl Boyd (also known as Nykki Starr), nephew, from his tree on 12 Oct 2021 on Ancestry.com.

Figure 225 Shirley PARKER[1479]

Figure 226 Hubert EVANS[1480]

[1479] Karl Boyd originally shared this on 11 Nov 2021 on *Ancestry.com*.
[1480] Karl Boyd originally shared this on 18 Aug 2023 on *Ancestry.com*.

Generation #11

Edward L. (Eddie) CULPEPPER (Rubell MALLET CULPEPPER, Fannie GAMBLE, Agnes Icy GUYTON GAMBLE, Pinkney, Aaron Whitaker, Aaron Steele, Joseph I, John I, Samuel II, Samuel I, John)

Edward L. (Eddie) CULPEPPER was the son of Rubell MALLETT (b. 20 Jul 1924 Leake Co., MS, d. 22 Jan 1998 Waterloo, Black Hawk Co., IA)[1481] and the Reverend George Louis CULPEPPER (b. 10 Jan 1927 Durant, Holmes Co., MS, d. 4 Aug 2000 Waterloo, Black Hawk Co., IA).[1482]

Edward was born on 3 Apr 1946 in Sallis, Attala Co., MS and died on 19 Jan 2015 Waterloo, Black Hawk Co., IA.[1483] He married Barbara Ruth SAFFOLD (b. 4 Jun 1948, d. Unknown)[1484] on 11 Jul 1964 Fillmore Co., MN.[1485] They later divorced.

Per Edward CULPEPPER's obituary (see Figure 227), he and Barbara had three children:

i   Gwenne CULPEPPER (Unknown).
ii   David CULPEPPER (Unknown).
iii Denise CULPEPPER (Unknown).

[1481] Rubell Bonita Mallett, grave marker, Fairview Cemetery, Waterloo, Black Hawk Co., IA, digital image s.v. "Rubell Bonita Culpepper," (birth 20 Jul 1924, death 22 Jan 1998), *FindaGrave.com*.
[1482] George Louis Culpepper, grave marker, Fairview Cemetery, Waterloo, Black Hawk Co., IA, digital image s.v. "Rev George Louis Culpepper," (birth 10 Jan 1927, death 4 Aug 2000), *FindaGrave.com*.
[1483] Edward L. (Eddie) Culpepper, grave marker, Fairview Cemetery, Waterloo, Black Hawk Co., IA, digital image s.v. "Edward L. Culpepper," (birth 3 Apr 1946, death 19 Jan 2015), *FindaGrave.com*.
[1484] "U.S., Public Records Index, 1950-1993, Volume 2," s.v. "Barbara R Culpepper-Schee," (birth 4 Jun 1948), *Ancestry.com*.
[1485] "Minnesota, U.S., Marriages from the Minnesota Official Marriage System, 1850-2022," s.v. "Barbara Ruth Saffold," (marriage 11 Jul 1964 to Edward Culpepper), *Ancestry.com*.

Edward L. "Eddie" Culpepper (1946-2015)

WATERLOO — Edward L. "Eddie" Culpepper, 68, of Waterloo, died at home Monday, Jan. 19.

He was born April 3, 1946, in Sallis, Miss., son of the Rev. George L. and Ruby Mallett Culpepper. He married Barbara Saffold in 1964 and they later divorced.

Eddie graduated from Waterloo East High School and Hawkeye Institute of Technology, earning an associate's degree in electrician training. He was the sector chief for the Federal Aviation Administration (FAA) at the Waterloo Regional Airport for many years, retiring in 2003.

Survived by: two daughters, Gwenne (John) Berry of Waterloo and Denise Culpepper Thomas of Des Moines; a son, David of Jacksonville, Fla.; four granddaughters; four brothers, Willie (Alice) of Le Claire, Martin (Terry) and Jerry (Sandy), both of Waterloo, and George of Rockford, Ill.; and four sisters, Elaine Culpepper of Colorado, Linda (Laverne) Harris of Waterloo, Betsy (Rory) Lucas of Minneapolis and Annette Culpepper of Los Angeles.

Preceded in death by: his parents; and two sisters, Mary Jean McCoy and Darlene Morgan.

Services: 11 a.m. Monday at Kearns Funeral Service Kimball Chapel, with burial in Fairview Cemetery. Visitation from 2 to 4 p.m. Sunday and an hour before services Monday at the funeral home.

Memorials: may be directed to Wounded Warriors Project, 230 W. Monroe St., Suite 200, Chicago 60606; or to the family at 3731 Pearl Lane, where visitors will be received.

Condolences can be expressed at www.KearnsFuneralService.com.

Eddie loved spending time with his family, particularly his granddaughters. He was an avid fisherman, enjoyed riding his motorcycle and playing the guitar. Most recently he resurrected his love for golf and began deer hunting.

Figure 227 Obituary of Edward L. CULPEPPER[1486]

[1486] "Edward L. 'Eddie' Culpepper (1946-2015)," *The Courier,* Fri, 23 Jan 2015, p. A12, digital image s.v. "Edward L. 'Eddie' Culpepper," *Newspapers.com.*

Rickey SIMMONS (LC SIMMONS, Callie Pairee GAMBLE SIMMONS, Agnes Icy GUYTON GAMBLE, Pinkney, Aaron Whitaker, Aaron Steele, Joseph I, John I, Samuel II, Samuel I, John)

Rickey SIMMONS is the son of L.C. SIMMONS (b. 15 Aug 1923 Attala Co., MS, d. 13 Jun 2009 Sallis, Attala Co, MS)[1487] and Lue Bertha WINDOMS (b. 22 May 1937, d. Unknown).[1488] Rickey was born on 4 Aug 1958 in Attala Co., MS, and is still living). See Figure 228. He had partnerships with (1) Carrie ROCKETT (Unknown), (2) UNKNOWN, and (3) UNKNOWN. His children, per a conversation, are as follows:

i   Rickey ROCKETT (b. 15 May 1977 MS, d. Living) with Carrie ROCKETT m. Shaleese Eugenia BEASLEY (b. 16 Jul 1982 IA, d. Living). See Figure 229. He has three sons: Rickey Rodney ROCKETT, Roman ROCKETT, and Reuben ROCKETT.
ii Crystal BYNDOM (b. ABT 1986, d. Living) with UNKNOWN. See Figure 230. She married Unknown HARMON.
iii Colby Von SIMMONS (b. ABT 1996 d. Living) m. with UNKNOWN. See Figure 231.

Figure 228 Rickey SIMMONS[1489]

Figure 229 Rickey ROCKETT

Figure 230 Crystal BYNDOM HARMON

Figure 231 Colby Von SIMMONS

[1487] "U.S., Social Security Death Index, 1935-2014," s.v. "Henry L. Simmons," (birth 5 Aug 1922, death 13 Jun 2009), Ancestry.com.
[1488] Personal conversation with their grandson, Rickey Simmons (b. abt 1958).
[1489] Photo from the Guyton family reunion in Kosciusko, Attala Co., MS in summer 2022.

Darlene MURPHY (Zenolia SIMMONS MURPHY, Callie Pairee GAMBLE SIMMONS, Agnes Icy GUYTON GAMBLE, Pinkney, Aaron Whitaker, Aaron Steele, Joseph I, John I, Samuel II, Samuel I, John)

Darlene MURPHY was the daughter of Zenolia SIMMONS (b. 9 Dec 1926 Kosciusko, Attala Co., MS, d. 19 Jan 2018 Eau Claire, Berrien Co., MI)[1490] and Ellon MURPHY (b. 20 Oct 1922 Kosciusko, Attala Co., MS, d. 20 Jul 1993 Berrien, Berrien Co., MI).[1491]

Darlene was born on 19 Jul 1945 in New York, NY, and died on 28 Dec 2010 in Benton Harbor, Berrien Co., MI.[1492] She married (1) James Edward DELANEY, Sr. and (2) Matthew Ashley SHARPE, Sr. (Unknown).[1493] She had five children:[1494]

i   Adrian DELANEY has one child: Nadia DELANEY.
ii   James DELANEY has four children: Shenise DELANEY, Sierra DELANEY, Serina DELANEY, and Sheyenne DELANEY.
iii Byron DELANEY, Sr., deceased, had two children: Brandy DELANEY, and Byron DELANEY, Jr.
iv   Brandon SHARPE, Sr. has three children: Brandon (BJ) SHARPE, Jr., Brianna SHARPE, and Kayden SHARPE.
v   Matthew SHARPE has two children: Destiny SHARPE and Trey SHARPE

Melvin MURPHY, Jr. (Zenolia SIMMONS MURPHY, Callie Pairee GAMBLE SIMMONS, Agnes Icy GUYTON GAMBLE, Pinkney, Aaron Whitaker, Aaron Steele, Joseph I, John I, Samuel II, Samuel I, John)

Melvin MURPHY, Jr. was the son of Zenolia SIMMONS (b. 9 Dec 1926 Kosciusko, Attala Co., MS, d. 19 Jan 2018 Eau Claire, Berrien Co., MI)[1495] and Ellon MURPHY (b. 20 Oct 1922 Kosciusko, Attala Co., MS, d. 20 Jul 1993 Berrien, Berrien Co., MI).[1496]

He had five children:[1497]

i   Chrystal MURPHY has at least five children: Darius DAWSON, Dejanae DAWSON, DeVonte DAWSON, Chico DAWSON, and Bumper UNKNOWN.
ii   Tonya MURPHY m. Unknown PETERS and has at least two children: Nookie PETERS and Kevon PETERS.
iii Pinto MURPHY.
iv   Max a Million MURPHY, deceased.
v   Chuckie MURPHY.

[1490] "U.S., Cemetery and Funeral Home Collection, 1847-Current," digital image s.v. "Zenolia Murphy Murphy," (birth 9 Dec 1926, death 19 Jan 2018), Ancestry.com.
[1491] "U.S., Social Security Applications and Claims Index, 1936-2007," s.v. "Ellon Murphy," (birth 20 Oct 1922, death 20 Jul 1993," Ancestry.com.
[1492] "U.S., Social Security Death Index, 1935-2014," s.v. "Darlene Sharpe," (birth 19 Jul 1945, death 28 Dec 2010), Ancestry.com.
[1493] Darlene Murphy had two sons who were juniors. I assumed the fathers carried the same names as seniors.
[1494] Per Rita McLean.
[1495] "U.S., Cemetery and Funeral Home Collection, 1847-Current," digital image s.v. "Zenolia Murphy Murphy," (birth 9 Dec 1926, death 19 Jan 2018), Ancestry.com.
[1496] "U.S., Social Security Applications and Claims Index, 1936-2007," s.v. "Ellon Murphy," (birth 20 Oct 1922, death 20 Jul 1993," Ancestry.com.
[1497] Per Rita McLean.

Marvin Ray MURPHY (Zenolia SIMMONS MURPHY, Callie Pairee GAMBLE SIMMONS, Agnes Icy GUYTON GAMBLE, Pinkney, Aaron Whitaker, Aaron Steele, Joseph I, John I, Samuel II, Samuel I, John)

Marvin Ray MURPHY was the son of Zenolia SIMMONS (b. 9 Dec 1926 Kosciusko, Attala Co., MS, d. 19 Jan 2018 Eau Claire, Berrien Co., MI)[1498] and Ellon MURPHY (b. 20 Oct 1922 Kosciusko, Attala Co., MS, d. 20 Jul 1993 Berrien, Berrien Co., MI).[1499]

He had three children:[1500]

i   Taj MURPHY had at least one child: Towa MURPHY.
ii   Keisha MURPHY, deceased, had at least three children: Sakaura RIMPSON, Briesha McGEE, and Miracle TRAVIS.
iii   Terria MURPHY had at least one child: Gabriel UNKNOWN.

Linda (Carol) MURPHY (Zenolia SIMMONS MURPHY, Callie Pairee GAMBLE SIMMONS, Agnes Icy GUYTON GAMBLE, Pinkney, Aaron Whitaker, Aaron Steele, Joseph I, John I, Samuel II, Samuel I, John)

Linda (Carol) MURPHY was the daughter of Zenolia SIMMONS (b. 9 Dec 1926 Kosciusko, Attala Co., MS, d. 19 Jan 2018 Eau Claire, Berrien Co., MI)[1501] and Ellon MURPHY (b. 20 Oct 1922 Kosciusko, Attala Co., MS, d. 20 Jul 1993 Berrien, Berrien Co., MI).[1502]

Carol (b. ABT 1948 IL, d. Living)[1503] m. (1) Curtis PINDER and (2) Neal YOUNG. She has four children:[1504]

i   Carolyn PINDER has at least one child: Robert BARNES.
ii   Darnelle PINDER, deceased, had at least one child: Crimson PINDER.
iii   Yolanda YOUNG m. Unknown TRAYLOR and had at least three children: Sarita TRAYLOR, Janay TRAYLOR, and Jacob TRAYLOR.
iv   Marcus YOUNG.

[1498] "U.S., Cemetery and Funeral Home Collection, 1847-Current," digital image s.v. "Zenolia Murphy Murphy," (birth 9 Dec 1926, death 19 Jan 2018), *Ancestry.com*.
[1499] "U.S., Social Security Applications and Claims Index, 1936-2007," s.v. "Ellon Murphy," (birth 20 Oct 1922, death 20 Jul 1993," *Ancestry.com*.
[1500] Per Rita McLean.
[1501] "U.S., Cemetery and Funeral Home Collection, 1847-Current," digital image s.v. "Zenolia Murphy Murphy," (birth 9 Dec 1926, death 19 Jan 2018), *Ancestry.com*.
[1502] "U.S., Social Security Applications and Claims Index, 1936-2007," s.v. "Ellon Murphy," (birth 20 Oct 1922, death 20 Jul 1993," *Ancestry.com*.
[1503] "1950 United States Federal Census," Chicago, Cook Co., IL, digital image s.v. "Caroline Murphy," (birth abt 1948), *Ancestry.com*.
[1504] Per Rita McLean.

Zenobia MURPHY (Zenolia SIMMONS MURPHY, Callie Pairee GAMBLE SIMMONS, Agnes Icy GUYTON GAMBLE, Pinkney, Aaron Whitaker, Aaron Steele, Joseph I, John I, Samuel II, Samuel I, John)

Zenobia MURPHY was the daughter of Zenolia SIMMONS (b. 9 Dec 1926 Kosciusko, Attala Co., MS, d. 19 Jan 2018 Eau Claire, Berrien Co., MI)[1505] and Ellon MURPHY (b. 20 Oct 1922 Kosciusko, Attala Co., MS, d. 20 Jul 1993 Berrien, Berrien Co., MI).[1506] Zenobia was born on 25 May 1949 in IL.[1507] She married Harry BROWN (deceased) and had two children:[1508]

- i   Tiffany BROWN has one child: Khari BROWN.
- ii   Abeni BROWN, adopted, has two children: Angelo BROWN and Aaron BROWN.

Murriel Delores MURPHY (Zenolia SIMMONS MURPHY, Callie Pairee GAMBLE SIMMONS, Agnes Icy GUYTON GAMBLE, Pinkney, Aaron Whitaker, Aaron Steele, Joseph I, John I, Samuel II, Samuel I, John)

Murriel Delores MURPHY was the daughter of Zenolia SIMMONS (b. 9 Dec 1926 Kosciusko, Attala Co., MS, d. 19 Jan 2018 Eau Claire, Berrien Co., MI)[1509] and Ellon MURPHY (b. 20 Oct 1922 Kosciusko, Attala Co., MS, d. 20 Jul 1993 Berrien, Berrien Co., MI).[1510] Murriel was born on 1 Oct 1952.[1511] She has two children:[1512]

- i   Christina GLENN.
- ii   Phillip GLENN.

[1505] "U.S., Cemetery and Funeral Home Collection, 1847-Current," digital image s.v. "Zenolia Murphy Murphy," (birth 9 Dec 1926, death 19 Jan 2018), *Ancestry.com*.

[1506] "U.S., Social Security Applications and Claims Index, 1936-2007," s.v. "Ellon Murphy," (birth 20 Oct 1922, death 20 Jul 1993," *Ancestry.com*.

[1507] "U.S. Public Records Index, 1950-1993, Volume 1," s.v. "Zenbioa Brown," (birth 25 May 1949), *Ancestry.com*.

[1508] Per Rita McLean.

[1509] "U.S., Cemetery and Funeral Home Collection, 1847-Current," digital image s.v. "Zenolia Murphy Murphy," (birth 9 Dec 1926, death 19 Jan 2018), *Ancestry.com*.

[1510] "U.S., Social Security Applications and Claims Index, 1936-2007," s.v. "Ellon Murphy," (birth 20 Oct 1922, death 20 Jul 1993," *Ancestry.com*.

[1511] "U.S., Public Records Index, 1950-1993, Volume 2," s.v. "Muriel Murphy," (birth 1 Oct 1952), *Ancestry.com*.

[1512] Per Rita McLean.

Patricia MURPHY (Zenolia SIMMONS MURPHY, Callie Pairee GAMBLE SIMMONS, Agnes Icy GUYTON GAMBLE, Pinkney, Aaron Whitaker, Aaron Steele, Joseph I, John I, Samuel II, Samuel I, John)

Patricia MURPHY was the daughter of Zenolia SIMMONS (b. 9 Dec 1926 Kosciusko, Attala Co., MS, d. 19 Jan 2018 Eau Claire, Berrien Co., MI)[1513] and Ellon MURPHY (b. 20 Oct 1922 Kosciusko, Attala Co., MS, d. 20 Jul 1993 Berrien, Berrien Co., MI).[1514] Patricia was born about 1961. Per her father's obituary, she married Kenneth HARPER, lived in Arizona, and has two children:[1515]

i   Amina HARPER.
ii   Anice HARPER m. Joseph SNYDER and had one child: Julian SNYDER.

Tony MURPHY, Sr. (Zenolia SIMMONS MURPHY, Callie Pairee GAMBLE SIMMONS, Agnes Icy GUYTON GAMBLE, Pinkney, Aaron Whitaker, Aaron Steele, Joseph I, John I, Samuel II, Samuel I, John)

Tony MURPHY was the son of Zenolia SIMMONS (b. 9 Dec 1926 Kosciusko, Attala Co., MS, d. 19 Jan 2018 Eau Claire, Berrien Co., MI)[1516] and Ellon MURPHY (b. 20 Oct 1922 Kosciusko, Attala Co., MS, d. 20 Jul 1993 Berrien, Berrien Co., MI).[1517] Per his father's obituary, Tony MURPHY lived in Michigan and has five children:[1518]

i   Tony MURPHY, Jr.
ii   Kazayh MURPHY.
iii Randon MURPHY.
iv Winter MURPHY.
v   NeVeah MURPHY, Jr.

[1513] "U.S., Cemetery and Funeral Home Collection, 1847-Current," digital image s.v. "Zenolia Murphy Murphy," (birth 9 Dec 1926, death 19 Jan 2018), *Ancestry.com*.
[1514] "U.S., Social Security Applications and Claims Index, 1936-2007," s.v. "Ellon Murphy," (birth 20 Oct 1922, death 20 Jul 1993," *Ancestry.com*.
[1515] Per Rita McLean.
[1516] "U.S., Cemetery and Funeral Home Collection, 1847-Current," digital image s.v. "Zenolia Murphy Murphy," (birth 9 Dec 1926, death 19 Jan 2018), *Ancestry.com*.
[1517] "U.S., Social Security Applications and Claims Index, 1936-2007," s.v. "Ellon Murphy," (birth 20 Oct 1922, death 20 Jul 1993," *Ancestry.com*.
[1518] Per Rita McLean.

Sheila MURPHY (Zenolia SIMMONS MURPHY, Callie Pairee GAMBLE SIMMONS, Agnes Icy GUYTON GAMBLE, Pinkney, Aaron Whitaker, Aaron Steele, Joseph I, John I, Samuel II, Samuel I, John)

Sheila MURPHY was the daughter of Zenolia SIMMONS (b. 9 Dec 1926 Kosciusko, Attala Co., MS, d. 19 Jan 2018 Eau Claire, Berrien Co., MI)[1519] and Ellon MURPHY (b. 20 Oct 1922 Kosciusko, Attala Co., MS, d. 20 Jul 1993 Berrien, Berrien Co., MI).[1520] Sheila was born after the 1950 Census. She married Unknown BROWN. She has three children:[1521]

- i   Zenola ROBINSON-McLEAN.
- ii   Derrick LaDAY.
- iii   Ronnie LaDAY.

Rita MURPHY (Zenolia SIMMONS MURPHY, Callie Pairee GAMBLE SIMMONS, Agnes Icy GUYTON GAMBLE, Pinkney, Aaron Whitaker, Aaron Steele, Joseph I, John I, Samuel II, Samuel I, John)

Rita MURPHY was the daughter of Zenolia SIMMONS (b. 9 Dec 1926 Kosciusko, Attala Co., MS, d. 19 Jan 2018 Eau Claire, Berrien Co., MI)[1522] and Ellon MURPHY (b. 20 Oct 1922 Kosciusko, Attala Co., MS, d. 20 Jul 1993 Berrien, Berrien Co., MI).[1523] Rita was born after the 1950 Census. She married L.C. McLEAN and had two children:[1524]

- i   Aaron McLEAN.
- ii   Levonna McLEAN.

[1519] "U.S., Cemetery and Funeral Home Collection, 1847-Current," digital image s.v. "Zenolia Murphy Murphy," (birth 9 Dec 1926, death 19 Jan 2018), *Ancestry.com*.
[1520] "U.S., Social Security Applications and Claims Index, 1936-2007," s.v. "Ellon Murphy," (birth 20 Oct 1922, death 20 Jul 1993," *Ancestry.com*.
[1521] Per Rita McLean.
[1522] "U.S., Cemetery and Funeral Home Collection, 1847-Current," digital image s.v. "Zenolia Murphy Murphy," (birth 9 Dec 1926, death 19 Jan 2018), *Ancestry.com*.
[1523] "U.S., Social Security Applications and Claims Index, 1936-2007," s.v. "Ellon Murphy," (birth 20 Oct 1922, death 20 Jul 1993," *Ancestry.com*.
[1524] Per Rita McLean.

Felicia MURPHY (Zenolia SIMMONS MURPHY, Callie Pairee GAMBLE SIMMONS, Agnes Icy GUYTON GAMBLE, Pinkney, Aaron Whitaker, Aaron Steele, Joseph I, John I, Samuel II, Samuel I, John)

Felicia MURPHY was the daughter of Zenolia SIMMONS (b. 9 Dec 1926 Kosciusko, Attala Co., MS, d. 19 Jan 2018 Eau Claire, Berrien Co., MI)[1525] and Ellon MURPHY (b. 20 Oct 1922 Kosciusko, Attala Co., MS, d. 20 Jul 1993 Berrien, Berrien Co., MI).[1526] Felicia was born after the 1950 Census. She married Unknown DAVIS. She has two children:

i   Cynthia MURPHY has four children: Jahya MURPHY, Jayden WALKER, Kemari MURPHY, and Kameron MURPHY.
ii   Felicia MURPHY PRYOR has four children: Isaiah PRYOR, Samuel PRYOR, Jeremiah PRYOR, and Nyla RWMANZI.

Larry MURPHY (Zenolia SIMMONS MURPHY, Callie Pairee GAMBLE SIMMONS, Agnes Icy GUYTON GAMBLE, Pinkney, Aaron Whitaker, Aaron Steele, Joseph I, John I, Samuel II, Samuel I, John)

Larry MURPHY was the son of Zenolia SIMMONS (b. 9 Dec 1926 Kosciusko, Attala Co., MS, d. 19 Jan 2018 Eau Claire, Berrien Co., MI)[1527] and Ellon MURPHY (b. 20 Oct 1922 Kosciusko, Attala Co., MS, d. 20 Jul 1993 Berrien, Berrien Co., MI).[1528] Larry MURPHY was born after the 1950 Census. He has three children:[1529]

i   Shakira MURPHY had at least two children: Javari UNKNOWN and Zafina UNKNOWN.
ii   Zavieria MURPHY.
iii   Nurso MURPHY.

[1525] "U.S., Cemetery and Funeral Home Collection, 1847-Current," digital image s.v. "Zenolia Murphy Murphy," (birth 9 Dec 1926, death 19 Jan 2018), *Ancestry.com*.
[1526] "U.S., Social Security Applications and Claims Index, 1936-2007," s.v. "Ellon Murphy," (birth 20 Oct 1922, death 20 Jul 1993," *Ancestry.com*.
[1527] "U.S., Cemetery and Funeral Home Collection, 1847-Current," digital image s.v. "Zenolia Murphy Murphy," (birth 9 Dec 1926, death 19 Jan 2018), *Ancestry.com*.
[1528] "U.S., Social Security Applications and Claims Index, 1936-2007," s.v. "Ellon Murphy," (birth 20 Oct 1922, death 20 Jul 1993," *Ancestry.com*.
[1529] Per Rita McLean.

Vincent MURPHY (Zenolia SIMMONS MURPHY, Callie Pairee GAMBLE SIMMONS, Agnes Icy GUYTON GAMBLE, Pinkney, Aaron Whitaker, Aaron Steele, Joseph I, John I, Samuel II, Samuel I, John)

Vincent MURPHY was the son of Zenolia SIMMONS (b. 9 Dec 1926 Kosciusko, Attala Co., MS, d. 19 Jan 2018 Eau Claire, Berrien Co., MI)[1530] and Ellon MURPHY (b. 20 Oct 1922 Kosciusko, Attala Co., MS, d. 20 Jul 1993 Berrien, Berrien Co., MI).[1531]

Vincent was born after the 1950 Census. He has three children:[1532]

i	Bryce MURPHY.	
ii	Chase MURPHY.	
iii	Trey MURPHY.	

Curtis MURPHY (Zenolia SIMMONS MURPHY, Callie Pairee GAMBLE SIMMONS, Agnes Icy GUYTON GAMBLE, Pinkney, Aaron Whitaker, Aaron Steele, Joseph I, John I, Samuel II, Samuel I, John)

Curtis MURPHY was the son of Zenolia SIMMONS (b. 9 Dec 1926 Kosciusko, Attala Co., MS, d. 19 Jan 2018 Eau Claire, Berrien Co., MI)[1533] and Ellon MURPHY (b. 20 Oct 1922 Kosciusko, Attala Co., MS, d. 20 Jul 1993 Berrien, Berrien Co., MI).[1534]

Curtis MURPHY was born after the 1950 Census, lives in Ghana, Africa, and has one son:

i Ahmad MURPHY, Sr. m. Krystal UNKNOWN and has two children: Ahmad MURPHY, Jr. and Ahmora MURPHY.

[1530] "U.S., Cemetery and Funeral Home Collection, 1847-Current," digital image s.v. "Zenolia Murphy Murphy," (birth 9 Dec 1926, death 19 Jan 2018), *Ancestry.com*.
[1531] "U.S., Social Security Applications and Claims Index, 1936-2007," s.v. "Ellon Murphy," (birth 20 Oct 1922, death 20 Jul 1993," *Ancestry.com*.
[1532] Per Rita McLean.
[1533] "U.S., Cemetery and Funeral Home Collection, 1847-Current," digital image s.v. "Zenolia Murphy Murphy," (birth 9 Dec 1926, death 19 Jan 2018), *Ancestry.com*.
[1534] "U.S., Social Security Applications and Claims Index, 1936-2007," s.v. "Ellon Murphy," (birth 20 Oct 1922, death 20 Jul 1993," *Ancestry.com*.

Karl Glenn BOYD (Icy Viola NASH BOYD, Lovie GAMBLE NASH PARKER, Agnes Icy GUYTON GAMBLE, Pinkney, Aaron Whitaker, Aaron Steele, Joseph I, John I, Samuel II, Samuel I, John)

Karl Glenn BOYD (AKA Nykki Lamarr STARR) is the son of Icy Viola NASH (b. 16 OCT 1935 Kosciusko, Attala Co., MS, 14 Oct 2009 in Naperville, DuPage Co., IL)[1535] and Thornton BOYD, Sr. (b. 5 Oct 1935, d. 1 Feb 2008).[1536] Karl (Nic) was born on 18 May 1959 in Chicago, Cook Co., IL, d. Living) m. (1) Cherry HILL (b. ABT 1958 Chicago, Cook Co., IL, d. Living) div., (2) Rosalind Lavon NORVELL (b. 6 Jan 1965 Temple, Bell Co., TX, d. Living) div., (3) partner Cynthia WILEY (b. Augusta, Richmond Co., GA, d. Living), (4) friend Dora Luzetta YOUNG (b. 17 Dec 1968 Philadelphia, Neshoba Co., MS, d. 11 Jun 2019 Philadelphia, Neshoba Co., MS, and (5) spouse Princess Monica WRIGHT (b. ABT 1959 Salisbury, MD, d. Living). See Figure 232, Figure 233, Figure 234, and Figure 235.

Figure 232 Karl BOYD as a Child[1537]

Figure 233 Karl BOYD in Classic Rock[1538]

Figure 234 Karl BOYD in the Army[1539]

Figure 235 Karl BOYD AKA Nykki Lamarr STARR About 2021[1540]

Karl is the owner of Young Voices United in Marietta, Cobb Co., GA. Its purpose is:[1541]

Young Voices United Performing Arts School (YVU) is a 501(c)(3) non-profit organization that is recognized as a provider of opportunities for the voices of our youth to be heard through the performing arts. YVU strives to be seen at the forefront of motivating our youth to be positive and successful members of society. Members of Young Voices United

---

[1535] "Icy Viola Nash," grave marker, Forest Home Cemetery, Forest Park, Cook Co., IL, digital image s.v. "Icy V Boyd," (birth 16 Oct 1935, death 14 Oct 2009), *FindaGrave.com*.
[1536] "U.S., Social Security Death Index, 1935-2014," s.v. "Thornton Boyd," (birth 5 Oct 1935, death 1 Feb 2008), *Ancestry.com*. "Cook County, Illinois Marriage Index, 1930-1960," s.v. "Icy Nash," (marriage to Thornton Boyd on 4 Mar 1960).
[1537] Karl Boyd originally shared this on 30 May 2022 on *Ancestry.com*.
[1538] Karl Boyd originally shared this on 30 May 2022 on *Ancestry.com*.
[1539] Karl Boyd originally shared this on 30 May 2022 on *Ancestry.com*. He writes, "Joined the military by bluffing Mom. Well, that didn't work out as I planned it!"
[1540] Karl Boyd originally shared this on 22 Dec 2021 on *Ancestry.com*.
[1541] *Young Voices United*, <https://www.youngvoicesunited.net/about>.

today will become positIve leaders and role modes in society tomorrow. We provide valued added classes in theatre, dance and vocal instruction. Our instructors are certified in each of their respectIve disciplines and our classes our modestly priced to serve the community of talented youth and adults who find it financially challenging to afford quality instruction. We are also one of two privately held institutions who hold a charter for the International Thespian Society, an honor society for performing artists. Young Voices United provides a caring family-oriented learning environment. Our students are national winners and phenomenal performers. Come join a place where we are making a positIve difference in the lives of our youth, that they might make a difference in the world...

Karl Glenn BOYD (Nykki Lamarr STARR) is the Artistic Director. "N.L. Starr is a performing artist, writer, director and producer, who constantly looks to the hills because he knows that's where his help comes from. Nic has graced the Atlanta stages with varying ranges of characters from those of the prolific playwright, August Wilson, to Charles Dickens' A Christmas Carol. You may have seen Nic on Survivor's Remorse, or The Banker. He is currently in production with the second season of Cherish the Day." His wife, Princess STARR, is the Managing Director. "Princess is an experienced and trained vocal coach and actor. She received her BA from Spelman College and her MFA from Barry UnIversity."

His children are:

i Karmeisha Kashaun BOYD (b. 17 Mar 1980 Bremen, Germany, d. Living) with Cherry HILL. See Figure 236.
ii Nykkiesha Lavon STARR (b. 17 Jul 1988 Bell Co., TX, d. Living) with Rosalind Lavon NORVELL. She is married to Nestor VERA (b. 11 Dec 1985 Venezuela, d. Living) and they have one child: Nikai Enrique STARR-VERA (b. 6 Jan 2020 Houston, Harris Co., TX, d. Living). See Figure 237.
iii Tayla Lashae STARR (b. 28 Jul 1995 Augusta, Richmond Co., Georgia, d. Living) with Cynthia WILEY. See Figure 238.
iv Nykki LaMarr STARR, Jr. (b. 26 Feb 1999 Meridian, Lauderdale Co., MS, d. Living) with Dora Luzetta YOUNG. See Figure 239.

Figure 236 Karmeisha Kashaun BOYD[1542]

Figure 237 Nykkiesha Lavon STARR[1543]

Figure 238 Tayla Lashae STARR[1544]

Figure 239 Nykki LaMarr STARR, Jr. [1545]

[1542] Karl Boyd originally shared this on 22 Oct 2020 on *Ancestry.com*.
[1543] Karl Boyd originally shared this on 22 Oct 2020 on *Ancestry.com*.
[1544] Karl Boyd originally shared this on 27 Dec 2021 on *Ancestry.com*.
[1545] Karl Boyd originally shared this on 27 Dec 2021 on *Ancestry.com*.

Felicia Cabrini BOYD (Icy Viola NASH BOYD, Lovie GAMBLE NASH PARKER, Agnes Icy GUYTON GAMBLE, Pinkney, Aaron Whitaker, Aaron Steele, Joseph I, John I, Samuel II, Samuel I, John)

Felicia Cabrini BOYD is the daughter of Icy Viola NASH (b. 16 Oct 1935 Kosciusko, Attala Co., MS, 14 Oct 2009 in Naperville, DuPage Co., IL[1546] and Thornton BOYD, Sr. (b. 5 Oct 1935, d. 1 Feb 2008).[1547] She was born in Aug 1960 in Chicago, Cook Co., IL, d. Living).[1548] She married Michael Terence MORAGHAN on 14 Feb 2000 in Albemarle Co., VA[1549] and divorced on 5 Aug 2005 in Augusta Co., VA.[1550] Felicia was a champion body builder, per her brother, Karl Glenn BOYD (Nykkie Lamarr STARR). She has acted as a Tina Turner impersonator for years. See Figure 240 and Figure 241.

Figure 240 Icy Felecia Cabrini BOYD Younger[1551]

Figure 241 Icy Felicia Cabrini BOYD Mature[1552]

Carmelita Sabrina BOYD (Icy Viola NASH BOYD, Lovie GAMBLE NASH PARKER, Agnes Icy GUYTON GAMBLE, Pinkney, Aaron Whitaker, Aaron Steele, Joseph I, John I, Samuel II, Samuel I, John)

Carmelita Sabrina BOYD is the daughter of Icy Viola NASH (b. 16 Oct 1935 Kosciusko, Attala Co., MS, 14 Oct 2009 in Naperville, DuPage Co., IL[1553] and Thornton BOYD, Sr. (b. 5 Oct 1935, d. 1 Feb 2008).[1554] Per her brother, Karl Glenn BOYD (AKA Nykki Lamarr STARR), Carmelita was born in Mar 1962 in Chicago,

---

[1546] "Icy Viola Nash," grave marker, Forest Home Cemetery, Forest Park, Cook Co., IL, digital image s.v. "Icy V Boyd," (birth 16 Oct 1935, death 14 Oct 2009), *FindaGrave.com*.

[1547] "U.S., Social Security Death Index, 1935-2014," s.v. "Thornton Boyd," (birth 5 Oct 1935, death 1 Feb 2008), *Ancestry.com*. "Cook County, Illinois Marriage Index, 1930-1960," s.v. "Icy Nash," (marriage to Thorton Boyd on 4 Mar 1960).

[1548] "U.S., Index to Public Records, 1994-2019," s.v. "Felicia Cabrini Boyd," (birth Aug 1960), *Ancestry.com*.

[1549] "Virginia, Marriage Records, 1936-2014," s.v. "Felecia Cabrini Boyd," (marriage 14 Feb 2000 to Michael Terence Moraghan), *Ancestry.com*.

[1550] "Virginia, U.S., Divorce Records, 1918-2014," s.v. "Felecia Moraghan," (divorce 5 Aug 2005), *Ancestry.com*.

[1551] "U.S., School Yearbooks, 1880-2012 Proviso East High School 1978," digital image s.v. "Felecia Boyd," *Ancestry.com*.

[1552] Karl Boyd originally shared this on 26 Mar 2021 on *Ancestry.com*.

[1553] "Icy Viola Nash," grave marker, Forest Home Cemetery, Forest Park, Cook Co., IL, digital image s.v. "Icy V Boyd," (birth 16 Oct 1935, death 14 Oct 2009), *FindaGrave.com*.

[1554] "U.S., Social Security Death Index, 1935-2014," s.v. "Thornton Boyd," (birth 5 Oct 1935, death 1 Feb 2008), *Ancestry.com*. "Cook County, Illinois Marriage Index, 1930-1960," s.v. "Icy Nash," (marriage to Thorton Boyd on 4 Mar 1960).

Cook Co., IL, d. Living).[1555] See Figure 242. She married (1) Craig OUSLEY (Unknown), (2) Kevin (Kippie) CAMPBELL (Unknown), (3) LeCurtis JOHNSON (Unknown). She has two children:

i   Jonte CAMPBELL, Sr. (b. 10 Mar 1980 Chicago, Cook Co., IL, d. Living) with Kevin (Kippie) CAMPBELL. Jonte is married to Ericka (b. 18 Oct 1986, d. Living) and has four children: James CAMPBELL, Ja'Niyah CAMPBELL, Jaida CAMPBELL, and Jonte CAMPBELL, Jr. See Figure 243.

ii   LaMar JOHNSON, Sr. (b. 5 Apr 1992, d. Living) with LeCurtis JOHNSON. He is married to Jessica McCLELLAN and has two children: LaMar JOHNSON, Jr. and LaMonte JOHNSON. See Figure 244.

Figure 242 Carmelita Sabrina STARR[1]

Figure 243 Jonte CAMPBELL[1]

Figure 244 LaMar JOHNSON[1]

Karl Glenn BOYD (aka Nykki Lamarr STARR) writes about his sister, Carmelita Sabrina BOYD:

    She was born March 31, 1962, in Chicago. She was our family's middle child, but middle child syndrome didn't quite sit well with her... she was, and still is, a force to be reckoned with! I have fought, it seems, all my life, but have never had an opponent who fought a harder battle than my sister, Carmelita, and truth be told, most of our battles - SHE WON! I'm not talking about physical battles, I'm talking mental, or psychological warfare. I later figured out, while I was playing checkers, Carmelita was playing Chess! Despite it all, she maintained a fierce loyalty to the family. What I love about her the most is her heart! She is the most loving and nurturing person I know. I truly admire her love and dedication to our parents, especially our dad. When he could no longer do for himself, she stepped in and took that task on herself... even now, she is the caretaker for our Uncle Sammy. I can't help but believe that there is a special place in Heaven for my Little Sister... I love you, Rabbit!

Her sister, Rhonda Larita BOYD, wrote:

My Carmie! What can I say other than the enemy has tried and at times was successful in separating us for WHATEVER reason! I'm GRATEFUL for recognizing what was happening

---

[1555] "U.S., Index to Public Records, 1994-2019," s.v. "Carmelita S Campbell," (born Mar 1962), Ancestry.com.

and making a decision NOT to allow distractions to change my heart! I've Loved You UNCONDITIONALLY and ALWAYS WILL. ~ Thank You for Your unselfish Love! Rhonda

Carmelita writes of herself:

My favorite thing to do for fun is traveling (it's personable). I love meeting new people from all over the world and I really get excited when I see that I can navigate a foreign country without a guide. Traveling helps me to understand ME better and put me in a great mental health space. Traveling boosts my self-awareness and problem-solving skills and improves my communication skills. Traveling has also afforded me the opportunity to experience some life-changing events (i.e. snorkeling, RV driving, mechanical bullriding, ziplining, skydiving, riding horses on the beach, parasailing and cave climbing). My favorite thing to learn while traveling is how other cultures live — especially what they eat ☺….. while traveling, everything/everywhere is new to me and that is exciting. I also love to hear the different languages spoken. Traveling helps me to not take life so seriously, puts me in a healthy comfortable state, and I am always happy to return home.

When I grow up, I want to be…ME!!!!! I LOVE being me ☺. I am a Mom to two (2) men who view me as their "No-Matter-What-Woman" – they actually think I can run the world. I am a Grumma to 5 extraordinary children and I have 2 bonus babes that keep me fascinated/growing/wondering and in awe. Through mishaps and missteps, I have learned the value and worth of having healthy friends, family, work ethics and the importance of life balance—I have learned that I can do anything as long as I keep (Him) in the equation. My best friend is Janice Henderson. We were friends for about 5 years, and we would always call each other Besties—then about nine years ago, we were at a house-party and we took a "know your best-friend" test. There were 20 questions---she got 18 answers correct and I got 16 answers correct-- ☺ she oozes integrity, dependability, honesty and care/concern — I love her!

Rhonda Larita BOYD (Icy Viola NASH BOYD, Lovie GAMBLE NASH PARKER, Agnes Icy GUYTON GAMBLE, Pinkney, Aaron Whitaker, Aaron Steele, Joseph I, John I, Samuel II, Samuel I, John)

Rhonda Larita BOYD is the daughter of Icy Viola NASH (b. 16 Oct 1935 Kosciusko, Attala Co., MS, 14 Oct 2009 in Naperville, DuPage Co., IL[1556] and Thornton BOYD, Sr. (b. 5 Oct 1935, d. 1 Feb 2008).[1557] Per her brother, Karl Glenn BOYD (AKA Nykki Lamarr STARR), Rhonda was born in Aug 1963 in Chicago, Cook Co., IL, and is living. See Figure 245. Rhonda married (1) Richard BALL (b. ABT 1965 Chicago, Cook Co., IL,

---

[1556] "Icy Viola Nash," grave marker, Forest Home Cemetery, Forest Park, Cook Co., IL, digital image s.v. "Icy V Boyd," (birth 16 Oct 1935, death 14 Oct 2009), *FindaGrave.com*.
[1557] "U.S., Social Security Death Index, 1935-2014," s.v. "Thornton Boyd," (birth 5 Oct 1935, death 1 Feb 2008), *Ancestry.com*. "Cook County, Illinois Marriage Index, 1930-1960," s.v. "Icy Nash," (marriage to Thorton Boyd on 4 Mar 1960).

d. Living), (2) Jeffrey Wayne BUCHANAN (b. ABT 1953 Chicago, Cook Co., IL, d. Living), (3) Ronald SHAW (b. ABT 1962, d. Living), (4) Michael TURNER (b. ABT 1960 Chicago, Cook Co., IL, d. Living).

Her children are as follows:

i   Kenyon J. BOYD (b. 18 Sep 1982 Maywood, Cook Co., IL, d. Living) with Jeffrey Wayne BUCHANAN. See Figure 246. Kenyon has two children: KaDen BOYD with Bria FELLOWS and Kamiyah BOYD with Latonya Y. HEMINGWAY.

ii   Lakeisha BOYD (b. 16 Jan 1979, d. Living) with Ronald SHAW. See Figure 247. Lakeisha has two children: Chyna HOLLINS with Robert HOLLINS and Amiri Naomi SELTZER with Charles SELTZER.

iii   Lakia Icy BOYD (b. 14 Nov 1985, d. Living) with Michael TURNER. See Figure 248. Lakia has two children: Ariana Lovie Viola WILLIAMS with Travis CORTEZ and Triniti Belle CHAIRES with Al Damontae CHAIRES.

Figure 245 Rhonda Larita BOYD[1558]

Figure 246 Kenyon BOYD[1559]

Figure 247 Lakeisha BOYD[1560]

Figure 248 Lakia Icy BOYD[1561]

[1558] Karl Boyd originally shared this on 27 Nov 2021 on *Ancestry.com*.
[1559] Karl Boyd originally shared this on 29 Oct 2021 on *Ancestry.com*.
[1560] Karl Boyd originally shared this on 27 Nov 2021 on *Ancestry.com*.
[1561] Karl Boyd originally shared this on 29 Oct 2021 on *Ancestry.com*.

Thornton BOYD, Jr. (Icy Viola NASH BOYD, Lovie GAMBLE NASH PARKER, Agnes Icy GUYTON GAMBLE, Pinkney, Aaron Whitaker, Aaron Steele, Joseph I, John I, Samuel II, Samuel I, John)

Thornton BOYD, Jr. aka Rikki STARR is the son of Icy Viola NASH (b. 16 Oct 1935 Kosciusko, Attala Co., MS, 14 Oct 2009 in Naperville, DuPage Co., IL[1562] and Thornton BOYD, Sr. (b. 5 Oct 1935, d. 1 Feb 2008).[1563] Thornton BOYD, Jr. (aka Rikki STARR) was born in Feb 1968 in Chicago, Cook Co., IL, and is living).[1564] See Figure 249**Error! Reference source not found.**.. He married (1) spouse Tabatha PETERSON (b. 18 Feb 1967 Chicago, Cook Co., IL, d. 21 Mar 2017 Allen, Collin Co., TX), (2) friend Oneko WHITE (b. ABT Mar 1971, d. Living), (3) spouse Cherylease M. PRATT (b. 20 Jul 1973, d. Living), (4) spouse Marcy L. RHONE (b. ABT 1973, d. Living), (5) spouse LaTonya Cheri SANDERS (b. 11 Feb 1972, d. Living), (6) spouse Tonya GREENE (Living), (7) partner Sarah CHOI (Living), (8) spouse Tracy GLOVER (Living), and (9) spouse Khankham (Candy) PHOMMAVONG (Living). He was adopted by his older brother, Karl Glenn BOYD (aka Nykki Lamarr STARR).

His children per his brother, Karl Glenn BOYD (aka Nykki Lamarr STARR), are as follows:

i   Tiana PETERSON (b. 8 Mar 1984 Chicago, Cook Co., IL, d. Living) with Tabatha PETERSON. See Figure 250. Tiana has two children: NiUnna PETERSON and Amar BOOKER.
ii   Shaina WHITE (b. 18 Apr 1991, d. Living) with Oneko WHITE. See Figure 251. She has one son: Aiden Lee WHITE.
iii   Riki STARR (male) (b. 2 Apr 1993, d. Living) with Cherylease M. PRATT. See Figure 252.
iv   Denzel RHONE (b. 27 Apr 1993, d. Living) with Marcy L. RHONE. See Figure 253. He is married to Chelsea RHONE and has three children: Nyla RHONE, Kareem RHONE, and Naima RHONE.
v   Amari Monét STARR (b. 4 Nov 1994, d. Living) with LaTonya Cheri SANDERS. See Figure 254. She is married to Ronnie THOMAS and has two children: Liliana Janae STARR and Amavi STARR-THOMAS.
vi   Kedary STARR (b. ABT 1995, d. Living) with Tonya GREENE. See Figure 255.
vii   Victoria Isabella CHOI (b. ABT 1996, d. Living) with Sarah CHOI. See Figure 256.
viii   Nia STARR (b. ABT 1998, d. Living) with Tracy GLOVER. See Figure 257.
ix   Aaliyah Icy STARR (b. ABT 2011, d. Living) with Khankham (Candy) PHOMMAVONG. See Figure 258.

[1562] "Icy Viola Nash," grave marker, Forest Home Cemetery, Forest Park, Cook Co., IL, digital image s.v. "Icy V Boyd," (birth 16 Oct 1935, death 14 Oct 2009), *FindaGrave.com*.
[1563] "U.S., Social Security Death Index, 1935-2014," s.v. "Thornton Boyd," (birth 5 Oct 1935, death 1 Feb 2008), *Ancestry.com*. "Cook County, Illinois Marriage Index, 1930-1960," s.v. "Icy Nash," (marriage to Thorton Boyd on 4 Mar 1960).
[1564] "U.S., Public Records Index, 1950-1993, Volume 1," s.v. "Rikki T Starr," (birth Feb 1968), *Ancestry.com*.

Figure 249 Thornton BOYD, Jr. aka Rikki STARR[1565]

Figure 250 Tiana PETERSON[1566]

Figure 251 Shaina WHITE[1567]

Figure 252 Riki STARR[1568]

Figure 253 Denzel RHONE[1569]

Figure 254 Amari Monet STARR[1570]

Figure 255 Kedary STARR[1571]

Figure 256 Victoria Isabella CHOI[1572]

Figure 257 Nia STARR[1573]

Figure 258 Aaliyah Icy STARR[1574]

[1565] Karl Boyd originally shared this on 23 Oct 2020 on *Ancestry.com*.
[1566] Karl Boyd originally shared this on 29 Nov 2021 on *Ancestry.com*.
[1567] Karl Boyd originally shared this on 29 Nov 2021 on *Ancestry.com*.
[1568] Karl Boyd originally shared this on 29 Nov 2021 on *Ancestry.com*.
[1569] Karl Boyd originally shared this on 29 Nov 2021 on *Ancestry.com*.
[1570] Karl Boyd originally shared this on 29 Nov 2021 on *Ancestry.com*.
[1571] Karl Boyd originally shared this on 26 Jul 2023 on *Ancestry.com*.
[1572] Karl Boyd originally shared this on 26 Jul 2023 on *Ancestry.com*.
[1573] Karl Boyd originally shared this on 26 Jul 2023 on *Ancestry.com*.
[1574] Karl Boyd originally shared this on 29 Nov 2021 on *Ancestry.com*.

Karl Glenn BOYD (aka Nykki Lamarr STARR) wrote the following about his brother:

    Rikki Thornton Boyd was born on February 15, 1968, in Chicago, Illinois. From birth, Lil' Brother was given nicknames. He was never called Thornton or Junior, he was called Box, and later, for various reasons, this morphed into Bam Bam, after the character from the Flintstones. This eventually turned to Bam, which is what most of the family still call him today. Of the Sibs, I'd say Bam was the one who had what I called "IT." This was something my father had, that I didn't understand till later. He had a hardness inside that he could turn off and on when he needed it. If you're straight with him, he's straight with you, but don't cross him. It would cost you. They never had to demand respect... they commanded it in the way that they carried themselves. Till this day, it wouldn't surprise me if my sisters felt like they had two big brothers. He handles his business unapologetically. He is a true Ride or Die... if you are good with him, you're good. He'll give you the shirt off his back, you call and he's there, no questions. If you're not, he simply doesn't bother with you, and your best bet is not to bother him. I have a lot of respect for my Lil' Brother, because it was him that came back to Chicago and positioned himself to buy a house and make a home for our mother. It was good to see her happy and secure, and with Bam, we didn't have to worry about her. Bam is a self-made Man, living by his own rules, his own code. A man with many talents, who could have done anything he wanted. He was an actor and a great musician. As a teen, he performed with me in different rock bands. It was great sharing the stage with him, probably my best experiences on stage. However, I wasn't on stage with him when he was performing in Vegas, and Prince came on stage and asked his guitarist if he could sit in! Yes, he once played with the Purple One... Prince! Like my father, my brother Bam is a self-made man, who has spent his life living by his own rules and being misunderstood. And when it's time to go to battle, I don't trust or want anyone else at my back! We've got us... Nic

Belynda MOORE [Lena Mae PARKER MOORE, Lovie GAMBLE NASH PARKER, Agnes Icy GUYTON GAMBLE, Pinkney, Aaron Whitaker, Aaron Steele, Joseph I, John I, Samuel II, Samuel I, John]

Belynda MOORE is the daughter of Lena Mae PARKER (b. ABT 1939 MS and her death, if it occurred, is unknown)[1575] and Herbert MOORE (b. 22 Jan 1932 Chicago, Cook Co., IL, d. 28 Oct 2001 Bellwood, Cook Co., IL).[1576] Belynda was born on 2 May 1959 Chicago, Cook Co., IL, d. Living).[1577] She married (1) Unknown LAMBERT and (2) Jethro Alexander HEAD (b. 10 Dec 1953, d. Living)[1578] on 31 Dec 1983 in Clark Co., NV.[1579] See Figure 259 for a photo of Belynda MOORE HEAD.

Figure 259 Beylynda MOORE HEAD

[1575] "1940 United States Federal Census," Holmes Co., MS, digital image s.v. "Lena M Parker," (birth abt 1939), *Ancestry.com*.
[1576] Per Karl Boyd, nephew to Lena Mae Parker, on his *Ancestry.com* tree.
[1577] "U.S., Public Records Index, 1950-1993, Volume 1," s.v. "Belynda Nmi Head," (birth 2 May 1959), *Ancestry.com*.
[1578] "U.S., Public Records Index, 1950-1993, Volume 1," s.v. "Jethro A Head," (birth 10 Dec 1953), *Ancestry.com*.
[1579] "Nevada, Marriage Index, 1956-2005," s.v. "Jethro A Head," (marriage 31 Dec 1983, recorded 5 Jan 1984 to Belynda Moore), *Ancestry.com*.

Cheryl Penny PARKER (Ilander PARKER, Jr., Lovie GAMBLE NASH PARKER, Agnes Icy GUYTON GAMBLE, Pinkney, Aaron Whitaker, Aaron Steele, Joseph I, John I, Samuel II, Samuel I, John)

Cheryl Penny PARKER is the daughter of Ilander PARKER, Jr. (b. 24 Aug 1941 Cruger, Holmes Co., Holmes Co., MS, d. 24 Oct 2005 Chicago, Cook Co., IL)[1580] and Katherine UNKNOWN (b. Jul 1942).[1581] Cheryl was born on 13 Aug 1963 and is living.[1582] See Figure 260. She married (1) Jerry BOONE (Unknown) (see Figure 261) and had one son, Kyler BOONE (b. Oct 1987, d. Living) (see Figure 262) and (2) Eric PARKER (b. 10 May Unknown) (see Figure 263) and they had one son, Ryan PARKER (b. Oct 2002, d. Living) (see Figure 264).

Figure 260 Cheryl Penny PARKER[1583]

Figure 261 Jerry BOONE[1584]

Figure 262 Kyler BOONE[1585]

Figure 263 Eric PARKER[1586]

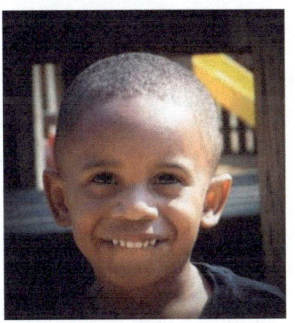

Figure 264 Ryan PARKER[1587]

[1580] "U.S., Social Security Death Index, 1935-2014," s.v. "Ilander Parker," (birth 24 Aug 1941, death 24 Oct 2005), *FindaGrave.com*.
[1581] Per Karl Boyd's tree on *Ancestry.com*. He was nephew of Ilander Parker, Jr.
[1582] "U.S. Public Records Index, 1950-1993, Volume 1," s.v. "Cheryl Parker Boone," (birth 13 Aug 1963), *Ancestry.com*.
[1583] Karl Boyd originally shared this on 21 Nov 2021 on *Ancestry.com*.
[1584] Karl Boyd originally shared this on 31 Jul 2023 on *Ancestry.com*.
[1585] Karl Boyd originally shared this on 31 Jul 2023 on Ancestry.com.
[1586] Karl Boyd originally shared this on 31 Jul 2023 on Ancestry.com.
[1587] Karl Boyd originally shared this on 31 Jul 2023 on Ancestry.com.

Chris PARKER (Ilander PARKER, Jr., Lovie GAMBLE NASH PARKER, Agnes Icy GUYTON GAMBLE, Pinkney, Aaron Whitaker, Aaron Steele, Joseph I, John I, Samuel II, Samuel I, John)

Chris PARKER is the son of Ilander PARKER, Jr. (b. 24 Aug 1941 Cruger, Holmes Co., MS, d. 24 Oct 2005 Chicago, Cook Co., IL)[1588] and Katherine UNKNOWN (b. Jul 1942).[1589] Chris was born in July 1964 and is living.[1590] See Figure 265. He married Yvette UNKNOWN (see Figure 266). They had one daughter, Charnelle PARKER. See Figure 267.

Figure 265 Chris PARKER[1591]

Figure 266 Yvette UNKNOWN PARKER[1592]

Figure 267 Charnelle PARKER[1593]

Sandy D. PARKER (Ilander PARKER, Jr., Lovie GAMBLE NASH PARKER, Agnes Icy GUYTON GAMBLE, Pinkney, Aaron Whitaker, Aaron Steele, Joseph I, John I, Samuel II, Samuel I, John)

Sandy D. PARKER is the daughter of Ilander PARKER, Jr. (b. 24 Aug 1941 Cruger, Holmes Co., MS, d. 24 Oct 2005 Chicago, Cook Co., IL)[1594] and Katherine UNKNOWN (b. Jul 1942).[1595] Sandy D. PARKER was born on 11 Mar 1966 and is living.[1596] See Figure 268. She married Isaac L. DUNSON (b. 23 Aug 1960).[1597] Her daughter, Britteny L. DUNSON (see Figure 269) was born in Feb 1988 and is living.[1598] Britteny married Raul SOTO (b. Unknown, d. Living).

[1588] "U.S., Social Security Death Index, 1935-2014," s.v. "Ilander Parker," (birth 24 Aug 1941, death 24 Oct 2005), *FindaGrave.com*.
[1589] Per Karl Boyd's tree on *Ancestry.com*. He was nephew of Ilander Parker, Jr.
[1590] The family information comes from Karl Boyd.
[1591] Karl Boyd originally shared this on 21 Nov 2021 on Ancestry.com.
[1592] Karl Boyd originally shared this on 31 Jul 2023 on Ancestry.com.
[1593] Karl Boyd originally shared this on 31 Jul 2023 on Ancestry.com.
[1594] "U.S., Social Security Death Index, 1935-2014," s.v. "Ilander Parker," (birth 24 Aug 1941, death 24 Oct 2005), *FindaGrave.com*.
[1595] Per Karl Boyd's tree on *Ancestry.com*. He was nephew of Ilander Parker, Jr.
[1596] "U.S. Public Records Index, 1950-1993, Volume 2," s.v. "Sandy D Dunson," (birth 11 Mar 1966), *Ancestry.com*.
[1597] "U.S. Public Records Index, 1950-1993, Volume 1," s.v. "Isaac L. Dunson," (birth 23 Aug 1960), *Ancestry.com*.
[1598] "U.S., Index to Public Records, 1994-2019," s.v. "Britteny L Dunson," (birth Feb 1988), *Ancestry.com*.

Figure 268 Sandy D. PARKER[1599]

Figure 269 Britteny L. DUNSON[1600]

Tera M. PARKER (Ilander PARKER, Jr., Lovie GAMBLE NASH PARKER, Agnes Icy GUYTON GAMBLE, Pinkney, Aaron Whitaker, Aaron Steele, Joseph I, John I, Samuel II, Samuel I, John)

Tera M. PARKER is the daughter of Ilander PARKER, Jr. (b. 24 Aug 1941 Cruger, Holmes Co., MS, d. 24 Oct 2005 Chicago, Cook Co., IL)[1601] and Katherine UNKNOWN (b. Jul 1942).[1602] Tera was born on 23 Apr 1967 and is living.[1603] See Figure 270. She married Steven S. MORRIS, Sr. (b. 11 Aug 1967, d. Living).[1604] See Figure 271. They had one son: Steven S. MORRIS, Jr. (b. 2 Jun 1997, d. Living). See Figure 272.

Figure 270 Tera M. PARKER[1605]

Figure 271 Steven S. MORRIS, Sr.[1606]

Figure 272 Steven S. MORRIS, Jr.[1607]

[1599] Karl Boyd originally shared this on 31 Jul 2023 on *Ancestry.com*.
[1600] Karl Boyd originally shared this on 31 Jul 2023 on *Ancestry.com*.
[1601] "U.S., Social Security Death Index, 1935-2014," s.v. "Ilander Parker," (birth 24 Aug 1941, death 24 Oct 2005), *FindaGrave.com*.
[1602] Per Karl Boyd's tree on *Ancestry.com*. He was nephew of Ilander Parker, Jr.
[1603] "U.S., Public Records Index, 1950-1993, Volume 2," s.v. "Tera M Parker-Morris," (birth 23 Apr 1967), *Ancestry.com*.
[1604] "U.S. Public Records Index, 1950-1993, Volume 1," s.v. "Steven S Morris," (birth 11 Aug 1967), *Ancestry.com*.
[1605] Karl Boyd originally shared this on 21 Nov 2021 on *Ancestry.com*.
[1606] Karl Boyd originally shared this on 1 Aug 2023 on *Ancestry.com*.
[1607] Karl Boyd originally shared this on 21 Nov 2021 on *Ancestry.com*.

Ollander (Odie) PARKER (Ilander PARKER, Jr., Lovie GAMBLE NASH PARKER, Agnes Icy GUYTON GAMBLE, Pinkney, Aaron Whitaker, Aaron Steele, Joseph I, John I, Samuel II, Samuel I, John)

Ollander (Odie) PARKER is the son of Ilander PARKER, Jr. (b. 24 Aug 1941 Cruger, Holmes Co., MS, d. 24 Oct 2005 Chicago, Cook Co., IL)[1608] and Katherine UNKNOWN (b. Jul 1942).[1609] Odie was born on 19 Jan 1971 and is living.[1610] See Figure 273. He married Lishon SEALS (b. Feb 1971, d. Living).[1611] See Figure 274. They have three children, per Karl Glenn BOYD (Nykki Lamarr STARR).

i   Nakai PARKER (male) (b. Unknown, d. Living).
ii   Nylah PARKER (female) (b. Unknown, d. Living).
iii Micah PARKER (male) (b. Unknown, d. Living).

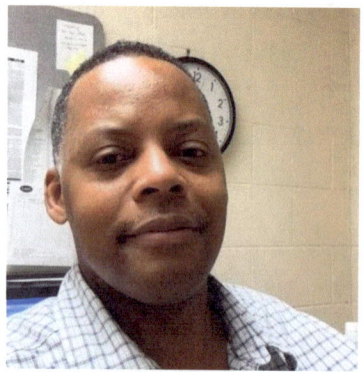

Figure 273 Ollander (Odie) PARKER[1612]

Figure 274 High School Photo of Lishon SEALS[1613]

[1608] "U.S., Social Security Death Index, 1935-2014," s.v. "Ilander Parker," (birth 24 Aug 1941, death 24 Oct 2005), *FindaGrave.com*.
[1609] Per Karl Boyd's tree on *Ancestry.com*. He was nephew of Ilander Parker, Jr.
[1610] "U.S., Public Records Index, 1950-1993, Volume 2," s.v. "Ollander Parker," (birth 19 Jan 1971), *Ancestry.com*.
[1611] "U.S., Index to Public Records, 1994-2019," s.v. "Lishon Seals," (birth Feb 1971), *Ancestry.com*.
[1612] Karl Boyd originally shared this on 21 Nov 2021 on *Ancestry.com*.
[1613] "U.S. School Yearbooks," digital image s.v. "Lishon Seals," (birth abt 1970, Sullivan High School, Chicago, Cook Co., IL), *Ancestry.com*.

LaTarshe (Toddy) PARKER (Ilander PARKER, Jr., Lovie GAMBLE NASH PARKER, Agnes Icy GUYTON GAMBLE, Pinkney, Aaron Whitaker, Aaron Steele, Joseph I, John I, Samuel II, Samuel I, John)

LaTarshe (Toddy) PARKER is the daughter of Ilander PARKER, Jr. (b. 24 Aug 1941 Cruger, Holmes Co., MS, d. 24 Oct 2005 Chicago, Cook Co., IL)[1614] and Katherine UNKNOWN (b. Jul 1942).[1615] Toddy was born on 23 Oct 1972 and is still living.[1616] See Figure 275. She married David L. JENKINS, Sr. (b. 20 Aug 1974 Chicago, Cook Co., IL, d. Living). They have one son, David (DJ) JENKINS, Jr. (b. Unknown, d. Living).

Figure 275 LaTarshe (Toddy) PARKER[1617]

Bernard PARKER (Ilander PARKER, Jr., Lovie GAMBLE NASH PARKER, Agnes Icy GUYTON GAMBLE, Pinkney, Aaron Whitaker, Aaron Steele, Joseph I, John I, Samuel II, Samuel I, John)

Bernard PARKER is the son of Ilander PARKER, Jr. (b. 24 Aug 1941 Cruger, Holmes Co., MS, d. 24 Oct 2005 Chicago, Cook Co., IL)[1618] and Katherine UNKNOWN (b. Jul 1942).[1619] Bernard was born on 28 Aug 1975 and is living.[1620] See Figure 276. He married Latisha GRANT (b. Jan 1977, d. Living). See Figure 277. They have three children, according to Karl Glenn BOYD (Nykki Lamarr STARR):

i   B.J. PARKER (male) (b. Unknown, d. Living).
ii   S'eance PARKER - TURNER (female) (b. Unknown, d. Living). See Figure 278.
iii   Makayla PARKER (b. Unknown, d. Living).

[1614] "U.S., Social Security Death Index, 1935-2014," s.v. "Ilander Parker," (birth 24 Aug 1941, death 24 Oct 2005), *FindaGrave.com*.
[1615] Per Karl Boyd's tree on *Ancestry.com*. He was nephew of Ilander Parker, Jr.
[1616] "U.S. Public Records Index, 1950-1993, Volume 1," s.v. "Latarshe Parker," (birth 23 Oct 1972), *Ancestry.com*.
[1617] Karl Boyd originally shared this on 21 Nov 2021 on *Ancestry.com*.
[1618] "U.S., Social Security Death Index, 1935-2014," s.v. "Ilander Parker," (birth 24 Aug 1941, death 24 Oct 2005), *FindaGrave.com*.
[1619] Per Karl Boyd's tree on *Ancestry.com*. He was nephew of Ilander Parker, Jr.
[1620] Per Karl Glenn Boyd.

Figure 276 Bernard PARKER[1621]    Figure 277 Latisha GRANT PARKER[1622]    Figure 278 S'eance PARKER-TURNER[1623]

Natasha PARKER (Shirley PARKER, Lovie GAMBLE NASH PARKER, Agnes Icy GUYTON GAMBLE, Pinkney, Aaron Whitaker, Aaron Steele, Joseph I, John I, Samuel II, Samuel I, John)

Natasha PARKER is the daughter of Shirley PARKER (b. 20 Oct 1954 Kosciusko, Attala Co., MS, d. 5 Jun 1992 Chicago, Cook Co., IL)[1624] and Hubert EVANS (Unknown). Natasha was born on 31 Oct 1974 and is living.[1625] See Figure 279. She married (1) Shannon R. SIMMONS (b. 4 May 1975, d. Living)[1626] (see Figure 280) and (2) De'Avlin V. OLGUIN (b. 18 Oct 1974, d. Living)[1627] (see Figure 281). She has one son:

i Shaun PARKER (b. Aug 1996, d. Living) (see Figure 282) m. Nova GRAY (b. abt 1995, d. Living). They have two children: Moon SIMMONS (male) and Jupiter Icy GRAY-GAMBLE (male). See Figure 282.

[1621] Karl Boyd originally shared this on 21 Nov 2021 on *Ancestry.com*.
[1622] Karl Boyd originally shared this on 21 Nov 2021 on *Ancestry.com*.
[1623] Karl Boyd originally shared this on 31 Jul 2023 on *Ancestry.com*.
[1624] Per Karl Boyd (also known as Nykki Starr), nephew, from his tree on 12 Oct 2021 on Ancestry.com.
[1625] "U.S., Public Records Index, 1950-1993, Volume 1," s.v. "Natasha Parker," (birth 31 Oct 1974), *Ancestry.com*.
[1626] "U.S. Public Records Index, 1950-1993, Volume 2," s.v. "Shannon R Simmon," (birth 4 May 1975), *Ancestry.com*.
[1627] "U.S. Public Records Index, 1950-1993, Volume 1," s.v. "Deavlin V Olguin," (birth 18 Oct 1974), *Ancestry.com*.

Figure 279 Natasha PARKER[1628]

Figure 280 Shannon R. SIMMONS[1629]

Figure 281 De'Avlin V. OLGUIN[1630]

Figure 282 Shaun SIMMONS[1631]

[1628] Karl Boyd originally shared this on 11 Nov 2021 on *Ancestry.com*.
[1629] Karl Boyd originally shared this on 23 Aug 2023 on *Ancestry.com*.
[1630] Karl Boyd originally shared this on 17 Jul 2022 on *Ancestry.com*.
[1631] Karl Boyd originally shared this on 11 Nov 2021 on *Ancestry.com*.

CHILD OF AARON WHITAKER GUYTON AND PATSY GIBSON: ELIJAH'S LINE

Generation #7

Elijah GUYTON (Aaron Whitaker, Aaron Steele, Joseph I, John I, Samuel II, Samuel I, John)

Elijah GUYTON is likely the son of Aaron Whitaker GUYTON and Patsy GIBSON. He was born about 1850 in Attala Co., MS, and died in 1901.[1632] He married two women: (1) Sarah RUSSELL (b. ABT 1856, d. 1893)[1633] about 1873 (when their first child was born) and (2) Tennessee (Tennie) FULLER (b. Oct 1869, d. 21 Oct 1939, St. Louis, MO).[1634] Tennie's parents were Henry FULLER and Lucy CONWAY, according to her death certificate. Lige married Tennie sometime around 1893 when Sarah RUSSELL died and before their first child was born. According to Karl Glenn BOYD (aka Nykki Lamarr STARR), Sarah's parents were Robert RUSSELL and Susan RUSSELL.

The 1850 U.S. Census Slave Schedules showed Aaron Whitaker GUYTON enslaved six people, ranging in age from 23 years to 6 months.[1635] See Figure 283. Enslaved persons were not named in the schedules. The three children, as described above, were likely Caroline (age 3), Pinkney (age 2), and Elijah (age 6 months). The two adult females (ages 21 and 20) could have been Sarah UNKNOWN/RUSSELL and Patsy GIBSON. See the section on Aaron Whitaker Guyton. There was also an adult male (age 23).

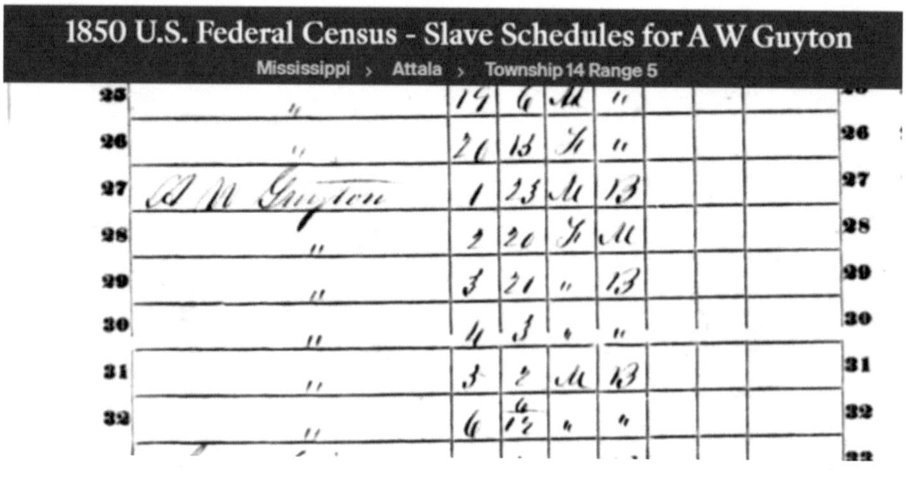
1850 U.S. Federal Census - Slave Schedules for A W Guyton
Mississippi › Attala › Township 14 Range 5

25	"	19	6	M	"	25
26	"	20	13	F	"	26
27	A W Guyton	1	23	M	B	27
28	"	2	20	F	M	28
29	"	3	21	"	B	29
30	"	4	3	"	"	30
31	"	5	2	M	B	31
32	"	6	6/12	"	"	32

Figure 283 1850 U.S. Census -- Slave Schedule for Aaron Whitaker GUYTON

1632 Elijah Guyton, grave marker, Russell Cemetery, Attala County, Mississippi, digital image s.v. "Lige Guyton," (1853-1901), *FindaGrave.com*.

1633 Sarah Russell, grave marker, Russell Cemetery, Attala County, Mississippi, digital image s.v. "Sarah Guyton," (1856-1893), *FindaGrave.com*.

1634 "Missouri, Death Certificates, 1910-1962," digital image s.v. "Tennie Geyton," (birth 15 Feb 1869, death 21 Oct 1939), *Ancestry.com*.

1635 "1850 United States Census: Slave Schedule," Township 14 Range 5, Attala County, Mississippi, digital image s.v. "A W Guyton," *Ancestry.com*.

The 1860 U.S. Census Slave Schedules likely listed the same adult male (age 30 – ages were not well-documented in the early census) and one of the same adult females (age 28).[1636] See Figure 284. The other adult female was not in the household. There were four children (again unnamed): probably Caroline (age 14), Pinkney (age 12), Elijah (age 10), and Adeline RAINEY (age 1). Adeline was sister to Artie RAINEY, Whit GUYTON's third partner, per Channie BROWN-CURRIE, genealogist for the Rainey descendants.

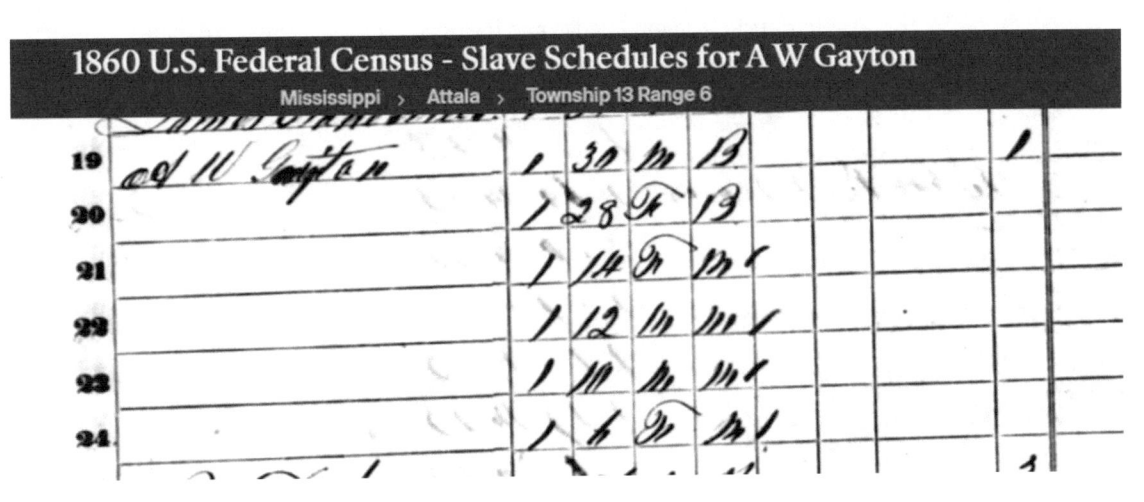

Figure 284 1860 U.S. Census -- Slave Schedule for Aaron Whitaker GUYTON

Pinkney (age 22) and Elijah (age 21) GUYTON lived in Aaron's household in Beat 4, Attala Co., MS.[1637] under their own names in the 1870 U.S. Census. Although the 1870 U.S. Census did not collect relationship information, it did collect race. The young men were shown as mulattoes, or of mixed race. Living with Whit was another young man, Allen BART, a 15-year-old mulatto, of unknown relationship with Whit. Allen's last name was likely Burt, rather than Bart.

On 1 Jan 1875, shortly before Elijah's marriage, Whit GUYTON conveyed 160 acres to Pink GUYTON and Elijah GUYTON in Land Deed Book O, p. 639.[1638]

In the 1880 U.S. Census, Lige (27) was married to Sarah RUSSELL (24) and they had four children: Orlena GUYTON (6), Doss GUYTON (3), Lindsay GUYTON (2), and Wade GUYTON (1).[1639] There is no surviving 1890 U.S. Census. Although Lige died in 1901, I do not find him in the 1900 U.S. Census.

Lige GUYTON and Sarah RUSSELL had at least the following children:

[1636] "1860 United States Census: Slave Schedule," Township 13 Range 6, Attala County, Mississippi, digital image s.v. "A W Guyton," *Ancestry.com*.

[1637] "1870 United States Census," Attala Co., MS, digital image s.v. "Penkey Guyton," (birth ABT 1848), *Ancestry.com*.

[1638] Source on *Ancestry.com* is given as: David F Guyton Springfield, 22 Lache Lane, Chester CH4 7LR, England E-mail: DFGuyton@compuserve.com Courtesy of Ann Breedlove genealogy librarian Attala County, Mississippi. In the posted document, the ultimate source of the information was a letter from John D. Guyton, written on 22 Jul 2002.

[1639] "1880 United States Census," Kosciusko, Attala Co., MS, digital image s.v. "Elijah Guyton," (birth 1853), *Ancestry.com*.

i   Orlena (Lena) GUYTON (b. 1873 MS, d. 1956 Kosciusko, Attala Co., MS)[1640] m. Turner FULLER, Sr. (b. Jan 1874 MS, d. 1948).[1641]

ii   Doss Ade GUYTON (b. ABT 1877 Kosciusko, Attala Co., MS, d. 30 Mar 1929 Battle Creek, MI)[1642] m. Emma CARR (b. 6 Mar 1887 Kosciusko, Attala Co., MS, d. Unknown).[1643]

iii   Lindsay Ford (Linzy) GUYTON, Sr. (b. Jan 1878 MS, d. Mar 1942 New Orleans, Orleans Parish, LA)[1644] m. Marceline G. LOCKETTE (b. ABT 1892, LA, d. 21 Apr 1928 New Orleans, Orleans Parish, LA).[1645]

iv   Wade Harvey GUYTON, Sr. (b. 7 May 1880 Kosciusko, Attala Co., MS, d. AFT 1942)[1646] m. (1) Callie BEAMAN (b. 25 Nov 1885 Kosciusko, Attala Co., MS, d. 8 May 1925 Detroit, Wayne Co., MI)[1647] married about 1906 based on the birth of their first child and (2) Mary Lovey Zinkey CARR (b. 26 Oct 1879 MS, d. 9 May 1980)[1648] on 16 Apr 1936 in Detroit, Wayne Co., MI and divorced on 15 Jan 1942 in Wayne Co., MI.[1649]

v   Adeline Susannah GUYTON (b. 24 Nov 1882 Kosciusko, Attala Co., MS, d. 11 Sep 1966 Kosciusko, Attala Co., MS)[1650] m. Ivery BURT, Sr. (b. 25 Dec 1876 MS, d. 25 Jun 1953 Attala Co., MS).[1651]

vi   Mattie GUYTON (b. Apr 1883 MS, d. Unknown).[1652]

vii   Shepard GUYTON (b. 15 Mar 1885 Kosciusko, Attala Co., MS, d. Unknown)[1653] m. Charlotte UNKNOWN (b. ABT 1888 MS, d. Unknown).[1654]

[1640] "1880 United States Census," Kosciusko, Attala Co., MS, digital image s.v. "Orlena Guyton," (birth 1874), *Ancestry.com*. Lena's grave marker contains a birth year of 1877 but the 1880 Census indicates Lena was six-years-old while Doss was 3-years-old. Lena Fuller, grave marker, Shelley Cemetery, Sallis, Attala Co., MS, digital image s.v. "Lena Fuller," (birth 1877, death 1956), *FindaGrave.com*.

[1641] Turner Fuller, Sr., grave marker, Shelley Cemetery, Sallis, Attala Co., MS, digital image s.v. "Turner Fuller," (death 1948), *FindaGrave.com*.

[1642] "1880 United States Census," Kosciusko, Attala Co., MS, digital image s.v. "Doss Guyton," (birth ABT 1877), *Ancestry.com*. "Michigan, Death Records, 1867-1952," digital image s.v. "Doss Guyton," (death 30 Mar 1929), *Ancestry.com*.

[1643] "1910 United States Census," Attala Co., MS, digital image s.v. "Emma Guyton," (birth about 1889), *Ancestry.com*.

[1644] "1910, United States Census," Kosciusko, Attala Co., MS, digital image s.v. "Lindsey F. Guyton," (birth Jan 1878), *Ancestry.com*. "New Orleans, Louisiana, Death Records Index, 1804-1949," Orleans Parish, LA, digital image s.v. "Linzy Guyton," (death Mar 1942), *Ancestry.com*.

[1645] "Louisiana, U.S., Statewide Death Index, 1819-1964," Orleans Parish, LA, s.v. "Marceline Guyton," (birth ABT 1895; death 21 Apr 1928), *Ancestry.com*.

[1646] "U.S., World War I Draft Registration Cards, 1917-1918," digital image s.v. "Wade Guyton," (birth 7 May 1880), *Ancestry.com*. He died sometime after his divorce from Lovey Carr in 1942.

[1647] "Michigan, Death Records, 1867-1952," digital image s.v. "Callie Guyton," (birth 25 Nov 1885; death 8 May 1925).

[1648] "U.S., FindaGrave Index, 1600s-Current," digital image s.v. "Love Zinkey Schropshire," (birth 26 Oct 1879; death 9 May 1980), *Ancestry.com*.

[1649] "Michigan, Divorce Records, 1897-1952," digital image s.v. "Wade Harvey Guyton," (marriage 1 Mar 1936; divorce 15 Jan 1942), *Ancestry.com*.

[1650] Adeline Guyton, grave marker, Bullock Cemetery, Attala Co., MS, digital image s.v. "Adeline Burt," (birth 24 Nov 1882; death 11 Sep 1966), *FindaGrave.com*.

[1651] Ivery Burt, Sr., grave marker, Bullock Cemetery, Attala Co., MS, digital image s.v. "Ivery Burt," (birth 25 Dec 1876; death 25 Jun 1953), *FindaGrave.com*.

[1652] "1900, United States Census," Kosciusko, Attala Co., MS, digital image s.v. "Mattie N. Guyton," (birth Apr 1883), *Ancestry.com*.

[1653] "U.S., Social Security Applications and Claims Index, 1936-2007," s.v. "Shepard Guyton," (born 15 Mar 1889), *Ancestry.com*.

[1654] "1940, United States Census," Lowndes Co., MS, digital image s.v. "Charlotte Guyton," (birth ABT 1888), *Ancestry.com*.

viii   Wiley Leach GUYTON (b. 12 Mar 1886 MS, d. 21 Jul 1978 Chicago, Cook Co., IL)[1655] m. Millie NASH (b. 16 Jun 1891 Leake Co., MS, d. 3 Jan 1978 Chicago, Cook Co., IL).[1656]

ix   Burt GUYTON (b. Jul 1887 MS. d. Unknown).[1657]

Lige GUYTON and Tennie FULLER had at least three children:

i   Fred L. GUYTON (b. 2 Sep 1893 Kosciusko, Attala Co., MS, d. 7 Nov 1957 St. Louis City, St. Louis Co., MO)[1658] m. Ethel Viola CURTIS (b. 14 Aug 1895 MO, d. 21 Oct 1966 St. Louis City, St. Louis Co., MS).[1659]

ii   Lottie GUYTON (b. Mar 1897 MS, d. 1924 MS)[1660] m. Charles MUNSON (b. 5 May 1895 MS, d. Jun 1969 IL).[1661]

iii   William GUYTON (b. Aug 1898 MS, d. Unknown).[1662]

[1655] "Social Security Death Index," Chicago, Cook Co., IL, s.v. "Leach Guyton," (birth 2 Mar 1886; death Jul 1978), *Ancestry.com*.

[1656] "Social Security Death Index," Chicago, Cook Co., IL, s.v. "Millie Guyton," (birth Millie Guyton 16 Jun 1891; death Jan 1978), *Ancestry.com*.

[1657] "1900, United States Census," Kosciusko, Attala Co., MS, digital image s.v. "Burt Guyton," (birth Jul 1887), *Ancestry.com*.

[1658] Fred L. Guyton, grave marker, Washington Park Cemetery (now at St. Peter's Cemetery), St. Louis, St. Louis, MO, digital image s.v. "Fred Guyton," (birth 2 Sep 1892; death 7 Nov 1957), *FindaGrave.com*.

[1659] Ethel Viola Curtis, grave marker, Washington Park Cemetery (now at St. Peter's Cemetery), St. Louis, St. Louis, MO, digital image s.v. "Ethel V. Guyton," (death 21 Oct 1966), *FindaGrave.com*.

[1660] "1900, United States Census," Kosciusko, Attala Co., MS, digital image s.v. "Lottie Guyton," (birth Mar 1897), Ancestry.com. "Mississippi, U.S., Index to Deaths, 1912-1943," digital image s.v. "Lottie Munsin," (death 1924), *Ancestry.com*.

[1661] "U.S., Social Security Death Index, 1935-2014," s.v. "Charlie Munson," (birth 5 May 1895; death Jul 1969), *Ancestry.com*.

[1662] 1900, United States Census," Kosciusko, Attala Co., MS, digital image s.v. "William Guyton," (birth Aug 1898), *Ancestry.com*.

Generation #8

Orlena (Lena) GUYTON (Elijah, Aaron Whitaker, Aaron Steele, Joseph I, John I, Samuel II, Samuel I, John)

Orlena (Lena) GUYTON was the daughter of Elijah (Lige) GUYTON (b. ABT 1849 Kosciusko, Attala Co., MS, d. ABT 1901 Kosciusko, Attala Co., MS)[1663] and Sarah RUSSELL.[1664] Lige married two women: (1) Sarah RUSSELL (b. ABT 1856, d. 1893)[1665] about 1873 (when their first child was born) and (2) Tennessee (Tennie) FULLER (b. Oct 1869, d. 21 Oct 1939 St. Louis, MO).[1666] Lige married Tennie sometime around 1893 after Sarah RUSSELL died and before their first child was born.

Lena was born in 1874 in MS and died in 1956 in Kosciusko, Attala Co., MS.[1667] She married Turner FULLER, Sr. (b. Jan 1874 MS, d. 1948) around 1895 (a year before the birth of their first child).[1668] Together, they had at least nine children:

i　　Lucius FULLER (b. 23 Jun 1896 MS, d. 28 Feb 1919).[1669] He died during military service, perhaps of the Spanish Flu.
ii　　Dannie W. FULLER (b. ABT 1897 MS, d. Unknown).[1670]
iii　　Ben FULLER (b. ABT 1898 MS, d. Unknown).[1671]
iv　　Leora FULLER (b. 19 Apr 1901 MS, d. 1 Feb 1926).[1672]
v　　Walter FULLER (b. 4 Mar 1904 MS, d. 18 Jul 1983).[1673]
vi　　Turner FULLER, Jr. (b. 22 Nov 1906 Attala Co., MS, d. Jan 1967)[1674] m. Lutie UNKNOWN (b. ABT 1910, d. Unknown).[1675]

[1663] Elijah Guyton, grave marker, Russell Cemetery, Attala County, Mississippi, digital image s.v. "Lige Guyton," (1853-1901), *FindaGrave.com*.

[1664] Sarah Russell, grave marker, Russell Cemetery, Attala County, Mississippi, digital image s.v. "Sarah Guyton," (1856-1893), *FindaGrave.com*.

[1665] Sarah Russell, grave marker, Russell Cemetery, Attala County, Mississippi, digital image s.v. "Sarah Guyton," (1856-1893), *FindaGrave.com*.

[1666] "Missouri, Death Certificates, 1910-1962," digital image s.v. "Tennie Geyton," (birth 15 Feb 1869, death 21 Oct 1939), *Ancestry.com*.

[1667] "1880 United States Census," Kosciusko, Attala Co., MS, digital image s.v. "Orlena Guyton," (birth 1874), *Ancestry.com*. Lena's grave marker contains a birth year of 1877 but the 1880 Census indicates Lena was six-years-old while Doss was 3-years-old. Lena Fuller, grave marker, Shelley Cemetery, Sallis, Attala Co., MS, digital image s.v. "Lena Fuller," (birth 1877, death 1956), *FindaGrave.com*.

[1668] Turner Fuller, Sr., grave marker, Shelley Cemetery, Sallis, Attala Co., MS, digital image s.v. "Turner Fuller," (death 1948), *FindaGrave.com*.

[1669] "Lucius Fuller," grave marker, Shelley Cemetery, Sallis, Attala Co., MS, digital image s.v. "Pvt Lucius Fuller," (birth 23 Jun 1896, death 28 Feb 1919), *FindaGrave.com*.

[1670] "1900 United States Census," Kosciusko, Attala Co., MS, digital image s.v. "Dannie W. Fuller," (birth ABT 1897), Ancestry.com.

[1671] "1910 United States Census," Beat 1, Attala Co., MS, digital image s.v. "Ben Fuller," (birth ABT 1898), Ancestry.com.

[1672] "Leora Fuller," grave marker, Shelley Cemetery, Sallis, Attala Co., MS, digital image s.v. "Leora Simmons," (birth 19 Apr 1901, death 1 Feb 1926), *FindaGrave.com*.

[1673] "Walter Fuller," grave marker, Shelley Cemetery, Sallis, Attala Co., MS, digital image s.v. "Walter Fuller," (birth 4 Mar 1904, death 18 Jul 1983), *FindaGrave.com*.

[1674] "U.S., Social Security Death Index, 1935-2014," s.v. "Turner Fuller," (birth 2 Nov 1906, death Jan 1967), *Ancestry.com*.

[1675] "1940 United States Census," Kosciusko, Attala Co., MS, digital image s.v. "Ludie Fuller," (birth ABT 1910), *Ancestry.com*.

vii		Elige FULLER (b. 7 Dec 1907 Attala Co., MS, d. 14 Sep 1998)[1676] m. Neria C. ESTES. (b. 23 Jul 1915 Kosciusko, Attala Co., MS, d. 4 Aug 2000).[1677]
viii		Lucie FULLER (b. ABT 1913 MS, d. Unknown).[1678]
ix		Velma FULLER (b. ABT 1916 MS, d. Unknown).[1679]

Doss Ade GUYTON (Elijah, Aaron Whitaker, Aaron Steele, Joseph I, John I, Samuel II, Samuel I, John)

Doss ADE GUYTON was the son of Elijah (Lige) GUYTON (b. ABT 1849 Kosciusko, Attala Co., MS, d. ABT 1901 Kosciusko, Attala Co., MS)[1680] and Sarah RUSSELL.[1681] Lige married two women: (1) Sarah RUSSELL (b. ABT 1856, d. 1893)[1682] about 1873 (when their first child was born) and (2) Tennessee (Tennie) FULLER (b. Oct 1869, d. 21 Oct 1939, St. Louis, MO).[1683] Lige married Tennie sometime around 1893 after Sarah RUSSELL died and before their first child was born.

Doss was born in Aug 1876 in Kosciusko, Attala Co., MS. He died on 30 Mar 1929 in Battle Creek, Calhoun Co., MI.[1684] He married Emma CARR (b. 6 Mar 1887 Kosciusko, Attala Co., MS, d. Unknown).[1685] See Figure 285 and Figure 286.

Doss and Emma had at least thirteen children.

i		Wilis Oliver GUYTON (b. ABT 1904 MS, d. Unknown).[1686]
ii		Limmie GUYTON (b. 30 Aug 1904 Kosciusko, Attala Co., MS, d. 22 Oct 2004 MI)[1687] m. John Canon FANT (b. 7 Apr 1901 Gainesville, GA, d. 23 May 1979 Detroit, Wayne Co., MI).[1688]

[1676] "Elige Fuller," grave marker, Shelley Cemetery, Sallis, Attala Co., MS, digital image s.v. "Elige Fuller," (birth 7 Dec 1907, death 14 Sep 1998), *FindaGrave.com*.

[1677] "Neria C. Estes," grave marker, Shelley Cemetery, Sallis, Attala Co., MS, digital image s.v. "Neria C. Fuller," (birth 23 Jul 1915, death 4 Aug 2000), *FindaGrave.com*.

[1678] "1920 United States Census," Kosciusko, Attala Co., MS, digital image s.v. "Lucie Fuller," (birth ABT 1913), *Ancestry.com*.

[1679] "1920 United States Census," Kosciusko, Attala Co., MS, digital image s.v. "Velmar Fuller," (birth ABT 1916), *Ancestry.com*.

[1680] Elijah Guyton, grave marker, Russell Cemetery, Attala County, MS, digital image s.v. "Lige Guyton," (1853-1901), *FindaGrave.com*.

[1681] Sarah Russell, grave marker, Russell Cemetery, Attala County, Mississippi, digital image s.v. "Sarah Guyton," (1856-1893), *FindaGrave.com*.

[1682] Sarah Russell, grave marker, Russell Cemetery, Attala County, MS, digital image s.v. "Sarah Guyton," (1856-1893), *FindaGrave.com*.

[1683] "Missouri, Death Certificates, 1910-1962," digital image s.v. "Tennie Geyton," (birth 15 Feb 1869, death 21 Oct 1939), *Ancestry.com*.

[1684] "Michigan, Death Records, 1867-1952," digital image s.v. "Doss Gnyton," (birth Aug 1876, death 30 Mar 1929), *Ancestry.com*.

[1685] "1910 United States Census," Beat 1, Attala Co., MS, digital image s.v. "Emma Guyton," (birth ABT 1889), *Ancestry.com*.

[1686] "1910 United States Census," Beat 1, Attala Co., MS, digital image s.v. "Wilis Guyton," (birth ABT 1904), *Ancestry.com*.

[1687] "Limmie Guyton," *Detroit Free Press*, Detroit, Wayne Co., MI, Thurs, 28 Oct 2004, p. 22, (birth 30 Aug 1904, death 30 Oct 2004), *Newspapers.com*.

[1688] "Michigan, U.S., Death Index, 1971-1996," s.v. "John C Fant," (birth 6 Apr 1901, death 23 May 1979), *Ancestry.com*.

iii		Lord Pankiel (Lazarky) GUYTON (b. ABT 1907 Kosciusko, Attala Co., MS, d. Unknown).[1689]
iv		Ophelia GUYTON (b. ABT 1908 MS, d. Unknown).[1690]
v		Blanche Gail GUYTON (b. 26 Feb 1910 Attala Co., MS, d. 19 Apr 2002 Detroit, Wayne Co., MI)[1691] m. (1) William E. LAMAR (b. 20 Apr 1908 IL, d. 1 Jan 2002) on 10 May 1934 Detroit, Wayne Co., MI,[1692] and (2) Robert A. WELLS (Unknown).[1693]
vi		Frank GUYTON (b. 21 Dec 1912 Kosciusko, Attala Co., MS, d. 27 Apr 1970)[1694] m. Emma ELLISON (b. ABT 1913, d. Unknown) in Detroit, Wayne Co., MI on 8 Feb 1931.[1695]
vii		James GUYTON (b. 26 Apr 1914 AR, d. 15 Jun 1990 Yates, Lake Co., MI)[1696] m. Mildred GIPSON (b. 11 Nov 1914 MI, d. 31 Jan 1993 Detroit, Wayne Co., MI).[1697] They had two daughters born in MI: Alfreda GUYTON (b. ABT 1938, d. BEF 1990 as her father survived her) and Darrelyn Lorraine GUYTON (b. Jan 1952, d. Unknown) m. Unknown ROBINSON (Unknown).[1698]
viii		Betty May GUYTON (b. 8 Jan 1916 Kosciusko, Attala Co., MS, d. 13 Jan 1994 Detroit, Wayne Co., MI)[1699] m. (1) Robert Nolan FREEMAN (b. 21 Sep 1913 Detroit, Wayne Co., MI, d. 4 Nov 1989 Los Angeles, Los Angeles Co., CA) on 20 Mar 1937 in Detroit, Wayne Co., MI and divorced 13 Mar 1951 in Wayne Co., MI[1700] and (2) Chances GOINS (b. Unknown, d. BEF 1994).[1701]
ix		Carrie J. GUYTON (b. 8 Jan 1916 Kosciusko, Attala Co., MS, d. 19 Nov 2004 Sun City, Maricopa Co., AZ)[1702] m. (1) Clarence Edward RUFF, Sr. (b. 19 May 1912 Columbia, SC, d., Unknown) on 3 Aug 1932 in Wood

---

[1689] "1910 United States Census," Beat 1, Attala Co., MS, digital image s.v. "Lord Pankiel Guyton," (birth ABT 1907), *Ancestry.com*.

[1690] "1910 United States Census," Beat 1, Attala Co., MS, digital image s.v. "Ophelia Guyton," (birth ABT 1908), *Ancestry.com*.

[1691] "U.S., Social Security Applications and Claims Index, 1936-2007," s.v. "Blanch Wells," (birth 26 Feb 1910, death 19 Apr 2002), *Ancestry.com*.

[1692] "Michigan, U.S., Marriage Records, 1867-1952," digital image s.v. "Blanche Guyton," (marriage 10 May 1934 to Mr William La Marr), *Ancestry.com*. "U.S., Social Security Applications and Claims Index, 1936-2007," s.v. "William Marr," (birth 20 Apr 1908, death 1 Jan 2002), *Ancestry.com*.

[1693] "Blanche Gail Wells Obituary," Conant Gardens Church of Christ, s.v. "Robert A. Wells," (married to Blanche Gail Wells," Jazlyn Anderson originally shared this on 31 May 2021, *Ancestry.com*.

[1694] Frank Guyton, grave marker, Westlawn Cemetery, Wayne County, MI, digital image s.v. "Sarah Guyton," (1856-1893), *FindaGrave.com*.

[1695] "Michigan, U.S., Marriage Records, 1867-1952," s.v. "Emma Ellison," (birth ABT 1913, marriage to Frank Guyton 8 Feb 1931), *Ancestry.com*.

[1696] "Michigan, U.S., Death Index, 1971-1996," s.v. "James D Guyton," (birth 26 Apr 1914, death 15 Jun 1990), *Ancestry.com*. "Michigan, Marriage Records, 1867-1952," digital image s.v. (marriage 25 Feb 1939 to Mildred G Gipson), *Ancestry.com*.

[1697] "Michigan, U.S., Death Index, 1971-1996," s.v., "Mildred L Guyton," (11 Nov 1914, death 31 Jan 1993), *Ancestry.com*.

[1698] Per Frank Guyton's funeral obituary program. "U.S., Index to Public Records, 1994-2019," s.v. "Darrelyn Lorraine Parker," (birth Jan 1952), *Ancestry.com*.

[1699] "Michigan, Death Index, 1971-1996," s.v. "Betty May Goins," (birth 8 Jan 1916, death 13 Jan 1994," *Ancestry.com*.

[1700] "Michigan, Marriage Records, 1867-1952," s.v. "Betty M Guyton," (marriage 20 Mar 1937 to Robert Freeman), *Ancestry.com*. "Michigan, U.S., Divorce Records, 1897-1952," s.v. "Betty May Freeman," (divorce 13 Mar 1951), *Ancestry.com*. "California, U.S., Death Index, 1940-1997," s.v. "Robert Freeman," (birth 21 Sep 1913, death 2 Nov 1989), *Ancestry.com*.

[1701] Obituary of Betty May Guyton, Jazlyn Anderson originally shared this on 31 May 2021 on *Ancestry.com*. Chances predeceased Betty.

[1702] Carrie J. Guyton, grave marker, Sunland Memorial Park, Sun City, Maricopa Co., AZ, digital image s.v. "Carrie J. Langford," (birth 8 Jan 1916, death 19 Nov 2004), *FindaGrave.com*.

	Co., OH and divorced on 20 May 1952 in Wayne Co., MI[1703] and (2) Lee William LANGFORD (b. 27 Sep 1917 Louisville, Jefferson Co., KY, d. 23 Oct 1993 Peoria, Maricopa Co., AZ) on 10 May 1952 at Detroit, Wayne Co., MI.[1704]
x	Christine GUYTON (b. 4 Jan 1918 MS, d. 14 Feb 1940 Detroit, Wayne Co., MI).[1705]
xi	Warren Harding GUYTON, Sr. (b. 3 Sep 1919 Kosciusko, Attala Co., MS, d. 8 Nov 1996 Inkster, Wayne Co., MI)[1706] m. (1) Dorothy CAVITT (b. 23 Jun 1920 Paris, Henry Co., TN, d. 24 Jun 1999) on 23 Mar 1940 and divorced on 12 Mar 1952 in Wayne Co., MI,[1707] and (2) Wilhelmina BROWN (b. 12 Nov 1927 Ashville, Buncombe Co., NC, d. 13 Feb 1998 Inkster, Wayne Co., MI).[1708]
xii	Georgia Lee GUYTON (b. 16 Jun 1925 MI, d. 12 Apr 2013 Westland, Wayne Co., MI)[1709] m. (1) Marvin Joseph WELLS, Jr. (b. ABT 1924 Detroit, Wayne Co., MI, d. 2 Dec 2021 MI)[1710] and (2) Unknown PEGRAM.[1711] She was raised by her sister Blanche Gail GUYTON and her husband William E. LAMAR.

[1703] "Ohio, U.S., County Marriage Records, 1774-1993," digital image s.v. "Carrie Guyton," (marriage 3 Aug 1932 Wood Co., OH to Clarence Ruff), *Ancestry.com*. "Michigan, U.S., Divorce Records, 1897-1952," s.v. "Carrie Ruff," (divorce 20 May 1952), *Ancestry.com*. "U.S., World War II Draft Cards Young Men, 1940-1947," digital image s.v. "Clarence Edward Ruff," (birth 19 May 1912), *Ancestry.com*.

[1704] Lee William Langford, grave marker, Sunland Memorial Park, Sun City, Maricopa Co., AZ, digital image s.v. "Lee William Langford," (birth 27 Sep 1917, death 23 Oct 1993), *FindaGrave.com*. "Michigan, U.S., Marriage Records, 1867-1952," s.v. "Lee Langoford Jr," (marriage to Carrie J. Guyton on 10 May 1952), *Ancestry.com*.

[1705] Christine Guyton, grave marker, Detroit Memorial Park East, Warren, Macomb Co., MI, digital image s.v. "Christine Guyton," (birth 4 Jan 1918, death 14 Feb 1940), *FindaGrave.com*.

[1706] "U.S. WWII Draft Cards Young Men, 1940-1947," digital image s.v. "Warren Harding Guyton," (birth 3 Sep 1919, Tilton, Lawrence Co., MS), *Ancestry.com*. "U.S., Social Security Applications and Claims Index, 1936-2007," s.v. "Warren Guyton," (birth 3 Sep 1919, death 8 Nov 1996), *Ancestry.com*.

[1707] "U.S., Social Security Applications and Claims Index, 1936-2007," s.v. "Dorothy Louise Guyton," (birth 23 Jun 1920, death 24 Jun 1999), *Ancestry.com*. "Ohio, U.S., County Marriage Records, 1774-1993," digital image s.v. "Warren Guyton," (marriage 23 Mar 1940), *Ancestry.com*. "Michigan, U.S., Divorce Records, 1897-1952," s.v. "Warren Guyton," (divorce 12 Mar 1952), *Ancestry.com*.

[1708] "Michigan, U.S., Marriage Records, 1867-1952," s.v. "Wilhelmena Brown," (marriage 19 Jan 1952 Wayne Co., MI), *Ancestry.com*. "U.S., Social Security Death Index, 1935-2014," s.v. Wilhelmina Guyton," (birth 12 Nov 1927, death 13 Feb 1998), *Ancestry.com*.

[1709] Georgia Lee Guyton, grave marker, United Memorial Gardens, Superior Township, Washtenaw Co., MI, digital image s.v. "Georgia Lee Pegram," (birth 16 Jun 1925, death 12 Apr 2013), *FindaGrave.com*.

[1710] Marvin Joseph Wells Jr., grave marker, Great Lakes National Cemetery, Holly, Oakland Co., MI, digital image s.v. "Marvin Joseph Wells Jr.," (birth 10 Jan 1924, death 2 Dec 2021), *FindaGrave.com*. "Michigan, U.S., Marriage Records, 1867-1952," digital image s.v. "Marvin Joseph Wells," (marriage 27 Jul 1946 to Georgia Lee Guyton), *Ancestry.com*.

[1711] "Celebrating the Life of Georgia Lee Pegram," Swanson Funeral Home, Detroit, MI, 20 Apr 2013.

Figure 285 Doss and Emma GUYTON with Child[1712]

Figure 286 Doss GUYTON[1713]

Lindsay Ford (Linzy) GUYTON, Sr. (Elijah, Aaron Whitaker, Aaron Steele, Joseph I, John I, Samuel II, Samuel I, John)

Lindsay Ford (Linzy) GUYTON, Sr. was the son of Elijah (Lige) GUYTON (b. ABT 1849 Kosciusko, Attala Co., MS, d. ABT 1901 Kosciusko, Attala Co., MS)[1714] and Sarah RUSSELL.[1715] Lige married two women: (1) Sarah RUSSELL (b. ABT 1856, d. 1893) about 1873 (when their first child was born) and (2) Tennessee (Tennie) FULLER (b. Oct 1869, d. 21 Oct 1939 St. Louis, MO).[1716] Lige married Tennie sometime around 1893 after Sarah RUSSELL died and before their first child was born.

Linzy GUYTON was born in Jan 1878 in MS and died in Mar 1942 in New Orleans, Orleans Parish, LA.[1717] He married Marceline G. LOCKETTE (b. ABT 1892, LA, d. 21 Apr 1928, New Orleans, Orleans Parish, LA).[1718] Marceline and Linzy had at least seven children:

[1712] Jazlyn Anderson originally shared this on 12 Jul 2022 on *Ancestry.com*.
[1713] Jazlyn Anderson originally shared this on 12 Jul 2022 on *Ancestry.com*.
[1714] Elijah Guyton, grave marker, Russell Cemetery, Attala County, Mississippi, digital image s.v. "Lige Guyton," (1853-1901), *FindaGrave.com*.
[1715] Sarah Russell, grave marker, Russell Cemetery, Attala County, Mississippi, digital image s.v. "Sarah Guyton," (1856-1893), *FindaGrave.com*.
[1716] "Missouri, Death Certificates, 1910-1962," digital image s.v. "Tennie Geyton," (birth 15 Feb 1869, death 21 Oct 1939), *Ancestry.com*.
[1717] "1900 United States Federal Census," digital image s.v. "Lindsey F Guyton," (birth Jan 1878), *Ancestry.com*. "New Orleans, Louisiana, Death Records Index, 1804-1949," digital image s.v. "Linzy Guyton," (death Mar 1942), *Ancestry.com*.
[1718] "New Orleans, Louisiana, U.S., Death Records Index, 1804-1949," s.v. "Marceline Guyton," (birth abt 1895, death 21 Apr 1928), *Ancestry.com*.

i   Sarah GUYTON (b. 10 Oct 1910 Bogalusa, Washington Parish, LA, d. 10 Feb 2006 New Orleans, Orleans Parish, LA) m. Charles LANE (Unknown).[1719]

ii   Lindsay (Linzy) GUYTON, Jr. (b. 11 Jun 1911 Bogalusa, Washington Parish, LA, d. 10 Dec 1991)[1720] m. (1) Leola JOSEPH (Unknown) in 1944 and separated by 1950[1721] and (2) Agnes BROWN (b. 10 Dec 1916 Natchez, Adams Co., MS, d. 29 Nov 2013 New Orleans, Orleans Parish, LA).[1722]

iii   Rosetta GUYTON (b. 15 Mar 1914 LA, d. 1 Apr 2008 San Jose, Santa Clara Co., CA)[1723] m. Curley FOUNTENBERRY, Sr. (b. 10 Aug 1911 Tylertown, Walthall Co., MS, d. 16 May 1999 New Orleans, Orleans Parish, LA).[1724]

iv   Eugene GUYTON, Sr. (b. 15 May 1916 Bogalusa, Washington Parish, LA, d. Aug 1984 Slidell, St Tammany Parish, LA)[1725] m. Lubertha LEWIS (b. 20 Oct 1925 New Orleans, Orleans Parish, LA, d. 22 Sep 2004) in May 1944[1726]

v   Irene GUYTON (b. 23 Apr 1919 Bogalusa, Washington Parish, LA, d. 29 Jun 2007).[1727]

vi   Robert Walter GUYTON (b. 22 Jan 1923 New Orleans, Orleans Parish, LA, d. 4 Mar 2009 New Orleans, Orleans Parish, LA)[1728] m. Ottilee PERRY (b. 14 Jun 1924 Hollyridge, Sunflower Co., MS, d. Jul 1988 New Orleans, Orleans Parish, LA).[1729]

vii   Lawrence Joseph GUYTON (b. 12 Apr 1928 New Orleans, Orleans Parish, LA, d. 12 Apr 1996 Slidell, Saint Tammany Parish, LA)[1730] m. Willie Beatrice McCOWAN (Unknown) in Oct 1951 in New Orleans, Orleans Parish, LA.[1731]

[1719] "New Orleans, Louisiana, Marriage Records Index, 1831-1964," New Orleans, Orleans Parish, LA, s.v. "Sarah Guyton," (marriage Apr 1941), *Ancestry.com*.

[1720] "U.S., Social Security Death Index, 1935-2014," s.v. "Linzy Guyton," (birth 11 Jun 1911, death 10 Dec 1991), *Ancestry.com*

[1721] "New Orleans, Louisiana, Marriage Records Index, 1831-1964," New Orleans, Orleans Parish, LA, s.v. "Linzy Guyton, Jr.," (marriage to Leola Joseph in Apr 1941), Ancestry.com. "1950 United States Census," New Orleans, Orleans, LA, digital image s.v. "Linzy Guiton," (separated by 1950), *Ancestry.com*.

[1722] "New Orleans, Louisiana, Marriage Records Index, 1831-1964," New Orleans, Orleans Parish, LA, s.v. "Linzy Guyton," (marriage to Agnes Brown in Apr 1951), Ancestry.com. Agnes Brown, grave marker, Lake Lawn Park Cemetery and Mausoleum, New Orleans, Orleans Parish, LA, digital image s.v. "Agnes Guyton," (birth 10 Dec 1916, death 29 Nov 2013), *FindaGrave*.

[1723] "U.S., Social Security Death Index, 1935-2014," s.v. "Rosetta G. Fountenberry," (birth 15 Mar 1914, death 1 Apr 2008), *Ancestry.com*.

[1724] "U.S., Veterans' Gravesites, ca.1775-2019," Metairie Cemetery, New Orleans, s.v. "Curley Fountenberry, Sr.," (birth 10 Aug 1911, death 16 May 1999), *Ancestry.com*.

[1725] "U.S., Social Security Death Index, 1935-2014," Slidell, Saint Tammany Parish, LA, s.v. "Eugene Guyton," (birth 15 May 1916, death Aug 1984), *Ancestry.com*.

[1726] "U.S., Social Security Death Index, 1935-2014," s.v. "Lubertha Johnson," (birth 20 Oct 1925, death 22 Sep 2004), *Ancestry.com*. "New Orleans, Louisiana, U.S., Marriage Records Index, 1831-1964," s.v. "Lubertha Lewis," (marriage to Eugene Guyton in May 1944), *Ancestry.com*.

[1727] "U.S., Social Security Death Index, 1935-2014," New Orleans, Orleans Parish, LA, s.v. "Irene Guyton," (birth 23 Apr 1919, death 29 Jun 2007), *Ancestry.com*.

[1728] "U.S., Social Security Death Index, 1935-2014," s.v. "Robert W. Guyton," (birth 22 Jan 1923, death 4 Mar 2009), *Ancestry.com*.

[1729] "U.S., Social Security Applications and Claims Index, 1936-2007," s.v. "Ottilee Marion Perry," (birth 14 Jun 1924, death Jul 1988), *Ancestry.com*.

[1730] "U.S., Social Security Applications and Claims Index, 1936-2007," s.v. "Lawrence J Guyton," (birth 12 Apr 1928, death 12 Apr 1996), *Ancestry.com*.

[1731] "New Orleans, Louisiana, U.S., Marriage Records Index, 1831-1964," s.v. "Willie Beatrice McCowan," (marriage Oct 1951 to Lawrence Joseph Guyton), *Ancestry.com*.

Wade Harvey GUYTON, Sr. (Elijah, Aaron Whitaker, Aaron Steele, Joseph I, John I, Samuel II, Samuel I, John)

Wade Harvey GUYTON, Sr. was the son of Elijah (Lige) GUYTON (b. ABT 1849 Kosciusko, Attala Co., MS, d. ABT 1901 Kosciusko, Attala Co., MS)[1732] and Sarah RUSSELL.[1733] Lige married two women: (1) Sarah RUSSELL (b. ABT 1856, d. 1893) about 1873 (when their first child was born) and (2) Tennessee (Tennie) FULLER (b. Oct 1869, d. 21 Oct 1939 St. Louis, MO).[1734] Lige married Tennie sometime around 1893 after Sarah RUSSELL died and before their first child was born.

Wade was born on 7 May 1880, Kosciusko, Attala Co., MS and died after 1942.[1735] He married (1) Callie BEAMAN (b. 25 Nov 1885, Kosciusko, Attala Co., MS, d. 8 May 1925, Detroit, Wayne Co., MI)[1736] about 1906 and (2) Mary Lovey Zinkey CARR (b. 26 Oct 1879 MS, d. 9 May 1980) on 16 Apr 1936 in Detroit, Wayne Co., MI and divorced her on 15 Jan 1942 in Wayne Co., MI.

Callie and Wade had at least seven children:

i   Coleman GUYTON (b. ABT 1907 Kosciusko, Attala Co., MS d. 25 Aug 1926 Detroit, Wayne Co., MI).[1737]

ii   Magnolia GUYTON (b. 30 Aug 1908 MS, d. 18 Sep 1974 Highland Park, Wayne Co., MI)[1738] m. John THOMAS (b. 21 Aug 1902 Baltimore, MD, d. Unknown).[1739]

iii   Percy Edward GUYTON (b. 22 Feb 1910 Kosciusko, Attala Co., MS, d. 28 Feb 1972 Chicago, Cook Co., IL).[1740]

iv   Preston Elijah GUYTON (b. 7 Dec 1911 Kosciusko, Attala Co., MS, d. 29 Mar 1995 Detroit, Wayne Co., MI)[1741] m. Frenzella JONES (b. ABT 1910, d. Unknown).[1742]

v   Elmira GUYTON (b. 10 May 1913 Kosciusko, Attala Co., MS, d. Oct 1993 Chicago, Cook Co., IL)[1743] m. Samuel WEATHERSLY (Unknown).[1744]

[1732] Elijah Guyton, grave marker, Russell Cemetery, Attala County, Mississippi, digital image s.v. "Lige Guyton," (1853-1901), *FindaGrave.com*.

[1733] Sarah Russell, grave marker, Russell Cemetery, Attala County, Mississippi, digital image s.v. "Sarah Guyton," (1856-1893), *FindaGrave.com*.

[1734] "Missouri, Death Certificates, 1910-1962," digital image s.v. "Tennie Geyton," (birth 15 Feb 1869, death 21 Oct 1939), *Ancestry.com*.

[1735] "U.S. World War II Draft Registration Cards, 1942," digital image s.v. "Wade Harvey Guyton," (birth 7 May 1884), *Ancestry.com*. "Michigan, Divorce Records, 1897-1952," digital image s.v. "Wade Harvey Guyton," (marriage 1 Mar 1936, divorce 15 Jan 1942). Wade died some time after his divorce.

[1736] "Michigan, Death Records, 1867-1952," digital image s.v. "Callie Guyton," (birth 25 Nov 1885, death 8 May 1925), *Ancestry.com*.

[1737] "Michigan, Death Records, 1867-1952," Detroit, Wayne Co., MI, s.v. "Celemon Guyton," (birth ABT 1907, death 25 Aug 1926), *Ancestry.com*.

[1738] "Michigan, Death Index, 1971-1996," Detroit, Wayne Co., MI, s.v. "Magnolia F Thomas," (birth 30 Aug 1908 death 18 Sep 1974), *Ancestry.com*.

[1739] "U.S. WWII Draft Cards Young Men, 1940-1947," Baltimore, MD, s.v. "John Thomas," (birth 21 Aug 1902), *Ancestry.com*.

[1740] "U.S., Department of Veterans Affairs BIRLS Death File, 1850-2010," s.v. "Percy Edward Guyton," (birth 22 Feb 1910, death 28 Feb 1972), *Ancestry.com*.

[1741] "U.S., Social Security Death Index, 1935-2014," s.v. "Preston E. Guyton," (birth 7 Dec 1911, death 29 Mar 1995), *Ancestry.com*.

[1742] "Ohio, County Marriage Records, 1774-1993," s.v. "Preston Guyton," (marriage to Frenzella Jones on 18 Jul 1941), *Ancestry.com*.

[1743] "Social Security Death Index U.S.," s.v. "Elmira Weathersby," (birth 10 May 1913, death Oct 1993), *Ancestry.com*.

[1744] "Cook County, Illinois Marriage Index, 1930-1960," s.v. "Elmira Guyton," (marriage to Samuel Weathersly on 14 Dec 1942), *Ancestry.com*.

vi   Valina GUYTON (b. ABT 1916 MS, d. AFT 1952)[1745] married and divorced Rufus GRISWOLD (b. 1911, d. Unknown). Marriage: 12 Jul 1937 Detroit, Wayne Co., Mi.[1746] Divorced: 13 May 1952 Wayne Co., MI.[1747]

vii   Wade Harvey GUYTON, Jr. (b. 5 Sep 1916 Kosciusko, Attala Co., MS, d. 4 Feb 2000 Saginaw, Saginaw Co., MI)[1748] m. and div. Edwina THOMPSON (b. 12 Jan 1917 AR, d. Aug 1974).[1749]

Adeline Susannah GUYTON (Elijah, Aaron Whitaker, Aaron Steele, Joseph I, John I, Samuel II, Samuel I, John)

Adeline Susannah GUYTON was the daughter of Elijah (Lige) GUYTON (b. ABT 1849 Kosciusko, Attala Co., MS, d. ABT 1901 Kosciusko, Attala Co., MS)[1750] and Sarah RUSSELL.[1751] Lige married two women: (1) Sarah RUSSELL (b. ABT 1856, d. 1893) about 1873 (when their first child was born) and (2) Tennessee (Tennie) FULLER (b. Oct 1869, d. 21 Oct 1939 St. Louis, MO).[1752] Lige married Tennie sometime around 1893 after Sarah RUSSELL died and before their first child was born.

Adeline's birth date varies by the reporter. According to *FindaGrave*, she was born on 24 Nov 1882 in Kosciusko, Attala Co., MS. She died on 11 Sep 1966 in the same town. She was buried in Bullock Cemetery.[1753] She married Ivery BURT, Sr., who was born on Christmas Day 1876 in MS and died on 25 Jun 1953 in Attala Co., MS.[1754]

[1745] "1920 United States Census," Detroit Ward 5, Wayne Co., MI, digital image s.v. "Valina Gyton," (birth ABT 1916), *Ancestry.com*.

[1746] "Michigan, Marriage Records, 1867-1952," digital image s.v. "Valina Guyton," (marriage 12 Jul 1937 to Rufus Griswold), *Ancestry.com*.

[1747] "Michigan, U.S., Divorce Records, 1897-1952," s.v. "Valina Griswold," (divorced 13 May 1952), *Ancestry.com*.

[1748] "U.S., Social Security Death Index, 1935-2014," Pawtucket, Providence, RI, s.v. "Wade H. Guyton," (birth 5 Sep 1916, d. 4 Feb 2000), *Ancestry.com*.

[1749] "U.S., Social Security Death Index, 1935-2014," s.v. "Edwina Guyton," (birth 12 Jan 1917, d. Aug 1974), *Ancestry.com*.

[1750] Elijah Guyton, grave marker, Russell Cemetery, Attala County, Mississippi, digital image s.v. "Lige Guyton," (1853-1901), *FindaGrave.com*.

[1751] Sarah Russell, grave marker, Russell Cemetery, Attala County, Mississippi, digital image s.v. "Sarah Guyton," (1856-1893), *FindaGrave.com*.

[1752] "Missouri, Death Certificates, 1910-1962," digital image s.v. "Tennie Geyton," (birth 15 Feb 1869, death 21 Oct 1939), *Ancestry.com*.

[1753] Adeline Susannah Guyton, grave marker, Bullock Cemetery, Attala Co., MS, digital image s.v. "Adeline Burt," (birth 24 Nov 1882, death 11 Sep 1966), *FindaGrave.com*. "Social Security Death Index," s.v. "Adeline Burt," (birth 30 Nov 1880, death Sep 1966), *Ancestry.com*.

[1754] Ivery Burt, Sr., grave marker, Bullock Cemetery, Attala Co., MS, digital image s.v. "Ivery Burt," (birth 25 Dec 1876 death 25 Jun 1953), *Ancestry.com*.

Adeline and Ivery had at least ten children:

i. Clara BURT (b. 24 Apr 1905 MS, d. 28 May 1972)[1755] m. Unknown SCOTT.
ii. Jodie Mae BURT (b. 20 Jan 1910 Attala Co., MS, d. 20 Jul 1994 Kosciusko, Attala Co., MS)[1756] m. Oscar LOVE, Sr. (b. 11 Apr 1911 Itta Bena, LeFlore Co., MS, d. 16 May 1989 Kosciusko, Attala Co., MS).[1757]
iii. Ivery BURT, Jr. (b. 30 Nov 1912 Kosciusko, Attala Co., MS, d. 21 Aug 1973 Chicago, Cook Co., IL).[1758]
iv. James A. BURT (b. ABT 1915 MS, d. Unknown).[1759]
v. Bob Green BURT (b. 7 Sep 1915 Attala Co., MS, d. 29 Nov 1999 Chicago, Cook Co., IL).[1760]
vi. Walter Mack BURT (b. 5 Oct 1916 Kosciusko, Attala Co., MS, d. 23 Sep 1990)[1761] m. Rosie REDD (b. 12 Apr 1926 Durant, Holmes Co., MS, d. 6 Sep 2003 Chicago, Cook Co., IL).[1762]
vii. Clinton L. BURT (b. 3 Jul 1919 Kosciusko, Attala Co., MS, d. 6 Oct 2005 Evanston, Cook Co., IL).[1763]
viii. Geneva BURT (b. 31 Mar 1920 Attala Co., MS, d. 29 Mar 2005 Chicago, Cook Co., IL)[1764] m. Brazie GUYTON (b. 6 Mar 1918 Attala Co., MS, d. 16 Dec 1998 Chicago, Cook Co., IL).[1765] Brazie was the grandson of Case GUYTON; Geneva was the granddaughter of Elijah GUYTON. The couple was second cousins.
ix. A.C. BURT (b. 26 Jun 1923 Attala Co., MS, d. 7 Jul 2005).[1766]
x. R.C. BURT (b. 13 Jan 1925 Kosciusko, Attala Co., MS, d. 25 Feb 2009 Kosciusko, Attala Co., MS)[1767] m. Julia CORRETHERS (b. 21 Apr 1919 Unknown, d. 12 Oct 2017 Kosciusko, Attala Co., MS).[1768]

[1755] Clara Burt, grave marker, Bullock Cemetery, Attala Co., MS, digital image s.v. "Clara Scott," (birth 24 Apr 1905 death 28 May 1972), *FindaGrave.com*.

[1756] Jodie Mae Burt, grave marker, Parkway Cemetery, Kosciusko, Attala Co., MS, digital image s.v. "Jodie Love," (birth 20 Jan 1910, death 20 Jul 1994), *FindaGrave.com*.

[1757] Oscar Love, Sr., grave marker, Parkway Cemetery, Kosciusko, Attala Co., MS, digital image s.v. "Oscar Love, Sr.," (birth 11 Apr 1911, death 16 May 1989), *FindaGrave.com*.

[1758] Ivery Burt, Jr., grave marker, Bullock Cemetery, Attala Co., MS, digital image s.v. Ivery Burt, Jr.," (birth 30 Nov 1912, death (21 Aug 1973), *FindaGrave.com*

[1759] "1930 United States Census," Beat 1, Attala Co., MS, digital image s.v. "James A. Burt," (birth ABT 1915), *Ancestry.com*.

[1760] "U.S., Social Security Death Index, 1935-2014," s.v. "Bob G. Burt," (birth 7 Sep 1914, death 29 Nov 1999), *Ancestry.com*.

[1761] Walter Mack Burt, grave marker, Oakridge-Glen Oak Cemetery, Hillside, Cook Co., IL, digital image s.v. "Walter M. Burt, Sr.," (birth 5 Oct 1916, death 23 Sep 1990), *FindaGrave.com*.

[1762] Rosie Redd, grave marker, Oakridge-Glen Oak Cemetery, Hillside, Cook Co., IL, digital image s.v. "Rosie Burt," (birth 12 Apr 1926, death 6 Sep 2003), *FindaGrave.com*.

[1763] Clinton L. Burt, grave marker, Bullock Cemetery, Attala Co., MS, digital image s.v. "Clinton Burt," (birth 3 Jul 1919, death 6 Oct 2005), *FindaGrave.com*.

[1764] "U.S., Social Security Death Index, 1935-2014," s.v. "Geneva Burt," (birth 31 Mar 1920, death 29 Mar 2005), *Ancestry.com*.

[1765] "U.S., World War II Draft Cards Young Men, 1940-1947," digital image s.v. "Brazie Guyton," (birth 6 Mar 1918, death 16 Dec 1998 per family trees), *Ancestry.com*.

[1766] A. C. Burt, grave marker, Bullock Cemetery, Attala Co., MS, digital image s.v. "A C Burt," (birth 1923, death 2005), *FindaGrave.com*.

[1767] R. C. Burt, grave marker, Bullock Cemetery, Attala Co., MS, digital image s.v. "R C Burt," (birth 13 Jan 1925, death 25 Feb 2009), *FindaGrave.com*.

[1768] Julie Correthers, grave marker, Bullock Cemetery, Attala Co., MS, digital image s.v. "Julia Burt," (death 12 Oct 2017), *FindaGrave.com*. "U.S., Public Records Index, 1950-1993, Volume 1," s.v. "Julia C. Burt," (birth 21 Apr 1919), *Ancestry.com*.

Mattie GUYTON (Elijah, Aaron Whitaker, Aaron Steele, Joseph I, John I, Samuel II, Samuel I, John)

Mattie GUYTON was the daughter of Elijah (Lige) GUYTON (b. ABT 1849 Kosciusko, Attala Co., MS, d. ABT 1901 Kosciusko, Attala Co., MS)[1769] and Sarah RUSSELL.[1770] Lige married two women: (1) Sarah RUSSELL (b. ABT 1856, d. 1893) about 1873 (when their first child was born) and (2) Tennessee (Tennie) FULLER (b. Oct 1869, d. 21 Oct 1939 St. Louis, MO).[1771] Lige married Tennie sometime around 1893 after Sarah RUSSELL died and before their first child was born.

Mattie GUYTON was born in Apr 1883 in Kosciusko, Attala Co., MS. Her death is unknown.[1772]

Shepard GUYTON (Elijah, Aaron Whitaker, Aaron Steele, Joseph I, John I, Samuel II, Samuel I, John)

Shepard GUYTON was the son of Elijah (Lige) GUYTON (b. ABT 1849 Kosciusko, Attala Co., MS, d. ABT 1901 Kosciusko, Attala Co., MS) and Sarah RUSSELL (b. ABT 1856, d. 1893), married about 1873 (when their first child was born). Lige married Tennessee (Tennie) FULLER (b. Oct 1869, d. 21 Oct 1939 St. Louis, MO) sometime around 1893 after Sarah RUSSELL died and before their first child was born.

Shepard was born on 15 Mar 1885 in Kosciusko, Attala Co., MS. His death is unknown but occurred after the 1950 U.S. Census.[1773] He married Charlotte UNKNOWN (b. ABT 1888, MS, d. after the 1950 Census).[1774] In the 1900 U.S. Census, Shepard (16) lived with his siblings and stepmother, Tennie. Because his parents were dead, Shepard lived in Kosciusko, Attala Co., MS with Doss Ade GUYTON (his brother), who served as head of household.[1775] In 1910, Shepard (25) had married Charlotte (27) and lived in Beat 2, Lowndes Co., MS with three of their children:[1776] Simon GUYTON (5), Lula GUYTON (3), and Malisa GUYTON (0). The Census indicated that the couple had been married for seven years. Shepard farmed on a rented farm. He was recorded as being able to read and write.

I could not find the family in the 1920 Census but in 1930 Shepard (52) and Charlotte (49) still lived in Beat 2, Lowndes Co., MS at 132 Aberdeen Road.[1777] Their ages are about a decade too old. They owned the farm they worked. They lived with children: Zollie GUYTON (14), Jonnie B. GUYTON (male) (11), Madesta GUYTON (9) and Ethelene GUYTON (4). The older children no longer lived at home. In

---

[1769] Elijah Guyton, grave marker, Russell Cemetery, Attala County, Mississippi, digital image s.v. "Lige Guyton," (1853-1901), *FindaGrave.com*.

[1770] Sarah Russell, grave marker, Russell Cemetery, Attala County, Mississippi, digital image s.v. "Sarah Guyton," (1856-1893), *FindaGrave.com*.

[1771] "Missouri, Death Certificates, 1910-1962," digital image s.v. "Tennie Geyton," (birth 15 Feb 1869, death 21 Oct 1939), *Ancestry.com*.

[1772] "1900 United States Federal Census," Kosciusko, Attala Co., MS, digital image s.v. "Mattie N Guyton," (birth Apr 1883), *Ancestry.com*.

[1773] "U.S., Social Security Applications and Claims Index, 1936-2007," s.v. "Shepard Guyton," (birth 15 Mar 1889), *Ancestry.com*.

[1774] "1940 United States Federal Census," MS, digital image s.v. "Charlotte Guyton," (birth ABT 1888), *Ancestry.com*.

[1775] "1900 United States Federal Census," Kosciusko, Attala Co., MS, digital image s.v. "Shepherd L Guyton," (birth Mar 1884), *Ancestry.com*.

[1776] "1910 United States Federal Census," Beat 2, Lowndes Co., MS, digital image s.v. "Shepard Guyton," (birth ABT 1885), *Ancestry.com*.

[1777] "1930 United States Federal Census," Beat 2, Lowndes Co., MS, digital image s.v. "Shepard Guyton," (birth ABT 1878), *Ancestry.com*. His birth year is significantly different than other documents record.

1940, the U.S. Census showed Shepard (53) and Charlotte (52) lived in Lowndes Co., MS on a farm the family owned.[1778] Their ages were recorded more accurately in the 1940 Census. Shepard was described as having completed the first year of high school. Living with them were Ethelene GUYTON (13), Madesta GUYTON LATHAM (19) (then married), and Madesta's daughter, Sarah L. LATHAM (3). Madesta is the age that Malisa should be.

Ten years later in 1950, Shepard was 66 and Charlotte was 64. Madesta GUYTON LATHAM (36) still lived with her parents and two daughters: Sarah L. LATHAM (13) and Mary A. LATHAM (6).[1779] She was separated from Unknown LATHAM. Madesta's age doesn't match what we expect for either Malisa or Madesta, but it is closer to the expected age of Malisa. Three other young children lived with the family, described as nieces and nephews: Charles A. LAGRONE (5), Betty L. LAGRONE (3), and James M. LAGRONE (2).

Together Shepard and Charlotte had seven children, according to Census records:

i   Simon GUYTON (b. ABT 1905, MS, d. Unknown).
ii Lula GUYTON (b. ABT 1907, MS, d. Unknown).
iii Malisa or Madesta GUYTON (b. ABT 1910 Beat 2, Lowndes Co., MS, d. Unknown) m. Unknown LATHAM (Unknown).[1780] It is possible that there are two daughters with the same name if Malisa/Madesta died young. Or it is possible that Malisa and Madesta are different daughters with some confusion on Madesta's birth date in some documents.
iv Zollie GUYTON (male) (b. 5 Mar 1917 Columbus, Lowndes Co., MS, d. Unknown)[1781] m. Eureka REVIS (b. 9 Jan 1907 Milam Co., TX, d. 9 Jun 1991, bur. Enid Cemetery, Enid, Garfield Co., OK)[1782] in 1946.[1783]
v   Jonnie B. GUYTON (male) (b. ABT 1919 MS, d. Unknown).[1784]
vi Medesta GUYTON (b. ABT 1921 Lowndes Co., MS, d. Unknown) m. Unknown LATHAM.[1785] It is possible that there are two daughters with the same name if Malisa/Madesta died young. Or it is possible that Malisa and Madesta are different daughters with some confusion on Madesta's birth date in some documents.
vii Ethel L. or Ethelene GUYTON (b. ABT 1926 Beat 2, Lowndes Co., MS, d. Unknown).[1786]

[1778] "1940 United States Federal Census," MS, digital image s.v. "Charlotte Guyton," (birth ABT 1888), *Ancestry.com*.

[1779] "1950 United States Federal Census," Beat 2, Lowndes Co., MS, digital image s.v. "Shepard Guyton," (birth ABT 1878), *Ancestry.com*. His birth year is significantly different than other documents record.

[1780] "1910 United States Federal Census," Lowndes Co., MS, digital image s.v. "Malisa Guyton," (birth ABT 1910), *Ancestry.com*. "1950 United States Federal Census," Lowndes Co., MS, digital image s.v. "Madesta Guyton," (married name Latham), separated), *Ancestry.com*.

[1781] "U.S. WWII Draft Cards Young Men, 1940-1947," digital image s.v. "Zollie Guyton," (birth 5 Mar 1917), *Ancestry.com*.

[1782] Eureka Guyton, grave marker, Enid Cemetery, Enid, Garfield Co., OK, digital image s.v. "Eureka I. Guyton," (birth 9 Jan 1907, death 9 Jun 1991), *FindaGrave.com*.

[1783] "Marriages," *The Enid Events*, Enid, OK, Fri, 29 Nov 1946, p. 7, digital image s.v. "Zollie Guyton," *Newspapers.com*.

[1784] "1930 United States Federal Census," Beat 2, Lowndes Co., MS, digital image s.v. "Jonnie B. Guyton," (birth ABT 1919), *Ancestry.com*.

[1785] "1930 United States Federal Census," Beat 2, Lowndes Co., MS, digital image s.v. "Medester Guyton," (birth ABT 1921), *Ancestry.com*.

[1786] "1930 United States Federal Census," Beat 2, Lowndes Co., MS, digital image s.v. "Ethel L. Guyton," (birth ABT 1926), *Ancestry.com*.

Wiley Leach GUYTON (Elijah, Aaron Whitaker, Aaron Steele, Joseph I, John I, Samuel II, Samuel I, John)

Wiley Leach GUYTON was the son of Elijah (Lige) GUYTON (b. ABT 1849 Kosciusko, Attala Co., MS, d. ABT 1901 Kosciusko, Attala Co., MS)[1787] and Sarah RUSSELL.[1788] Lige married two women: (1) Sarah RUSSELL (b. ABT 1856, d. 1893) about 1873 (when their first child was born) and (2) Tennessee (Tennie) FULLER (b. Oct 1869 d. 21 Oct 1939, St. Louis, MO).[1789] Lige married Tennie sometime around 1893 after Sarah RUSSELL died and before their first child was born.

Leach GUYTON was born on 12 Mar 1886 in MS and died on 21 Jul 1978 in Chicago, Cook Co., IL.[1790] See Figure 287. He married Millie NASH, who was born on 16 Jun 1891 in Leake Co., MS. She died about six months before Leach did, on 3 Jan 1978 in Chicago, Cook Co., IL.[1791]

Figure 287 Millie NASH GUYTON[1792]

Wiley and Millie had seven children:

i Cleveland Davis GUYTON (b. 7 Nov 1907 MS, d. 19 Mar 1984 Houston, Harris Co., TX).[1793] There is more than one Davis GUYTON. One was married to Mallie and one was married to Florida.
ii Sarah Lee GUYTON (b. 3 Feb 1910 Attala Co., MS, d. 23 Apr 2003 Detroit, Wayne Co., MI)[1794] m. Tom Jordan GAMLIN, Sr. (15 Jan 1910 Kosciusko, Attala Co., MS, d. 21 Mar 1991 Detroit, Wayne Co., MI).[1795]

[1787] Elijah Guyton, grave marker, Russell Cemetery, Attala County, Mississippi, digital image s.v. "Lige Guyton," (1853-1901), *FindaGrave.com*.
[1788] Sarah Russell, grave marker, Russell Cemetery, Attala County, Mississippi, digital image s.v. "Sarah Guyton," (1856-1893), *FindaGrave.com*.
[1789] "Missouri, Death Certificates, 1910-1962," digital image s.v. "Tennie Geyton," (birth 15 Feb 1869, death 21 Oct 1939), *Ancestry.com*.
[1790] "Social Security Death Index," s.v. "Leach Guyton," (birth 12 Mar 1886, death Jul 1978), *Ancestry.com*.
[1791] "U.S., Social Security Death Index, 1935-2014," s.v. "Millie Guyton," (birth 16 Jun 1891, death Jan 1978), *Ancestry.com*.
[1792] gloriaff originally shared this on 14 Feb 2015, *Ancestry.com*.
[1793] "U.S., Social Security Death Index, 1935-2014," s.v. "Davis Guyton," (birth 21 Nov 1907, death Mar 1984), *Ancestry.com*.
[1794] "U.S., Social Security Death Index, 1935-2014," s.v. "Sarah L. Gamlin," (birth 3 Feb 1910, death 23 Apr 2003), *Ancestry.com*.
[1795] "U.S., Social Security Death Index, 1935-2014," s.v. "Tom J. Gamlin," (birth 15 Jan 1910, death 21 Mar 1991), *Ancestry.com*.

iii   Mary Lee GUYTON (b. 3 Feb 1910 MS, d. 13 Feb 1939 Chicago, Cook Co., IL)[1796] m. Marvin BOTTOM (Unknown).

iv   Andy GUYTON (b. 7 Jan 1912 Kosciusko, Attala Co., MS, d. 31 Jul 1986 Southfield, Oakland Co., MI)[1797] m. Helen TERRY (b. 15 Jun 1913 MS, d. 20 Jun 1997 MI).[1798] Her sister, Vera LaVern TERRY, was married to Willie Clayton (WC) GUYTON, Sr.

v   Virner GUYTON (b. 30 Jan 1914 Kosciusko, Attala Co., MS, d. 29 Jul 2002 Flushing, Queens, NY).[1799]

vi   Emma Kate GUYTON (b. 24 Feb 1916 Kosciusko Beat 1, Attala Co., MS, d. 21 Jun 1976 Detroit, Wayne Co., MI)[1800] m. (1) Kaley Henry (Kelcy) SUDDUTH (b. 25 Jan 1911 Sallis, Attala Co., MS, d. 7 Apr 1994 Chicago, Cook Co., IL, div.)[1801] and (2) John Paul CLARK (b. ABT 1916, d. Unknown, div.).[1802]

vii   Chatmon GUYTON (b. 21 Dec 1926 Attala Co., MS, d. 8 Nov 2009 Ferndale, Oakland Co., MI).[1803]

Fred L. GUYTON (Elijah, Aaron Whitaker, Aaron Steele, Joseph I, John I, Samuel II, Samuel I, John)

Fred L. GUYTON was the son of Elijah (Lige) GUYTON (b. ABT 1849 Kosciusko, Attala Co., MS, d. ABT 1901 Kosciusko, Attala Co., MS)[1804] and Tennie FULLER. Lige married two women: (1) Sarah RUSSELL (b. ABT 1856, d. 1893)[1805] about 1873 (when their first child was born) and (2) Tennessee (Tennie) FULLER (b. Oct 1869, d. 21 Oct 1939 St. Louis, MO).[1806] Lige married Tennie sometime around 1893 after Sarah RUSSELL died and before their first child was born.

[1796] "1910 United States Federal Census," Beat 1, Attala Co., MS, digital image s.v. "Mary Lee Guyton," (birth ABT 1910), Ancestry.com. "Illinois, Deaths and Stillbirths Index, 1916-1947," s.v. "Mary Lee Bottom (death 13 Feb 1939), Ancestry.com. See the death index to see Marvin Bottom's name as spouse.

[1797] "U.S., Social Security Death Index, 1935-2014," s.v. "Andy Guyton," (birth 7 Jan 1912, death Jul 1986), Ancestry.com.

[1798] "U.S., Social Security Death Index, 1935-2014," s.v. "Helen Guyton," (birth 15 Jun 1913, death 20 Jun 1997), Ancestry.com.

[1799] "U.S., Social Security Death Index, 1935-2014," s.v. "Virner Guyton," (birth 30 Jan 1914, death 29 Jul 2002), Ancestry.com.

[1800] "Michigan, Death Index, 1971-1996," s.v. "Emma K. Guyton," (birth 24 Feb 1916, death 21 Jun 1976), Ancestry.com.

[1801] "U.S., Social Security Death Index, 1935-2014," s.v. "Kelcy Sudduth," (birth 25 Jan 1911, death 7 Apr 1994), Ancestry.com. "1940 United States Federal Census," Rankin Co., MS, digital image s.v. "Kaley A Sudduth," (married to Emma K. Sudduth), Ancestry.com.

[1802] "Michigan, U.S., Divorce Records, 1897-1952," s.v. "John P Clark," (marriage 28 May 1949 Ohio, divorce 14 Jun 1950 Wayne Co., MI), Ancestry.com.

[1803] "U.S., Social Security Death Index, 1935-2014," s.v. "Chatmon Guyton," (birth 21 Dec 1926, death 8 Nov 2009), Ancestry.com.

[1804] Elijah Guyton, grave marker, Russell Cemetery, Attala County, Mississippi, digital image s.v. "Lige Guyton," (1853-1901), FindaGrave.com.

[1805] Sarah Russell, grave marker, Russell Cemetery, Attala County, Mississippi, digital image s.v. "Sarah Guyton," (1856-1893), FindaGrave.com.

[1806] "Missouri, Death Certificates, 1910-1962," digital image s.v. "Tennie Geyton," (birth 15 Feb 1869, death 21 Oct 1939), Ancestry.com.

Fred was born on 2 Sep 1893 in Kosciusko, Attala Co., MS and died on 7 Nov 1957 in St. Louis City, St. Louis, MO).[1807] He married Ethel Viola CURTIS (b. 14 Aug 1895 MO, d. 21 Oct 1966, St. Louis City, St. Louis, MO).[1808] His uncle Case GUYTON lived with Fred in St. Louis at the end of Case's life.

Viola and Fred had one child:

i   Mildred GUYTON (b. ABT 1929, MO, d. Unknown).[1809]

Lottie GUYTON (Elijah, Aaron Whitaker, Aaron Steele, Joseph I, John I, Samuel II, Samuel I, John)

Lottie GUYTON was the daughter of Elijah (Lige) GUYTON (b. ABT 1849 Kosciusko, Attala Co., MS, d. ABT 1901 Kosciusko, Attala Co., MS)[1810] and Tennie FULLER. Lige married two women: (1) Sarah RUSSELL (b. ABT 1856, d. 1893) about 1873[1811] (when their first child was born) and (2) Tennessee (Tennie) FULLER (b. Oct 1869, d. 21 Oct 1939 St. Louis, MO).[1812] Lige married Tennie sometime around 1893 after Sarah RUSSELL died and before their first child was born.

Lottie was born in Mar 1897 in MS. She was only 27 when she died in 1924 in Attala Co., MS.[1813] Her youngest child, Howard MUNSON, was born on 1 Oct 1924. Perhaps Lottie died in childbirth or because of injuries incurred during childbirth. She married Charles MUNSON, who was born on 5 May 1895 in MS and died in Jun 1969 in IL.[1814]

Lottie and Charles had four children before Lottie died.

i   Alma Lee MUNSON (b. 23 Sep 1916 MS, d. 4 Jul 1951 Ann Arbor, Washtenaw Co., MI)[1815] m. I. C. HUNTER, Sr. (b. 9 Mar 1913 Terry., Hinds Co., MS, d. 3 Jul 1951 Superior Twsp, Washtenaw Co., MI).[1816] They both died one day apart. Perhaps they were in a car accident or house fire. They were both in their thirties. According to Marie MUNSON's obituary, she and her husband, John Henry HUNTER, raised her sister's children. John HUNTER was I.C. HUNTER's brother.

[1807] Fred L. Guyton, grave marker, Washington Park Cemetery (now at St. Peter's Cemetery), St. Louis, St. Louis, MO, digital image s.v. "Fred Guyton," (birth 2 Sep 1892; death 7 Nov 1957), *FindaGrave.com*.

[1808] Ethel Viola Curtis, grave marker, Washington Park Cemetery (now at St. Peter's Cemetery), St. Louis, St. Louis, MO, digital image s.v. "Ethel V. Guyton," (death 21 Oct 1966), *FindaGrave.com*.

[1809] "1940 United States Census," St Louis, St Louis City, MO, digital image s.v. "Mildred Guiton," (birth ABT 1929), *Ancestry.com*.

[1810] Elijah Guyton, grave marker, Russell Cemetery, Attala County, Mississippi, digital image s.v. "Lige Guyton," (1853-1901), *FindaGrave.com*.

[1811] Sarah Russell, grave marker, Russell Cemetery, Attala County, Mississippi, digital image s.v. "Sarah Guyton," (1856-1893), *FindaGrave.com*.

[1812] "Missouri, Death Certificates, 1910-1962," digital image s.v. "Tennie Geyton," (birth 15 Feb 1869, death 21 Oct 1939), *Ancestry.com*.

[1813] "1900, United States Census," Kosciusko, Attala Co., MS, digital image s.v. "Lottie Guyton," (birth Mar 1897), Ancestry.com. "Mississippi, U.S., Index to Deaths, 1912-1943," digital image s.v. "Lottie Munsin," (death 1924), *Ancestry.com*.

[1814] "U.S., Social Security Death Index, 1935-2014," s.v. "Charlie Munson," (birth 5 May 1895; death Jul 1969), *Ancestry.com*.

[1815] "Michigan, Death Records, 1867-1952," s.v. "Alma Hunter," (birth 23 Sep 1916, death 4 Jul 1951), *Ancestry.com*.

[1816] "Michigan, Death Records, 1867-1952," s.v. "I C Hunter," (birth 9 Mar 1913, death 4 Jul 1951), *Ancestry.com*.

ii   Marie MUNSON (b. 2 Mar 1919 Kosciusko, Attala Co., MS, d. 25 Oct 2012 Ann Arbor, Washtenaw Co., MI)[1817] m. John Henry HUNTER (b. 29 Jul 1918 Shelby Co., MS, d. 5 Jun 1991 Superior, Washtenaw Co., MI).[1818]

iii   Christine MUNSON (b. ABT 1923 MS, d. Unknown).[1819]

iv   Howard MUNSON (b. 18 Oct 1924 Kosciusko, Attala Co., MS, d. 9 May 1997 Ann Arbor, Washtenaw Co., MI).[1820]

[1817] Marie MUNSON, grave marker, Fairview Cemetery, Ann Arbor, Washtenaw Co., MI, digital image s.v. "Marie Hunter," (birth 2 Mar 1919, death 25 Oct 2012), *FindaGrave.com*.

[1818] "U.S., Social Security Death Index, 1935-2014," s.v. "John H. Hunter," (birth 29 Jul 1917, death 5 Jun 1991), *Ancestry.com*.

[1819] "1930 United States Federal Census," Beat 3, Bolivar Co., MS, digital image s.v. "Christine Munson," (birth ABT 1923), *Ancestry.com*.

[1820] "Social Security Death Index," s.v. "Howard Munson," (birth 18 Oct 1924, death 9 May 1997), *Ancestry.com*.

Generation #9

Elige (Lige) Fuller (Orlena (Lena) GUYTON FULLER, Elijah, Aaron Whitaker, Aaron Steele, Joseph I, John I, Samuel II, Samuel I, John)

Elige (Lige) FULLER was the son of Orlena (Lena) GUYTON (b. 1874 MS, d. 1956 Kosciusko, Attala Co., MS)[1821] and Turner FULLER, Sr. (b. Jan 1874 MS, d. 1948) around 1895 (a year before the birth of their first child).[1822] Lige, named for his grandfather, was born on 7 Dec 1907 in Attala Co., MS, and died on 14 Sep 1998).[1823] He married Neria C. ESTES (b. 23 Jul 1915 Kosciusko, Attala Co., MS, d. 4 Aug 2000).[1824]

In the 1940 U.S. Federal Census, Lige (32) was married to Neria (24) and they lived in Kosciusko, Attala Co., MS.[1825] They lived with their children: Henry Niles FULLER (8), Lacy C. FULLER (6), Dorothy FULLER (5), Will Ernest FULLER (3), and Elmira FULLER (1). Lige was working on a rented farm. He had a seventh-grade education; Neria went to school for six years.

Lige's physical description on his draft registration indicated he was 5'10", weighed 185 lbs., had a dark brown complexion, black hair, and brown eyes.[1826]

By the 1950 U.S. Census, Lige (42) and Neria (34) lived on McAdams Road near Kosciusko, Attala Co., MS with ten of their children and Lige's mother, Lena.[1827] The children were Henry Niles FULLER (18), Lacy FULLER (15), Dorothy FULLER (14), Will Ernest FULLER (12), Elmira FULLER (11), Bernice FULLER (8), Juanita FULLER (6), Jimmy L. FULLER (4), Claude FULLER (2), and Joyce FULLER (less than 1). The Census transcription incorrectly reports that Joyce was 29 years old. Lena, then widowed, was 75. Lige and Henry worked 64 hours per week on the farm; Lacey worked 24 hours per week.

In the early 1990s, Lige lived in Jackson, MS. They lived at several addresses: 303 E Myers St., 159 York Dr., and 4016 N State St.[1828] See Figure 288 and Figure 289. Lige's obituary is in Figure 290.

[1821] "1880 United States Census," Kosciusko, Attala Co., MS, digital image s.v. "Orlena Guyton," (birth 1874), *Ancestry.com*. Lena's grave marker contains a birth year of 1877 but the 1880 Census indicates Lena was six-years-old while Doss was 3-years-old. Lena Fuller, grave marker, Shelley Cemetery, Sallis, Attala Co., MS, digital image s.v. "Lena Fuller," (birth 1877, death 1956), *FindaGrave.com*.
[1822] Turner Fuller, Sr., grave marker, Shelley Cemetery, Sallis, Attala Co., MS, digital image s.v. "Turner Fuller," (death 1948), *FindaGrave.com*.
[1823] "Elige Fuller," grave marker, Shelley Cemetery, Sallis, Attala Co., MS, digital image s.v. "Elige Fuller," (birth 7 Dec 1907, death 14 Sep 1998), *FindaGrave.com*.
[1824] "Neria C. Estes," grave marker, Shelley Cemetery, Sallis, Attala Co., MS, digital image s.v. "Neria C. Fuller," (birth 23 Jul 1915, death 4 Aug 2000), *FindaGrave.com*.
[1825] "1940 United States Federal Census," Kosciusko, Attala Co., MS, digital image s.v. "Lige Fuller," (birth abt 1908), *Ancestry.com*.
[1826] "U.S., World War II Draft Cards Young Men, 1940-1947," digital image s.v. "Lige Fuller," (registration date 16 Oct 1940), *Ancestry.com*.
[1827] "1950 United States Federal Census," Kosciusko, Attala Co., MS, digital image s.v. "Lige Fuller," (birth abt 1908), *Ancestry.com*.
[1828] "U.S., Public Records Index, 1950-1993, Volume 1," s.v. "Elige Fuller," (addresses: 303 E Myers St and 4016 N State St), *Ancestry.com*.

Figure 288 159 York Dr., Jackson, MS (Google Earth)

Figure 289 4016 N. State St., Jackson, MS (Google Earth)

Elige Fuller

Services for Elige Fuller, 90, of Sallis were held Saturday at 11 a.m. at Palestine Baptist Church with burial in Shelly Cemetery.

Fuller, a retired farmer and custodian, died Sept. 14, 1998 at Montfort Jones Memorial Hospital.

He is survived by his wife, Mrs. Neria C. Estes Fuller of Sallis; four sons, Lacey Fuller of Chicago, Ill., Jimmy Fuller, Jackie Fuller and Will Fuller, all of Kosciusko; daughters, Ms. Dorothy Jones of Chicago, Mrs. Joyce Rush of Kosciusko, Ms. Brinda Willis of Atlanta, Ga., Mrs. Linda Walker, Mrs. Phyllis Robinson of Jackson, Mrs. Juanita Guyton of Maywood, Ill., and Mrs. Burnice Lenior of Chicago; a brother, Roosevelt Simmons of Chicago; 33 grandchildren, and 22 great-grandchildren.

Winters Funeral Home was in charge of arrangements.

Figure 290 Elige FULLER Obituary[1829]

[1829] "Obituary of Elige Fuller," *The Star-Herald,* Kosciusko, Attala Co., MS, "Elige Fuller," Thu, 24 Sep 1998, p. 6, *Newspapers.com*.

Lige and Neria's children, highlighted in Lige's obituary above, are shown below.

i   Henry Niles FULLER (b. 22 Dec 1931 Kosciusko, Attala Co., MS, d. 10 May 1995 Maywood, Cook Co., IL)[1830] m. Unknown. He had two sons: Cedric FULLER (Unknown) and Lorenzo FULLER (Unknown).

ii   Lacy C. FULLER (b. 22 May 1934 MS, d. 4 Jan 2012).[1831]

iii   Dorothy L. FULLER (b. abt 1935 MS, d. Unknown)[1832] m. Unknown JONES.

iv   Juanita FULLER (b. 18 Jul 1936 MS, d. 23 Jan 2014 Hayward, Alameda Co., CA) m. Unknown GUYTON (Unknown).[1833]

v   Will Ernest FULLER (b. 13 Jan 1937 Sallis, Attala Co., MS, d. 24 Nov 2014 Chicago, Cook Co., IL).[1834]

vi   Elmira (Bobby) FULLER (b. 29 Jan 1939 Sallis, Attala Co., MS, d. 7 Apr 1998 Chicago, Cook Co., IL).[1835] She was a teacher in Chicago. She had three children: Darryl FULLER who lived in Atlanta in 1998; Jacinda McGILL and Racquel McGILL both of Chicago.

vii   Bernice FULLER, Jr. (b. 19 Apr 1942 MS, d. Unknown)[1836] m. (1) Willie LENOIR (b. 18 Oct 1925, d. Unknown) ABT 1987 in Venice, IL) and (2) Unknown JACKSON.

viii   James (Jimmy) L. FULLER (b. 26 Jul 1945 Kosciusko, Attala Co., MS, d. 6 Oct 2023 Jackson, Hinds Co., MS).[1837]

ix   Claude FULLER (18 Jul 1947 Sallis, Attala Co., MS, d. 18 Jul 1981 Kosciusko, Attala Co., MS).[1838]

x   Joyce FULLER (b. Aug 1949 MS, d. Unknown) m. Unknown RUSH (Unknown).[1839]

xi   Phyllis FULLER (Unknown) m. Unknown ROBINSON (Unknown).

xii   Linda FULLER (b. AFT 1950, d. Unknown) m. (1) Unknown WILLIAMS and (2) Sylvester WALKER (Unknown) on 28 Aug 1982 in Jackson, Hinds Co., MS.[1840]

xiii   Jackie FULLER (b. 19 Mar 1952 MS, d. Unknown).[1841]

xiv   Brinda FULLER (b. 13 Jan 1953 MS, d. Unknown) m. Unknown WILLIS (Unknown).[1842]

[1830] "U.S., Social Security Death Index, 1935-2014," s.v. "Henry N. Fuller," (birth 22 Dec 1931, death 7 May 1995), *Ancestry.com*. "Henry Niles Fuller," grave marker, Shelley Cemetery, Sallis, Attala Co., MS, digital image s.v. "Henry Niles Fuller," (birth 22 Dec 1931, death 7 May 1995), *FindaGrave.com*. His obituary lists his children on the *FindaGrave* site.

[1831] "U.S., Social Security Death Index, 1935-2014," s.v. "Lacy Fuller," (birth 22 May 1934, death 4 Jan 2012), *Ancestry.com*.

[1832] "1940 United States Federal Census," Kosciusko, Attala Co., MS, digital image s.v. "Dorothy Fuller," (birth abt 1935), *Ancestry.com*.

[1833] "Juanita Fuller," grave marker, Rolling Hills Memorial Park, Richmond, Contra Costa Co., CA, digital image s.v. "Juanita Guyton," (birth 18 Jul 1936, death 23 Jan 2014), *FindaGrave.com*.

[1834] "U.S., Social Security Applications and Claims Index, 1936-2007," s.v. "Will Ernest Fuller," (birth 13 Jan 1937, death 24 Nov 2004), *Ancestry.com*.

[1835] "Elmira Fuller," grave marker, Shelley Cemetery, Sallis, Attala Co., MS, digital image s.v. "Elmira Fuller," (birth 29 Jan 1939, death 7 Apr 1998), *FindaGrave.com*. Her obituary lists her children on the *FindaGrave* site.

[1836] "U.S., Public Records Index, 1950-1993, Volume 2," s.v. "Bernice Lenoir," (birth 19 Apr 1942), *Ancestry.com*. "U.S., Newspapers.com™ Marriage Index, 1800s-current," s.v. "Bernice Jackson," (marriage abt 1987 to Willie Lenoir), *Ancestry.com*.

[1837] "James (Jimmy) Fuller," grave marker, Shelley Cemetery, Sallis, Attala Co., MS, digital image s.v. "Jimmy Fuller," (birth 26 Jul 1945, death 6 Oct 2023), *FindaGrave.com*.

[1838] "Claude Fuller," grave marker, Presley Cemetery, Sallis, Attala Co., MS, digital image s.v. "Claude Fuller," (birth 18 Jul 1947, death 18 Jul 1981), *FindaGrave.com*.

[1839] "U.S., Index to Public Records, 1994-2019," s.v. "Joyce F Rush," (birth Aug 1949), *Ancestry.com*.

[1840] "U.S., Newspapers.com™ Marriage Index, 1800s-current," s.v. "Linda Williams," (marriage 28 Aug 1982 to Sylvester Walker), *Ancestry.com*.

[1841] "U.S., Public Records Index, 1950-1993, Volume 1," s.v. "Jackie Fuller," (birth 19 Mar 1952), *Ancestry.com*.

[1842] "U.S., Public Records Index, 1950-1993, Volume 1," s.v. "Brinda F Willis," (birth 13 Jan 1953), *Ancestry.com*.

Limmie GUYTON (Doss Ade, Elijah, Aaron Whitaker, Aaron Steele, Joseph I, John I, Samuel II, Samuel I, John)

Limmie GUYTON was the daughter of Doss Ade GUYTON (b. Aug 1876 Kosciusko, Attala Co., MS, d. 30 Mar 1929, Battle Creek, Calhoun Co., MI)[1843] and Emma CARR (b. 6 Mar 1887, Kosciusko, Attala Co., MS, d. Unknown).[1844] Limmie was born on 30 Aug 1904 in Kosciusko, Attala Co., MS, and died on 22 Oct 2004 in Idlewild, Lake Co., MI.[1845] She married John Canon FANT (b. 7 Apr 1901 Gainesville, Hall Co., GA, d. 23 May 1979 Detroit, Wayne Co., MI).[1846] The couple married on 16 Jan 1924 in Detroit, Wayne Co., MI.[1847]

In the 1930 U.S. Federal Census, Limmie and John were married about five years. They lived on 4755 Williams Street in Detroit, Wayne Co., MI.[1848] The house no longer exists. John worked in the foundry of an auto factory. The couple lived with their four sons: John Henry (5), Edward William, Sr. (4), Robert (2), and Jerome (2 months). By the 1940 U.S. Federal Census, John and Limmie owned their home at 5692 24th Street in Detroit. John worked as a molder in an auto factory, making $900 per year.[1849] The Census reported that Limmie had a seventh-grade education. The family lived with their four sons: John Henry (15), Edward William, Sr. (14), Robert (12), and Jerome (10). In 1950, the U.S. Census showed that John (49) and Limmie (44) lived at 5696 24th Street in Detroit.[1850] I'm unsure whether the couple moved down the street between 1940 and 1950 or whether one of the Census records had an incorrect house number. John and Jerome (20) worked on the assembly line at an auto factory. Limmie worked as an assembler at an auto factory. Edward (23) was unemployed.

i   John Henry FANT (b. 16 Nov 1924 Detroit, Wayne Co., MI, d. 20 Dec 2007)[1851] m. (1) Delphine UNKNOWN[1852] and (2) Anna FLOYD (b. 4 Aug 1927, d. 30 Sep 2016).[1853] They are buried at Ft. Custer National Cemetery. John served in the U.S. Navy during WWII.

[1843] "Michigan, Death Records, 1867-1952," digital image s.v. "Doss Gnyton," (birth Aug 1876, death 30 Mar 1929), *Ancestry.com*.

[1844] "1910 United States Census," Beat 1, Attala Co., MS, digital image s.v. "Emma Guyton," (birth abt 1889), *Ancestry.com*.

[1845] "Limmie Guyton," *Detroit Free Press*, Detroit, Wayne Co., MI, Thurs, 28 Oct 2004, p. 22, (birth 30 Aug 1904, death 30 Oct 2004), *Newspapers.com*.

[1846] "Michigan, U.S., Death Index, 1971-1996," s.v. "John C Fant," (birth 6 Apr 1901, death 23 May 1979), *Ancestry.com*.

[1847] "Michigan, U.S., Marriage Records, 1867-1952," s.v. "Limmie Guyton," (marriage 16 Jan 1924 to John C Fant), *Ancestry.com*.

[1848] "1930 United States Federal Census," Detroit, Wayne Co., MI, s.v. "Limmie Fant," (birth abt 1905), *Ancestry.com*.

[1849] "1940 United States Federal Census," Detroit, Wayne Co., MI, s.v. "Linnie H Fant," (birth abt 1905), *Ancestry.com*.

[1850] "1950 United States Federal Census," Detroit, Wayne Co., MI, s.v. "Limmie H Fant," (birth abt 1906), *Ancestry.com*.

[1851] "U.S. Veterans Gravesites, ca.1775-2006," s.v. "John Henry Fant," (birth 16 Nov 1924, death 20 Dec 2007), *Ancestry.com*.

[1852] "1950 United States Federal Census," Detroit, Wayne Co., MI, s.v. "Delphine Funt," (birth abt 1926), *Ancestry.com*.

[1853] "U.S. Veterans Gravesites, ca.1775-2006," s.v. "Anna Floyd Fant," (birth 4 Aug 1927, death 30 Sep 2016), *Ancestry.com*.

ii   Edward William FANT, Sr. (b. 6 Apr 1926 Detroit, Wayne Co., MI, d. 16 Jun 2009 Detroit, Wayne Co., MI)[1854] m. Hetty (or Hedy) LAMAR (Unknown). They had one child: Edward William FANT, Jr. (Unknown).

iii   Robert Canon FANT (b. 28 Jul 1927 Detroit, Wayne Co., MI, d. AFT 1993, perhaps in Sun City West, Maricopa Co., AZ)[1855] m. Josephine Doris CHAPMAN (b. 16 Dec 1928 Detroit, Wayne Co., MI, d. 11 Feb 2015 perhaps in Sun City West, Maricopa Co., AZ because she lived there beginning in the 1990s)[1856] on 26 Jul 1947 in Detroit, Wayne Co., MI.[1857] They had at least one child: Brenda C. FANT (b. ABT 1949, d. Unknown).

iv   Jerome (Romeo) FANT (b. 21 Oct 1929 Detroit, Wayne Co., MI, d. Dec 1967)[1858] m. Vera Mae McLENDON (b. 10 Dec 1930 Detroit, Wayne Co., MI, d. 8 Apr 1995 Detroit, Wayne Co., MI).[1859]

Blanche Gail GUYTON (Doss Ade, Elijah, Aaron Whitaker, Aaron Steele, Joseph I, John I, Samuel II, Samuel I, John)

Blanche Gail GUYTON was the daughter of Doss Ade GUYTON (b. Aug 1876 Kosciusko, Attala Co., MS, d. 30 Mar 1929, Battle Creek, Calhoun Co., MI)[1860] and Emma CARR (b. 6 Mar 1887, Kosciusko, Attala Co., MS, d. Unknown).[1861] Blanche was born on 26 Feb 1910 in Attala Co., MS, and died on 19 Apr 2002 in Detroit, Wayne Co., MI).[1862] She married (1) William E. LAMAR (b. 20 Apr 1908 IL, d. 1 Jan 2002) on 10 May 1934 Detroit, Wayne Co., MI,[1863] and (2) Robert A. WELLS (Unknown).[1864] See Figure 291.

In 1920, the U.S. Federal Census recorded Blanche (age 10) lived with her family in Beat 3, Bolivar, Bolivar Co., MS.[1865] By 1930, she lived with her mother, Emma, and her siblings in Detroit, Wayne Co.,

---

[1854] "U.S., Social Security Death Index, 1935-2014," s.v. "Edward W. Fant," (birth 6 Apr 1926, death 16 Jun 2009), *Ancestry.com*. See also his funeral program that names his wife and son.

[1855] "U.S., World War II Draft Cards Young Men, 1940-1947," digital image s.v. "Robert Canon Fant," (birth 28 Jul 1927), *Ancestry.com*. In 1993, Robert lived in Sun City West, Maricopa Co., AZ with Josephine. "U.S. Public Records Index, 1950-1993, Volume 1," s.v. "Robert C Fant," (address 18214 N 129th Dr., Sun City West, AZ), *Ancestry.com*. I don't see any records for Robert after 1993.

[1856] "U.S., Cemetery and Funeral Home Collection, 1847-Current," s.v. "Josephine Doris Fant," (birth 16 Dec 1928, death 11 Feb 2015), *Ancestry.com*.

[1857] "Michigan, U.S., Marriage Records, 1867-1952," s.v. "Robert Fant," (marriage 26 Jul 1947 to Josephine Chapman), *Ancestry.com*.

[1858] "U.S., Social Security Applications and Claims Index, 1936-2007," s.v. "Jerome Fant," (birth 21 Oct 1929, death Dec 1967), *Ancestry.com*.

[1859] "Michigan, U.S., Death Index, 1971-1996," s.v. "Thelma Ver-Mae Fant," (birth 10 Dec 1930, death 8 Apr 1995), *Ancestry.com*.

[1860] "Michigan, Death Records, 1867-1952," digital image s.v. "Doss Gnyton," (birth Aug 1876, death 30 Mar 1929), *Ancestry.com*.

[1861] "1910 United States Census," Beat 1, Attala Co., MS, digital image s.v. "Emma Guyton," (birth abt 1889), *Ancestry.com*.

[1862] "U.S., Social Security Applications and Claims Index, 1936-2007," s.v. "Blanch Wells," (birth 26 Feb 1910, death 19 Apr 2002), *Ancestry.com*.

[1863] "Michigan, U.S., Marriage Records, 1867-1952," digital image s.v. "Blanche Guyton," (marriage 10 May 1934 to Mr William La Marr), *Ancestry.com*. "U.S., Social Security Applications and Claims Index, 1936-2007," s.v. "William Marr," (birth 20 Apr 1908, death 1 Jan 2002), *Ancestry.com*.

[1864] "Blanche Gail Wells Obituary," Conant Gardens Church of Christ, s.v. "Robert A. Wells," (married to Blanche Gail Wells," Jazlyn Anderson originally shared this on 31 May 2021, *Ancestry.com*.

[1865] "1920 United States Federal Census," Bolivar, Bolivar Co., MS, digital image s.v. "Blanch Geiyton," (birth abt 1910), *Ancestry.com*

MS.[1866] At nineteen, she was the oldest child in the Detroit household: James (15), Carry (14), Carrie's twin, Betty, (14), Christine (12), Warren (8), and Georgia Lee (4). They lived at 3028 Stanley Ave. in Detroit.

The 1940 U.S. Federal Census reported Blanche (29) as married to William E. LAMAR (31) and lived with her father-in-law as head of household, Emanuel LAMAR (68), William and Blanche's daughter, Patricia Ruth LAMAR (two months old), and William's niece, Sylvia J. GRISBY (8).[1867] The Census noted that Blanche had an eighth-grade education. The family lived at 6414 Iroquois Avenue in Detroit. Their home no longer exists. The Census in 1950 indicated that the family lived in the same house. William E. LAMAR (42) ranked as the head of household. Living with him were Blanche (40), Patricia (10), Emanuel (80) and Sylvia J. GRIGSBY (18).[1868]

William and Blanche raised William's niece, Sylvia, their two daughters, Patricia Ruth LAMAR and Deborah Gail LAMAR, Blanche's youngest sister, Georgia Lee GUYTON, "special daughter, Desi MITCHELL (SIMPSON)," and numerous foster children.[1869] Blanche was known for her devotion to the Church of Christ, baking cakes and her famous dinner rolls, and sewing. Sometime after William died, Blanche married Robert A. WELLS, who survived her. Deborah LAMAR must have been born after the 1950 U.S. Census.

i   Patricia Ruth LAMAR (b. ABT 1940) m. Unknown ROBINSON (Unknown).
ii   Deborah Gail LAMAR (b. AFT 1950) m. Unknown BALDWIN (Unknown).

[1866] "1930 United States Federal Census," Detroit, Wayne Co., MI, digital image s.v. "Blanch Geiyton," (birth abt 1911), *Ancestry.com*.

[1867] "1940 United States Federal Census," Detroit, Wayne Co., MI, digital image s.v. "Blancke Lamarr," (birth abt 1911), *Ancestry.com*.

[1868] "1950 United States Federal Census," Detroit, Wayne Co., MI, digital image s.v. "Blanche G Lamar," (birth abt 1910), *Ancestry.com*.

[1869] Per Blanche Gail Guyton's funeral obituary program.

Figure 291 Photo Album of Blanche GUYTON LAMAR WELLS[1870]

Betty May GUYTON (Doss Ade, Elijah, Aaron Whitaker, Aaron Steele, Joseph I, John I, Samuel II, Samuel I, John)

Betty May GUYTON was the daughter of Doss Ade GUYTON (b. Aug 1876 Kosciusko, Attala Co., MS, d. 30 Mar 1929, Battle Creek, Calhoun Co., MI)[1871] and Emma CARR (b. 6 Mar 1887, Kosciusko, Attala Co., MS, d. Unknown).[1872] Betty was born on 8 Jan 1916 in Kosciusko, Attala Co., MS, and died on 13 Jan 1994 in Detroit, Wayne Co., MI).[1873] She was born a twin of Carrie J. GUYTON. She married (1) Robert Nolan FREEMAN (b. 21 Sep 1913 Detroit, Wayne Co., MI, d. 4 Nov 1989 Los Angeles, Los Angeles Co., CA) on 20 Mar 1937 in Detroit, Wayne Co., MI and divorced 13 Mar 1951 in Wayne Co., MI[1874] and (2) Chances GOINS (b. Unknown, d. BEF 1994)[1875] after 1950.[1876]

According to Betty and Robert's divorce record, they had no children. Betty's funeral obituary program does not mention children either. In the 1950 Census, she worked as a home domestic.

[1870] Jazlyn Anderson originally shared this on 31 May 2021 on *Ancestry.com*.
[1871] "Michigan, Death Records, 1867-1952," digital image s.v. "Doss Gnyton," (birth Aug 1876, death 30 Mar 1929), *Ancestry.com*.
[1872] "1910 United States Census," Beat 1, Attala Co., MS, digital image s.v. "Emma Guyton," (birth abt 1889), *Ancestry.com*.
[1873] "Michigan, Death Index, 1971-1996," s.v. "Betty May Goins," (birth 8 Jan 1916, death 13 Jan 1994," *Ancestry.com*.
[1874] "Michigan, Marriage Records, 1867-1952," s.v. "Betty M Guyton," (marriage 20 Mar 1937 to Robert Freeman), *Ancestry.com*. "Michigan, U.S., Divorce Records, 1897-1952," s.v. "Betty May Freeman," (divorce 13 Mar 1951), *Ancestry.com*. "California, U.S., Death Index, 1940-1997," s.v. "Robert Freeman," (birth 21 Sep 1913, death 2 Nov 1989), *Ancestry.com*.
[1875] Obituary of Betty May Guyton, Jazlyn Anderson originally shared this on 31 May 2021 on *Ancestry.com*. Chances predeceased Betty. Betty was separated from Robert Freeman in the 1950 U.S. Census.
[1876] "1950 United States Federal Census," Detroit, Wayne Co., MI, digital image s.v. "Betty M Freeman," (marital status separated), *Ancestry.com*.

Carrie J. GUYTON (Doss Ade, Elijah, Aaron Whitaker, Aaron Steele, Joseph I, John I, Samuel II, Samuel I, John)

Carrie J. GUYTON was the daughter of Doss Ade GUYTON (b. Aug 1876 Kosciusko, Attala Co., MS, d. 30 Mar 1929, Battle Creek, Calhoun Co., MI)[1877] and Emma CARR (b. 6 Mar 1887, Kosciusko, Attala Co., MS, d. Unknown).[1878] Carrie was born on 8 Jan 1916 in Kosciusko, Attala Co., MS, and died on 19 Nov 2004 in Sun City, Maricopa Co., AZ).[1879] She was born a twin of Betty May GUYTON. She married (1) Clarence Edward RUFF, Sr. (b. 19 May 1912 Columbia, SC, d. Unknown) on 3 Aug 1932 in Wood Co., OH and divorced on 20 May 1952 in Wayne Co., MI,[1880] and (2) Lee William LANGFORD (b. 27 Sep 1917 Louisville, Jefferson Co., KY, d. 23 Oct 1993 Peoria, Maricopa Co., AZ) on 10 May 1952 in Detroit, Wayne Co., MI.[1881]

In the 1940 U.S. Federal Census, Carrie (24) and Clarence (27) lived at 6537 Stanford Street in Detroit with their two sons, Clarence Edward RUFF, Jr. (7) and John (Bogie) William RUFF (5).[1882] Carrie's twin sister, Betty May GUYTON FREEMAN (24), and her husband, Robert Nolan FREEMAN (28), also lived with them. In 1950, the U.S. Census recorded that Carrie and Clarence were separated.[1883] Carrie lived at the same address as in 1940 with her two sons.

i   Clarence Edward RUFF, Jr. (b. 24 Dec 1932 Detroit, Wayne Co., MI, d. 4 Jun 1990 Detroit, Wayne Co., MI).[1884]

ii   John (Bogie) William RUFF (b. 31 Jul 1934 Detroit, Wayne Co., MI, d. 2 Jan 1991 Detroit, Wayne Co., MI).[1885]

[1877] "Michigan, Death Records, 1867-1952," digital image s.v. "Doss Gnyton," (birth Aug 1876, death 30 Mar 1929), *Ancestry.com*.

[1878] "1910 United States Census," Beat 1, Attala Co., MS, digital image s.v. "Emma Guyton," (birth abt 1889), *Ancestry.com*.

[1879] Carrie J. Guyton, grave marker, Sunland Memorial Park, Sun City, Maricopa Co., AZ, digital image s.v. "Carrie J. Langford," (birth 8 Jan 1916, death 19 Nov 2004), *FindaGrave.com*.

[1880] "Ohio, U.S., County Marriage Records, 1774-1993," digital image s.v. "Carrie Guyton," (marriage 3 Aug 1932 Wood Co., OH to Clarence Ruff), *Ancestry.com*. "Michigan, U.S., Divorce Records, 1897-1952," s.v. "Carrie Ruff," (divorce 20 May 1952), *Ancestry.com*. "U.S., World War II Draft Cards Young Men, 1940-1947," digital image s.v. "Clarence Edward Ruff," (birth 19 May 1912), *Ancestry.com*.

[1881] Lee William Langford, grave marker, Sunland Memorial Park, Sun City, Maricopa Co., AZ, digital image s.v. "Lee William Langford," (birth 27 Sep 1917, death 23 Oct 1993), *FindaGrave.com*. "Michigan, U.S., Marriage Records, 1867-1952," s.v. "Lee Langoford Jr," (marriage to Carrie J. Guyton on 10 May 1952), *Ancestry.com*.

[1882] "1940 United States Census," Detroit, Wayne Co., MI, digital image s.v. "Carrie Ruff," (birth abt 1935), *Ancestry.com*.

[1883] "1950 United States Federal Census," Detroit, Wayne Co., MI, digital image s.v. "Carrie Kuff," (marital status separated), *Ancestry.com*.

[1884] "Michigan, U.S., Death Index, 1971-1996," s.v. "Clarence Ruff," (birth 24 Dec 1932, death 4 Jun 1990), *Ancestry.com*.

[1885] "Michigan, U.S., Death Index, 1971-1996," s.v. "John W Ruff," (birth 31 Jul 1934, death 2 Jan 199), *Ancestry.com*.

Warren Harding GUYTON, Sr. (Doss Ade, Elijah, Aaron Whitaker, Aaron Steele, Joseph I, John I, Samuel II, Samuel I, John)

Warren GUYTON, Sr. was the son of Doss Ade GUYTON (b. Aug 1876 Kosciusko, Attala Co., MS, d. 30 Mar 1929, Battle Creek, Calhoun Co., MI)[1886] and Emma CARR (b. 6 Mar 1887, Kosciusko, Attala Co., MS, d. Unknown).[1887] Warren was born on 3 Sep 1919 in Kosciusko, Attala Co., MS, and died on 8 Nov 1996 in Inkster, Wayne Co., MI).[1888] See Figure 292. He married (1) Dorothy CAVITT (b. 23 Jun 1920 Paris, Henry Co., TN, d. 24 Jun 1999) on 23 Mar 1940 and divorced on 12 Mar 1952 in Wayne Co., MI,[1889] and (2) Wilhelmina BROWN (b. 12 Nov 1927 Ashville, Buncombe Co., NC, d. 13 Feb 1998 Inkster, Wayne Co., MI).[1890]

The 1940 U.S. Census recorded Warren (21) and Dorothy (19) lived as lodgers at 5726 Williams St. in Detroit. Warren had two years of high school education. He worked as a chipper at an auto factory. The 1950 U.S. Census reported Warren (30) and Dorothy (29) lived at 566 Hague Street in Detroit, Wayne Co., MI. Warren worked as a furnace operator at a gasket factory. Dorothy worked as a material trimmer for the lining of car doors at an auto factory.[1891] The couple had no children reported in the Census and they divorced in 1952.

Warren and Wilhelmina BROWN married on 19 Jan 1952 in Wayne Co., MI. The date of Warren's marriage to Wilhelmina (19 Jan 1952) comes before the date his divorce was finalized with Dorothy (12 Mar 1952). Warren and Wilhelmina had at least five children, according to the *Ancestry.com* tree of Jazlyn ANDERSON. She identifies only two, twins Rose GUYTON LOTMAN and Ronald (Ronnie) GUYTON. See Figure 293.

i   Ronald (Ronnie) GUYTON (28 Nov 1957 Detroit, Wayne Co., MI, d. 24 Aug 2020 Inkster, Wayne Co., MI).[1892]

[1886] "Michigan, Death Records, 1867-1952," digital image s.v. "Doss Gnyton," (birth Aug 1876, death 30 Mar 1929), *Ancestry.com*.

[1887] "1910 United States Census," Beat 1, Attala Co., MS, digital image s.v. "Emma Guyton," (birth abt 1889), *Ancestry.com*.

[1888] "U.S. WWII Draft Cards Young Men, 1940-1947," digital image s.v. "Warren Harding Guyton," (birth 3 Sep 1919, Tilton, Lawrence Co., MS), *Ancestry.com*. "U.S., Social Security Applications and Claims Index, 1936-2007," s.v. "Warren Guyton," (birth 3 Sep 1919, death 8 Nov 1996), *Ancestry.com*.

[1889] "U.S., Social Security Applications and Claims Index, 1936-2007," s.v. "Dorothy Louise Guyton," (birth 23 Jun 1920, death 24 Jun 1999), *Ancestry.com*. "Ohio, U.S., County Marriage Records, 1774-1993," digital image s.v. "Warren Guyton," (marriage 23 Mar 1940), *Ancestry.com*. "Michigan, U.S., Divorce Records, 1897-1952," s.v. "Warren Guyton," (divorce 12 Mar 1952), *Ancestry.com*.

[1890] "Michigan, U.S., Marriage Records, 1867-1952," s.v. "Wilhelmena Brown," (marriage 19 Jan 1952 Wayne Co., MI), *Ancestry.com*. "U.S., Social Security Death Index, 1935-2014," s.v. Wilhelmina Guyton," (birth 12 Nov 1927, death 13 Feb 1998), *Ancestry.com*.

[1891] "1950 United States Census," Detroit, Wayne Co., MI, digital image s.v. "Warren G. Guyton," (birth abt 1920), *Ancestry.com*.

[1892] Ronald (Ronnie) Guyton, grave marker, Detroit Memorial Park West, Redford, Wayne Co., MI, digital image s.v. "Ronald Guyton," (birth 1957, death 2020), *FindaGrave.com*. Specific dates of birth and death from Jazlyn Anderson's *Ancestry.com* tree.

ii   Rose Guyton (b. 28 Nov 1957 Detroit, Wayne Co., MI, d. Unknown) m. Unknown LOTMAN.[1893]

Figure 292 Warren Harding GUYTON, Sr.[1894]

Figure 293 Twins Rose GUYTON and Ronald GUYTON[1895]

Georgia Lee GUYTON (Doss Ade, Elijah, Aaron Whitaker, Aaron Steele, Joseph I, John I, Samuel II, Samuel I, John)

Georgia Lee GUYTON was the daughter of Doss Ade GUYTON (b. Aug 1876 Kosciusko, Attala Co., MS, d. 30 Mar 1929, Battle Creek, Calhoun Co., MI)[1896] and Emma CARR (b. 6 Mar 1887, Kosciusko, Attala Co., MS, d. Unknown).[1897] Georgia was born on 16 Jun 1925 in MI, and died on 12 Apr 2013 in Westland, Wayne Co., MI).[1898] See Figure 294. She married (1) Marvin Joseph WELLS, Jr. (b. ABT 1924 Detroit, Wayne Co., MI, d. 2 Dec 2021 MI)[1899] and (2) Unknown PEGRAM.[1900] She was raised by her sister Blanche Gail GUYTON and her husband William E. LAMAR after her mother died. Her father died when she was four years old.

[1893] Per her daughter, Jazlyn Anderson, Rose is a twin of Ronald Guyton. See Jazlyn Anderson's *Ancestry.com* tree. Her tree shows her paternal grandfather carried the name of Lotman and she has an *Ancestry.com* tree under the last name of Lotman.
[1894] Jazlyn Lotman originally shared this on 13 Nov 2015 on *Ancestry.com*.
[1895] Jazlyn Anderson originally shared this on 12 Jul 2022 on *Ancestry.com*.
[1896] "Michigan, Death Records, 1867-1952," digital image s.v. "Doss Gnyton," (birth Aug 1876, death 30 Mar 1929), *Ancestry.com*.
[1897] "1910 United States Census," Beat 1, Attala Co., MS, digital image s.v. "Emma Guyton," (birth abt 1889), *Ancestry.com*.
[1898] Georgia Lee Guyton, grave marker, United Memorial Gardens, Superior Township, Washtenaw Co., MI, digital image s.v. "Georgia Lee Pegram," (birth 16 Jun 1925, death 12 Apr 2013), *FindaGrave.com*.
[1899] Marvin Joseph Wells Jr., grave marker, Great Lakes National Cemetery, Holly, Oakland Co., MI, digital image s.v. "Marvin Joseph Wells Jr.," (birth 10 Jan 1924, death 2 Dec 2021), *FindaGrave.com*. "Michigan, U.S., Marriage Records, 1867-1952," digital image s.v. "Marvin Joseph Wells," (marriage 27 Jul 1946 to Georgia Lee Guyton), *Ancestry.com*.
[1900] "Celebrating the Life of Georgia Lee Pegram," Swanson Funeral Home, Detroit, MI, 20 Apr 2013.

Georgia had four children per her funeral obituary program. Georgia and Marvin Joseph WELLS, Jr. had two children:

i   Marvin WELLS (Unknown).
ii   Dwight WELLS (Unknown).

Georgia and Unknown PEGRAM had two children:

i   Rosalyn PEGRAM (Unknown).
ii   Thomas PEGRAM (Unknown).

Figure 294 Georgia Lee GUYTON WELLS PEGRAM[1901]

Rosetta GUYTON (Lindsay (Linzy), Elijah, Aaron Whitaker, Aaron Steele, Joseph I, John I, Samuel II, Samuel I, John)

Rosetta GUYTON was the daughter of Lindsay Ford (Linzy) GUYTON, Sr. (b. Jan 1878 MS, d. Mar 1942 New Orleans, Orleans Parish, LA)[1902] and Marceline G. LOCKETTE (b. ABT 1892, LA, d. 21 Apr 1928, New Orleans, Orleans Parish, LA).[1903] Rosetta GUYTON was born on 15 Mar 1914 in LA, and died on 1 Apr 2008 in San Jose, Santa Clara Co., CA).[1904] She married Curley FOUNTENBERRY, Sr. (b. 10 Aug 1911 Tylertown, Walthall Co., MS, d. 16 May 1999 New Orleans, Orleans Parish, LA).[1905]

The couple had at least three children:

i   Curley Eugene FOUNTENBERRY, Jr. (b. 17 Feb 1935 New Orleans, Orleans Parish, LA, d. 1 Sep 2005 New Orleans, Orleans Parish, LA)[1906] m. Myrtle Vivian DEVORE (15 Sep 1934, d. Unknown)[1907] in Sep 1959 in

---

[1901] Per Georgia Lee Guyton's funeral obituary program.
[1902] "1900 United States Federal Census," digital image s.v. "Lindsey F Guyton," (birth Jan 1878), *Ancestry.com*. "New Orleans, Louisiana, Death Records Index, 1804-1949," digital image s.v. "Linzy Guyton," (death Mar 1942), *Ancestry.com*.
[1903] "New Orleans, Louisiana, U.S., Death Records Index, 1804-1949," s.v. "Marceline Guyton," (birth abt 1895, death 21 Apr 1928), *Ancestry.com*.
[1904] "U.S., Social Security Death Index, 1935-2014," s.v. "Rosetta G. Fountenberry," (birth 15 Mar 1914, death 1 Apr 2008), *Ancestry.com*.
[1905] "U.S., Veterans' Gravesites, ca.1775-2019," Metairie Cemetery, New Orleans, s.v. "Curley Fountenberry, Sr.," (birth 10 Aug 1911, death 16 May 1999), *Ancestry.com*.
[1906] "U.S., Social Security Applications and Claims Index, 1936-2007," s.v. "Curley Eugene Fountenberry Jr," (birth 17 Feb 1935, death 1 Sep 2005), *Ancestry.com*.
[1907] "U.S., Public Records Index, 1950-1993, Volume 1," s.v. "Myrtle D Fountenberry," (birth 15 Sep 1934), *Ancestry.com*.

New Orleans, Orleans Parish, LA and later divorced.[1908] Curley lost his position as a junior high school guidance counsellor due to a charge of arranging for a 15-year-old girl to act in a pornographic film.[1909]

ii   Marceline Audrey FOUNTENBERRY (b. 15 Jun 1936 LA, d. Unknown)[1910] m. (1) Reuben Evariste BROWN (b. Sep 1935, d. Unknown)[1911] on 16 Nov 1957 in Westwego, Jefferson Parish, LA[1912] and divorced in Apr 1970 in San Mateo Co., CA[1913] and (2) Alfred JEFFERSON (b. 19 Oct 1935 Harris Co., TX, d. 15 Jul 1987 San Joaquin Co., CA)[1914] on 6 Jan 1973 in Alameda City., Alameda Co., CA.[1915]

iii   Ronald FOUNTENBERRY(b. Jan 1938 LA, d. Unknown)[1916] m. Carolyn Mellisa WILKINS (b. 24 Jul 1942 Houston, Harris Co., TX, d. Unknown)[1917] on 12 Jun 1965 in Houston, Harris Co., TX[1918] and divorced in Oct 1973 in San Mateo Co., CA).[1919]

Eugene GUYTON, Sr. (Lindsay (Linzy), Elijah, Aaron Whitaker, Aaron Steele, Joseph I, John I, Samuel II, Samuel I, John)

Eugene GUYTON, Sr. was the son of Lindsay Ford (Linzy) GUYTON, Sr. (b. Jan 1878 MS, d. Mar 1942 New Orleans, Orleans Parish, LA)[1920] and Marceline G. LOCKETTE (b. abt 1892, LA, d. 21 Apr 1928, New Orleans, Orleans Parish, LA).[1921] Eugene GUYTON was born on 15 May 1916 in Bogalusa, Washington Parish, LA, and died in Aug 1984 in Slidell, St Tammany Parish, LA).[1922] He married Lubertha LEWIS (b. 20 Oct 1925 New Orleans, Orleans Parish, LA, d. 22 Sep 2004) in May 1944.[1923]

[1908] "New Orleans, Louisiana, U.S., Marriage Records Index, 1831-1964," s.v. "Myrtle vivian Devore," (marriage Sep 1959 to Curley Eugene Fountenberry), Ancestry.com.

[1909] "Porno Case Involving Counselor: Cops Locate Girl," digital image s.v. "Curley E. Fountenberry," *The Post Standard,* Syracuse, NY, 14 Apr 1977, Thu, p. 9, Newspapers.com.

[1910] "U.S., Public Records Index, 1950-1993, Volume 1," s.v. "Marceline A Jefferson," (birth 15 Jun 1936), Ancestry.com.

[1911] "U.S., Index to Public Records, 1994-2019," s.v. "Reuben E Brown Sr," (birth Sep 1935), Ancestry.com.

[1912] "Louisiana, U.S., Compiled Marriage Index, 1718-1925," s.v. "M A Fountenbrry," (marriage 16 Nov 1957 to Reuben E Brown," Ancestry.com.

[1913] "California, U.S., Divorce Index, 1966-1984," s.v. "Marcelin A Fountainber," (divorced Apr 1970 from Reuben E Brown), Ancestry.com.

[1914] "California, U.S., Death Index, 1940-1997," s.v. "Alfred Jefferson," (birth 19 Oct 1935, death 15 Jul 1987), Ancestry.com.

[1915] "California, Marriage Index, 1960-1985," s.v. "Alfred Jefferson," (marriage 6 Jan 1973 to Marcelin A Brown), Ancestry.com.

[1916] "U.S., Index to Public Records, 1994-2019," s.v. "Ronald R Fountenberry," (birth Jan 1938), Ancestry.com.

[1917] "Texas Birth Index, 1903-1997," s.v. "Carolyn Mellisa Wilkins," (birth 24 Jul 1942), Ancestry.com.

[1918] "U.S., Newspapers.com™ Marriage Index, 1800s-current," s.v. "Ronald Fountenberry," (marriage 12 Jun 1965 to Carolyn Mellisa Wilkins," Ancestry.com.

[1919] "California, Divorce Index, 1966-1984," s.v. "Ronald Fountenberr," (divorce Oct 1973 from Carolyn M Wilkins), Ancestry.com.

[1920] "1900 United States Federal Census," digital image s.v. "Lindsey F Guyton," (birth Jan 1878), Ancestry.com. "New Orleans, Louisiana, Death Records Index, 1804-1949," digital image s.v. "Linzy Guyton," (death Mar 1942), Ancestry.com.

[1921] "New Orleans, Louisiana, U.S., Death Records Index, 1804-1949," s.v. "Marceline Guyton," (birth abt 1895, death 21 Apr 1928), Ancestry.com.

[1922] "U.S., Social Security Death Index, 1935-2014," Slidell, Saint Tammany Parish, LA, s.v. "Eugene Guyton," (birth 15 May 1916, death Aug 1984), Ancestry.com.

[1923] "U.S., Social Security Death Index, 1935-2014," s.v. "Lubertha Johnson," (birth 20 Oct 1925, death 22 Sep 2004), Ancestry.com. "New Orleans, Louisiana, U.S., Marriage Records Index, 1831-1964," s.v. "Lubertha Lewis," (marriage to Eugene Guyton in May 1944), Ancestry.com.

In the 1950 U.S. Census, Eugene (33) was married to Lubertha (24). They lived with their three children, Eugene GUYTON, Jr. (3), Donald T. GUYTON, Sr. (2), and Tyrone Linzy GUYTON, Sr. (less than one year old), and Lubertha's mother, Bertha LEWIS (40). They lived at 1353 Lafreniere St. in New Orleans, Orleans Parish, LA.[1924]

The couple may have had more children after the 1950 Census, but I could not find a death notice for either Eugene or Lubertha, which might have detailed their offspring.

i   Eugene GUYTON, Jr. (b. ABT 1947 LA, d. Unknown).[1925]
ii   Donald T. GUYTON, Sr. (b. Dec 1947 LA, d. Unknown). He moved to California.[1926]
iii   Tyrone Linzy GUYTON, Sr. (b. 15 Jun 1949 LA, d. Unknown).[1927]

In 1956, the New Orleans telephone directory included them. Eugene worked as a lift operator at American Sugar Refining.[1928] They lived at 1628 Hendee Rd. It appears the couple divorced before 1969 when Lubertha went by the name Lubertha JOHNSON.[1929]

Robert Walter GUYTON, Sr. (Lindsay (Linzy), Elijah, Aaron Whitaker, Aaron Steele, Joseph I, John I, Samuel II, Samuel I, John)

Robert Walter GUYTON, Sr. was the son of Lindsay Ford (Linzy) GUYTON, Sr.(b. Jan 1878 MS, d. Mar 1942 New Orleans, Orleans Parish, LA)[1930] and Marceline G. LOCKETTE (b. ABT 1892 LA, d. 21 Apr 1928, New Orleans, Orleans Parish, LA).[1931] He was born on 22 Jan 1923 in New Orleans, Orleans Parish, LA, and died on 4 Mar 2009 in New Orleans, Orleans Parish, LA).[1932] He married Ottilee PERRY (b. 14 Jun 1924 Hollyridge, Sunflower Co., MS, d. Jul 1988 New Orleans, Orleans, LA).[1933]

[1924] "1950 United States Census," New Orleans, Orleans Parish, LA, digital image s.v. "Eugene Guyton Sr.," (birth abt 1917), *Ancestry.com*.
[1925] "1950 United States Census," New Orleans, Orleans Parish, LA, digital image s.v. "Eugene Guyton Jr.," (birth abt 1947), *Ancestry.com*.
[1926] "U.S., Index to Public Records, 1994-2019," s.v. "Donald T Guyton," (birth Dec 1947), *Ancestry.com*.
[1927] "U.S. Public Records Index, 1950-1993, Volume 1," s.v. "Tyrone L Guyton," (birth 15 Jun 1949), *Ancestry.com*.
[1928] "U.S., City Directories, 1822-1995: Louisiana, New Orleans, 1956," digital image s.v. "Eug (Lubertha) Guyton," *Ancestry.com*.
[1929] "U.S., Social Security Applications and Claims Index, 1936-2007," s.v. "Lubertha Lewis Guyton," (name recorded by Social Security Apr 1969), *Ancestry.com*.
[1930] "1900 United States Federal Census," digital image s.v. "Lindsey F Guyton," (birth Jan 1878), *Ancestry.com*. "New Orleans, Louisiana, Death Records Index, 1804-1949," digital image s.v. "Linzy Guyton," (death Mar 1942), *Ancestry.com*.
[1931] "New Orleans, Louisiana, U.S., Death Records Index, 1804-1949," s.v. "Marceline Guyton," (birth abt 1895, death 21 Apr 1928), *Ancestry.com*.
[1932] "U.S., Social Security Death Index, 1935-2014," s.v. "Robert W. Guyton," (birth 22 Jan 1923, death 4 Mar 2009), *Ancestry.com*.
[1933] "U.S., Social Security Applications and Claims Index, 1936-2007," s.v. "Ottilee Marion Perry," (birth 14 Jun 1924, death Jul 1988), *Ancestry.com*.

They had at least nine children:[1934]

i	Diane Luberta GUYTON (b. 30 Jun 1946 San Francisco Co., CA, d. 13 Mar 2021).[1935]
ii	Russell GUYTON (Unknown).
iii	Roland GUYTON (Unknown).
iv	Reginald GUYTON (Unknown).
v	Andrea GUYTON (Unknown).
vi	Joyce GUYTON (Unknown).
vii	Ronald GUYTON (Unknown).
viii	Richard GUYTON (Unknown).
ix	Robert GUYTON (Unknown).

Magnolia GUYTON (Wade Harvey Sr., Elijah, Aaron Whitaker, Aaron Steele, Joseph I, John I, Samuel II, Samuel I, John)

Magnolia GUYTON was the daughter of Wade Harvey GUYTON, Sr. (b. 7 May 1880 Kosciusko, Attala Co., MS, d. AFT 1942)[1936] and Callie BEAMAN (b. 25 Nov 1885 Kosciusko, Attala Co., MS, d. 8 May 1925 Detroit, Wayne Co., MI)[1937] married about 1906. Magnolia was born on 30 Aug 1908 in MS and died on 18 Sep 1974 in Highland Park, Wayne Co., MI.[1938] She married John THOMAS, Sr. on 3 Oct 1934.[1939] John was born on 21 Aug 1902 in Baltimore, MD. I did not find his death date.[1940] At the time of their marriage, John worked as a driver.

In the 1940 U.S. Census, Magnolia (31) and John (37) lived on the first floor of 1503 Lyman Avenue in Detroit, Wayne Co., MI.[1941] They lived with their children: Delores THOMAS (8), John THOMAS, Jr. (7), Marvin THOMAS (5), Gwendolyn THOMAS (4), and Diane THOMAS (2). John was seeking work as a truck driver. John and Magnolia had 2 and 8 years of education, respectively.

By the time of the 1950 U.S. Census, the couple was separated.[1942] Magnolia (41) lived with her children, Marvin THOMAS (15), Gwendolyn THOMAS (14), Diane THOMAS (12), and three of her

---

[1934] "U.S., Obituary Collection, 1930-Current," s.v. "Robert Walter Guyton Sr.," (birth abt 1923, death 4 Mar 2009), *Ancestry.com*.

[1935] "U.S., Obituary Collection, 1930-Current," s.v. "Diane Luberta Guyton," (birth 30 Jun 1946, death 13 Mar 2021), *Ancestry.com*. "California Birth Index, 1905-1995," s.v. "Diane Luberta Guyton," (birth 30 Jun 1946 in San Francisco Co., CA), *Ancestry.com*.

[1936] "U.S. World War II Draft Registration Cards, 1942," digital image s.v. "Wade Harvey Guyton," (birth 7 May 1884), *Ancestry.com*. "Michigan, Divorce Records, 1897-1952," digital image s.v. "Wade Harvey Guyton," (marriage 1 Mar 1936, divorce 15 Jan 1942). Wade died some time after his divorce.

[1937] "Michigan, Death Records, 1867-1952," digital image s.v. "Callie Guyton," (birth 25 Nov 1885, death 8 May 1925), *Ancestry.com*.

[1938] "Michigan, Death Index, 1971-1996," s.v. "Magnolia F Thomas," (birth 30 Aug 1908, death 18 Sep 1974), *Ancestry.com*.

[1939] "Michigan, Marriage Records, 1867-1952," digital image s.v. "Magnolia Guyton," (marriage 3 Oct 1934 to Mr John Thomas), *Ancestry.com*.

[1940] "U.S. WWII Draft Cards Young Men, 1940-1947," digital image s.v. "John Thomas," (birth 21 Aug 1902), *Ancestry.com*.

[1941] "1940 United States Census," Detroit, Wayne Co., MI, digital image s.v. "Magnolia Thomas," (birth abt 1909), *Ancestry.com*

[1942] "1950 United States Census," Detroit, Wayne Co., MI, digital image s.v. "Magnolia Thomas," (birth abt 1909), *Ancestry.com*

brothers, Percy GUYTON (40), Preston Elijah GUYTON (37), and Harvey GUYTON (33). They lived at 11625 Russell in Detroit. Percy worked as a grinder in a steel plant; Preston was a janitor at a service station; and Harvey worked in a round house at the railroad.

According to the 1940 and 1950 U.S. Censuses, John and Magnolia's children were:

i	Delores THOMAS (b. ABT 1932 MI, d. Unknown).
ii	John THOMAS (b. ABT 1933 MI, d. Unknown).
iii	Marvin THOMAS (b. ABT 1934 MI, d. Unknown).
iv	Gwendolyn THOMAS (b. 1 Feb 1936 Detroit, Wayne Co., MI, d. 4 Nov 2003)[1943] m. Unknown TAYLOR (Unknown). Her Social Security record showed the change in her surname in Nov 1965).
v	Diane THOMAS (b. ABT 1938 MI, d. Unknown).

Wade Harvey GUYTON, Jr. (Wade Harvey Sr., Elijah, Aaron Whitaker, Aaron Steele, Joseph I, John I, Samuel II, Samuel I, John)

Wade Harvey GUYTON, Jr. was the son of Wade Harvey GUYTON, Sr. (b. 7 May 1880, Kosciusko, Attala Co., MS, d. after 1942)[1944] and Callie BEAMAN (b. 25 Nov 1885, Kosciusko, Attala Co., MS, d. 8 May 1925, Detroit, Wayne Co., MI)[1945] married about 1906. Harvey, as he was frequently called in documents, was born on 5 Sep 1916 in Kosciusko, Attala Co., MS, and died on 4 Feb 2000 in Saginaw, Saginaw Co., MI).[1946] He was nine years old when his mother died. He married (and divorced Edwina THOMPSON (b. 12 Jan 1917 AR, d. Aug 1974).[1947] They married on 20 Dec 1934 in Wayne Co., MI and divorced in the same place on 14 Jan 1946.[1948]

In the 1930 U.S. Census, Harvey GUYTON, Jr. (13) lived with his father, Wade GUYTON, Sr. (53), and five of his siblings: Magnolia GUYTON (22), Percy GUYTON (20), Preston Elijah GUYTON (18), Elmira GUYTON (16), and Valina GUYTON (15).[1949] They lived in Detroit, Wayne Co., MI at 11527 Russell Avenue. In 1940, Wade (23) was married to Edwina THOMPSON (22). They lived in Detroit at 8443 Cameron Avenue. Wade attended school through the third year of high school and worked as a laborer at an auto

---

[1943] "U.S., Social Security Applications and Claims Index, 1936-2007," s.v. "Gwendolyn Thomas," (birth 1 Feb 1936, death 4 Nov 2003), *Ancestry.com*.
[1944] "U.S. World War II Draft Registration Cards, 1942," digital image s.v. "Wade Harvey Guyton," (birth 7 May 1884), *Ancestry.com*. "Michigan, Divorce Records, 1897-1952," digital image s.v. "Wade Harvey Guyton," (marriage 1 Mar 1936, divorce 15 Jan 1942). Wade died some time after his divorce.
[1945] "Michigan, Death Records, 1867-1952," digital image s.v. "Callie Guyton," (birth 25 Nov 1885, death 8 May 1925), *Ancestry.com*.
[1946] "U.S., Social Security Death Index, 1935-2014," Pawtucket, Providence, RI, s.v. "Wade H. Guyton," (birth 5 Sep 1916, d. 4 Feb 2000), *Ancestry.com*.
[1947] "U.S., Social Security Death Index, 1935-2014," s.v. "Edwina Guyton," (birth 12 Jan 1917, d. Aug 1974), *Ancestry.com*.
[1948] "Michigan, U.S., Divorce Records, 1897-1952," s.v. "Wade H Guyton," (marriage 20 Dec 1934; divorce 14 Jan 1946), *Ancestry.com*.
[1949] "1930 United States Census," Detroit, Wayne Co., MI, digital image s.v. "Harvey Guyton," (birth abt 1917), *Ancestry.com*.

factory. The couple lived with three of their children: Donna Jean GUYTON (4), Martha GUYTON (3), Phyllis GUYTON (1), and two lodgers.[1950]

In the 1950 U.S. Census, Harvey (33) lived with Magnolia's (his sister) family with his brothers, Percy GUYTON (40) and Preston GUYTON (37).[1951] Harvey and Edwina were divorced at this point but Harvey's record indicated he was separated. Edwina THOMPSON (32) lived at 4856 Stockton in Detroit with their four children: Donna J. GUYTON (14), Martha GUYTON (13), Phyllis Lorraine GUYTON (11), Wade Harvey GUYTON III (9), and a lodger. Edwina's Census entry indicated she was single and never married, rather than divorced. She was not working.

Their children, per Edwina GUYTON's 1950 U.S. Census entry:

i   Donna Jean GUYTON (b. 19 Jun 1935 Detroit, Wayne Co., MI, d. 24 Jul 2001)[1952] m. Unknown ROGERS.
ii   Martha GUYTON (b. ABT 1938, d. Unknown).
iii   Phyllis Lorraine GUYTON (b. ABT 1939, d. Unknown).
iv   Wade Harvey GUYTON, III (b. 27 Nov 1940 MI, d. Jan 1983 MI).[1953]

See photos of the children (Figure 295, Figure 296, and Figure 297).

Figure 295 Donna Jean GUYTON[1954]

Figure 296 Martha GUYTON[1955]

Figure 297 Phyllis GUYTON[1956]

[1950] "1940 United States Census," Detroit, Wayne Co., MI, digital image s.v. "Harvey Guyton," (birth abt 1917), *Ancestry.com*.
[1951] "1950 United States Census," Detroit, Wayne Co., MI, digital image s.v. "Harvey Guyton," (birth abt 1917), Ancestry.com.
[1952] "U.S., Social Security Applications and Claims Index, 1936-2007," s.v. "Donna Jean Guyton," (birth 19 Jun 1935, death 24 Jul 2001), *Ancestry.com*. The record indicates that Mar 1955, she changed her surname to Rogers.
[1953] "U.S., Social Security Death Index, 1935-2014," s.v. "Wade III Guyton III," (birth 27 Nov 1940, death Jan 1983), *Ancestry.com*.
[1954] Naya Jones originally shared this on 9 Jun 2023 on *Ancestry.com*.
[1955] "U.S. School Yearbooks," Pershing High School, Detroit, MI, s.v. "Martha Guyton," *Ancestry.com*.
[1956] "U.S. School Yearbooks," Pershing High School, Detroit, MI, s.v. "Phyllis Loraine Guyton," *Ancestry.com*.

Jodie Mae BURT [Adeline Susannah GUYTON BURT, Elijah, Aaron Whitaker, Aaron Steele, Joseph I, John I, Samuel II, Samuel I, John]

Jodie Mae BURT was the daughter of Adeline Susannah GUYTON (b 24 Nov 1882 Kosciusko, Attala Co., MS, d. 11 Sep 1966 Kosciusko, Attala Co., MS). She was buried in Bullock Cemetery[1957] and Ivery BURT, Sr. (b. 25 Dec 1876 MS, d. 25 Jun 1953 Attala Co., MS).[1958] Jodie was born on 20 Jan 1910 in Attala Co., MS, and died on 20 Jul 1994 in Kosciusko, Attala Co., MS).[1959] She married Oscar LOVE, Sr. (b. 11 Apr 1911 Itta Bena, LeFlore Co., MS, d. 16 May 1989 Kosciusko, Attala Co., MS).[1960] They had one son, Oscar LOVE, Jr. (b. 20 Dec 1941 MS, d. Unknown)[1961] who married Fannie Mae EPPS. Fannie worked in education. According to an article in the *Star-Herald,* she joined the elementary school staff in Kosciusko from a position in Holmes County schools.[1962]

In the 1950 U.S. Census, Jodie (32) and Oscar (38) lived in Kosciusko, Attala Co., MS with their son, Oscar LOVE, Jr. (8).[1963] Oscar worked as a laborer in the feed industry and Jodie worked as a domestic.

Geneva BURT [Adeline Susannah GUYTON BURT, Elijah, Aaron Whitaker, Aaron Steele, Joseph I, John I, Samuel II, Samuel I, John]

Geneva BURT was the daughter of Adeline Susannah GUYTON (b 24 Nov 1882 Kosciusko, Attala Co., MS, d. 11 Sep 1966 Kosciusko, Attala Co., MS)[1964] and Ivery BURT, Sr. (b. 25 Dec 1876 MS, d. 25 Jun 1953 Attala Co., MS).[1965] Geneva was born on 31 Mar 1920 in Attala Co., MS, and died on 29 Mar 2005 in Chicago, Cook Co., IL).[1966] She married Brazie GUYTON (b. 6 Mar 1918 Attala Co., MS, d. 16 Dec 1998

[1957] Adeline Susannah Guyton, grave marker, Bullock Cemetery, Attala Co., MS, digital image s.v. "Adeline Burt," (birth 24 Nov 1882, death 11 Sep 1966), *FindaGrave.com*. "Social Security Death Index," s.v. "Adeline Burt," (birth 30 Nov 1880, death Sep 1966), *Ancestry.com*.
[1958] Ivery Burt, Sr., grave marker, Bullock Cemetery, Attala Co., MS, digital image s.v. "Ivery Burt," (birth 25 Dec 1876, death 25 Jun 1953), *Ancestry.com*.
[1959] Jodie Mae Burt, grave marker, Parkway Cemetery, Kosciusko, Attala Co., MS, digital image s.v. "Jodie Love," (birth 20 Jan 1910, death 20 Jul 1994), *FindaGrave.com*.
[1960] Oscar Love, Sr., grave marker, Parkway Cemetery, Kosciusko, Attala Co., MS, digital image s.v. "Oscar Love, Sr.," (birth 11 Apr 1911, death 16 May 1989), *FindaGrave.com*.
[1961] "U.S., Public Records Index, 1950-1993, Volume 1," s.v. "Oscar Jr Love Jr," (birth 20 Dec 1941), *Ancestry.com*.
[1962] "Principals Named for City Schools: East Side, High Get New Officials," Kosciusko, Attala Co., MS, *The Star-Herald*, Thu, 23 Apr 1970, p. 1 and 12, s.v. "Mrs. Fannie Epps Love," *Newspapers.com*.
[1963] "1950 United States Federal Census," Kosciusko, Attala Co., MS, digital image s.v. "Jodie M Love," (birth abt 1918), *Ancestry.com*.
[1964] Adeline Susannah Guyton, grave marker, Bullock Cemetery, Attala Co., MS, digital image s.v. "Adeline Burt," (birth 24 Nov 1882, death 11 Sep 1966), *FindaGrave.com*. "Social Security Death Index," s.v. "Adeline Burt," (birth 30 Nov 1880, death Sep 1966), *Ancestry.com*.
[1965] Ivery Burt, Sr., grave marker, Bullock Cemetery, Attala Co., MS, digital image s.v. "Ivery Burt," (birth 25 Dec 1876, death 25 Jun 1953), *Ancestry.com*.
[1966] "U.S., Social Security Death Index, 1935-2014," s.v. "Geneva Burt," (birth 31 Mar 1920, death 29 Mar 2005), *Ancestry.com*.

Chicago, Cook Co., IL).[1967] Brazie was the grandson of Case GUYTON; Geneva was the granddaughter of Elijah GUYTON. They were second cousins. I could find one child: James Earl BURT (b. and d. 1949, Chicago, Cook Co., IL).

R.C. BURT (Adeline Susannah GUYTON BURT, Elijah, Aaron Whitaker, Aaron Steele, Joseph I, John I, Samuel II, Samuel I, John)

R.C. BURT was the son of Adeline Susannah GUYTON (b 24 Nov 1882 Kosciusko, Attala Co., MS, d. 11 Sep 1966 Kosciusko, Attala Co., MS). She was buried in Bullock Cemetery[1968] and Ivery BURT, Sr.(b. 25 Dec 1876 MS, d. 25 Jun 1953 Attala Co., MS).[1969] R.C. BURT was born on 13 Jan 1925 in Kosciusko, Attala Co., MS, and died on 25 Feb 2009 in Kosciusko, Attala Co., MS).[1970] He married Julia CORRETHERS (b. 21 Apr 1919 Unknown, d. 12 Oct 2017 Kosciusko, Attala Co., MS).[1971]

According to Julia's obituary, she was a retired teacher.[1972] See Figure 298. She and R.C. had four children:

i   Linda BURT (b. Unknown) m. Unknown COOPERWOOD (Unknown). They lived in Memphis when Julia died.
ii Sheron BURT (b. Unknown) lived in Jackson, Hinds Co., MS.
iii Lisa Alesia BURT (b. 7 Sep 1960 d. Unknown) m. (1) James Michael JONES (b. 27 Jan 1958, d. Unknown)[1973] on 12 Oct 1981 and divorced on 1 May 1985;[1974] and (2) Unknown WALTON (Unknown) lived in Glen Allen, VA.
iv Isaac BURT (b. 2 Jan 1962 Kosciusko, Attala Co., MS,[1975] d. 7 Sep 1996 Chicago, Cook Co., IL, bur. Bullock Cemetery, Attala Co., MS)[1976] His obituary reported a surviving son, Dentonio ALLEN.

[1967] "U.S., World War II Draft Cards Young Men, 1940-1947," digital image s.v. "Brazie Guyton," (birth 6 Mar 1918, death 16 Dec 1998 per family trees), *Ancestry.com*.
[1968] Adeline Susannah Guyton, grave marker, Bullock Cemetery, Attala Co., MS, digital image s.v. "Adeline Burt," (birth 24 Nov 1882, death 11 Sep 1966), *FindaGrave.com*. "Social Security Death Index," s.v. "Adeline Burt," (birth 30 Nov 1880, death Sep 1966), *Ancestry.com*.
[1969] Ivery Burt, Sr., grave marker, Bullock Cemetery, Attala Co., MS, digital image s.v. "Ivery Burt," (birth 25 Dec 1876, death 25 Jun 1953), *Ancestry.com*.
[1970] R. C. Burt, grave marker, Bullock Cemetery, Attala Co., MS, digital image s.v. "R C Burt," (birth 13 Jan 1925, death 25 Feb 2009), *FindaGrave.com*.
[1971] Julie Correthers, grave marker, Bullock Cemetery, Attala Co., MS, digital image s.v. "Julia Burt," (death 12 Oct 2017), *FindaGrave.com*. "U.S., Public Records Index, 1950-1993, Volume 1," s.v. "Julia C. Burt," (birth 21 Apr 1919), *Ancestry.com*.
[1972] "Obituary for Julia Carrethers Burt," digital image s.v. "Julia Correthers Burt," *The Star-Herald*, 16 Oct 2017, (death 12 Oct 2017), *FindaGrave*.
[1973] "Virginia, U.S., Marriage Records, 1936-2014," digital image s.v. "Lisa Alesia Burt," (marriage 12 Oct 1981 to James Michael Jones), *Ancestry.com*.
[1974] "Virginia, U.S., Divorce Records, 1918-2014," digital image s.v. "James Michael Jones," (divorce 1 May 1985, birth of James Michael Jones 9 Jul 1960), *Ancestry.com*.
[1975] Isaac Burt, grave marker, Bullock Cemetery, Attala Co., MS, digital image s.v. "Isaac Burt," (birth 2 Jan 1962, death 7 Sep 1996), *FindaGrave.com*.
[1976] "Isaac Burt Obituary," *The Star-Herald*," Kosciusko, MS, 19 Sep 1996, p. 6, digital image s.v. "Isaac Burt," (death 7 Sep 1996).

Figure 298 Julia CORRETHERS BURT[1977]

Madesta GUYTON (Shepard, Elijah, Aaron Whitaker, Aaron Steele, Joseph I, John I, Samuel II, Samuel I, John)

Madesta (or Malisa) GUYTON was the daughter of Shepard GUYTON (b. 15 Mar 1885 Kosciusko, Attala Co., MS, d. AFT 1950, likely in Lowndes Co., MS)[1978] and Charlotte UNKNOWN (b. ABT 1888, MS, d. AFT 1950, likely in Lowndes Co., MS).[1979] Malisa or Madesta GUYTON was born about 1921 in Beat 2, Lowndes Co., MS. Her death date is unknown.[1980] She married Unknown LATHAM (Unknown).[1981] It is possible that there are two daughters with the same name if Malisa/Madesta died young. Or it is possible that Malisa and Madesta are different daughters with some confusion on Madesta's birth date in some documents.

In the 1930 U.S. Census, Madesta (9) lived with her parents and three siblings: Zollie GUYTON (14), Jonnie B. GUYTON (male) (11), and Ethelene GUYTON (4).[1982] By the time the 1940 U.S. Census was taken, Madesta GUYTON (19) lived with her parents and was married to Unknown LATHAM, who did not live with her. Madesta had a daughter named Sarah L. LATHAM (3). In the 1950 U.S. Census, Madesta GUYTON LATHAM was reported as 36-years-old, rather than 29-years-old. She lived with her parents and two daughters: Sarah L. LATHAM (13) and Mary A. LATHAM (6).[1983] She was separated from Unknown LATHAM.

[1977] Anita Martin Briggs originally shared this on 21 Jul 2023 on *Ancestry.com*.
[1978] "U.S., Social Security Applications and Claims Index, 1936-2007," s.v. "Shepard Guyton," (birth 15 Mar 1889), *Ancestry.com*.
[1979] "1940 United States Federal Census," MS, digital image s.v. "Charlotte Guyton," (birth abt 1888), *Ancestry.com*.
[1980] "1910 United States Federal Census," Lowndes Co., MS, digital image s.v. "Malisa Guyton," (birth abt 1910), *Ancestry.com*.
[1981] "1950 United States Federal Census," Lowndes Co., MS, digital image s.v. "Madesta Guyton," (married name Latham), separated), *Ancestry.com*.
[1982] "1930 United States Federal Census," Beat 2, Lowndes Co., MS, digital image s.v. "Medester Guyton," (birth ABT 1921), *Ancestry.com*.
[1983] "1950 United States Federal Census," Lowndes Co., MS, digital image s.v. "Madesta Lathan," (birth abt 1914), *Ancestry.com*.

| i | Sarah L. LATHAM (b. ABT 1937, likely Lowndes Co., MS, d. Unknown). |
| ii | Mary A. LATHAM (b. ABT 1944, likely Lowndes Co., MS, d. Unknown). |

Sarah Lee GUYTON (Wiley Leach, Elijah, Aaron Whitaker, Aaron Steele, Joseph I, John I, Samuel II, Samuel I, John)

Sarah Lee GUYTON was the daughter of Wiley Leach GUYTON (b. 12 Mar 1886 in MS, d. 21 Jul 1978 in Chicago, Cook Co., IL)[1984] and Millie NASH (b. 16 Jun 1891 Leake Co., MS, d. 3 Jan 1978 Chicago, Cook Co., IL).[1985] Sarah was born on 3 Feb 1910 in Attala Co., MS, and died on 23 Apr 2003 in Detroit, Wayne Co., MI.[1986] She married Tom Jordan GAMLIN, Sr. (b. 15 Jan 1910 Kosciusko, Attala Co., MS, d. 21 Mar 1991 Detroit, Wayne Co., MI).[1987] See Figure 299 and Figure 300.

Figure 299 Tom Jordan GAMLIN, Sr.[1988]

Figure 300 Sarah Lee GUYTON GAMLIN[1989]

In the 1930 U.S. Census, Sarah Lee was single, 20-years-old, and lived with her family in Beat 1, Attala Co., MS. She contributed to the family as an unpaid farm worker. She had attended school.[1990] By the 1940 US. Census, Sarah (30) was married to Tom Jordan GAMLIN, Sr. (30). They lived in a rural area near Kosciusko, Attala Co., MS. Sarah had an education through the fourth year of high school. Tom worked as a laborer in a milk plant. They lived with their children: Tom Jordan GAMLIN, Jr. (5), Howard

---

[1984] "Social Security Death Index," s.v. "Leach Guyton," (birth 12 Mar 1886, death Jul 1978), *Ancestry.com*.
[1985] "U.S., Social Security Death Index, 1935-2014," s.v. "Millie Guyton," (birth 16 Jun 1891, death Jan 1978), *Ancestry.com*.
[1986] "U.S., Social Security Death Index, 1935-2014," s.v. "Sarah L. Gamlin," (birth 3 Feb 1910, death 23 Apr 2003), *Ancestry.com*.
[1987] "U.S., Social Security Death Index, 1935-2014," s.v. "Tom J. Gamlin," (birth 15 Jan 1910, death 21 Mar 1991), *Ancestry.com*.
[1988] Reginald Gamlin originally shared this on 26 Jan 2023 on *Ancestry.com*.
[1989] Reginald Gamlin originally shared this on 26 Jan 2023 on *Ancestry.com*.
[1990] "1930 United States Federal Census," Beat 1, Attala Co., MS, digital image s.v. "Sarah L. Guyton," (birth abt 1910), *Ancestry.com*.

GAMLIN (3), and Claude GAMLIN (1), along with Tom's father and sisters.[1991] A marriage notice suggests another child, Jason GAMLIN.[1992]

The couple had at least four children per the 1940 U.S. Census:

i   Tom Jordan GAMLIN, Jr. (b. 3 Jan 1935 MS, d. 10 Apr 2020 MI).[1993]
ii   Howard GAMLIN (b. ABT 1937 MS, d. 30 Jul 2017 Kosciusko, Attala Co., MS).[1994]
iii   Claude GAMLIN (b. ABT 1939 MS, d. Unknown).
iv   Jason GAMLIN (b. AFT 1940 MS, d. Unknown).[1995]

Andy GUYTON (Wiley Leach, Elijah, Aaron Whitaker, Aaron Steele, Joseph I, John I, Samuel II, Samuel I, John)

Andy GUYTON was the son of Wiley Leach GUYTON (b. 12 Mar 1886 in MS, d. 21 Jul 1978 in Chicago, Cook Co., IL)[1996] and Millie NASH (b. 16 Jun 1891 Leake Co., MS, d. 3 Jan 1978 Chicago, Cook Co., IL).[1997] Andy was born 7 Jan 1912 in Kosciusko, Attala Co., MS, and died on 31 Jul 1986 in Southfield, Oakland Co., MI).[1998] He married Helen TERRY (b. 15 Jun 1913 MS, d. 20 Jun 1997 MI).[1999] Her sister, Vera LaVern TERRY, was married to Willie Clayton (WC) GUYTON, Sr.

In the 1930 U.S. Census, Andy was single, 18-years-old and lived with his family in Beat 1, Attala Co., MS. He contributed to the family as an unpaid farm worker. He had not attended school but could read and write.[2000] By the 1940 U.S. Census, Andy (28) was married to Helen TERRY (27). They lived on a farm (likely a dairy farm, based on information in Andy's obituary) the family owned on Burt Road near Kosciusko, Attala Co., MS. Andy had a sixth-grade elementary school education. The couple lived with

---

[1991] "1940 United States Federal Census," Kosciusko, Attala Co., MS, digital image s.v. "Sarah Gamlin," (birth abt 1910), *Ancestry.com*.
[1992] "Marriage of Brown/Gamlin," *The Courier-Journal*, Louisville, KY, Sun, 7 Aug 1977, p. 126, digital image s.v. "Tom Gamlin Sr.," *Newspapers.com,* <https://www.newspapers.com/image/110820995/?article=e6d73daf-0fc0-4417-81e2-3b40ffe69fb6&focus=0.010017045,0.28310743,0.17813699,0.37812218&xid=3398>.
[1993] Tom Jordan Gamlin, Jr., grave marker, Great Lakes National Cemetery, Holly, Oakland County, Mi, digital image s.v. "Tom Jordan Gamlin Jr," (birth 3 Jan 1935, death 10 Apr 2020), *FindaGrave.com*.
[1994] "1940 United States Federal Census," Kosciusko, Attala Co., MS, digital image s.v. "Howard Gamier," (birth abt 1937), *Ancestry.com*. "Death Notices Howard L. Gamlin," *The Star-Herald,* Kosciusko, Attala Co., MS, Thu, 3 Aug 2017, p. A5, *Newspapers.com,* <https://www.newspapers.com/article/the-star-herald-death-notice-howard-l-g/149865736/>.
[1995] "Marriage of Brown/Gamlin," *The Courier-Journal*, Louisville, KY, Sun, 7 Aug 1977, p. 126, digital image s.v. Jason Camlin," *Newspapers.com,* <https://www.newspapers.com/image/110820995/?article=e6d73daf-0fc0-4417-81e2-3b40ffe69fb6&focus=0.010017045,0.28310743,0.17813699,0.37812218&xid=3398>.
[1996] "Social Security Death Index," s.v. "Leach Guyton," (birth 12 Mar 1886, death Jul 1978), *Ancestry.com*.
[1997] "U.S., Social Security Death Index, 1935-2014," s.v. "Millie Guyton," (birth 16 Jun 1891, death Jan 1978), *Ancestry.com*.
[1998] "U.S., Social Security Death Index, 1935-2014," s.v. "Andy Guyton," (birth 7 Jan 1912, death Jul 1986), *Ancestry.com*.
[1999] "U.S., Social Security Death Index, 1935-2014," s.v. "Helen Guyton," (birth 15 Jun 1913, death 20 Jun 1997), *Ancestry.com*.
[2000] "1930 United States Federal Census," Beat 1, Attala Co., MS, digital image s.v. "Andy Guyton," (birth abt 1912), *Ancestry.com*.

their child, Marvin GUYTON (4).²⁰⁰¹ In the 1950 U.S. Census, the family lived on 135 Guyton Road in Kosciusko, Attala Co., MS. Andy (38) and Helen (36) owned and operated his own sawmill business. They lived with three children: Marvin GUYTON (14), Jerelyn GUYTON (8), and Vivian GUYTON (7).²⁰⁰²

In 1954, the family moved to Detroit, Wayne Co., MI where Andy GUYTON worked for Copper Brazing, Inc. He was active in the Baptist Church. See his obituary in Figure 301.

Andy Guyton

Services for Andy Guyton, 74, of Detroit, Mi., former resident of Kosciusko, were held Aug. 4, at 11 a.m. at King David Missionary Baptist Church in Detroit.

Guyton owned and operated a sawmill and dairy farm while living in Kosciusko and was a member of Palestine Missionary Baptist Church where he served as Sunday School superintendent for a number of years.

He moved to Detroit in 1954 and was employed with Copper Brazzing Inc. until he retired. He served on the trustee board of King David Missionary Baptist Church.

He leaves wife, Helen Terry Guyton; two sons, Marvin and Quinton Guyton; two daughters, Jerlene Douglas and Vivian Agnew and five grandchildren.

Figure 301 Andy GUYTON's Obituary

Andy and Helen Terry GUYTON had four children per Andy's obituary and the 1950 US. Census:

i   Marvin GUYTON (b. 3 Jul 1935 MS, d. 23 Jul 2006 Detroit, Wayne Co., MI)²⁰⁰³ m. Ann Ada LEROY (b. 16 Jan 1935 MI, d. 26 Mar 1988 Detroit, Wayne Co., MI).²⁰⁰⁴

ii   Jerelyn GUYTON (b. ABT 1942 MS, d. Unknown) m. Unknown DOUGLAS (Unknown).²⁰⁰⁵

[2001] "1940 United States Federal Census," Kosciusko, Attala Co., MS, digital image s.v. "Andy Guyton," (birth abt 1912), *Ancestry.com.*

[2002] "1950 United States Federal Census," Kosciusko, Attala Co., MS, digital image s.v. "Andy Guyton," (birth abt 1912), *Ancestry.com.*

[2003] "U.S., Social Security Death Index, 1935-2014," s.v. "Marvin Guyton," (birth 15 Jul 1935, death 23 Jul 2006), *Ancestry.com.*

[2004] "Michigan, U.S., Death Index, 1971-1996," s.v. "Ann A Guyton," (birth 16 Jan 1935, death 26 Mar 1988), *Ancestry.com.*

[2005] "1940 United States Federal Census," Kosciusko, Attala Co., MS, digital image s.v. "Howard Gamier," (birth abt 1937), *Ancestry.com.* "Death Notices Howard L. Gamlin," *The Star-Herald,* Kosciusko, Attala Co., MS, Thu, 3 Aug

iii   Vivian GUYTON (b. 28 Jan 1943 Kosciusko, Attala Co., MS, d. 23 Jan 2005 Las Vegas, Clark Co., NV) m. (1) Unknown DENNIS ABT Jul 1966 and (2) Unknown AGNEW ABT Aug 1981.[2006]

iv   Quinton Leach GUYTON II (b. Oct 1952 MS, d. Unknown).[2007]

Alma Lee MUNSON (Lottie, Elijah, Aaron Whitaker, Aaron Steele, Joseph I, John I, Samuel II, Samuel I, John)

Alma Lee MUNSON was the daughter of Lottie GUYTON (b. Mar 1897 MS, d. 1924 Attala Co., MS[2008] and Charles MUNSON (b. 5 May 1895 MS, d. Jun 1969 IL).[2009] Alma Lee MUNSON was born on 23 Sep 1916 in MS, and died on 4 Jul 1951 in Ann Arbor, Washtenaw Co., MI).[2010] She married I.C. HUNTER, Sr. (b. 9 Mar 1913 Terry, Hinds Co., MS, d. 3 Jul 1951 Superior Twsp, Washtenaw Co., MI).[2011] They died one day apart. Perhaps they were in a car accident or house fire. They were both in their thirties. According to Marie MUNSON's obituary (she was Alma Lee's younger sister), Marie and her husband, John Henry HUNTER (brother of I.C. HUNTER, Sr.), raised Alma's and Charles' children.

In the 1940 U.S. Census, I.C. and Alma were married and lived in Bolivar Co., MS. They operated a rented farm. They lived with their two children: I.C. HUNTER, Jr. (2) and Ruby Lee HUNTER (1).[2012] By 1950, I.C. (36) and Alma (33) had moved to Ann Arbor, Washtenaw Co., MI and lived at 516 Felch St. I.C. worked as a porter at a drug store. They lived with their four children: I.C Hunter, Jr. (11), Ruby Lee HUNTER (10), Mary HUNTER (8), and Robert Lee (Robbie) HUNTER (6).[2013]

Their four children are shown below:

i   I.C. HUNTER, Jr.(b. 30 Jan 1938 Shelby, Bolivar Co., MS, d. 19 Jan 2017 Ypsilanti, Washtenaw Co., MI)[2014] m. UNKNOWN. He had at least one son: Robin Joseph HUNTER (b. 16 Jul 1961, d. 2 Sep 1988 Superior, Washtenaw Co., MI).[2015]

2017, p. A5, *Newspapers.com,* <https://www.newspapers.com/article/the-star-herald-death-notice-howard-l-g/149865736/>.

[2006] "U.S., Social Security Applications and Claims Index, 1936-2007," s.v. "vivian Guyton," (birth 28 Jan 1943, death 23 Jan 2005), *Ancestry.com.*

[2007] "U.S., Index to Public Records, 1994-2019," s.v. "Quinton Leach Guyton II," (birth Oct 1952), *Ancestry.com.*

[2008] "1900, United States Census," Kosciusko, Attala Co., MS, digital image s.v. "Lottie Guyton," (birth Mar 1897), Ancestry.com. "Mississippi, U.S., Index to Deaths, 1912-1943," digital image s.v. "Lottie Munsin," (death 1924), *Ancestry.com.*

[2009] "U.S., Social Security Death Index, 1935-2014," s.v. "Charlie Munson," (birth 5 May 1895; death Jul 1969), *Ancestry.com.*

[2010] "Michigan, Death Records, 1867-1952," s.v. "Alma Hunter," (birth 23 Sep 1916, death 4 Jul 1951), *Ancestry.com.*

[2011] "Michigan, Death Records, 1867-1952," s.v. "I C Hunter," (birth 9 Mar 1913, death 4 Jul 1951), *Ancestry.com.*

[2012] "1940, United States Census," Bolivar Co., MS, digital image s.v. "I C. Hunter," (birth abt 1913), Ancestry.com.

[2013] "1950, United States Census," Ann Arbor, Washtenaw, MI, digital image s.v. "J C. Hunter," (birth abt 1914), Ancestry.com.

[2014] I. C. Hunter, Jr., grave marker, Forest Hill Cemetery, Ann Arbor, Washtenaw Co., MI, digital image s.v. "I. C. Hunter Jr," (birth 30 Jan 1938, death 19 Jan 2017), *FindaGrave.com.*

[2015] "Michigan, U.S., Death Index, 1971-1996," s.v. "Robin J. Hunter," (birth 16 Jul 1961, death 2 Sep 1988), *Ancestry.com.*

ii   Ruby Lee HUNTER (b. 2 Dec 1939 Shelby, Bolivar Co., MS, d. 8 Dec 1999 Ann Arbor, Washtenaw Co., MI)[2016] m. Patrick Duwane TAYLOR, Sr. (b. 21 Jul 1940 Ann Arbor, Washtenaw Co., MI, d. 19 Sep 2002 San Mateo Co., CA) and divorced.[2017]

iii   Mary HUNTER (b. ABT 1942 MS, d. Unknown).[2018]

iv   Robert Lee (Robbie) HUNTER (b. 26 Sep 1943 Shelby, Bolivar Co., MS, d. 21 May 1995 Superior, Washtenaw Co., MI).[2019]

Marie MUNSON (Lottie, Elijah, Aaron Whitaker, Aaron Steele, Joseph I, John I, Samuel II, Samuel I, John)

Marie MUNSON was the daughter of Lottie GUYTON (b. Mar 1897 MS, d. 1924 Attala Co., MS[2020] and Charles MUNSON (b. 5 May 1895 MS, d. Jun 1969 IL).[2021] Marie was born on 2 Mar 1919 in Kosciusko, Attala Co., MS, and died on 25 Oct 2012 in Ann Arbor, Washtenaw Co., MI.[2022] See Figure 302. She married John Henry HUNTER (b. 29 Jul 1918 Shelby, Boliver Co., MS, d. 5 Jun 1991 Superior, Washtenaw Co., MI).[2023] When Marie's sister, Alma Lee, died along with her husband, I.C. HUNTER, Sr. (John Henry's brother), they raised their children.

In the 1940 U.S. Census, Marie (20) was single and lived with her father, Charles MUNSON (43) and brother, Howard MUNSON (15) in Bolivar Co., MS. Marie worked on her father's farm.[2024] By 1950, Marie was 33, never married, and lived in Willow Run., Washtenaw Co., MI. She lived with her children: Blondean MUNSON (5) (seeFigure 303), Frederick MUNSON (2), and Thurman MUNSON (less than one year). Marie was not working.[2025]

[2016] "U.S., Social Security Applications and Claims Index, 1936-2007," s.v. "Ruby L Hunter," (birth 2 Dec 1939, death 8 Dec 1999), *Ancestry.com*.

[2017] Patrick Duwane Taylor, Sr., grave marker, burial details reported as unknown (perhaps scattered cremains), digital image s.v. "Patrick Duwane Taylor," (birth 21 Jul 1940, death 19 Sep 2002), *FindaGrave.com*.

[2018] "1950, United States Census," Ann Arbor, Washtenaw, MI, digital image s.v. "Mary Hunter," (birth abt 1942), *Ancestry.com*.

[2019] "U.S., Social Security Applications and Claims Index, 1936-2007," s.v. "Robbie Lee Hunter," (birth 26 Sep 1943, death 21 May 1995), *Ancestry.com*.

[2020] "1900, United States Census," Kosciusko, Attala Co., MS, digital image s.v. "Lottie Guyton," (birth Mar 1897), *Ancestry.com*. "Mississippi, U.S., Index to Deaths, 1912-1943," digital image s.v. "Lottie Munsin," (death 1924), *Ancestry.com*.

[2021] "U.S., Social Security Death Index, 1935-2014," s.v. "Charlie Munson," (birth 5 May 1895; death Jul 1969), *Ancestry.com*.

[2022] "United States Obituary Collection," s.v. "Marie Hunter," (birth 2 Mar 1919, death 25 Oct 2012), *Ancestry.com*.

[2023] "Michigan, Death Records, 1971-1996," s.v. "John H Hunter," (birth 29 Jul 1918, death 5 Jun 1991), *Ancestry.com*.

[2024] "1940, United States Census," Bolivar Co., MS, digital image s.v. "Marie Munson," (birth abt 1920), *Ancestry.com*.

[2025] "1950, United States Census," Ann Arbor, Washtenaw, MI, digital image s.v. "J C. Hunter," (birth abt 1914), *Ancestry.com*.

Figure 302 Marie MUNSON HUNTER[2026]

Figure 303 Blondean MUNSON[2027]

Marie's three children from the 1950 Census are shown below:

i   Blondeen MUNSON (b. 5 Oct 1944 Kosciusko, Attala Co., MS, d. 25 Jan 2014 Washtenaw Co., MI).[2028] Her obituary indicated that she had four children: Jessica BURNS, Stacy HENDERSON, Charese WOODS, and Christina Marie DENNIS.
ii   Frederick MUNSON (b. ABT 1948 MI, d. Unknown).[2029]
iii Thurman MUNSON (b. ABT 1942 MS, d. Unknown).[2030]

[2026] Photo added by PKEngle to Marie Hunter's *Findagrave* entry, Memorial ID 99621608.
[2027] revchristina originally shared this on 8 Feb 2018 on *Ancestry.com*.
[2028] "U.S., Obituary Collection, 1930-Current," s.v. "Blondeen Munson," (birth 5 Oct 1944, death 25 Jan 2014), *Ancestry.com*.
[2029] "1950, United States Census," Willow Run, Washtenaw Co., MI, digital image s.v. "Frederick Munson," (birth abt 1948), *Ancestry.com*.
[2030] "1950, United States Census," Willow Run, Washtenaw Co., MI, digital image s.v. "Thurman Hunter," (birth abt 1950), *Ancestry.com*.

CHILD OF AARON WHITAKER GUYTON AND ARTIE RAINEY: ANDREW'S LINE

Generation #7

Andrew J. GUYTON (Aaron Whitaker, Aaron Steele, Joseph I, John I, Samuel II, Samuel I, John)

Andrew (A. J.) GUYTON was the son of Aaron Whitaker GUYTON and Artie RAINEY. He was born on 18 Jan 1866 in Attala Co., MS and died on 18 Jan 1923 in Attala Co., MS.[2031] He was buried in Russell Cemetery. A.J. married Gwen UNKNOWN, who was born about 1867 in Attala Co., MS.[2032] Her death is Unknown. I cannot find the family in the 1900, 1910, or 1920 U.S. Censuses. Therefore, I cannot determine whether Andrew owned land free and clear. Together, A.J. and Gwen had two daughters:

i   Annie Bell GUYTON (b. 1889 Sallis, Attala Co., MS., d. ABT 1971 Chicago, Cook Co., IL)[2033] m. Harvey ELLIS (b. ABT 1887 Attala Co., MS, d. 31 May 1961 Chicago, Cook Co., IL).[2034]

ii   Letha GUYTON (b. ABT 1892, likely Sallis, Attala Co., MS, d. 29 Nov 1962 Cook Co., IL)[2035] m. (1) Unknown BROWN (b. 6 Mar 1887 Kosciusko, Attala Co., MS, d. Unknown)[2036] about 1912 and (2) Willie FITZPATRICK (b. 25 Sep 1889 Chickasaw Co., MS, d. 5 Aug 1941 Proviso Township, Cook Co., IL)[2037] on 19 Dec 1917 in Phillips, AR.[2038]

[2031] Andrew Rainey Guyton, grave marker, Russell Cemetery, Attala Co., MS, s.v. "Andrew Rainey," (1866-1923), *FindaGrave.com*.

[2032] Per undocumented trees in *Ancestry.com*.

[2033] "1900 United States Federal Census," Newport, Attala Co., MS, digital image s.v. "Annie B. Guyton," (birth Apr 1889), *Ancestry.com*. Death information from Channie Brown Currie.

[2034] "1900 United States Census," Newport, Attala Co., MS, digital image s.v. "Harvey Ellis," (birth Mar 1887), *Ancestry.com*. "Cook County, Illinois Death Index, 1908-1988," s.v. "Harvey Ellis," (death 31 May 1961), *Ancestry.com*.

[2035] "1920 United States Federal Census," Beat 4, Tunica Co., MS, digital image s.v. "Leather Fitzpatrick," (birth ABT 1892), *Ancestry.com*. "Cook County, Illinois Death Index, 1908-1988," s.v. "Letha Fitzpatrick," (death 29 Nov 1962), *Ancestry.com*.

[2036] "Arkansas, County Marriages Index, 1837-1957," s.v. "Letha Brown," (marriage to William Fitzpatrick on Will Fitzpatrick on 19 Dec 1917), *Ancestry.com*.

[2037] "Illinois, U.S., Deaths and Stillbirths Index, 1916-1947," digital image s.v. "Willie Fitzpatrick," (birth 5 Aug 1941; death 9 Aug 1941), *Ancestry.com*.

[2038] "Illinois, U.S., Deaths and Stillbirths Index, 1916-1947," s.v. "Willie Fitzpatrick," (birth 25 Sep 1889, death 5 Aug 1941), *Ancestry.com*.

Generation #8

Annie Bell GUYTON (Andrew, Aaron Whitaker, Aaron Steele, Joseph I, John I, Samuel II, Samuel I, John)

Annie Bell GUYTON was the daughter of Andrew (A.J.) GUYTON (b. 18 Jan 1866 Attala Co., MS, d. 18 Jan 1923 Attala Co., MS)[2039] and Gwen UNKNOWN (b. 1867 Attala Co., MS, d. Unknown).[2040] Annie Bell was born in 1889 in Sallis, Attala Co., MS. Her death is unknown.[2041] See Figure 304. She married Harvey ELLIS, who was born about 1887 in Attala Co., MS. He died on 31 May 1961 in Chicago, Cook Co., IL.[2042]

Annie and Harvey had three children:

i   Mable ELLIS (b. 28 Sep 1910 Clarksdale, Coahoma Co., MS, d. 29 Dec 1998 Chicago, Cook Co., IL)[2043] m. Aaron Garmon HARRIS (b. 24 Jan 1901, Canton, MS, d. 27 Jun 1942 Chicago, Cook Co., IL)[2044]
ii   Earnest ELLIS (b. Unknown Chicago, Cook Co., IL, d. Unknown Chicago, Cook Co., IL)[2045]
iii Letha ELLIS (Unknown).[2046]

Figure 304 Annie Bell GUYTON ELLIS[2047]

[2039] Andrew Rainey Guyton, grave marker, Russell Cemetery, Attala Co., MS, s.v. "Andrew Rainey," (1866-1923), *FindaGrave.com*.
[2040] Per undocumented trees in *Ancestry.com*.
[2041] "1900 United States Federal Census," Newport, Attala Co., MS, digital image s.v. "Annie B. Guyton," (birth Apr 1889), *Ancestry.com*.
[2042] "1900 United States Census," Newport, Attala Co., MS, digital image s.v. "Harvey Ellis," (birth Mar 1887), *Ancestry.com*. "Cook County, Illinois Death Index, 1908-1988," s.v. "Harvey Ellis," (death 31 May 1961), *Ancestry.com*.
[2043] "Social Security Death Index," s.v. "Mabel E. Harris," (birth 28 Sep 1910, death 29 Dec 1998), *Ancestry.com*. "Iowa, Marriage Records, 1880-194," digital image s.v. "Mable Eller," (birth abt 1910 Clarksdale, MS), *Ancestry.com*.
[2044] "Illinois, U.S., Deaths and Stillbirths Index, 1916-1947," s.v. "Aaron G. Harris," birth 24 Jan 1901, death 27 Jun 1942), *Ancestry.com*.
[2045] Per Channie BROWN CURRIE.
[2046] Per Channie BROWN CURRIE.
[2047] chancurri originally shared this on 19 Dec 2016, *Ancestry.com*.

Letha GUYTON (Andrew, Aaron Whitaker, Aaron Steele, Joseph I, John I, Samuel II, Samuel I, John)

Letha GUYTON was the daughter of Andrew (A. J.) GUYTON (b. 18 Jan 1866 Attala Co., MS, d. 18 Jan 1923 Attala Co., MS)[2048] and Gwen UNKNOWN (b. 1867 Attala Co., MS, d. Unknown).[2049] Letha was born about 1892, likely in Sallis, Attala Co., MS. She died on 29 Nov 1962 in Cook Co., IL).[2050] She appears to have had two husbands: (1) Unknown BROWN (b. 6 Mar 1887, Kosciusko, Attala Co., MS, d. Unknown) about 1912[2051] and (2) Willie FITZPATRICK (b. 25 Sep 1889 Chickasaw Co., MS, d. 5 Aug 1941 Proviso Township, Cook Co., IL) on 19 Dec 1917 in Phillips, AR.[2052] She had one son, Andrew BROWN, 1913-1932.

[2048] Andrew Rainey Guyton, grave marker, Russell Cemetery, Attala Co., MS, s.v. "Andrew Rainey," (1866-1923), *FindaGrave.com*.

[2049] Per undocumented trees in *Ancestry.com*.

[2050] "1920 United States Federal Census," Beat 4, Tunica Co., MS, digital image s.v. "Leather Fitzpatrick," (birth ABT 1892), *Ancestry.com*. "Cook County, Illinois Death Index, 1908-1988," s.v. "Letha Fitzpatrick," (death 29 Nov 1962), *Ancestry.com*.

[2051] "Arkansas, County Marriages Index, 1837-1957," s.v. "Letha Brown," (marriage to William Fitzpatrick on Will Fitzpatrick on 19 Dec 1917), *Ancestry.com*.

[2052] "Illinois, U.S., Deaths and Stillbirths Index, 1916-1947," s.v. "Willie Fitzpatrick," (birth 25 Sep 1889, death 5 Aug 1941), *Ancestry.com*.

Generation #9

Mable ELLIS (Annie Bell GUYTON ELLIS, Andrew, Aaron Whitaker, Aaron Steele, Joseph I, John I, Samuel II, Samuel I, John)

Mable ELLIS was the daughter of Annie Bell GUYTON (b. ABT 1889 Sallis, Attala Co., MS, d. Unknown)[2053] and Harvey ELLIS (b. ABT 1887 Attala Co., MS, d. 31 May 1961 Chicago, Cook Co., IL).[2054] Mable was born on 28 Sep 1910 in Clarksdale, Coahoma Co., MS, and died on 29 Dec 1998 in Chicago, Cook Co., IL.[2055] She married Aaron Garmon HARRIS, who was born on 24 Jan 1901 in Canton, MS, and died on 27 Jun 1942 in Chicago, Cook Co., IL.[2056] They were married in Iowa, perhaps Waterloo, on 8 Aug 1930.[2057] Aaron described his occupation as a laborer.

In the 1940 U.S. Census, Aaron and Mable lived in Chicago, Cook Co., IL at 5359 Prairie Avenue.[2058] Per *Google Earth,* today it is an empty lot with what looks like a large garden plot next door, close to apartment buildings. Mabel (27) reported having two years of high school education and did not work. Aaron (39) reported 8 years of schooling and worked as a pork cutter, likely in a meat packing plant. Living with them were three children: Yvonne HARRIS (5), Milton HARRIS (2), and Brunetta HARRIS (1).

They also lived with four lodgers: Elmira GUYTON (from Mississippi, 26-years-old, married, with 3 years of high school education, and working as a seamstress in a dress factory); Robert LEE (from Arkansas, 26-years old, single, with 8 years of education, and working as a bus boy in a restaurant); Johnny LEE (from Arkansas, 22-years old, single, with 8 years of education, and working as a porter in a retail store; and Grady JONES (from Alabama, 24-years-old, married, with 8 years of education, and working as a retail salesman in poultry). Mable and Elmira were distant cousins (4th cousin 1x removed). I wonder if they knew each other as children.

Aaron died in 1942 in Chicago and was buried in Elmwood Cemetery in Waterloo, Black Hawk Co., IA.[2059] In the 1950 U.S. Census, Mable was reported as separated but Aaron had died.[2060] She still went by the Harris last name. Had she remarried? She lived at 4142 South Park Blvd in Chicago. It is an area with nice homes now. It appears that Mable (42) lived alone in an apartment in a complex. She usually

---

[2053] "1900 United States Federal Census," Newport, Attala Co., MS, digital image s.v. "Annie B. Guyton," (birth Apr 1889), *Ancestry.com.*
[2054] "1900 United States Census," Newport, Attala Co., MS, digital image s.v. "Harvey Ellis," (birth Mar 1887), *Ancestry.com.* "Cook County, Illinois Death Index, 1908-1988," s.v. "Harvey Ellis," (death 31 May 1961), *Ancestry.com.*
[2055] "Social Security Death Index," s.v. "Mabel E. Harris," (birth 28 Sep 1910, death 29 Dec 1998), *Ancestry.com.* "Iowa, Marriage Records, 1880-194," digital image s.v. "Mable Eller," (birth abt 1910 Clarksdale, MS), *Ancestry.com.*
[2056] "Illinois, U.S., Deaths and Stillbirths Index, 1916-1947," s.v. "Aaron G. Harris," birth 24 Jan 1901, death 27 Jun 1942), *Ancestry.com.*
[2057] "Iowa, U.S., Marriage Records, 1880-1948," digital image s.v. "Mable Eller," (marriage 8 Aug 1930), *Ancestry.com.*
[2058] "1940 United States Census," Chicago, Cook Co, IL, digital image s.v. "Mabel Harris," (birth abt 1913), *Ancestry.com.*
[2059] Aaron Garmon Harris, grave marker, Elmwood Cemetery, Waterloo, Black Hawk Co., IA, digital image s.v. "Aaron G. Harris," (birth 1901, death 28 Jun 1942), *FindaGrave.com.*
[2060] "1950 United States Census," Chicago, Cook Co, IL, digital image s.v. "Mabel Harris," (birth abt 1908), *Ancestry.com.*

worked as a presser for a laundry but was unemployed when the census was taken. No children were living with her, although Yvonne HARRIS would have been 15, Milton HARRIS 12, and Brunetta 11. Brunetta lived with her uncle and aunt, Jordan and Laurie VORTICE in Gary, Lake Co., IN in the 1950 U.S. Census. Her guardians were likely from her father's side of the family. Were the other children similarly with other guardians? If so, why? Mable had another daughter in 1944, Joyce Lee HARRIS, or perhaps she went by a different last name.[2061] See details below.

Mable and Aaron had three children:

i   Yvonne HARRIS (b. 28 Sep 1934 Cook Co., IL, d. 22 Oct 1992 Chicago, Cook Co., IL)[2062] m. Eugene BUTLER (b. 2 Feb 1931 Kemper Springs, Kemper Co., MS, d. 5 Feb 1994, Chicago, Cook Co., IL[2063]

ii   Milton HARRIS (b. ABT 1937 Chicago, Cook Co., IL, d. 16 Apr 1999)[2064] m. Jeannie UNKNOWN.[2065]

iii   Brunetta HARRIS (b. ABT 1939 Chicago, Cook Co., IL, d. Unknown).[2066]

Mable had at least one other child:

i   Joyce Lee HARRIS, or other last name (b. 18 Mar 1944 Chicago, Cook Co., IL, d. 8 Dec 2008 Hammond, Cook Co., IN) m. Johnnie SMITH (b. and d. Chicago, Cook Co., IL and died before Joyce).[2067]

[2061] "Indiana, Death Certificates, 1899-2011," digital image s.v. "Joyce Lee Smith," (birth 18 Mar 1944, death 8 Dec 2008, mother Mabel Ellis), *Ancestry.com*.

[2062] "Cook County, Illinois Birth Index, 1916-1935," s.v. "Yvonne Harris," (birth 28 Sep 1934), *Ancestry.com*. Death information from the *Ancestry.com* tree of her daughter, Stephanie Butler.

[2063] "Social Security Death Index, 1935-2014," s.v. "Eugene Butler," (birth 2 Feb 1931, death 5 Feb 1994), *Ancestry.com*.

[2064] "Social Security Applications and Claims Index, 1936-2007," s.v. "Milton Harris," (birth 18 Oct 1937, death 16 Apr 1999), *Ancestry.com*.

[2065] Per Channie Brown-Currie.

[2066] "1940 United States Federal Census," Chicago, Cook Co., IL, digital image s.v. "Brunette Harris," (birth abt 1939), *Ancestry.com*.

[2067] Per Channie Brown-Currie.

CHILD OF AARON WHITAKER GUYTON AND ARTIE RAINEY: JAMES T'S LINE

Generation #7

James T. GUYTON (Aaron Whitaker, Aaron Steele, Joseph I, John I, Samuel II, Samuel I, John)

James T. GUYTON was the son of Aaron Whitaker GUYTON and Artie RAINEY. He was born about 1868 in Sallis, Attala Co., MS and died about 1882 in Sallis.[2068] He is buried in Russell Cemetery. James died too young to determine if he ever owned any land free and clear.

[2068] "1870 United States Census," Beat 4, Attala Co., MS, digital image s.v. "James Rainey," (birth ABT 1866), *Ancestry.com*.

CHILD OF AARON WHITAKER GUYTON AND ARTIE RAINEY: CASE'S LINE

Generation #7

Case GUYTON (Aaron Whitaker, Aaron Steele, Joseph I, John I, Samuel II, Samuel I, John)

Case GUYTON (son of Aaron Whitaker GUYTON and Artemesia (Artie) RAINEY) was born in Jan 1869 in Attala Co., MS. See Figure 305. He died on 24 Apr 1936 in St. Louis, St. Louis Co., MO.[2069] In 1910, Case and his younger brother, Ike, lived with their mother in Beat 4, Attala Co., MS. They were engaged in farming on a farm owned without a mortgage by Artie and/or by her sons. The Census indicates that Case could not read or write but that Artie and Ike could.[2070]

By the 1920 U.S. Census, Case lived with his nephew, Fred L. GUYTON, and Fred's wife, Ethel Viola CURTIS GUYTON.[2071] They lived in St. Louis, MO, Ward 7 at 1535 and 1537 Papin St.[2072] See Figure 306. Fred L. GUYTON was the son of Lige GUYTON. By recognizing each other as uncle and nephew, Case and Fred give additional evidence that Pinkney and Lige are the sons of Aaron Whitaker GUYTON, contrary to the traditions of Artie Rainey descendants. In 1920, Case worked in a car shop as a laborer.

Figure 305 Case GUYTON[2073]

[2069] Case Guyton, grave marker, Russell Cemetery, Attala Co., MS, s.v. "Case Rainey," (1869- 24 Apr 1936), *FindaGrave.com*.
[2070] "1910 United States Census," Attala Co., MS, digital image s.v. "Emma Guyton," (birth about 1889), *Ancestry.com*.
[2071] "1920 United States Census," St. Louis, St. Louis Co., MO, digital image s.v. "Case Guyton," (birth about 1865), *Ancestry.com*.
[2072] "U.S., City Directories, 1822-1995 for Case Guyton in 1920," digital image s.v. "Case Guyton," (address r1535 Papin St.), *Ancestry.com*.
[2073] Posted by Channie Brown-Currie as Chancuuri, 18 May 2013, *Ancestry.com*.

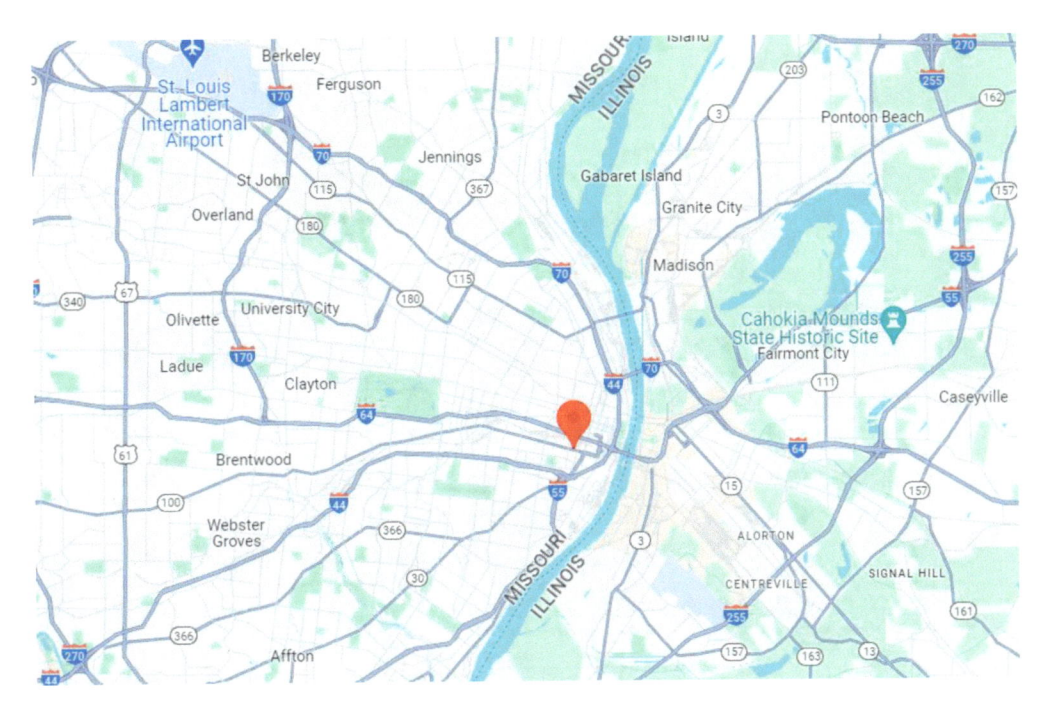

Figure 306 Map of 1535 Papin St in St. Louis, MO

It appears from Case GUYTON's death certificate that he still lived with his nephew, Fred L. GUYTON.[2074] See Figure 307. They lived at 1808 Papin St., near their home in the 1920 U.S. Census. Case worked as a laborer for the railroad at his death.

[2074] "Missouri, U.S., Death Certificates, 1910-1969 for Case Guyton," digital image s.v. "Case Guyton," death (24 Apr 1936), *Ancestry.com*.

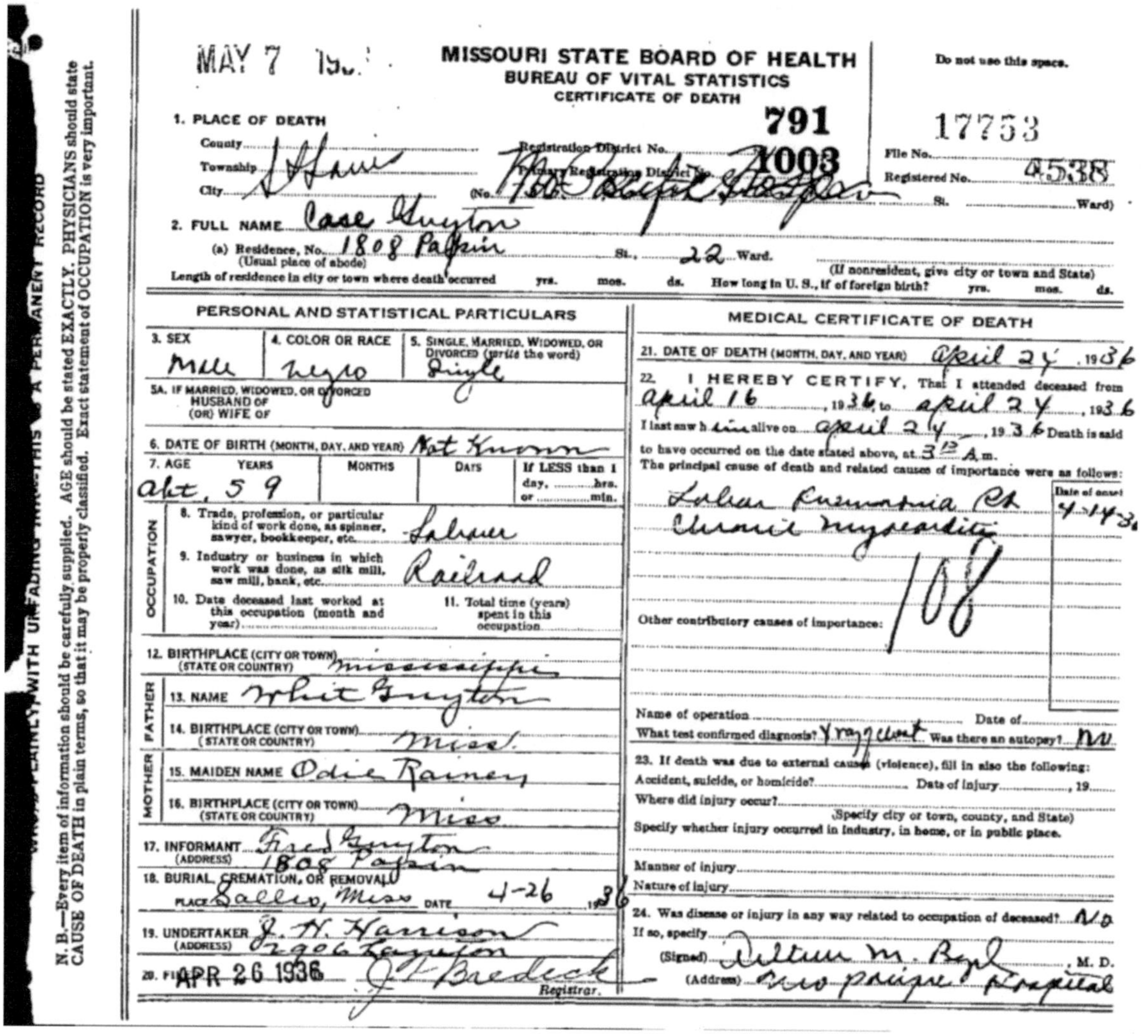
MAY 7 193

MISSOURI STATE BOARD OF HEALTH
BUREAU OF VITAL STATISTICS
CERTIFICATE OF DEATH

Do not use this space.

791 17753

1. PLACE OF DEATH
County St Louis Registration District No. 1003 File No.
Township Primary Registration District Registered No. 4538
City (No. 1750 Pacific Hospital St. Ward)
2. FULL NAME Case Guyton
(a) Residence, No. 1808 Papin St., 22 Ward.
(Usual place of abode) (If nonresident, give city or town and State)
Length of residence in city or town where death occurred yrs. mos. ds. How long in U. S., if of foreign birth? yrs. mos. ds.

PERSONAL AND STATISTICAL PARTICULARS
3. SEX Male
4. COLOR OR RACE Negro
5. SINGLE, MARRIED, WIDOWED, OR DIVORCED (write the word) Single
5A. IF MARRIED, WIDOWED, OR DIVORCED HUSBAND OF (OR) WIFE OF
6. DATE OF BIRTH (MONTH, DAY, AND YEAR) Not Known
7. AGE YEARS abt. 59 MONTHS DAYS If LESS than 1 day, hrs. or min.
OCCUPATION
8. Trade, profession, or particular kind of work done, as spinner, sawyer, bookkeeper, etc. Laborer
9. Industry or business in which work was done, as silk mill, saw mill, bank, etc. Railroad
10. Date deceased last worked at this occupation (month and year)
11. Total time (years) spent in this occupation
12. BIRTHPLACE (CITY OR TOWN) (STATE OR COUNTRY) Mississippi
FATHER
13. NAME Whit Guyton
14. BIRTHPLACE (CITY OR TOWN) (STATE OR COUNTRY) Miss.
MOTHER
15. MAIDEN NAME Odie Rainey
16. BIRTHPLACE (CITY OR TOWN) (STATE OR COUNTRY) Miss.
17. INFORMANT Fred Guyton
(ADDRESS) 1808 Papin
18. BURIAL, CREMATION, OR REMOVAL
PLACE Sallis, Miss. DATE 4-26 1936
19. UNDERTAKER J. H. Harrison
(ADDRESS) 2906 Lawton
20. FILED APR 26 1936 J F Bredeck Registrar.

MEDICAL CERTIFICATE OF DEATH
21. DATE OF DEATH (MONTH, DAY, AND YEAR) April 24 1936
22. I HEREBY CERTIFY, That I attended deceased from April 16 1936, to April 24 1936
I last saw h im alive on April 24 1936 Death is said to have occurred on the date stated above, at 3 12 A.m.
The principal cause of death and related causes of importance were as follows: Date of onset
Lobar Pneumonia Rt 4-14-36
Chronic myocarditis
108
Other contributory causes of importance:
Name of operation Date of
What test confirmed diagnosis? X ray Was there an autopsy? no
23. If death was due to external causes (violence), fill in also the following:
Accident, suicide, or homicide? Date of injury 19
Where did injury occur? (Specify city or town, county, and State)
Specify whether injury occurred in industry, in home, or in public place.
Manner of injury
Nature of injury
24. Was disease or injury in any way related to occupation of deceased? No
If so, specify
(Signed) William M. Boyd M. D.
(Address) Mo. Pacific Hospital

N. B.—Every item of information should be carefully supplied. AGE should be stated EXACTLY. PHYSICIANS should state CAUSE OF DEATH in plain terms, so that it may be properly classified. Exact statement of OCCUPATION is very important.
WRITE PLAINLY, WITH UNFADING INK—THIS IS A PERMANENT RECORD

Figure 307 Case GUYTON's Death Certificate

Case appears to have had several partners/wives by whom he had children. It is difficult to determine which children were born to which partners and opinions differ. The birth dates of the children suggest that Case may have been having relationships with more than one women at the same time. On this topic, I rely on my own research, the research conducted by David F. GUYTON,[2075] and an Aaron Whitaker GUYTON genealogy book by Channie BROWN-CURRIE.[2076] Case's first known partner was Vina (Vinnie) ELLINGTON (b. ABT 1872 Sallis, Attala Co., MS, d. Unknown, Sallis, Attala Co., MS).[2077] Vina and Case likely partnered around 1891 because their son, Willie GUYTON, Sr. was born in 1892. Willie lived with Vina ELLINGTON's family in the 1900 U.S. Census and is designated as the grandson of the head of household, Bird ELLINGTON.[2078]

2075 David F. Guyton shared his four-generation tree for Case Guyton with me on 7 Apr 2024.
2076 Channie Brown-Currie, *The Descendants of Artie Rainey and Aaron W. Guyton,"* Guyton Family Reunion, 2017.
2077 "1880 United States Federal Census," Attala, Co., MS, digital image s.v. "Vina Elington," (birth ABT 1872), *Ancestry.com*. Death location from Channie Brown Currie.
2078 "1900 United States Census," Newport, Attala Co., MS, digital image s.v. "Willie Guytin," (birth Mar 1892), *Ancestry.com.*

i   Willie GUYTON, Sr. (b. 31 Mar 1892, Sallis, Attala Co., MS., d. 7 Jun 1979 Chicago, Cook Co., IL)[2079] m. Etta BROWN (b. 1 Nov 1892 Sallis, Attala Co., MS, d. 28 Mar 1944, buried at Hill Springs Cemetery, Sallis, Attala Co., MS).[2080]

Case's second partner was Susie UNKNOWN but she adopted the last name of her stepfather, William STINGLEY. After her relationship with Case GUYTON, she partnered or married a man named Fred LUCKETT[2081] and had children with him. In the 1910 U.S. Census, Susie's last name has been written over. Her name may have been GREEN or GREER. She was living with her mother and stepfather with at least two of her Guyton children. She was shown as Susie STINGLEY, however, in the 1900 U.S. Census.[2082] She was born on 16 Feb 1880 in Sallis, Attala Co., MS to Mollie UNKNOWN. Susie died on 26 Dec 1962 in Sallis, Attala Co., MS.[2083] She lived with her son, Shelton N. GUYTON, and his family when the 1950 U.S. Census was recorded.[2084] Her children were likely:

i   Zelma GUYTON (b. 1 Sep 1902 Attala Co., MS, d. 11 Jan 1995 Kosciusko, Attala Co., MS)[2085] m. (1) Charlie EVANS (b. 9 Apr 1900, d. 27 Jan 1946 Attala Co., MS);[2086] (2) Jesse WILLIAMS (Unknown); and (3) Unknown BURT (Unknown).[2087]

ii   John L. GUYTON (b. ABT 1904 Attala Co., MS, d. Unknown)[2088]

iii   James (Jim) GUYTON (b. 2 Sep 1905 Sallis, Attala Co., MS, d. 1956 Sallis and New Port, Attala Co., MS)[2089] m. Lillie Wardean ROBY (b. 17 Nov 1909 Sallis, Attala Co., MS, d. 27 Oct 2003 Chicago, Cook Co., IL)[2090] about 1925 before their first child was born. Lillie was the granddaughter of Pinkney GUYTON. James was the son of Case GUYTON, Pinkney's half-brother.

[2079] Will Guyton, Sr., grave marker, Sunset Memorial Lawns, Northbrook, Cook Co., IL, digital image s.v. "Deacon Will Guyton, Sr," (birth 31 Mar 1892, death 7 Jun 1979), *FindaGrave.com*.

[2080] Etta Brown Guyton, grave marker, Hill Springs Cemetery, Sallis, Attala Co., MS, digital image s.v. "Etter Guyton," (birth 1 Nov 1892, death 28 Mar 1944), *FindaGrave.com*.

[2081] Lula Avery Guyton, Funeral Program, Toinette Ducksworth originally shared this on 28 Mar 2023, *Ancestry.com*.

[2082] "1900 United States Census," Newport, Attala Co., MS, digital image s.v. "Susie Stingley," (birth ABT 1882), *Ancestry.com*. "1910 United States Census," Newport, Attala Co., MS, digital image s.v. "Susie Green," (birth about 1888), *Ancestry.com*.

[2083] Susie Stingley Luckett, grave marker, Barlow United Methodist Church Cemetery, Sallis, Attala Co., MS, digital image s.v. "Susie Luckett," (birth 16 Feb 1880, death 26 Dec 1962), *FindaGrave.com*.

[2084] "1950 United States Federal Census," Newport, Attala Co., MS, digital image s.v. "Susan Stingley," (birth ABT 1882), *Ancestry.com*.

[2085] Zelma Guyton, grave marker, Parkway Cemetery, Kosciusko, Attala Co., MS, digital image s.v. "Zelma Evans Burt," (birth 1 Sep 1902, death 11 Jan 1995), *FindaGrave.com*.

[2086] Charlie Evans, grave marker, Bullock Cemetery, Attala Co., MS, digital image s.v. "Charlie Evans," (birth 9 Apr 1900, death 27 Jan 1946), *FindaGrave.com*.

[2087] Zelma Guyton, grave marker, ParkwayCemetery, Kosciusko, Attala Co., MS, digital image s.v. "Zelma Evans Burt," (birth 1 Sep 1902, death 11 Jan 1995), *FindaGrave.com*.

[2088] "1910 United States Census," Beat 4, Attala Co., MS, digital image s.v. "John L. Guyton," (birth ABT 1904), *Ancestry.com*.

[2089] "U.S., World War II Draft Cards Young Men, 1940-1947," digital image s.v. "Jim Guyton," (birth 2 Sep 1905), *Ancestry.com*. David F. Guyton, personal correspondence, Jim Guyton's death was 1956 in Newton and Sallis, Attala, MS, 2024.

[2090] Lillie Wardean Roby, grave marker, Burr Oak Cemetery, Alsip, Cook Co., IL, digital image s.v. "Lillie Wardean Guyton," (birth 17 Nov 1909; d. 27 Oct 2003), *FindaGrave.com*.

iv   Shelton N. GUYTON (b. 12 Mar 1909 Sallis, Attala Co., MS, d. 30 May 1984 Sallis, Attala Co., MS)[2091] m. Vamis (Vammie) ROBY (b. ABT 1919 Sallis, Attala Co., MS, d. BEF 1950 Sallis, Attala Co., MS).[2092]

v   Percy GUYTON (b. ABT 1911 MS,[2093] d. 1 Feb 1993 Jackson, Hinds Co., MS)[2094] m. Maudie M. WILLIAMS (Unknown).

vi   Lula Avery (Doll Baby) GUYTON (b. 14 Oct 1914 Sallis, Attala Co., MS., d. 16 Feb 2013 Los Angeles Co., CA)[2095] m. (1) Joe JOHNSON (Unknown) ABT 1932 in Attala Co., MS and (2) Lawrence LEFFUE (b. 15 Jun 1916 Arkansas, d. 10 Apr 1974 Contra Costa Co., CA)[2096] on 29 Nov 1961 in Alameda, CA.[2097]

Case's third partner's name is not known with certainty. Fannie is known by the following last names: WILDER, WISE, and GREER.[2098] Her children with Case are shown below:

i   Lillie GUYTON (b. ABT 1906 likely in Attala Co., MS, d. Unknown).[2099]

ii   John Henry GUYTON (b. ABT 1909, d. 12 May 1989, Atlanta, Fulton Co., GA).[2100]

iii   Annie Pearl GUYTON (b. 9 Jun 1910 Sallis, Attala Co., MS, d. 27 May 1983 Sallis, Attala Co., MS)[2101] m. Jim Bell RILEY (b. 6 Apr 1906 Sallis, Attala Co., MS, d. 10 Sep 1991 Chicago, Cook Co., IL)[2102] about 1929 before the birth of their first child.

iv   Fred GUYTON (b. 3 Jul 1912 Kosciusko, Attala Co., MS, d. 13 Dec 1998 Sallis, Attala Co., MS)[2103] m. (1) UNKNOWN and (2) Unknown ALLEN. Fred had two sons: Joe Frank ALLEN and Robert GUYTON, per his obituary.

[2091] "U.S., Social Security Death Index, 1935-2014," s.v. "Shelton Guyton," (birth 12 Mar 1909, death May 1984), *Ancestry.com*. Shelton N. Guyton, grave marker, Russell Cemetery, Attala Co., MS, digital image s.v. "Shelton N. Guyton," (death 30 May 1984), *FindaGrave.com*.

[2092] "1920 United States Census," Attala Co., MS, digital image s.v. "Vama Roby," (birth ABT 1918), *Ancestry.com*. She died sometime after 1940 when she was entered as a contact in Shelton Guyton's WWII Draft Registration.

[2093] Per Channie Brown-Currie.

[2094] "Percy Guyton Ex-Cement Company Employee," *Clarion-Ledger*, Jackson, MS, Fri, Feb 05 Feb 1993, pp. 15-16, *Newspapers.com*. The article says Percy was 81 years old, making his birth around 1912. He died on the Monday before the obituary was published, 1 Feb 1993.

[2095] Lula Avery Guyton, grave marker, Holy Cross Cemetery, Culver City, Los Angeles Co., CA, digital image s.v. "Lulavery Guyton Johnson Leffue," (birth 14 Oct 1914; d. 16 Feb 2013), *FindaGrave.com*.

[2096] "California, U.S., Death Index, 1940-1997," s.v. "Lawrence Leffue," (birth 15 Jun 1916; death 10 Apr 1974), *Ancestry.com*.

[2097] "California, U.S., Marriage Index, 1960-1985," digital image s.v. "Lawrence Leffue," (marriage 29 Nov 1961), *Ancestry.com*.

[2098] Fannie is shown as part of the Wilder family in the 1910 U.S. Census in Beat 4, Attala Co., MS. In the "U.S., Social Security Applications and Claims Index, 1936-2007," on *Ancestry.com*, she is known as Fannie Wise. And in *FindaGrave*, she is shown as Fannie Greer (Memorial ID 119468651 in Russell Cemetery).

[2099] "1910 United States Census," Beat 4, Attala Co., MS, digital image s.v. "Lillie Guyton," (birth ABT 1906), *Ancestry.com*.

[2100] "Georgia Deaths, 1919-98," s.v. "John H. Guyton," (birth ABT 1909, death 12 May 1989), *Ancestry.com*. Channie Brown Currie writes that he died in Atlanta.

[2101] Annie Pearl Guyton, grave marker, Russell Cemetery, Attala Co., MS, digital image s.v. "Pearl Riley," (birth ABT 12 Jun 1910; d. 27 May 1983), *FindaGrave.com*.

[2102] Jim Riley, grave marker, Russell Cemetery, Attala Co., MS, digital image s.v. "Jim Riley," (birth ABT 6 Apr 1906; death 10 Sep 1991), *FindaGrave.com*.

[2103] Fred Guyton, grave marker, Russell Cemetery, Attala Co., MS, digital image s.v. "Fred Guyton," (birth 3 Jul 1912; death 13 Dec 1998), *FindaGrave.com*. "Fred Guyton," *The Star-Herald*, Kosciusko, MS, Thu, Dec 24, 1998, p. 6, *Newspapers.com*. The obituary indicates that Lula Avery (Louaves) Johnson, living in Los Angeles, CA, is a surviving sister. He is also survived by sister, Mrs. Rose B. Edwards. In *FindaGrave*, Mrs. Rosie Bell Greer Edwards was born 6 Sep 1915, in Leake Co., MS to Kelly and Fannie Greer.

Lillie, John Henry, and Annie Pearl GUYTON were listed in the 1910 U.S. Census living with Fannie Wilder.

Generation #8

Willie GUYTON, Sr. (Case, Aaron Whitaker, Aaron Steele, Joseph I, John I, Samuel II, Samuel I, John)

Willie Guyton, Sr.'s father was Case GUYTON (b. Jan 1869 Attala Co., MS, d. 24 Apr 1936, St. Louis, St. Louis City, MO).[2104] Case had several known partners. His first known partner was Vina (Vinnie) ELLINGTON (b. ABT 1872 Sallis, Attala Co., MS, death Unknown).[2105] Vina and Case likely partnered around 1891 because their son, Willie GUYTON, Sr., was born in 1892. Willie lived with Vina ELLINGTON's family in the 1900 U.S. Census and is designated as the grandson of the head of household, Bird ELLINGTON.[2106]

Willie was born on 31 Mar 1892 in Sallis, Attala Co., MS. He died on 7 Jun 1979 in Chicago, Cook Co., IL.[2107] See Figure 308. He is buried in Sunset Memorial Lawns in Northbrook, IL. See Figure 309. He married Etta BROWN, who was born on 1 Nov 1892 in Sallis, Attala Co., MS. She died on 28 Mar 1944 and is buried at Hill Springs Cemetery in Sallis, Attala Co., MS.[2108] It appears that Willie moved to Chicago after Etta died. I first saw him in Chicago in 1952.

Figure 308 Willie GUYTON, Sr.

Figure 309 Sunset Memorial Lawns, Northbrook, Cook Co., IL

Reported in the 1950 U.S. Census, Willie was widowed and lived on Coon Trail Road in Kosciusko, Attala Co., MS.[2109] Coon Trail Road, according to *Google Maps*, is some subset of Attala Road 3034.

[2104] Case Guyton, grave marker, Russell Cemetery, Attala Co., MS, s.v. "Case Rainey," (1869- 24 Apr 1936), *FindaGrave.com*.

[2105] "1880 United States Federal Census," Attala, Co., MS, digital image s.v. "Vina Elington," (birth ABT 1872), *Ancestry.com*

[2106] "1900 United States Federal Census," New Port, Attala, Co., MS, digital image s.v. "Willie Guytin," (birth Mar 1892), *Ancestry.com*

[2107] Will Guyton, Sr., grave marker, Sunset Memorial Lawns, Northbrook, Cook Co., IL, digital image s.v. "Deacon Will Guyton, Sr," (birth 31 Mar 1892, death 7 Jun 1979), *FindaGrave.com*.

[2108] Etta Brown Guyton, grave marker, Hill Springs Cemetery, Sallis, Attala Co., MS, digital image s.v. "Etter Guyton," (birth 1 Nov 1892, death 28 Mar 1944), *FindaGrave.com*.

[2109] "1950 United States Federal Census," Kosciusko, Attala, Co., MS, digital image s.v. "Will Guyton," (birth ABT 1893), *Ancestry.com*

According to family genealogist Channie BROWN-CURRIE, Will GUYTON, Sr. was associated with Hill Spring MB Church. He was one of the founding members in Attala Co., MS.

Willie and Etta had at least eleven children:

i   Annie May GUYTON (b. 29 May 1912 Sallis, Attala Co., MS, d. 19 Oct 1997 Chicago, Cook Co., IL)[2110] m. Frank Ellis WALTERS (b. 4 Apr 1914 Attala Co., MS, d. 21 Oct 1982).[2111]

ii   Essie Dee GUYTON (b. 15 Sep 1916 Sallis, Attala Co., MS, d. 8 Aug 2005 Chicago, Cook Co., IL)[2112] m. Rollegge Newell (Rollie) BROWN (b. 29 Jan 1912 Sallis, Attala Co., MS, d. 4 Nov 1994 Chicago, Cook Co., IL).[2113]

iii   Brazie GUYTON (b. 6 Mar 1918 Attala Co., MS, d. 16 Dec 1998 Chicago, Cook Co., IL)[2114] m. Geneva BURT (b. 31 Mar 1920 Attala Co., MS, d. 29 Mar 2005 Chicago, Cook Co., IL).[2115] Brazie was the grandson of Case GUYTON; Geneva was the granddaughter of Elijah GUYTON. The couple was second cousins.

iv   Fannie Louise GUYTON (b. 15 May 1920 Sallis, Attala Co., MS, d. 16 Dec 1998 Southfield., Oakland Co., MI)[2116] m. Ollie BELL, Jr. (b. 12 Feb 1920 Kosciusko, Attala Co., MS, d. 30 Jan 2018 Southfield, Oakland Co., MI).[2117]

v   Willie GUYTON, Jr. (b. 22 Apr 1922 Sallis, Attala Co., MS, d. 1 Mar 1980 Chicago, Cook Co., IL)[2118] m. (1) Louvenia GREEN (b. 2 Oct 1928 AL, d. Unknown),[2119] (2) Lucille BARRETT (b. 8 Oct 1925 AR, d. 2022),[2120] and (3) Mildred CLAIBORNE (b. 1917, d. 2016 Chicago, Cook Co., IL).[2121]

vi   Elvie GUYTON (b. 11 May 1924 Sallis, Attala Co., MS, d. 14 Oct 2012 Detroit, Wayne Co., MI)[2122] m. Flemmie Buford TERRY (b. 18 Jun 1924 Kosciusko, Attala Co., MS, d. 20 Apr 2007 Detroit, Wayne Co., MI).[2123]

[2110] Birth and death dates and death location were provided by undocumented trees, *Ancestry.com*. She is not buried in the Kosciusko City Cemetery with her husband and daughter, making *FindaGrave* unhelpful.

[2111] Frank Ellis Walters, grave marker, Kosciusko City Cemetery, Kosciusko, Attala Co., MS, digital image s.v. "Frank Ellis Walters," (birth 4 Apr 1914, death 21 Oct 1982), *FindaGrave.com*.

[2112] "U.S., Social Security Death Index, 1935-2014," s.v. "Essie Brown," (birth 11 Sep 1915, death 8 Aug 2005), *Ancestry.com*. Sources vary as to the year of her birth, either 1915 or 1916.

[2113] "U.S., Social Security Death Index, 1935-2014," s.v. "Rollie Brown," (birth 29 Feb 1912, death 4 Nov 1994), *Ancestry.com*. His birth in February may be a mistake as it is shown as January in public records, his *FindaGrave* entry, his draft registration, etc.

[2114] "U.S., World War II Draft Cards Young Men, 1940-1947," digital image s.v. "Brazie Guyton," (birth 6 Mar 1918, death 16 Dec 1998 per family trees), *Ancestry.com*.

[2115] "U.S., Social Security Death Index, 1935-2014," s.v. "Geneva Burt," (birth 31 Mar 1920, death 29 Mar 2005), *Ancestry.com*.

[2116] "U.S., Social Security Death Index, 1935-2014," s.v. "Fannie Bell," (birth 20 May 1920, death 16 Dec 1998), *Ancestry.com*. The U.S., Social Security Applications and Claims Index, 1936-2007, on *Ancestry.com* indicates her birthday was 15 May 1920.

[2117] Ollie Bell, Jr., grave marker, United Memorial Gardens, Superior Township, Washtenaw Co., MI, digital image s.v. "Ollie Bell," (birth 16 Mar 1920, death 30 Jan 2018), *FindaGrave.com*. His WWII Draft Card indicates his birthdate was 12 Feb 1920.

[2118] "U.S., Department of Veterans Affairs BIRLS Death File, 1850-2010," s.v. "William Guyton," (birth 22 Apr 1922, death Mar 1980), *Ancestry.com*.

[2119] "Ohio, U.S., County Marriage Records, 1774-1993," digital image, "Louvenie Green," (marriage with Will Guyton on 9 Nov 1946, birth ABT 1922), *Ancestry.com*.

[2120] Undocumented tree on *Ancestry.com*.

[2121] Mildred Claiborne was married to Willie Guyton, Jr. at his death in 2016. "Illinois, Cook County Deaths, 1871-1998," s.v. Will Guyton," *FamilySearch*.

[2122] Elvie Guyton, grave marker, Westlawn Cemetery, Wayne, Wayne Co., MI, digital image s.v. "Elve Terry," (birth 11 May 1924, death 14 Oct 2012), *FindaGrave.com*.

[2123] "U.S., Social Security Death Index, 1935-2014," s.v. "Flemmie B. Terry," (birth 18 Jun 1924, death 20 Apr 2007), *Ancestry.com*.

vii Willie Clayton (WC) GUYTON, Sr. (b. 10 Jul 1926 Sallis, Attala Co., MS, d. 16 May 2011 Chicago, Cook Co., IL)[2124] m. Vera LaVern TERRY (b. 8 May 1930 Kosciusko, Attala Co., MS, d. 1 Aug 2018 Bolingbrook, Will Co., IL).[2125]

viii Rev. Clarence GUYTON, Sr. (b. 12 Sep 1928 Kosciusko, Attala Co., MS, d. 17 Aug 1998 Chicago, Cook Co., IL)[2126] m. (1) Nulugia SMITH (b. 30 Apr 1934 MS, d. Unknown)[2127] on 22 Jan 1953 in Chicago,[2128] and (2) Lessie V. JAMES (b. 7 Feb 1926 MS, d. 26 May 2011 Chicago, Cook Co., IL).[2129]

ix Claude GUYTON (b. Mar 1931 MS, d. 9 Aug 1952 Cook Co., IL)[2130] m. Helen HEMP (Unknown).

x Mary Lynn GUYTON (b. ABT 1934 Attala Co., MS, d. Unknown)[2131] m. James SMITH (Unknown).[2132]

xi Vernon T. (Vearn) GUYTON, Sr. (b. Jul 1936 MS, d. Unknown)[2133] m. Ollie J. Peteet (b. 31 Jan 1942 MS, d. Unknown).[2134]

Zelma GUYTON (Case, Aaron Whitaker, Aaron Steele, Joseph I, John I, Samuel II, Samuel I, John)

Zelma GUYTON's father was Case GUYTON (b. Jan 1869 Attala Co., MS, d. 24 Apr 1936 St. Louis, St. Louis City, MO).[2135] Case had several known partners. His second partner was Susie UNKNOWN, Zelma's mother. Susie adopted the last name of her stepfather, William STINGLEY. After her relationship with Case GUYTON, she partnered or married a man named Fred LUCKETT[2136] and had children with him. In the 1910 U.S. Census, Susie's last name had been written over. Her name may have been GREEN or GREER. She was living with her mother and stepfather with at least two of her Guyton children. She was shown as Susie STINGLEY, however, in the 1900 U.S. Census.[2137] She was born on 16 Feb 1880 in Sallis, Attala Co., MS to Mollie UNKNOWN. Susie died on 26 Dec 1962 in Sallis, Attala Co., MS.[2138]

[2124] "U.S., Social Security Death Index, 1935-2014," s.v. "W.C. Guyton," (birth 10 Jul 1926, death 16 May 2011), *Ancestry.com*.

[2125] "1950 United States Federal Census," MS, digital image s.v. "Vera L. Guyton," (birth ABT 1931), *Ancestry.com*. The other dates come from undocumented trees in *Ancestry.com*.

[2126] "U.S., Social Security Death Index, 1935-2014," s.v. "Clarence Guyton," (birth 12 Sep 1928, death 17 Aug 1998), *Ancestry.com*.

[2127] "U.S., Public Records Index, 1950-1993, Volume 1," s.v. "Nequlia Guyton," (birth 30 Apr 1934), *Ancestry.com*.

[2128] "Cook County, Illinois Marriage Index, 1930-1960," s.v. "Clarence Guyton," (marriage to Nugulia Smith on 22 Jan 1953 in Cook Co., IL), *Ancestry.com*.

[2129] "U.S., Social Security Death Index, 1935-2014," s.v. "Lessie V. Guyton," (birth 7 Feb 1926, death 26 May 2011), *Ancestry.com*.

[2130] "U.S., Index to Public Records, 1994-2019," s.v. "Claude L. Guyton," (birth Mar 1931), *Ancestry.com*. "Cook County, Illinois Death Index, 1908-1988," s.v. Claude Guyton," (death 9 Aug 1952), *Ancestry.com*.

[2131] "1950 United States Federal Census," Kosciusko, Attala Co., MS, digital image s.v. "Mary L. Guyton," (birth ABT 1934), *Ancestry.com*.

[2132] Per Channie Brown-Currie.

[2133] "U.S., Index to Public Records, 1994-2019," s.v. "Vearn T Guyton," (birth Jul 1936), *Ancestry.com*. "Cook County, Illinois Marriage Index, 1930-1960," s.v. "Ollie Peteet," (marriage to Vearn T. Gayton on 14 Aug 1959), *Ancestry.com*.

[2134] "U.S., Public Records Index, 1950-1993, Volume 2," s.v. "Ollie J Guyton," (birth 31 Jan 1942), *Ancestry.com*.

[2135] Case Guyton, grave marker, Russell Cemetery, Attala Co., MS, digital image s.v. "Case Rainey," (1869- 24 Apr 1936), *FindaGrave.com*.

[2136] Lula Avery Guyton, Funeral Program, Toinette Ducksworth originally shared this on 28 Mar 2023, *Ancestry.com*.

[2137] "1900 United States Census," Newport, Attala Co., MS, digital image s.v. "Susie Stingley," (birth ABT 1882), *Ancestry.com*. "1910 United States Census," Newport, Attala Co., MS, digital image s.v. "Susie Green," (birth about 1888), *Ancestry.com*.

[2138] Susie Stingley Luckett, grave marker, Barlow United Methodist Church Cemetery, Sallis, Attala Co., MS, digital image s.v. "Susie Luckett," (birth 16 Feb 1880, death 26 Dec 1962), *FindaGrave.com*.

Zelma GUYTON was born on 1 Sep 1902 in Attala Co., MS. She died on 11 Jan 1995 in Kosciusko, Attala Co., MS.[2139] See Figure 310. She may have had three husbands. The first was Charlie EVANS (b. 9 Apr 1900, d. 27 Jan 1946 Attala Co., MS), who died at age 45.[2140] She may have married or partnered with Jesse WILLIAMS (Unknown)[2141] shortly after Charlie EVANS died. Zelma and Jesse's daughter was born in 1947. Her third husband was Unknown BURT (Unknown). I believe he was her last husband because she used his name last on her headstone in Parkway Cemetery in Kosciusko, MS. She was recorded as Zelma GUYTON EVANS BURT.

Figure 310 Zelma GUYTON EVANS BURT

[2139] Zelma Guyton, grave marker, Parkway Cemetery, Kosciusko, Attala Co., MS, digital image s.v. "Zelma Evans Burt," (birth 1 Sep 1902, death 11 Jan 1995), *FindaGrave.com*.

[2140] Charlie Evans, grave marker, Bullock Cemetery, Attala Co., MS, digital image s.v. "Charlie Evans," (birth 9 Apr 1900, death 27 Jan 1946), *FindaGrave.com*.

[2141] The only way we know Jesse's name is through his daughter's *FindaGrave* page. Birttie Williams, grave marker, Parkway Cemetery, Kosciusko, Attala Co., MS, digital image s.v. "Birttie Evans Scott," (birth 31 Jul 1947, death 11 Oct 2018), *FindaGrave.com*.

With Charlie EVANS, Zelma had at least five children:

i   Edward (Cornine) EVANS (b. 21 Nov 1924 Attala Co., MS, d. AFT 1995 when his mother died).[2142]

ii   Earl EVANS (b. 18 Dec 1927 Kosciusko, Attala Co., MS, d. 26 Jan 1995 Milwaukee, Milwaukee Co., WI)[2143] m. Lily Mae BURT (b. 17 Dec 1929 Kosciusko, Attala Co., MS, d. ABT 2021 Milwaukee, Milwaukee Co., WI).[2144]

iii   Tillie Mae EVANS (b. 30 Jul 1930 Kosciusko, Attala Co., MS, d. 8 Jun 2019 Waterloo, Black Hawk Co., IA)[2145] m. (1) Tommie ELLIS, Sr. (b. ABT 1926 MS, d. BEF 1955 when she married M.L. SMITH)[2146] and (2) M.L. SMITH (b. Unknown, d. BEF 2019 when Tillie died).[2147]

iv   Charlie Ray EVANS (b. ABT 1935 MS, d. Unknown) m. Rosemary TATUM (b. ABT 1945, d. Unknown).[2148] Per his mother's obituary in 1995, Charlie lived in Los Angeles, CA.

v   Avery Lou EVANS (b. 21 Apr 1938 MS, d. Unknown). Based on one obituary of Harold L. PATTERSON, Sr. (b. 21 Apr 1938 Waterloo, Black Hawk Co., IA, d. 2 Jul 2020, Waterloo, Black Hawk Co., IA), Avery and Harold were "significant others."[2149] In *FindaGrave*, four children are mentioned associated with the couple but their names are not clear enough to understand who was their biological father. They were Sheila, Harold Jr., Kevin Lamar, and Airkas (Billy) JENKINS.

Zelma GUYTON had a child with Jesse WILLIAMS. She was:

i   Brittie WILLIAMS EVANS (b. 31 Jul 1947 St. Louis City, MO, d. 11 Oct 2018 Jackson, Hinds Co., MS)[2150] m. Thomas SCOTT (Unknown) in 1994. See Figure 311 and Figure 312.

[2142] "U.S. Public Records Index, 1950-1993, Volume 1," s.v. "Cornine Edward Evans," (birth 21 Nov 1924), *Ancestry.com*.

[2143] "U.S., Social Security Death Index, 1935-2014," s.v. "Earl Evans," (birth 18 Dec 1927, death 26 Jan 1995), *Ancestry.com*.

[2144] Undocumented trees on *Ancestry.com*.

[2145] "Tillie Smith," *The Courier*, Waterloo, IA, Sun, 16 Jun 2019, p. B7, *Newspapers.com*. Her birth date is given as 31 July 1930. Her death occurred on 8 Jun 2019.

[2146] "1950 United States Federal Census," Waterloo, Black Hawk Co., IA, digital image s.v. "Tommie Ellis," (birth ABT 1926 – shown on census but not on transcription), *Ancestry.com*.

[2147] "Minnesota, U.S., Marriages from the Minnesota Official Marriage System, 1850-2022," s.v. "Tillie Mae Ellis," (married M.L. Smith on 8 Oct 1955 in Fillmore, MN), *Ancestry.com*.

[2148] "California, Marriage Index, 1960-1985," s.v. "Charlie R. Evans," (marriage to Rosemary Tatum on 20 Nov 1966 in Los Angeles, Charlie born about 1935, Rosemary born about 1945), *Ancestry.com*.

[2149] "Harold L. Patterson Obituary, <https://www.echovita.com/us/obituaries/ia/waterloo/harold-l-patterson-11084745>, accessed 6 May 20224. Harold L. Patterson, Sr., grave marker, Garden of Memories, Waterloo, Black Hawk Co., IA, digital image s.v. "Harold L. Patterson," (birth 21 Apr 1938, death 2 Jul 2020), *FindaGrave.com*.

[2150] Brittie Williams, grave marker, Parkway Cemetery, Kosciusko, Attala Co., MS, digital image s.v. "Birttie Evans Scott," (birth 31 Jul 1947, death 11 Oct 2018), *FindaGrave.com*.

Figure 311 Young Brittie WILLIAMS EVANS

Figure 312 Mature Brittie WILLIAMS EVANS

James (Jim) GUYTON (Case, Aaron Whitaker, Aaron Steele, Joseph I, John I, Samuel II, Samuel I, John)

Jim GUYTON's father was Case GUYTON (b. Jan 1869 Attala Co., MS, d. 24 Apr 1936 St. Louis, St. Louis City, MO).[2151] Case had several known partners. His second partner was Susie UNKNOWN, Jim's mother. Susie adopted the last name of her stepfather, William STINGLEY. After her relationship with Case GUYTON, she partnered or married a man named Fred LUCKETT[2152] and had children with him. In the 1910 U.S. Census, Susie's last name had been written over. Her name may have been GREEN or GREER. She was living with her mother and stepfather with at least two of her Guyton children. She was shown as Susie STINGLEY, however, in the 1900 U.S. Census.[2153] She was born on 16 Feb 1880 in Sallis, Attala Co., MS to Mollie UNKNOWN. Susie died on 26 Dec 1962 in Sallis, Attala Co., MS.[2154]

James (Jim) GUYTON was born on 2 Sep 1905 Sallis, Attala Co., MS and died in 1956 in Sallis, Attala Co., MS.[2155] He married Lillie Wardean ROBY, who was born on 17 Nov 1909 in Sallis, Attala Co., MS, and she died on 27 Oct 2003 Chicago, Cook Co., IL.[2156] Jim GUYTON was related to Lillie as he was the son of Case GUYTON (son of Aaron Whitaker GUYTON and Artie RAINEY) and Susie STINGLEY. Lillie was the

---

[2151] Case Guyton, grave marker, Russell Cemetery, Attala Co., MS, digital image s.v. "Case Rainey," (1869- 24 Apr 1936), *FindaGrave.com*.

[2152] Lula Avery Guyton, Funeral Program, Toinette Ducksworth originally shared this on 28 Mar 2023, *Ancestry.com*.

[2153] "1900 United States Census," Newport, Attala Co., MS, digital image s.v. "Susie Stingley," (birth ABT 1882), *Ancestry.com*. "1910 United States Census," Newport, Attala Co., MS, digital image s.v. "Susie Green," (birth about 1888), *Ancestry.com*.

[2154] Susie Stingley Luckett, grave marker, Barlow United Methodist Church Cemetery, Sallis, Attala Co., MS, digital image s.v. "Susie Luckett," (birth 16 Feb 1880, death 26 Dec 1962), *FindaGrave.com*.

[2155] "U.S., World War II Draft Cards Young Men, 1940-1947," digital image s.v. "Jim Guyton," (birth 2 Sep 1905), *Ancestry.com*. David F. Guyton, personal correspondence, Jim Guyton's death was 1956 in Newton and Sallis, Attala, MS, 2024.

[2156] Lillie Wardean Roby, grave marker, Burr Oak Cemetery, Alsip, Cook Co., IL, digital image s.v. "Lillie Wardean Guyton," (birth 17 Nov 1909; d. 27 Oct 2003), *FindaGrave.com*.

daughter of Patsy J. GUYTON (b. Aug 1877 Sallis, Attala Co., MS, d. after 1950, likely in Sallis, Attala Co., MS)[2157] and William (Willie) ROBY (b. Mar 1876, MS, d. Unknown).[2158]

Jim (23) and Lillie (21) were married in the 1930 U.S. Census.[2159] They had been married when Jim was 18 and Lillie was 16. Jim worked as a general farmer. Lillie's father, Will ROBY (53), lived with them on Goodman Highway in Beat 4, Attala Co., Mississippi. Also living with them were two children: Casey Glenn GUYTON, Sr. (4) and Rozell J. GUYTON (2). Jim could read and write but Lillie could not.

When the 1940 U.S. Census was taken, Jim (40) and Lillie (29) – ages are way off – lived in New Port., Attala Co., Mississippi.[2160] Their reported educational status had drastically changed. Jim had two years of school and Lillie had six. The couple then had six children and Will ROBY no longer lived with them. Their children were: Casey Glenn GUYTON, Sr. (14), Rozell J. GUYTON (13), Genova GUYTON (10), Lovell GUYTON (9), Mary Belle (Maebell) GUYTON (5), and Lucy GUYTON (3). Jim was working his own farm and had supplemental income.

The 1950 U.S. Census indicated that the family was heavily involved in the family farm.[2161] Jim (46), Lillie (40), Maebelle GUYTON (16), Lucy GUYTON (14), Susie Jean GUYTON (13), and Jimmie Ruth GUYTON (12) reportedly each worked fifty hours per week on the farm in the week preceding the Census. The younger children were presumably at school or too young to attend school. These were: Joe Troy GUYTON (7), Ray (Ike?) GUYTON (4), Caaye GUYTON (male, 1), and Lanell GUYTON (female, 1).

Information on the children is shown below:

i   Casey Glenn GUYTON, Sr. (b. 13 Jan 1926 Sallis, Attala Co., MS, d. 7 Jul 2018 Chicago Cook Co.[2162] m. Mildred TATE (b. 1 Mar 1928 Kosciusko, Attala Co., MS d. 7 May 2008 Milwaukee, Milwaukee Co., WI)[2163] on 8 Aug 1952 in Cook Co., IL.[2164]

ii   Rozell J. GUYTON (b. 1 Mar 1928 Kosciusko Attala Co., MS, d. 7 May 2008 Milwaukee, Milwaukee Co., WI)[2165] m. Ollie D. Riley, Sr. (b. 17 Sep 1921 Sallis, Attala Co., MS, d. 31 Dec 1993, Milwaukee, Milwaukee Co., WI).[2166]

[2157] "1900 United States Census," Kosciusko, Attala Co., MS, digital image s.v. "Patsy J Roby," (birth Aug 1877), *Ancestry.com*.

[2158] "1900 United States Census," Kosciusko, Attala Co., MS, digital image s.v. "Will Roby," (birth Mar 1876), *Ancestry.com*.

[2159] "1930 United States Census," Beat 4, Attala Co., MS, digital image s.v. "Jim Gyton," (birth ABT 1907), *Ancestry.com*.

[2160] "1940 United States Census," New Port, Attala Co., MS, digital image s.v. "Jenie Guyton," (birth ABT 1900), *Ancestry.com*.

[2161] "1950 United States Census," New Port, Attala Co., MS, digital image s.v. "Jim Guyton," (birth ABT 1904), *Ancestry.com*.

[2162] "World War II Draft Cards Young Men, 1940-1947," digital image s.v. "Casey Glenn Guyton," (birth 13 Jan 1926, residence, Chicago, IL), *Ancestry.com*.

[2163] "U.S., Social Security Applications and Claims Index, 1936-2007," s.v. "James Willie Perkins," (birth 12 May 1928, death 7 May 1996), *Ancestry.com*.

[2164] "Cook County, Illinois Marriage Index, 1930-1960," s.v. "Kasey Guyton," (marriage 8 Aug 1952 to Mildred Tate), *Ancestry.com*.

[2165] Rozell J. Roby, grave marker, Parkway Cemetery, Kosciusko, Attala Co., MS, digital image s.v. "Rozell J. Riley," (birth 1 Mar 1928, death 7 May 2008), *FindaGrave.com*.

[2166] Ollie D. Riley, grave marker, Parkway Cemetery, Kosciusko, Attala Co., MS, digital image s.v. "Ollie D Riley," (birth 17 Sep 1921, death 31 Dec 1993), *FindaGrave.com*.

iii   Genova GUYTON (b. 20 May 1930, Sallis, Attala Co., MS, d. 17 Jun 2023 Chicago, Cook Co., IL)[2167] m. (1) Ben GUYTON (b. 2 Apr 1920 Sallis, Attala Co., MS, d. 8 Nov 1996 Sallis, Attala Co., MS)[2168] and (2) Daniel WALKER (b. 23 Jul 1934 Port Gibson, Claiborne Co., MS, d. 2 Dec 2002, Chicago, Cook Co., IL).[2169] Genova was first cousin to Ben GUYTON, who was Ike GUYTON's son.

iv   Lovell GUYTON (b. 16 Oct 1933 Sallis, Attala Co., MS, d. 22 May 2009 Milwaukee, Milwaukee Co., WI)[2170] m. Albert BEAMON (b. 22 Dec 1928, d. 22 Sep 1978).[2171] See Figure 313.

v   Maebell GUYTON (b. ABT 1934 MS, d. Unknown).[2172]

vi   Lucy GUYTON (b. ABT 1936 MS, d. Unknown).[2173]

vii   Susie Jean GUYTON (b. ABT 1937 MS, d. Unknown).[2174]

viii   Jimmie Ruth GUYTON (b. ABT 1938 MS, Unknown).[2175]

ix   Joe Troy GUYTON (b. Nov 1945, d. Unknown).[2176]

x   Ray GUYTON (b. ABT 1946 MS, d. Unknown).[2177]

xi   Lanell GUYTON (female) (b. ABT 1949 MS, d. Unknown).[2178]

xii   Caaye GUYTON (male) (b. ABT 1949 MS, d. Unknown).[2179]

Figure 313 Lovell GUYTON and Albert BEAMON

[2167] Per Channie Brown-Currie.

[2168] Per Channie Brown-Currie.

[2169] Per Channie Brown-Currie.

[2170] Lovell GUYTON, grave marker, Lincoln Memorial Cemetery, Milwaukee, Milwaukee Co., WI, digital image s.v. "Mrs. Lovell Beamon," (birth 16 Oct 1933, death 22 May 2009), *FindaGrave.com*.

[2171] Albert Beamon, grave marker, Lincoln Memorial Cemetery, Milwaukee, Milwaukee Co., WI, digital image s.v. "Albert Beamon," (birth 22 Dec 1928, death 22 Sep 1978), *FindaGrave.com*.

[2172] "1950 United States Federal Census," Newport, Attala Co., MS, digital image s.v. "May Guyton," (birth ABT 1934), *Ancestry.com*.

[2173] "1950 United States Federal Census," Newport, Attala Co., MS, digital image s.v. "Lucy Guyton," (birth ABT 1936), *Ancestry.com*.

[2174] "1950 United States Federal Census," Newport, Attala Co., MS, digital image s.v. "Jean Guyton," (birth ABT 1937), *Ancestry.com*.

[2175] "1950 United States Federal Census," Newport, Attala Co., MS, digital image s.v. "Ruth Guyton," (birth ABT 1937), *Ancestry.com*.

[2176] "U.S., Index to Public Records, 1994-2019" s.v. "Joe Troy Guyton," (birth Nov 1945), *Ancestry.com*.

[2177] "1950 United States Federal Census," Newport, Attala Co., MS, digital image s.v. "Ray Guyton," (birth ABT 1946), *Ancestry.com*.

[2178] "1950 United States Federal Census," Newport, Attala Co., MS, digital image s.v. "Lanell Guyton," (birth ABT 1949), *Ancestry.com*.

[2179] "1950 United States Federal Census," Newport, Attala Co., MS, digital image s.v. "Caaye Guyton," (birth ABT 1949), *Ancestry.com*.

Shelton N. GUYTON (Case, Aaron Whitaker, Aaron Steele, Joseph I, John I, Samuel II, Samuel I, John)

Shelton GUYTON's father was Case GUYTON (b. Jan 1869, Attala Co. MS, d. 24 Apr 1936 St. Louis, St. Louis City, MO).[2180] Case had several known partners. His second partner was Susie UNKNOWN, Shelton's mother. Susie adopted the last name of her stepfather, William STINGLEY. After her relationship with Case GUYTON, she partnered or married a man named Fred LUCKETT[2181] and had children with him. In the 1910 U.S. Census, Susie's last name had been written over. Her name may have been GREEN or GREER. She was living with her mother and stepfather with at least two of her Guyton children. She was shown as Susie STINGLEY, however, in the 1900 U.S. Census.[2182] She was born on 16 Feb 1880 in Sallis, Attala Co., MS to Mollie UNKNOWN. Susie died on 26 Dec 1962 in Sallis, Attala Co., MS.[2183] She lived with her son, Shelton N. GUYTON, and his family when the 1950 U.S. Census was recorded.[2184]

Shelton was born on 12 Mar 1909 in Sallis, Attala Co., MS, and died on 30 May 1984 in the same town.[2185] He married Vamis (Vammie) ROBY (b. ABT 1919 Sallis, Attala Co., MS, d. BEF 1950 Sallis, Attala Co., MS).[2186] Shelton and Vammie were cousins. Shelton's grandparents were Aaron Whitaker GUYTON and Artie RAINEY. Vammie is the great-granddaughter of Aaron Whitaker GUYTON and Patsy GIBSON.

More information about the family can be found in the section on Vamis (Vammie) ROBY.

Percy GUYTON (Case, Aaron Whitaker, Aaron Steele, Joseph I, John I, Samuel II, Samuel I, John)

Percy GUYTON's father was Case GUYTON (b. Jan 1869 Attala Co., MS, d. 24 Apr 1936 St. Louis, St. Louis Co., MO).[2187] Case had several known partners. His second partner was Susie UNKNOWN, Percy's mother. Susie adopted the last name of her stepfather, William STINGLEY. After her relationship with Case GUYTON, she partnered or married a man named Fred LUCKETT[2188] and had children with him. In the 1910 U.S. Census, Susie's last name had been written over. Her name may have been GREEN or GREER. She was living with her mother and stepfather with at least two of her Guyton children. She was

---

[2180] Case Guyton, grave marker, Russell Cemetery, Attala Co., MS, digital image s.v. "Case Rainey," (1869- 24 Apr 1936), *FindaGrave.com*.

[2181] Lula Avery Guyton, Funeral Program, Toinette Ducksworth originally shared this on 28 Mar 2023, *Ancestry.com*.

[2182] "1900 United States Census," Newport, Attala Co., MS, digital image s.v. "Susie Stingley," (birth ABT 1882), *Ancestry.com*. "1910 United States Census," Newport, Attala Co., MS, digital image s.v. "Susie Green," (birth about 1888), *Ancestry.com*.

[2183] Susie Stingley Luckett, grave marker, Barlow United Methodist Church Cemetery, Sallis, Attala Co., MS, digital image s.v. "Susie Luckett," (birth 16 Feb 1880, death 26 Dec 1962), *FindaGrave.com*.

[2184] "1950 United States Federal Census," Newport, Attala Co., MS, digital image s.v. "Susan Stingley," (birth ABT 1882), *Ancestry.com*.

[2185] "U.S., Social Security Death Index, 1935-2014," s.v. "Shelton Guyton," (birth 12 Mar 1909, death May 1984), *Ancestry.com*. Shelton N. Guyton, grave marker, Russell Cemetery, Attala Co., MS, digital image s.v. "Shelton N. Guyton," (death 30 May 1984), *FindaGrave.com*.

[2186] "1920 United States Census," Attala Co., MS, digital image s.v. "Vama Roby," (birth ABT 1918), *Ancestry.com*. She died sometime after 1944 when her child Buddy Guyton was born and before the 1950 U.S. Census.

[2187] Case Guyton, grave marker, Russell Cemetery, Attala Co., MS, digital image s.v. "Case Rainey," (1869- 24 Apr 1936), *FindaGrave.com*.

[2188] Lula Avery Guyton, Funeral Program, Toinette Ducksworth originally shared this on 28 Mar 2023, *Ancestry.com*.

shown as Susie STINGLEY, however, in the 1900 U.S. Census.[2189] She was born on 16 Feb 1880 in Sallis, Attala Co., MS to Mollie UNKNOWN. Susie died on 26 Dec 1962 in Sallis, Attala Co., MS. She lived with her son, Shelton N. GUYTON, and his family when the 1950 U.S. Census was recorded.[2190]

Percy GUYTON (b. ABT 1912 Sallis, Attala Co., MS, d. 1 Feb 1993 Jackson, Hinds Co., MS)[2191] m. Maudie M. WILLIAMS (Unknown).

Lula Avery GUYTON (Case, Aaron Whitaker, Aaron Steele, Joseph I, John I, Samuel II, Samuel I, John)

Lula Avery GUYTON's father was Case GUYTON (b. Jan 1869 Attala Co., MS, d. 24 Apr 1936 St. Louis, St. Louis Co., MO).[2192] Case had several known partners. His second partner was Susie UNKNOWN, Avery's mother. Susie adopted the last name of her stepfather, William STINGLEY. After her relationship with Case GUYTON, she partnered or married a man named Fred LUCKETT[2193] and had children with him. In the 1910 U.S. Census, Susie's last name had been written over. Her name may have been GREEN or GREER. She was living with her mother and stepfather with at least two of her Guyton children. She was shown as Susie STINGLEY, however, in the 1900 U.S. Census.[2194] She was born on 16 Feb 1880 in Sallis, Attala Co., MS to Mollie UNKNOWN. Susie died on 26 Dec 1962 in Sallis, Attala Co., MS.[2195] She lived with her son, Shelton N. GUYTON, and his family when the 1950 U.S. Census was recorded.[2196]

Lula Avery (Doll Baby) GUYTON was born on 14 Oct 1914 in Sallis, Attala Co., MS., and died on 16 Feb 2013 in Los Angeles Co., CA.[2197] See Figure 314 and Figure 315. She married (1) Joe JOHNSON (Unknown) about 1932 in Attala Co., MS and (2) Lawrence LEFFUE (b. 15 Jun 1916 Arkansas, d. 10 Apr 1974 Contra Costa Co., CA)[2198] on 29 Nov 1961 in Alameda, CA.[2199] Joe and Avery had one child:

[2189] "1900 United States Census," Newport, Attala Co., MS, digital image s.v. "Susie Stingley," (birth ABT 1882), Ancestry.com. "1910 United States Census," Newport, Attala Co., MS, digital image s.v. "Susie Green," (birth about 1888), Ancestry.com.
[2190] "1950 United States Federal Census," Newport, Attala Co., MS, digital image s.v. "Susan Stingley," (birth ABT 1882), Ancestry.com.
[2191] "Percy Guyton Ex-Cement Company Employee," Clarion-Ledger, Jackson, MS, Fri, Feb 05 Feb 1993, pp. 15-16, Newspapers.com. The article says Percy was 81 years old, making his birth around 1912. He died on the Monday before the obituary was published, 1 Feb 1993.
[2192] Case Guyton, grave marker, Russell Cemetery, Attala Co., MS, digital image s.v. "Case Rainey," (1869- 24 Apr 1936), FindaGrave.com.
[2193] Lula Avery Guyton, Funeral Program, Toinette Ducksworth originally shared this on 28 Mar 2023, Ancestry.com.
[2194] "1900 United States Census," Newport, Attala Co., MS, digital image s.v. "Susie Stingley," (birth ABT 1882), Ancestry.com. "1910 United States Census," Newport, Attala Co., MS, digital image s.v. "Susie Green," (birth about 1888), Ancestry.com.
[2195] Susie Stingley Luckett, grave marker, Barlow United Methodist Church Cemetery, Sallis, Attala Co., MS, digital image s.v. "Susie Luckett," (birth 16 Feb 1880, death 26 Dec 1962), FindaGrave.com.
[2196] "1950 United States Federal Census," Newport, Attala Co., MS, digital image s.v. "Susan Stingley," (birth ABT 1882), Ancestry.com.
[2197] Lula Avery Guyton, grave marker, Holy Cross Cemetery, Culver City, Los Angeles Co., CA, digital image s.v. "Lulavery Guyton Johnson Leffue," (birth 14 Oct 1914; d. 16 Feb 2013), FindaGrave.com.
[2198] "California, U.S., Death Index, 1940-1997," s.v. "Lawrence Leffue," (birth 15 Jun 1916; death 10 Apr 1974), Ancestry.com.
[2199] "California, U.S., Marriage Index, 1960-1985," digital image s.v. "Lawrence Leffue," (marriage 29 Nov 1961), Ancestry.com.

i   Charles JOHNSON (b. ABT 1936 Sallis, Attala Co., MS, d. Unknown)[2200] m. Sheila UNKNOWN (Unknown). According to Lula's obituary below, Charles and Sheila had a son named Brian JOHNSON. Brian JOHNSON and UNKNOWN had three children: Genesis, Brian II, and Keilani.

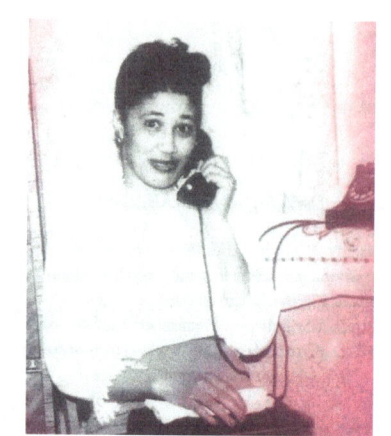

Figure 314 Lula Avery GUYTON on Phone

Figure 315 Lula Avery GUYTON Dressed Up

Lula's obituary is quoted in its entirety:

> On October 14, 1914, Ms. Lula Avery GUYTON JOHNSON LEFFUE was the seventh of the Guyton children, namely Jim, Will, Percy, Shelton, Thomas, Zelma, born to Susie and Case GUYTON in Attala County, Mississippi.
>
> Later, her mother Ms. Susie GUYTON met and married Mr. Fred LUCKETT and was blessed with four additional children, namely Waudeen, O.C., J.C. and R.L. LUCKETT. Lula was educated in the Attala County school system. Her first Christian experience was at Cedar Grove M.B. Church in Attala County.
>
> Lula was 18 when she married Joe JOHNSON in Attala and from this union bore Charles her one and only son. After the death of Joe, she soon left Attala for St. Louis, Missouri to find work. She was revered as an excellent worker with exemplary work ethics at Forest Drug Store. She sent for her son only to find that he wanted to join the Korean conflict as a marine. She met Lawrence LEFFUE and they married and migrated to the west coast, Richmond, California where they bought a home and settled down. She carried her worth ethic to Richmond, California. She worked for the Contra Costa School System and retired after twenty years at John. F. Kennedy High School and was honored for her achievements. She was always available for extra work and monitored the State SAT exams at her school. She traveled to Hawaii and to Yosemite National State Park with the students. The children loved and honored her and she will always be remembered

---

[2200] Charles is mentioned in his mother's obituary but there was no vital information about him.

by her students. She was a Christian woman. She united with North Richmond M.B. Church where she served as an usher for years until her health failed.

She had a sense of humor but a no-nonsense attitude. She was skilled in 'soul food' culinary arts. Her potato pies, lemon cake, greens with turkey butts were legendary. She had a passion for sports, particularly baseball. She loved the News, Joe Leno and Dr. Phil. People the world call hustlers, all came to Ms. Lula for a handout -- $2 if they watered her lawn or some other errand. She excelled in caregiving for many children and seniors. Her husband, Lawrence, suffered a debilitating illness and preceded her in death.

Her special love was reserved for each member of her family and in particular her son Charles, who spent his last days with her until God called his name. Losing Brian, and Keilani [Charles' son] was hard for everyone, but we persevered through the heartache. We'll remember him through his child, Brian II, and grandchildren, Brian II, Keilani who celebrated her birthdays together and Genesis. On Saturday, February 16, 2013, 2:40 a.m., Lulavery, Lula, Lue, LA, Doll Baby, and "Bi" made her transition from mortality to immortality.

Lula leaves to remember her life her grandsons, Quinton Pierre JOHNSON of Los Angeles, CA, Antonio RILEY of Chicago, IL; her great grandson Brian Renard JOHNSON (Jasmine) of Los Angeles, CA her great grandchildren, her nephews Charlie Ray EVANS (Rosemary) Acadia; Edward EVANS, Kosciusko, MS; nieces; Tellie SMITH (Waterloo, Iowa) Avery Lou PATTERSON (Harold) Waterloo, Iowa; Brittie SCOTT (Tom) Sturdevant, Wisconsin; many great nieces and nephews, relatives, great neighbors, caretakers and friends. Special thanks to my caretaker and daughter-in-law, Charlesetta and Sheila who wanted me to look my best.

Annie Pearl GUYTON (Case, Aaron Whitaker, Aaron Steele, Joseph I, John I, Samuel II, Samuel I, John)

Annie Pearl GUYTON's father was Case GUYTON (b. Jan 1869 Attala Co., MS, d. 24 Apr 1936 St. Louis, St. Louis City, MO).[2201] Case had several known partners. Not much is known about Case's third partner, Annie's mother, Fannie. Her name is not known with certainty. Fannie is known by the following last names: WILDER, WISE, and GREER.

Annie was born on 9 Jun 1910 in Sallis, Attala Co., MS. She died on 27 May 1983 in the same town.[2202] She married Jim Bell RILEY about 1929 before the birth of their first child. Jim was born on 6 Apr 1906 in Sallis, Attala Co., MS. He died on 10 Sep 1991 in Chicago, Cook Co., IL.[2203] See Figure 316, Figure 317, and Figure 318.

[2201] Case Guyton, grave marker, Russell Cemetery, Attala Co., MS, digital image s.v. "Case Rainey," (1869- 24 Apr 1936), FindaGrave.com.
[2202] Annie Pearl Guyton, grave marker, Russell Cemetery, Attala Co., MS, digital image s.v. "Pearl Riley," (birth ABT 12 Jun 1910; d. 27 May 1983), FindaGrave.com.
[2203] Jim Riley, grave marker, Russell Cemetery, Attala Co., MS, digital image s.v. "Jim Riley," (birth ABT 6 Apr 1906; death 10 Sep 1991), FindaGrave.com.

In 1930, at the age of twenty, Annie lived with her husband, Jim, and daughter, Lorine RILEY, in Beat 4, Attala Co., MS, on the Sallis and Zemuly Road. Jim was farming and Lorine was a newborn.[2204] In 1940, the couple lived in New Port, Attala Co., MS with two daughters: Lorine RILEY (10) and Collean RILEY (8).[2205] By 1950, Jim and Annie lived in New Port, Attala Co., MS. The family consisted of Jim (40), Annie (38), and Collean RILEY (16). The spelling of the girls' names varied greatly across all documents.[2206]

Figure 316 Annie Pearl GUYTON[2207]

Figure 317 Jim Bell RILEY[2208]

Jim and Annie Pearl had just the two daughters:

i   Lorine RILEY (b. 1 Nov 1930 Sallis, Attala Co., MS, d. 4 Feb 2007 Chicago, Cook Co., IL)[2209] m. James Willie PERKINS (b. 12 May 1928 Goodman, Holmes Co., MS, d. 7 May 1996 Chicago, Cook Co., IL).[2210]

ii   Collean RILEY (b. 27 Dec 1932 Attala Co., MS, d. Unknown)[2211] m. John L. FULLER (Unknown) on 22 Jul 1959 in Cook Co., IL.

[2204] "1930 United States Federal Census," Beat 4, Attala Co., MS, digital image s.v. "Annie Pearl Riley," (birth ABT 1913), *Ancestry.com*.

[2205] "1940 United States Federal Census," New Port, Attala Co., MS, digital image s.v. "Annie Pearle Rilley," (birth ABT 1915), *Ancestry.com*.

[2206] "1950 United States Federal Census," New Port, Attala Co., MS, digital image s.v. "Annie Riley," (birth ABT 1912), *Ancestry.com*.

[2207] cocucenacane6 originally shared this on 25 Sep 2010 on *Ancestry.com*.

[2208] cocucenacane6 originally shared this on 25 Sep 2010 on *Ancestry.com*.

[2209] "U.S., Social Security Death Index, 1935-2014," s.v. "Lorine Perkins," (birth 1 Nov 1929, death 4 Feb 2007), *Ancestry.com*.

[2210] "U.S., Social Security Applications and Claims Index, 1936-2007," s.v. "James Willie Perkins," (birth 12 May 1928, death 7 May 1996), *Ancestry.com*.

[2211] "U.S. Public Records Index, 1950-1993, Volume 1," s.v. "Collean Fuller," (birth 27 Dec 1932), *Ancestry.com*. "Cook County, Illinois Marriage Index, 1930-1960," s.v. "John L. Fuller," (marriage to Collean Riley on 22 Jul 1959 in Cook Co., IL), *Ancestry.com*.

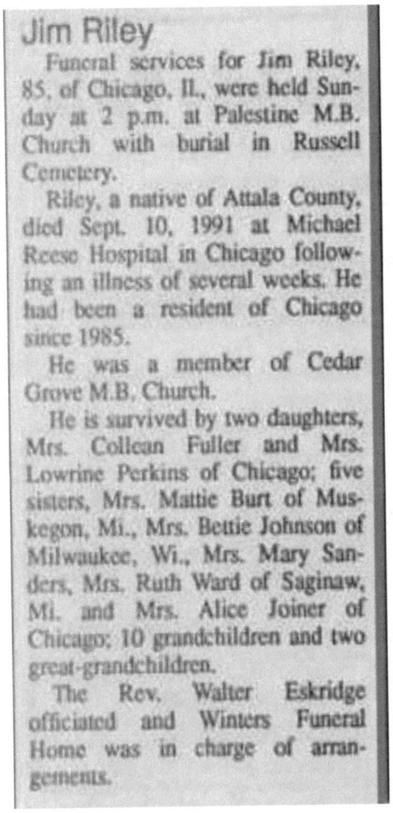

Jim Riley

Funeral services for Jim Riley, 85, of Chicago, Il., were held Sunday at 2 p.m. at Palestine M.B. Church with burial in Russell Cemetery.

Riley, a native of Attala County, died Sept. 10, 1991 at Michael Reese Hospital in Chicago following an illness of several weeks. He had been a resident of Chicago since 1985.

He was a member of Cedar Grove M.B. Church.

He is survived by two daughters, Mrs. Colleen Fuller and Mrs. Lowrine Perkins of Chicago; five sisters, Mrs. Mattie Burt of Muskegon, Mi., Mrs. Bettie Johnson of Milwaukee, Wi., Mrs. Mary Sanders, Mrs. Ruth Ward of Saginaw, Mi. and Mrs. Alice Joiner of Chicago; 10 grandchildren and two great-grandchildren.

The Rev. Walter Eskridge officiated and Winters Funeral Home was in charge of arrangements.

Figure 318 Jim Bell RILEY's Obituary in Chicago, IL[2212]

Fred GUYTON (Case, Aaron Whitaker, Aaron Steele, Joseph I, John I, Samuel II, Samuel I, John)

Fred GUYTON's father was Case GUYTON (b. Jan 1869 Attala Co., MS, d. 24 Apr 1936 St. Louis, St. Louis City, MO).[2213] Case had several known partners. Not much is known about Case's third partner, Fred's mother, Fannie. Her name is not known with certainty. Fannie is known by the following last names: WILDER, WISE, and GREER.

Fred GUYTON was born on 3 Jul 1912 in Kosciusko, Attala Co., MS. He died on 13 Dec 1998 in Sallis, Attala Co., MS.[2214] See Figure 319. He married (1) UNKNOWN and (2) Unknown ALLEN. Fred had two sons: Joe Frank ALLEN and Robert GUYTON, per his obituary. See Figure 320.

[2212] "Jim Riley," *The Star-Herald*, Kosciusko, Attala Co., MS, Thu, Sep 19, 1991, p. 8, *Newspapers.com.*

[2213] Case Guyton, grave marker, Russell Cemetery, Attala Co., MS, digital image s.v. "Case Rainey," (1869- 24 Apr 1936), *FindaGrave.com*.

[2214] Fred Guyton, grave marker, Russell Cemetery, Attala Co., MS, digital image s.v. "Fred Guyton," (birth 3 Jul 1912; death 13 Dec 1998), *FindaGrave.com*. "Fred Guyton," *The Star-Herald*, Kosciusko, MS, Thu, Dec 24, 1998, p. 6, *Newspapers.com.* The obituary indicates that Lula Avery (Louaves) Johnson, living in Los Angeles, CA, is a surviving sister. He is also survived by sister, Mrs. Rose B. Edwards. In *FindaGrave*, Mrs. Rosie Bell Greer Edwards was born 6 Sep 1915, in Leake Co., MS to Kelly and Fannie Greer.

Figure 319 Fred GUYTON[2215]

Fred Guyton

Services for Fred Guyton, 90, of Kosciusko were held Saturday at 1 p.m. at Cedar Grove Baptist Church with burial in Russell Cemetery.

Guyton, a retired farmer and construction worker, died Dec. 13, 1998 at his residence. He was a native of Attala County and a member of Galilee M.B. Church.

He is survived by sons, Robert Guyton of Kosciusko and Joe Frank Allen of Sallis; sisters, Mrs. Grace Sandifer, Mrs. Rose B. Edwards of Sallis and Mrs. Louaves Johnson of Los Angeles, Calif.

The Rev. Osie Grays officiated and Winters Funeral Home was in charge of arrangements.

Figure 320 Fred GUYTON's Obituary[2216]

[2215] chancurri originally shared this on 29 Jul 2016 on *Ancestry.com*.
[2216] "Fred Guyton," *The Star-Herald*, Kosciusko, MS, Thu, Dec 24, 1998, p. 6, *Newspapers.com*.

Generation #9

Annie May Guyton (Willie, Sr., Case, Aaron Whitaker, Aaron Steele, Joseph I, John I, Samuel II, Samuel I, John)

Annie May GUYTON was the daughter of Willie GUYTON, Sr. (b. 31 Mar 1892 Sallis, Attala Co., MS, d. 7 Jun 1979 Chicago, Cook Co., IL)[2217] and Etta BROWN (b. 1 Nov 1892 Sallis, Attala Co., MS, d. 28 Mar 1944, bur. Hill Springs Cemetery Sallis, Attala Co., MS).[2218] Annie May was born on 29 May 1912 in Sallis, Attala Co., MS, and died on 19 Oct 1997 in Chicago, Cook Co., IL.[2219] She married Frank Ellis WALTERS (b. 4 Apr 1914 Attala Co., MS, d. 21 Oct 1982, buried Kosciusko City Cemetery).[2220]

In the 1930 U.S. Census, Annie May (17) lived in Beat 4, Attala Co., MS with her parents (Willie GUYTON, Sr., 38, and Etta BROWN, 38) and her siblings.[2221] In 1940, the U.S. Census reported that Annie May (28) was married to Frank Ellis WALTERS (27) and had two children: Annie Catherine WALTERS (1), and Jerry Willie (Jerry) WALTERS (3 months old). Annie had a 4th year high school education.[2222] They lived in New Port, Attala Co., MS on a farm that the family owned. Frank had a 7th grade education.

In 1950, the family still lived in New Port, MS on their owned farms and the family had enlarged considerably: Frank WALTERS (36), Annie M. WALTERS (37), Annie Catherine WALTERS (11), Jerry W. WALTERS (10), Dora Ellis WALTERS (8), James Roy WALTERS (6), Earl D. WALTERS (5), Perry WALTERS (4), Bonnie Dean WALTERS (written Bernadine in the Census) (2), and Bobbie Joe WALTERS (1).

The couple had at least a dozen children per the 1950 U.S. Census. Information about these children and other children not found in the 1950 Census was provided by Channie BROWN-CURRIE:[2223]

i   Annie Catherine WALTERS (b. ABT 1939 New Port, Attala Co., MS, d. Unknown) m. (1) James A. DILLARD (Unknown) and (2) Joseph MADISON (Unknown).
ii   Jerry Willie WALTERS (b. ABT 1940 New Port, Attala Co., MS, d. Unknown).
iii   Dora Ellis WALTERS (b. Oct 1941 New Port, Attala Co., MS, d. Unknown)[2224] m. MacArthur VAUGHN (Unknown).
iv   James Roy WALTERS (b. ABT 1944 New Port, Attala Co., MS, d. Unknown) m. Ruby Jean UNKNOWN (Unknown).

[2217] Will Guyton, Sr., grave marker, Sunset Memorial Lawns, Northbrook, Cook Co., IL, digital image s.v. "Deacon Will Guyton, Sr," (birth 31 Mar 1892, death 7 Jun 1979), *FindaGrave.com*.
[2218] Etta Brown Guyton, grave marker, Hill Springs Cemetery, Sallis, Attala Co., MS, digital image s.v. "Etter Guyton," (birth 1 Nov 1892, death 28 Mar 1944), *FindaGrave.com*.
[2219] Birth and death dates and death location were provided by undocumented trees, *Ancestry.com*. She is not buried in the Kosciusko City Cemetery with her husband and daughter, making *FindaGrave* unhelpful.
[2220] Frank Ellis Walters, grave marker, Kosciusko City Cemetery, Kosciusko, Attala Co., MS, digital image s.v. "Frank Ellis Walters," (birth 4 Apr 1914, death 21 Oct 1982), *FindaGrave.com*.
[2221] "1930 United States Federal Census," Newport, Attala Co., MS, digital image s.v. "Annie May Walters," (birth abt 1912), *Ancestry.com*.
[2222] "1940 United States Federal Census," Newport, Attala Co., MS, digital image s.v. "Annie May Walters," (birth abt 1912), *Ancestry.com*.
[2223] "1950 United States Federal Census," Newport, Attala Co., MS, digital image s.v. "Annie M Walter," (birth abt 1913), *Ancestry.com*. Birth dates are based on the 1950 Census. Middle names, marriages, birth places, and death places are per Channie Brown-Currie.
[2224] "U.S., Index to Public Records, 1994-2019," s.v. "Dora E E Vaughn," (birth Oct 1941), *Ancestry.com*.

v	Earl D. WALTERS (b. 23 Sep 1944 Goodman, Attala Co., MS, d. 9 May 2007 Cook Co., IL).[2225]
vi	Perry WALTERS (b. ABT 1946 New Port, Attala Co., MS, d. Unknown) m. Gerri UNKNOWN (Unknown).
vii	Bonnie Dean WALTERS (b. 2 Nov 1947 Sallis, Attala Co., MS, d. Unknown)[2226] m. James PRITCHETT (Unknown).
viii	Bobbie Joe WALTERS (b. ABT 1949 New Port, Attala Co., MS, d. Unknown) m. Dr. Haywood Larence BROWN (b. 16 Nov 1952 Pantego, Beaufort Co., NC, d. Unknown).[2227] Bobbie Joe was a nurse and nursing educator at the college level, including at the University of Tennessee at Knoxville. She received her M.S. degree in nursing at the University of Mississippi. Haywood received his MD from Wake Forest University and completed his residency in obstetrics and gynecology at the University of Tennessee Center for Health Sciences in June 1982. They married on 20 Mar 1982 in Knoxville, Knox Co., TN.[2228]
ix	Lue [like Louie] Arthur WALTERS (b. 17 Jan 1952 Sallis, Attala Co., MS, d. Unknown)[2229] m. JoAnn E. UNKNOWN (Unknown).
x	Frankie Jean WALTERS (b. 22 Aug 1954 Sallis, Attala Co., MS, d. 18 May 1968 likely in Attala Co., MS).[2230]
xi	Bettye Kate WALTERS (b. AFT 1950 Sallis, Attala Co., MS, d. Unknown).
xii	Eddie Lee WALTERS (b. AFT 1950 Sallis, Attala Co., MS, d. Unknown) m. Gwen UNKNOWN.[2231]

Essie Dee Guyton (Willie, Sr., Case, Aaron Whitaker, Aaron Steele, Joseph I, John I, Samuel II, Samuel I, John)

Esther Essie Dee GUYTON was the daughter of Willie GUYTON, Sr. (b. 31 Mar 1892 Sallis, Attala Co., MS, d. 7 Jun 1979 Chicago, Cook Co., IL)[2232] and Etta BROWN (b. 1 Nov 1892 Sallis, Attala Co., MS, d. 28 Mar 1944, bur. Hill Springs Cemetery Sallis, Attala Co., MS).[2233] Essie was born on 15 Sep 1916 in Sallis, Attala Co., MS, and died on 8 Aug 2005 in Chicago, Cook Co., IL.[2234] She married Rollegge Newell (Rollie) BROWN (b. 29 Jan 1912 Sallis, Attala Co., MS, d. 4 Nov 1994 Chicago, Cook Co., IL).[2235] See Figure 321.

[2225] "Social Security Death Index," s.v. "Earl D. Walters," (birth 23 Sep 1944, death 9 May 2007).

[2226] "U.S., Public Records Index, 1950-1993, Volume 1," s.v. "Bonnie W. Pritchett," (birth 2 Nov 1947), *Ancestry.com*.

[2227] "North Carolina, U.S., Birth Indexes, 1800-2000," digital image s.v. "Haywood Larence Brown," (birth 16 Nov 1952), *Ancestry.com*.

[2228] "Bobbie Walters weds Dr. Ha[y]wood Brown," *The Greenwood Commonwealth*, Greenwood, MS, Sun, 21 Mar 1982, p. 14, *Newspapers.com*. "Walters-Brown Vows Planned," *The Star-Herald*, Kosciusko, MS, Thur, 18 Mar 1982, p. 25, *Newspapers.com*.

[2229] "U.S., Public Records Index, 1950-1993, Volume 1," s.v. "Lue A Walters," (birth 17 Jan 1952), *Ancestry.com*.

[2230] Frankie Jean Walters, grave marker, Kosciusko City Cemetery, Kosciusko, Attala Co., MS, digital image s.v. "Frankie Jean Walters," (birth 22 Aug 1954, death 18 May 1968), *FindaGrave.com*.

[2231] Per Channie Brown-Currie.

[2232] Will Guyton, Sr., grave marker, Sunset Memorial Lawns, Northbrook, Cook Co., IL, digital image s.v. "Deacon Will Guyton, Sr," (birth 31 Mar 1892, death 7 Jun 1979), *FindaGrave.com*.

[2233] Etta Brown Guyton, grave marker, Hill Springs Cemetery, Sallis, Attala Co., MS, digital image s.v. "Etter Guyton," (birth 1 Nov 1892, death 28 Mar 1944), *FindaGrave.com*.

[2234] "U.S., Social Security Death Index, 1935-2014," s.v. "Essie Brown," (birth 11 Sep 1915, death 8 Aug 2005), *Ancestry.com*. Sources vary as to the year of her birth, either 1915 or 1916.

[2235] "U.S., Social Security Death Index, 1935-2014," s.v. "Rollie Brown," (birth 29 Feb 1912, death 4 Nov 1994), *Ancestry.com*. His birth in February may be a mistake as it is shown as January in public records, his *FindaGrave* entry, his draft registration, etc.

Figure 321 Rollie and Essie Dee GUYTON BROWN[2236]

In the 1940 U.S. Census, Rollie (28) and Essie (24) were married, living in New Port, Attala Co., MS on a farm owned by the family. They had one son, Willie D. (W.D.) BROWN (6). Essie had a 7th grade education.[2237] By the time of the 1950 Census, the couple had moved to Chicago. They lived with Essie's sister, Vera LaVern GUYTON, and her husband, WC GUYTON, Sr. Rollie and Essie had two sons, Willie D. BROWN (16) and Lon T. (L.T.) BROWN (9). Rollie worked as an assembler in a window frame factory; Essie filled powder puffs in a powder factory. Also living at the home were two of WC GUYTON's brothers.[2238]

Rollie and Essie's children were:

i   Willie D. (W.D.) BROWN (b. 26 May 1933 Sallis, Attala Co., MS, d. 24 Sep 1995 Hammond, Lake Co., IN)[2239] m. (1) Connie Mae Thompson (b. 8 Oct 1935 Sallis, Attala Co., MS, d. 11 Oct 2013 Matteson, Cook Co., IL)[2240] on 9 Nov 1953 in Cook Co., IL[2241] and (2) Odester W. UNKNOWN (Unknown) who survived him in Chicago. W.D. had at least one child: Alfred BROWN (b. 15 Jun 1954 Chicago, Cook Co., IL, d. 8 Nov 2007 Dixon, Lee Co., IL).[2242]

ii   Lon T. (L.T.) BROWN (b. 7 Jun 1940 Sallis, Attala Co., MS, d. 9 Apr 2014 Chicago, Cook Co., IL)[2243] m. Vera M. McLIN (Unknown).[2244]

[2236] chancurri originally shared this on 2 Jun 2011 on *Ancestry.com*.
[2237] "1940 United States Federal Census," Newport, Attala Co., MS, digital image s.v. "Essie Dee Brown," (birth abt 1916), *Ancestry.com*.
[2238] "1950 United States Federal Census," Chicago, Cook Co., IL, digital image s.v. "Esther Brown," (birth abt 1917), *Ancestry.com*.
[2239] "Indiana, U.S., Death Certificates, 1899-2011," digital image s.v. "Willie D Brown," (birth 26 May 1933 MS, death 24 Sep 1995 IN), *Ancestry.com*.
[2240] Per stingraay's tree, accessed 1 Sep 2024, *Ancestry.com*.
[2241] "Cook County, Illinois Marriage Index, 1930-1960," s.v. "Connie Mae Thompson," (marriage 9 Nov 1953), *Ancestry.com*.
[2242] Alfred Brown, grave marker, Oakridge-Glen Oak Cemetery, Hillside, Cook Co., IL, digital image s.v. "Alfred Brown," (birth 15 Jun 1954, death 8 Nov 2007), *FindaGrave.com*.
[2243] "U.S., Cemetery and Funeral Home Collection, 1847-Current," s.v. "Lon Brown," (birth 7 Jun 1940, death 22 Apr 2014), *Ancestry.com*.
[2244] "U.S., Cemetery and Funeral Home Collection, 1847-Current," s.v. "Lon Brown," (birth 7 Jun 1940, death 22 Apr 2014), Ancestry.com.

Brazie Guyton (Willie, Sr., Case, Aaron Whitaker, Aaron Steele, Joseph I, John I, Samuel II, Samuel I, John)

Brazie GUYTON was the son of Willie GUYTON, Sr. (b. 31 Mar 1892 Sallis, Attala Co., MS, d. 7 Jun 1979 Chicago, Cook Co., IL)[2245] and Etta BROWN (b. 1 Nov 1892 Sallis, Attala Co., MS, d. 28 Mar 1944, bur. Hill Springs Cemetery Sallis, Attala Co., MS).[2246] Brazie was born on 6 Mar 1918 in Attala Co., MS, and died on 16 Dec 1998 in Chicago, Cook Co., IL.[2247] He married Geneva BURT (b. 31 Mar 1920 Attala Co., MS, d. 29 Mar 2005 Chicago, Cook Co., IL).[2248] Brazie and Geneva were second cousins. Brazie was the grandson of Case GUYTON; Geneva was the granddaughter of Elijah GUYTON.

In the 1940 U.S. Census, Brazie was 21-years-old, lived in Kosciusko, Attala Co., MS, and worked as a yard boy with 2 years of high school education.[2249] He lived with his sister, Fannie Louise GUYTON BELL's family. I could not find the 1950 U.S. Census for Brazie and Geneva, which makes it difficult to know much about them or to identify their children born in the 1940s.

According to Channie BROWN-CURRIE, Brazie and Geneva had the following children:

i   James Earl GUYTON (b. and d. 1949, Chicago, Cook Co., IL).
ii Mary Van GUYTON (Unknown) m. Unknown WHITEHEAD (Unknown).
iii Annie F. GUYTON (Unknown) m. Unknown AUSTIN (Unknown).
iv Unknown Male GUYTON (Unknown).
v   Ricky GUYTON (Unknown) m. Belinda UNKNOWN (Unknown).

[2245] Will Guyton, Sr., grave marker, Sunset Memorial Lawns, Northbrook, Cook Co., IL, digital image s.v. "Deacon Will Guyton, Sr," (birth 31 Mar 1892, death 7 Jun 1979), *FindaGrave.com*.
[2246] Etta Brown Guyton, grave marker, Hill Springs Cemetery, Sallis, Attala Co., MS, digital image s.v. "Etter Guyton," (birth 1 Nov 1892, death 28 Mar 1944), *FindaGrave.com*.
[2247] "U.S., World War II Draft Cards Young Men, 1940-1947," digital image s.v. "Brazie Guyton," (birth 6 Mar 1918, death 16 Dec 1998 per family trees), *Ancestry.com*.
[2248] "U.S., Social Security Death Index, 1935-2014," s.v. "Geneva Burt," (birth 31 Mar 1920, death 29 Mar 2005), *Ancestry.com*.
[2249] "1940 United States Federal Census," Kosciusko, Attala Co., MS, digital image s.v. "Brezie Guyton," (birth abt 1919), *Ancestry.com*.

Fannie Louise Guyton (Willie, Sr., Case, Aaron Whitaker, Aaron Steele, Joseph I, John I, Samuel II, Samuel I, John)

Fannie Louise GUYTON was the daughter of Willie GUYTON, Sr. (b. 31 Mar 1892 Sallis, Attala Co., MS, d. 7 Jun 1979 Chicago, Cook Co., IL)[2250] and Etta BROWN (b. 1 Nov 1892 Sallis, Attala Co., MS, d. 28 Mar 1944, bur. Hill Springs Cemetery Sallis, Attala Co., MS).[2251] Fannie was born on 15 May 1920 in Sallis, Attala Co., MS, and died on 16 Dec 1998 in Southfield, Oakland Co., MI).[2252] She married Ollie BELL, Jr. (b. 12 Feb 1920 Kosciusko, Attala Co., MS, d. 30 Jan 2018 Southfield, Oakland Co., MI).[2253] See Figure 322 for a photo of Ollie BELL and Figure 323 for a photo of his son, Frederick Douglas BELL.

Figure 322 Ollie BELL, Jr.[2254]

Figure 323 Frederick Douglas BELL[2255]

In the 1940 U.S. Census, Fannie (19) and Ollie (21) lived on South Street in Kosciusko, Attala Co., MS.[2256] The Census recorded that Fannie had completed one year of high school. They lived with their son, Ollie BELL, III (1). Ollie, Jr. reported he had worked 65 hours in the week prior to the Census as a cook at a café. Fannie's brother, Brazie GUYTON (21) lived with the family along with Maylene GUYTON. Maylene was described as Ollie's sister-in-law, but her age was given as 1-year-old. There is some type of error in the Census for Maylene.

[2250] Will Guyton, Sr., grave marker, Sunset Memorial Lawns, Northbrook, Cook Co., IL, digital image s.v. "Deacon Will Guyton, Sr," (birth 31 Mar 1892, death 7 Jun 1979), *FindaGrave.com*.

[2251] Etta Brown Guyton, grave marker, Hill Springs Cemetery, Sallis, Attala Co., MS, digital image s.v. "Etter Guyton," (birth 1 Nov 1892, death 28 Mar 1944), *FindaGrave.com*.

[2252] "U.S., Social Security Death Index, 1935-2014," s.v. "Fannie Bell," (birth 20 May 1920, death 16 Dec 1998), *Ancestry.com*. The U.S., Social Security Applications and Claims Index, 1936-2007, on *Ancestry.com* indicates her birthday was 15 May 1920.

[2253] Ollie Bell, Jr., grave marker, United Memorial Gardens, Superior Township, Washtenaw Co., MI, digital image s.v. "Ollie Bell," (birth 16 Mar 1920, death 30 Jan 2018), *FindaGrave.com*. His WWII Draft Card indicates his birthdate was 12 Feb 1920.

[2254] scoobeee48 originally shared this on 18 Dec 2018 on *Ancestry.com*.

[2255] scoobeee48 originally shared this on 18 Dec 2018 on *Ancestry.com*.

[2256] "1940 United States Federal Census," Kosciusko, Attala Co., MS, digital image s.v. "Fannie L Bell," (birth abt 1921), *Ancestry.com*.

In the 1950 U.S. Census, Ollie BELL, Jr. (30), Fannie Louise GUYTON (29), and Ollie BELL, III (10) lived in Detroit, Wayne Co., MI at 2011 McDougal St.[2257] See Figure 324. Ollie, Jr. worked in the printing department of a medical supply company. Fannie was a homemaker. The house was full of other family members, too. Included in the household were: Flemmie Buford TERRY (Elvie's husband) (24), Elvie GUYTON TERRY (Fannie's sister) (24), Clemenie TERRY (their son) (3), Sylvia TERRY (daughter) (1), Willie ROBINSON (brother-in-law to Ollie BELL, Jr.) (24), Clarence M. BELL (Ollie's brother) (20), and James BELL (Ollie's brother) (33). To comfortably fit ten people in one home, the house needed to be large. The house is a duplex that is very deep.

Figure 324 2011 McDougall in Detroit, the BELL Home

According to Lynn A. Fisher (Bell)--Parks/Sales Family (scoobeee48) on *Ancestry.com*, Ollie and Fannie GUYTON BELL had a second son:

i   Ollie BELL, III (b. 17 Jan 1939 MS, d. Unknown)[2258] m. Martha Elizabeth GLADNEY (b. 19 Aug 1948, d. 14 Jul 2018 Wetumpka, Elmore Co., AL).[2259]

ii   Frederick Douglas BELL (b. 3 Apr 1955 Detroit, Wayne Co., MI, d. Living) m. Lynn A. FISHER.[2260] See Figure 323.

Willie GUYTON, Jr. (Willie, Sr., Case, Aaron Whitaker, Aaron Steele, Joseph I, John I, Samuel II, Samuel I, John)

Willie GUYTON, Jr. was the son of Willie GUYTON, Sr. (b. 31 Mar 1892 Sallis, Attala Co., MS, d. 7 Jun 1979 Chicago, Cook Co., IL)[2261] and Etta BROWN (b. 1 Nov 1892 Sallis, Attala Co., MS, d. 28 Mar 1944, bur. Hill Springs Cemetery Sallis, Attala Co., MS).[2262] Willie was born on 22 Apr 1922 in Sallis, Attala Co., MS,

---

[2257] "1950 United States Federal Census," Detroit, Wayne Co., MI, digital image s.v. "Fannie Bell," (birth abt 1921), *Ancestry.com*.

[2258] "U.S. Public Records Index, 1950-1993, Volume 2," s.v. "Ollie Bell 3d," (birth 17 Jan 1939), *Ancestry.com*.

[2259] "U.S., Public Records Index, 1950-1993, Volume 1," s.v. "Martha E Gladney," (birth 19 Aug 1948), *Ancestry.com*. According to Lynn A. Fisher (Bell)--Parks/Sales Family (scoobeee48) on *Ancestry.com*.

[2260] Per Channie Brown-Currie.

[2261] Will Guyton, Sr., grave marker, Sunset Memorial Lawns, Northbrook, Cook Co., IL, digital image s.v. "Deacon Will Guyton, Sr," (birth 31 Mar 1892, death 7 Jun 1979), *FindaGrave.com*.

[2262] Etta Brown Guyton, grave marker, Hill Springs Cemetery, Sallis, Attala Co., MS, digital image s.v. "Etter Guyton," (birth 1 Nov 1892, death 28 Mar 1944), *FindaGrave.com*.

and died on 1 Mar 1980 in Chicago, Cook Co., IL.[2263] He married (1) Louvenia GREEN (b. 2 Oct 1928 AL, d. Unknown),[2264] (2) Lucille BARRETT (b. 8 Oct 1925 AR, d. 2022),[2265] and (3) Mildred CLAIBORNE (b. 1917, d. 2016 Chicago, Cook Co., IL).[2266]

In the 1940 U.S. Census, Willie (18) was single and lived with his parents in New Port, Attala Co., MS. He had an eighth-grade education.[2267] In the 1950 U.S. Census, Willie (28) had married Louvenia GREEN (23). They lived at 3608 Michigan in Hamtramck, Wayne Co., MI with their four children: Willie James GUYTON (3), Tyrone GUYTON (2), Melvin GUYTON (1), and Beatrice GUYTON (less than one year old).[2268]

Louvenia and Willie GUYTON, Jr. had the following children:

i   Willie James GUYTON (b. 14 Feb 1947 Hamtramck, Wayne Co., MI, d. 26 Apr 2003 Detroit, Wayne Co., MI).[2269] See Figure 325.
ii   Tyrone GUYTON (b. 23 Dec 1947 Hamtramck, Wayne Co., MI, d. 21 Nov 2000 Detroit, Wayne Co., MI).[2270] SeeFigure 326.
iii Melvin GUYTON (b. 23 Dec 1949 MI, d. 11 Mar 1969 VIETNAM).[2271] See Figure 327. He was buried at Detroit Memorial Park Cemetery in Warren, Macombs Co., MI. He was killed by an enemy booby trap.[2272] See Figure 329. He had two daughters: Pat RICHARDS and Paulette MARTIN.
iv   Beatrice GUYTON (b. ABT 1950, d. Unknown).[2273] See Figure 328.
v   Bernice GUYTON (Unknown).[2274]

[2263] "U.S., Department of Veterans Affairs BIRLS Death File, 1850-2010," s.v. "William Guyton," (birth 22 Apr 1922, death Mar 1980), *Ancestry.com*.
[2264] "Ohio, U.S., County Marriage Records, 1774-1993," digital image, "Louvenie Green," (marriage with Will Guyton on 9 Nov 1946, birth abt 1922), *Ancestry.com*.
[2265] Undocumented tree on *Ancestry.com*.
[2266] Mildred Claiborne was married to Willie Guyton, Jr. at his death in 2016. "Illinois, Cook County Deaths, 1871-1998," s.v. Will Guyton," *FamilySearch*.
[2267] "1940 United States Federal Census," Kosciusko, Attala Co., MS, digital image s.v. "Will Bell," (birth abt 1922), *Ancestry.com*.
[2268] "1950 United States Federal Census," Hamtramck, Wayne Co., MI, digital image s.v. "Guyton Moore, Jr.," (birth abt 1922), *Ancestry.com*.
[2269] "U.S., Social Security Applications and Claims Index, 1936-2007," s.v. "Willie James Guyton," (birth 14 Feb 1947, death 26 Apr 2003), *Ancestry.com*.
[2270] "U.S., Social Security Applications and Claims Index, 1936-2007," s.v. "Tyrone Guyton," (birth 13 Dec 1947, death 21 Nov 2000), *Ancestry.com*.
[2271] Melvin Guyton, grave marker, Detroit Memorial Park East, Warren, McComb Co., MI, digital image s.v. "Cpl Melvin Guyton," (birth 23 Dec 1948, death 11 Mar 1969), *FindaGrave.com*.
[2272] "3 Chicago Area Service Men Killed in viet," *Chicago Tribune*, Chicago, Cook Co., IL, Tues, 18 Mar 1969, p. 28, *Newspapers.com*.
[2273] "1950 United States Federal Census," Hamtramck, Wayne Co., MI, digital image s.v. "Beatrice Moore," (birth abt 1950), *Ancestry.com*.
[2274] See Melvin's obituary.

Figure 325 Willie James GUYTON[2275]  Figure 326 Tyrone GUYTON[2276]  Figure 327 Melvin GUYTON[2277]  Figure 328 Beatrice GUYTON[2278]

PFC. Melvin Guyton Killed; Had Signed With Tigers

Obituaries

Services for Army Pfc. Melvin Guyton, killed in action March 11 in Vietnam, will be at 11 a.m. Thursday at the Leland Missionary Baptist Church, 2432 Finley, Hamtramck.

Pfc. Guyton, 19, was the son of Mr. and Mrs. Will Guyton of 3227 Denton, Hamtramck.

He signed a contract with the Detroit Tigers last year and was training with the team when he was drafted in July. He went to Vietnam last December.

He had been a star baseball player for Hamtramck High School before being signed by the Tigers.

Surviving also are two sisters, Beatrice and Bernice, and three brothers, Willie, Tyrone and Clarence.

Burial will be in Detroit Memorial Park Cemetery.

auxiliary of the House of Providence.

Services will be at 10 a.m. Thursday in St. Peter and Paul Church. Burial will be in Mt. Elliott Cemetery.

Rosary will be at 8 p.m. Wednesday in the Howe-Peterson Funeral Home, 22546 Michigan, Dearborn.

Paul F. Tocco, Roseville Resident

Services for Paul F. Tocco, head dispatcher for Metropolitan Delivery Inc. of Highland Park, will be at 9:30 a.m. Saturday at the Bagnasco Funeral Home,

seph; two daughter, Mrs. Pat Richards and Mrs. Paulette Martin, four sisters, three brothers and six grandchildren.

Burial will be in Mt. Olivet Cemetery.

Pvt. Jerry E. Ewing, Killed in Vietnam

Services are pending for Pvt. Jerry E. Ewing, 20, of Detroit, killed Friday in Vietnam by artillery fragments during an engagement at an aircraft landing zone.

A gradute of Northwestern High School, Pvt. Ewing was the son of Mrs. Hattie Ewing of 5204 Roosevelt and Hobert R. Ewing, of 3767 Townsend.

Pvt. Ewing enlisted in the Army in November, 1967, and arrived in Vietnam in May, 1968.

Figure 329 PFC. Melvin GUYTON Killed in Vietnam[2279]

[2275] "U.S. School Yearbooks," Hamtramck High School, Hamtramck, Wayne Co., MI, digital image s.v. "Willie Guyton," (birth abt 1950), *Ancestry.com*.

[2276] "U.S. School Yearbooks," Hamtramck High School, Hamtramck, Wayne Co., MI, digital image s.v. "Tyronne Guyton," (birth abt 1950), *Ancestry.com*.

[2277] See his *Findagrave* entry above.

[2278] "U.S. School Yearbooks," Hamtramck High School, Hamtramck, Wayne Co., MI, digital image s.v. "Beatrice Guyton," (birth abt 1950), *Ancestry.com*.

[2279] "PFC. Melvin Guyton Killed; Had Signed with Tigers," *Detroit Free Press,* Detroit, Wayne Co., MI, Wed, 26 Mar, 1969, p. 14, *Newspapers.com*.

Willie GUYTON, Jr. and Lucille BARRETT had one son:

i   Clarence William GUYTON (b. 29 Apr 1955 MI, d. Unknown).[2280]

Elvie GUYTON (Willie, Sr., Case, Aaron Whitaker, Aaron Steele, Joseph I, John I, Samuel II, Samuel I, John)

Elvie GUYTON was the daughter of Willie GUYTON, Sr. (b. 31 Mar 1892 Sallis, Attala Co., MS, d. 7 Jun 1979 Chicago, Cook Co., IL)[2281] and Etta BROWN (b. 1 Nov 1892 Sallis, Attala Co., MS, d. 28 Mar 1944, bur. Hill Springs Cemetery Sallis, Attala Co., MS).[2282] Elvie was born on 11 May 1924 in Sallis, Attala Co., MS, and died in 14 Oct 2012 in Detroit, Wayne Co., MI.[2283] She married Flemmie Buford TERRY (b. 18 Jun 1924 Kosciusko, Attala Co., MS, d. 20 Apr 2007 Detroit, Wayne Co., MI).[2284]

In the 1940 U.S. Census, Elvie (16) was single and lived with her parents and siblings in New Port, Attala Co., MS.[2285] She had an eighth-grade education. In the 1950 U.S. Census, Elvie (24) and Flemmie (24) and their two daughters, Clemenie TERRY (Male - 3) and Sylvia TERRY (1) lived in Detroit, Wayne Co., MI at 2011 McDougal St.[2286] with Elvie's sister, Fannie Louise GUYTON (29), and her husband, Ollie BELL, Jr. (30). See the section on Fannie Louise GUYTON for the complete list of household members. Elvie was a homemaker while Flemmie worked as a janitor at a chemical company.

The couple had at least the two children listed in the 1950 Census and two others according to Channie BROWN-CURRIE:

i   Clemenie TERRY (male) (b. ABT 1947 MS, d. Unknown).
ii   Sylvia TERRY (b. ABT 1949 MI, d. Unknown) m. Unknown WRIGHT (Unknown).
iii   Brenda TERRY (b. 23 Oct 1953 Detroit, Wayne Co., MI, d. Unknown) m. Unknown MILLINER (Unknown).
iv   Kenneth Matthew TERRY (b. 15 Nov 1962 Detroit, Wayne Co., MI, d. 27 Sep 1992 Detroit, Wayne Co., MI).[2287]

[2280] "U.S., Public Records Index, 1950-1993, Volume 2," s.v. "Clarence W Guyton," (birth 29 Apr 1955), *Ancestry.com*.
[2281] Will Guyton, Sr., grave marker, Sunset Memorial Lawns, Northbrook, Cook Co., IL, digital image s.v. "Deacon Will Guyton, Sr," (birth 31 Mar 1892, death 7 Jun 1979), *FindaGrave.com*.
[2282] Etta Brown Guyton, grave marker, Hill Springs Cemetery, Sallis, Attala Co., MS, digital image s.v. "Etter Guyton," (birth 1 Nov 1892, death 28 Mar 1944), *FindaGrave.com*.
[2283] Elvie Guyton, grave marker, Westlawn Cemetery, Wayne, Wayne Co., MI, digital image s.v. "Elve Terry," (birth 11 May 1924, death 14 Oct 2012), *FindaGrave.com*.
[2284] "U.S., Social Security Death Index, 1935-2014," s.v. "Flemmie B. Terry," (birth 18 Jun 1924, death 20 Apr 2007), *Ancestry.com*.
[2285] "1940 United States Federal Census," Kosciusko, Attala Co., MS, digital image s.v. "L B Bell," (birth abt 1924), *Ancestry.com*.
[2286] "1950 United States Federal Census," Detroit, Wayne Co., MI, digital image s.v. "Elve Terry," (birth abt 1926), *Ancestry.com*.
[2287] "Michigan, U.S., Death Index, 1971-1996," s.v. "Kenneth M Terry," (birth 15 Nov 1962, death 27 Sep 1992), *Ancestry.com*.

Willie Clayton (WC) GUYTON, Sr. (Willie, Sr., Case, Aaron Whitaker, Aaron Steele, Joseph I, John I, Samuel II, Samuel I, John)

Willie Clayton (WC) GUYTON, Sr. was the son of Willie GUYTON, Sr. (b. 31 Mar 1892 Sallis, Attala Co., MS, d. 7 Jun 1979 Chicago, Cook Co., IL)[2288] and Etta BROWN (b. 1 Nov 1892 Sallis, Attala Co., MS, d. 28 Mar 1944, bur. Hill Springs Cemetery Sallis, Attala Co., MS).[2289] WC was born on 10 Jul 1926 in Sallis, Attala Co., MS, and died on 16 May 2011 in Chicago, Cook Co., IL.[2290] He married Vera LaVern TERRY (b. 8 May 1930 Kosciusko, Attala Co., MS, d. 1 Aug 2018 Bolingbrook, Will Co., IL).[2291] Vera was the sister of Flemmie Buford TERRY, the husband of Elvie GUYTON. See Figure 330 and Figure 331.

By the time of the 1950 Census, WC (23) and Vera (19) had moved to Chicago and lived at 92 Monroe Street.[2292] The Census indicated WC was the head of household. The couple lived with WC's sister, Essie Dee GUYTON BROWN, and her husband, Rollegge Newell (Rollie) BROWN, the Browns' two children, and two of WC GUYTON's brothers – Claude GUYTON and Clarence GUYTON, Sr. Also living with them were WC and Vera's children: Willie Clayton GUYTON, Jr. (5) and Ada Vera GUYTON (2). WC worked as an assembler at window assembly factory. Vera was a homemaker.

Figure 330 Willie Clayton (WC) GUYTON, Sr.[2293]

Figure 331 Vera LaVern TERRY GUYTON[2294]

[2288] Will Guyton, Sr., grave marker, Sunset Memorial Lawns, Northbrook, Cook Co., IL, digital image s.v. "Deacon Will Guyton, Sr," (birth 31 Mar 1892, death 7 Jun 1979), *FindaGrave.com*.

[2289] Etta Brown Guyton, grave marker, Hill Springs Cemetery, Sallis, Attala Co., MS, digital image s.v. "Etter Guyton," (birth 1 Nov 1892, death 28 Mar 1944), *FindaGrave.com*.

[2290] "U.S., Social Security Death Index, 1935-2014," s.v. "W.C. Guyton," (birth 10 Jul 1926, death 16 May 2011), *Ancestry.com*.

[2291] "1950 United States Federal Census," MS, digital image s.v. "Vera L. Guyton," (birth abt 1931), *Ancestry.com*. The other dates come from undocumented trees in *Ancestry.com*. "Obituary of Ollie B. Terry," *The Star-Herald*, Kosciusko, Attala Co., MS, Thu, 31 Jan 1991, p. 8, *Newspapers.com*, <https://www.newspapers.com/image/268658440/?article=93153db4-2874-4ca9-9c48-9fad120357e3&focus=0.81250685,0.16715112,0.9795659,0.35185516&xid=3355>.

[2292] "1950 United States Federal Census," Chicago, Cook Co., IL, digital image s.v. "W C Gryton," (birth abt 1927), *Ancestry.com*.

[2293] DorChaune Peteet originally shared this on 19 Aug 2018 on *Ancestry.com*.

[2294] DorChaune Peteet originally shared this on 19 Aug 2018 on *Ancestry.com*.

The couple had two children included in the 1950 U.S. Census:

i Willie Clayton GUYTON, Jr. (b. 15 Mar 1945 Chicago, Cook Co., IL, d. 1 Feb 2017 Chicago, Cook Co., IL)[2295] m. (1) Carol Ann SYKES (b. ABT 1948, d. Unknown) on 30 Jun 1972 in Chester Co., TN[2296] and (2) Ellenore Shirley CARTMAN (b. 29 Jan 1948 Nuremberg, Germany, d. 25 Sep 2001 White Plains, Charles Co., MD).[2297]
ii Ada Vera GUYTON (b. ABT 1948 Chicago, Cook Co., IL, d. Unknown).
iii Etta GUYTON (b. AFT 1950, d. Unknown). Channie BROWN-CURRIE named her as a child of Willie Clayton GUYTON, Sr. She may be a child with Ellenore Shirley CARTMAN. Or Ada and Etta may be the same person.

Clarence GUYTON, Sr. (Willie, Sr., Case, Aaron Whitaker, Aaron Steele, Joseph I, John I, Samuel II, Samuel I, John)

Clarence GUYTON, Sr. was the son of Willie GUYTON, Sr. (b. 31 Mar 1892 Sallis, Attala Co., MS, d. 7 Jun 1979 Chicago, Cook Co., IL)[2298] and Etta BROWN (b. 1 Nov 1892 Sallis, Attala Co., MS, d. 28 Mar 1944, bur. Hill Springs Cemetery Sallis, Attala Co., MS).[2299]

The Reverend Clarence GUYTON, Sr. was born on 12 Sep 1928 in Kosciusko, Attala Co., MS. He died on 17 Aug 1998 in Chicago, Cook Co., IL.[2300] He married (1) Nugulia SMITH (b. 30 Apr 1934 MS, d. Unknown)[2301] on 22 Jan 1953 in Chicago,[2302] and perhaps (2) Lessie V. JAMES (b. 7 Feb 1926 MS, d. 26 May 2011 Chicago, Cook Co., IL).[2303]

In the 1950 Census, Clarence GUYTON, Sr. lived with his brother, WC (23), and WC's wife, Vera (19). The couple had moved to Chicago and lived at 92 Monroe Street.[2304] The Census indicated WC was the head of household. The couple also lived with WC's sister, Essie Dee GUYTON BROWN, and her husband, Rollegge Newell (Rollie) BROWN, the Browns' two children, and another brother of WC's, Claude GUYTON.

[2295] Willie Clayton Guyton, Sr., grave marker, Abraham Lincoln National Cemetery, Elwood, Will Co., IL, digital image s.v. "Willie Clayton Guyton," (birth 15 Mar 1945, death 1 Feb 2017), *FindaGrave.com*.
[2296] "Tennessee, U.S., Marriage Records, 1780-2002," digital image s.v. "Carol Ann Sykes," (birth abt 1948, marriage 30 Jun 1972 to Willie Clayton Guyton), *Ancestry.com*.
[2297] Joylita Lynch, Family Tree of Shirley E. Cartman Family, accessed 1 Sep 2024, *Ancestry.com*.
[2298] Will Guyton, Sr., grave marker, Sunset Memorial Lawns, Northbrook, Cook Co., IL, digital image s.v. "Deacon Will Guyton, Sr," (birth 31 Mar 1892, death 7 Jun 1979), *FindaGrave.com*.
[2299] Etta Brown Guyton, grave marker, Hill Springs Cemetery, Sallis, Attala Co., MS, digital image s.v. "Etter Guyton," (birth 1 Nov 1892, death 28 Mar 1944), *FindaGrave.com*.
[2300] "U.S., Social Security Death Index, 1935-2014," s.v. "Clarence Guyton," (birth 12 Sep 1928, death 17 Aug 1998), *Ancestry.com*.
[2301] "U.S., Public Records Index, 1950-1993, Volume 1," s.v. "Nequlia Guyton," (birth 30 Apr 1934), *Ancestry.com*.
[2302] "Cook County, Illinois Marriage Index, 1930-1960," s.v. "Clarence Guyton," (marriage to Nugulia Smith on 22 Jan 1953 in Cook Co., IL), *Ancestry.com*.
[2303] "U.S., Social Security Death Index, 1935-2014," s.v. "Lessie V. Guyton," (birth 7 Feb 1926, death 26 May 2011), *Ancestry.com*.
[2304] "1950 United States Federal Census," Chicago, Cook Co., IL, digital image s.v. "W C Gryton," (birth abt 1927), *Ancestry.com*.

Channie BROWN-CURRIE's list of Clarence's children is associated with Nugulia SMITH. She does not mention wife, Lessie JAMES GUYTON. It is possible that Lessie was not a wife of Clarence GUYTON, Sr.

i		Mary Louise GUYTON (b. AFT 1953 Chicago, Cook Co., IL), d. Unknown).
ii		Clarence GUYTON, Jr. (b. AFT 1953, d. Unknown).
iii		Lawrence GUYTON (b. AFT 1953, d. Unknown) m. Crystal UNKNOWN (Unknown).
iv		Cheryl Shuvetta GUYTON (b. AFT 1953, d. Unknown) m. Eizy DIXON (Unknown).
v		Oreatha GUYTON (b. AFT 1953, d. Unknown) m. Unknown WINSTON (Unknown).

Claude GUYTON (Willie, Sr., Case, Aaron Whitaker, Aaron Steele, Joseph I, John I, Samuel II, Samuel I, John)

Claude GUYTON was the son of Willie GUYTON, Sr. (b. 31 Mar 1892 Sallis, Attala Co., MS, d. 7 Jun 1979 Chicago, Cook Co., IL)[2305] and Etta BROWN (b. 1 Nov 1892 Sallis, Attala Co., MS, d. 28 Mar 1944, bur. Hill Springs Cemetery Sallis, Attala Co., MS).[2306]

Claude GUYTON was born on Mar 1931 in MS, and died on 9 Aug 1952 in Cook Co., IL.[2307] According to Channie BROWN-CURRIE, he married Helen HEMP (Unknown). They had two children:

i		Claudia GUYTON (b. AFT 1953 Detroit, Wayne Co., MI, d. Unknown) m. Unknown WILKINSON (Unknown).
ii		Caroline GUYTON (b. AFT 1953 Detroit, Wayne Co., MI, d. Unknown) m. Unknown CAMPBELL (Unknown).

In the 1950 Census, Claude GUYTON lived with his brother, WC (23), and WC's wife, Vera (19). The couple had moved to Chicago and lived at 92 Monroe Street.[2308] The Census indicated WC was the head of household. The couple also lived with WC's sister, Essie Dee GUYTON BROWN, and her husband, Rollegge Newell (Rollie) BROWN, the Browns' two children, and another brother of WC's, Clarence GUYTON.

[2305] Will Guyton, Sr., grave marker, Sunset Memorial Lawns, Northbrook, Cook Co., IL, digital image s.v. "Deacon Will Guyton, Sr," (birth 31 Mar 1892, death 7 Jun 1979), *FindaGrave.com*.
[2306] Etta Brown Guyton, grave marker, Hill Springs Cemetery, Sallis, Attala Co., MS, digital image s.v. "Etter Guyton," (birth 1 Nov 1892, death 28 Mar 1944), *FindaGrave.com*.
[2307] "U.S., Index to Public Records, 1994-2019," s.v. "Claude L. Guyton," (birth Mar 1931), *Ancestry.com*. "Cook County, Illinois Death Index, 1908-1988," s.v. Claude Guyton," (death 9 Aug 1952), *Ancestry.com*.
[2308] "1950 United States Federal Census," Chicago, Cook Co., IL, digital image s.v. "W C Gryton," (birth abt 1927), *Ancestry.com*.

Mary Lynn GUYTON (Willie, Sr., Case, Aaron Whitaker, Aaron Steele, Joseph I, John I, Samuel II, Samuel I, John)

Mary Lynn GUYTON was the daughter of Willie GUYTON, Sr. (b. 31 Mar 1892 Sallis, Attala Co., MS, d. 7 Jun 1979 Chicago, Cook Co., IL)[2309] and Etta BROWN (b. 1 Nov 1892 Sallis, Attala Co., MS, d. 28 Mar 1944, bur. Hill Springs Cemetery Sallis, Attala Co., MS).[2310]

Mary Lynn GUYTON was born ABT 1934 in Attala Co., MS, and her death is unknown.[2311] She married James SMITH (Unknown).[2312] They had at least one child:[2313]

i   Sheri Lynn SMITH (Unknown).

Vernon T. (Vearn) GUYTON, Sr. (Willie, Sr., Case, Aaron Whitaker, Aaron Steele, Joseph I, John I, Samuel II, Samuel I, John)

Vernon T. (Vearn) GUYTON, Sr. was the son of Willie GUYTON, Sr. (b. 31 Mar 1892 Sallis, Attala Co., MS, d. 7 Jun 1979 Chicago, Cook Co., IL)[2314] and Etta BROWN (b. 1 Nov 1892 Sallis, Attala Co., MS, d. 28 Mar 1944, bur. Hill Springs Cemetery Sallis, Attala Co., MS).[2315] See Figure 332.

Vernon T. (Vearn) GUYTON, Sr. was born in Jul 1936 in MS, and his death is unknown.[2316] He married Ollie J. Peteet, who was born on 31 Jan 1942 MS, and her death is unknown.[2317] They had at least two children:[2318]

i   Vernon T. GUYTON, Jr. (b. Chicago, Cook Co., IL, d. Unknown).
ii   Ebony GUYTON (b. Chicago, Cook Co., IL, d. Unknown).

[2309] Will Guyton, Sr., grave marker, Sunset Memorial Lawns, Northbrook, Cook Co., IL, digital image s.v. "Deacon Will Guyton, Sr," (birth 31 Mar 1892, death 7 Jun 1979), *FindaGrave.com*.
[2310] Etta Brown Guyton, grave marker, Hill Springs Cemetery, Sallis, Attala Co., MS, digital image s.v. "Etter Guyton," (birth 1 Nov 1892, death 28 Mar 1944), *FindaGrave.com*.
[2311] "1950 United States Federal Census," Kosciusko, Attala Co., MS, digital image s.v. "Mary L. Guyton," (birth ABT 1934), *Ancestry.com*.
[2312] Per Channie Brown-Currie.
[2313] Per Channie Brown-Currie.
[2314] Will Guyton, Sr., grave marker, Sunset Memorial Lawns, Northbrook, Cook Co., IL, digital image s.v. "Deacon Will Guyton, Sr," (birth 31 Mar 1892, death 7 Jun 1979), *FindaGrave.com*.
[2315] Etta Brown Guyton, grave marker, Hill Springs Cemetery, Sallis, Attala Co., MS, digital image s.v. "Etter Guyton," (birth 1 Nov 1892, death 28 Mar 1944), *FindaGrave.com*.
[2316] "U.S., Index to Public Records, 1994-2019," s.v. "Vearn T Guyton," (birth Jul 1936), *Ancestry.com*. "Cook County, Illinois Marriage Index, 1930-1960," s.v. "Ollie Peteet," (marriage to Vearn T. Gayton on 14 Aug 1959), *Ancestry.com*.
[2317] "U.S., Public Records Index, 1950-1993, Volume 2," s.v. "Ollie J Guyton," (birth 31 Jan 1942), *Ancestry.com*.
[2318] Per Channie Brown-Currie.

Figure 332 Vearn GUYTON, Sr.

Casey Glenn GUYTON, Sr. (James, Case, Aaron Whitaker, Aaron Steele, Joseph I, John I, Samuel II, Samuel I, John)

Casey Glenn GUYTON, Sr. was the son of James (Jim) GUYTON (b. 2 Sep 1905 Sallis, Attala Co., MS and died in 1956 in Sallis, Attala Co., MS)[2319] and Lillie Wardean ROBY (b. 17 Nov 1909 in Sallis, Attala Co., MS, d. 27 Oct 2003 Chicago, Cook Co., IL).[2320] Jim GUYTON was related to Lillie as he was the son of Case GUYTON (son of Aaron Whitaker GUYTON and Artie RAINEY) and Susie STINGLEY. Lillie was the daughter of Patsy J. GUYTON[2321] and William (Willie) ROBY.[2322]

See section of the book on Lillie Wardean ROBY for their descendants.

Lorine RILEY (Annie Pearl GUYTON RILEY, Case, Aaron Whitaker, Aaron Steele, Joseph I, John I, Samuel II, Samuel I, John)

Lorine RILEY was the daughter of Annie Pearl GUYTON (b. 9 Jun 1910 Sallis, Attala Co., MS, d. 27 May 1983 in Sallis)[2323] and Jim Bell RILEY (b. 6 Apr 1906 Sallis, Attala Co., MS, d. 10 Sep 1991 Chicago, Cook Co., IL).[2324] Lorine RILEY was born on 1 Nov 1930 on Sallis, Attala Co., MS, and died on 4 Feb 2007 in Chicago, Cook Co., IL.[2325] She married James Willie PERKINS (b. 12 May 1928 Goodman, Holmes Co., MS, d. 7 May 1996 Chicago, Cook Co., IL).[2326] See Figure 333 and Figure 334.

[2319] "U.S., World War II Draft Cards Young Men, 1940-1947," digital image s.v. "Jim Guyton," (birth 2 Sep 1905), *Ancestry.com*. David F. Guyton, personal correspondence, Jim Guyton's death was 1956 in Newton and Sallis, Attala, MS, 2024.

[2320] Lillie Wardean Roby, grave marker, Burr Oak Cemetery, Alsip, Cook Co., IL, digital image s.v. "Lillie Wardean Guyton," (birth 17 Nov 1909; d. 27 Oct 2003), *FindaGrave.com*.

[2321] "1900 United States Census," Kosciusko, Attala Co., MS, digital image s.v. "Patsy J Roby," (birth Aug 1877), *Ancestry.com*.

[2322] "1900 United States Census," Kosciusko, Attala Co., MS, digital image s.v. "Will Roby," (birth Mar 1876), *Ancestry.com*.

[2323] Annie Pearl Guyton, grave marker, Russell Cemetery, Attala Co., MS, digital image s.v. "Pearl Riley," (birth 12 Jun 1910; d. 27 May 1983), *FindaGrave.com*.

[2324] Jim Riley, grave marker, Russell Cemetery, Attala Co., MS, digital image s.v. "Jim Riley," (birth abt 6 Apr 1906; death 10 Sep 1991), *FindaGrave.com*.

[2325] "U.S., Social Security Death Index, 1935-2014," s.v. "Lorine Perkins," (birth 1 Nov 1929, death 4 Feb 2007), *Ancestry.com*.

[2326] "U.S., Social Security Applications and Claims Index, 1936-2007," s.v. "James Willie Perkins," (birth 12 May 1928, death 7 May 1996), *Ancestry.com*.

Figure 333 Lorine RILEY PERKINS[2327]

Figure 334 James Willie PERKINS[2328]

Lorine and James had at least three children together:[2329]

i Fannie Bea PERKINS (b. 21 Apr 1955 Chicago, Cook Co., IL, d. 13 Feb 2021 Chicago, Cook Co., IL). She had three children: Donte PERKINS, Eddie PERKINS, and Angela PERKINS. See Figure 335
ii Arey PERKINS (male) (b. 17 Jun 1957 Chicago, Cook Co., IL, d. 15 May 1983 Chicago, Cook Co., IL). See Figure 336.
iii Bennie Lee PERKINS (b. 28 Sep 1959 Chicago, Cook Co., IL, d. 4 Jun 2009 Maywood, Cook Co., IL). See Figure 337.

Figure 335 Fannie Bea PERKINS[2330]

Figure 336 Arey PERKINS[2331]

Figure 337 Bennie Lee PERKINS[2332]

[2327] chancurri originally shared this on 28 May 2013 on *Ancestry.com*.
[2328] cocucenacane6 originally shared this on 25 Sep 2010 on *Ancestry.com*.
[2329] cocucenacane6, Perkins-Clifton Family Tree, *Ancestry.com*.
[2330] cocucenacane6 originally shared this on 17 Feb 2021 on *Ancestry.com*.
[2331] cocucenacane6 originally shared this on 31 May 2014 on *Ancestry.com*.
[2332] cocucenacane6 originally shared this on 31 May 2014 on *Ancestry.com*.

CHILD OF AARON WHITAKER GUYTON AND ARTIE RAINEY: MAGGIE'S LINE

Generation #7

Maggie GUYTON (Aaron Whitaker, Aaron Steele, Joseph I, John I, Samuel II, Samuel I, John)

Maggie GUYTON was the daughter of Aaron Whitaker GUYTON and Artemesia (Artie) RAINEY. She was born about 1874 in Attala Co., MS. She died on 4 May 1919 in Mississippi City, Harrison Co., MS.[2333] She married Thomas (Tom) STINGLEY about 1902 before their first child was born. Tom was born in Apr 1875 in Attala Co., MS and died in 1957 in Kosciusko, Attala Co., MS.[2334] See Figure 338.

Figure 338 Maggie GUYTON STINGLEY[2335]

In the 1880 U.S. Census, Maggie was 7-years-old, and lived in New Port, Attala Co., MS with her mother and siblings.[2336] Her father, Whit GUYTON, was 72-years-old; Artie was about 32-years-old. Whit died sometime between 1881 and 1883. According to the 1900 U.S. Census, Maggie was single and lived with her mother, some siblings, and some of their children. The family still lived in New Port.[2337] In 1910, Maggie and Tom were married and lived in Beat 4, Attala Co., MS. Tom owned their farm without a

---

[2333] Maggie Guyton, grave marker, Russell Cemetery, Attala Co., MS, digital image s.v. "Maggie Stingley Guyton," (birth ABT 1874; death 4 May 1919), *FindaGrave.com*. "1880 United States Census," Newport, Attala Co., MS, digital image s.v. "Maggie Delpha," (birth ABT 1871), *Ancestry.com*.

[2334] Thomas Stingley, grave marker, Russell Cemetery, Attala Co., MS, digital image s.v. "Tom Stingley," (birth ABT 1875; death ABT 1957), *FindaGrave.com*.

[2335] Channie Brown-Currie (Chancurri), posted on 6 May 2013 on *Ancestry.com*.

[2336] "1880 United States Federal Census," Newport, Attala Co., MS, digital image s.v. "Maggy Delpha," (birth ABT 1873), *Ancestry.com*.

[2337] "1900 United States Federal Census," Newport, Attala Co., MS, digital image s.v. "Mag Guyton," (birth May 1871), *Ancestry.com*.

mortgage.[2338] Maggie worked as a wage-earning farm laborer and both Tom and Maggie were able to read and write. She and Tom already had five children: Herman STINGLEY, Louria STINGLEY, Lottie STINGLEY, Mayvell STINGLEY, and Guyton STINGLEY. Maggie and Tom had two more children before Maggie died in 1919: Mannie Whitt STINGLEY and John Ike STINGLEY, who was only six-years-old when she died. In the 1950 U.S. Census, Tom lived as a widower with his son, Whitt. They both worked on the farm that Tom owned free and clear.

Tom and Maggie's children were:

i   Herman STINGLEY (b. 14 Sep 1903 MS, d. 15 Sep 1964 Orleans Parish, LA)[2339] m. Pearline ALLEN (b. ABT 1909 LA, d. Unknown)[2340] in Jun 1929 in New Orleans, Orleans Parish, LA.[2341]
ii Louria STINGLEY (b. 30 Dec 1904 MS, d. 23 Dec 1988 Kosciusko, Attala Co., MS)[2342] m. Lee Boston TURNER (b. ABT 1877 Kosciusko, Attala Co., MS, d. 1941 Kosciusko, Attala Co., MS).[2343]
iii Lottie STINGLEY (b. 1907 MS, d. 14 Apr 1946 Attala Co., MS).[2344]
iv Mayvell STINGLEY (b. 2 Dec 1907 Attala Co., MS, d. 28 May 1994 Kosciusko, Attala Co., MS)[2345] m. Joe Howard SUDDUTH (b. 27 Sep 1898 Sallis, Attala Co., MS, d. 10 Nov 1987 Sallis, Attala Co., MS).[2346]
v   Guyton STINGLEY (b. 15 Jul 1911 Attala Co., MS, d. 6 Sep 1950 Korea).[2347]
vi Mannie Whitt STINGLEY (b. 31 May 1912 Attala Co., MS, d. 19 Jul 1979 Kosciusko, Attala Co., MS)[2348] m. Dorotha JENKINS (b. 25 Sep 1925 Sallis, Attala Co., MS, d. 23 Aug 1988 Kosciusko, Attala Co., MS).[2349]
vii John Ike STINGLEY (b. 18 Mar 1913 Sallis, Attala Co., MS, d. 5 Nov 1988 Chicago, Cook Co., IL)[2350] m. Quincy Thelma (Q.T.) SUDDUTH (b. 25 Jul 1917 Attala Co., MS, d. 23 Jan 2011 Maywood, Cook Co., IL).[2351]

[2338] "1910 United States Federal Census," Beat 4, Attala Co., MS, digital image s.v. "Maggie Stingley," (birth 1875), *Ancestry.com*.
[2339] Herman Stingley, grave marker, Russell Cemetery, Attala Co., MS, digital image s.v. "Herman Stingley," (birth 14 Sep 1903, death 15 Sep 1964), *FindaGrave.com*.
[2340] "1940 United States Census," New Orleans, Orleans Parish, LA, MS, digital image s.v. "Pauline Stingley," (birth ABT 1909), *Ancestry.com*.
[2341] "New Orleans, Louisiana, Marriage Records Index, 1831-1964," s.v. "Herman Stingley (marriage Jun 1929), *Ancestry.com*.
[2342] "Social Security Death Index," s.v. "Louria S. Turner," (birth 30 Dec 1904, death 23 Dec 1988), *Ancestry.com*.
[2343] Lee Boston Turner, grave marker, Kosciusko City Cemetery, Kosciusko, Attala Co., MS, digital image s.v. "Lee Boston Turner," (birth 1877, death 1941), *FindaGrave.com*.
[2344] Lottie Stingley, grave marker, Russell Cemetery, Kosciusko, Attala Co., MS, digital image s.v. "Lottie Stingley," (birth 1907, death 14 Apr 1946), *FindaGrave.com*.
[2345] Mayvell Stingley, grave marker, Russell Cemetery, Kosciusko, Attala Co., MS, digital image s.v. "Mayvell Sudduth," (birth 2 Dec 1907, death 28 May 1994), *FindaGrave.com*.
[2346] Joe Howard Sudduth, grave marker, Russell Cemetery, Kosciusko, Attala Co., MS, digital image s.v. "Joe Howard Sudduth," (birth 27 Sep 1898, death 10 Nov 1987), *FindaGrave.com*.
[2347] "U.S., Headstone Applications for Military Veterans, 1925-1963, digital image s.v. "Guyton Stingley," (birth 15 Jul 1911, death 6 Sep 1950), Russell Cemetery, Sallis, Attala Co., MS.
[2348] Whitt Stingley, grave marker, Kosciusko City Cemetery, Kosciusko, Attala Co., MS, digital image s.v. "Whitt Stingley," (birth 31 May 1911, d. 19 Jul 1979), *FindaGrave.com*.
[2349] Dorotha Jenkins, grave marker, Kosciusko City Cemetery, Kosciusko, Attala Co., MS, digital image s.v. "Dorotha Stingley," (birth 25 Sep 1925, d. 23 Aug 1988), *FindaGrave.com*.
[2350] John Ike Stingley, grave marker, Russell Cemetery, Kosciusko, Attala Co., MS, digital image s.v. "John Ike Stingley," (birth 18 Mar 1913, d. 5 Nov 1988), *FindaGrave.com*
[2351] Quincy Thelma Sudduth, grave marker, Russell Cemetery, Kosciusko, Attala Co., MS, digital image s.v. "Quincy Thelma Stingley," (b. 25 Jul 1917, d. 23 Jan 2011), *FindaGrave.com*.

The children in this family were extremely well-educated for the times. In the 1940 U.S. Federal Census, all six younger children were single and lived at home with their father.[2352] They ranged in age from 35 to 24. Their father, Tom, had only a third-grade education. We don't know Maggie's level of education. See the table below for a summary.

Child	Education Level	Job
Louria	4 years of high school	Teacher
Lottie	4 years of high school	Teacher
Mayvell	4 years of high school	Housekeeper
Guyton	1 year of college	Teacher
Whitt	4 years of high school	Teacher
John Ike	3 years of high school	In School

[2352] "1940 United States Federal Census," Newport, Attala Co., MS, digital image s.v. "Tom Stingley," (birth ABT 1880), Ancestry.com.

Generation #8

Herman STINGLEY (Maggie, Aaron Whitaker, Aaron Steele, Joseph I, John I, Samuel II, Samuel I, John)

Herman STINGLEY was the son of Maggie GUYTON (b. ABT 1874 Attala Co., MS, d. 4 May 1919 Mississippi City, Harrison Co., MS)[2353] and Thomas (Tom) STINGLEY (b. Apr 1875 Attala Co., MS, d. 1957 Kosciusko, Attala Co., MS).[2354] He was born on 14 Sep 1903 in MS, and died on 15 Sep 1964 in Orleans Parish, LA.[2355] Herman's draft registration and the 1940 and 1950 U.S. Censuses indicated that Herman was born in Louisiana but other sources indicated Mississippi. He married Pearline ALLEN (b. ABT 1909 LA, d. Unknown)[2356] in Jun 1929 in New Orleans, Orleans Parish, LA.[2357]

In the 1940 U.S. Federal Census, Herman (32) and Pearline (31) lived in a rented home in New Orleans, at 1701 Spain Street. See Figure 339. Herman worked as a truck driver. Pearline did not work, and they had no children. They lived in the same home in the 1950 U.S. Census. Four nieces and nephews lived with them in 1950.[2358]

Figure 339 1701 Spain Street, Home of Herman STINGLEY

[2353] Maggie Guyton, grave marker, Russell Cemetery, Attala Co., MS, digital image s.v. "Maggie Stingley Guyton," (birth ABT 1874; death 4 May 1919), *FindaGrave.com*. "1880 United States Census," Newport, Attala Co., MS, digital image s.v. "Maggie Delpha," (birth ABT 1871), *Ancestry.com*.

[2354] Thomas Stingley, grave marker, Russell Cemetery, Attala Co., MS, digital image s.v. "Tom Stingley," (birth ABT 1875; death ABT 1957), *FindaGrave.com*.

[2355] Herman Stingley, grave marker, Russell Cemetery, Attala Co., MS, digital image s.v. "Herman Stingley," (birth 14 Sep 1903, death 15 Sep 1964), *FindaGrave.com*.

[2356] "1940 United States Census," New Orleans, Orleans Parish, LA, digital image s.v. "Pauline Stingley," (birth ABT 1909), *Ancestry.com*.

[2357] "New Orleans, Louisiana, Marriage Records Index, 1831-1964," s.v. "Herman Stingley (marriage Jun 1929), *Ancestry.com*.

[2358] "1940 United States Census," New Orleans, Orleans Parish, LA, digital image s.v. "Herman Stingley," (birth ABT 1908), *Ancestry.com*. "1950 United States Census," New Orleans, Orleans Parish, LA, digital image s.v. "Herman Stingley," (birth ABT 1904), *Ancestry.com*.

In Herman's February 1942 draft registration in New Orleans, the government recorded his height at 5'8" and weight at 140 lbs. He worked for Douglas Transfer Company.[2359]

Louria STINGLEY (Maggie, Aaron Whitaker, Aaron Steele, Joseph I, John I, Samuel II, Samuel I, John)

Louria STINGLEY was the daughter of Maggie GUYTON (b. ABT 1874 Attala Co., MS, d. 4 May 1919 Harrison Co., MS)[2360] and Thomas (Tom) STINGLEY, Sr. (b. Apr 1875 Attala Co., MS, d. 1957 Kosciusko, Attala Co., MS).[2361] Louria was born on 30 Dec 1904 in Mississippi, and died on 23 Dec 1988 in Kosciusko, Attala Co., MS.[2362] She married Lee Boston TURNER (b. 14 Feb 1877 Kosciusko, Attala Co., MS, d. 1941 Kosciusko, Attala Co., MS).[2363] Note that Lee was 27 years older than Louria; he was closer to her parents' age. Lee was a widower and had children. Louria and Lee did not have children together. See Figure 340 and Figure 341.

Figure 340 Louria STINGLEY and Lee Boston TURNER[2364]

Figure 341 Obituary for Louria STINGLEY TURNER[2365]

[2359] "U.S., World War II Draft Cards Young Men, 1940-1947," digital image s.v. "Herman Stingley (draft registration February 16, 1942), *Ancestry.com*.
[2360] Maggie Guyton, grave marker, Russell Cemetery, Attala Co., MS, digital image s.v. "Maggie Stingley Guyton," (birth ABT 1874; death 4 May 1919), *FindaGrave.com*. "1880 United States Census," Newport, Attala Co., MS, digital image s.v. "Maggie Delpha," (birth ABT 1871), *Ancestry.com*.
[2361] Thomas Stingley, grave marker, Russell Cemetery, Attala Co., MS, digital image s.v. "Tom Stingley," (birth ABT 1875; death ABT 1957), *FindaGrave.com*.
[2362] "Social Security Death Index," s.v. "Louria S. Turner," (birth 30 Dec 1904, death 23 Dec 1988), *Ancestry.com*.
[2363] Lee Boston Turner, grave marker, Kosciusko City Cemetery, Kosciusko, Attala Co., MS, digital image s.v. "Lee Boston Turner," (birth 1877, death 1941), *FindaGrave.com*. "U.S., World War I Draft Registration Cards, 1917-1918," digital image s.v. "Lee B. Turner," (birth 14 Feb 1877), *Ancestry.com*.
[2364] stingraay originally shared this on 7 Jul 2016 on *Ancestry.com*.
[2365] "Mrs. Louria Stingley Turner," *The Star-Herald*, 29 Dec 1988, p. 13; digital image, s.v. "Mrs. Louria Stingley Turner," *Newspapers.com* <https://www.newspapers.com/article/the-star-herald-obituary-for-louria-stin/129956996/>.

In the 1930 U.S. Federal Census, Louria was single, living with her family, and working on the family farm. By 1940, she still lived in New Port, Attala Co., MS with her family, was single, and she worked as a teacher. She had completed a 4-year high school diploma. In 1950, Louria was married to Lee Boston TURNER, lived in Kosciusko, and worked as an elementary school teacher in the city.[2366]

Lee worked as a manager/operator in a funeral home in 1950 at the age of 73. He and Louria lived at 200 College Street. Lee was a very educated man. According to his 1940 U.S. Census, he completed a four-year college degree.[2367] His WWI draft registration indicated that he was a teacher at Central Mississippi College in Kosciusko on 12 Sep 1918.[2368] Central Mississippi College was a segregated school for African American students established in 1893 by Baptist associations in Kosciusko, Attala Co., MS. The school was a grammar school, high school, and normal school in its early history. Later, it was a junior college (college extension school).[2369]

According to Evan Howard ASHFORD, Lee Boston TURNER was a graduate of Central Mississippi College and a professor there. Lee wrote in the *Oklahoma Safeguard,* [2370]

> If Negroes are ever to become anything more than drudges for other races they must both establish and support more high schools and colleges, and see that they are attended regularly. From time to time wise and good people, inspired by the xpressed [sic] above and realizing that the public schools of the South are inadequate to meet the needs of the Colored people, have established schools of higher grade.

[2366] "1930 United States Federal Census," Beat 4, Attala Co., MS, digital image s.v. "Loui Stingley," (birth ABT 1905), *Ancestry.com*. "1940 United States Census," Newport, Attala Co., MS, digital image s.v. "Lauria Stingley," (birth ABT 1915), *Ancestry.com*. "1950 United States Census," Kosciusko, Attala Co., MS, digital image s.v. "Louria S. Turner," (birth ABT 1905), *Ancestry.com*.
[2367] "1940 United States Federal Census," Kosciusko, Attala Co., MS, digital image s.v. "Lee B. Turner," (birth ABT 1875), *Ancestry.com*. "1950 United States Federal Census," Kosciusko, Attala Co., MS, digital image s.v. "Lee B. Turner," (birth ABT 1877), *Ancestry.com*.
[2368] "U.S., World War I Draft Registration Cards, 1917-1918," digital image s.v. "Lee B. Turner," (birth 14 Feb 1877), *Ancestry.com*.
[2369] "Central Mississippi College," *Wikipedia,* last edited 16 April 2024 <https://en.wikipedia.org/wiki/Central_Mississippi_College>.
[2370] Evan Howard Ashford, "Mississippi Zion: The Struggle for Liberation in Attala County, 1865–1915," Mississippi: Univ. Press of Mississippi, 2022 <https://books.google.com/books?id=PXR4EAAAQBAJ&pg=RA2-PA1858#v=onepage&q&f=false>.

Lottie STINGLEY (Maggie, Aaron Whitaker, Aaron Steele, Joseph I, John I, Samuel II, Samuel I, John)

Lottie STINGLEY was the daughter of Maggie GUYTON (b. ABT 1874 Attala Co., MS, d. 4 May 1919 Mississippi City, Harrison Co., MS)[2371] and Thomas (Tom) STINGLEY (b. Apr 1875 Attala Co., MS, d. 1957 Kosciusko, Attala Co., MS).[2372] She was born about 1907 in MS and died on 14 Apr 1946 in Attala Co., MS.[2373] See Figure 342.

Like her sister, Louria STINGLEY, Lottie was well-educated. She had a 4-year high school diploma and taught school.[2374] She did not marry or have children.

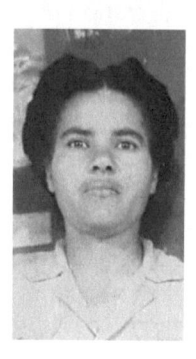

Figure 342 Lottie STINGLEY[2375]

Mayvell STINGLEY (Maggie, Aaron Whitaker, Aaron Steele, Joseph I, John I, Samuel II, Samuel I, John)

Mayvell STINGLEY was the daughter of Maggie GUYTON (b. ABT 1874 Attala Co., MS, d. 4 May 1919 Mississippi City, Harrison Co., MS)[2376] and Thomas (Tom) STINGLEY (b. Apr 1875 Attala Co., MS, d. 1957 Kosciusko, Attala Co., MS).[2377] She was born on 2 Dec 1907 in Attala Co., MS, and died on 28 May 1994 in Kosciusko, Attala Co., MS.[2378] She married Joe Howard SUDDUTH (b. 27 Sep 1898 Sallis, Attala Co., MS, d. 10 Nov 1987 Sallis, Attala Co., MS).[2379] They had no children. See Figure 343, Figure 344, and Figure 345.

[2371] Maggie Guyton, grave marker, Russell Cemetery, Attala Co., MS, digital image s.v. "Maggie Stingley Guyton," (birth ABT 1874; death 4 May 1919), *FindaGrave.com*. "1880 United States Census," Newport, Attala Co., MS, digital image s.v. "Maggie Delpha," (birth ABT 1871), *Ancestry.com*.

[2372] Thomas Stingley, grave marker, Russell Cemetery, Attala Co., MS, digital image s.v. "Tom Stingley," (birth ABT 1875; death ABT 1957), *FindaGrave.com*.

[2373] Lottie Stingley, grave marker, Russell Cemetery, Kosciusko, Attala Co., MS, digital image s.v. "Lottie Stingley," (birth 1907, death 14 Apr 1946), *FindaGrave.com*.

[2374] "1940 United States Census," Newport, Attala Co., MS, digital image s.v. "Lattie Stingley," (birth ABT 1906), *Ancestry.com*.

[2375] chancurri originally shared this on 30 Jun 2016 on *Ancestry.com*.

[2376] Maggie Guyton, grave marker, Russell Cemetery, Attala Co., MS, digital image s.v. "Maggie Stingley Guyton," (birth ABT 1874; death 4 May 1919), *FindaGrave.com*. "1880 United States Census," Newport, Attala Co., MS, digital image s.v. "Maggie Delpha," (birth ABT 1871), *Ancestry.com*.

[2377] Thomas Stingley, grave marker, Russell Cemetery, Attala Co., MS, digital image s.v. "Tom Stingley," (birth ABT 1875; death ABT 1957), *FindaGrave.com*.

[2378] Mayvell Stingley, grave marker, Russell Cemetery, Kosciusko, Attala Co., MS, digital image s.v. "Mayvell Sudduth," (birth 2 Dec 1907, death 28 May 1994), *FindaGrave.com*.

[2379] Joe Howard Sudduth, grave marker, Russell Cemetery, Kosciusko, Attala Co., MS, digital image s.v. "Joe Howard Sudduth," (birth 27 Sep 1898, death 10 Nov 1987), *FindaGrave.com*.

In the 1930 U.S. Federal Census, Mayvell was about 22 years old and lived with her father and siblings.[2380] In 1940, she still lived at home, working as a housekeeper for the family. She was equally well-educated as her sisters Louria and Lottie – a 4-year high school diploma. The 1950 U.S. Federal Census reported that Joe Howard and Mayvell SUDDUTH lived in New Port, Attala Co., MS. Joe farmed and Mayvell kept house.

Figure 343 Mayvell STINGLEY SUDDUTH[2381]

Figure 344 Obituary of Mayvell STINGLEY SUDDUTH[2382]

Figure 345 Joe Howard SUDDUTH[2383]

Guyton STINGLEY (Maggie, Aaron Whitaker, Aaron Steele, Joseph I, John I, Samuel II, Samuel I, John)

Guyton STINGLEY was the son of Maggie GUYTON (b. ABT 1874 Attala Co., MS, d. 4 May 1919 Mississippi City, Harrison Co., MS)[2384] and Thomas (Tom) STINGLEY (b. Apr 1875 Attala Co., MS, d. 1957 Kosciusko, Attala Co., MS).[2385] Guyton was born on the 15th of July 1911 in Attala Co., MS, and died in action in Korea on 6 Sep 1950. Guyton was well-educated like his siblings; he received his college degree in civil engineering. See Figure 346.

[2380] "1930 United States Federal Census," Beat 4, Attala Co., MS, digital image s.v. "May B Stingley," (birth ABT 1908), *Ancestry.com*. "1940 United States Census," Newport, Attala Co., MS, digital image s.v. "Mary Valle Stingley," (birth ABT 1910), *Ancestry.com*. "1950 United States Census," Kosciusko, Attala Co., MS, digital image s.v. "Louria S. Turner," (birth ABT 1905), *Ancestry.com*.
[2381] chancurri originally shared this on 30 Jun 2016 on *Ancestry.com*.
[2382] "Mrs. Mayvell S. Sudduth," *The Star-Herald*, Kosciusko, MS, 9 Jun 1994, p. 6; digital image, s.v. "Mrs. Mayvell S. Sudduth," Newspapers.com <https://www.newspapers.com/article/the-star-herald/36777088/>.
[2383] chancurri originally shared this on 30 Jun 2016 on *Ancestry.com*.
[2384] Maggie Guyton, grave marker, Russell Cemetery, Attala Co., MS, digital image s.v. "Maggie Stingley Guyton," (birth ABT 1874; death 4 May 1919), *FindaGrave.com*. "1880 United States Census," Newport, Attala Co., MS, digital image s.v. "Maggie Delpha," (birth ABT 1871), *Ancestry.com*.
[2385] Thomas Stingley, grave marker, Russell Cemetery, Attala Co., MS, digital image s.v. "Tom Stingley," (birth ABT 1875; death ABT 1957), *FindaGrave.com*.

Cpl. Guyton Stingley To Be Buried With Full Military Honors Sunday

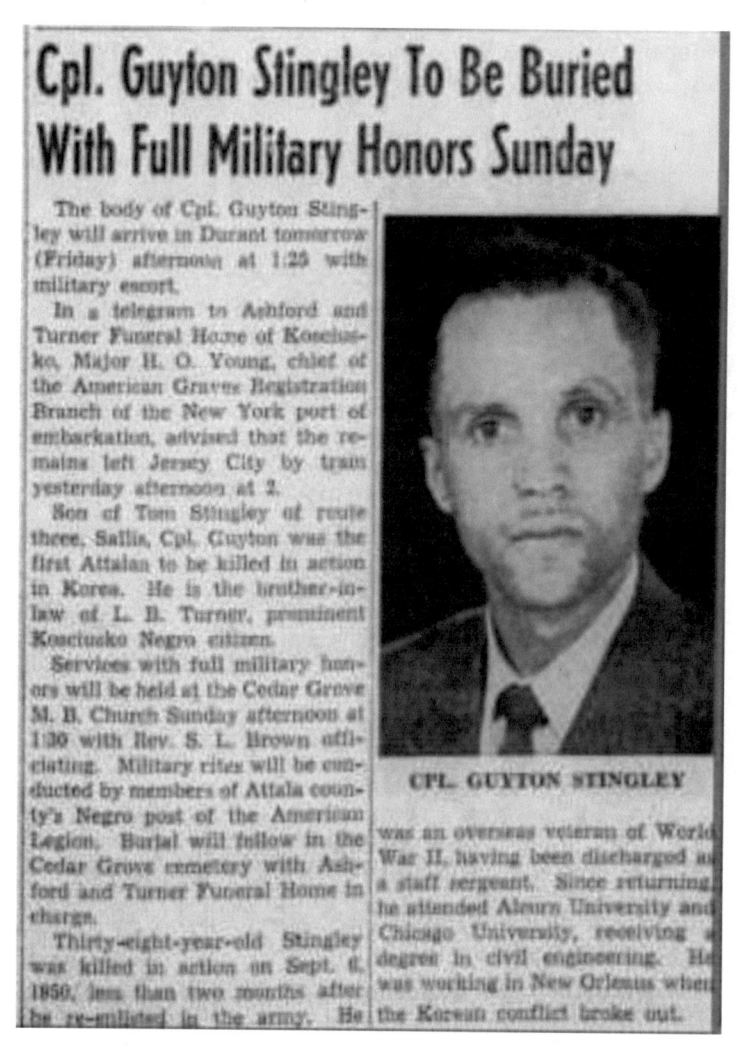

The body of Cpl. Guyton Stingley will arrive in Durant tomorrow (Friday) afternoon at 1:25 with military escort.

In a telegram to Ashford and Turner Funeral Home of Kosciusko, Major H. O. Young, chief of the American Graves Registration Branch of the New York port of embarkation, advised that the remains left Jersey City by train yesterday afternoon at 2.

Son of Tom Stingley of route three, Sallis, Cpl. Guyton was the first Attalan to be killed in action in Korea. He is the brother-in-law of L. B. Turner, prominent Kosciusko Negro citizen.

Services with full military honors will be held at the Cedar Grove M. B. Church Sunday afternoon at 1:30 with Rev. S. L. Brown officiating. Military rites will be conducted by members of Attala county's Negro post of the American Legion. Burial will follow in the Cedar Grove cemetery with Ashford and Turner Funeral Home in charge.

Thirty-eight-year-old Stingley was killed in action on Sept. 6, 1950, less than two months after he re-enlisted in the army. He was an overseas veteran of World War II, having been discharged as a staff sergeant. Since returning, he attended Alcorn University and Chicago University, receiving a degree in civil engineering. He was working in New Orleans when the Korean conflict broke out.

Figure 346 Death of Guyton STINGLEY in Korea[2386]

Corporal STINGLEY was a medic with the Medical Detachment, 21st Anti-Aircraft Artillery (Automatic Weapons) Battalion, 25th Infantry Division. He was Killed in Action while tending his wounded comrades in South Korea on September 6, 1950. Corporal STINGLEY was awarded the Purple Heart, the Korean Service Medal, the United Nations Service Medal, the National Defense Service Medal, the Korean Presidential Unit Citation, and the Republic of Korea War Service Medal.[2387]

[2386] "Cpl. Guyton Stingley to be Buried with Full Military Honors Sunday," *The Star-Herald*, Kosciusko, MS, 26 Jul 1951, p. 1; digital image, s.v. "Cpl. Guyton Stingley," Newspapers.com <https://www.newspapers.com/article/the-star-herald-obituary-guyton-stingley/129960365/>.

[2387] "WWI, WWII, and Korean War Casualty Listings," s.v. "Guyton Stingley," (killed in action 6 Sep 1950), *Ancestry.com*.

Mannie Whitt (Whitt) STINGLEY (Maggie, Aaron Whitaker, Aaron Steele, Joseph I, John I, Samuel II, Samuel I, John)

Whitt STINGLEY was the son of Maggie GUYTON (b. ABT 1874 Attala Co., MS, d. 4 May 1919 Mississippi City, Harrison Co., MS)[2390] and Thomas (Tom) STINGLEY (b. Apr 1875 Attala Co., MS, d. 1957 Kosciusko, Attala Co., MS).[2391] Whitt was born on 31 May 1912 in Attala Co., MS, and died on 19 Jul 1979 in Kosciusko, Attala Co., MS.[2392] He married Dorotha JENKINS (b. 25 Sep 1925 Sallis, Attala Co., MS, d. 23 Aug 1988 Kosciusko, Attala Co., MS).[2393] See Figure 347, Figure 348, Figure 349, and Figure 350.

Figure 347 Mannie Whitt STINGLEY[2388]

Figure 348 Dorotha JENKINS STINGLEY[2389]

[2388] chancurri originally shared this on 30 Jun 2016 on *Ancestry.com*.
[2389] stingraay originally shared this on 7 Jul 2016 on *Ancestry.com*.
[2390] Maggie Guyton, grave marker, Russell Cemetery, Attala Co., MS, digital image s.v. "Maggie Stingley Guyton," (birth ABT 1874; death 4 May 1919), *FindaGrave.com*. "1880 United States Census," Newport, Attala Co., MS, digital image s.v. "Maggie Delpha," (birth ABT 1871), *Ancestry.com*.
[2391] Thomas Stingley, grave marker, Russell Cemetery, Attala Co., MS, digital image s.v. "Tom Stingley," (birth ABT 1875; death ABT 1957), *FindaGrave.com*.
[2392] Mannie Whitt Stingley, grave marker, Kosciusko City Cemetery, Attala Co., MS, digital image s.v. "Whitt Stingley," (birth 31 May 1911, death 19 Jul 1979), *FindaGrave.com*.
[2393] Dorotha Jenkins, grave marker, Kosciusko City Cemetery, Attala Co., MS, digital image s.v. "Dorotha Stingley," (birth 25 Sep 1925, death 23 Aug 1988), FindaGrave.com.

Mrs. Dorotha J. Stingley

Mrs. Dorotha Jenkins Stingley, 63, a retired teacher, died Aug. 23, 1989, at St. Dominic Hospital following a short illness.

Funeral services were held Sunday at 4 p.m. at Christian Liberty M. B. Church with burial in the city cemetery. The Rev. R. B. Harris officiated.

Mrs. Stingley was a native of Attala County, a member of Christian Liberty M. B. Church, the Retired Teachers Association, the National Council of Negro Women and Community Services Unlimited.

She leaves a daughter, Ms. Louria L. Stingley of Kosciusko; a son, Martin L. Stingley of Kosciusko; a sister, Mrs. Ruth M. McFadden of Kosciusko; a brother, John Jenkins of West; one grandson.

Pallbearers were John Bayne, Mack Clark, James Latiker, Jerry Redmond, Leslie Walker and Henry Turnbo.

Figure 349 Obituary for Dorotha JENKINS STINGLEY[2394]

Whitt Stingley Services Held On Monday

Funeral services were held at 2 p.m. Monday at Kosciusko's Liberty MB Church for Whitt Stingley who died Thursday at Veteran's Hospital in Jackson following a prolonged illness.

Stingley, 68, was a native of Sallis and a graduate of Alcorn A&M with a master's degree in sciencse from Tuskegee Institute. He also studied at Tougaloo College.

He was involved in a number of organizations including the Attala County Improvement Club, in which he was executive director, the Lone Star Masonic Lodge 51 and Christian Liberty Church where he was a deacon and Sunday School teacher.

Stingley served several years as a teacher in Attala and Holmes Counties and for 11 years was assistant director at Winters and Stingley Funeral Home, now Winters Funeral Home.

Survivors include his wife, Mrs. Dorotha Jenkins Stingley, a daughter, Louria Lorraine Stingley and a son, Martin Luther Stingley, all of Kosciusko.

Also among Stingley's survivors are two sisters, Mrs. Louria Turner, Kosciusko, and Mrs. Mayvell Sudduth of Sallis, and a brother, John Ike Stingley of Maywood Ill.

Interment was at Kosciusko City Cemetery. Pallbearers were fellow Masons and honorary pall bearers were deacons from Christian Liberty.

Figure 350 Obituary for Mannie Whitt STINGLEY[2395]

[2394] "Obituary for Mrs. Dorotha J. Stingley," *The Star-Herald*, Kosciusko, MS, 31 Aug 1989, p. 7; digital image, s.v. "Mrs. Dorotha J. Stingley," *Newspapers.com* <https://www.newspapers.com/article/the-star-herald-obituary-for-dorotha-jen/129962261/>.

According to Whit STINGLEY'S obituary, he earned a bachelor's degree from Alcorn State University and a master's degree in science from Tuskegee Institute. He also studied at Tougaloo College.[2396] See Figure 351. Tougaloo College was founded in 1869 as an independent, historically Black, coeducational four-year liberal arts institution, located on the northern border of Jackson, Mississippi. Tougaloo College has historically produced over 40% of the African American physicians and dentists, practicing in the state of Mississippi, more than 33% of the state's African American attorneys and educators including teachers, principals, school superintendents, college/university faculty and administrators.[2397]

Alcorn State University (Figure 352) is the oldest public historically Black land-grant institution in the United States and the second-oldest state-supported institution of higher learning in Mississippi. Alcorn State University was founded in 1871 because people of Mississippi exerted efforts to educate the descendants of formerly enslaved Africans. It was named in honor of the sitting governor of Mississippi, James L. ALCORN. Alcorn is situated in Claiborne County, Mississippi, seven miles west of Lorman, 80 miles south of the capital city of Jackson, 45 miles south of Vicksburg, and 40 miles north of Natchez.

Figure 351 Woodworth Chapel, Tougaloo College

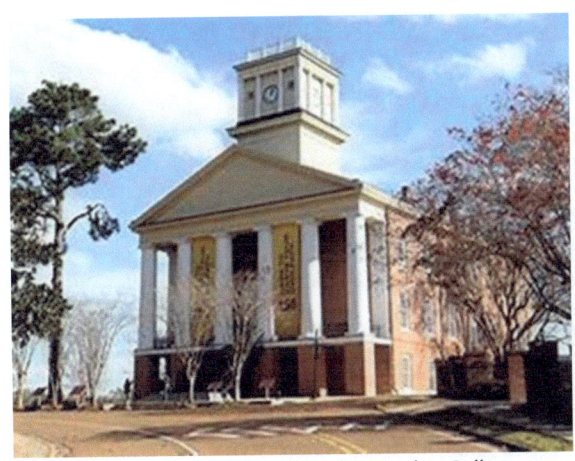

Figure 352 Alcorn State University's Oakland Chapel

[2395] "Whitt Stingley Services Held on Monday," *The Star-Herald*, Kosciusko, MS, 26 Jul 1979, p. 10; digital image, s.v. "Whitt Stingley," *Newspapers.com* <https://www.newspapers.com/article/the-star-herald-obituary-for-whitt-sting/129956106/>.

[2396] "Whitt Stingley Services Held on Monday," *The Star-Herald*, Kosciusko, MS, 26 Jul 1979, p. 10; digital image, s.v. "Whitt Stingley," *Newspapers.com* <https://www.newspapers.com/article/the-star-herald-obituary-for-whitt-sting/129956106/>.

[2397] "Tougaloo College: Home, About Tougaloo College, Tougaloo College Facts," 2024, <https://www.tougaloo.edu/about-tougaloo-college/quick-facts>.

Like many of his siblings, Whitt worked as a teacher. He also worked for eleven years at the Winters and Stingley Funeral Home, now Winters Funeral Home. It is likely this is the same funeral home owned and operated by his brother-in-law, Lee Boston TURNER (husband of his sister, Louria STINGLEY).

John Ike STINGLEY (Maggie, Aaron Whitaker, Aaron Steele, Joseph I, John I, Samuel II, Samuel I, John)

John Ike STINGLEY was the son of Maggie GUYTON (b. ABT 1874 Attala Co., MS, d. 4 May 1919 Mississippi City, Harrison Co., MS)[2398] and Thomas (Tom) STINGLEY (b. Apr 1875 Attala Co., MS, d. 1957 Kosciusko, Attala Co., MS).[2399] John Ike STINGLEY was born on 18 Mar 1913 in Sallis, Attala Co., MS. He died on 5 Nov 1988 in Chicago, Cook Co., IL.[2400] He married Quincy Thelma (Q.T.) SUDDUTH (b. 25 Jul 1917 Attala Co., MS. d. 23 Jan 2011 Maywood, Cook Co., IL).[2401] The couple was buried in Russell Cemetery in Attala Co., MS. See Figure 353**Error! Reference source not found.**, Figure 354, Figure 355, Figure 356, and Figure 357.[2402]

John Ike Stingley

John Ike Stingley, 75, of Maywood, Il., died Nov. 5, 1988, at the Veterans Hospital in Chicago, Il. following an illness of several years.

Funeral services for the Attala County native were held Saturday at 1 p.m. at Christian Liberty M. B. Church with burial in Russell Cemetery at Sallis.

The Rev. R. B. Harris officiated and Winters Funeral Home was in charge of arrangements.

He is survived by his wife, Mrs. Quincy T. Stingley of Maywood, Il; a daughter, Mrs. Dona S. Montgomery of San Pedro, Ca.; a son, Tommie Stingley of San Francisco, Ca.; two sisters, Mrs. Louria S. Turner of Kosciusko and Mrs. Maybelle Sudduth of Sallis; four grandchildren.

He was a member of Maywood Metropolitan Baptist Church, a deacon, a club leader, trustee and veteran.

Nephews served as pallbearers.

Figure 353 John Ike STINGLEY's Obituary

[2398] Maggie Guyton, grave marker, Russell Cemetery, Attala Co., MS, digital image s.v. "Maggie Stingley Guyton," (birth ABT 1874; death 4 May 1919), *FindaGrave.com*. "1880 United States Census," Newport, Attala Co., MS, digital image s.v. "Maggie Delpha," (birth ABT 1871), *Ancestry.com*.

[2399] Thomas Stingley, grave marker, Russell Cemetery, Attala Co., MS, digital image s.v. "Tom Stingley," (birth ABT 1875; death ABT 1957), *FindaGrave.com*.

[2400] John Ike Stingley, grave marker, Russell Cemetery, Attala Co., MS, digital image s.v. "John Ike Stingley," (birth 18 Mar 1913; death 5 Nov 1988), *FindaGrave.com*.

[2401] Quincy Thelma Sudduth, grave marker, Russell Cemetery, Attala Co., MS, digital image s.v. "Quincy Thelma Stingley," (birth 25 Jul 1917, death 23 Jan 2011), *FindaGrave.com*.

[2402] "Obituary of John Ike Stingley," *The Star-Herald*, Kosciusko, MS, 17 Nov 1988, p. 12; digital image, s.v. "John Ike Stingley," *Newspapers.com* <https://www.newspapers.com/article/the-star-herald-john-ike-stingley-obitua/129966749/>.

Figure 354 John Ike STINGLEY[2403]

Figure 355 Quincy Thelma SUDDUTH[2404]

In the 1940 U.S. Federal Census, John had completed 3 years of high school and was still in school, although he was 22.[2405] He and Quincy lived in Chicago in the 1950 U.S. Census. He cut steel in a steel factory for a living. The family lived at 2315 Washington Blvd. in Chicago.[2406]

Quincy and John had at least two children who were listed in John's obituary.[2407]

i   Iona (or Dona) STINGLEY (b. ABT 1946 Chicago, Cook Co., IL, d. Unknown)[2408] m. Unknown MONTGOMERY (Unknown).[2409]

ii   Tommy STINGLEY (b. Unknown, Chicago, Cook Co., IL after the 1950 U.S. Census).[2410]

[2403] stingraay originally shared this on 7 Jul 2016 on *Ancestry.com*.
[2404] Chancurri originally shared this on 16 Nov 2015 on *Ancestry.com*.
[2405] "1940 United States Census," Newport, Attala Co., MS, digital image s.v. "John Ike Stingley," (birth ABT 1916), *Ancestry.com*.
[2406] "1950 United States Federal Census," Chicago, Cook Co., IL, digital image s.v. "John Stingley," (birth ABT 1913), *Ancestry.com*.
[2407] "Obituary of John Ike Stingley," *The Star-Herald*, Kosciusko, MS, 17 Nov 1988, p. 12; digital image, s.v. "John Ike Stingley," *Newspapers.com* <https://www.newspapers.com/article/the-star-herald-john-ike-stingley-obitua/129966749/>.
[2408] "1950 United States Federal Census," Chicago, Cook Co., IL, digital image s.v. "Iona C Stingley," (birth ABT 1946), *Ancestry.com*. Born in Chicago per Channie Brown-Currie.
[2409] See John Ike Stingley's obituary.
[2410] See John Ike Stingley's obituary.

Figure 356 John Ike STINGLEY's Memorial Program[2411]

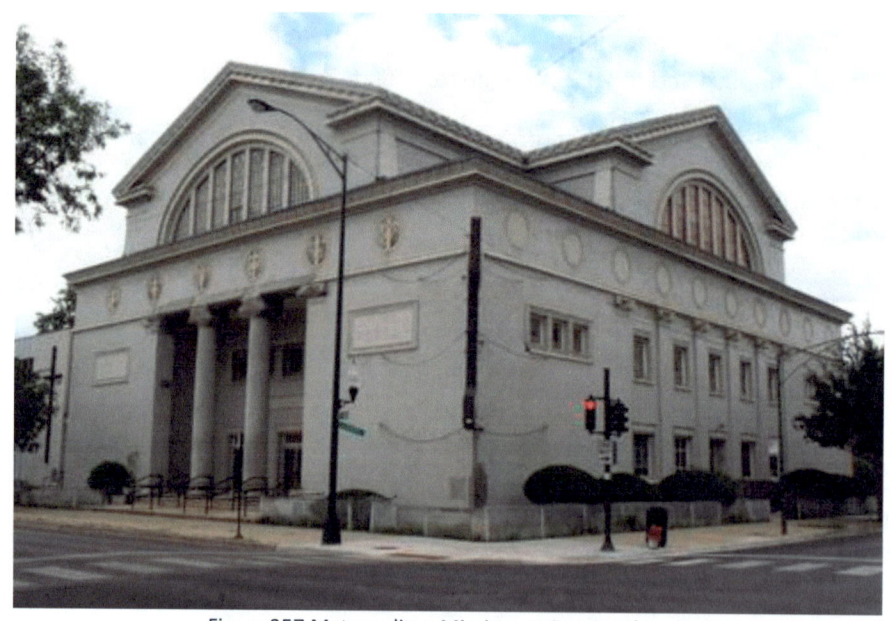

Figure 357 Metropolitan Missionary Baptist Church

[2411] chancurri originally shared this on 6 Dec 2014 on *Ancestry.com*.

CHILD OF AARON WHITAKER GUYTON AND ARTIE RAINEY: AMANDA'S LINE

Generation #7

Amanda (Annie B.) GUYTON (Aaron Whitaker, Aaron Steele, Joseph I, John I, Samuel II, Samuel I, John)

Amanda GUYTON was the daughter of Aaron Whitaker GUYTON and Artemesia (Artie) RAINEY. She was born in Aug 1872 in Sallis, Attala Co., MS, and she died in 1933 in Sallis, Attala Co., MS. See Figure 358. She married Joseph Thomas (Joe) TERRY around 1892, according to the 1910 U.S. Census. Joe was born about 1874 in Sallis, Attala Co., MS. I don't find a date of death for Joe but both he and Amanda are buried in Russell Cemetery, Attala Co., MS.[2412] Joe was included in the 1940 U.S. Census.

There is some confusion over Amanda's. name. Her family all know her by the name of Amanda. Channie BROWN-CURRIE is the family genealogist for Artie RAINEY's family. Channie conversed with the grandchildren of Aaron Whitaker GUYTON and Artie RAINEY. They all know her as Amanda. Most records, however, report her as Annie B. I refer to her as Amanda in the book with notations of her other known name, Annie B.

Figure 358 Amanda (Annie B.) GUYTON TERRY[2413]

In the 1900 U.S. Census, Amanda was married and using the last name TERRY, but she lived with her brother, Case, and her oldest child, Lela TERRY, in New Port, Attala Co., MS.[2414] Amanda could read

---

[2412] Amanda Guyton and Joseph Thomas (Joe) Terry, grave marker, Russell Cemetery, Attala Co., MS, digital image s.v. "Annie Terry," and "Joseph Terry," (Memorial ID 107273730 and 201392258, FindaGrave.com.
[2413] Received from Channie Brown-Currie.
[2414] "1900 United States Census," Newport, Attala Co., MS, digital image s.v. "Ann Terry," (birth Aug 1872), Ancestry.com.

and write. In 1910, Amanda lived with Joe TERRY in Beat 1, Attala Co., MS.[2415] The family lived on their farm which they owned free and clear. The Census indicates they had been married for eighteen years and had three children: Lela TERRY (11), Quesada TERRY (9), and Carnes Fred TERRY (2). Joe TERRY could read and write.

In 1920, the family lived on New Port Road, Kosciusko, Attala Co., MS.[2416] Living with Amanda and Joe on the farm were Carnes Fred TERRY (10) and Stella Mae TERRY (8). The 1930 U.S. Census shows Amanda and Joe lived on their owned farm with Lela TERRY (a 38-year-old married woman but with no children living with her) and her younger brother, Carnes TERRY (22).[2417] Carnes helped Joe farm the property. In 1940, Joe and Amanda lived on the farm with their son, Carnes, his wife Callie Beatrice McMICHAEL, and the younger couple's two children, Yvonne TERRY and Bernice Marie TERRY.[2418]

Joe and Amanda GUYTON TERRY had at least four children:

i Lela TERRY (b. Apr 1892 MS, d. Unknown).[2419]
ii Quesada TERRY (b. ABT 1901 MS, d. Unknown).[2420]
iii Carnes Fred TERRY (b. 7 Oct 1907 Sallis, Attala Co., MS, d. Jun 1973 Jackson, Hinds Co., MS)[2421] m. Callie Beatrice McMICHAEL (b. 20 Sep 1915 Attala Co., MS, d. 19 May 1979 Memphis, Shelby Co., TN).[2422]
iv Stella Mae TERRY (b. 17 Aug 1912 Sallis, Attala Co., MS, d. 1 Jan 1993 Lexington, Holmes Co., MS)[2423] m. Joe Dale (Joe D.) GUYTON (b. 24 Dec 1901 MS, d. Dec 1967 Sallis, Attala Co., MS).[2424] Joe D. was the son of Simon GUYTON, Sr. and Viola GUYTON. He was a cousin to Stella Mae.

Joe and Amanda's children and their descendants are reported in Caroline's line.

[2415] "1910 United States Census," Beat 1, Attala Co., MS, digital image s.v. "Annie B. Terry," (birth ABT 1874), *Ancestry.com*.
[2416] "1920 United States Census," Kosciusko, Attala Co., MS, digital image s.v. "Annie Terry," (birth ABT 1880), *Ancestry.com*.
[2417] "1930 United States Census," Natchez Trace Road, Beat 1, Attala Co., MS, digital image s.v. "Anne Terry," (birth ABT 1880), *Ancestry.com*.
[2418] "1940 United States Census," Goodman Road, Kosciusko, Attala Co., MS, digital image s.v. "Annie Grory," (birth ABT 1880), *Ancestry.com*.
[2419] "1900 United States Census," Newport, Attala Co., MS, digital image s.v. "Lela Terry," (birth Apr 1892), *Ancestry.com*.
[2420] "1910 United States Census," Beat 1, Attala Co., MS, digital image s.v. "Quesada Terry," (birth ABT 1901), *Ancestry.com*.
[2421] "Social Security Death Index," s.v. "Fred Terry," (birth 7 Oct 1907, death Jun 1973), *Ancestry.com*.
[2422] Callie Beatrice McMichael, grave marker, Hollywood Cemetery, Memphis, Shelby Co., TN, digital image s.v. "Callie Beatrice Terry Anthony," (birth 20 Sep 1915, death 19 May 1979), *FindaGrave.com*.
[2423] Stella Mae Terry, grave marker, Mallett Cemetery, Attala Co., MS, digital image s.v. "Stella Mae Guyton," (birth 17 Aug 1912, death 1 Jan 1993), *FindaGrave.com*.
[2424] "Social Security Death Index," s.v. "Joe Guyton," (birth 24 Dec 1901, death Dec 1967), *Ancestry.com*.

CHILD OF AARON WHITAKER GUYTON AND ARTIE RAINEY: SIMON'S LINE

Generation #7

Simon GUYTON, Sr. (Aaron Whitaker, Aaron Steele, Joseph I, John I, Samuel II, Samuel I, John)

Simon GUYTON, Sr. was the son of Aaron Whitaker GUYTON and Artemesia (Artie) RAINEY. He was born on 15 Jan 1876 in Sallis, Attala Co., MS, but it is not clear when he died. He is buried in Russell Cemetery in Sallis, Attala Co., MS. See Figure 359. He married Viola UNKNOWN (perhaps WILDER).[2425] She was born about 1880 in MS and her death is unknown.[2426]

Figure 359 Simon GUYTON[2427]

In the 1900 U.S. Census, Simon was 24 and Viola was 21. They were just married in 1900 but they already had two children: Brad (4) and Pomfrey (2). They lived in New Port, Attala Co., MS on a farm that

---

[2425] "Social Security Applications and Claims Index, 1936-2007," s.v. "Simon Guyton," (birth 15 Jan 1876), *Ancestry.com*.
[2426] "1920 United States Census," Newport, Attala Co., MS, digital image s.v. "Viola Guyton," (birth ABT 1880), *Ancestry.com*.
[2427] Image shared by Twanda Gary on 30 Nov 2021 on *Ancestry.com*.

Simon owned free and clear.[2428] Neither Simon nor Viola could read or write. In 1910, Simon and Viola lived on the farm described as in Beat 4, Attala Co., MS. Besides farming, Simon worked as a laborer earning wages at a public school. The Census indicates they had been married for ten years and had seven children living with them, none of whom were called Brad or Pomfrey: Simon GUYTON, Jr. (13), who was likely called Brad in the earlier Census; Jimmy (12), who is likely Pomfrey; Frankie (10); Joe Dale (Joe D.) (8); Hattie Irene (5); Callie (3); and Robbie Lee (written as Robitine in the Census) (0).[2429]

In 1920, the family lived on a farm owned free and clear in New Port, Attala Co., MS.[2430] Simon was no longer working as a laborer. He and Viola lived with children Percy GUYTON (17), whose name shows up for the first time; Hattie GUYTON (14); Callie A. GUYTON (12); Robbie Lee (written Robby King in the Census) GUYTON (9); Annie GUYTON (7); Mary Maggie GUYTON (7); Steele GUYTON (4 2/12); and Casey Jones GUYTON (1 6/12). The 1930 U.S. Census indicated that Simon and Viola lived on a rented farm on the Sallis and Zemuly Road in Beat 4, Attala Co., MS. Simon worked as a laborer in a sawmill. The children still living at home were Robbie Lee (17); Annie (14); Maggie (14), Steele (13); and Casey Jones (12).[2431]

The 1940 Census reflects that Simon was farming again on a farm he owned. It was in New Port, Attala Co., MS. He lived with Viola (68), Casey Jones (21, attended school through the 4th grade); Robbie GUYTON TEAGUE (23, a widow, attended school through the 6th grade); Allie Mae TEAGUE (Robbie's daughter, 6); Maggie (24, attended school through the 4th grade); and two grandsons, Billy HARMON (1) and Earnest G. TERRY (2). Casey Jones worked as a laborer at a sawmill. Robbie and Maggie helped with the farm work. I cannot readily find the parents of Billy HARMON and Earnest G. TERRY.[2432]

i		Simon (Brad) GUYTON, Jr.(b. Apr 1896 MS, d. Unknown).[2433] He is shown as Brazee GUYTON in Channie BROWN-CURRIE's book.
ii		Pomfrey (Jimmy) GUYTON (b. Mar 1898 MS, d. Unknown).[2434]
iii		Frankie GUYTON (b. Apr 1900 MS, d. Dec 1972 Sallis, Attala Co., MS).[2435]
iv		Joe Dale (Joe D.) GUYTON (b. 24 Dec 1901 MS, d. Dec 1967 Sallis, Attala Co., MS) [2436] m. Stella Mae TERRY (b. 17 Aug 1912 Sallis, Attala Co., MS, d. 1 Jan 1993 Sallis, Attala Co., MS).[2437] Stella Mae was the daughter of Joe and Amanda (Annie B.) GUYTON TERRY. She was a first cousin to Joe D.

[2428] "1900 United States Census," Newport, Attala Co., MS, digital image s.v. "Simon Guyton," (birth Feb 1876), *Ancestry.com*.

[2429] "1910 United States Census," Beat 4, Attala Co., MS, digital image s.v. "Simon Guyton," (birth ABT 1883), *Ancestry.com*.

[2430] "1920 United States Census," Kosciusko, Attala Co., MS, digital image s.v. "Simon Guyton," (birth ABT 1875), *Ancestry.com*.

[2431] "1930 United States Census," Sallis and Zemuly Road, Beat 4, Attala Co., MS, digital image s.v. "Simon Gyton," (birth ABT 1876), *Ancestry.com*.

[2432] "1940 United States Census," Newport, Attala Co., MS, digital image s.v. "Simon Guyton," (birth ABT 1873), *Ancestry.com*.

[2433] See Simon Guyton's 1900 and 1910 U.S. Census above.

[2434] See Simon Guyton's 1900 and 1910 U.S. Census above.

[2435] "Social Security Death Index," s.v. "Frank Guyton," (birth 3 Apr 1900, death Dec 1972), *Ancestry.com*.

[2436] "Social Security Death Index," s.v. "Joe Guyton," (birth 24 Dec 1901, death Dec 1967), *Ancestry.com*.

[2437] Stella Mae Terry, grave marker, Mallett Cemetery, Attala Co., MS, digital image s.v. "Stella Mae Guyton," (birth 17 Aug 1912, death 1 Jan 1993), *FindaGrave.com*.

v		Percy GUYTON (b. ABT 1903 MS, d. Unknown).[2438] He is not included in Channie BROWN-CURRIE's book.
vi		Hattie Irene GUYTON (b. 18 May 1904 MS, d. 22 Aug 1973 Chicago, Cook Co., IL)[2439] m Dave (Fat Dave) SUDDUTH (b. 12 Oct 1901 Attala Co., MS, d. 24 Jun 1965 Chicago, Cook Co., IL).[2440]
vii		Callie A. GUYTON (b. ABT 1907 MS, d. Unknown).[2441]
viii		Robbie Lee GUYTON (b. 20 Mar 1911 Sallis, Attala Co., MS, d. 22 Dec 2002 Oak Park, Cook Co., IL)[2442] m (1) Booker T. TEAGUE (b. ABT 1910 MS, d. Dec 1933 MS)[2443] and (2) Edward Fletcher (Shine) BURT (b. 20 Mar 1913 MS, d. 27 May 1987 Sallis, Attala Co., MS).[2444]
ix		Mary (Maggie) GUYTON (b. ABT 1913 MS, d. Unknown)[2445] m. Leon HARMON (b. Unknown Sallis, Attala Co., MS, d. Unknown).[2446]
x		Annie GUYTON (b. ABT 1913 MS, d. Unknown)[2447] m. Leon TERRY (b. 26 Nov 1911 Sallis, Attala Co., MS, d. 30 Aug 1991 Sallis, Attala Co., MS).[2448] She may be known as Annie (Eudy) in Channie BROWN-CURRIE's book.
xi		Steele GUYTON (b. 16 Jul 1915 MS, d. 25 Dec 1994 Chicago, Cook Co., IL)[2449] m. Minnie GUYTON (b. 22 May 1918 Sallis, Attala Co., MS, d. 10 Nov 1976 Chicago, Cook Co., IL).[2450] Minnie was the daughter of Ike GUYTON and Ida RILEY GUYTON. That makes Minnie and Steele first cousins.
xii		Casey Jones GUYTON (b. 21 Jul 1917 MS, d. AFT 6 Oct 1940).[2451] He had four children: Bruce GUYTON (b. ABT 1950), Penny GUYTON, Charlie GUYTON, and Tipp GUYTON.[2452]

[2438] "1920 United States Census," Newport, Attala Co., MS, digital image s.v. "Percy Guyton," (birth ABT 1903), *Ancestry.com*. "Social Security Death Index," s.v. "Hattie Sudduth," (birth 18 May 1904, death Aug 1973), *Ancestry.com*.
[2439] "Social Security Death Index," s.v. "Hattie Sudduth," (birth 18 May 1904, death Aug 1973), *Ancestry.com*.
[2440] "Social Security Death Index," s.v. "Dave Sudduth," (birth 12 Oct 1901, death Jun 1965), *Ancestry.com*.
[2441] "1910 United States Census," Beat 4, Attala Co., MS, digital image s.v. "Callie Guyton," (birth ABT 1907), *Ancestry.com*.
[2442] "Social Security Death Index," s.v. "Robbie Burt," (birth 20 Mar 1910, death 22 Dec 2002), *Ancestry.com*.
[2443] Booker Teague, grave marker, New Bethel Cemetery, Sallis, Attala Co., MS, digital image s.v. "Booker Teague," (birth ABT 1910, death Dec 1933), *FindaGrave.com*.
[2444] Edward Fletcher Burt, grave marker, Bullock Cemetery, Attala Co., MS, digital image s.v. "Edward Fletcher Burt," (birth 20 Mar 1914, death 27 May 1987), *FindaGrave.com*.
[2445] "1920 United States Census," Newport, Attala Co., MS, digital image s.v. "Maggie Guyton," (birth ABT 1913), *Ancestry.com*.
[2446] Per Channie Brown-Currie.
[2447] "1920 United States Census," Newport, Attala Co., MS, digital image s.v. "Annie Guyton," (birth ABT 1913), *Ancestry.com*.
[2448] Per Channie Brown-Currie.
[2449] "Social Security Death Index," s.v. "Steel Guyton," (birth 16 Jul 1915, death Dec 1994), *Ancestry.com*.
[2450] "Social Security Death Index," s.v. "Minnie Guyton," (birth 22 May 1918, death Nov 1976), *Ancestry.com*.
[2451] "1920 United States Census," Newport, Attala Co., MS, digital image s.v. "Racy Jones Guyton," (birth ABT 1919), *Ancestry.com*. "U.S., World War II Draft Cards Young Men, 1940-1947," Newport, Attala Co., MS, digital image s.v. "Case Jones Guyton," (signed 6 Oct 1940).
[2452] Per Channie Brown Currie.

Generation #8

Mary (Maggie) Guyton (Simon, Aaron Whitaker, Aaron Steele, Joseph I, John I, Samuel II, Samuel I, John)

Mary (Maggie) GUYTON was the daughter of Simon GUYTON, Sr. (b. 15 Jan 1876 Sallis, Attala Co., MS, d. Unknown)[2453] and Viola UNKNOWN (perhaps WILDER) (b. ABT 1880 MS, d. Unknown).[2454] Mary (Maggie) GUYTON was born about 1913 in MS, and her death is unknown.[2455] She married Leon HARMON (b. Sallis, Attala Co., MS, d. Unknown).[2456] They had two children:

i   Maggie Ruth HARMON (Unknown).
ii   Jessie D. HARMON (Unknown) m. Ollie M. UNKNOWN (Unknown).

Frankie Guyton (Simon, Aaron Whitaker, Aaron Steele, Joseph I, John I, Samuel II, Samuel I, John)

Frankie GUYTON was the son of Simon GUYTON, Sr. (b. 15 Jan 1876 Sallis, Attala Co., MS, d. Unknown)[2457] and Viola UNKNOWN (perhaps WILDER) (b. ABT 1880 MS, d. Unknown).[2458] Frankie GUYTON was born in Apr 1900 in MS, and died in Dec 1972 in Sallis, Attala Co., MS.[2459] He married Lula SAMPLE, who was born 9 Feb 1906 in MS and died in Oct 1984.[2460]

By the 1920 U.S. Federal Census, Frank and Lula were married and lived at a rented home at 29 Main Street in Goodman, Holmes Co., MS.[2461] Frank worked as a laborer in a sawmill and they were 22 and 18, respectively. In the 1930 U.S. Census, Lula had children: Lillie GUYTON (10), Fleming GUYTON (6), May GUYTON (4), and Inez GUYTON (3).[2462] She and the children lived with Lula's father, Aaron SAMPLE, and family. The Census reported that Lula was divorced and using her maiden name. The children, however, were Guytons. Lula and Frank must have gotten back together because in the 1940

[2453] "Social Security Applications and Claims Index, 1936-2007," s.v. "Simon Guyton," (birth 15 Jan 1876), *Ancestry.com*.
[2454] "1920 United States Census," Newport, Attala Co., MS, digital image s.v. "Viola Guyton," (birth ABT 1880), *Ancestry.com*.
[2455] "1920 United States Census," Newport, Attala Co., MS, digital image s.v. "Maggie Guyton," (birth ABT 1913), *Ancestry.com*.
[2456] Per Channie Brown-Currie.
[2457] "Social Security Applications and Claims Index, 1936-2007," s.v. "Simon Guyton," (birth 15 Jan 1876), *Ancestry.com*.
[2458] "1920 United States Census," Newport, Attala Co., MS, digital image s.v. "Viola Guyton," (birth ABT 1880), *Ancestry.com*.
[2459] "Social Security Death Index," s.v. "Frank Guyton," (birth 3 Apr 1900, death Dec 1972), *Ancestry.com*.
[2460] "U.S., Social Security Death Index, 1935-2014," s.v. "Lula Guyton," (birth 9 Feb 1906, death Oct 1984), *Ancestry.com*.
[2461] "1920 United States Federal Census," Goodman, Holmes Co., MS, digital image s.v. "Lula Guyton," (birth ABT 1902), *Ancestry.com*.
[2462] "1930 United States Federal Census," Beat 2, Holmes Co., MS, digital image s.v. "Lula Sample," (birth ABT 1905), *Ancestry.com*.

U.S. Census, Frank and Lula lived in New Port, Attala Co., MS. Frank worked as a farmer on a rented farm.[2463] They lived with their six children.

Lula and Frank had at least six children:

i   Lillie GUYTON (b. ABT 1920, MS, d. Unknown).[2464]
ii Fleming Alexander GUYTON (b. 4 Apr 1923 Sallis, Attala Co., MS, d. 25 Sep 2012)[2465] m. Emma ROBY (b. 28 Jun 1928 Goodman, Holmes Co., MS, d. 13 Jul 2019 Kosciusko, Attala Co., MS).[2466]
iii May Lee GUYTON (b. ABT 1926 MS, d. Unknown)[2467] m. Unknown LITTLE, per Fleming Alexander GUYTON's obituary.
iv Inez GUYTON (b. 9 Feb 1926 Kosciusko, Attala Co., MS, d. 29 Sep 2007 Kosciusko, Attala Co., MS)[2468] m. Leon ANDERSON (b. 10 Aug 1922 Attala Co., MS, d. 7 Dec 1997 Durant, Holmes Co., MS).[2469]
v   Dorothy Mae GUYTON (b. ABT 1934 MS, d. Unknown)[2470] m. Unknown SANDIFER.
vi Athie (Athel) GUYTON (b. ABT 1936 MS, d. Unknown) m. Unknown GRIFFIN.[2471]

Annie Guyton (Simon, Aaron Whitaker, Aaron Steele, Joseph I, John I, Samuel II, Samuel I, John)

Annie GUYTON was the daughter of Simon GUYTON, Sr. (b. 15 Jan 1876 Sallis, Attala Co., MS, d. Unknown)[2472] and Viola UNKNOWN (perhaps WILDER) (b. ABT 1880 MS, d. Unknown).[2473]

I am somewhat confused about Annie GUYTON. Some call her Annie B. Some call her Eudy. I hope I have the correct Annie here. Annie was born about 1913, likely in Sallis, Attala Co., MS. Her death is unknown.[2474] She married Leon TERRY (b. 26 Nov 1911 Sallis, Attala Co., MS, d. 30 Aug 1991 Sallis, Attala Co., MS).[2475]

[2463] "1940 United States Federal Census," New Port, Attala Co., MS, digital image s.v. "Frank Guyton," (birth ABT 1901), *Ancestry.com*.
[2464] "1930 United States Federal Census," Beat 2, Holmes Co., MS, digital image s.v. "Lillie Guyton," (birth ABT 1920), *Ancestry.com*.
[2465] Fleming Alexander Guyton, grave marker, Parkway Cemetery, Kosciusko, Attala Co., MS, digital image s.v. "Fleming Guyton," (birth 4 Apr 1923, death 25 Sep 2012), *FindaGrave.com*.
[2466] Emma Roby, grave marker, Parkway Cemetery, Kosciusko, Attala Co., MS, digital image s.v. "Emma Guyton," (birth 28 Jun 1928, death 13 Jul 2019), *FindaGrave.com*.
[2467] "1930 United States Federal Census," Beat 2, Holmes Co., MS, digital image s.v. "May Guyton," (birth ABT 1925), *Ancestry.com*.
[2468] Inez Guyton, grave marker, St. Mark Cemetery, Attala Co., MS, digital image s.v. "Inez Anderson," (birth 9 Feb 1926, death 29 Sep 2007), *FindaGrave.com*.
[2469] "U.S., Social Security Applications and Claims Index, 1936-2007," s.v. "Leander Anderson," (birth 10 Aug 1922 Death 7 Dec 1997), *Ancestry.com*.
[2470] "1940 United States Federal Census," Newport, Attala Co., MS, digital image s.v. "Dorothy Mae Guyton," (birth ABT 1934), *Ancestry.com*.
[2471] "1940 United States Federal Census," Newport, Attala Co., MS, digital image s.v. "Athie Guyton," (birth ABT 1936), *Ancestry.com*.
[2472] "Social Security Applications and Claims Index, 1936-2007," s.v. "Simon Guyton," (birth 15 Jan 1876), *Ancestry.com*.
[2473] "1920 United States Census," Newport, Attala Co., MS, digital image s.v. "Viola Guyton," (birth ABT 1880), *Ancestry.com*.
[2474] "1920 United States Census," Newport, Attala Co., MS, digital image s.v. "Annie Guyton," (birth ABT 1913), *Ancestry.com*.
[2475] Per Channie Brown-Currie.

In the 1940 U.S. Census, Annie (24) and Leon (26) were married.[2476] They lived on Goodman Road in Attala Co., MS. Annie had a 6th grade education; Leon had a 4th grade education. Leon worked as a laborer in a saw mill, while Annie kept house. Living with the couple were Leon's brother, Earl, and two of Leon's sisters, Dashie and Lillian, as well as the couple's three children: Leon (Vince) TERRY (4), Earnest G. TERRY (1), and Simon Andy TERRY (3 months). I could not find the family in the 1950 U.S. Census.

Annie and Leon had five children:[2477]

i   Leon (Vince) TERRY (b. ABT 1936, MS, d. Unknown).
ii Earnest G. TERRY (b. 20 Jul 1938 Sallis, Attala Co., MS, d. Jan 1973).[2478]
iii Simon Andy TERRY (b. 8 Feb 1940 Sallis, Attala Co., MS, d. 23 Jul 2005).[2479]
iv Earl Denison TERRY, Sr. (b. 10 Jan 1948 Kosciusko, Attala Co., MS, d. 12 Aug 2016 Surprise, Maricopa Co., AZ).[2480] He married Dorothy J. UNKNOWN (Unknown).
v   Clinton TERRY, Sr. (b. AFT 1940 Census, d. AFT 2016 when Earl died) m. Rhonda UNKNOWN (Unknown).

Joe Dale (Joe D.) Guyton (Simon, Aaron Whitaker, Aaron Steele, Joseph I, John I, Samuel II, Samuel I, John)

Joe Dale GUYTON was the son of Simon GUYTON, Sr. (b. 15 Jan 1876 Sallis, Attala Co., MS, d. Unknown)[2481] and Viola UNKNOWN (perhaps WILDER) (b. ABT 1880 MS, d. Unknown).[2482] Joe Dale (Joe D.) GUYTON was born on 24 Dec 1901 in MS, and died in Dec 1967 in Sallis, Attala Co., MS.[2483] He married Stella Mae TERRY (b. 17 Aug 1912 Sallis, Attala Co., MS, d. 1 Jan 1993 Sallis, Attala Co., MS).[2484] Stella Mae TERRY was the daughter of Joe and Amanda GUYTON TERRY. She was a first cousin once-removed to Joe D. For more information about the family, please see the section on Stella Mae GUYTON.

[2476] "1940 United States Census," Kosciusko, Attala Co., MS, digital image s.v. "Leon Terry," (birth ABT 1914), *Ancestry.com*.
[2477] Based on the 1940 U.S. Census and Channie Brown-Currie.
[2478] "Social Security Applications and Claims Index, 1936-2007," s.v. "Earnest G Terry," (birth 20 Jul 1938, death Jan 1973), *Ancestry.com*.
[2479] "Social Security Applications and Claims Index, 1936-2007," s.v. "Simon Lee Terry," (birth 8 Feb 1940, death 23 Jul 2005), *Ancestry.com*.
[2480] "U.S. Cemetery and Funeral Home Collection," s.v. "Earl Denison Terry," (birth 10 Jan 1948, death 12 Aug 2016), *Ancestry.com*.
[2481] "Social Security Applications and Claims Index, 1936-2007," s.v. "Simon Guyton," (birth 15 Jan 1876), *Ancestry.com*.
[2482] "1920 United States Census," Newport, Attala Co., MS, digital image s.v. "Viola Guyton," (birth ABT 1880), *Ancestry.com*.
[2483] "Social Security Death Index," s.v. "Joe Guyton," (birth 24 Dec 1901, death Dec 1967), *Ancestry.com*.
[2484] Stella Mae Terry, grave marker, Mallett Cemetery, Attala Co., MS, digital image s.v. "Stella Mae Guyton," (birth 17 Aug 1912, death 1 Jan 1993), *FindaGrave.com*.

Hattie Irene Guyton (Simon, Aaron Whitaker, Aaron Steele, Joseph I, John I, Samuel II, Samuel I, John)

Hattie Irene GUYTON was the daughter of Simon GUYTON, Sr. (b. 15 Jan 1876 Sallis, Attala Co., MS, d. Unknown)[2485] and Viola UNKNOWN (perhaps WILDER) (b. ABT 1880 MS, d. Unknown).[2486] She was born on 18 May 1904 in MS, and died on 22 Aug 1973 in Chicago, Cook Co., IL.[2487] See Figure 360. She married Dave (Fat Dave) SUDDUTH (b. 12 Oct 1901 Attala Co., MS, d. 24 Jun 1965 Chicago, Cook Co., IL).[2488]

In the 1930 U.S. Census, Hattie and Dave lived in Beat 4, Attala Co., MS, engaged in farming.[2489] They had been married for four years and had one son, Frank Young SUDDUTH, age 2. In the 1940 U.S. Census, the family had moved to Rankin Co., MS. Dave worked as a laborer at a blacksmith business.[2490] By 1950, the family lived in Chicago. Dave worked as a salesman for a carmaker.[2491] Hattie was a printer for a tile company, and Frank was a mill operator for a steel shop. Living next door to them was her brother's family: Steele GUYTON, his wife Minnie GUYTON GUYTON, and children Katherine GUYTON, Fred Steele GUYTON, and Laclain GUYTON, along with Hattie and Steele's sister, Mary (Maggie) GUYTON. See the sections on Steele GUYTON and Minnie GUYTON.

Hattie and Dave had only one child:

i   Frank Young SUDDUTH (b. 1 Sep 1927 Kosciusko, Attala Co., MS, d. 27 Nov 1977 Chicago, Cook Co., IL)[2492] m. Arlene WEST (b. 29 Apr 1934, Unknown d. 18 Oct 2011 Chicago, Cook Co., IL).[2493]

[2485] "Social Security Applications and Claims Index, 1936-2007," s.v. "Simon Guyton," (birth 15 Jan 1876), *Ancestry.com*.
[2486] "1920 United States Census," Newport, Attala Co., MS, digital image s.v. "Viola Guyton," (birth ABT 1880), *Ancestry.com*.
[2487] "Social Security Death Index," s.v. "Hattie Sudduth," (birth 18 May 1904, death Aug 1973), *Ancestry.com*.
[2488] "Social Security Death Index," s.v. "Dave Sudduth," (birth 12 Oct 1901, death Jun 1965), *Ancestry.com*.
[2489] "1930 United States Federal Census," Beat 4, Attala Co., MS, digital image s.v. "Hattie Suddeth," (birth ABT 1905), *Ancestry.com*.
[2490] "1940 United States Federal Census," Rankin Co., MS, digital image s.v. "Hattie Sudduth," (birth ABT 1906), *Ancestry.com*.
[2491] "1950 United States Federal Census," Chicago, Cook Co., IL, digital image s.v. "Hattie Sudduth," (birth ABT 1906), *Ancestry.com*.
[2492] "Social Security Death Index," s.v. "Frank Sudduth," (birth 21 Sep 1927, death Nov 1977), *Ancestry.com*.
[2493] "Cook County, Illinois Marriage Index, 1930-1960," s.v. "Frank Y. Sudduth," (marriage to Arlene West on 26 Apr 1957), *Ancestry.com*. "U.S., Obituary Collection, 1930-Current," s.v. "Arlene Sudduth," (birth 29 Apr 1934, death 18 Oct 2011), *Ancestry.com*.

Figure 360 Hattie GUYTON SUDDUTH[2494]

Robbie Lee Guyton (Simon, Aaron Whitaker, Aaron Steele, Joseph I, John I, Samuel II, Samuel I, John)

Robbie Lee GUYTON was the daughter of Simon GUYTON, Sr. (b. 15 Jan 1876 Sallis, Attala Co., MS, d. Unknown) [2495] and Viola UNKNOWN (perhaps WILDER) (b. ABT 1880 MS, d. Unknown).[2496] Robbie was born on 20 Mar 1911 in Sallis, Attala Co., MS, and died on 22 Dec 2002 in Oak Park, Cook Co., IL).[2497] She married (1) Booker T. TEAGUE (b. ABT 1910 MS, d. Dec 1933 MS) likely in early 1933[2498] and (2) Edward Fletcher (Shine) BURT (b. 20 Mar 1913 MS, d. 27 May 1987 Sallis, Attala Co., MS).[2499] See Figure 361 and Figure 362.

In 1940, Robbie lived with her parents, some of her siblings, and her daughter, Allie Mae TEAGUE, in New Port, Attala Co., MS.[2500] She married Edward Fletcher (Shine) BURT around 1940 based on the birth of their first child, Erma Jean BURT.

[2494] chancurri originally shared this on 9 Sep 2016 on *Ancestry.com*.
[2495] "Social Security Applications and Claims Index, 1936-2007," s.v. "Simon Guyton," (birth 15 Jan 1876), *Ancestry.com*.
[2496] "1920 United States Census," Newport, Attala Co., MS, digital image s.v. "Viola Guyton," (birth ABT 1880), *Ancestry.com*.
[2497] "Social Security Death Index," s.v. "Robbie Burt," (birth 20 Mar 1910, death 22 Dec 2002), *Ancestry.com*.
[2498] Booker Teague, grave marker, New Bethel Cemetery, Sallis, Attala Co., MS, digital image s.v. "Booker Teague," (birth ABT 1910, death Dec 1933), *FindaGrave.com*. Brenda Guyton originally shared this on 4 Jul 2022
[2499] Edward Fletcher Burt, grave marker, Bullock Cemetery, Attala Co., MS, digital image s.v. "Edward Fletcher Burt," (birth 20 Mar 1914, death 27 May 1987), *FindaGrave.com*. The couple married before Booker's death and the birth of their daughter, Allie Mae Teague.
[2500] "1940 United States Federal Census," Newport, Attala Co., MS, digital image s.v. "Robbie Teague," (birth ABT 1917), *Ancestry.com*.

Figure 361 Obituary of Robbie GUYTON BURT[2501]

Figure 362 Robbie GUYTON ROBY[2502]

Robbie GUYTON and Booker T. TEAGUE had one child together before Booker's death in 1933.

i   Allie Mae TEAGUE (b. 4 Jul 1934 Sallis, Attala Co., MS, d. Unknown)[2503] m. Prince Lamar (Sonny Man) THURMAN (b. ABT 1936 Sallis, Attala Co., MS, d. 3 Feb 1999 Milwaukee Co., WI).[2504]

Robbie GUYTON and Edward Fletcher (Shine) BURT had at least four children together.

i   Erma Jean BURT (b. AFT the 1940 Census, d. Unknown) m. Robert SCOTT (Unknown).[2505] They had at least two children: Kesha S. SCOTT (b. Chicago, Cook Co., IL, d. Unknown) m. Victor PHILLIPS (Unknown); and Thaddious S. SCOTT (b. Chicago, Cook Co., IL, d. Unknown).
ii   Charles Edward BURT (b. 11 May 1954 MS, d. 12 Mar 2014 Sallis, Attala Co.). He married Carolyn UNKNOWN.
iii   Fannie BURT (Unknown) m. Unknown WARD.
iv   Alice Edna BURT (Unknown) m. Nelson TRIPLETT.

[2501] "Obituary of Robbie Guyton," *The Star-Herald*, Kosciusko, MS, 2 Jan 2003, p. 6; digital image, s.v. "Robert L. Burt," *Newspapers.com*, <https://www.newspapers.com/article/the-star-herald-obituary-for-robbie-l-b/130031965/>.
[2502] Brenda Guyton originally shared this on 4 Jul 2022 on *Ancestry.com*.
[2503] "1940 United States Federal Census," Newport, Attala Co., MS, digital image s.v. "Allie Mae Teague," (birth ABT 1934), *Ancestry.com*.
[2504] Prince Lamar Thurman, grave marker, Graceland Cemetery, Milwaukee, Milwaukee Co., WI, digital image s.v. "Prince L. Thurman," (birth ABT 1936, death 1999), *FindaGrave.com*.
[2505] Marriage and children information from Channie Brown-Currie.

Steele Guyton (Simon, Aaron Whitaker, Aaron Steele, Joseph I, John I, Samuel II, Samuel I, John)

Steele GUYTON was the son of Simon GUYTON, Sr. (b. 15 Jan 1876 Sallis, Attala Co., MS, d. Unknown) and Viola UNKNOWN (perhaps WILDER) (b. ABT 1880 MS, d. Unknown). Steele GUYTON was born on 16 Jul 1915 in MS, and died on Christmas Day 1994 in Chicago, Cook Co., IL. He married Minnie GUYTON (b. 22 May 1918 Sallis, Attala Co., MS, d. 10 Nov 1976 Chicago, Cook Co., IL). Minnie was the daughter of Ike and Ida RILEY GUYTON. That makes Minnie and Steele first cousins. See Figure 363 and Figure 364.

Figure 363 Minnie GUYTON GUYTON

Figure 364 Steele GUYTON

The family moved to Chicago in the early 1940s, between the births of Fred and Laclain. In the 1950 U.S. Census, Steele worked as a spotter in a cleaning business. Mary (Maggie) GUYTON, Steele's sister, lived with the family in 1950. Steele's family lived next door to another sister, Hattie Irene GUYTON.

They had at least three children:

i   Katherine GUYTON (b. 7 Nov 1938 Sallis, Attala Co., MS, d. 31 Dec 1989 Chicago, Cook Co., IL)[2506] m. Leroy ERVIN (Unknown). See Figure 365.

ii   Fred Steele GUYTON, Sr.(b. 14 Jun 1941 Brandon, Rankin Co., MS, d. 19 Sep 2005 Calumet City, Cook Co., IL)[2507] m. Gladys UNKNOWN (Unknown). See Figure 366.

iii   Laclain GUYTON (b. 8 Oct 1945 Chicago, Cook Co., IL, d. 22 Oct 2008)[2508] m. Doris GIBSON (Unknown) on 18 Jun 1977 in Chicago, Cook Co., IL.[2509] See Figure 367.

[2506] Katherine Guyton, grave marker, Burr Oak Cemetery, Chicago, Cook County, IL, digital image s.v. "Katherine Ervin," (birth 7 Nov 1938, death 7 May 1990), *FindaGrave.com*.

[2507] "Fred Steele Guyton, Sr., grave marker, Abraham Lincoln National Cemetery, Elwood, Will Co., IL, digital image s.v. "Fred Steele Guyton, Sr," (birth 14 Jun 1941, death 19 Sep 2005), *FindaGrave.com*.

[2508] "Laclain GUYTON, grave marker, Abraham Lincoln National Cemetery, Elwood, Will Co., IL, digital image s.v. "Laclain GUYTON," (birth 8 Oct 1945, death 22 Oct 2008), *FindaGrave.com*.

[2509] Per Channie Brown-Currie.

Figure 365 Katherine GUYTON ERVIN[2510]

Figure 366 Fred Steele GUYTON and Fred Steele GUYTON, Jr.[2511]

Figure 367 Laclain GUYTON[2512]

[2510] chancurri originally shared this on 10 Jun 2013 on *Ancestry.com*.
[2511] Pguyton911 originally shared this on 29 Aug 2020 on *Ancestry.com*.
[2512] chancurri originally shared this on 27 May 2013 on *Ancestry.com*.

Generation #9

Fleming Alexander GUYTON (Frankie, Simon, Aaron Whitaker, Aaron Steele, Joseph I, John I, Samuel II, Samuel I, John)

Fleming Alexander GUYTON was the son of Frankie GUYTON (b. Apr 1900 MS, d. Dec 1972 Sallis, Attala Co., MS)[2513] and Lula SAMPLE (b. 9 Feb 1906 in MS, d. Oct 1984).[2514] He was born on 4 Apr 1923 in Sallis, Attala Co., MS, and died on 25 Sep 2012.[2515] He married Emma ROBY (b. 28 Jun 1928 Goodman, Holmes Co., MS, d. 13 Jul 2019 Kosciusko, Attala Co., MS).[2516]

In the 1940 U.S. Federal Census, Fleming (15) was single and lived with his father, Frank (39), and mother, Lula (27), and siblings: Mary Lee GUYTON (18), Inez GUYTON (13), Dorothy Mae GUYTON (6), and Athie GUYTON (4).[2517] Fleming had a fifth-grade education, worked as a farm laborer for his father, and put in 60 hours of work the week the before the Census was taken.

I found two newspaper notices in which Fleming and Emma's property was seized to pay debts. The first notice was the Kosciusko, Attala Co., MS *The Star-Herald* on 28 Mar 1963.[2518] The land was sold for back taxes of $23.29. See Figure 368. Etux means "and wife." The terminology used in these sales are based on the standard division of land in the U.S. Basically, the land in the U.S. was divided into squares (townships), which were then divided into smaller squares (sections), which were again divided into then smaller squares (quarters). See Figure 369 and Figure 370.

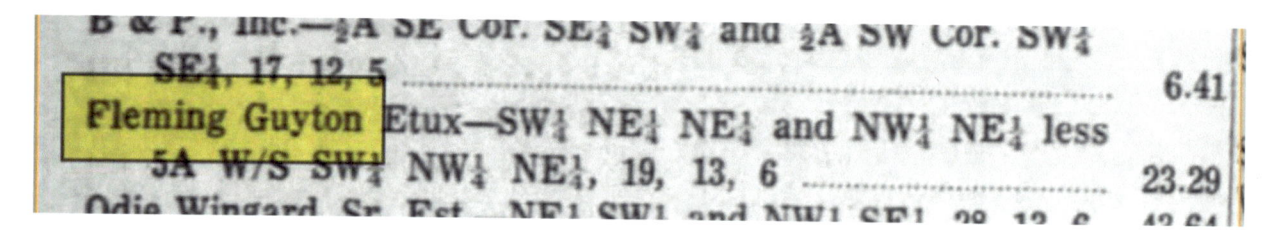

Figure 368 Fleming and Emma GUYTON Loss of Land 1963

[2513] "Social Security Death Index," s.v. "Frank Guyton," (birth 3 Apr 1900, death Dec 1972), *Ancestry.com*.
[2514] "U.S., Social Security Death Index, 1935-2014," s.v. "Lula Guyton," (birth 9 Feb 1906, death Oct 1984), *Ancestry.com*.
[2515] Fleming Alexander Guyton, grave marker, Parkway Cemetery, Kosciusko, Attala Co., MS, digital image s.v. "Fleming Guyton," (birth 4 Apr 1923, death 25 Sep 2012), *FindaGrave.com*.
[2516] Emma Roby, grave marker, Parkway Cemetery, Kosciusko, Attala Co., MS, digital image s.v. "Emma Guyton," (birth 28 Jun 1928, death 13 Jul 2019), *FindaGrave.com*.
[2517] "1940 United States Federal Census," Newport, Attala Co., MS, digital image s.v. "Fleming Guyton," (birth abt 1925), *Ancestry.com*.
[2518] "Sheriff Sale of Lands for Taxes, Attala County," *The Star-Herald*, Kosciusko, Attala Co., MS, Thu, 28 Mar 1963, p. 12, *Newspapers.com*, <https://www.newspapers.com/article/the-star-herald-fleming-guytons-propert/147940381/>.

Figure 371 shows how a township is divided into sections and how sections are broken down into quarters (northeast, northwest, southwest, and southeast). Then each of these quarters are broken into quarters, also northeast, northwest, southwest, and southeast.

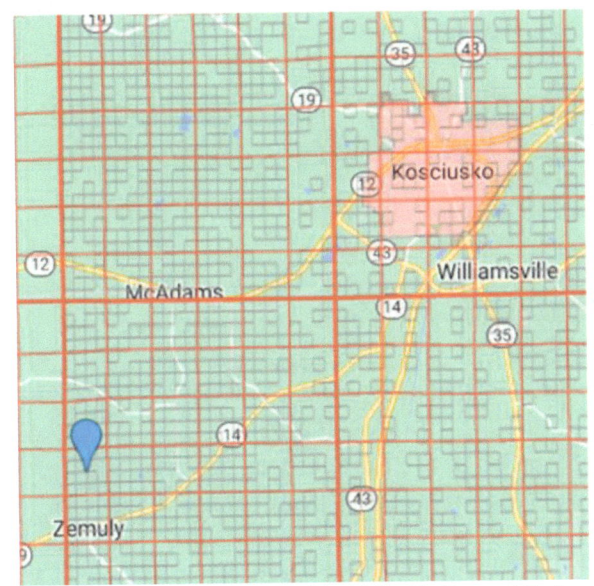

Figure 369 Section 19, Township 13 North, Range 6 East, Choctaw Principal Meridian, Mississippi, Blue Pin (randymajors.org)

Figure 370 Section 19, Township 13 North, Range 6 East, Closer view. See Section 19 in Yellow.[2519]

SECTIONS IN A TOWNSHIP

6	5	4	3	2	1
7	8	9	10	11	12
18	17	16	15	14	13
19	20	21	22	23	24
30	29	28	27	26	25
31	32	33	34	35	36

DIVISIONS OF A SECTION

Figure 371 Illustration of how Townships, Sections, and Quarters are Divided

---

[2519] *Earthstar Geographics: Compiled by the Bureau of Land Management,* PLSS Map viewer, Section 19, Township 13 North, Range 6 East, Choctaw Principal Meridian, Mississippi, <https://www.arcgis.com/apps/view/index.html?appid=019dd6f39fda4d3b811abfab0878b63b>.

Figure 372 is a section of an article from the Kosciusko *The Star-Herald* on the sale of Fleming and Emma's property for failure to pay a debt.

> The NW¼ of the NE¼ less five (5) acres off the entire West side of the SW¼ of the NW¼ of the NE¼; and the SW¼ of the NE¼; of the NE¼ all in Secion 19, Township 13 North, Range 6 East. This being the same land conveyed to Fleming Guyton and wife by deed from Robbie Burt.

Figure 372 Fleming and Emma GUYTON Land Loss Due to Non-payment of Debt[2520]

Figure 373 and Figure 374 represent my best interpretation of their property losses from information given in the newspaper articles. The property descriptions are somewhat vague.

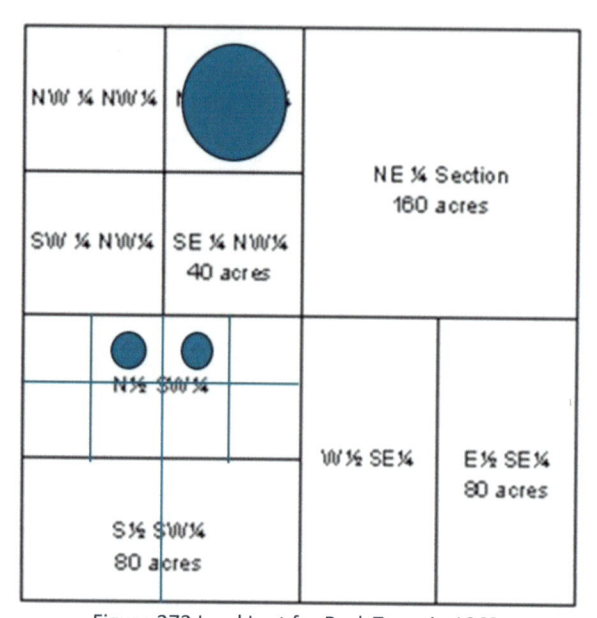

Figure 373 Land Lost for Back Taxes in 1963

Figure 374 Land Lost for Loan Default

[2520] "State of Mississippi, County of Attala, Notice of Substitute Trustees Sale," digital image s.v. "Fleming Guyton," *The Star-Herald*, Kosciusko, Attala Co., MS, Thu, 2 Jul 1964, p. 8, *Newspapers.com*, <https://www.newspapers.com/image/274555340/?clipping_id=150120143&fcfToken=eyJhbGciOiJIUzI1NiIsInR5c CI6IkpXVCJ9.eyJmcmVlLXZpZXctaWQiOjI3NDU1NTM0MCwiaWF0IjoxNzE5NDQ0NjY0LCJleHAiOjE3MTk1MzEwNjR9. pvIRjPMiFpRc0s87O_ZuT7UIRB4CESB4WZRgD96FN34>.

Fleming GUYTON's obituary is available on his *FindaGrave* site. It includes the following:

Along with his parents, Mr. GUYTON was preceded in death by (2) sisters, Mary LITTLE and Inez ANDERSON; (1) brother, Fred Henry GUYTON; granddaughter, Kissy GUYTON; and son-in-law, Rufus HALL. He departed this life on Tuesday, September 25, 2012, at the Attala County Nursing Center in Kosciusko, MS. Mr. Fleming GUYTON leaves to cherish his memories a loving and devoted wife of 68 years, Mrs. Emma GUYTON; children, Sarah HALL Detroit, MI; Florence (Percy) BURT Milwaukee, WI; Edward GUYTON McAdams, MS; Bobbie GUYTON Detroit, MI; Lucille GUYTON Milwaukee, WI; Emma P. GUYTON Milwaukee, WI; Johnny (Kim) GUYTON Waterford, WI; David (Dorothy) GUYTON West, MS; and Earl (Michele) GUYTON Milwaukee, WI. He also leaves 13 grandchildren, 9 great-grandchildren, 2 great-great-grandchildren, 2 sisters, Athel GRIFFIN, and Dorothy SANDIFER; 3 brothers, Joe GUYTON, Fred (Ora) GUYTON, and Simon (Alean) GUYTON; a host of nieces, nephews, cousins relatives and friends.

Fleming and Emma had nine children, per Flemmie's obituary:

i	Sarah GUYTON (b. ABT 1945 MS, d. Unknown) m. Rufus HALL (Unknown).	
ii	James Edward GUYTON (b. 10 Jan 1949 MS, d. 30 Dec 2015 Jackson, Hinds Co., MI).[2521]	
iii	Earl GUYTON (b. Unknown, d. Unknown) m. Michele UNKNOWN.	
iv	David GUYTON (b. Unknown, d. Unknown) m. Dorothy UNKNOWN.	
v	Johnny GUYTON (b. Unknown, d. Unknown) m. Kim UNKNOWN.	
vi	Emma P. GUYTON (b. Unknown, d. Unknown).	
vii	Lucille GUYTON (b. Unknown, d. Unknown).	
viii	Bobbie GUYTON (b. Unknown, d. Unknown).	
ix	Florence Sarah GUYTON (b. Sallis, Attala Co., MS, d. Unknown) m. Percy Earl BURT (b. 16 Jun 1946, d. likely Milwaukee, WI).[2522]	

[2521] James Edward Guyton, grave marker, Parkway Cemetery, Kosciusko, Attala Co., MS, digital image s.v. "James Edward Guyton," (birth 10 Jan 1949, death 30 Dec 2015), *FindaGrave.com*.
[2522] "U.S., Index to Public Records, 1994-2019," s.v. "Florence S Burt," (birth Mar 1947), *Ancestry.com*. "U.S. Public Records Index, 1950-1993, Volume 1," s.v. "Percy E Burt," (birth 16 Jun 1946), *Ancestry.com*.

Inez GUYTON (Frankie, Simon, Aaron Whitaker, Aaron Steele, Joseph I, John I, Samuel II, Samuel I, John)

Inez GUYTON was the daughter of Frankie GUYTON (b. Apr 1900 MS, d. Dec 1972 Sallis, Attala Co., MS)[2523] and Lula SAMPLE (b. 9 Feb 1906 in MS, d. Oct 1984).[2524] Inez was born on 9 Feb 1926 in Kosciusko, Attala Co., MS, and died on 29 Sep 2007 Kosciusko, Attala Co., MS.[2525] She married Leon ANDERSON (b. 10 Aug 1922 Attala Co., MS, d. 7 Dec 1997 Durant, Holmes Co., MS).[2526]

The couple had at least five children based on Leon ANDERSON's obituary:[2527]

i   Dorothy Nell ANDERSON (b. Oct 1946 Kosciusko, Attala Co.,MS, d. Unknown).[2528]
ii   Dorothy Jean ANDERSON (16 Jul 1948 Kosciusko, Attala Co., MS, d. 29 Jul 2019 Jackson, Hinds Co., MS) m. Edward (Poot) LEAVY (Unknown) on 15 Dec 1971.[2529] They had one child: Edward Vanardale (Donald) LEAVY (b. 31 Jul 1972 Sallis, Attala Co., MS, d. 25 Feb 1997 Kosciusko, Attala Co., MS).[2530] Donald's obituary on his *FindaGrave* entry indicates he had a daughter: Kamisha Zartessia LEAVY-JONES.
iii   Sallye ANDERSON (b. 1 Sep 1953 Kosciusko, Attala Co.,MS, d. Unknown)[2531] m. Joseph Lawrence LEAVY, Jr. (b. 26 Aug 1953 Attala Co., MS, d. Unknown).[2532]
iv   Laura L. ANDERSON (b. 28 Feb 1958 Kosciusko, Attala Co., MS, d. Unknown).[2533]
v   Arthur Lee ANDERSON, II (b. Kosciusko, Attala Co., d. Unknown) m. Dorothy UNKNOWN (Unknown).

Earl Denison Terry, Sr. (Annie GUYTON TERRY, Simon, Aaron Whitaker, Aaron Steele, Joseph I, John I, Samuel II, Samuel I, John)

Earl Denison Terry, Sr. was the son of Annie GUYTON (b. ABT 1913, likely in Sallis, Attala Co., MS, d. Unknown).[2534] She married Leon TERRY (b. 26 Nov 1911 Sallis, Attala Co., MS, d. 30 Aug 1991 Sallis, Attala Co., MS).[2535]

[2523] "Social Security Death Index," s.v. "Frank Guyton," (birth 3 Apr 1900, death Dec 1972), *Ancestry.com*.
[2524] "U.S., Social Security Death Index, 1935-2014," s.v. "Lula Guyton," (birth 9 Feb 1906, death Oct 1984), *Ancestry.com*.
[2525] Inez Guyton, grave marker, St. Mark Cemetery, Attala Co., MS, digital image s.v. "Inez Anderson," (birth 9 Feb 1926, death 29 Sep 2007), *FindaGrave.com*.
[2526] "U.S., Social Security Applications and Claims Index, 1936-2007," s.v. "Leander Anderson," (birth 10 Aug 1922 Death 7 Dec 1997), *Ancestry.com*.
[2527] "Obituary of Leon Anderson," digital image, s.v. "Leon Anderson," *The Star-Herald*, Kosciusko, Attala Co., MS, Thu, 18 Dec 1997, p. 6, *Newspapers.com*, <https://www.newspapers.com/image/304818353/?focus=0.026834367%2C0.2567003%2C0.19596045%2C0.47472&xid=3355>.
[2528] "U.S., Index to Public Records, 1994-2019," s.v. "Dorothy Nell Anderson," (birth Oct 1946), *Ancestry.com*.
[2529] Dorothy Jean Guyton, grave marker, Pleasant Grove Cemetery, Jackson, HindsCo., MS, digital image s.v. "Dorothy Jean Leavy," (birth 16 Jul 1948, death 29 Jul 2019), *FindaGrave.com*.
[2529] "U.S., Social Security Applications and Claims
[2530] Edward Varnardale Leavy, grave marker, Pleasant Grove Cemetery, Jackson, HindsCo., MS, digital image s.v. "Edward Varnasdale Leavy," (birth 31 Jul 1972, death 25 Feb 1997), *FindaGrave.com*.
[2531] "U.S., Public Records Index, 1950-1993, Volume 1," s.v. "Sallye Leavy," (birth 1 Sep 1953), *Ancestry.com*.
[2532] "U.S. Public Records Index, 1950-1993, Volume 1," s.v. "Joseph Leavy Jr," (birth 26 Aug 1953), *Ancestry.com*.
[2533] "U.S. Public Records Index, 1950-1993, Volume 2," s.v. "Laura L Anderson," (b. 28 Feb 1958), *Ancestry.com*.
[2534] "1920 United States Census," Newport, Attala Co., MS, digital image s.v. "Annie Guyton," (birth ABT 1913), *Ancestry.com*.
[2535] Per Channie Brown-Currie.

Earl was born on 10 Jan 1948 in Kosciusko, Attala Co., MS, and died on 12 Aug 2016 in Surprise, Maricopa Co., AZ).[2536] See Figure 375. He married Dorothy J. UNKNOWN (Unknown) with whom he had three children:

i   Earl Denison TERRY, Jr. (Unknown).
ii   Jarrett TERRY (Unknown).
iii   Twylla TERRY (Unknown) m. Unknown HOLLOWAY (Unknown).
iv   Brandon TERRY (Unknown).

Figure 375 Earl Denison TERRY, Sr.

Clinton TERRY, Sr. (Annie GUYTON TERRY, Simon, Aaron Whitaker, Aaron Steele, Joseph I, John I, Samuel II, Samuel I, John)

Clinton TERRY, Sr. was the son of Annie GUYTON (b. ABT 1913, likely in Sallis, Attala Co., MS, d. unknown).[2537] She married Leon TERRY (b. 26 Nov 1911 Sallis, Attala Co., MS, d. 30 Aug 1991 Sallis, Attala Co. , MS).[2538]

Clinton was born after the 1940 Census and died after 2016 when his brother, Earl, died). He married Rhonda UNKNOWN (Unknown). They had six children: [2539]

i   Jamari TERRY (Unknown).
ii   Yalonda TERRY (Unknown) m. Unknown BRAY (Unknown).
iii   Eleane TERRY (Unknown) m. Elmer TANNER (Unknown).
iv   Clinton TERRY, Jr. (Unknown).
v   Timothy TERRY (Unknown).
vi   Unknown TERRY (Unknown).

[2536] "U.S. Cemetery and Funeral Home Collection," s.v. "Earl Denison Terry," (birth 10 Jan 1948, death 12 Aug 2016), *Ancestry.com*.
[2537] "1920 United States Census," Newport, Attala Co., MS, digital image s.v. "Annie Guyton," (birth ABT 1913), *Ancestry.com*.
[2538] Per Channie Brown-Currie.
[2539] Per Channie Brown-Currie.

Allie Mae TEAGUE (Robbie GUYTON TEAGUE, Simon, Aaron Whitaker, Aaron Steele, Joseph I, John I, Samuel II, Samuel I, John)

Allie Mae TEAGUE was the daughter of Robbie Lee GUYTON (b. 20 Mar 1911 Sallis, Attala Co., MS, d. 22 Dec 2002 Oak Park, Cook Co., IL)[2540] and Booker T. TEAGUE (b. ABT 1910 MS, d. Dec 1933 MS) around 1933.[2541] Robbie had a second husband (and perhaps a third): Edward Fletcher (Shine) BURT (b. 20 Mar 1913 MS, d. 27 May 1987 Sallis, Attala Co., MS).[2542]

Allie Mae TEAGUE was born on 4 Jul 1934 in Sallis, Attala Co., MS, and died on 5 Nov 2020 Milwaukee Co., WI.[2543] See Figure 376. She married Prince Lamar (Sonny Man) THURMAN (b. ABT 1936 Sallis, Attala Co., MS, d. 3 Feb 1999 Milwaukee, WI).[2544] See Figure 377.

Figure 376 Allie Mae TEAGUE[2545]

Figure 377 Prince Lamar THURMAN[2546]

Allie Mae had a son with an unknown husband:

i   Rickey Nelson TEAGUE (b. 19 Jun 1959 Milwaukee Co., WI, d. 2020 Milwaukee Co., WI)[2547] m. Carolyn Ann LAMBERT (b. 16 Jan 1955, d. Unknown)[2548] on 16 Feb 1982 in Milwaukee Co., WI.[2549] See Figure 378.

[2540] "Social Security Death Index," s.v. "Robbie Burt," (birth 20 Mar 1910, death 22 Dec 2002), *Ancestry.com*.
[2541] Booker Teague, grave marker, New Bethel Cemetery, Sallis, Attala Co., MS, digital image s.v. "Booker Teague," (birth abt 1910, death Dec 1933), *FindaGrave.com*. Brenda Guyton originally shared this on 4 Jul 2022
[2542] Edward Fletcher Burt, grave marker, Bullock Cemetery, Attala Co., MS, digital image s.v. "Edward Fletcher Burt," (birth 20 Mar 1914, death 27 May 1987), *FindaGrave.com*. The couple married before Booker's death and the birth of their daughter, Allie Mae Teague.
[2543] "1940 United States Federal Census," Newport, Attala Co., MS, digital image s.v. "Allie Mae Teague," (birth abt 1934), *Ancestry.com*. LaVonte Rogers, LaVonte Rogers Family Tree, *Ancestry.com*.
[2544] Prince Lamar Thurman, grave marker, Graceland Cemetery, Milwaukee, Milwaukee Co., WI, digital image s.v. "Prince L. Thurman," (birth abt 1936, death 1999), *FindaGrave.com*.
[2545] Brenda Guyton originally shared this on 20 Dec 2021 on *Ancestry.com*.
[2546] Brenda Guyton originally shared this on 17 Dec 2021 on *Ancestry.com*.
[2547] LaVonte Rogers, LaVonte Rogers Family Tree, *Ancestry.com*.
[2548] "U.S., Public Records Index, 1950-1993, Volume 1," s.v. "Carol A. Teague," (birth 16 Jan 1955), *Ancestry.com*.
[2549] "Wisconsin, U.S., Marriage Index, 1973-1997," digital image s.v. "Carol Ann Lambert," (marriage 16 Feb 1982 to Ricky Nelson Teague), *Ancestry.com*.

She had two daughters with Prince Lamar THURMAN:[2550]

i   Mary THURMAN (b. Milwaukee, Milwaukee Co., WI, d. Unknown). See Figure 379.
ii   Sandra THURMAN (b. Milwaukee., Milwaukee Co., WI, d. Unknown).

Figure 378 Rickey Nelson TEAGUE with Perhaps Carol LAMBERT[2551]

Figure 379 Mary THURMAN and Allie Mae TEAGUE THURMAN[2552]

Charles Edward Burt (Robbie GUYTON TEAGUE, Simon, Aaron Whitaker, Aaron Steele, Joseph I, John I, Samuel II, Samuel I, John)

Charles Edward BURT was the son of Robbie GUYTON (b. 20 Mar 1911 in Sallis, Attala Co., MS, d. 22 Dec 2002 in Oak Park, Cook Co., IL)[2553] and Edward Fletcher (Shine) BURT (b. 20 Mar 1913 MS, d. 27 May 1987 Sallis, Attala Co., MS).[2554]

Charles was born on 11 May 1954 in MS and died on 12 Mar 2014 in Sallis, Attala Co. See Figure 380. He married Carolyn UNKNOWN and they had five children:[2555]

i   Alexis BURT (b. MS, d. Unknown) m. Unknown ROYAL.
ii   Chassie BURT (b. MS, d. Unknown) m. Unknown ROYAL.
iii   Pamela BURT (b. MS, d. Unknown) m. Unknown GREENWOOD.
iv   Charleston BURT (b. MS, d. Unknown).
v   Marcus BURT (b. MS, d. Unknown).

[2550] Chancurri, Guyton Family Tree, *Ancestry.com*.
[2551] Brenda Guyton originally shared this on 30 Dec 2021 on *Ancestry.com*.
[2552] Brenda Guyton originally shared this on 11 Jan 2022 on Ancestry.com.
[2553] "Social Security Death Index," s.v. "Robbie Burt," (birth 20 Mar 1910, death 22 Dec 2002), *Ancestry.com*.
[2554] Edward Fletcher Burt, grave marker, Bullock Cemetery, Attala Co., MS, digital image s.v. "Edward Fletcher Burt," (birth 20 Mar 1914, death 27 May 1987), *FindaGrave.com*. The couple married before Booker's death and the birth of their daughter, Allie Mae Teague.
[2555] Per Channie Brown-Currie.

Figure 380 Charles Edward BURT (with Carolyn?)[2556]

Fannie Burt (Robbie GUYTON TEAGUE, Simon, Aaron Whitaker, Aaron Steele, Joseph I, John I, Samuel II, Samuel I, John)

Fannie BURT was the daughter of Robbie GUYTON (b. 20 Mar 1911 in Sallis, Attala Co., MS, d. 22 Dec 2002 in Oak Park, Cook Co., IL)[2557] and Edward Fletcher (Shine) BURT (b. 20 Mar 1913 MS, d. 27 May 1987 Sallis, Attala Co., MS).[2558]

Fannie BURT's birth and death are unknown. She married an Unknown WARD. Fannie had at least three children:[2559]

i   Charles BURT (b. Chicago, Cook Co., IL, d. Unknown).
ii   Tonia BURT (b. Chicago, Cook Co., IL, d. Unknown).
iii   Felicia NELSON (b. Chicago, Cook Co., IL, d. Unknown) m. Sean SIPP.

Erma Jean Burt (Robbie GUYTON TEAGUE, Simon, Aaron Whitaker, Aaron Steele, Joseph I, John I, Samuel II, Samuel I, John)

Erma Jean BURT was the daughter of Robbie GUYTON (b. 20 Mar 1911 in Sallis, Attala Co., MS, d. 22 Dec 2002 in Oak Park, Cook Co., IL)[2560] and Edward Fletcher (Shine) BURT (b. 20 Mar 1913 MS, d. 27 May 1987 Sallis, Attala Co., MS).[2561]

She was born after the 1940 Census and her death is unknown. She married Robert SCOTT (Unknown).[2562] They had at least two children:

[2556] Brenda Guyton originally shared this on 4 Jul 2022 on *Ancestry.com*.
[2557] "Social Security Death Index," s.v. "Robbie Burt," (birth 20 Mar 1910, death 22 Dec 2002), *Ancestry.com*.
[2558] Edward Fletcher Burt, grave marker, Bullock Cemetery, Attala Co., MS, digital image s.v. "Edward Fletcher Burt," (birth 20 Mar 1914, death 27 May 1987), *FindaGrave.com*. The couple married before Booker's death and the birth of their daughter, Allie Mae Teague.
[2559] Per Channie Brown-Currie.
[2560] "Social Security Death Index," s.v. "Robbie Burt," (birth 20 Mar 1910, death 22 Dec 2002), *Ancestry.com*.
[2561] Edward Fletcher Burt, grave marker, Bullock Cemetery, Attala Co., MS, digital image s.v. "Edward Fletcher Burt," (birth 20 Mar 1914, death 27 May 1987), *FindaGrave.com*. The couple married before Booker's death and the birth of their daughter, Allie Mae Teague.
[2562] Marriage and children information from Channie Brown-Currie.

i   Kesha S. SCOTT (b. Chicago, Cook Co., IL, d. Unknown) m. Unknown PHILLIPS (Unknown).
ii Thaddious S. SCOTT (b. Chicago, Cook Co., IL, d. Unknown).

Alice Edna Burt (Robbie GUYTON TEAGUE, Simon, Aaron Whitaker, Aaron Steele, Joseph I, John I, Samuel II, Samuel I, John)

Alice Edna BURT was the daughter of Robbie GUYTON (b. 20 Mar 1911 in Sallis, Attala Co., MS, d. 22 Dec 2002 in Oak Park, Cook Co., IL)[2563] and Edward Fletcher (Shine) BURT (b. 20 Mar 1913 MS, d. 27 May 1987 Sallis, Attala Co., MS).[2564]

Alice was born in Sallis, Attala Co., MS, and her death is unknown. She married Nelson TRIPLETT (Unknown). They had one child:[2565]

i   Jean TRIPLETT (b. Louisville, Winston Co., MS, d. Unknown) who married Unknown JIMMERSON (Unknown).

Fred Steele GUYTON, Sr. (Steele, Simon, Aaron Whitaker, Aaron Steele, Joseph I, John I, Samuel II, Samuel I, John)

Fred Steele GUYTON, Sr. was the son of Steele GUYTON (b. 16 Jul 1915 MS, d. Christmas Day 1994 Chicago, Cook Co., IL and Minnie GUYTON (b. 22 May 1918 Sallis, Attala Co., MS, d. 10 Nov 1976 Chicago, Cook Co., IL).[2566] Minnie was the daughter of Ike and Ida RILEY GUYTON. That makes Minnie and Steele first cousins.

Fred Steele GUYTON, Sr. was born on 14 Jun 1941 in Brandon, Rankin Co., MS, and died on 19 Sep 2005 in Calumet City, Cook Co., IL.[2567] See Figure 381. He married Gladys UNKNOWN (Unknown). They had at least two children:[2568]

i   Fred Steele GUYTON, Jr. (b. 29 May 1964 Chicago, Cook Co., IL d. Unknown).[2569]
ii Richard GUYTON (b. ABT 1970 Chicago, Cook Co., IL, d. Unknown) m. LaLesia UNKNOWN (Unknown).[2570]

[2563] "Social Security Death Index," s.v. "Robbie Burt," (birth 20 Mar 1910, death 22 Dec 2002), *Ancestry.com*.
[2564] Edward Fletcher Burt, grave marker, Bullock Cemetery, Attala Co., MS, digital image s.v. "Edward Fletcher Burt," (birth 20 Mar 1914, death 27 May 1987), *FindaGrave.com*. The couple married before Booker's death and the birth of their daughter, Allie Mae Teague.
[2565] Per Channie Brown-Currie.
[2566] "Social Security Death Index," s.v. "Steel Guyton," (birth 16 Jul 1915, death Dec 1994), Ancestry.com. "Social Security Death Index," s.v. "Minnie Guyton," (birth 22 May 1918, death Nov 1976), Ancestry.com.
[2567] "Fred Steele Guyton, Sr., grave marker, Abraham Lincoln National Cemetery, Elwood, Will Co., IL, digital image s.v. "Fred Steele Guyton, Sr," (birth 14 Jun 1941, death 19 Sep 2005), *FindaGrave.com*.
[2568] Per Channie Brown-Currie.
[2569] "U.S. Public Records Index, 1950-1993, Volume 2," s.v. "Frederick S. Guyton," (birth 29 May 1964), *Ancestry.com*.
[2570] Per Channie Brown-Currie.

Figure 381 Fred Steele GUYTON, Sr. and Fred Steele GUYTON, Jr [2571]

[2571] Pguyton911 originally shared this on 29 Aug 2020 on *Ancestry.com*.

CHILD OF AARON WHITAKER GUYTON AND ARTIE RAINEY: IKE'S LINE

Generation #7

Ike GUYTON (Aaron Whitaker, Aaron Steele, Joseph I, John I, Samuel II, Samuel I, John)

Ike GUYTON was the son of Aaron Whitaker GUYTON and Artemesia (Artie) RAINEY. He was born on 12 May 1878 in Sallis, Attala Co., MS and died on 10 Feb 1953 in Sallis, Attala Co., MS.[2572] He partnered with Ida RILEY, who was born in 1887 in Sallis, Attala Co., MS and died on 18 May 1951 in Sallis, Attala Co., MS.[2573] See Figure 382, Figure 383, and Figure 384.

In the 1900 U.S. Census, Ike (age 22 and single) lived with his mother, Artie, and siblings Case, Maggie, and Amanda. Amanda's daughter, Lela, lived with them as did a nephew (John H. GUYTON) and a niece (Annie Bell GUYTON). Case was listed as the head of household. Ike worked as a farm laborer for his brother. He could read and write.[2574] In 1910, Ike was still single and lived with Case and Artie, but he worked as a railroad laborer.[2575] Note that his children Mary Georgia (6), Isadora (5), and Gus Davis GUYTON (1) were already born in 1910 and being raised as Guytons. They lived with their single mother Ida RILEY, who lived with her widowed mother, Belle RILEY, on a mortgaged farm.[2576] Ike and Ida did not live far from each other because their entries in the 1910 Census were only three pages apart.

The 1920 U.S. Census listed Ike as the head of household, a married man living with his mother, Artie. He was farming land that was owned without a mortgage.[2577] Ike's wife, Ida, still listed herself as single (aged 35) living with her mother, Belle RILEY, and sister, Jimmie RILEY. Ida and Ike's children also lived with her: Mary Georgia (14), Isadora (11), Gus (9), Joe Frank (7), Annie Frances (5), Minnie (Census says Maggie) (2), and Ben (0). It seems like a very strange arrangement that Ike should still live with his mother while his family grew in a separate household.[2578]

[2572] Ike Guyton, grave marker, Russell Cemetery, Attala Co., MS, digital image s.v. "Ike Guyton," (birth 12 May 1878, death 10 Feb 1953), *FindaGrave.com*.

[2573] Ida Riley, grave marker, Russell Cemetery, Attala Co., MS, digital image s.v. "Ida Riley," (birth ABT 1887, death 18 May 1951), *FindaGrave.com*.

[2574] "1900 United States Census," Newport, Attala Co., MS, digital image s.v. "Isac Guyton," (birth May 1878), *Ancestry.com*.

[2575] "1910 United States Census," Beat 4, Attala Co., MS, digital image s.v. "Ike Guyton," (birth May 1882), *Ancestry.com*.

[2576] "1910 United States Census," Beat 4, Attala Co., MS, digital image s.v. "Ida Riley," (birth May 1886), *Ancestry.com*.

[2577] "1920 United States Census," Newport, Attala Co., MS, digital image s.v. "Ike Guyton," (birth May 1878), *Ancestry.com*.

[2578] "1920 United States Census," Newport, Attala Co., MS, digital image s.v. "Ida Riley," (birth May 1885), *Ancestry.com*.

Figure 382 Ike GUYTON[2579]

Figure 383 Ida RILEY[2580]

Figure 384 Ida RILEY with Grandchildren, June 1962[2581]

    In 1930, the Census recorded Artie as the head of the household, living with Ike who is identified as single. He farmed the land for his mother.[2582] Neither Ida nor his children lived with him. Ida's mother must have passed away because Ida was then the head of household at her mother's farm. She was listed as single and added two more children to the family: Lil (Alice, who was 5) and Claude (4). Her farm was located on the Sallis and Zemuly Road in Beat 4, Attala Co., MS.[2583] Not much changed in the 1940 U.S. Census. Ike still lived with his mother, working her farm that was owned free and clear. He

---

[2579] Chancurri. 7 Jun 2013. Posted on *Ancestry.com*.
[2580] Cpack1218. 26 Apr 2014. Posted on *Ancestry.com. Photo taken in June 1962.*
[2581] Chancurri. 15 Feb 2014. Posted on *Ancestry.com*.
[2582] "1930 United States Census," Beat 4, Attala Co., MS, digital image s.v. "Isaac Guyton," (birth ABT 1877), *Ancestry.com*.
[2583] "1930 United States Census," Beat 4, Attala Co., MS, digital image s.v. "Ida Riley," (birth ABT 1880), *Ancestry.com*.

was listed as a single man who lived in New Port, Attala Co., MS. Artie was 92-years-old; Ike was 62.[2584] Ida RILEY was also single and lived in New Port. She worked on a rented farm and had a fourth-grade education. Most of the children had left her household except for Mary (35), Ben (18), Alice (15), and Claude (14). The year 1950 revealed Ida RILEY had never been married. She kept house at a farm that appears to be on Bullis and Thomastown Road in New Port. She lived with her sons Ben and Claude and with Ben's wife. The men worked the farm.[2585]

By 1950, Artie RAINEY had passed away. The Census found Ike lived with his son, Joe Frank (36), Joe's wife, Mildred (30), and grandchildren: Katherine (12), Doris (4), Leeander (2), and Edwin (newborn). Ike was reported as widowed and working for his son, Joe Frank, as an unpaid farm worker. Joe Frank lived next door to his mother, Ida RILEY, implying that Ike no longer lived at his mother's farm that was held free and clear.[2586]

The Zemuly Road and Thomastown Road intersection may be captured in this *Google Map* below in Figure 385:

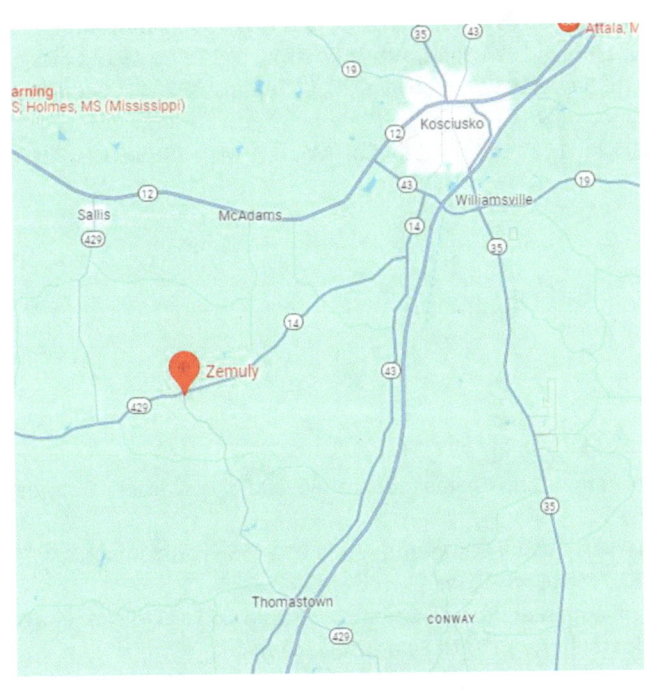

Figure 385 Map of Zemuly and Thomastown Road Intersection

[2584] "1940 United States Census," Newport, Attala Co., MS, digital image s.v. "Ike Guyton," (birth ABT 1878), *Ancestry.com*.

[2585] "1940 United States Census," Newport, Attala Co., MS, digital image s.v. "Ida Riley," (birth ABT 1890), *Ancestry.com*.

[2586] "1950 United States Census," Newport, Attala Co., MS, digital image s.v. "Ida Riley," (birth ABT 1890), *Ancestry.com*. "1950 United States Census," Newport, Attala Co., MS, digital image s.v. "Ike Guyton," (birth ABT 1879), *Ancestry.com*.

The couple had at least nine children:

i   Mary Georgia GUYTON (b. 10 Dec 1905 Kosciusko, Attala Co., MS, d. 18 Mar 1996 Sallis, Attala Co., MS).[2587] See Figure 386 of Alice, Mary, Annie, and Isadora.

ii   Isadora GUYTON (b. 30 Dec 1906 Sallis, Attala Co., MS, d. 14 Feb 1985 Sallis, Attala Co., MS)[2588] m. Antney Wesley BROWN (b. 4 Jul 1909 Sallis, Attala Co., MS, d. 13 Aug 1977 Sallis, Attala Co., MS).[2589] See Figure 386 of Alice, Mary, Annie, and Isadora.

iii   Gus Davis GUYTON (b. 3 Mar 1909 Sallis, Attala Co., MS, d. 8 Jul 1990 Cook Co., IL)[2590] m. Ruth Lee (Ruthie) ROBY (b. 7 May 1916 Sallis, Attala Co., MS, d. 13 Jan 1996 Wauwatosa, Milwaukee Co., WI).[2591]

iv   Joe Frank GUYTON (b. 10 Sep 1912 Sallis, Attala Co., MS, d. 23 Aug 1994 Sallis, Attala Co., MS)[2592] m. Mildred Irene WINGARD (b. 11 Mar 1917 MS, d. 17 Apr 2016 Chicago Heights, Cook Co., IL).[2593]

v   Annie Frances GUYTON (b. 28 Feb 1916 Kosciusko, Attala Co., MS, d. 17 Oct 1995 Chicago, Cook Co., IL)[2594] m. Allen Leroy (Gipp) EVANS, Sr. (29 Dec 1912 Sallis, Attala Co., MS, d. Jun 1972 Chicago, Cook Co., IL).[2595] See Figure 386 of Alice, Mary, Annie, and Isadora.

vi   Minnie GUYTON (b. 22 May 1918 Sallis, Attala Co., MS, d. 10 Nov 1976 Chicago, Cook Co., IL)[2596] m. Steele GUYTON (b. 16 Jul 1915 MS, d. 25 Dec 1994 Chicago, Cook Co., IL).[2597] Steele was the son of Simon and Viola WILDER GUYTON. That makes Minnie and Steele first cousins.

vii   Ben GUYTON (b. 2 Apr 1920 Sallis, Attala Co., MS, d. 8 Nov 1996 Sallis, Attala Co., MS).[2598]

viii   Alice Lee GUYTON (b. 10 May 1924 Sallis, Attala Co., MS, d. 11 Feb 1992 Chicago, Cook Co., IL)[2599] m. Oliver DeBois WEBB (b. 3 Aug 1912 Greenville, SC, d. 16 Jan 1992).[2600] See Figure 386 of Alice, Mary, Annie, and Isadora.

ix   Claude GUYTON (b. 5 Mar 1927 Sallis, Attala Co., MS, d. 1 May 1985 Sallis, Attala Co., MS).[2601]

[2587] "U.S., Social Security Applications and Claims Index, 1936-2007," s.v. "Mary Georgia Guyton," (birth 10 Dec 1905, death 18 Mar 1996).

[2588] Isadora Guyton, grave marker, Russell Cemetery, Attala Co., MS, digital image s.v. "Isadora Brown," (birth 30 Dec 1906, death 14 Feb 1985), *FindaGrave.com*.

[2589] Antney Wesley Brown, grave marker, Russell Cemetery, Attala Co., MS, digital image s.v. "Antney Wesley Brown," (birth 14 Jul 1909, death 13 Aug 1977), *FindaGrave.com*.

[2590] "Social Security Death Index," s.v. "Gus D. Guyton," (birth 3 Mar 1909, death 8 Jul 1990), *Ancestry.com*.

[2591] "Social Security Death Index," s.v. "Ruth Guyton," (birth 7 May 1916, death 13 Jan 1996), *Ancestry.com*.

[2592] "Social Security Death Index," s.v. "Joe Guyton," (birth 10 Sep 1912, death 23 Aug 1994), *Ancestry.com*.

[2593] Mildred Irene Wingard, grave marker, Russell Cemetery, Attala Co., MS, digital image s.v. "Mildred Irene Guyton," (birth 11 Mar 1917, death 17 Apr 2016), *FindaGrave.com*.

[2594] "Social Security Death Index," s.v. "Annie Evans," (birth 28 Feb 1916, death 17 Oct 1995), *Ancestry.com*.

[2595] Allen Leroy Evans, Sr., grave marker, Restvale Cemetery, Alsip, Cook Co., IL, digital image s.v. "Allen Leroy Evans," (birth 29 Dec 1912, death 14 Jun 1972), *FindaGrave.com*.

[2596] "Social Security Death Index," s.v. "Minnie Guyton," (birth 22 May 1918, death Nov 1976), *Ancestry.com*.

[2597] "Social Security Death Index," s.v. "Steel Guyton," (birth 16 Jul 1915, death Dec 1994), *Ancestry.com*.

[2598] "Social Security Death Index," s.v. "Ben Guyton," (birth 2 Apr 1920, death 8 Nov 1996), *Ancestry.com*.

[2599] "Social Security Death Index," s.v. "Alice Webb," (birth 10 May 1924, death 11 Feb 1992), *Ancestry.com*.

[2600] Oliver DeBois Webb, grave marker, Oakland Memory Lanes, Dolton, Cook Co., IL, digital image s.v. "Oliver Debois Webb," (birth 3 Aug 1912, death 16 Jan 1992), *FindaGrave.com*.

[2601] Claude L. Guyton, grave marker, Russell Cemetery, Attala Co., MS, digital image s.v. "Claude L. Guyton," (birth 5 Mar 1927, death 1 May 1985), *FindaGrave.com*.

Figure 386 Ida RILEY's Daughters: L to R Alice, Mary, Annie, and Isadora[2602]

[2602] chancurri originally shared this on 15 Feb 2014 on *Ancestry.com*.

Generation #8

Mary Georgia Guyton (Ike, Aaron Whitaker, Aaron Steele, Joseph I, John I, Samuel II, Samuel I, John)

Mary Georgia GUYTON was the daughter of Ike GUYTON (b. 12 May 1878 Sallis, Attala Co., MS, d. 10 Feb 1953 Sallis, Attala Co., MS)[2603] and Ida RILEY (b. 1887 Sallis, Attala Co., MS, d. 18 May 1951 Sallis, Attala Co., MS).[2604] Mary Georgia GUYTON was born on 10 Dec 1905 in Kosciusko, Attala Co., MS and died on 18 Mar 1996 in Sallis, Attala Co., MS.[2605] See Figure 387 and Figure 388.

Figure 387 Mary Georgia GUYTON

Figure 388 Obituary of Mary Georgia GUYTON[2606]

In the 1930 U.S. Census, Mary Georgia GUYTON lived with her mother, Ida RILEY, and her siblings.[2607] The nature of the relationship between her parents, Ida and Ike, is unclear. Ike always lived with his mother in various censuses. Ida RILEY and her children were recorded in the 1930 Census as Rileys, not Guytons. They lived on the Sallis and Zemuly Road in Beat 4, Attala Co. Mary Georgia was the oldest child and supposedly never attended school, although all her younger siblings did. At 22 years old in 1930, it is surprising that the Census indicated that none of the children were employed. Children who work on the family farm were usually indicated as such. Ida was a farmer.

[2603] Ike Guyton, grave marker, Russell Cemetery, Attala Co., MS, digital image s.v. "Ike Guyton," (birth 12 May 1878, death 10 Feb 1953), *FindaGrave.com*.

[2604] Ida Riley, grave marker, Russell Cemetery, Attala Co., MS, digital image s.v. "Ida Riley," (birth ABT 1887, death 18 May 1951), *FindaGrave.com*.

[2605] "U.S., Social Security Applications and Claims Index, 1936-2007," s.v. "Mary Georgia Guyton," (birth 10 Dec 1905, death 18 Mar 1996).

[2606] "Obituary of Ms. Mary G. Guyton," *The Star-Herald*, Kosciusko, MS, 28 Mar 1996, Thu, p. 6; digital image, s.v. "Ms. Mary G. Guyton," *Newspapers.com*, <https://www.newspapers.com/image/276509935/?article=85bf258f-eceb-48e8-91b5-c6f465e6dd0b&focus=0.34338963,0.4274018,0.50740737,0.51537186&xid=3355>.

[2607] "1930 United States Census," Beat 4, Attala Co., MS, digital image s.v. "Mary George Riley," (birth ABT 1908), *Ancestry.com*.

The reported information changed in the 1940 U.S. Census. Mary Georgia lived with her mother and three of her siblings – Ben GUYTON, Alice GUYTON, and Claude GUYTON.[2608] Mary was an unpaid farm assistant to her mother, Ida. While Ida still went by the last name Riley, the children were labeled Guytons. The Census indicated that Mary had a 6th grade education. Mary did not live with her mother in the 1950 U.S. Census, but I could not find her elsewhere. Her obituary suggests that she never married or had children.

Isadora Guyton (Ike, Aaron Whitaker, Aaron Steele, Joseph I, John I, Samuel II, Samuel I, John)

Isadora GUYTON was the daughter of Ike GUYTON (b. 12 May 1878 Sallis, Attala Co., MS, d. 10 Feb 1953 Sallis, Attala Co., MS)[2609] and Ida RILEY (b. 1887 Sallis, Attala Co., MS, d. 18 May 1951 Sallis, Attala Co., MS).[2610]

Isadora GUYTON was born on 30 Dec 1906 in Sallis, Attala Co., MS. She died on 14 Feb 1985 in Sallis, Attala Co., MS).[2611] She and Antney Wesley BROWN (b. 4 Jul 1909 Sallis, Attala Co., MS, d. 13 Aug 1977 Sallis, Attala Co., MS[2612] were married on 8 Oct 1931 in Sallis.[2613] See Figure 389, Figure 390, Figure 391, Figure 392, Figure 393, and Figure 394.

In the 1930 U.S. Census, Isadore lived with her mother, Ida RILEY, and her siblings.[2614] The nature of the relationship between her parents, Ida and Ike, is unclear. Ike always lived with his mother in various censuses. Ida RILEY and her children were recorded in the 1930 Census as Rileys, not Guytons. They lived on the Sallis and Zemuly Road in Beat 4, Attala Co.. Isadore was the second oldest child at age 20. She reportedly attended school, although her older sister, Mary Georgia GUYTON, supposedly did not. At 20 years old in 1930, it is surprising that the Census indicated that none of the children were employed in farming with their mother, Ida.

The 1940 U.S. Census indicated that Isadore and Antney were married.[2615] Antney owned his own farm and Isadore worked as a homemaker. They had three children by this time: Charlie Willie BROWN (6), Evvie BROWN (4), and Emma BROWN (2). By 1950, the family was composed of Charles Willie

---

[2608] "1940 United States Census," New Port, Attala Co., MS, digital image s.v. "Mary Guyton," (birth ABT 1905), *Ancestry.com*.
[2609] Ike Guyton, grave marker, Russell Cemetery, Attala Co., MS, digital image s.v. "Ike Guyton," (birth 12 May 1878, death 10 Feb 1953), *FindaGrave.com*.
[2610] Ida Riley, grave marker, Russell Cemetery, Attala Co., MS, digital image s.v. "Ida Riley," (birth ABT 1887, death 18 May 1951), *FindaGrave.com*.
[2611] Isadora Guyton, grave marker, Russell Cemetery, Attala Co., MS, digital image s.v. "Isadora Brown," (birth 30 Dec 1906, death 14 Feb 1985), *FindaGrave.com*.
[2612] Antney Wesley Brown, grave marker, Russell Cemetery, Attala Co., MS, digital image s.v. "Antney Wesley Brown," (birth 14 Jul 1909, death 13 Aug 1977), *FindaGrave.com*.
[2613] Marriage date per their daughter, Channie Brown Currie.
[2614] "1930 United States Census," Beat 4, Attala Co., MS, digital image s.v. "Isadore Riley," (birth 1906), *Ancestry.com*.
[2615] "1940 United States Census," New Port, Attala Co., MS, digital image s.v. "Isadore Brown," (birth abt 1910), *Ancestry.com*.

BROWN (16), Eva BROWN (13), Emma BROWN (11), Shelay Mae BROWN (9), and Channie M. BROWN (7). The family lived near New Port, Attala Co., MS.[2616]

Figure 389 An Older Isadore GUYTON BROWN[2617]

Figure 390 A Young Antney Wesley BROWN[2618]

Figure 391 Antney Wesley BROWN Plowing the Field[2619]

Figure 392 BROWN Family in Aug 1963[2620]

[2616] "1950 United States Census," New Port, Attala Co., MS, digital image s.v. "Isadora Brown," (birth abt 1910), *Ancestry.com*.
[2617] chancurri originally shared this on 25 Jan 2014 on *Ancestry.com*.
[2618] chancurri originally shared this on 23 Feb 2019 on *Ancestry.com*.
[2619] Chancurri originally shared this on 29 Jan 2014 on *Ancestry.com*.
[2620] Chancurri originally shared this on 29 Jan 2014 on *Ancestry.com*.

Figure 393 Daughters Eva, Channie, and Emma[2621]

Figure 394 Shelay BROWN Class of 1960

Isadora and Antney had at least five children per Channie BROWN-CURRIE:[2622]

i   Charles Willie BROWN (b. 14 Nov 1933 Sallis, Attala Co., MS, d. 31 Jul 1985 Chicago, Cook Co., IL)[2623] m. Eula Mae UNKNOWN. See Figure 395.

ii   Eva BROWN (b. 19 Jul 1936 Sallis, Attala Co., MS, d. 7 Nov 2003 Chicago, Cook Co., IL)[2624] m. Flozell ROGERS (b. Tupelo, Lee Co., MS, d. Unknown). See Figure 396.

iii   Emma M. BROWN (b. 20 Jul 1938 Sallis, Attala Co., MS, d. Unknown)[2625] m. Freddie C. EVANS, Sr. (b. Sallis, Attala Co., MS, d. Unknown). See Figure 397.

iv   Shelay Mae BROWN (b. 16 Nov 1940 Sallis, Attala Co., MS, d. 27 Sep 1990 Chicago, Cook Co., IL).[2626] See Figure 398.

v   Channie M. BROWN (21 Oct 1942 Sallis, Attala Co., MS, d. Living) m. Stanley Neal CURRIE, Sr. (b. 30 Nov 1946 Jackson, Hinds Co., MS (Unknown) on 12 May 1966 in Jackson, Hinds Co., MS. See Figure 399.

[2621] chancurri originally shared this on 2 Mar 2019 on *Ancestry.com*.
[2622] Channie Brown-Currie, "Descendants of Artie Rainey and Aaron W. Guyton," 2017 Guyton Family Reunion, copy shared by the author.
[2623] Charles Willie Brown, grave marker, Russell Cemetery, Attala Co., MS, digital image s.v. "Charles Willie Brown," (birth 14 Nov 1933, death 31 Jul 1985), *FindaGrave.com*.
[2624] Eva Brown, grave marker, Saint Mary Catholic Cemetery and Mausoleum, Evergreen Park, Cook Co., IL, digital image s.v. "Eva Rogers," (birth 19 Jul 1936, death 7 Nov 2003), *FindaGrave.com*.
[2625] Channie Brown-Currie, "Descendants of Artie Rainey and Aaron W. Guyton," 2017 Guyton Family Reunion, copy shared by the author.
[2626] Shelay Mae Brown, grave marker, Saint Mary Catholic Cemetery and Mausoleum, Evergreen Park, Cook Co., IL, digital image s.v. "Shelay Mae Brown," (birth 16 Nov 1940, death 27 Sep 1990), *FindaGrave.com*.

Figure 395 Charles and Eula BROWN[2627]

Figure 396 Eva BROWN ROGERS[2628]

Figure 397 Emma M. BROWN EVANS[2629]

Figure 398 Shelay Mae BROWN[2630]

Figure 399 Channie BROWN CURRIE[2631]

Gus Davis Guyton (Ike, Aaron Whitaker, Aaron Steele, Joseph I, John I, Samuel II, Samuel I, John)

Gus Davis GUYTON was the son of Ike GUYTON (b. 12 May 1878 Sallis, Attala Co., MS, d. 10 Feb 1953 Sallis, Attala Co., MS)[2632] and Ida RILEY (b. 1887 Sallis, Attala Co., MS, d. 18 May 1951 Sallis, Attala Co., MS.[2633] Gus was born on 3 Mar 1909 in Sallis, Attala Co., MS, and died on 8 Jul 1990 in Cook Co.,

---

[2627] chancurri originally shared this on 16 May 2013 on *Ancestry.com*. I do not know the relationship between Charles and Eula.
[2628] chancurri originally shared this on 23 Feb 2019 on *Ancestry.com*.
[2629] chancurri originally shared this on 2 Mar 2019 on *Ancestry.com*.
[2630] chancurri originally shared this on 16 May 2013 on *Ancestry.com*.
[2631] Chancurri on *Ancestry.com* has made major contributions to this book through the photos she has provided.
[2632] Ike Guyton, grave marker, Russell Cemetery, Attala Co., MS, digital image s.v. "Ike Guyton," (birth 12 May 1878, death 10 Feb 1953), *FindaGrave.com*.
[2633] Ida Riley, grave marker, Russell Cemetery, Attala Co., MS, digital image s.v. "Ida Riley," (birth ABT 1887, death 18 May 1951), *FindaGrave.com*.

IL).[2634] He married Ruth Lee (Ruthie) ROBY (b. 7 May 1916 Sallis, Attala Co., MS, d. 13 Jan 1996 Wauwatosa, Milwaukee Co., WI).[2635]

In the 1930 U.S. Census, Gus Davis lived with his mother, Ida RILEY, and his siblings.[2636] The nature of the relationship between his parents, Ida and Ike, is unclear. Ike always lived with his mother in various censuses. Ida RILEY and her children were recorded in the 1930 Census as Rileys, not Guytons. They lived on the Sallis and Zemuly Road in Beat 4, Attala Co. Gus was the third child and oldest son at age 17. He was attending school. At 20 years old in 1930, it is surprising that the Census indicated that none of the children were employed in farming with their mother, Ida.

In the 1940 U.S. Census Gus was married to Ruthie ROBY. Gus worked on his own farm while Ruthie was a homemaker. They had four children by this time: Earline GUYTON (6), Irene GUYTON (4), Curtis GUYTON (2), and Joan (showns as Jae Ann) GUYTON (11/12). Also living with them was Will ROBY (56), Ruthie's father.[2637] By 1950, the family was composed of Earline GUYTON (16), Irene GUYTON (14), Curtis GUYTON (12), Joan GUYTON (10), Arthur David (Buddy) GUYTON (8), Billie Ruth GUYTON (5), and Barbara GUYTON (2). The family lived near New Port, Attala Co., MS.[2638] See Figure 400, Figure 401, and Figure 402.

Figure 400 Gus Davis GUYTON[2639]

Figure 401 Ruthie ROBY GUYTON[2640]

I could not find them in the 1950 U.S. Census, but I noted that Gus predeceased Ruthie. His obituary indicated that he died in Chicago when Ruthie lived in Milwaukee, Milwaukee Co., WI. Were they separated?

[2634] "Social Security Death Index," s.v. "Gus D. Guyton," (birth 3 Mar 1909, death 8 Jul 1990), *Ancestry.com*.
[2635] "Social Security Death Index," s.v. "Ruth Guyton," (birth 7 May 1916, death 13 Jan 1996), *Ancestry.com*.
[2636] "1930 United States Federal Census," Beat 4, Attala Co., MS, digital image s.v. "Gus Riley," (birth ABT 1913), *Ancestry.com*.
[2637] "1940 United States Federal Census," Newport, Attala Co., MS, digital image s.v. "Gus Guyton," (birth ABT 1910), *Ancestry.com*.
[2638] "1950 United States Federal Census," Newport, Attala Co., MS, digital image s.v. "Gus Guyton," (birth ABT 1910), *Ancestry.com*.
[2639] Nathaniel Guyton originally shared this on 25 May 2014 on *Ancestry.com*.
[2640] chancurri originally shared this on 27 May 2013 on *Ancestry.com*.

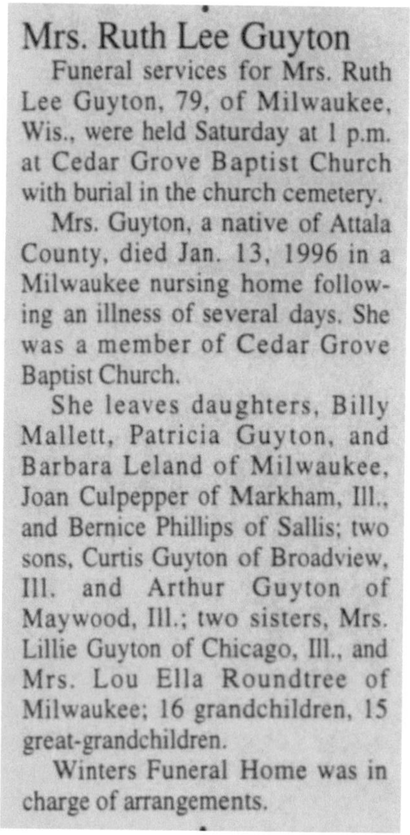

> **Mrs. Ruth Lee Guyton**
>
> Funeral services for Mrs. Ruth Lee Guyton, 79, of Milwaukee, Wis., were held Saturday at 1 p.m. at Cedar Grove Baptist Church with burial in the church cemetery.
>
> Mrs. Guyton, a native of Attala County, died Jan. 13, 1996 in a Milwaukee nursing home following an illness of several days. She was a member of Cedar Grove Baptist Church.
>
> She leaves daughters, Billy Mallett, Patricia Guyton, and Barbara Leland of Milwaukee, Joan Culpepper of Markham, Ill., and Bernice Phillips of Sallis; two sons, Curtis Guyton of Broadview, Ill. and Arthur Guyton of Maywood, Ill.; two sisters, Mrs. Lillie Guyton of Chicago, Ill., and Mrs. Lou Ella Roundtree of Milwaukee; 16 grandchildren, 15 great-grandchildren.
>
> Winters Funeral Home was in charge of arrangements.

Figure 402 Obituary of Ruth Lee ROBY GUYTON[2641]

Gus and Ruth's children per Ruth's obituary and Channie BROWN-CURRIE:[2642]

i   Earlene GUYTON (b. 19 Aug 1933 Sallis, Attala Co., MS, d. 22 May 1965 Cook Co., IL)[2643] m. Otha LANDINGHAM (b. 31 Oct 1922, d. 19 May 1981).[2644]

ii   Bernice GUYTON (17 Jun 1935 Attala Co., MS, d. 14 Dec 2002 McAdams, Attala Co., MS)[2645] m. Joseph Lee PHILLIPS, Sr. in Cook Co., IL.[2646]

[2641] "Obituary of Mrs. Ruth Lee Guyton," *The Star-Herald*, Kosciusko, MS, 25 Jan 1996, p. 6; digital image, s.v. "Mrs. Ruth Lee Guyton," *Newspapers.com*, <https://www.newspapers.com/image/276503363/?article=a2a904a0-aa81-43a4-b01b-7750d52b4373&focus=0.18792301,0.18902864,0.34821227,0.36937332&xid=3355>.

[2642] "Obituary of Mrs. Ruth Lee Guyton," *The Star-Herald*, Kosciusko, MS, 25 Jan 1996, p. 6; digital image, s.v. "Mrs. Ruth Lee Guyton," *Newspapers.com*, <https://www.newspapers.com/image/276503363/?article=a2a904a0-aa81-43a4-b01b-7750d52b4373&focus=0.18792301,0.18902864,0.34821227,0.36937332&xid=3355>.

[2643] Earlene Guyton, grave marker, Russell Cemetery, Attala Co., MS, digital image s.v. "Earlene Landingham," (birth 19 Aug 1933, death 22 May 1965), *FindaGrave.com*.

[2644] Otha Landingham, grave marker, Restvale Cemetery, Chicago, Cook Co., IL, digital image s.v. "Otha Landingham," (birth 31 Oct 1922, death 19 May 1981), *FindaGrave.com*.

[2645] Bernice Guyton, grave marker, Russell Cemetery, Attala Co., MS, digital image s.v. "Bernice Phillips," (birth 17 Jun 1935, death 14 Dec 2002), *FindaGrave.com*.

[2646] "Cook County, Illinois Marriage Index, 1930-1960," s.v. "Joseph L. Phillips," (marriage to Bernice Guyton on 29 Oct 1957).

iii		Irene (Polly) GUYTON (b. ABT 1936 MS, d. Unknown).[2647]
iv		Curtis GUYTON (b. 29 Jul 1937 Sallis, Attala Co., MS, d. Unknown)[2648] m. Hattie BANKS (b. Sallis, Attala Co., MS, d. Unknown).[2649]
v		Joan GUYTON (b. 2 Jul 1939 Sallis, Attala Co., MS, d. Unknown)[2650] m. Frederick CULPEPPER, Sr. (b. Sallis, Attala Co., MS, d. Unknown) on 17 May 1958 in Chicago, Cook Co., IL.[2651]
vi		Arthur David (Buddy) GUYTON (b. 30 Mar 1942 Sallis, Attala Co., MS, d. 19 Apr 2014 Maywood, Cook Co., IL)[2652] m. Juanita FULLER (b. Sallis, Attala Co., MS, d. Unknown).[2653]
viii		Barbara Louise GUYTON (b. ABT 1948 New Port, Attala Co., MS, d. Unknown)[2654] m. Gene LELAND (b. ABT 1947 MS, d. Unknown).[2655]
ix		Patricia GUYTON (b. ABT 1952 Sallis, Attala Co., MS, d. Unknown).[2656]
x		Margaret GUYTON (Unknown).

Joe Frank Guyton (Ike, Aaron Whitaker, Aaron Steele, Joseph I, John I, Samuel II, Samuel I, John)

Joe Frank GUYTON was the son of Ike GUYTON (b. 12 May 1878 Sallis, Attala Co., MS, d. 10 Feb 1953 Sallis, Attala Co., MS)[2657] and Ida RILEY (b. 1887 Sallis, Attala Co., MS, d. 18 May 1951 Sallis, Attala Co., MS).[2658] He was born on 10 Sep 1912 in Sallis, Attala Co., MS, and died on 23 Aug 1994 in Sallis, Attala Co., MS.[2659] He married Mildred Irene WINGARD (b. 11 Mar 1917 MS, d. 17 Apr 2016 Chicago Heights, Cook Co., IL).[2660] See Figure 403, Figure 404, Figure 405, and Figure 406.

The 1940 U.S. Census showed Joe Frank lodged in New Port, Attala Co., MS with his sister, Annie Frances GUYTON EVANS, and her family. He was farming with the family. He indicated on the 1940 Census that he lived in Chicago, Cook Co., IL in 1935.[2661] By the 1950 U.S. Census, Joe Frank and Mildred were married and living in New Port, Attala Co., MS. Living with the couple were Joe Frank's father, Ike

---

[2647] "1940 United States Federal Census," Newport, Attala Co., MS, digital image s.v. "Irene Guyton," (birth ABT 1936), *Ancestry.com*.
[2648] "U.S. Public Records Index, 1950-1993, Volume 1," s.v. "Curtis M. Guyton," (birth 29 Jul 1937), *Ancestry.com*.
[2649] Per Channie Brown-Currie.
[2650] "U.S., Public Records Index, 1950-1993, Volume 1," s.v. "Joan Culpepper," (birth 2 Jul 1939), *Ancestry.com*.
[2651] "Cook County, Illinois Marriage Index, 1930-1960," s.v. "Fred Culpepper," (marriage 17 May 1958 to Joan Guyton), *Ancestry.com*.
[2652] "Arthur David Guyton, grave marker, Oakridge-Glen Oak Cemetery, Hillside, Cook Co., IL, digital image s.v. "Arthur David Guyton," (birth 30 Mar 1942, death 19 Apr 2014), *FindaGrave.com*.
[2653] Per Channie Brown-Currie.
[2654] "1950 United States Federal Census," Newport, Attala Co., MS, digital image s.v. "Barbara Luyton," (birth ABT 1948), *Ancestry.com*.
[2655] Per Channie Brown-Currie.
[2656] Date and place of birth per Channie Brown-Currie.
[2657] Ike Guyton, grave marker, Russell Cemetery, Attala Co., MS, digital image s.v. "Ike Guyton," (birth 12 May 1878, death 10 Feb 1953), *FindaGrave.com*.
[2658] Ida Riley, grave marker, Russell Cemetery, Attala Co., MS, digital image s.v. "Ida Riley," (birth ABT 1887, death 18 May 1951), *FindaGrave.com*.
[2659] "Social Security Death Index," s.v. "Joe Guyton," (birth 10 Sep 1912, death 23 Aug 1994), *Ancestry.com*.
[2660] Mildred Irene Wingard, grave marker, Russell Cemetery, Attala Co., MS, digital image s.v. "Mildred Irene Guyton," (birth 11 Mar 1917, death 17 Apr 2016), *FindaGrave.com*.
[2661] "1940 United States Federal Census," Newport, Attala Co., MS, digital image s.v. "Joe Guyton," (birth ABT 1914), *Ancestry.com*.

(age 71), and the couple's children: Katherine GUYTON (12), Doris Nell GUYTON (4), Leander GUYTON (2), Edwin GUYTON (Nov).[2662]

Figure 403 Young Joe Frank GUYTON[2663]

Figure 404 Older Joe Frank GUYTON[2664]

Figure 405 Mildred Irene WINGARD GUYTON[2665]

According to Joe Frank's obituary, he and Mildred had the following children:[2666]

i   Katherine RILEY GUYTON (ABT 1938 MS, d. Unknown)[2667] m. Otis RUSH (Unknown).[2668] Katherine may be the daughter of a man named RILEY. Katherine and her mother lived with Mildred's father in the 1940 U.S. Census. Mildred's last name was WINGARD; Katherine's was RILEY.
ii   Doris Nell GUYTON (b. ABT 1946 MS, d. Unknown)[2669] m. Unknown THOMAS (Unknown).
iii Leander (Lee) GUYTON (b. ABT 1948 MS, d. Unknown)[2670] m. Serita UNKNOWN (Unknown).
iv   Edwin GUYTON (b. 3 Nov 1949 Sallis, Attala Co., MS, d. 4 Aug 2007 Sallis, Attala Co., MS).[2671]

[2662] "1950 United States Federal Census," Newport, Attala Co., MS, digital image s.v. "Joe Gustan," (birth ABT 1914), *Ancestry.com*.
[2663] Nathaniel Guyton originally shared this on 25 May 2014 on *Ancestry.com*.
[2664] chancurri originally shared this on 15 Feb 2014 on *Ancestry.com*.
[2665] chancurri originally shared this on 1 Jul 2016 on *Ancestry.com*.
[2666] "Obituary of Joe Frank Guyton," *The Star-Herald*, Kosciusko, MS, 1 Sep 1994, p. 6; digital image, s.v. "Joe Guyton," *Newspapers.com*, <https://www.newspapers.com/image/276594373/?article=62303f3d-2bb4-4b43-baf7-b3efd9a0d859&focus=0.19185807,0.21945038,0.3505045,0.42690027&xid=3355>.
[2667] "1940 United States Federal Census," Newport, Attala Co., MS, digital image s.v. "Catherine Riley," (birth ABT 1934), *Ancestry.com*.
[2668] "Cook County, Illinois Marriage Index, 1930-1960," s.v. "Katherine Guyton," (marriage to Otis Rush on 30 Jun 1959), *Ancestry.com*.
[2669] "1950 United States Federal Census," Newport, Attala Co., MS, digital image s.v. "Doris Guyton," (birth ABT 1946), *Ancestry.com*.
[2670] "1950 United States Federal Census," Newport, Attala Co., MS, digital image s.v. "Leearden Guyton," (birth ABT 1948), *Ancestry.com*.
[2671] "Edwin Guyton, grave marker, Russell Cemetery, Sallis, Attala Co., MS, digital image s.v. "Edwin Guyton," (birth 3 Nov 1949, death 4 Aug 2007), *FindaGrave.com*.

v   Linda Bell GUYTON (b. 13 Jan 1952 Sallis, Attala Co., MS, d. 13 Apr 2002 Sallis, Attala Co., MS).[2672]
vi Brenda Dell GUYTON (b. 13 Jan 1952 Sallis, Attala Co., MS, d. 10 Oct 2019 Sallis, Attala Co., MS)[2673] m. Charles (Charlie) William CARR (Unknown).[2674]
vii Bonnie GUYTON (AFT 1950, d. Unknown) m. Nathaniel WILDER (Unknown).
viii Sarah GUYTON (b. AFT 1950, d. Unknown).

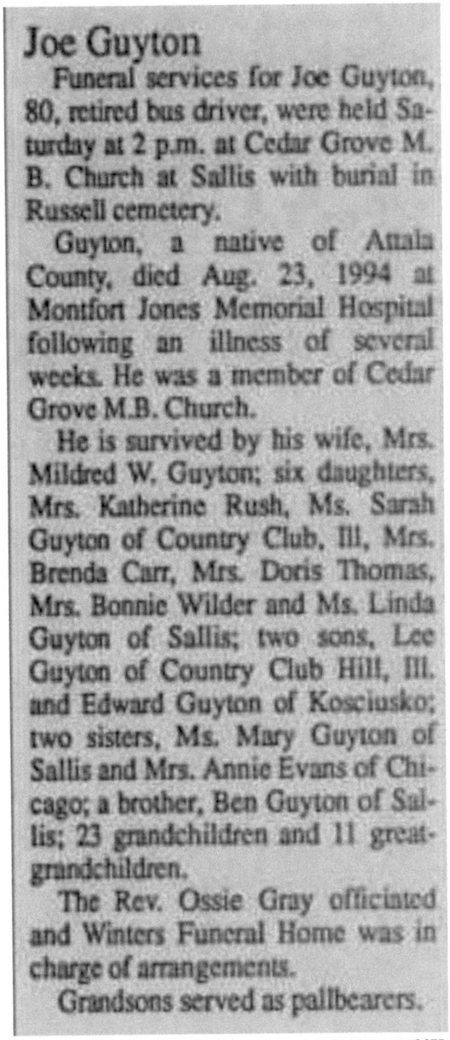

Joe Guyton

Funeral services for Joe Guyton, 80, retired bus driver, were held Saturday at 2 p.m. at Cedar Grove M. B. Church at Sallis with burial in Russell cemetery.

Guyton, a native of Attala County, died Aug. 23, 1994 at Montfort Jones Memorial Hospital following an illness of several weeks. He was a member of Cedar Grove M.B. Church.

He is survived by his wife, Mrs. Mildred W. Guyton; six daughters, Mrs. Katherine Rush, Ms. Sarah Guyton of Country Club, Ill, Mrs. Brenda Carr, Mrs. Doris Thomas, Mrs. Bonnie Wilder and Ms. Linda Guyton of Sallis; two sons, Lee Guyton of Country Club Hill, Ill. and Edward Guyton of Kosciusko; two sisters, Ms. Mary Guyton of Sallis and Mrs. Annie Evans of Chicago; a brother, Ben Guyton of Sallis; 23 grandchildren and 11 great-grandchildren.

The Rev. Ossie Gray officiated and Winters Funeral Home was in charge of arrangements.

Grandsons served as pallbearers.

Figure 406 Obituary of Joe Frank GUYTON[2675]

[2672] "Linda Bell Guyton, grave marker, Russell Cemetery, Sallis, Attala Co., MS, digital image s.v. "Linda Bell Guyton," (birth 13 Jan 1952, death 13 Apr 2002), *FindaGrave.com*.
[2673] "Brenda Dell Guyton, grave marker, Russell Cemetery, Sallis, Attala Co., MS, digital image s.v. "Brenda Dell Carr," (birth 13 Jan 1952, death 10 Oct 2019), *FindaGrave.com*.
[2674] Per Channie Brown Currie's *Ancestry.com* tree.
[2675] "Obituary of Joe Frank Guyton," *The Star-Herald*, Kosciusko, MS, 1 Sep 1994, p. 6; digital image, s.v. "Joe Guyton," *Newspapers.com*, <https://www.newspapers.com/image/276594373/?article=62303f3d-2bb4-4b43-baf7-b3efd9a0d859&focus=0.19185807,0.21945038,0.3505045,0.42690027&xid=3355>.

Annie Frances Guyton (Ike, Aaron Whitaker, Aaron Steele, Joseph I, John I, Samuel II, Samuel I, John)

Annie GUYTON was the daughter of Ike GUYTON (b. 12 May 1878 Sallis, Attala Co., MS, d. 10 Feb 1953 Sallis, Attala Co., MS)[2676] and Ida RILEY (b. 1887 Sallis, Attala Co., MS, d. 18 May 1951 Sallis, Attala Co., MS).[2677] Annie was born on 28 Feb 1916 in Kosciusko, Attala Co., MS, and died on 17 Oct 1995 in Chicago, Cook Co., IL.[2678] She married Allen Leroy (Gipp) EVANS, Sr. (b. 29 Dec 1912 Sallis, Attala Co., MS, d. Jun 1972 Chicago, Cook Co., IL).[2679] See Figure 407.

Figure 407 Annie GUYTON EVANS[2680]

In the 1930 U.S. Census, Annie was 14 and lived with her mother on the Sallis and Zemuly Road in Beat 4, Attala Co., MS.[2681] By 1940, she and Gipp were married and had two sons: Willie Edward EVANS (7) and Terry Leroy EVANS (4).[2682] Joe Frank GUYTON, Annie's brother, lived with them during the census. He had lived in Chicago in 1935. The family farmed around New Port, Attala Co., MS. At the 1950 Census, Annie and Gipp lived west of Sallis, Attala Co., MS.[2683] They had five children living with them: Willie Edward EVANS (17), Terry Leroy EVANS (14), Gene Arthur EVANS (5), Gloria Jean EVANS (3), and Darlene EVANS (1). Allen was a farmer and Willie was his helper.

[2676] Ike Guyton, grave marker, Russell Cemetery, Attala Co., MS, digital image s.v. "Ike Guyton," (birth 12 May 1878, death 10 Feb 1953), *FindaGrave.com*.

[2677] Ida Riley, grave marker, Russell Cemetery, Attala Co., MS, digital image s.v. "Ida Riley," (birth ABT 1887, death 18 May 1951), *FindaGrave.com*.

[2678] "Social Security Death Index," s.v. "Annie Evans," (birth 28 Feb 1916, death 17 Oct 1995), *Ancestry.com*.

[2679] Allen Leroy Evans, Sr., grave marker, Restvale Cemetery, Alsip, Cook Co., IL, digital image s.v. "Allen Leroy Evans," (birth 29 Dec 1912, death 14 Jun 1972), *FindaGrave.com*.

[2680] Chancurri originally shared this on 6 May 2013 on Ancestry.com.

[2681] "1930 United States Federal Census," Beat 4, Attala Co., MS, digital image s.v. "Nan Riley," (birth ABT 1916), *Ancestry.com*.

[2682] "1940 United States Federal Census," Newport, Attala Co., MS, digital image s.v. "Annie Evans," (birth ABT 1916), *Ancestry.com*.

[2683] "1950 United States Federal Census," Newport, Attala Co., MS, digital image s.v. "Annie Evans," (birth ABT 1916), *Ancestry.com*.

Annie and Allen Leroy (Gipp) EVANS, Sr. had at least six children:

i   Willie Edward EVANS (b. 16 Jan 1933 Sallis, Attala Co., MS, d. 15 May 1995 Chicago, Cook Co., IL).[2684]
ii   Terry Leroy EVANS (b. 27 Oct 1935 Sallis, Attala Co., MS, d. 3 Aug 1996 Elgin, Kane Co., IL).[2685]
iii   Gene Arthur (Pie Joe) EVANS (b. ABT 1945 MS).[2686] See Figure 408.
iv   Gloria Jean EVANS (b. 4 Jan 1947 Sallis, Attala Co., MS, d. 26 Jun 2014 Chicago, Cook Co., IL).[2687]
v   Darlene EVANS (b. 9 Mar 1949 Sallis, Attala Co., MS, d. 9 Sep 1991 Chicago, Cook Co., IL).[2688] See Figure 409.
vi   Allen Leroy EVANS, Jr. (b. 6 Oct 1952 Sallis, Attala Co., MS, d. 4 Apr 2015 Chicago, Cook Co., IL).[2689] See Figure 410.

All the children moved to Chicago and the Chicago area.

Figure 408 Gene Arty (Pie Joe) EVANS[2690]

Figure 409 Darlene EVANS[2691]

Figure 410 Allen Leroy EVANS, Jr.[2692]

[2684] Willie Edward Evans, grave marker, Lakewood Memorial Park, Elgin, Cook Co., IL, digital image s.v. "Willie Edward Evans," (birth 16 Jan 1933, death 3 May 1995), *FindaGrave.com*.
[2685] Terry Leroy Evans, grave marker, Lakewood Memorial Park, Elgin, Cook Co., IL, digital image s.v. "Terry Evans," (birth 27 Oct 1935, death 3 Aug 1996), *FindaGrave.com*.
[2686] "1950 United States Federal Census," Newport, Attala Co., MS, digital image s.v. "Jean Arthur Evans," (birth ABT 1945), *Ancestry.com*.
[2687] "U.S. Public Records Index, 1950-1993, Volume 1," s.v. "Gloria J Evans," (birth 4 Jan 1947), *Ancestry.com*. Channie Brown-Currie, "Descendants of Artie Rainey and Aaron W. Guyton,"2017 Guyton Family Reunion, (death 26 Jun 2014).
[2688] Darlene Evans, grave marker, Burr Oak Cemetery, Elgin, Cook Co., IL, digital image s.v. "Darlene Evans," (birth 9 Mar 1949, death 9 Sep 1995), *FindaGrave.com*.
[2689] "Allen Leroy Evans, Jr., funeral program. chancurri originally shared this on 6 May 2015 on *Ancestry.com*.
[2690] chancurri originally shared this on 23 May 2013 on *Ancestry.com*.
[2691] chancurri originally shared this on 19 May 2015 on *Ancestry.com*.
[2692] chancurri originally shared this on 6 May 2015 on *Ancestry.com*.

Minnie Guyton (Ike, Aaron Whitaker, Aaron Steele, Joseph I, John I, Samuel II, Samuel I, John)

Minnie GUYTON was the daughter of Ike GUYTON (b. 12 May 1878 Sallis, Attala Co., MS, d. 10 Feb 1953 Sallis, Attala Co., MS)[2693] and Ida RILEY (b. 1887 Sallis, Attala Co., MS, d. 18 May 1951 Sallis, Attala Co., MS).[2694] Minnie was born on 22 May 1918 in Sallis, Attala Co., MS, and died on 10 Nov 1976 in Chicago, Cook Co., IL.[2695] She married Steele GUYTON (b. 16 Jul 1915 MS, d. 25 Dec 1994 Chicago, Cook Co., IL).[2696] Steele was the son of Simon GUYTON, Sr. and Viola WILDER GUYTON. That makes Minnie and Steele first cousins. See the section on Steele GUYTON for more information about the family.

Ben Guyton (Ike, Aaron Whitaker, Aaron Steele, Joseph I, John I, Samuel II, Samuel I, John)

Ben GUYTON was the son of Ike GUYTON (b. 12 May 1878 Sallis, Attala Co., MS, d. 10 Feb 1953 Sallis, Attala Co., MS)[2697] and Ida RILEY (b. 1887 Sallis, Attala Co., MS, d. 18 May 1951 Sallis, Attala Co., MS).[2698] He was born on 2 Apr 1920 in Sallis, Attala Co., MS, and died on 8 Nov 1996 Sallis, Attala Co., MS.[2699] See Figure 411.

The 1930, 1940, and 1950 U.S. Censuses reported Ben lived with his mother.[2700] In the 1930 and 1950 Census, he was recorded as a Riley; in the 1940 Census he went by the name Guyton. He farmed with his mother. The 1950 Census indicated that he was married but his wife's first name is missing. Channie BROWN-CURRIE reports that he married his cousin Genova GUYTON (b. 20 May 1930 Sallis, Attala Co., MS, d. 17 Jun 2023, Chicago, Cook Co., IL).[2701] See Figure 412. Ben was first cousin to Genova GUYTON, who was Case GUYTON's daughter. There is no mention of her in Ben's *FindaGrave* entry.[2702]

[2693] Ike Guyton, grave marker, Russell Cemetery, Attala Co., MS, digital image s.v. "Ike Guyton," (birth 12 May 1878, death 10 Feb 1953), *FindaGrave.com*.
[2694] Ida Riley, grave marker, Russell Cemetery, Attala Co., MS, digital image s.v. "Ida Riley," (birth ABT 1887, death 18 May 1951), *FindaGrave.com*.
[2695] "Social Security Death Index," s.v. "Minnie Guyton," (birth 22 May 1918, death Nov 1976), *Ancestry.com*.
[2696] "Social Security Death Index," s.v. "Steel Guyton," (birth 16 Jul 1915, death Dec 1994), *Ancestry.com*.
[2697] Ike Guyton, grave marker, Russell Cemetery, Attala Co., MS, digital image s.v. "Ike Guyton," (birth 12 May 1878, death 10 Feb 1953), *FindaGrave.com*.
[2698] Ida Riley, grave marker, Russell Cemetery, Attala Co., MS, digital image s.v. "Ida Riley," (birth ABT 1887, death 18 May 1951), *FindaGrave.com*.
[2699] "Social Security Death Index," s.v. "Ben Guyton," (birth 2 Apr 1920, death 8 Nov 1996), *Ancestry.com*.
[2700] "1930 United States Federal Census," Beat 4, Attala Co., MS, digital image s.v. "Ben Riley," (birth ABT 1923), *Ancestry.com*. "1940 United States Federal Census," Newport, Attala Co., MS, digital image s.v. "Ben Guyton," (birth ABT 1922), *Ancestry.com*. "1950 United States Federal Census," Newport, Attala Co., MS, digital image s.v. "Ben Riley," (birth ABT 1925), *Ancestry.com*.
[2701] Per Channie Brown-Currie.
[2702] Ben Guyton, grave marker, Russell Cemetery, Attala Co., MS, digital image s.v. "Ben Guyton," (birth 2 Apr 1920, death 8 Nov 1996), *FindaGrave.com*.

Figure 411 Ben GUYTON[2703]

Figure 412 Genova GUYTON[2704]

Alice Lee Guyton (Ike, Aaron Whitaker, Aaron Steele, Joseph I, John I, Samuel II, Samuel I, John)

Alice Lee GUYTON was the daughter of Ike GUYTON (b. 12 May 1878 Sallis, Attala Co., MS, d. 10 Feb 1953 Sallis, Attala Co., MS)[2705] and Ida RILEY (b. 1887 Sallis, Attala Co., MS, d. 18 May 1951 Sallis, Attala Co., MS).[2706] Alice was born on 10 May 1924 in Sallis, Attala Co., MS, and died on 11 Feb 1992 in Chicago, Cook Co., IL.[2707] She married Oliver DeBois WEBB (b. 3 Aug 1912 Greenville, SC, d. 16 Jan 1992).[2708] See Figure 413, Figure 414, and Figure 415.

[2703] Chancurri originally shared this on 15 Feb 2014 on *Ancestry.com*.
[2704] Chancurri originally shared this on 15 May 2013 on *Ancestry.com*.
[2705] Ike Guyton, grave marker, Russell Cemetery, Attala Co., MS, digital image s.v. "Ike Guyton," (birth 12 May 1878, death 10 Feb 1953), *FindaGrave.com*.
[2706] Ida Riley, grave marker, Russell Cemetery, Attala Co., MS, digital image s.v. "Ida Riley," (birth ABT 1887, death 18 May 1951), *FindaGrave.com*.
[2707] "Social Security Death Index," s.v. "Alice Webb," (birth 10 May 1924, death 11 Feb 1992), *Ancestry.com*.
[2708] Oliver DeBois Webb, grave marker, Oakland Memory Lanes, Dolton, Cook Co., IL, digital image s.v. "Oliver Debois Webb," (birth 3 Aug 1912, death 16 Jan 1992), *FindaGrave.com*.

Figure 413 Young Alice GUYTON WEBB[2709]

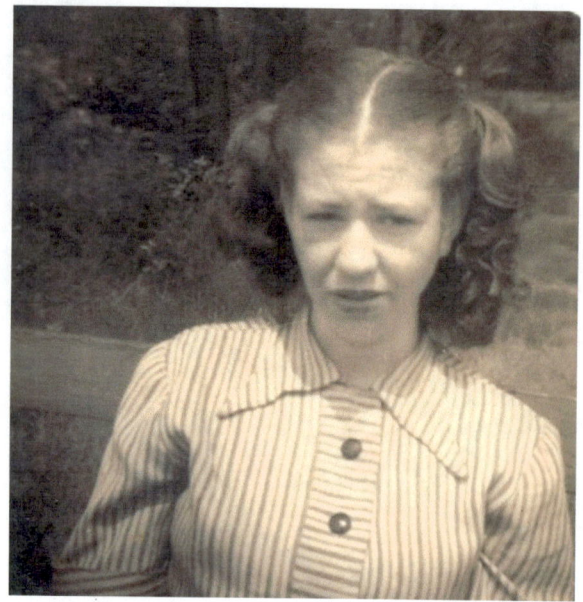

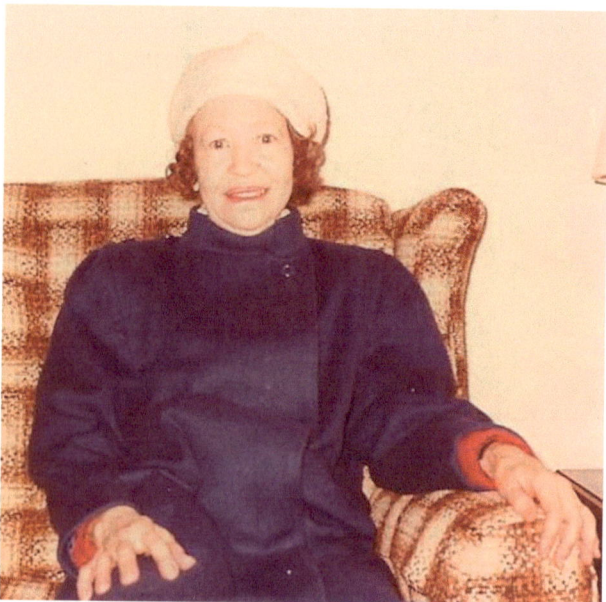

Figure 414 Older Alice GUYTON WEBB[2710]

In the 1930 and 1940 U.S. Censuses, Alice lived with her mother, Ida RILEY. In 1930, she was recorded using the last name Riley; in 1940, she was labeled as a Guyton. In 1950, the Census showed her married to Oliver DeBois WEBB and living in Chicago.[2711] The Census indicated that Alice made lamp shades at a lamp shade factory, but no job was listed for Oliver. He was listed as unable to work.

The couple had at least two children:

i   Oliver WEBB, Jr. (b. ABT 1946 Chicago, Cook Co., IL, d. ABT 1950 Chicago, Cook Co., IL).[2712]
ii   Bonnie WEBB (b. 27 Oct 1948 Chicago, Cook Co., IL, d. Unknown)[2713] m. James Lee NORTH, Sr. (b. 27 Oct 1931 Nashville, Davidson Co., TN, d. 17 Apr 2008 Lansing, Cook Co., IL).[2714]

[2709] osj9582 originally shared this on 9 Oct 2017 on *Ancestry.com*.
[2710] Chancurri originally shared this on 15 Feb 2014 on *Ancestry.com*.
[2711] "1930 United States Federal Census," Beat 4, Attala Co., MS, digital image s.v. "Lil Riley," (birth ABT 1925), *Ancestry.com*. "1940 United States Federal Census," Newport, Attala Co., MS, digital image s.v. "Alice Guyton," (birth ABT 1925), *Ancestry.com*. "1950 United States Federal Census," Chicago, Cook Co., IL, digital image s.v. "Alice Webb," (birth ABT 1926), *Ancestry.com*.
[2712] "1950 United States Federal Census," Chicago, Cook Co., IL, digital image s.v. "Oliver Webb, Jr.," (birth ABT 1948), *Ancestry.com*. Information also from Channie Brown-Currie.
[2713] "1950 United States Federal Census," Chicago, Cook Co., IL, digital image s.v. "Barney Webb [sic]," (birth ABT 1949), *Ancestry.com*.
[2714] Marriage per Channie Brown Currie.

Figure 415 Oliver Debois WEBB and son Oliver (Butch) WEBB[2715]

Claude Guyton (Ike, Aaron Whitaker, Aaron Steele, Joseph I, John I, Samuel II, Samuel I, John)

Claude GUYTON was the son of Ike GUYTON (b. 12 May 1878 Sallis, Attala Co., MS, d. 10 Feb 1953 Sallis, Attala Co., MS)[2716] and Ida RILEY (b. 1887 Sallis, Attala Co., MS, d. 18 May 1951 Sallis, Attala Co., MS).[2717] He was born on 5 Mar 1927 in Sallis, Attala Co., MS, and died on 1 May 1985 in Sallis, Attala Co., MS).[2718] See Figure 416 and Figure 417.

The 1930, 1940, and 1950 U.S. Censuses reported Claude lived with his mother. In the 1930 and 1950 Census, he is recorded as a Riley; in the 1940 Census he went by the name Guyton. He farmed with his mother.[2719]

[2715] Chancurri originally shared this on 19 May 2015 on *Ancestry.com*.
[2716] Ike Guyton, grave marker, Russell Cemetery, Attala Co., MS, digital image s.v. "Ike Guyton," (birth 12 May 1878, death 10 Feb 1953), *FindaGrave.com*.
[2717] Ida Riley, grave marker, Russell Cemetery, Attala Co., MS, digital image s.v. "Ida Riley," (birth ABT 1887, death 18 May 1951), *FindaGrave.com*.
[2718] Claude L. Guyton, grave marker, Russell Cemetery, Attala Co., MS, digital image s.v. "Claude L. Guyton," (birth 5 Mar 1927, death 1 May 1985), *FindaGrave.com*.
[2719] "1930 United States Federal Census," Beat 4, Attala Co., MS, digital image s.v. "Claude Riley," (birth ABT 1926), *Ancestry.com*. "1940 United States Federal Census," Newport, Attala Co., MS, digital image s.v. "Claude Guyton," (birth ABT 1926), *Ancestry.com*. "1950 United States Federal Census," Chicago, Cook Co., IL, digital image s.v. "Clovid Riley," (birth ABT 1928), *Ancestry.com*.

Figure 416 Claude GUYTON and Bonnie WEBB[2720]

Claude Guyton

Claude Guyton, 58, of Sallis died May 1 at Montfort Jones Memorial Hospital.

Funeral services were conducted by the Rev. A. C. Nash at 11 a.m. May 5 at Hills Springs M. B. Church. Interment was in Russell Cemetery.

Survivors are three sisters, Mrs. Mary Alice Webb, Mrs. Ann Evans, both of Chicago, Il., and Miss Mary Guyton of Sallis; three brothers, Guss Guyton, Joe Guyton and Ben Guyton, all of Sallis.

Handling arrangements was Winters Funeral Home.

Figure 417 Obituary of Claude GUYTON[2721]

[2720] Chancurri originally shared this on 6 May 2013 on *Ancestry.com*.
[2721] "Obituary of Claude Guyton," *The Star-Herald*, Kosciusko, MS, 9 May 1985, p. 12; digital image, s.v. "Claude Guyton," *Newspapers.com*, <https://www.newspapers.com/article/the-star-herald-obituary-for-claude-guyt/131123396/>.

Generation #9

Charles Willie BROWN (Isadora GUYTON BROWN, Ike, Aaron Whitaker, Aaron Steele, Joseph I, John I, Samuel II, Samuel I, John)

Charles Willie BROWN was the son of Isadora GUYTON (b. 30 Dec 1906 Sallis, Attala Co., MS, d. 14 Feb 1985 Sallis, Attala Co., MS)[2722] and Antney Wesley BROWN (b. 4 Jul 1909 Sallis, Attala Co., MS, d. 13 Aug 1977 Sallis, Attala Co., MS).[2723] They were married on 8 Oct 1931 in Sallis.[2724]

Charles was born on 14 Nov 1933 in Sallis, Attala Co., MS, and died on 31 Jul 1985 in Chicago, Cook Co., IL).[2725] He married Eula Mae UNKNOWN. See Figure 418. Charles had two daughters:[2726]

i   Emma YATES (Unknown).
ii   Shirley Jean YATES (Unknown).

Figure 418 Charlies Willie and Eula Mae BROWN

[2722] Isadora Guyton, grave marker, Russell Cemetery, Attala Co., MS, digital image s.v. "Isadora Brown," (birth 30 Dec 1906, death 14 Feb 1985), *FindaGrave.com*.
[2723] Antney Wesley Brown, grave marker, Russell Cemetery, Attala Co., MS, digital image s.v. "Antney Wesley Brown," (birth 14 Jul 1909, death 13 Aug 1977), *FindaGrave.com*.
[2724] Marriage date per their daughter, Channie Brown Currie.
[2725] Charles Willie Brown, grave marker, Russell Cemetery, Attala Co., MS, digital image s.v. "Charles Willie Brown," (birth 14 Nov 1933, death 31 Jul 1985), *FindaGrave.com*.
[2726] "Beta: Newspapers.com Obituary Index, 1940-1955," s.v. "Emma Yates and Shirley Jean Yates," (children of Charles Willie Brown), *Ancestry.com*.

Emma M. BROWN (Isadora GUYTON BROWN, Ike, Aaron Whitaker, Aaron Steele, Joseph I, John I, Samuel II, Samuel I, John)

Emma M. BROWN was the daughter of Isadora GUYTON (b. 30 Dec 1906 Sallis, Attala Co., MS, d. 14 Feb 1985 Sallis, Attala Co., MS)[2727] and Antney Wesley BROWN (b. 4 Jul 1909 Sallis, Attala Co., MS, d. 13 Aug 1977 Sallis, Attala Co., MS).[2728] They were married on 8 Oct 1931 in Sallis.[2729]

Emma was born on 20 Jul 1938 in Sallis, Attala Co., MS, and her death is unknown.[2730] She married Freddie C. EVANS, Sr. (b. Sallis, Attala Co., MS, d. Unknown).[2731] They had two children: [2732]

i   Freddie C. EVANS, Jr. (b. Milwaukee, Milwaukee Co., WI, d. Unknown).
ii   Dale Fitzgerald EVANS (b. Milwaukee, Milwaukee Co., WI, d. Unknown).

Channie M. BROWN (Isadora GUYTON BROWN, Ike, Aaron Whitaker, Aaron Steele, Joseph I, John I, Samuel II, Samuel I, John)

Channie M. BROWN-CURRIE is the daughter of Isadora GUYTON (b. 30 Dec 1906 Sallis, Attala Co., MS, d. 14 Feb 1985 Sallis, Attala Co., MS)[2733] and Antney Wesley BROWN (b. 4 Jul 1909 Sallis, Attala Co., MS, d. 13 Aug 1977 Sallis, Attala Co., MS).[2734] They were married on 8 Oct 1931 in Sallis.[2735]

Channie M. BROWN was born on 21 Oct 1942 in Sallis, Attala Co., MS, d. Living).[2736] She married Stanley Neal CURRIE, Sr. (b. 30 Nov 1946 Jackson, Hinds Co., MS (Unknown) on 12 May 1966 in Jackson, Hinds Co., MS.[2737] They have two children:[2738]

i   Stanley Neal CURRIE, Jr. (b. 14 Nov 1966 Jackson, Hinds Co., MS, d. Living) m. Kenyette SAUNDERS (b. Harlem, NY, d. Living).
ii   Felicia Michelle CURRIE (b. 9 Feb 1970 New London, New London Co. CT, d. Living).

[2727] Isadora Guyton, grave marker, Russell Cemetery, Attala Co., MS, digital image s.v. "Isadora Brown," (birth 30 Dec 1906, death 14 Feb 1985), *FindaGrave.com*.
[2728] Antney Wesley Brown, grave marker, Russell Cemetery, Attala Co., MS, digital image s.v. "Antney Wesley Brown," (birth 14 Jul 1909, death 13 Aug 1977), *FindaGrave.com*.
[2729] Marriage date per their daughter, Channie Brown Currie.
[2730] Channie Brown-Currie, "Descendants of Artie Rainey and Aaron W. Guyton," 2017 Guyton Family Reunion, copy shared by the author.
[2731] Per Channie Brown-Currie.
[2732] Information from Channie Brown-Currie.
[2733] Isadora Guyton, grave marker, Russell Cemetery, Attala Co., MS, digital image s.v. "Isadora Brown," (birth 30 Dec 1906, death 14 Feb 1985), *FindaGrave.com*.
[2734] Antney Wesley Brown, grave marker, Russell Cemetery, Attala Co., MS, digital image s.v. "Antney Wesley Brown," (birth 14 Jul 1909, death 13 Aug 1977), *FindaGrave.com*.
[2735] Marriage date per their daughter, Channie Brown Currie.
[2736] Channie Brown-Currie, "Descendants of Artie Rainey and Aaron W. Guyton," 2017 Guyton Family Reunion, copy shared by the author.
[2737] Per Channie Brown-Currie.
[2738] Per Channie Brown-Currie.

Channie CURRIE-BROWN's contributions to this book on the descendants of Aaron Whitaker GUYTON and Artemesia (Artie) RAINEY were invaluable. I am deeply indebted to her.

Figure 419 Channie BROWN-CURRIE

Earlene GUYTON (Gus Davis, Ike, Aaron Whitaker, Aaron Steele, Joseph I, John I, Samuel II, Samuel I, John)

Earlene GUYTON was the daughter of Gus Davis GUYTON (b. 3 Mar 1909 Sallis, Attala Co., MS, d. 8 Jul 1990 Cook Co., IL)[2739] and Ruth Lee (Ruthie) ROBY (b. 7 May 1916 Sallis, Attala Co., MS, d. 13 Jan 1996 Wauwatosa, Milwaukee Co., WI.[2740] See Figure 420.

Earlene was born on 19 Aug 1933 in Sallis, Attala Co., MS, and died on 22 May 1965 Cook Co., IL).[2741] She married Otha LANDINGHAM (b. 31 Oct 1922, d. 19 May 1981).[2742] They had two children:[2743]

i   Susie LANDINGHAM (b. Sallis, Attala Co., MS, d. Living) m. John CALVIN (Unknown).
ii Linda Faye O'HARA (b. Chicago, Cook Co. IL, d. Living) m. Ronnie O'HARA (Unknown).

Figure 420 Earlene GUYTON LANDINGHAM[2744]

[2739] "Social Security Death Index," s.v. "Gus D. Guyton," (birth 3 Mar 1909, death 8 Jul 1990), *Ancestry.com*.
[2740] "Social Security Death Index," s.v. "Ruth Guyton," (birth 7 May 1916, death 13 Jan 1996), *Ancestry.com*.
[2741] Earlene Guyton, grave marker, Russell Cemetery, Attala Co., MS, digital image s.v. "Earlene Landingham," (birth 19 Aug 1933, death 22 May 1965), *FindaGrave.com*.
[2742] Otha Landingham, grave marker, Restvale Cemetery, Chicago, Cook Co., IL, digital image s.v. "Otha Landingham," (birth 31 Oct 1922, death 19 May 1981), *FindaGrave.com*.
[2743] Per Channie Brown-Currie.
[2744] chancurri originally shared this on 16 May 2013 on *Ancestry.com*.

Bernice GUYTON (Gus Davis, Ike, Aaron Whitaker, Aaron Steele, Joseph I, John I, Samuel II, Samuel I, John)

Bernice GUYTON was the daughter of Gus Davis GUYTON (b. 3 Mar 1909 Sallis, Attala Co., MS, d. 8 Jul 1990 Cook Co., IL)[2745] and Ruth Lee (Ruthie) ROBY (b. 7 May 1916 Sallis, Attala Co., MS, d. 13 Jan 1996 Wauwatosa, Milwaukee Co., WI).[2746]

She was born on 17 Jun 1935 in Sallis, Attala Co., MS, and died on 14 Dec 2002 in McAdams, Attala Co., MS.[2747] See Figure 421. She married Joseph Lee PHILLIPS, Sr. (b. 1924 Sallis, Attala Co., MS, d. 2001 Sallis, Attala Co., MS) in Cook Co., IL.[2748] The couple had five children:[2749]

i   Jackie PHILLIPS (b. Sallis, Attala Co., MS, d. Living).
ii   Yolanda PHILLIPS (b. 1977 Sallis, Attala Co., MS, d. Living).
iii Joseph Lee PHILLIPS, Jr. (b. Sallis, Attala Co., MS, d. Living).
iv Darren PHILLIPS (b. Sallis, Attala Co., MS, d. Living) m. Lamonica UNKNOWN (Unknown).
v   Patrick PHILLIPS (b. Sallis, Attala Co., MS, d. Living) m. Jacqueling UNKNOWN (Unknown).

Figure 421 Bernice GUYTON PHILLIPS[2750]

Curtis GUYTON (Gus Davis, Ike, Aaron Whitaker, Aaron Steele, Joseph I, John I, Samuel II, Samuel I, John)

Curtis GUYTON was the son of Gus Davis GUYTON (b. 3 Mar 1909 Sallis, Attala Co., MS, d. 8 Jul 1990 Cook Co., IL)[2751] and Ruth Lee (Ruthie) ROBY (b. 7 May 1916 Sallis, Attala Co., MS, d. 13 Jan 1996 Wauwatosa, Milwaukee Co., WI).[2752]

Curtis was born on 29 Jul 1937 in Sallis, Attala Co., MS, and his death is unknown.[2753] He married Hattie BANKS (b. Sallis, Attala Co., MS, d. Unknown).[2754] They had at least two children:[2755]

i   Hiram GUYTON (b. Chicago, Cook Co., IL).
ii   Karla GUYTON (b. Chicago, Cook Co., IL).

[2745] "Social Security Death Index," s.v. "Gus D. Guyton," (birth 3 Mar 1909, death 8 Jul 1990), *Ancestry.com*.
[2746] "Social Security Death Index," s.v. "Ruth Guyton," (birth 7 May 1916, death 13 Jan 1996), *Ancestry.com*.
[2747] Bernice Guyton, grave marker, Russell Cemetery, Attala Co., MS, digital image s.v. "Bernice Phillips," (birth 17 Jun 1935, death 14 Dec 2002), *FindaGrave.com*.
[2748] "Cook County, Illinois Marriage Index, 1930-1960," s.v. "Joseph L. Phillips," (marriage to Bernice Guyton on 29 Oct 1957).
[2749] Per Channie Brown-Currie.
[2750] chancurri originally shared this on 23 May 2013 on *Ancestry.com*.
[2751] "Social Security Death Index," s.v. "Gus D. Guyton," (birth 3 Mar 1909, death 8 Jul 1990), *Ancestry.com*.
[2752] "Social Security Death Index," s.v. "Ruth Guyton," (birth 7 May 1916, death 13 Jan 1996), *Ancestry.com*.
[2753] "U.S. Public Records Index, 1950-1993, Volume 1," s.v. "Curtis M. Guyton," (birth 29 Jul 1937), *Ancestry.com*.
[2754] Per Channie Brown-Currie.
[2755] Per Channie Brown-Currie.

Joan GUYTON (Gus Davis, Ike, Aaron Whitaker, Aaron Steele, Joseph I, John I, Samuel II, Samuel I, John)

Joan GUYTON was the daughter of Gus Davis GUYTON (b. 3 Mar 1909 Sallis, Attala Co., MS, d. 8 Jul 1990 Cook Co., IL)[2756] and Ruth Lee (Ruthie) ROBY (b. 7 May 1916 Sallis, Attala Co., MS, d. 13 Jan 1996 Wauwatosa, Milwaukee Co., WI).[2757]

Joan was born on 2 Jul 1939 Sallis, Attala Co., MS, and her death is unknown.[2758] She married Frederick CULPEPPER, Sr. (b. Sallis, Attala Co., MS, d. Unknown) on 17 May 1958 in Chicago, Cook Co., IL.[2759] They had at least three children:[2760]

i   Monica CULPEPPER (b. Chicago, Cook Co., IL, d. Unknown) m. Norman NITMAN (Unknown).
ii Adoratia CULPEPPER (b. Chicago, Cook Co., IL, d. Unknown) m. Kevin PURDY (Unknown).
iii Frederick CULPEPPER, Jr. (b. Chicago, Cook Co., IL, d. Unknown) m. Elain UNKNOWN (Unknown).

Arthur David (Buddy) GUYTON (Gus Davis, Ike, Aaron Whitaker, Aaron Steele, Joseph I, John I, Samuel II, Samuel I, John)

Arthur David (Buddy) GUYTON was the son of Gus Davis GUYTON (b. 3 Mar 1909 Sallis, Attala Co., MS, d. 8 Jul 1990 Cook Co., IL)[2761] and Ruth Lee (Ruthie) ROBY (b. 7 May 1916 Sallis, Attala Co., MS, d. 13 Jan 1996 Wauwatosa, Milwaukee Co., WI).[2762]

Buddy GUYTON was born on 30 Mar 1942 Sallis, Attala Co., MS, d. 19 Apr 2014 Maywood, Cook Co., IL.[2763] See Figure 422. He married Juanita FULLER (b. Sallis, Attala Co., MS, d. Unknown).[2764] They had at least four children:[2765]

i   Jerome GUYTON (b. Chicago, Cook Co., IL, d. Unknown).
ii Tammie GUYTON (b. Chicago, Cook Co., IL, d. Unknown).
iii Marketta GUYTON (b. Chicago, Cook Co., IL, d. Unknown).
iv Maurice GUYTON (b. Chicago, Cook Co., IL, d. Unknown).

[2756] "Social Security Death Index," s.v. "Gus D. Guyton," (birth 3 Mar 1909, death 8 Jul 1990), *Ancestry.com*.
[2757] "Social Security Death Index," s.v. "Ruth Guyton," (birth 7 May 1916, death 13 Jan 1996), *Ancestry.com*.
[2758] "U.S., Public Records Index, 1950-1993, Volume 1," s.v. "Joan Culpepper," (birth 2 Jul 1939), *Ancestry.com*.
[2759] "Cook County, Illinois Marriage Index, 1930-1960," s.v. "Fred Culpepper," (marriage 17 May 1958 to Joan Guyton), *Ancestry.com*.
[2760] Per Channie Brown-Currie.
[2761] "Social Security Death Index," s.v. "Gus D. Guyton," (birth 3 Mar 1909, death 8 Jul 1990), *Ancestry.com*.
[2762] "Social Security Death Index," s.v. "Ruth Guyton," (birth 7 May 1916, death 13 Jan 1996), *Ancestry.com*.
[2763] "Arthur David Guyton, grave marker, Oakridge-Glen Oak Cemetery, Hillside, Cook Co., IL, digital image s.v. "Arthur David Guyton," (birth 30 Mar 1942, death 19 Apr 2014), *FindaGrave.com*.
[2764] Per Channie Brown-Currie.
[2765] Per Channie Brown-Currie.

Figure 422 Buddy and Juanita FULLER GUYTON[2766]

Katherine RILEY GUYTON (Joe Frank, Ike, Aaron Whitaker, Aaron Steele, Joseph I, John I, Samuel II, Samuel I, John)

Katherine RILEY GUYTON was the daughter of Joe Frank GUYTON (b. 10 Sep 1912 in Sallis, Attala Co., MS, d. 23 Aug 1994 in Sallis, Attala Co., MS)[2767] and Mildred Irene WINGARD (b. 11 Mar 1917 MS, d. 17 Apr 2016 Chicago Heights, Cook Co., IL).[2768] Katherine may be the daughter of a man named RILEY. Katherine and her mother lived with Mildred's father in the 1940 U.S. Census. Mildred's last name was WINGARD; Katherine's was RILEY.

Katherine was born about 1938 in MS, and her death is unknown.[2769] She married Otis RUSH (Unknown) in Chicago on 30 Jun 1959.[2770] It is unlikely she married the famous Chicago Blues musician by that same name! The couple had four children:[2771]

i   Tony RUSH (b. Chicago, Cook Co., IL, d. Unknown).
ii   Rickey RUSH (b. Chicago, Cook Co., IL, d. Unknown).
iii Renetta RUSH (b. Chicago, Cook Co., IL, d. Unknown).
iv   Diane RUSH (b. Chicago, Cook Co., IL, d. Chicago, Cook Co., IL).

[2766] chancurri originally shared this on 23 Jun 2015 on *Ancestry.com*.
[2767] "Social Security Death Index," s.v. "Joe Guyton," (birth 10 Sep 1912, death 23 Aug 1994), *Ancestry.com*.
[2768] Mildred Irene Wingard, grave marker, Russell Cemetery, Attala Co., MS, digital image s.v. "Mildred Irene Guyton," (birth 11 Mar 1917, death 17 Apr 2016), *FindaGrave.com*.
[2769] "1940 United States Federal Census," Newport, Attala Co., MS, digital image s.v. "Catherine Riley," (birth ABT 1934), *Ancestry.com*.
[2770] "Cook County, Illinois Marriage Index, 1930-1960," s.v. "Katherine Guyton," (marriage to Otis Rush on 30 Jun 1959), *Ancestry.com*.
[2771] Per Channie Brown-Currie.

Doris Nell GUYTON (Joe Frank, Ike, Aaron Whitaker, Aaron Steele, Joseph I, John I, Samuel II, Samuel I, John)

Doris Nell GUYTON was the daughter of Joe Frank GUYTON (b. 10 Sep 1912 in Sallis, Attala Co., MS, d. 23 Aug 1994 in Sallis, Attala Co., MS)[2772] and Mildred Irene WINGARD (b. 11 Mar 1917 MS, d. 17 Apr 2016 Chicago Heights, Cook Co., IL).[2773]

Doris was born about 1946 in MS, and her death is unknown.[2774] At some point, she married Unknown THOMAS because she went by that last name in her father's obituary. She had three children who carried the Guyton surname:[2775]

i	Andrea GUYTON (b. Chicago, Cook Co., IL, d. Unknown).
ii	Dantae GUYTON (b. Chicago, Cook Co., IL, d. Unknown).
iii	Corey GUYTON (b. Chicago, Cook Co., IL, d. Unknown).

Leander (Lee) GUYTON (Joe Frank, Ike, Aaron Whitaker, Aaron Steele, Joseph I, John I, Samuel II, Samuel I, John)

Leander (Lee) GUYTON was the son of Joe Frank GUYTON (b. 10 Sep 1912 in Sallis, Attala Co., MS, d. 23 Aug 1994 in Sallis, Attala Co., MS)[2776] and Mildred Irene WINGARD (b. 11 Mar 1917 MS, d. 17 Apr 2016 Chicago Heights, Cook Co., IL).[2777]

Leander GUYTON was born on 6 Jun 1948 in MS, d. Unknown.[2778] He married Serita UNKNOWN (b. 9 Apr 1951, d. Unknown).[2779] They had at least two children:[2780]

i	Lavelle GUYTON (b. Chicago, Cook Co., IL, d. Unknown).
ii	Lee GUYTON, Jr. (b. Chicago, Cook Co., IL, d. Unknown).

[2772] "Social Security Death Index," s.v. "Joe Guyton," (birth 10 Sep 1912, death 23 Aug 1994), *Ancestry.com*.
[2773] Mildred Irene Wingard, grave marker, Russell Cemetery, Attala Co., MS, digital image s.v. "Mildred Irene Guyton," (birth 11 Mar 1917, death 17 Apr 2016), *FindaGrave.com*.
[2774] "1950 United States Federal Census," Newport, Attala Co., MS, digital image s.v. "Doris Guyton," (birth ABT 1946), *Ancestry.com*.
[2775] Per Channie Brown-Currie.
[2776] "Social Security Death Index," s.v. "Joe Guyton," (birth 10 Sep 1912, death 23 Aug 1994), *Ancestry.com*.
[2777] Mildred Irene Wingard, grave marker, Russell Cemetery, Attala Co., MS, digital image s.v. "Mildred Irene Guyton," (birth 11 Mar 1917, death 17 Apr 2016), *FindaGrave.com*.
[2778] "U.S. Public Records Index, 1950-1993, Volume 2," s.v. "Lee Guyton," (birth 6 Jun 1948), *Ancestry.com*.
[2779] "U.S. Public Records Index, 1950-1993, Volume 1," s.v. "Serita Guyton," (birth 9 Apr 1951), *Ancestry.com*.
[2780] Per Channie Brown-Currie.

Edwin GUYTON (Joe Frank, Ike, Aaron Whitaker, Aaron Steele, Joseph I, John I, Samuel II, Samuel I, John)

Edwin GUYTON was the son of Joe Frank GUYTON (b. 10 Sep 1912 in Sallis, Attala Co., MS, d. 23 Aug 1994 in Sallis, Attala Co., MS)[2781] and Mildred Irene WINGARD (b. 11 Mar 1917 MS, d. 17 Apr 2016 Chicago Heights, Cook Co., IL).[2782]

Edwin GUYTON was born on 3 Nov 1949 in Sallis, Attala Co., MS, and died on 4 Aug 2007 in Sallis, Attala Co., MS.[2783] He had two children by an unknown woman, per Channie BROWN-CURRIE:

i   Amy Lee TOLLIVER (b. Sallis, Attala Co., MS, d. Unknown).
ii Frederick TOLLIVER (b. Sallis, Attala Co., MS, d. Unknown).

Brenda Dell GUYTON (Joe Frank, Ike, Aaron Whitaker, Aaron Steele, Joseph I, John I, Samuel II, Samuel I, John)

Brenda Dell GUYTON was the twin daughter of Joe Frank GUYTON (b. 10 Sep 1912 in Sallis, Attala Co., MS, d. 23 Aug 1994 in Sallis, Attala Co., MS)[2784] and Mildred Irene WINGARD (b. 11 Mar 1917 MS, d. 17 Apr 2016 Chicago Heights, Cook Co., IL).[2785]

She was born on 13 Jan 1952 in Sallis, Attala Co., MS and died on 10 Oct 2019 Sallis, Attala Co., MS.[2786] Her twin was Linda Bell GUYTON. See Figure 424 and Figure 425. She married Charles (Charlie) William CARR (b. ABT 1938, d. ABT 2011).[2787] Brenda had five children:[2788]

i   Lawanda GUYTON-CARR (b. Sallis, Attala Co., MS, d. Unknown). Lawanda used both Guyton and Carr as her surname. She married Kevin Maurice HOWARD on 1 May 2004.[2789] She earned an accounting degree from the University of Southern Mississippi and worked as a tax accountant when she married. See Figure 423.
ii   Luther GUYTON (b. Sallis, Attala Co., MS, d. Unknown).
iii C.J. GUYTON (b. Kosciusko, Attala Co., MS, d. Unknown).
iv   Tony GUYTON (b. Kosciusko, Attala Co., MS, d. Unknown).
v   Jeremy GUYTON (b. Kosciusko, Attala Co., MS, d. Unknown).

[2781] "Social Security Death Index," s.v. "Joe Guyton," (birth 10 Sep 1912, death 23 Aug 1994), *Ancestry.com*.
[2782] Mildred Irene Wingard, grave marker, Russell Cemetery, Attala Co., MS, digital image s.v. "Mildred Irene Guyton," (birth 11 Mar 1917, death 17 Apr 2016), *FindaGrave.com*.
[2783] "Edwin Guyton, grave marker, Russell Cemetery, Sallis, Attala Co., MS, digital image s.v. "Edwin Guyton," (birth 3 Nov 1949, death 4 Aug 2007), *FindaGrave.com*.
[2784] "Social Security Death Index," s.v. "Joe Guyton," (birth 10 Sep 1912, death 23 Aug 1994), *Ancestry.com*.
[2785] Mildred Irene Wingard, grave marker, Russell Cemetery, Attala Co., MS, digital image s.v. "Mildred Irene Guyton," (birth 11 Mar 1917, death 17 Apr 2016), *FindaGrave.com*.
[2786] "Brenda Dell Guyton, grave marker, Russell Cemetery, Sallis, Attala Co., MS, digital image s.v. "Brenda Dell Carr," (birth 13 Jan 1952, death 10 Oct 2019), *FindaGrave.com*.
[2787] Death per Channie Brown Currie's *Ancestry.com* tree. "1950 United States Federal Census," Humphreys Co., MS, digital image s.v. "Charlie W. Carr," (birth ABT 1938), *Ancestry.com*.
[2788] Per Channie Brown-Currie.
[2789] "Guyton-Howard Vows Set in May," *The Star-Herald*," Kosciusko, MS, Thu, 18 Mar 2004, p. 20, digital image s.v. "Lawanda Michelle Guyton," (marriage set for 1 May 2004).

Figure 423 Lawanda GUYTON and Kevin HOWARD Engagement Photo

Figure 424 Brenda Dell GUYTON CARR[2790]

Figure 425 Linda Bell GUYTON[2791]

Linda Bell GUYTON (Joe Frank, Ike, Aaron Whitaker, Aaron Steele, Joseph I, John I, Samuel II, Samuel I, John)

Linda Bell GUYTON was the twin daughter of Joe Frank GUYTON (b. 10 Sep 1912 in Sallis, Attala Co., MS, d. 23 Aug 1994 in Sallis, Attala Co., MS)[2792] and Mildred Irene WINGARD (b. 11 Mar 1917 MS, d. 17 Apr 2016 Chicago Heights, Cook Co., IL).[2793]

Linda was born on 13 Jan 1952 in Sallis, Attala Co., MS and died on 13 Apr 2002 Sallis, Attala Co., MS).[2794] See Figure 424 and Figure 425. Her twin sister was Brenda Dell GUYTON. Linda had one child:[2795]

i   Stephanie GUYTON (b. Sallis, Attala Co., MS, d. Unknown).

Bonnie GUYTON (Joe Frank, Ike, Aaron Whitaker, Aaron Steele, Joseph I, John I, Samuel II, Samuel I, John)

Bonnie GUYTON was the daughter of Joe Frank GUYTON (b. 10 Sep 1912 in Sallis, Attala Co., MS, d. 23 Aug 1994 in Sallis, Attala Co., MS)[2796] and Mildred Irene WINGARD (b. 11 Mar 1917 MS, d. 17 Apr 2016 Chicago Heights, Cook Co., IL).[2797]

Bonnie was born after the 1950 U.S. Census in Sallis, Attala Co., MS[2798] and her death is unknown. She married Nathaniel WILDER (Unknown). Bonnie had four children, who go by the Guyton surname:[2799]

[2790] chancurri originally shared this on 23 May 2013 on *Ancestry.com*.
[2791] chancurri originally shared this on 23 May 2013 on *Ancestry.com*.
[2792] "Social Security Death Index," s.v. "Joe Guyton," (birth 10 Sep 1912, death 23 Aug 1994), *Ancestry.com*.
[2793] Mildred Irene Wingard, grave marker, Russell Cemetery, Attala Co., MS, digital image s.v. "Mildred Irene Guyton," (birth 11 Mar 1917, death 17 Apr 2016), *FindaGrave.com*.
[2794] "Linda Bell Guyton, grave marker, Russell Cemetery, Sallis, Attala Co., MS, digital image s.v. "Brenda Dell Carr," (birth 13 Jan 1952, death 13 Apr 2002), *FindaGrave.com*.
[2795] Per Channie Brown-Currie.
[2796] "Social Security Death Index," s.v. "Joe Guyton," (birth 10 Sep 1912, death 23 Aug 1994), *Ancestry.com*.
[2797] Mildred Irene Wingard, grave marker, Russell Cemetery, Attala Co., MS, digital image s.v. "Mildred Irene Guyton," (birth 11 Mar 1917, death 17 Apr 2016), *FindaGrave.com*.
[2798] Per Channie Brown-Currie.
[2799] Per Channie Brown-Currie.

i	Sherrie GUYTON (b. Sallis, Attala Co., MS, d. Unknown) m. Christopher ARCHER (b. Sallis, Attala Co., MS, d. Unknown).
ii	Jada GUYTON (b. Kosciusko, Attala Co., MS, d. Unknown).
iii	Trevon GUYTON (b. Kosciusko, Attala Co., MS, d. Unknown).
iv	Nathan GUYTON (b. Kosciusko, Attala Co., MS, d. Unknown).

Sarah GUYTON (Joe Frank, Ike, Aaron Whitaker, Aaron Steele, Joseph I, John I, Samuel II, Samuel I, John)

Sarah GUYTON was the daughter of Joe Frank GUYTON (b. 10 Sep 1912 in Sallis, Attala Co., MS, d. 23 Aug 1994 in Sallis, Attala Co., MS)[2800] and Mildred Irene WINGARD (b. 11 Mar 1917 MS, d. 17 Apr 2016 Chicago Heights, Cook Co., IL).[2801]

Sarah GUYTON was born sometime after the 1950 U.S. Census. She has one child:[2802]

i	Shawana GUYTON (b. Chicago, Cook Co., IL, d. Unknown).

Willie Edward EVANS (Annie GUYTON EVANS, Ike, Aaron Whitaker, Aaron Steele, Joseph I, John I, Samuel II, Samuel I, John)

Willie Edward EVANS was the son of Annie Frances GUYTON (b. 28 Feb 1916 Kosciusko, Attala Co., MS, d. 17 Oct 1995 in Chicago, Cook Co., IL)[2803] and Allen Leroy (Gipp) EVANS, Sr. (b. 29 Dec 1912 Sallis, Attala Co., MS, d. Jun 1972 Chicago, Cook Co., IL).[2804]

Willie was born on 16 Jan 1933 in Sallis, Attala Co., MS, and died on 15 May 1995 in Chicago, Cook Co., IL).[2805] See Figure 426. His wife's name is unknown. They had at least eleven children:[2806]

i	Mark EVANS, Sr. (b. Chicago, Cook Co., IL, d. Unknown) m. Angel UNKNOWN.
ii	Emma Jean EVANS (b. Chicago, Cook Co., IL, d. Unknown).
iii	Emma Lean EVANS (b. Chicago, Cook Co., IL, d. Unknown).
iv	Dorothy EVANS (b. Sallis, Attala Co., MS, d. Unknown).
v	Rev. Alvin EVANS (b. Chicago, Cook Co., IL, d. Unknown).
vi	Jerry EVANS (b. Chicago, Cook Co., IL, d. Unknown).
vii	Betty EVANS (b. Chicago, Cook Co., IL, d. Unknown).
viii	Ricky EVANS (b. Chicago, Cook Co., IL, d. Unknown).
ix	Willie Earl EVANS (b. Chicago, Cook Co., IL, d. Unknown).
x	Willie Claude EVANS (b. Chicago, Cook Co., IL, d. Unknown).
xi	James EVANS (b. Chicago, Cook Co., IL, d. Unknown).

[2800] "Social Security Death Index," s.v. "Joe Guyton," (birth 10 Sep 1912, death 23 Aug 1994), *Ancestry.com*.
[2801] Mildred Irene Wingard, grave marker, Russell Cemetery, Attala Co., MS, digital image s.v. "Mildred Irene Guyton," (birth 11 Mar 1917, death 17 Apr 2016), *FindaGrave.com*.
[2802] Per Channie Brown-Currie.
[2803] "Social Security Death Index," s.v. "Annie Evans," (birth 28 Feb 1916, death 17 Oct 1995), *Ancestry.com*.
[2804] Allen Leroy Evans, Sr., grave marker, Restvale Cemetery, Alsip, Cook Co., IL, digital image s.v. "Allen Leroy Evans," (birth 29 Dec 1912, death 14 Jun 1972), *FindaGrave.com*.
[2805] Willie Edward Evans, grave marker, Lakewood Memorial Park, Elgin, Cook Co., IL, digital image s.v. "Willie Edward Evans," (birth 16 Jan 1933, death 3 May 1995), *FindaGrave.com*.
[2806] Per Channie Brown-Currie.

Figure 426 Willie Edwards EVANS[2807]

Terry Leroy EVANS (Annie GUYTON EVANS, Ike, Aaron Whitaker, Aaron Steele, Joseph I, John I, Samuel II, Samuel I, John)

Terry Leroy EVANS was the son of Annie Frances GUYTON (b. 28 Feb 1916 Kosciusko, Attala Co., MS, d. 17 Oct 1995 in Chicago, Cook Co., IL).[2808] and Allen Leroy (Gipp) EVANS, Sr. (b. 29 Dec 1912 Sallis, Attala Co., MS, d. Jun 1972 Chicago, Cook Co., IL).[2809]

Terry was born on 27 Oct 1935 in Sallis, Attala Co., MS, and died on 3 Aug 1996 in Elgin, Kane Co., IL.[2810] See Figure 427. He married Ozella (Sugar Baby) WILLIAMS (b. TN, d. Unknown).[2811] They had at least six children:

i	Sheron EVANS (b. 11 Nov. 1964 Elgin, Cook Co., IL, d. Unknown) m. Unknown WILLIAMS (Unknown).
ii	Cynthia EVANS (b. 7 Apr 1968 Elgin, Cook Co., IL, d. Unknown) m. Unknown SPATES (Unknown).
iii	Terri EVANS (b. 23 Sep 1969 Elgin, Cook Co., IL, d. Unknown) m. Sheldon SMITH (Unknown).
iv	Demitri EVANS (b. 22 May 1973 Elgin, Cook Co., IL, d. Unknown).
v	Diane EVANS (b. Sallis, Attala Co., IL, d. Unknown) m. Willie BENTLEY (Unknown).
vi	Makeya EVANS (b. 1 May 1979 Elgin, Cook Co., IL, d. Unknown).

[2807] chancurri originally shared this on 23 May 2013 on *Ancestry.com*.
[2808] "Social Security Death Index," s.v. "Annie Evans," (birth 28 Feb 1916, death 17 Oct 1995), *Ancestry.com*.
[2809] Allen Leroy Evans, Sr., grave marker, Restvale Cemetery, Alsip, Cook Co., IL, digital image s.v. "Allen Leroy Evans," (birth 29 Dec 1912, death 14 Jun 1972), *FindaGrave.com*.
[2810] Terry Leroy Evans, grave marker, Lakewood Memorial Park, Elgin, Cook Co., IL, digital image s.v. "Terry Evans," (birth 27 Oct 1935, death 3 Aug 1996), *FindaGrave.com*.
[2811] Per Channie Brown-Currie.

Figure 427 Terry Leroy EVANS[2812]

Gloria Jean EVANS (Annie GUYTON EVANS, Ike, Aaron Whitaker, Aaron Steele, Joseph I, John I, Samuel II, Samuel I, John)

Gloria Jean EVANS was the daughter of Annie Frances GUYTON (b. 28 Feb 1916 Kosciusko, Attala Co., MS, d. 17 Oct 1995 in Chicago, Cook Co., IL).[2813] and Allen Leroy (Gipp) EVANS, Sr. (b. 29 Dec 1912 Sallis, Attala Co., MS, d. Jun 1972 Chicago, Cook Co., IL).[2814] See Figure 428.

Gloria was born on 4 Jan 1947 in Sallis, Attala Co., MS, d. 26 Jun 2014 Chicago, Cook Co., IL).[2815] She had two children:[2816]

i   Kesha EVANS (b. 20 Jan 1965 Chicago, Cook Co., IL, d. 19 Sep 1996 Chicago, Cook Co., IL) m. Andre WILSON (Unknown) on 23 Dec 1965 in Chicago.
ii   LaToya EVANS (Unknown).

Figure 428 Gloria Jean EVANS[2817]

[2812] chancurri originally shared this on 6 Dec 2014 on *Ancestry.com*.
[2813] "Social Security Death Index," s.v. "Annie Evans," (birth 28 Feb 1916, death 17 Oct 1995), *Ancestry.com*.
[2814] Allen Leroy Evans, Sr., grave marker, Restvale Cemetery, Alsip, Cook Co., IL, digital image s.v. "Allen Leroy Evans," (birth 29 Dec 1912, death 14 Jun 1972), *FindaGrave.com*.
[2815] "U.S. Public Records Index, 1950-1993, Volume 1," s.v. "Gloria J Evans," (birth 4 Jan 1947), *Ancestry.com*. Channie Brown-Currie, "Descendants of Artie Rainey and Aaron W. Guyton," 2017 Guyton Family Reunion, (death 26 Jun 2014).
[2816] Per Channie Brown-Currie.
[2817] chancurri originally shared this on 23 May 2013 on *Ancestry.com*.

Bonnie WEBB (Alice GUYTON WEBB, Ike, Aaron Whitaker, Aaron Steele, Joseph I, John I, Samuel II, Samuel I, John)

Bonnie WEBB was the daughter of Alice Lee GUYTON (b. 10 May 1924 Sallis, Attala Co., MS, d. 11 Feb 1992 in Chicago, Cook Co., IL)[2818] and Oliver DeBois WEBB (b. 3 Aug 1912 Greenville, SC, d. 16 Jan 1992).[2819]

Bonnie was born on 27 Oct 1948 in Chicago, Cook Co., IL, d. Unknown.[2820] She married James Lee NORTH, Sr. (b. 27 Oct 1931 Nashville, Davidson Co., TN, d. 17 Apr 2008 Lansing, Cook Co., IL).[2821] Bonnie had at least two children with Unknown JENKINS (Unknown):[2822]

i   Kenya JENKINS (b. 16 May 1978 Chicago, Cook Co., IL, d. Unknown)[2823] m. James WRIGHT (b. Chicago, Cook Co., IL , d. Unknown).

ii   Kimberly JENKINS (b. 5 Jul 1980 Chicago, Cook Co., IL, d. Unknown).[2824]

[2818] "Social Security Death Index," s.v. "Alice Webb," (birth 10 May 1924, death 11 Feb 1992), *Ancestry.com*.
[2819] Oliver DeBois Webb, grave marker, Oakland Memory Lanes, Dolton, Cook Co., IL, digital image s.v. "Oliver Debois Webb," (birth 3 Aug 1912, death 16 Jan 1992), *FindaGrave.com*.
[2820] "1950 United States Federal Census," Chicago, Cook Co., IL, digital image s.v. "Barney Webb," (birth ABT 1949), *Ancestry.com*.
[2821] Marriage per Channie Brown Currie.
[2822] Per Channie Brown-Currie.
[2823] Per Channie Brown-Currie.
[2824] Per Channie Brown-Currie.

CHILD OF AARON WHITAKER GUYTON AND ARTIE RAINEY: BABY JAMES

Generation #7

James (Baby James) GUYTON (Aaron Whitaker, Aaron Steele, Joseph I, John I, Samuel II, Samuel I, John)

James (Baby James) GUYTON was the son of Aaron Whitaker GUYTON and Artemesia (Artie) RAINEY. He was born about 1880 in Kosciusko, Beat 4, Attala Co., MS, and died about 1882 Sallis, Attala Co., MS) from drowning.[2825]

[2825] Per Channie Brown-Currie.

INDEX

A.D. Murphy Plantation, 114, 115
ADAMS
   Catherine, 17, 30
   Katran, 30
AFRICA, 65
   Ghana, 241, 266
AGEE
   James, 117
   Vernice, 117
AGNEW
   Unknown, 325
AIKENS
   Frederick, 132
   Ira G., 132
AKIN
   Mrs. Ernest, 83
ALABAMA, 33, 40, 61, 63, 98, 100, 101, 103, 105, 106
   Birmingham, 112
   Elmore Co., 360
   Ethelsville, 33, 60
   Fayette Co., 60
   Greene Co., 53
   Lamar Co., 61
   Marion Co., 52
   Montgomery, 117, 140
   Montgomery Co., 117, 140
   Pickens Co., 33, 40, 50, 52, 53, 54, 60, 61, 65
   Wetumpka, 360
Alabama State Legislature, 60, 63
ALCORN
   James L., 381
Alcorn State University, 381
ALFRED
   Alexander Paul, 222
   Genet, 222
   Paul Wilton, 222
ALLEN
   Addison D., 155, 168, 170, 179, 181, 183
   Anna Louise, 183
   Asher, 169
   Buster Brown Clinton, 168, 169
   Clara F., 168, 169
   Daisy J., 135
   Dentonio, 320
   Dorothy May, 183
   Edna Alma, 168, 169
   Emma, 154, 155, 168, 179, 181, 183
   Ethel S., 168, 169, 181, 182
   Fred, 183
   Iola E., 168, 169
   Joe Frank, 353
   Johnnie, 135
   Johnnie Amzy, 168, 169
   Judy Kate, 123, 150, 151
   Martha, 168
   Nola J., 168, 169, 179, 180, 219
   Otha B., 168, 169
   Pearline, 371, 373
   Stella E., 168, 169
   Unknown, 338, 353
   Willie Mae, 183
   Willie Walter, 168, 169, 183
ANDERSON
   Arthur Lee, II, 402
   Dorothy, 402
   Dorothy Jean, 402
   Dorothy Nell, 402
   Frances Virginia, 60, 63
   Inez, 390, 391, 398, 401, 402
   Laura L., 402
   Leon, 391, 402
   Rufus King, 61, 63
   Sallye, 402
ANTHONY
   Dorothy J., 235
   Henrietta, 120
   Unknown, 235
ARCHER

Christopher, 440
Sherrie, 440
ARIZONA
   Maricopa Co., 290, 291, 307, 310, 392, 403
   Peoria, 291, 310
   Sun City, 290, 310
   Sun City West, 307
   Surprise, 392, 403
ARKANSAS, 104, 124, 349
   Marked Tree, 190, 225
   Monticello, 112
   Phillips, 328, 330
   Poinsett Co., 190, 225
   St. Francis Co., 65
ARNOLD
   Ethel S., 168, 169, 181, 182
   Jimmy Dale, 181, 182
   Leroy, Jr., 181, 182
   Leroy, Sr., 169, 181, 182
   Mabel (Maybell), 181, 182
   Myrtis, 181, 182
   Otho James, 181, 182
   Robert L., 181, 182
   Willis C., 181, 182
ASHFORD
   Evan, 67, 69, 71, 72, 76, 375
ASHMORE
   John D., 49
ATKINSON
   Eugenia, 83
AUSTIN
   Annie F., 358
   Unknown, 358
BALDWIN
   Patricia Ruth, 308
BALL
   Rhonda Larita, 270, 271
   Richard, 244, 271
BALLARD
   C.A., 80
BANKHEAD
   Luvenia N., 52
BANKS
   Hattie, 421, 434
BARBADOS, 31
BARNES
   Robert, 261
BARRETT
   Lucille, 341, 361, 363
BART
   Allen, 71, 153, 285
BARTON
   Luria, 108, 129, 130
   Willie D., 108, 130
Battle of Blackstocks, 47
Battle of Cowpens, 38, 47, 50
Battle of Eutaw Springs, 47, 50
Battle of Kings Mountain, 38
Battle of Purrysburg, 47
Battle of Williamson's Plantation, 47
Battle of Wofford's Iron Works, 47
BEAMON
   Albert, 186, 347
   Callie, 286, 294, 316, 317
   Lovell, 186, 346, 347
BEASLEY
   Shaleese Eugenia, 259
BELL
   Charles, 79
   Clarence M., 360
   Fannie Louise, 341, 358, 359, 360, 363
   Frederick Douglas, 360
   James, 360
   Lynn A., 360
   Martha Elizabeth, 360
   Ollie, III, 359, 360
   Ollie, Jr., 341, 359, 360, 363
   R.J., 79
BENTLEY
   Diane, 441
   Willie, 441
BERKLEY
   William, 23
BLACKMAN
   Ocelee, 116, 138
BOATMAN
   Mae D. or Mary or Mardell, 202, 203

BODDEN
 Louella, 222
BOOKER
 Amar, 273
BOONE
 Cheryl Penny, 277
 Jerry, 277
 Kyler, 277
BOTTOM
 Marvin, 300
 Sarah Lee, 300
Bottom Road, 27
Bounty Land Warrant, 50
BOYD
 Carmelita Sabrina, 244, 269, 270, 271
 Cherry, 244
 Cherylease M., 273
 Felicia Cabrini, 244, 269
 Icy Viola, 76, 243, 244, 267, 269, 271, 273
 KaDen, 272
 Kamiyah, 272
 Karl Glenn, v, 1, 76, 77, 153, 156, 160, 163, 205, 207, 243, 244, 246, 248, 249, 250, 253, 255, 267, 268, 269, 270, 273, 275, 280, 281, 284
 Kenyon J., 272
 Khankham (Candy), 273
 Lakeisha, 272
 Lakia Icy, 272
 LaTonya Cheri, 273
 Marcy L., 273
 Princess Monica, 244
 Rhonda Larita, 270, 271
 Rosalind Lavon, 244
 Tabatha, 273
 Thornton, Jr., 244, 273, 275
 Thornton, Sr., 243, 267, 269, 271, 273
 Tony, 273
 Tracy, 273
BOYETT
 Eula, 97, 102
 Eva, 102
BRATTON
 Thomas, 47

BRAY
 Unknown, 403
 Yalonda, 403
BRAZELL, 115
BREEDLOVE
 Ann, 160, 163
British Navy, 40
BROOKS
 Shannon, 224
BROWN
 Aaron, 262
 Abeni, 262
 Agnes, 293
 Alfred, 357
 Andrew, 330
 Angelo, 262
 Antney Wesley, 412, 415, 417, 431, 432
 Bobbie Joe, 355, 356
 Channie, v, 1, 68, 146, 187, 336, 341, 355, 358, 363, 365, 366, 385, 388, 389, 416, 417, 426, 432, 433
 Charles Willie, 415, 416, 417, 431
 Connie Mae, 357
 Ella, 79
 Emma, 415, 416, 417, 432
 Essie Dee, 341, 356, 357, 364, 365, 366
 Estelle, 180, 219
 Etta, 337, 340, 341, 355, 356, 358, 359, 360, 363, 364, 365, 366, 367
 Eula Mae, 417, 431
 Eva, 415, 416, 417
 Harry, 262
 Haywood Larence, Dr., 356
 Isadora, 409, 412, 415, 417, 431, 432
 J.A., 79
 Jessie, 219
 Khari, 262
 Letha, 328, 330
 Lon T. (L.T.), 357
 Marceline Audrey, 314
 Odester W., 357
 Reuben Evariste, 314
 Rollege Newell (Rollie), 341, 356, 357, 364, 365, 366

Sheila, 241, 264
Shelay Mae, 416, 417
Tiffany, 262
Unknown, 240, 241, 264, 328, 330
Vera M., 357
Wilhelmina, 291, 311
Willie D. (W.D.), 357
Zenobia, 240, 262

BRUTON
Frances Virginia, 60, 63

BUCHANAN
Jeffrey Wayne, 244, 272
Rhonda Larita, 270, 271

BURDINE
Mary Elizabeth, 60

BURNS
Jessica, 327

BURNSIDE
Anthony, 145
Bernice Marie, 101, 120, 144, 145, 386
Charles, 145
Curtis Lee, 120, 135, 144, 145
Mary, 135
Willie, 145

BURT
A.C., 296
Adeline Susannah, 286, 295, 296, 319, 320
Alexis, 405
Alice Edna, 395, 407
Bob Green, 296
Carolyn, 395, 405
Charles, 406
Charles Edward, 395, 405
Charleston, 405
Chassie, 405
Clara, 296
Clinton L., 296
Douglas, 143
Edward Fletcher (Shine), 389, 394, 404, 405, 406, 407
Erma Jean, 394, 395, 406
Fannie, 395, 406
Florence Sarah, 401

Geneva, 296, 319, 320, 341, 358
George Allen, 143
Irma Jean, 119, 143
Isaac, 320
Ivery, Jr., 296
Ivery, Sr., 286, 295, 296, 319, 320
James A., 296
James Earl, 320
Jodie Mae, 296, 319
Julia, 296, 320
Lily Mae, 344
Linda, 320
Lisa Alesia, 320
Marcus, 405
Mary, 96, 98, 99, 107, 110, 111, 117, 118
Pamela, 405
Percy Earl, 401
R.C., 296, 320
Richard, 143
Robbie, 404
Robbie Lee, 388, 389, 394, 405, 406, 407
Rosie, 296
Sheron, 320
Terrance, 143
Tonia, 406
Unknown, 119, 143, 337, 343
Walter Mack, 296
Zelma, 337, 342, 343

BUSH
Mabel (Maybell), 181, 182
William Samuel, 182

BUTLER
Eugene, 332
Ruth Mae, 180
Yvonne, 331, 332

BYNDOM
Crystal, 259

CALIFORNIA
Alameda, 338, 349
Alameda City, 314
Alameda Co., 305, 314
Contra Costa Co., 178, 338, 349
Hayward, 305
Los Angeles, 90, 290, 309, 344, 351

Los Angeles Co., 290, 309, 338, 349
Richmond, 178, 350
San Francisco Co., 140
San Joaquin Co., 314
San Jose, 293, 313
San Mateo Co., 314, 326
Santa Clara, 293, 313

CALVIN
John, 3, 433
Susie, 433
Unknown, 225

Camden District Regiment, 47

CAMPBELL
Carmelita Sabrina, 269, 270
Caroline, 366
Ericka, 270
Ja'Niyah, 270
Jaida, 270
James, 270
Jonte, Jr., 270
Jonte, Sr., 270
Kevin (Kippie), 270
Unknown, 366

CARR
Brenda Dell, 423, 438
Charles (Charlie) William, 423, 438
Emma, 286, 289, 306, 307, 309, 310, 311, 312
Lawanda, 438
Mary Lovey Zinkey, 286, 294

CARTER
Glenn James, 242
Lois, 197
Theresa, 242

CARTMAN
Ellenore Shirley, 365

CAVITT
Dorothy, 291, 311

Cedar Grove M.B. Church, 350
Cedar Grove Negro Public School, 82

CEMETERIES
Bullock Cemetery, 83, 295, 319, 320
Coleman Cemetery, 80
Dear Cemetery, 80
Detroit Memorial Park Cemetery, 361
Ellington Cemetery, 64, 83
Elmwood Cemetery, 331
Enid Cemetery, 298
Ethel Cemetery, 79
Fort Hill Cemetery, 46
Ft. Custer National Cemetery, 306
Georgia Veterans Memorial Cemetery, 151
Guyton Cemetery, 19, 20, 32, 33, 40
Harmon Cemetery, 83
Hill Springs Cemetery, 83, 337, 340, 355, 356, 358, 359, 360, 363, 364, 365, 366, 367
Isaacs Cemetery, 80
John Smith Cemetery, 33
Kosciusko City Cemetery, 355
Mallett Cemetery, 83, 150, 160
Martin Cemetery, 33, 60, 61
McMillan Cemetery, 80
Nash Cemetery, 83
Parker Cemetery, 33
Parkway Cemetery, 343
Roby Cemetery, 83
Russell Cemetery, 83, 87, 96, 98, 100, 102, 118, 119, 328, 333, 382, 385, 387
Sallis Cemetery, 83
Shelley Cemetery, 305
Shelley Cemetery 1, 83
Shelley Cemetery 2, 83
Stonewall Cemetery, 79
Sunset Memorial Lawns, 340
Wood National Cemetery, 228
Woodlawn Cemetery, 142
Wright Cemetery, 155, 177, 236

Central Mississippi College, 375

CHAIRES
Al Damontae, 272
Triniti Belle, 272

CHAPMAN
Josephine Doris, 307

Charles I, 13
Chicago Race Riot of 1919, 91

CHILDRESS

    James C., 34, 63
    Sarah, 34, 63
CHOI
    Sarah, 244, 273
    Victoria Isabella, 273
Church of England, 13
Church of England in Maryland, 28
Civil War, 54, 55
CLAIBORNE
    Mildred, 341, 361
CLAITOR, 79
    W.S., 79
CLARK
    Emma Kate, 300
    John Paul, 300
    Lula M., 201
    Mable Ethel, 173, 175, 208
    Thomas Eugene (Uncle Bud), Sr., 175, 208
    Thomas Eugene, Jr., 210
CLAYTON
    Betty Janell, 176, 215
    Emma Evester, 176, 211, 212
    John Wesley, 176, 211, 215
COFFEE
    Shirley, 194, 236
    Unknown, 236
COLE
    Nancy, 32, 46, 47
COLEMAN
    Dorla, 53, 163
    Leroy, 104
    Samuel, 80
COLLIER
    Catherine, 47
COLLINS
    J.S., 79
Commodity Program, 115
CONNECTICUT
    New London, 432
    New London Co., 432
CONWAY
    Alice, 112
    Alvin, 138
    Charles, 116
    Daniel, 140
    Earl, 112, 116
    Ethel Lavelle, 112, 116, 136
    Frenetter, 117, 140
    James, 112, 113
    James Welmer, Jr., 140
    James Welmer, Sr., 117, 139
    Jerry Leon, 140
    Katie Mae, 116, 139
    Lenard, 112, 115, 116, 137, 138
    Leon, 116
    Lucy, 112
    Lucy, 284
    Major Alvin, 111, 112, 113, 115, 116, 136, 137, 138, 139, 140
    Major, Sr., 111
    Mary Eugenia, 112, 116
    Melinda, 111, 112
    Nealie Eugene, 92, 98, 99, 111, 112, 116, 136, 137, 138, 139
    Ocelee, 116, 138
    Ollie, 112, 117
    Porter, 112
    Richard, 112
    Ruth Elizabeth, 112, 116, 117
    Sally, 112
    Vernice, 112, 117
    William Major Alvin, 116
    William Major, Jr., 111, 112, 113, 115, 116, 136, 137, 138, 139, 140
    William Major, Sr., 99, 111, 136, 137, 138, 139
    Willie, 112, 117
    Willie, 112
    Willie M., 112
COOK
    Gertrude, 124
    Julius, 124
    Julius D., 104, 124
    Ruth G., 103, 104, 124
COOPERWOOD
    Linda, 320
    Unknown, 320
CORNWALLIS

Lord, 47
CORRETHERS
　Julia, 296, 320
CORTEZ
　Travis, 272
COTTON
　Diana, 238
　Justin Simmons, 238
　Unknown, 238
CRANE
　Gertrude, 104, 124, 151
CROSS
　Faye, 146
　Ira Mae, 109, 132
　June, 146
　Kate Emma, 232
　Marie, 146
　Richard V., 232
　Unknown, 123, 146
　Velma Ruth, 123, 146, 150
CULPEPPER
　Adoratia, 435
　Alice, 230
　Annette, 231
　Barbara Ruth, 230, 257
　Betsy L., 231
　Darlene, 231
　David, 257
　Denise, 257
　Earl, 229
　Edward L. (Eddie), 230, 257
　Elain, 435
　Frederick, Jr., 435
　Frederick, Sr., 421, 435
　George Lewis, Jr., 231
　George Louis, 194, 229, 230, 257
　Gwenne, 257
　Jerry L., 231
　Joan, 419, 421, 435
　Katie K., 193, 194, 232
　Linda M., 231
　Martin L., 229, 230
　Mary Jean, 231
　Monica, 435
　Rubell (Ruby) Bonita, 193, 194, 229, 230, 257
　Ruby, 231
　Terry, 230
　Willy J., 229, 230
CURRIE
　Channie, v, 1, 68, 146, 187, 336, 341, 355, 358, 363, 365, 366, 385, 388, 389, 416, 417, 426, 432, 433
　Felicia Michelle, 432
　Kenyette, 432
　Stanley Neal, Jr., 432
　Stanley Neal, Sr., 417, 432
CURTIS
　Ethel Viola, 287, 301, 334
DAVIS
　Bertha Marie, 180
　Felicia, 241, 265
　Unknown, 241, 265
DAWSON
　Chico, 260
　Darius, 260
　Dejanae, 260
　DeVonte, 260
DELANEY
　Adrian, 260
　Brandy, 260
　Byron, Jr., 260
　Byron, Sr., 260
　Callie Jean, 197
　Darlene, 240, 260
　James, 260
　James Edward, Sr., 240, 260
　Jim, 197
　Nadia, 260
　Serina, 260
　Shenise, 260
　Sheyenne, 260
　Sierra, 260
DENNIS
　Christina Marie, 327
　Unknown, 325
Detroit Riot of 1943, 91
DEVORE

Myrtle Vivian, 313
DILLARD
   Annie Catherine, 355
   James A., 355
DOTSON
   Danny, 150
   Diane, 150
   Ernest, 149
   Ernie Vedel, 150
   Esther, 150
   Evell, 123, 149
   Jerome, 123
   Johnnie Lavelle, 123
   Ruby, 150
   Stellie Rose, 123, 149, 150
   Tina, 123
   Unknown, 123
DOUGLAS
   Unknown, 324
DUCKWORTH
   Hester, 48
   Sarah Matilda (Sally), 49
DUNSON
   Britteny L., 278
   Isaac L., 278
   Mary Jean, 231
   Sandy D., 278
   Unknown, 231
DURHAM
   Odell (Pink), 153, 160, 171, 172
   Unknown, 172
DUTCH REPUBLIC, 4
Dutch Revolt, 4
DYE
   Amey, 20, 21
Edict of Fontainebleau, 4
Edict of Nantes, 3, 4
Edict of Tolerance, 4
EDWARD
   Ernest, 132
   Ira Mae, 132
   Ivery L. (Ive), 107
   Mary Emma, 128
   Ruth Griffin, 132

   Ulysses (Julious), 130
EDWARDS
   Betty Mae, 109
   Carol, 132
   Della, 107, 108
   E.J., 132
   Effie, 107, 108, 129
   Emma Jane, 132
   Ernest, 107, 109, 131, 132
   Ernestine, 133
   Estella (Stella), 107
   Fannie, 107, 132
   Frances M. (Fannie), 131
   Geneva, 131
   Grace Ora, 108, 128
   Ira G., 132
   Ira Mae, 109, 132
   Ivery L. (Ive), 107
   James, 133
   James R. (Jim), 99, 107, 128, 129, 130, 131
   Jimmie Kyles, 132
   John H., 107
   Johnnie C., 131
   Kile King, 109
   Linda J., 132
   Loni, 107, 109
   Lucious James (L.J.), 132
   Luegene, 108, 130
   Luria, 107, 108, 129, 130
   Malina, 107
   Mark, 132
   Mary Emma, 98, 99, 107, 129, 130, 131
   Mary Lou, 130
   Minda Lou (Malina), 109
   Minnie L., 107, 109
   Pearlie M., 107, 131
   Rosa (Rosie), 107
   Ruth Griffin, 109, 132
   Stella, 107
   Thomas (Tommie), 107
   Ulysses (Julious), 107, 108, 130
   Unknown, 136
   Vickie Lynn, 136

Walter, 107, 109
Wiley W., 131
Will E., 132
Willie, 107
Willie D., 131
Willie H., 107, 108, 128
Willie Ray, 130
Elizabeth I, 4
ELKIN
   F.A., 79
ELLINGTON
   Bird, 336, 340
   Duke, 90
   Vina (Vinnie), 336, 340
ELLIS
   Annie Bell, 328, 329, 331, 409
   Earnest, 329
   Harvey, 328, 329, 331
   Letha, 329
   M.L., 344
   Mable, 329, 331, 332
   Martha Patsy, 33, 52
   Patsy, 33
   Tillie Mae, 344
   Tommie, Sr., 344
ELLISON
   Emma, 290
ENGLAND, 4, 6, 13, 31
   Essex, 3
   Gayton, 2, 5
   Norfolk Co., 13
   Norwich Castle, 7
   Norwich Cathedral, 7, 11
   Norwich, Norfolk Co., 4, 5, 6, 7, 8, 9, 11, 12, 13, 14, 15, 16, 17, 18, 19, 20, 30
   Trowse, Norfolk Co., 12, 15, 16
EPPS
   Fannie Mae, 319
ERVIN
   Katherine, 393, 396
   Leroy, 396
ESTERS
   Fannie Mae, 117, 142
   Lamar, 142
   Leport, 117, 142
   Sarah L., 142
ESTES
   Neria C., 289, 303, 305
EVANS
   Allen Leroy (Gipp), Sr., 412, 424, 425, 440, 441, 442
   Allen Leroy, Jr., 425
   Alvin, Rev., 440
   Angel, 440
   Annie Frances, 409, 412, 421, 424, 425, 440, 441, 442
   Avery Lou, 344, 351
   Bessie Mae, 110
   Betty, 440
   Bobbie, 236
   Brenda, 225
   Brittie, 344, 351
   Charlie, 337, 343, 344
   Charlie Ray, 344, 351
   Cynthia, 441
   Dale Fitzgerald, 432
   Darlene, 424, 425
   Demitri, 441
   Diane, 441
   Dorla, 53, 163
   Dorothy, 440
   Earl, 344
   Edward, 351
   Edward (Cornine), 344
   Emma, 417, 432
   Emma Jean, 440
   Emma Lean, 440
   Freddie C., Jr., 432
   Freddie C., Sr., 417, 432
   Gene Arthur (Pie Joe), 424, 425
   Gloria Jean, 424, 425, 442
   Hubert, 255, 282
   James, 440
   Jerry, 440
   Kesha, 442
   LaToya, 442
   Lily Mae, 344
   Maebell, 224

Makeya, 441
Mark, Sr., 440
Ricky, 440
Rosemary, 344, 351
Sheron, 441
Shirley, 255
Terri, 441
Terry Leroy, 424, 425, 441
Tillie Mae, 344
Tony, 225
Unknown, 110
Willie Claude, 440
Willie Earl, 440
Willie Edward, 424, 425, 440
Zelma, 337, 342, 343, 344, 350
FAGAN
　Katie K., 232
　Leonard, 232
　Mary Gordon, 232
　Patricia, 232
　William (Sleepy), Sr., 194, 232
　William, Jr., 232
FANT
　Anna, 306
　Brenda C., 307
　Delphine, 306
　Edward William, Jr., 307
　Edward William, Sr., 306, 307
　Hetty (or Hedy), 307
　Jerome (Romeo), 306, 307
　John Canon, 289, 306
　John Henry, 306
　Josephine Doris, 307
　Limmie, 289, 306
　Robert Canon, 306, 307
　Vera Mae, 307
FELLOWS
　Bria, 272
FENWICK
　Mrs. E.C., 83
FERGUSON
　Diane, 150
　Unknown, 150
FISHER
　Lynn A., 360
FITZPATRICK
　Annie Bell, 328, 330
　Letha, 330
　Willie, 328, 330
Fleming Place, 112
FLOOD
　Inet, 178
FLOYD
　Anna, 306
FONDREN
　Hannah, 32
　Matthew, 46
FORD
　Agnes Louise, 180
　Alberta, 179, 180
　Bertha Marie, 180
　David Cicero, 179, 180
　Douglas, 179, 180
　Emmett, 179, 180
　Ernestine, 219
　Estelle, 180, 219
　Fannie Lee, 179, 180
　Frank, 219
　Grace, 179
　Joseph, 179, 180
　Luvenia, 179
　Maggie Jean, 219
　Mary, 180
　Mary Ann, 219
　Matthew, 179
　Nelson, 179
　Nola Ann, 179, 180
　Nola J., 168, 169, 179, 180, 219
　Ruth Mae, 180
　Ruthie, 179, 180
　Samuel Alonzo, Sr., 179, 180, 219
　Sherman, 169, 179, 180, 219
　Susan, 179
　Tena, 179
　Verian Louise, 219
FOSTER
　Margaret, 30
　Samuel, 30

FOUNTENBERRY
  Carolyn Mellisa, 314
  Curley, Jr., 313
  Curley, Sr., 293, 313
  Marceline Audrey, 314
  Myrtle Vivian, 313
  Ronald, 314
  Rosetta, 293, 313
FOUT
  Lydia, 31
  Unknown, 31
FRANCISCO
  Buvern, III., 254
  Buvern, Jr., 254
  Charlene, 254, 255
  Tonya Lashun, 254
Fred's Dollar Store, 134
FREEMAN
  Betty May, 290, 308, 309, 310
  Robert Nolan, 290, 309, 310
Freemen of Norwich, 7, 8, 9
French and Indian War, 21, 22
French Wars of Religion, 3
FRIERSON
  Gideon, 63
FULLER
  Ben, 288
  Bernice, Jr., 303, 305
  Brinda, 305
  Cedric, 305
  Claude, 303, 305
  Collean, 352
  Dannie W., 288
  Darryl, 305
  Dorothy L., 303, 305
  Elige (Lige), 289, 303, 305
  Elmira (Bobby), 303, 305
  Henry, 112, 284
  Henry Niles, 303, 305
  Jackie, 305
  James (Jimmy) L., 303, 305
  John L., 352
  Joyce, 303, 305
  Juanita, 303, 305, 421, 435
  Lacy C., 303, 305
  Leora, 288
  Linda, 305
  Lorenzo, 305
  Lucie, 289
  Lucius, 288
  Lutie, 288
  Neria C., 289, 303, 305
  Orleana (Lena), 285, 286, 288, 303
  Phyllis, 305
  Tennie, 70, 284, 287, 288, 289, 292, 294, 295, 297, 299, 300, 301
  Turner, Jr., 288
  Turner, Sr., 286, 288, 303
  Velma, 289
  Walter, 288
  Will Ernest, 303, 305
G. Loewenburg & Co., 156
GAMBLE
  Agnes Isolome (Icy), 154, 155, 173, 174, 193, 195, 200, 201, 202, 203, 205, 208
  Albert, 155, 173, 174, 193, 195, 200, 201, 202, 203, 205, 208
  Betty, 173, 174
  Callie Pairee, 173, 174, 195, 196, 237, 240
  Ella Mae, 174, 201
  Estelle, 200
  Eva May, 201
  Fannie, 193
  Fannie B., 173, 174, 193, 228, 229, 232, 234, 236
  Fred (Big Baby), 173, 174, 201
  Josephine, 201
  Katie D. (KD), 173, 175, 203, 204, 242
  Lovie, 173, 175, 205, 207, 208, 243, 246, 249, 250, 251, 254, 255
  Lula M., 201
  Mable Ethel, 173, 175, 208
  Mitchell, 201
  Nathan Eugene, 173, 174, 200
  Nola Mae, 173, 175, 202
GAMLIN
  Claude, 323
  Howard, 323

Jason, 323
Sarah Lee, 299, 322
Tom Jordan, Jr., 322, 323
Tom Jordan, Sr., 299, 322
GASTON
    Ruby Lee, 127
    Unknown, 127
GAYTON, 2
GEORGIA, 40, 78
    Atlanta, 160, 268, 305, 338
    Augusta, 65, 244, 268
    Bartow Co., 65
    Bibb Co., 46
    Cobb Co., 231
    Dublin, 46
    Fulton Co., 338
    Gainesville, 289, 306
    Glennville, 151
    Hall Co., 49, 68, 306
    Hinesville, 125, 151
    Johnson Co., 65
    Laurens Co., 47, 65
    Macon, 46
    Macon Co., 177, 218
    Marietta, 231
    Richmond Co., 65, 244, 268
    Thomas Co., 65
GERMANY
    Nuremberg, 365
GIBSON
    Doris, 396
    Patsy, 1, 67, 68, 69, 70, 76, 153, 185, 192,
        221, 222, 223, 224, 284, 348
    Patsy J., 368
GILMORE
    Marie, 146
    Robert, 146
GIPSON
    Mildred, 290
GITON
    Elizabeth, 11, 12, 15, 16
    John, 4, 7, 8, 9, 10, 11
    Margaret, 7, 9
    Samuel I, 5, 7, 10, 11, 12, 13, 14, 15, 16

    Samuel II, 11
GLADNEY
    Martha Elizabeth, 360
GLASS
    Fannie, 107
GLENN
    Christina, 262
    Phillip, 262
Glorious Revolution, 18
GLOVER
    Tracy, 244, 273
GOINS
    Betty May, 290, 308, 309, 310
    Chances, 290, 309
GOODWIN
    Clara F., 168, 169
    Unknown, 169
GRANT
    Latisha, 281
GRAY
    John, 29, 30
    Nova, 282
GRAY-GAMBLE
    Jupiter Icy, 282
GREAT BRITAIN, 21, 22, 39, 40
Great Migration, 76, 89, 90, 91, 92, 93
GREEN
    Louvenia, 341, 361
GREENE
    Nathanael, Major Gen., 39
    Tonya, 244, 273
GREENWOOD
    Pamela, 405
    Unknown, 405
GREER
    Fannie, 338, 339, 351, 353
GREGORY
    A.E., 79
    E.M., 79
GRIFFIN
    Athie (Athel), 391, 398, 401
    Dora, 97, 105
    Gertie Mae, 127
    Harriett N., 54

Unknown, 127, 391
GRISBY
   Sylvia J., 308
GRISWOLD
   Elmira, 295
   Rufus, 295
   Valina, 317
GUITON, 2, 3, 4
GUITTON, 2
   John de, 3
GUYTON, 2, 3, 4
   A. J., 73, 74, 75, 93, 328, 329, 330
   Aaron Steele, 32, 39, 47, 48, 50, 64, 72
   Aaron Whitaker, 1, 2, 19, 49, 64, 65, 66, 67, 68, 69, 70, 71, 72, 73, 74, 75, 76, 77, 78, 83, 85, 91, 93, 94, 95, 96, 100, 153, 154, 156, 160, 163, 166, 172, 185, 190, 192, 221, 222, 223, 224, 225, 226, 284, 285, 328, 333, 334, 336, 345, 348, 368, 370, 385, 387, 409, 433, 444
   Abraham, 20, 29, 30, 33, 52, 53
   Abraham J. (Bud), 53, 54
   Abraham P., 53
   Ada Vera, 364, 365
   Adaline, 54
   Adel, 176
   Adeline, 71, 74, 96
   Adeline Susannah, 286, 295, 296, 319, 320
   Agnes, 293
   Agnes Isolome (Icy), 154, 155, 173, 174, 193, 195, 200, 201, 202, 203, 205, 208
   Alean, 401
   Alfreda, 290
   Alice Lee, 410, 411, 412, 415, 427, 428, 443
   Allene, 123, 147, 148
   Amanda, 73, 74, 75, 93, 96, 100, 101, 119, 120, 121, 385, 386, 388, 392, 409
   Amashire, 65
   Amelia, 31
   Amershire, 65
   Andrea, 316, 437
   Andrew, 73, 74, 75, 93
   Andrew J., 328, 329, 330
   Andy, 300, 323, 324
   Angelia, 150, 151
   Ann Ada, 324
   Anne, 17
   Annie, 388, 389, 391, 392, 402, 403
   Annie (Eudy), 389
   Annie B., 73, 74, 75, 93, 96, 100, 101, 119, 120, 121, 385, 386, 388, 392, 409
   Annie Bell, 328, 329, 331, 409
   Annie F., 358
   Annie Frances, 409, 412, 421, 424, 425, 440, 441, 442
   Annie May, 341, 355
   Annie Pearl, 338, 339, 351, 352, 368
   Arthur David (Buddy), 419, 421, 435
   Athie (Athel), 391, 398, 401
   Baby James, 74, 444
   Barbara Louise, 419, 421
   Beatrice, 361
   Belinda, 358
   Ben, 186, 347, 409, 411, 412, 415, 426
   Benjamin A., Dr., 27
   Benjamin I, 16, 17, 18, 19, 21, 22, 23, 24, 30, 31
   Benjamin II, 31
   Bernice, 226, 361, 420, 434
   Betty, 192
   Betty Janell, 176, 215
   Betty May, 290, 308, 309, 310
   Billie Ruth, 419
   Blanche Gail, 290, 291, 307, 308, 312
   Bobbie, 401
   Bonnie, 423, 439
   Brazee, 388
   Brazie, 296, 319, 320, 341, 358, 359
   Brenda Dell, 423, 438
   Bruce, 389
   C.J., 438
   Caaye, 187, 346, 347
   Callie, 286, 294, 316, 317
   Callie A., 388, 389
   Carol Ann, 365

Caroline, 69, 70, 71, 93, 95, 96, 98, 100, 101, 103, 105, 106, 284, 285, 366, 386
Carrie J., 290, 308, 309, 310
Case, 73, 74, 75, 93, 100, 172, 185, 221, 222, 223, 224, 296, 301, 320, 334, 335, 336, 337, 338, 340, 341, 342, 345, 348, 349, 350, 351, 353, 358, 368, 385, 409, 426
Casey Glenn, Sr., 186, 221, 346, 368
Casey Jones, 388, 389
Catherine, 17, 30, 47, 52
Charles Saxon, 47
Charlie, 389
Charlotte, 286, 297, 298, 321
Chatmon, 300
Cherry Mae, 176, 210, 213
Christine, 291, 308
Cintha Susan (Sue C.), 54
Clarence (Buddy), 192
Clarence William, 363
Clarice, 123
Claude, 342, 364, 365, 366, 410, 411, 412, 415, 429
Claudia, 366
Cleveland Davis, 299
Coleman, 294
Corey, 437
Curtis, 191, 419, 421, 434
Dantae, 437
Darrelyn Lorraine, 290
David, 123, 150, 401
David F., 1, 5, 7, 8, 9, 11, 12, 16, 65, 69, 70, 71, 72, 74, 93, 96, 336
Davis, 299
Diane Luberta, 316
Donald T., Sr., 315
Donna J., 318
Doris, 396, 411
Doris Nell, 422, 437
Dorothy, 291, 311, 401
Dorothy Ann, 221
Dorothy Jean, 192
Dorothy Mae, 391, 398, 401

Doss Ade, 102, 285, 286, 289, 297, 306, 307, 309, 310, 311, 312
Drucilla L. H., 53, 54
Earl, 401
Earlene, 190, 225, 419, 420, 433
Ebony, 367
Edwin, 411, 422, 438
Edwina, 295, 317, 318
Elijah, 69, 70, 71, 96, 153, 154, 284, 285, 287, 288, 289, 292, 294, 295, 296, 297, 299, 300, 301, 320, 334, 341
Elijah (Lige), 303
Elisa, 163
Elizabeth, 11, 12, 13, 15, 16, 17, 47, 53, 177, 210, 218
Elizabeth (Betsey), 33, 48, 63
Elizabeth Eleander, 31
Ellene Sue, 148
Ellenore Shirley, 365
Elmina Horn, 47
Elmira, 294, 317, 331
Elvie, 341, 360, 363, 364
Emma, 154, 155, 168, 179, 181, 183, 286, 289, 290, 306, 307, 309, 310, 311, 312, 391, 398, 400, 401
Emma Evester, 176, 211, 212, 215
Emma Kate, 300
Emma P., 401
Epaphras, 17
Ernest, 221
Essie Dee, 341, 356, 357, 364, 365, 366
Ethel L., 297, 298, 321
Ethel Viola, 287, 301, 334
Ethelene, 297, 298, 321
Etta, 337, 340, 341, 355, 356, 358, 359, 360, 363, 364, 365, 366, 367
Eugene, Jr., 315
Eugene, Sr., 293, 314, 315
Eureka, 298
Fannie, 70, 153, 154, 155, 156, 160, 164, 168, 170, 173, 176, 177, 338, 339, 351, 353
Fannie Douglas, 177, 210, 217
Fannie Louise, 341, 358, 359, 360, 363

Fleming Alexander, 390, 391, 398, 400, 401
Flora, 65
Florence Sarah, 401
Florida, 299
Frances, 20
Frank, 290
Frankie, 388, 390, 391, 398, 402
Fred, 338, 353
Fred Henry, 401
Fred L., 287, 300, 301, 334, 335
Fred Steele, Jr., 407
Fred Steele, Sr., 393, 396, 407
Frenzella, 294
General John Washington, 49
Geneva, 296, 319, 320, 341, 358
Genova, 186, 346, 347, 426
Georgia Lee, 291, 308, 312, 313
Gilly L. H., 53, 54
Gladys, 396, 407
Gloria, 221
Gus Davis, 172, 190, 225, 226, 409, 412, 418, 419, 420, 433, 434, 435
Guyton, 49
Gwen, 73, 328, 329, 330
Gyte, 49
Hannah, 32, 33, 35, 40, 46, 48, 50, 60, 61, 63
Hannah Lyon, 19, 32, 34, 35, 40, 46, 48, 52, 53, 60, 64
Harriett N., 54
Harvey, 317
Hattie, 421, 434
Hattie Irene, 388, 389, 393, 396
Helen, 300, 323, 324, 342, 366
Henry, 31
Hester, 48
Hiram, 434
Hubert, 123, 150, 151, 187
Ida, 74, 172, 389, 396, 407, 409, 410, 411, 414, 415, 418, 419, 421, 424, 426, 427, 428, 429

Ike, 74, 75, 93, 172, 186, 334, 347, 389, 396, 407, 409, 410, 411, 414, 415, 418, 419, 421, 424, 426, 427, 429
Ike Roby, 187
Ike Young, 123, 147, 148
Inez, 390, 391, 398, 401, 402
Irene, 123, 147, 148, 293
Irene (Polly), 419, 421
Isaac, 20, 29, 30, 52, 53
Isadora, 409, 412, 415, 417, 431, 432
Isaiah P., 54
J. T., 73, 74, 75
J. W. S., 74, 75, 76
Jacob, 20, 29, 30
Jada, 440
James, 73, 74, 75, 290, 308, 444
James (Baby James), 444
James (Jim), 172, 185, 221, 222, 223, 224, 337, 345, 346, 350, 368
James Earl, 358
James Edward, 401
James T., 333
James T. (Baby James), 94
James William Sunderland, 74, 75, 76
Jane Malissa, 48
Jean, 163
Jerelyn, 324
Jeremiah, 123
Jeremy, 438
Jerome, 435
Jimmie Dell, 123
Jimmie Ruth, 186, 223, 346, 347
Jimmy Dell, 150
Joan, 419, 421, 435
Joe, 401
Joe Dale (Joe D.), 101, 122, 146, 147, 148, 149, 150, 386, 388, 392
Joe Frank, 123, 147, 148, 150, 338, 409, 411, 412, 421, 422, 424, 436, 437, 438, 439, 440
Joe Frank, Sr., 123, 147
Joe Troy, 186, 346, 347
John, 4, 7, 8, 9, 10, 11, 46
John Ellis, 52

John H., 409
John Henry, 338, 339
John I, 16, 18, 19, 20, 21, 22, 23, 24, 25, 29, 30, 31, 32
John II, 19, 20, 24, 29, 30
John L., 337
John Luther, 54
John Washington, 49
Johnnie Lavelle, 123
Johnny, 150, 151, 401
Jonnie B., 297, 298, 321
Joseph, 17, 18, 47
Joseph A., 1, 49, 64, 69, 72, 76, 85
Joseph B., 52
Joseph I, 19, 29, 30, 32, 33, 34, 35, 39, 40, 43, 46, 48, 50, 52, 53, 60, 64, 65
Joseph II, 33, 52, 53, 54, 55, 56, 57, 58, 59
Joseph William (Whit), 54
Joshua, 20, 25, 29, 30
Joyce, 316
Juanita, 305, 421, 435
Judith Saxon, 46
Judy, 146
Judy Kate, 123, 150, 151
Karla, 434
Kasey Glen, Jr., 221
Katherine, 393, 396, 411, 422, 436
Kennedy, 148
Kim, 401
Kissy, 401
Lacey, 176, 210, 211, 213, 216, 217, 218
Laclain, 393, 396
LaLesia, 407
Lanell, 187, 346, 347
Lavelle, 437
Lawanda, 438
Lawrence Joseph, 293
Lawson, 71, 72, 153
Leander (Lee), 411, 422, 437
Lee, Jr., 437
Lela, 386
Leo, 146
Leola, 293
Lessie V., 342, 365, 366

Letha, 328, 330
Lige, 69, 70, 71, 96, 153, 154, 284, 285, 287, 288, 289, 292, 294, 295, 296, 297, 299, 300, 301, 320, 334, 341
Lillie, 338, 339, 390, 391
Lillie Wardean, 171, 172, 185, 221, 222, 223, 224, 337, 345, 346, 368
Limmie, 289, 306
Limmie Mae Douglas, 155, 176, 210, 211, 213, 215, 216, 217, 218
Linda, 163
Linda Bell, 423, 439
Lindsay (Linzy), Jr., 293
Lindsay Ford (Linzy), Sr., 285, 286, 292, 313, 314, 315
Lisa, 163
Lord Pankiel (Lazarky), 290
Lottie, 287, 301, 325, 326
Louvenia, 341, 361
Lovell, 186, 346, 347
Lubertha, 293, 314, 315
Lucille, 341, 361, 363, 401
Lucy, 186, 224, 346, 347
Lula, 297, 298, 390, 391, 398, 402
Lula Avery, 338, 349, 350, 351
Luther, 438
Luther C., 52
Luvenia N., 52
Lydia, 31
Lydie (Lydia), 17
Madesta, 297, 298, 321
Maebell, 186, 224, 346, 347
Maggie, 73, 74, 75, 93, 370, 371, 372, 373, 374, 376, 377, 379, 382, 409
Magnolia, 294, 316, 317
Malisa, 297, 298, 321
Mallie, 299
Marceline G., 286, 292, 313, 314, 315
Margaret, 7, 9, 11, 15, 16, 19, 30, 48, 50, 64, 421
Margaret Catherine (Molly), 34
Margaret Watson, 49
Maria (Mariah), 33, 53
Marketta, 435

Martha, 318
Martha Patsy, 33, 52
Martha Patsy (Passy), 52
Marvin, 324
Mary, 19, 20, 24, 29, 30, 32, 46, 54
Mary (Maggie), 388, 389, 390, 393, 396
Mary Georgia, 409, 411, 412, 414, 415
Mary Lee, 300, 398, 401
Mary Lovey Zinkey, 286, 294
Mary Lynn, 342, 367
Mary McRee (Polly), 48
Mary Nancy, 52
Mary Van, 358
Mattie, 286, 297
Maudie M., 338, 349
Maurice, 435
May Lee, 390, 391
Maylene, 359
Melvin, 123, 361
Michele, 401
Mildred, 186, 221, 290, 301, 341, 346, 361
Mildred Irene, 411, 412, 421, 422, 436, 437, 438, 439, 440
Millie, 287, 299, 322, 323
Minnie, 389, 393, 396, 407, 409, 412, 426
Minnie Guyton, 389, 393, 396, 407, 409, 412, 426
Moses I, 32, 39, 46, 47, 50
Moses II, 47
Nancy, 20, 32, 46, 47
Nancy M., 53, 54
Nathan, 440
Nathaniel, 17, 20, 29, 30
Nugulia, 342, 365, 366
Ollie J., 342, 367
Ophelia, 290
Ora, 401
Orlena (Lena), 285, 286, 288, 303
Ottilee, 293, 315
Patience, 48
Patricia, 421
Patsy, 33

Patsy J., 154, 155, 170, 171, 184, 185, 187, 189, 190, 192, 221, 222, 223, 224, 346
Patsy Martha (Passy), 53
Pauline, 192
Penny, 389
Percy, 317, 318, 338, 348, 349, 350, 388, 389
Percy Edward, 294
Phyllis Lorraine, 318
Pink, 77
Pink West (PW), 176, 210, 216
Pinkney, 1, 69, 70, 71, 77, 96, 153, 154, 155, 156, 158, 160, 163, 164, 168, 170, 172, 173, 176, 177, 284, 285, 334, 337
Pomfrey (Jimmy), 387, 388
Preston Elijah, 294, 317, 318
Prissilla, 31
Quinton Leach II, 325
R.C., 320
Ray, 186, 346, 347
Reginald, 316
Rev. Clarence, Sr., 342, 364, 365, 366
Richard, 316, 407
Ricky, 358
Robbie Lee, 388, 389, 394, 404, 405, 406, 407
Robert, 316, 338, 353
Robert McCurdy, 48
Robert Walker, Sr., 315
Robert Walter, 293
Roland, 316
Ronald, 316
Ronald (Ronnie), 311
Rose, 311, 312
Rosetta, 293, 313
Rozell J., 186, 222, 346
Russell, 316
Ruth Lee (Ruthie), 171, 172, 190, 225, 226, 412, 419, 420, 433, 434, 435
Sadie, 123, 150
Sam, 163
Samuel, 19, 25, 29, 30
Samuel I, 4, 5, 7, 10, 11, 12, 13, 14, 15, 16

Samuel II, 11, 12, 15, 16, 18, 19, 21, 30
Samuel III, 17, 18
Sarah, 11, 20, 29, 30, 31, 32, 33, 47, 54, 70, 284, 285, 288, 289, 292, 293, 294, 295, 297, 299, 300, 301, 401, 423, 440
Sarah Ann, 49
Sarah Lee, 299, 322
Sarah Matilda (Sally), 49
Serita, 422, 437
Shawana, 440
Shelton N., 172, 192, 337, 338, 348, 349, 350
Shepard, 286, 297, 298, 321
Sherrie, 440
Shirley, 187
Simon, 297, 298, 401
Simon (Brad), Jr., 387, 388
Simon, Sr., 74, 75, 94, 101, 122, 149, 150, 386, 387, 388, 390, 391, 392, 393, 394, 396, 412, 426
Steele, 388, 389, 393, 396, 407, 412, 426
Stella Mae, 101, 121, 122, 146, 147, 148, 149, 150, 386, 388, 392
Stellie Rose, 123, 149, 150
Stephanie, 439
Sue C., 54
Suegene, 155, 177
Susie, 73, 172, 185, 221, 222, 223, 224, 225, 337, 342, 345, 348, 349, 350, 368
Susie Jean, 186, 346, 347
Tabitha, 32, 46, 47
Tammie, 435
Tennie, 70, 284, 287, 288, 289, 292, 294, 295, 297, 299, 300, 301
Theresa, 150, 151
Thomas, 350
Thomas Mitchel, 29, 30
Tipp, 389
Tony, 438
Trevon, 440
Tyrone, 361
Tyrone Linzy, Sr., 315
Underwood, 31
Unknown, 305

Unknown Male, 358
Valina, 295, 317
Vamis (Vammie), 171, 172, 192, 338, 348
Velma Ruth, 123, 146, 150
Vera LaVern, 300, 323, 342, 357, 364, 365, 366
Verner, 300
Vernon T. (Vearn), Sr., 342, 367
Vernon T., Jr., 367
Vina (Vinnie), 336, 340
Viola, 74, 94, 101, 122, 149, 150, 386, 387, 388, 390, 391, 392, 393, 394, 396, 412, 426
Violet, 54
Vivian, 324, 325
Wade Harvey, III, 318
Wade Harvey, Jr., 295, 317, 318
Wade Harvey, Sr., 285, 286, 294, 316, 317
Warren Harding, Sr., 291, 308, 311
Whitaker W., 52
Wiley Leach, 287, 299, 322, 323
Wilhelmina, 291, 311
Wilis Oliver, 289
William, 17, 287
William Amzy, Jr., 176, 215
William Amzy, Sr., 154, 155, 156, 176, 210, 211, 213, 215, 216, 217, 218
Willie Beatrice, 293
Willie Clayton (WC), Sr., 300, 323, 342, 357, 364, 365, 366, 367
Willie Clayton, Jr., 364, 365
Willie James, 361
Willie, Jr., 341, 360, 361, 363
Willie, Sr., 336, 337, 340, 341, 350, 355, 356, 358, 359, 360, 363
Zelma, 337, 342, 343, 344, 350
Zemuely, 49
Zemuely McClusky, 64, 85
Zollie, 297, 298, 321
GUYTON REES
  Helen, 20, 22, 29, 48, 50
Guyton's Addition, 25
Guyton's Prospect, 24, 25
Guyton's Road, 27

GY
  John le, 3
GYTON
  Elizabeth, 11, 12, 13, 15, 16
  John, 4, 7, 8, 9, 10, 11
  Margaret, 7, 9
  Samuel I, 5, 7, 10, 11, 12, 13, 14, 15, 16
  Samuel II, 11
  Thomas, 2
HALL
  Benjamin Harrison, 126
  Bernice, 126
  Jalisa, 242
  Rufus, 401
  Sarah, 401
  Unknown, 242
HAMLETT, 115
Hamlett Plantation, 115
HARMAN
  Ellene Sue, 148
  Gladys, 102
  Roy, 148
HARMON
  Andrew, 103
  Arvin Howard, 118
  Bessie Mae, 110
  Billy, 388
  Bonnie Jean, 110, 134, 135, 136
  Brenda, 135
  Daisy J., 135
  Dolores Augusta, 117, 142
  Edna F., 103
  Edward, 118
  Esre, 110
  Ethel, 98, 99, 110
  Eula M., 110
  Fannie Mae, 117, 142
  Jackie, 135
  Janice (or Janie), 136
  Jessie D., 390
  Jim Roger, 110, 134, 135
  Jimmie, 135
  John, 99, 110, 133, 134
  Johnnie, 110, 133
  Johnnie M., 99
  Kattie M., 118
  Larry Wade, Sr., 135
  Leila, 117, 140
  Leila Mae, 118, 143
  Leon, 389, 390
  Louis, 118
  Maggie Ruth, 390
  Mary, 135
  Mary (Maggie), 389, 390
  Mildred, 134, 136
  Murie (Murray), 118, 143
  Ollie Clara, 135
  Ollie M., 390
  Queen T., 133
  Queen T., Jr., 99
  Roy Willie, 110
  Sarah Mae, 118
  Sarah V., 99, 100, 117
  Sharon, 136
  Unknown, 259
  Vickie Lynn, 136
  Walter, 100, 117, 140, 142, 143
  Walter Alvin, 117, 142
  Willie Ray, 118
  Youngs, 118
HARPER
  Anice, 263
  Patricia, 241, 263
  Unknown, 241, 263
HARPER
  Amina, 263
HARRIS
  Aaron Garmon, 329, 331, 332
  Brunetta, 331, 332
  Jeannie, 332
  Joyce Lee, 332
  Katie Mae, 116, 139
  Mable, 329, 331, 332
  Milton, 331, 332
  Yvonne, 331, 332
HARRISON
  Grace Ora, 108, 128
HAYWOOD

Lorene, 148
HEAD
   Belynda, 249, 276
   Jethro Alexander, 249, 276
Head Start School, 134
HEALD
   J.T., 79
HECHAVARRIA
   Unknown, 235
   Vergie, 235
HEMINGWAY
   Latonya Y., 272
HEMP
   Helen, 342, 366
HENDERSON
   Stacy, 327
Henry IV, 3
Henry VIII, 13
HEWETT
   Lula, 99
HILL
   Cherry, 244
   Everlean, 195, 196
   George Van, Jr., 196
   Jimmie Ruth, 186, 223
   Keshia, 224
   Michael, 224
   Shannon, 224
   Wardell, 223
Hit or Miss, 35
HOLLINS
   Chyna, 272
   Robert, 272
HOLLOWAY
   Twylla, 403
   Unknown, 403
HOLT
   Sarah, 31
HOOKER
   Dremetris, 238
HOPSON
   Michael Octavius, 136
   Vickie Lynn, 136
HOWARD
   Henry, 136
   Janice (or Janie), 136
   Kevin Maurice, 438
   Lawanda, 438
Howell's Ferry, 54
HUDDELSTON
   T.J., 115, 116
Huddleston Plantation, 115
HUGHES
   Langston, 90
   Lillian, 189
Huguenots, 3, 4
HUNTER
   Alma Lee, 301, 325, 326
   I.C., Jr., 325
   I.C., Sr., 301, 325, 326
   John Henry, 301, 302, 325, 326
   Marie, 301, 302, 325, 326, 327
   Mary, 325, 326
   Robert Lee (Robbie), 325, 326
   Robin Joseph, 325
   Ruby Lee, 325, 326
HURSTON
   Zora Neale, 90
HUTCHINS
   Allene, 123, 147, 148
   Dan, Sr., 108, 129
   Effie, 108, 129
   Irene, 123, 147, 148
ILLINOIS
   Bellwood, 249, 276
   Bolingbrook, 342, 364
   Calumet City, 396, 407
   Chicago, 76, 90, 91, 103, 117, 141, 150, 155, 160, 168, 169, 170, 172, 175, 179, 180, 181, 183, 185, 186, 190, 197, 204, 205, 207, 208, 219, 221, 222, 223, 224, 225, 243, 244, 246, 249, 250, 251, 252, 254, 255, 267, 269, 270, 271, 272, 273, 275, 276, 277, 278, 279, 280, 281, 282, 287, 294, 296, 299, 300, 305, 319, 320, 322, 323, 328, 329, 331, 332, 337, 338, 340, 341, 342, 345, 346, 347, 351, 352, 355, 356, 357, 358, 359, 360, 361, 363,

364, 365, 366, 367, 368, 369, 371, 382, 383, 389, 393, 395, 396, 406, 407, 412, 417, 419, 421, 424, 425, 426, 427, 428, 431, 433, 434, 435, 436, 437, 440, 441, 442, 443
Chicago Heights, 412, 421, 436, 437, 438, 439, 440
Cook Co., 103, 117, 137, 141, 155, 168, 169, 172, 174, 175, 179, 180, 181, 183, 185, 186, 190, 191, 195, 196, 197, 204, 205, 207, 208, 219, 221, 222, 223, 224, 225, 226, 237, 240, 243, 244, 246, 249, 250, 251, 252, 254, 255, 267, 269, 270, 271, 272, 273, 276, 277, 278, 279, 280, 281, 282, 287, 294, 296, 299, 300, 305, 319, 320, 322, 323, 328, 329, 330, 331, 332, 337, 338, 340, 341, 342, 345, 346, 347, 351, 352, 355, 356, 357, 358, 359, 360, 361, 363, 364, 365, 366, 367, 368, 369, 371, 382, 383, 389, 393, 394, 395, 396, 404, 405, 406, 407, 412, 417, 418, 420, 421, 424, 425, 426, 427, 428, 431, 433, 434, 435, 436, 437, 438, 439, 440, 441, 442, 443
Dixon, 357
DuPage Co., 207, 243, 267, 269, 271, 273
Edwardsville, 104, 124, 151
Elgin, 425, 441
Evanston, 296
Kane Co., 425, 441
Lansing, 428, 443
Lee Co., 357
Madison Co., 104, 124, 151
Matteson, 357
Maywood, 174, 191, 195, 237, 240, 272, 305, 369, 371, 382, 421, 435
Naperville, 207, 243, 267, 269, 271, 273
Northbrook., 340
Oak Park, 389, 394, 404, 405, 406, 407
Proviso Township, 328, 330
Rockford, 169, 181, 182
Venice, 305
Will Co., 342, 364
Winnebago Co., 169, 181, 182

Indentured Servant, 21
INDIANA
  Cook Co., 332
  Gary, 332
  Hammond, 332, 357
  Indianapolis, 100, 118, 119, 143
  Lake Co., 332, 357
  Marion Co., 100, 118, 119, 143
IOWA
  Black Hawk Co., 194, 229, 230, 231, 232, 234, 235, 257, 331, 344
  Burnsville, 231
  Iowa Co., 231
  Waterloo, 76, 91, 194, 229, 230, 231, 232, 234, 235, 257, 331, 344, 351
ISLAND
  Beatrice, 99, 100, 118, 143
JACKSON
  Prissilla, 31
  Unknown, 305
Jacob Chapel School, 134
JAMES
  Lessie V., 342, 365, 366
James II, 18
JAMISON
  Ardess (Dutch), 129
  Ardice, 107
  Charles, 107, 129
  Effie, 108, 129
  Unknown, 108, 129
JEFFERIES
  Harriett N., 54
JEFFERSON
  Alfred, 314
  Marceline Audrey, 314
JENKINS
  Airkas (Billy), 344
  David (DJ), Jr., 281
  David L., Sr., 281
  Dorotha, 371
  Kenya, 443
  Kimberly, 443
  LaTarshe (Toddy), 281
  Unknown, 443

JIMMERSON
   Jean, 407
   Unknown, 407
JOHNSON
   Bernice Marie, 386
   Bernice Marie, 101, 120, 144, 145
   Brian, 350, 351
   Brian II, 350, 351
   Brian Renard, 351
   Carmelita Sabrina, 244, 269, 270, 271
   Charles, 350, 351
   Charlesetta, 351
   Genesis, 350, 351
   Jasmine, 351
   Jessica, 270
   Joe, 338, 349, 350
   Kate Emma, 232
   Katie K., 193, 194, 232
   Keilani, 350, 351
   LaMar, Jr., 270
   LaMar, Sr., 270
   LaMonte, 270
   LeCurtis, 270
   Leroy, 232
   Lubertha, 293, 314, 315
   Lula Avery, 338, 349, 350, 351
   Quinton Pierre, 351
   Sarah, 54
   Sheila, 350, 351
   Thomas, 194
   Thomas J., Sr., 232
   Thomas, Jr., 232
   Thomas, Sr., 232
   Vernon, Jr., 145
   Vernon, Sr., 120, 144, 145
JOINER
   Claude (Pretty Boy), Sr., 175
   Claude, Jr., 204
   Claude, Sr., 203, 204, 242
   Dorothy Jean, 204
   Icy Dean, 204
   Katie D. (KD), 173, 175, 203, 204, 242
   Percy Lee (Sunny), 204
   Vernestine (Susie), 204, 242

JONES
   Dorothy L., 303, 305
   Frenzella, 294
   Grady, 331
   James Michael, 320
   Kamisha Zartessia, 402
   Leavernard, Sr., 120, 144
   Lisa Alesia, 320
   Nola Ann, 180
   Unknown, 305
   Yvonne Jacquline, 101, 120, 144, 386
JORDAN
   Allen, 169
   John, 169
   Johnnie Amzy, 168, 169
JOSEPH
   Leola, 293
KENNEDY
   Elizabeth, 53
   Unknown, 53
KENTUCKY, 63
   Jefferson Co., 207, 291, 310
   Louisville, 291, 310
KERN
   Alice, 141
   Alton Ralph, 141
   Leila, 117, 140
   Olton Ray, 141
   Otis, 117, 141
   Owen Reed, 141
Knights and Daughters of Tabor, 115
KOREA, 180, 236, 350, 371, 377, 378
Korean Presidential Unit Citation, 378
Korean Service Medal, 378
Kosciusko Baptist Church, 83
LaDAY
   Derrick, 264
   Ronnie, 264
LAFLORE
   Susie Jean, 186
LaGRONE
   Betty L., 298
   James M., 298
LAGRONE

Charles A., 298
LAMAR
   Blanche Gail, 290, 291, 307, 308, 312
   Deborah Gail, 308
   Emanuel, 308
   Hetty (or Hedy), 307
   Patricia Ruth, 308
   William E., 290, 291, 307, 308, 312
LAMBERT
   Belynda, 276
   Carolyn Ann, 404
   Unknown, 276
LAMPKIN
   Sudie, 83
LANDINGHAM
   Earlene, 190, 225, 419, 420, 433
   Linda Faye, 433
   Otha, 190, 225, 420, 433
   Susie, 225, 433
LANE
   Charles, 293
   Sarah, 293
LANE, Mr., 79
LANGDON
   P. F., 52
LANGFORD
   Carrie J., 290, 308, 309, 310
   Lee William, 291, 310
LANGSTON
   Willie M., 112
LATHAM
   Madesta, 298, 321
   Mary A., 298, 321, 322
   Sarah L., 298, 321, 322
   Unknown, 298, 321
LEAVY
   Dorothy Jean, 402
   Edward (Poot), 402
   Edward Vanardale (Donald), 402
   Joseph Lawrence, Jr., 402
   Kamisha Zartessia, 402
   Sallye, 402
LEE
   Johnny, 331
   Robert, 331
LEECH
   Joseph W., Sr., 54
   Mary, 54
LEFFUE
   Lawrence, 338, 349, 350
   Lula Avery, 338, 349, 350, 351
LEFLORE
   Judy A., 235
   Lincoln, 235
LELAND
   Barbara Louise, 419, 421
   Gene, 421
LENOIR
   Willie, 305
LEVY
   Archie (Bud), 185
   Eva, 104, 126
   Velma Mae, 185
LEWIS
   Bertha, 315
   Lubertha, 293, 314, 315
LINDSAY
   Susie I., 202, 203
   Unknown, 203
LITTLE
   Decekka Diante, 238
   Mary Lee, 398, 401
   May Lee, 390, 391
   Sadie, 123, 150
   Unknown, 123, 391
   Willie Mae, 183
LLOYD
   Larry Jason, 251
LOCKETTE
   Marceline G., 286, 292, 313, 314, 315
LONG
   Everlean, 195, 196
LONGS
   Bernice, 126
   Calvin Vernon, 126
Lord Baltimore, 25, 35
LOTMAN
   Rose, 311, 312

Unknown, 312
Louis XIV, 4
Louis XVI, 4
LOUISIANA
   Bogalusa, 293, 314
   Good Pine, 108, 128
   Jefferson Parish, 314
   La Salle Parish, 108, 128
   Madison Parish, 178
   New Orleans, 286, 292, 293, 313, 314, 315, 371, 373, 374
   Orleans Parish, 286, 292, 293, 313, 314, 315, 371, 373
   Slidell, 293, 314
   St. Tammany Parish, 293, 314
   Tallulah, 178
   Washington Parish, 293, 314
   Westwego, 314
LOVE
   Drucilla L. H., 53, 54
   Fannie Mae, 319
   Gilly L. H., 53, 54
   Jodie Mae, 296, 319
   Oscar, Jr., 319
   Oscar, Sr., 296, 319
LOW COUNTRIES, 4
LOWE
   Bob, 112
LUCAS
   Betsy L., 231
   Rory, 231
LUCKETT
   Fred, 337, 342, 345, 348, 349, 350
   J.C., 350
   O.C., 350
   R.L., 350
   Susie, 73, 172, 185, 221, 222, 223, 224, 337, 342, 345, 348, 349, 350, 368
   Waudeen, 350
MACOMSON
   David, 34
   Rachel, 34
MADISON
   Annie Catherine, 355
   Joseph, 355
MALLETT
   Adeline, 71, 74, 96, 285
   Alphonzo L. (A.L.), 194, 236
   Beulah, 212
   Billie Ruth, 419
   Bobbie, 236
   Brenda, 194, 236
   Christian or Christine, 194
   Clara, 228, 229
   Dock Jeremiah, 193, 194
   Dock M., 174, 193, 212, 228, 229, 232, 234, 236
   Dorothy J., 235
   Fannie, 195
   Fannie B., 173, 174, 193, 228, 229, 232, 234, 236
   Fred, 193, 194, 230, 234, 235
   Frederick J., 235
   Georgia, 229
   Gloria, 235
   J.C., 193, 194, 228, 229
   Jessie, 195
   Judy A., 235
   Katherine, 194
   Katie K., 193, 194, 232
   Linda G., 184
   Louis or Louise, 194
   Ollie, 195
   R.D., 194
   Rubell (Ruby) Bonita, 193, 194, 229, 230, 257
   Shirley, 194, 236
   Vergie, 235
   Vergie Lee, 234, 235
Mallett School, 74
MARTIN
   Alexander, 33, 40, 50, 60, 61, 63
   Frances Virginia, 60, 63
   Hannah, 33, 35, 40, 50, 60, 61, 63
   John, 61
   Joseph, 60
   Mary Elizabeth, 60
   Patsey, 188

Paulette, 361
Unknown, 188
MARYLAND, 19, 20, 21, 23, 24, 25, 28, 29, 31, 34, 35
  Aberdeen Proving Grounds, 34
  Baltimore, 21, 22, 28, 294, 316
  Baltimore Co., 17, 19, 20, 22, 24, 27, 28, 30, 31, 32, 33, 34, 35, 46, 48
  Calvert Cliffs State Park, 22
  Calvert Co., 22, 23, 24, 31, 34, 35
  Calvertown, 23
  Charles Co., 365
  Deniston, 35
  Gunpowder Falls State Park, 27
  Gunpowder Hundred, 29
  Gunpowder Manor, 25
  Harford Co., 16, 19, 20, 22, 24, 25, 29, 32, 33, 34, 35
  Joppa, 27, 28, 29, 30, 31
  Kingsville, 29
  Michaelsville, 34
  My Lady's Manor, 19, 25
  Perryman, 29, 32, 34
  Salisbury, 244
  Upper Hundred Cliffs, 22
  White Plains, 365
Maryland Alien Property Commission, 25
MAXWELL
  Henrietta, 120
McADAMS
  Josiah, 80
McBRIDE
  W.W., 79
McBRYDE
  W.P., 79
McCABE
  Margaret, 50
McCALL
  Viola, 148
McCLELLAN
  Jessica, 270
McCLUSKY
  Zemuely, 49, 64, 85
McCOWAN
  Willie Beatrice, 293
McCOY
  Amaris Vania, 231
  John, 231
  Mary Jean, 231
McCURDY
  Margaret, 48, 50, 64
McDONALD
  John, 29, 30
McGEE
  Briesha, 261
McGILL
  Jacinda, 305
  Racquel, 305
McKELLAR
  Jeanette, 238
  Marcus Simmons, 238
  Unknown, 238
McLEAN
  Aaron, 264
  L.C., 241, 264
  Levonna, 264
  Rita, v, 1, 241, 264
McLENDON
  Vera Mae, 307
McLIN
  Vera M., 357
McMICHAEL
  Callie Beatrice, 101, 119, 120, 144, 146, 386
MERKSON
  Rebecca, 197
  Unknown, 197
MICHIGAN
  Ann Arbor, 301, 302, 325, 326
  Battle Creek, 286, 289, 306, 307, 309, 310, 311, 312
  Benton Harbor, 240, 260
  Berrien, 196, 260, 261, 262, 263, 264, 265, 266
  Berrien Co., 196, 240, 260, 261, 262, 263, 264, 265, 266
  Calhoun Co., 289, 306, 307, 309, 310, 311, 312

Dearborn, 150
Detroit, 76, 90, 91, 99, 100, 104, 107, 108, 117, 118, 126, 127, 128, 129, 130, 131, 140, 141, 142, 143, 150, 176, 177, 194, 210, 211, 212, 213, 214, 215, 216, 217, 218, 228, 229, 286, 289, 290, 291, 294, 295, 299, 300, 306, 307, 308, 309, 310, 311, 312, 316, 317, 318, 322, 324, 341, 360, 361, 363, 366, 401
Eau Claire, 196, 240, 260, 261, 262, 263, 264, 265, 266
Ecourse, 149, 150
Ferndale, 300
Hamtramck, 361
Highland Park, 294, 316
Idlewild, 306
Inkster, 291, 311
Lake Co., 290, 306
Lincoln Park, 123, 149
Macomb Co., 126
Macombs Co., 361
Northville, 117, 142
Oakland Co., 300, 323, 341, 359
Saginaw, 295, 317
Saginaw Co., 295, 317
Southfield, 300, 323, 341, 359
Superior Township, 301, 302, 325, 326
Warren, 361
Washtenaw Co., 301, 302, 325, 326, 327
Wayne Co., 99, 100, 104, 107, 108, 117, 118, 123, 126, 127, 128, 129, 130, 131, 140, 141, 142, 143, 149, 150, 176, 177, 194, 210, 211, 213, 214, 215, 216, 217, 218, 228, 229, 286, 289, 290, 291, 294, 295, 299, 300, 306, 307, 309, 310, 311, 312, 316, 317, 318, 322, 324, 341, 360, 361, 363, 366
Westland, 291, 312
Willow Run, 326
Yates, 290
Ypsilanti, 325

MIDDLEBROOK
T.J., 79

MILES
Esther, 150

MILLINER
Brenda, 363
Unknown, 363

MINNESOTA
Fillmore Co., 230, 257

MISSISSIPPI, 48, 104, 105, 168, 288
Adams Co., 66, 194, 232, 293
Alcorn, 381
Attala Co., 49, 64, 65, 68, 69, 70, 73, 74, 75, 78, 79, 80, 81, 83, 85, 93, 94, 95, 96, 97, 98, 99, 100, 101, 102, 103, 104, 105, 106, 107, 108, 109, 110, 111, 112, 116, 117, 118, 119, 120, 121, 122, 123, 124, 128, 129, 130, 131, 132, 133, 134, 135, 136, 138, 139, 140, 141, 142, 143, 144, 146, 147, 148, 149, 150, 153, 154, 155, 156, 158, 160, 168, 169, 170, 171, 172, 173, 174, 175, 176, 177, 178, 179, 180, 181, 182, 183, 184, 185, 186, 187, 188, 189, 190, 191, 192, 193, 194, 195, 196, 197, 200, 201, 202, 203, 204, 205, 207, 208, 210, 211, 213, 215, 216, 217, 218, 221, 222, 223, 224, 225, 226, 228, 229, 230, 232, 234, 236, 237, 238, 240, 242, 243, 246, 249, 250, 251, 254, 255, 257, 259, 260, 261, 262, 263, 264, 265, 266, 267, 269, 271, 273, 282, 284, 285, 286, 287, 288, 289, 290, 291, 292, 294, 295, 296, 297, 299, 300, 301, 302, 303, 305, 306, 307, 309, 310, 311, 312, 316, 317, 319, 320, 321, 322, 323, 324, 325, 326, 327, 328, 329, 330, 331, 333, 334, 336, 337, 338, 340, 341, 342, 343, 344, 345, 346, 347, 348, 349, 350, 351, 352, 353, 355, 356, 357, 358, 359, 360, 361, 363, 364, 365, 366, 367, 368, 370, 371, 373, 374, 375, 376, 377, 379, 382, 385, 386, 387, 388, 389, 390, 391, 392, 393, 394, 395, 396, 398, 401, 402, 403, 404, 405, 406, 407, 409, 410, 411, 412, 414, 415, 416, 417, 418, 419, 420, 421, 422, 423, 424, 425, 426, 427, 429, 431, 432,

433, 434, 435, 436, 437, 438, 439, 440, 441, 442, 443, 444
Attalaville, 81
Bluff Springs, 81
Bolivar, 307
Bolivar Co., 99, 111, 112, 116, 117, 136, 137, 138, 139, 140, 307, 325, 326
Bolton, 169, 179, 180
Brandon, 396, 407
Camp Shelby, 228
Canton, 329, 331
Carthage, 109, 131
Center, 107, 117, 120, 144
Chickasaw Co., 328, 330
Choctaw Co., 78
Claiborne, 136
Claiborne Co., 186, 347, 381
Clarksdale, 116, 138, 329, 331
Clinton, 80, 180
Coahoma Co., 116, 137, 138, 329, 331
Columbus, 85, 298
Conway, 108, 129
Cruger, 126, 175, 249, 251, 254, 255, 277, 278, 279, 280, 281
Dundee, 99, 111, 116, 136, 137, 138, 139
Durant, 83, 134, 169, 179, 180, 194, 229, 257, 296, 391, 402
Ethel, 78, 79, 80
George Co., 177
Goodman, 352, 356, 368, 390, 391, 398
Greenwood, 249
Gulfport, 132, 175, 202
Harrison Co., 132, 175, 202, 370, 373, 374, 376, 377, 379, 382
Hinds Co., 101, 110, 119, 120, 123, 134, 144, 146, 147, 148, 150, 169, 171, 175, 179, 180, 184, 194, 203, 204, 219, 238, 242, 301, 305, 320, 325, 338, 344, 349, 386, 401, 402, 417, 432
Hollyridge, 293, 315
Holmes Co., 78, 101, 103, 104, 122, 124, 126, 146, 147, 148, 149, 150, 169, 175, 179, 180, 181, 183, 194, 205, 207, 208, 219, 229, 246, 249, 250, 251, 254, 255, 257, 277, 278, 279, 280, 281, 296, 319, 352, 368, 386, 390, 391, 398, 402
Hushpuckena, 112, 113
Indianola, 176, 211
Itta Bena, 296, 319
Jackson, 101, 110, 119, 120, 123, 134, 144, 146, 147, 148, 150, 169, 175, 194, 203, 204, 238, 242, 303, 305, 320, 338, 344, 349, 381, 386, 401, 402, 417, 432
Joseph, 83, 85
Kemper Springs, 332
Kemper Springs Co., 332
Kosciusko, 1, 74, 78, 81, 82, 83, 85, 96, 97, 98, 99, 101, 102, 104, 105, 106, 107, 108, 110, 112, 116, 117, 118, 119, 120, 123, 124, 128, 129, 130, 131, 132, 133, 134, 135, 136, 138, 142, 143, 144, 147, 148, 153, 155, 158, 160, 163, 164, 168, 169, 171, 173, 174, 175, 176, 177, 183, 184, 186, 188, 193, 194, 195, 196, 200, 201, 202, 203, 204, 205, 210, 228, 229, 232, 234, 236, 237, 238, 240, 242, 243, 249, 251, 254, 255, 260, 261, 262, 263, 264, 265, 266, 269, 273, 282, 286, 287, 288, 289, 290, 291, 292, 294, 295, 296, 297, 299, 300, 301, 302, 303, 305, 306, 307, 309, 310, 311, 312, 316, 317, 319, 320, 321, 322, 323, 324, 325, 326, 327, 328, 330, 337, 338, 340, 341, 342, 343, 344, 346, 351, 353, 358, 359, 363, 364, 365, 370, 371, 373, 374, 375, 376, 377, 379, 382, 386, 391, 392, 393, 398, 400, 402, 403, 412, 414, 424, 438, 440, 441, 442, 444
Leake Co., 78, 82, 108, 109, 126, 129, 131, 175, 193, 194, 197, 202, 205, 212, 229, 236, 243, 246, 257, 287, 299, 322, 323
Lee Co., 417
LeFlore Co., 249, 296, 319
Lexington, 101, 122, 146, 147, 148, 149, 150, 183, 386
Lorman, 381
Louisville, 407

495

Lowndes Co., 65, 297, 298, 321, 322
Lula, 115, 116, 137
Madison Co., 78
McAdams, 80, 81, 99, 100, 117, 120, 134, 136, 140, 142, 143, 146, 172, 187, 190, 226, 401, 420, 434
McCool, 78
McVille, 80, 81, 197, 204
Mississippi City, 370, 373, 376, 377, 379, 382
Montgomery Co., 78
Mt. Salus, 80
Natchez, 293, 381
Neshoba Co., 135, 244
New Port, 81, 82, 83, 94, 100, 101, 102, 105, 168, 171, 173, 179, 181, 183, 200, 337, 346, 352, 355, 356, 357, 361, 363, 370, 375, 377, 385, 387, 388, 391, 394, 411, 416, 419, 421, 424
Noxubee Co., 155, 173, 193, 195, 200, 201, 202, 203, 205, 208
Ofahoma, 126
Philadelphia, 244
Pickens, 104, 126
Port Gibson, 186, 347
Rankin Co., 393, 396, 407
Richland, 103
Sallis, 49, 64, 73, 74, 78, 80, 81, 82, 85, 96, 99, 100, 101, 103, 110, 117, 119, 121, 122, 123, 134, 135, 136, 140, 142, 143, 144, 146, 147, 148, 149, 150, 153, 155, 168, 169, 170, 171, 172, 175, 179, 182, 183, 184, 185, 186, 187, 188, 189, 190, 191, 192, 196, 203, 208, 219, 221, 222, 223, 224, 225, 226, 230, 237, 242, 257, 259, 300, 305, 328, 329, 330, 331, 333, 336, 337, 338, 340, 341, 342, 345, 346, 347, 348, 349, 350, 351, 352, 353, 355, 356, 357, 358, 359, 360, 363, 364, 365, 366, 367, 368, 371, 376, 379, 382, 385, 386, 387, 388, 389, 390, 391, 392, 393, 394, 395, 396, 398, 401, 402, 403, 404, 405, 406, 407, 409, 412, 414, 415, 417, 418, 419, 420, 421, 422, 423, 424, 425, 426, 427, 429, 431, 432, 433, 434, 435, 436, 437, 438, 439, 440, 441, 442, 443, 444
Shelby, 112, 116, 138, 325, 326
Shuqualak, 155, 173, 193, 195, 200, 201, 202, 203, 205, 208
Smith Co., 48
Stallo, 120, 135, 144
Sunflower Co., 176, 211, 293, 315
Tallahatchie Co., 176
Terry, 301, 325
Thomastown, 80, 81, 193, 194, 212, 236, 411
Tippah Co., 52, 65, 153
Tunica Co., 99, 111, 116, 136, 137, 138, 139
Tupelo, 417
Tylertown, 293, 313
Vicksburg, 381
Walthall Co., 293, 313
West, 401
Winston Co., 78, 407
Yazoo, 115
Zemuly, 82, 85
Mississippi State University, 134
MISSOURI
Kansas City, 137
St. Louis, 70, 73, 76, 91, 104, 117, 124, 125, 142, 151, 163, 169, 182, 284, 287, 288, 289, 292, 294, 295, 297, 299, 300, 301, 334, 340, 342, 344, 345, 348, 349, 350, 351, 353
St. Louis Co., 104, 124, 151, 169, 182, 287, 301, 334, 348
MITCHELL
Desi, 308
Ella Mae, 174, 201
Mary Elizabeth, 104, 124, 151
Sarah, 20
Violet, 54
William, 54
MIZELL
Elmina Horn, 47
MONTGOMERY

Iona (or Dona), 383
Robert, 47
Unknown, 383
MOORE
   Belynda, 249, 276
   Herbert F., Jr., 249
   Herbert F., Sr., 249, 276
   Lena Mae, 249, 276
   Michael Anthony, 249
   Rodney, 238
   Timothy (Tim Man), 249
MORAGHAN
   Felicia Cabrini, 269
   Michael Terence, 269
MORGAN
   Charlie, 82
   Darlene, 231
   Lynn D., 231
   Sarah Lynn, 231
   Zemuly, 82
Morgan School, 82
MORRIS
   Tera M., 279
MUNSON
   Alma Lee, 301, 325, 326
   Blondean, 326, 327
   Charles, 287, 301, 325, 326
   Christine, 302
   Frederick, 326, 327
   Howard, 301, 302, 326
   Lottie, 287, 301, 325, 326, 371
   Marie, 301, 302, 325, 326, 327
   Thurman, 326, 327
MURPHY
   A.D., 113, 114, 115
   Ahmad, Jr., 266
   Ahmad, Sr., 266
   Ahmora, 266
   Bryce, 266
   Carol, 240, 261
   Chase, 266
   Chrystal, 260
   Curtis, 241, 266
   Cynthia, 265
   Darlene, 240, 260
   Ellon, 196, 240, 260, 261, 262, 263, 264, 265, 266
   Felicia, 241, 265
   Gabriel, 261
   Jahya, 265
   Javari, 265
   Kameron, 265
   Kazayn, 263
   Keisha, 261
   Kemari, 265
   Krystal, 266
   Larry, 241, 265
   Linda (Carol), 261
   Marvin, 241
   Marvin Ray, 261
   Max a Million, 260
   Melvin, Jr., 240, 260
   Murriel Delores, 241, 262
   NeVeah, 263
   Nurso, 265
   Patricia, 241, 263
   Pinto, 260
   Randon, 263
   Rita, v, 1, 241, 264
   Shakira, 265
   Sheila, 241, 264
   Taj, 261
   Terria, 261
   Tony, Jr., 263
   Tony, Sr., 241, 263
   Tonya, 260
   Towa, 261
   Trey, 266
   Vincent, 241, 266
   Winter, 263
   Zafina, 265
   Zavieria, 265
   Zenobia, 240, 262
   Zenolia, 195, 196, 240, 260, 261, 262, 263, 264, 265, 266
NAACP, 91, 134
NASH
   Christine, 148

Emma Jane, 132
George W., 246
Icy Viola, 76, 243, 244, 267, 269, 271, 273
Limmie Mae Douglas, 155, 176, 210, 211, 213, 215, 216, 217, 218
Lovie, 173, 175, 205, 207, 208, 243, 246, 249, 250, 251, 254, 255
Millie, 287, 299, 322, 323
Rev. W.W., 83
Vergie Lee, 234, 235
Woodrow Wilson, 175, 205, 207, 243, 246

National Defense Service Medal, 378

NAYLOR
Beatrice F., 143
Eugene, 119, 143
Francis, 143
Irma Jean, 119, 143
Priscilla, 143

NEAL
Eva May, 201

NELSON
Felicia, 406

NETHERLANDS, 13

NEVADA
Clark Co., 249, 276, 325
Las Vegas, 325

New Deal, 93

NEW YORK
Flushing, 300
New York, 240, 260
New York City, 90, 300
Queens, 300

NEWELL
Henry, 110, 133
Johnnie, 110, 133

NITMAN
Monica, 435
Norman, 435

NORMAN
Barbra Ann, 251

NORTH
Bonnie, 428, 443
James Lee, Sr., 428, 443

NORTH CAROLINA
Ashville, 291, 311
Beaufort Co., 356
Buncombe Co., 291, 311
Maxton, 231
Pantego, 356
Robeson Co., 231

North Richmond M.B. Church, 351

NORVELL
Rosalind Lavon, 244

O'HARA
Linda Faye, 433
Robert, 433
Unknown, 225

Oath of Fidelity, 29

OHIO
Lucas Co., 177
Toledo, 177
Wood Co., 291, 310

OKLAHOMA
Enid, 298
Garfield Co., 298

OLGUIN
De'Avlin, 255, 282
Natasha, 255, 282

OUSLEY
Carmelita Sabrina, 244, 269, 270, 271
Craig, 270

PAGETT
John Luke, 48

PARKER
Aaron, 33
Arthur Lee, 251
B.J., 281
Barbra Ann, 251
Bernard, 281
Charlene, 254, 255
Charnelle, 278
Cheryl Penny, 277
Chris, 278
Elizabeth (Betsey), 33, 63
Eric, 277
Hannah, 33

Ilander N., Jr., 250, 277, 278, 279, 280, 281
Ilander N., Sr., 175, 205, 207, 208, 249, 250, 251, 254, 255
Isaac G., 33
John, 33
Joseph, 34
LaTarshe (Toddy), 281
Latisha, 281
Lena Mae, 249, 276
Lishon, 280
Lovie, 173, 175, 205, 207, 208, 243, 246, 249, 250, 251, 254, 255
Makayla, 281
Micah, 280
Nakai, 280
Natasha, 255, 282
Nova, 282
Nylah, 280
Ollander (Odie), 280
Rachel, 34
Rosemary, 251
Ryan, 277
S'eance, 281
Sandy D., 278
Sarah, 34, 63
Shaun, 282
Shirley, 255
Steven S., Jr., 279
Steven S., Sr., 279
Tera M., 279

PARROTT
Rev., 79

PATTERSON
Avery Lou, 344, 351
Bessie Mae, 110
Harold L., Jr., 344
Harold L., Sr., 344, 351
Kevin Lamar, 344
Shaneka Latrisha, 238
Sheila, 344
Unknown, 110
Vertrishe, 238
William, 29, 30

PATTON
Carrie, 178

PEGRAM
Georgia Lee, 291, 308, 312, 313
Rosalyn, 313
Thomas, 313
Unknown, 312, 313

PENNSYLVANIA
Delaware Co., 124
Upland, 124

PERKINS
Andrew, 176, 213
Anetha, 120, 146
Angela, 369
Arey, 369
Bennie Lee, 369
Cherry Mae, 176, 210, 213
Donte, 369
Eddie, 369
Fannie Bea, 369
James Willie, 352, 368, 369
Lorine, 352, 368, 369
Unknown, 120

PERNELL
Judy, 146
Tony, 146

PERRY
Ottilee, 293, 315

PERTEET
Icy Dean, 204
Unknown, 204

PETEET
Ollie J., 342, 367

PETERS
Kevon, 260
Nookie, 260
Tonya, 260
Unknown, 260

PETERSON
NiUnna, 273
Tabatha, 244, 273
Tiana, 273

PHILLIPS
Bernice, 226, 420, 434

Darren, 226, 434
Jackie, 434
Jacqueline, 226
Jacqueling, 434
Joseph Lee, Jr., 226, 434
Joseph Lee, Sr., 226, 420, 434
Kesha S., 395, 407
Lamonica, 434
Patrick, 226, 434
Unknown, 407
Victor, 395
Yolanda, 226, 434
PHOMMAVONG
Khankham (Candy), 244, 273
PINDER
Carolyn, 261
Crimson, 261
Curtis, 261
Darnelle, 261
PINK
Keith Anthony, 251
Rosemary, 251
Toya, 251
Plantation Act of 1740, 21
Planters' Academy, 81
POINTER
Edna Alma, 168, 169
Stella E., 168, 169
Unknown, 168
POPE
W.R., 79
PRATT
Cherylease M., 244, 273
PRIDMORE
Maria (Mariah), 33, 53
PRITCHETT
Bonnie Dean, 355, 356
James, 356
Protestant Reformation, 6, 13
PRYOR
Felicia, 265
Isaiah, 265
Jeremiah, 265
Samuel, 265

Public Works Authority, 115
PURDY
Adoratia, 435
Kevin, 435
Puritans, 23
PURYEAR
H.H., 79
Quakers, 23, 24
Queen Mary, 13
RABERN
Charles, 79
RAINEY
A. J., 73, 74, 75, 93, 328, 329, 330
Adeline, 74, 96, 285
Amanda, 73, 74, 75, 93, 96, 100, 101, 119, 120, 121, 385, 386, 388, 392, 409
Andrew, 73, 74, 75, 93
Andrew J., 328, 329, 330
Annie B., 73, 74, 75, 93, 96, 100, 101, 119, 120, 121, 385, 386, 388, 392, 409
Artie, 1, 67, 68, 71, 72, 73, 74, 75, 76, 93, 100, 172, 185, 192, 221, 222, 223, 224, 285, 328, 333, 334, 345, 348, 368, 370, 385, 387, 409, 410, 411, 433, 444
Baby James, 74, 444
Case, 73, 74, 75, 93, 100, 172, 185, 221, 222, 223, 224, 296, 301, 320, 334, 335, 336, 337, 338, 340, 341, 342, 345, 348, 349, 350, 351, 353, 358, 368, 385, 409, 426
Ike, 74, 75, 93, 172, 186, 334, 347, 389, 396, 407, 409, 410, 411, 414, 415, 418, 419, 421, 424, 426, 427, 429
J. T., 73, 74, 75
James, 73, 74, 75, 444
James T., 333
Maggie, 73, 74, 75
Simon, Sr., 74, 75, 94, 101, 122, 149, 150, 386, 387, 388, 390, 391, 392, 393, 394, 396, 412, 426
RAY
Burris, 79
John, Rev., 79
REDD

Rosie, 296
REDMOND
    Courtney Malone, 238
REES
    Helen GUYTON, 20, 22, 29, 48, 50
Republic of Korea War Service Medal, 378
REVIS
    Eureka, 298
Revolutionary War, 22, 25, 32, 38, 40, 47, 50
RHONE
    Chelsea, 273
    Denzel, 273
    Kareem, 273
    Marcy L., 244, 273
    Naima, 273
    Nyla, 273
Richard I, 8
Richard the Lionheart, 8
RICHARDS
    Pat, 361
RILEY
    Annie B., 385
    Annie Pearl, 338, 339, 351, 352, 368
    Antonio, 351
    Belle, 409
    Brenda, 194, 236
    Charlie E., 202, 203
    Collean, 352
    Damon, 175, 202
    Donnie, 203
    Emma A., 202, 203
    Genet, 222
    Gloria, 235
    Ida, 74, 172, 389, 396, 407, 409, 410, 411, 414, 415, 418, 419, 421, 424, 426, 427, 428, 429
    J.R., 79
    James E., 202, 203
    Jim Bell, 338, 351, 352, 368
    Jimmie, 409
    Katherine, 411, 422, 436
    Locile, 102
    Lorine, 352, 368, 369

    Mae D. or Mary or Mardell, 202, 203
    Nola Mae, 173, 175, 202
    Ollie D., Jr., 222
    Ollie D., Sr., 186, 222, 346
    Ronnie, 203
    Rosie Jean, 222
    Rozell J., 186, 222, 346
    Susie I., 202, 203
    Unknown, 222, 235
    Willie Claude, 222
RIMPSON
    Sakaura, 261
RINGWOOD
    Linda, 163
    Tom, 163
ROBINSON
    Darrelyn Lorraine, 290
    Patricia Ruth, 308
    Phyllis, 305
    Unknown, 290, 305
    Willie, 360
Robinson's Rest, 23, 24
ROBINSON-McLEAN
    Zenola, 264
ROBY
    Earnest Mitchell, 171, 184
    Edna, 171, 172
    Elmer, 171, 172
    Elmer Gene, 189
    Emma, 391, 398, 400, 401
    Homer, 171
    James Lamar, 185
    Joyrosea, 185
    Katie, 184
    Lillian, 189
    Lillie Wardean, 171, 172, 185, 221, 222, 223, 224, 337, 345, 346, 368
    Linnie B., 184, 185
    Louella, 171, 172, 187
    Mitchell, 184
    Odell (Pink), 153, 160, 171, 172
    Patsy J., 154, 155, 170, 171, 184, 185, 187, 189, 190, 192, 221, 222, 223, 224, 346

Pleas W., 171
Ruth Lee (Ruthie), 171, 172, 190, 225, 226, 412, 419, 420, 433, 434, 435
Vamis (Vammie), 171, 172, 192, 338, 348
Velma, 189
Velma Lizzie, 171, 184
Velma Mae, 185
Vernon L., 185
Will, 419
William (Willie), 155, 170, 171, 184, 185, 187, 189, 190, 192, 346, 368
Willie Charles, 185
Wilmer Dean, 189

ROCKETT
Carrie, 238, 259
Reuben, 259
Rickey, 259
Rickey Rodney, 259
Roman, 259

RODGERS
Judge Henry, 196

ROGERS
Donna J., 318
Eva, 415, 416, 417
Unknown, 318, 417

ROTH
Elisa, 163
Lisa, 163
William, 163

ROUNDTREE
Andrew, 188
Annie Christine, 188
Bobbie Jean, 188
Cleotha, 188
Clyde Wade, 188
Jessie D., 188
July Jean, 188
Louella, 171, 172, 187
Mary Lee, 188
Othar, 172, 187
Patsey, 188
Ulla Mae, 188
Vellar, 188

ROYAL
Alexis, 405
Chassie, 405
Unknown, 405

RUBENS
Johnnie Lavelle, 123
Unknown, 123

RUFF
Carrie J., 290, 308, 309, 310
Clarence Edward, Jr., 310
Clarence Edward, Sr., 290, 310
John (Bogie) William, 310

RUSH
Joyce, 303, 305
Katherine, 411, 422, 436
Otis, 422, 436
Rickey, 436
Tony, 436
Unknown, 305

RUSSELL
Ellen, 72, 153
Green, 69, 70, 74, 95, 96
Robert, 284
Sarah, 67, 68, 69, 70, 74, 95, 96, 100, 284, 285, 288, 289, 292, 294, 295, 297, 299, 300, 301
Susan, 284

Rust College, 134

RWMANZI
Nyla, 265

SAFFOLD
Barbara Ruth, 230, 257

Saint Jr. College, 134

SALLIS
Fannie, 70, 153, 154, 155, 156, 160, 164, 168, 170, 173, 176, 177
J.G., 81

SAMPLE
Aaron, 390
Lula, 390, 391, 398, 402

SANCHEZ
Johnnie Amzy, 168, 169
Sixto Cruz, 169

SANDERS
Ellen, 153

LaTonya Cheri, 244, 273
Rev., 115
SANDIFER
    Bonnie Jean, 110, 134, 135, 136
    Dorothy Mae, 391, 398, 401
    Mattie, 134
    Unknown, 391
SAUNDERS
    Kenyette, 432
SAXON
    Tabitha, 32, 46
SCARFF
    Amelia, 31
SCOTT
    Brittie, 344, 351
    Clara, 296
    Erma Jean, 394, 395, 406
    Kesha S., 395, 407
    Robert, 395, 406
    Thaddious S., 395, 407
    Thomas (Tom), 344, 351
    Unknown, 296
SEALS
    Lishon, 280
SELTZER
    Amiri Naomi, 272
    Charles, 272
Sharecropping, 92, 93
SHARPE
    Brandon (BJ), Jr., 260
    Brandon, Sr., 260
    Brianna, 260
    Darlene, 240, 260
    Destiny, 260
    Kayden, 260
    Matthew, 260
    Matthew Ashley, Sr., 240, 260
    Trey, 260
SHAW
    Rhonda Larita, 270, 271
    Ronald, 244, 272
SHERRILL
    Mary McRee (Polly), 48
Siege of Ninety-Six, 47, 50

SIMMONS
    Bobo, 238
    Callie Jean, 197
    Callie Pairee, 173, 174, 195, 196, 237, 240
    Clara, 197
    Diana, 238
    Everlean, 195, 196
    Felicia, 238
    Henry (L. C.), 195, 196, 237, 238, 259
    Henry Porterwood, 174, 195, 237, 240
    Iola, 195, 197
    Ishida, 238
    Jeanette, 238
    Jeanie Mae, 238
    Joyce, 238
    Katie, 238
    Larry Lamar, 238
    Lester (Tot), 197
    Lois, 195, 197
    Lona Mae, 197
    Lovie (Mae), 197
    Lue Bertha, 237
    Moon, 282
    Natasha, 255, 282
    Rebecca, 197
    Rickey, 1, 160, 237, 238, 259
    Robert, 197
    S. Thomas (S.T.), 197
    Shaneka Latrisha, 238
    Shannon R., 255, 282
    Tracey, 238
    Tracey Lebron, 238
    Tracvon, 238
    Travis, 238
    Trayvon, 238
    Vertrishe, 238
    Wakeco, 238
    Zenolia, 195, 196, 240, 260, 261, 262, 263, 264, 265, 266
SIMON
    Mrs. M., 156
SIMPSON
    Desi, 308
SIPP

Felicia, 406
Sean, 406
SMARR
William Peyton, 53, 54
SMART
Loretha Vernetia, 125
SMITH
Alexander, 31
Ann, 17
Benjamin, 17
Chandra Valencia, 218
Elizabeth, 17, 177, 210, 218
Elizabeth Eleander, 31
Ernest, Jr., 177, 218
Frances Virginia, 60, 63
Hannah, 33
James, 33, 342, 367
John, 22
Johnnie, 332
Jonathan, 34
Joyce Lee, 332
Margaret Catherine (Molly), 34
Mary Lynn, 342, 367
Nathan Alexander, 61, 63
Nugulia, 342, 365, 366
Ollie Clara, 135
Sheldon, 441
Sheri Lynn, 367
Tellie, 351
Terri, 441
Thomas, 135
Tillie Mae, 344
Wyatt, 48
SNOW
Ernest Jim, 184, 185
Katie, 184
Linnie B., 184, 185
Oscar, 184, 185
SNYDER
Joseph, 263
Julian, 263
SOTO
Britteny L., 278
Raul, 278

SOUTH CAROLINA, 21, 32, 33, 35, 38, 40, 42, 43, 54, 60, 61, 69
Anderson Co., 48, 49, 54, 64, 65, 153
Anderson District, 32, 50
Cambridge, 39
Charleston, 32, 46
Cherokee Co., 19, 20, 32, 33, 38, 40, 42, 53, 54
Columbia, 290, 310
Cowpens National Battlefield, SC, 42
Gaffney, 19, 32, 33, 35, 38, 39, 40, 42
Greenville, 412, 427, 443
Hickory Grove, 33
Low Country, 38
Marion Co., 60
Ninety-Six District, 32, 35, 39, 50
Oconee Co., 49
Pendleton District, 50
Spartanburg Co., 32, 42, 46, 47
Union District, 20, 32, 33, 42, 43, 50, 52, 53, 54, 60, 65
Up Country, 38
York Co., 33, 42, 54, 65
York District, 50
Yorktown, 47
South Carolina Legislature, 49
South Dakota
Meade, 222
South Union School, 82
Spartanburg Regiment, 47
SPATES
Cynthia, 441
Unknown, 441
St. George Tombland Church, 11
St. George's Spesutia Parish Church, 29, 32, 34
St. George's Tombland, 11, 15
St. Gregory's Church, 15
St. James' Episcopal Church, 20, 25
St. James' Episcopal Church Cemetery, 19
St. John M. B. Church, 134
St. John's Gunpowder Parish Church, 20, 27, 29, 30, 31
St. Laurence's Church, 17

St. Martin at Oak Church, 17
St. Martin at Palace Church, 11, 12, 16, 17, 19, 20, 30
St. Michael at Coslany Church, 17
St. Michael at Plea Church, 11
St. Paul's Church, 7, 8
St. Peter Parmentergate Church, 9, 10, 11, 12
Stamp Act, 22
STARR
    Aaliyah Icy, 273
    Amari Monét STARR, 273
    Amavi, 273
    Cherylease M., 273
    Kedary, 273
    Khankham (Candy), 273
    LaTonya Cheri, 273
    Liliana Janae, 273
    Marcy L., 273
    Nia, 273
    Nykki Lamarr, v, 1, 76, 77, 153, 156, 160, 163, 205, 207, 243, 244, 246, 248, 249, 250, 253, 255, 267, 268, 269, 270, 273, 275, 280, 281, 284
    Nykki Lamarr, Jr., 268
    Princess, 1
    Riki, 273
    Rikki, 244, 273, 275
    Tabatha, 273
    Tonya, 273
    Tracy, 273
STEELE
    William Love, 49
STEEN
    James, 47
STEVENSON
    Leila Mae, 118, 143
STEWART
    Angelia, 150, 151
    Unknown, 151
STINGLEY
    Dorotha, 371
    Guyton, 371, 372, 377, 378
    Herman, 371, 373, 374

    Iona (or Dona), 383
    John Ike, 371, 372, 382, 383
    Lottie, 301, 371, 372, 376, 377
    Louria, 371, 372, 374, 375, 376, 377, 382
    Maggie, 73, 74, 75, 93, 370, 371, 372, 373, 374, 376, 377, 379, 382, 409
    Mannie Whitt (Whitt), 371, 372, 379, 381, 382
    Mayvell, 371, 372, 376, 377
    Pearline, 371, 373
    Quincy Thelma, 371, 382, 383
    Susie, 172, 185, 221, 222, 223, 224, 337, 342, 345, 348, 349, 350, 368
    Thomas (Tom), 73, 93, 370, 371, 372, 373, 374, 376
    Tommy, 383
    Velma Lizzie, 171, 184
    William, 337, 342, 345, 348, 349
STONE
    William, 23
STRAUSS
    Jeanie Mae, 238
    Tiffany Simmons, 238
    Unknown, 238
SUDDUTH
    Arlene, 393
    Dave (Fat Dave), 389, 393
    Emma Kate, 300
    Frank Young, 393
    Hattie Irene, 388, 389, 393, 396
    Joe Howard, 371, 376, 377
    Kaley Henry (Kelcy), 300
    Mayvell, 371, 372, 376, 377
    Quincy Thelma, 371, 382, 383
SUMMERS
    Dolores Augusta, 117, 142
Sunderland All Saints' Church, 24
SYKES
    Carol Ann, 365
TANNER
    Eleane, 403
    Unknown, 403
TATE
    Mildred, 186, 221, 346

TATUM
   Rosemary, 344
TAUL
   Thomas P., 63
TAYLOR
   Emma A., 202, 203
   Gwendolyn, 316, 317
   Patrick Duwane, Sr., 326
   Ruby Lee, 325, 326
   Unknown, 203, 317
TEAGUE
   Allie Mae, 388, 394, 395, 404
   Anthony, 168, 169
   Booker T., 389, 394, 404
   Brenda, 135
   Carolyn Ann, 404
   Edna Alma, 168, 169
   Rickey Nelson, 404
   Robbie Lee, 388, 389, 394, 404, 405, 406, 407
   Unknown, 135
TENNESSEE, 33, 63
   Chester Co., 365
   Davidson Co., 428, 443
   Henry Co., 291, 311
   Knox Co., 356
   Knoxville, 356
   Memphis, 96, 98, 99, 101, 104, 107, 110, 111, 117, 118, 119, 120, 124, 125, 144, 146, 149, 175, 208, 320, 386
   Nashville, 428, 443
   Paris, 291, 311
   Rutherford Co., 52
   Shelby Co., 96, 98, 99, 101, 104, 107, 110, 111, 117, 118, 119, 120, 124, 125, 144, 146, 149, 175, 208, 302, 386
TERRY
   Alexander, 100
   Amanda, 73, 74, 75, 93, 96, 100, 101, 119, 120, 121, 385, 386, 388, 392, 409
   Andrew, 103, 104, 126
   Anetha, 120, 146
   Annie, 389, 391, 392, 402, 403
   Annie B., 73, 74, 75, 93, 96, 100, 101, 119, 120, 121, 385, 386, 388, 392, 409
   Annie Z., 119
   Beatrice, 99, 100, 118, 143
   Bernice, 126
   Bernice Marie, 101, 120, 144, 145, 386
   Blanche, 102, 103
   Brandon, 403
   Brenda, 363
   Bryford Andre, 152
   Callie Beatrice, 101, 119, 120, 144, 146, 386
   Carnes Fred, 101, 119, 120, 144, 146, 386
   Caroline, 69, 70, 71, 93, 95, 96, 98, 100, 101, 103, 105, 106, 284, 285, 386
   Clemenie, 360, 363
   Clinton, Jr., 403
   Clinton, Sr., 392, 403
   Dashie, 392
   Delgardo, 152
   Dora, 97, 105
   Dorothy J., 392, 403
   Earl, 392
   Earl Denison, Jr., 403
   Earl Denison, Sr., 392, 402, 403
   Earnest G., 388, 392
   Edna F., 102, 103
   Eleane, 403
   Elizabeth, 104, 126
   Elvie, 341, 360, 363, 364
   Ernest, 127
   Ethel, 98, 99, 110
   Eula, 97, 102
   Eva, 104, 126
   Flemmie Buford, 341, 360, 363, 364
   Frank, 102
   Fred Steele, Sr., 407
   Gertie Mae, 127
   Gertrude, 104, 124, 151
   Gladys, 102
   Green, 97, 103, 104, 124, 126
   Grover, 102, 103
   Hattie, 105
   Helen, 300, 323, 324

Howard, 103, 104
Howard Lee, 127
Irma Jean, 119, 143
Isaac H., 102
Jacob G. (Jake), 97, 105, 106
Jamari, 403
Jarrett, 403
John, 97, 101, 102
Johnnie, 103, 104
Joseph, 103, 104
Joseph Thomas (Joe), 73, 93, 96, 100, 101, 105, 119, 120, 121, 385, 386, 388
Kenneth Matthew, 363
L.I. or L.J., 104
Lela, 100, 101, 385, 386, 409
Leon, 105, 389, 391, 392, 402, 403
Leon (Vince), 392
Lillian, 103, 104, 392
Lillian P., 125
Lockett J., 127
Lockett Joseph, Jr., 125
Lockett Joseph, Sr., 103, 104, 124, 125, 151
Loretha Vernetia, 125
Lula, 99, 100
Lula Cladis, 102
Magnolia, 125
Magnolia (Maggie), 97, 103, 104, 124, 126
Margaret, 125
Mary, 96, 97, 98, 99, 107, 110, 111, 117, 118
Mary Elizabeth, 104, 124, 151
Mary Emma, 98, 99, 107, 128, 129, 130, 131
Michael, 152
Michael Joseph, Jr., 152
Michael Joseph, Sr., 125, 151
Minnie, 105
Nealie Eugene, 92, 98, 99, 111, 112, 116, 136, 137, 138, 139
Patsy, 97
Peat, 104
Quesada, 101, 386

Retha, 102, 103
Rhonda, 392, 403
Romie, Jr., 127
Romie, Sr., 103, 104, 126
Ruby, 104
Ruby Lee, 127
Ruth G., 103, 104, 124
Sarah Ann, 127
Sarah Elizabeth, 152
Sarah J. (Sallie), 97
Sarah V., 99, 100, 117
Shirley A., 125
Simon Andy, 392
Stella Mae, 101, 121, 122, 146, 147, 148, 149, 150, 386, 388, 392
Sylvia, 360, 363
Taffanye Michel, 152
Tertis or Gert, 103, 105
Thomas P., 80
Timothy, 403
Tommie, 103, 104
Twylla, 403
Unknown, 403
Vera LaVern, 300, 323, 342, 357, 364, 365, 366
Vincent, 69, 71, 93, 95, 96, 98, 100, 101, 102, 103, 105, 106
Vincent Green, 125
Vinson, 69, 71, 93, 95, 96, 98, 100, 101, 102, 103, 105, 106
Walter, 105
Walter G., 99
Walter G., Sr., 97, 105
Wiley F., 103, 105
William M., Sr., 96, 98, 99, 110, 111, 117, 118
William Vinson, Jr., 99, 100, 118, 143
Yalonda, 403
Yvonne Jacquline, 101, 120, 144, 386
TEXAS, 33, 61
   Allen, 244, 273
   Bell Co., 244
   Camp Co., 125
   Collin Co., 244, 273

Harris Co., 222, 268, 299, 314
Harrison Co., 63
Henderson, 34
Houston, 268, 299, 314
Milam Co., 298
Rusk Co., 34
Temple, 244
Walker, 222
Washington Co., 52, 53, 65

THOMAS
Amavi, 273
Delores, 316, 317
Diane, 316, 317
Doris, 411
Doris Nell, 422, 437
Elizabeth, 177, 210, 218
Gwendolyn, 316, 317
John, 294
John, Jr., 316, 317
John, Sr., 316, 317
Magnolia, 294, 316, 317
Marvin, 316, 317
Osceola, 137
Ronnie, 273
Unknown, 437
Willie James, 177, 218

THOMPSON
Connie Mae, 357
Edwina, 295, 317, 318

Thompson's Plantation, 112, 113

THURMAN
Allie Mae, 388, 394, 395, 404
Anita, 224
John Lee, 186, 224
Linda, 224
Lucy, 186, 224
Mary, 224, 405
Prince Lamar (Sonny Man), 395, 404, 405
Sandra, 405

THWEATT
Uriah, 80

TOLL
Thomas P., 63

TOLLIVER
Amy Lee, 438
Frederick, 438

Toplin School House, 107
Tougaloo College, 134, 381

TOUT
Lydia, 31
Unknown, 31

TRAVIS
Miracle, 261

TRAYLOR
Jacob, 261
Janay, 261
Sarita, 261
Unknown, 261
Yolanda, 261

TRIPLETT
Alice Edna, 395, 407
Jean, 407
Nelson, 395, 407

TRUSS
Johnnie, 110, 133
Johnnie Mae, 133
Unknown, 110, 133

TUBBS
June, 146
Lee, 146

TUCKER
Elmina Horn, 47

TURNER
Lee Boston, 371, 374, 375, 382
Louria, 371, 372, 374, 375, 376
Michael, 244, 272
Rhonda Larita, 270, 271
S'eance, 281

Tuskegee Institute, 381

UNDERHILL
Mary, 19, 29, 30

UNDERWOOD
Margaret, 11, 15, 16, 19, 30

United Nations Service Medal, 378

UNKNOWN
Alean, 401
Alice, 230
Angel, 440

Belinda, 358
Bobbie, 194
Bumper, 260
Carolyn, 395, 405
Charlotte, 286, 297, 298, 321
Clarice, 123
Delphine, 306
Dorothy, 401, 402
Dorothy J., 392, 403
Elain, 435
Elizabeth, 11, 12, 13, 15, 16, 104, 126
Ellen, 153
Emma Jane, 132
Ericka, 270
Estelle, 200
Eula M., 110
Eula Mae, 417, 431
Fannie, 132
Frances, 20
Gabriel, 261
Gerri, 356
Gladys, 396, 407
Gwen, 73, 328, 329, 330, 356
Jackie, 135
Jacqueling, 434
Javari, 265
Jeannie, 332
JoAnn E., 356
Josephine, 201
Kim, 401
Krystal, 266
LaLesia, 407
Lamonica, 434
Luegene, 108, 130
Lutie, 288
Luvenia, 179
Magnolia (Maggie), 97, 103, 104, 124, 126
Margaret, 7, 9
Martha, 168
Mary, 19, 24, 29, 30, 32, 180
Michele, 401
Mollie, 337, 342, 345, 348, 349
Nancy, 20

Nancy M., 53, 54
Odester W., 357
Ollie M., 390
Ora, 401
Rhonda, 392, 403
Ruby Jean, 355
Sarah, 67, 68, 69, 70, 74, 95, 96, 100, 284
Serita, 422, 437
Sheila, 350
Susie, 73, 172, 185, 221, 222, 223, 224, 337, 342, 345, 348, 349, 350, 368
Terry, 230
Viola, 74, 94, 101, 122, 149, 150, 386, 387, 388, 390, 391, 392, 393, 394, 396, 412, 426
Yvette, 278
Zafina, 265
VAUGHN
  Dora Ellis, 355
  MacArthur, 355
VEASLEY
  Ruth Griffin, 109, 132
VIETNAM, 182
VIRGINIA, 23, 46, 61
  Albemarle Co., 269
  Augusta Co., 269
  Chesapeake, 21
  Colony, 21
  Glen Allen, 320
  Norfolk, 118, 143
VORTICE
  Jordan, 332
  Laurie, 332
WALKER
  Daniel, 186, 347
  Genova, 186, 346, 347, 426
  Jayden, 265
  Linda, 305
  Sylvester, 305
WALLS
  Alexis, 254
  Jarrette, 254
  Kennedy, 254
  Tonya Lashun, 254

WALTERS
   Annie Catherine, 355
   Annie May, 341, 355
   Bettye Kate, 356
   Bobbie Joe, 355, 356
   Bonnie Dean, 355, 356
   Dora Ellis, 355
   Earl D., 355, 356
   Eddie Lee, 356
   Frank Ellis, 341, 355
   Frankie Jean, 356
   Gerri, 356
   Gwen, 356
   James Roy, 355
   Jerry Willie, 355
   JoAnn E., 356
   Lue Arthur, 356
   Perry, 355, 356
   Ruby Jean, 355
WALTON
   Lisa Alesia, 320
   Lovie (Mae), 197
   Unknown, 197, 320
War of 1812, 40, 49
WARD
   Ethel Lavelle, 112, 116, 136
   Fannie, 395, 406
   Felton, 116, 137
   Johnny Howard, 116, 136
   Oscela, 116
   Osceola, 137
   Unknown, 395, 406
   Willie James, 137
WASHINGTON
   Augustine Sr., 21
   George, 21, 47
WATTERS
   James, 31
   Lydia, 31
WEATHERSLY
   Elmira, 294, 317, 331
   Samuel, 294
WEBB
   Alice Lee, 410, 411, 412, 415, 427, 428, 443
   Bonnie, 428, 443
   Elizabeth (Betsey), 48
   Oliver DeBois, 412, 427, 428, 443
   Oliver, Jr., 428
   William, 48
WEBBER
   Joseph, 46
WELLBORN
   Sarah Ann, 49
WELLS
   Blanche Gail, 290, 291, 307, 308, 312
   Dwight, 313
   Georgia Lee, 291, 308, 312, 313
   Marvin, 313
   Marvin Joseph, Jr., 291, 312, 313
   Robert A., 290, 307, 308
Wesley M.E. Church, 102
WEST
   Arlene, 393
WHISONANT
   Adaline, 54
WHITAKER
   Hannah Lyon, 19, 32, 34, 35, 40, 46, 48, 52, 53, 60, 64
   Mary, 19
WHITE
   Aiden Lee, 273
   Oneko, 244, 273
   Shaina, 273
WHITEHEAD
   Mary Van, 358
   Unknown, 358
WHITTINGTON
   Frenetter, 117, 140
WILDER
   Bonnie, 423, 439
   Fannie, 338, 339, 351, 353
   Nathaniel, 423, 439
   Viola, 74, 94, 101, 122, 149, 150, 386, 387, 388, 390, 391, 392, 393, 394, 396, 412, 426
WILEY

Cynthia, 244
WILKINS
  Carolyn Mellisa, 314
WILKINSON
  Claudia, 366
  Unknown, 366
William II, 13
William, Prince of Orange, 18
WILLIAMS
  Ariana Lovie Viola, 272
  Bessie Mae, 110
  Brittie, 344, 351
  Jeremy Juawon, 238
  Jesse, 337, 343, 344
  Linda, 305
  Maudie M., 338, 349
  Ozella (Sugar Baby), 441
  Sheron, 441
  Unknown, 110, 305, 441
  Vertrishe, 238
  Zelma, 337, 342, 343, 344, 350
WILLIS
  Brinda, 305
  Unknown, 305
WILSON
  Andre, 442
  Bessie Mae, 110
  Kesha, 442
  Unknown, 110
WINDOMS
  Bertha, 259
  Lue Bertha, 196, 237
WINGARD
  Debra, 242
  Luther D. (Rabbit), 204, 242
  Mildred Irene, 411, 412, 421, 422, 436, 437, 438, 439, 440
  Sonji F. (Lisa), 242
  Stacy, 242
  Theresa, 242
  Timothy, 242
  Tony, 242
  Tracy, 242
  Tremesha, 242

Vernestine (Susie), 204, 242
WINTERS
  Reverend, 112
Winters and Stingley Funeral Home, 382
Winters Funeral Home, 382
WISCONSIN
  Adams Co., 231
  Milwaukee, 76, 90, 91, 108, 129, 132, 148, 150, 185, 186, 188, 194, 204, 222, 224, 228, 344, 346, 347, 401, 404, 405, 419, 432
  Milwaukee Co., 108, 129, 132, 172, 186, 188, 190, 194, 204, 222, 224, 225, 226, 228, 344, 346, 347, 395, 404, 405, 412, 419, 432, 433, 434, 435
  Monroe, 231
  Sturdevant, 351
  Wauwatosa, 172, 190, 225, 226, 412, 419, 433, 434, 435
WISE
  Fannie, 338, 339, 351, 353
  Judy A., 235
  Willie N., Jr., 235
WOODS
  Cintha Susan (Sue C.), 54
  Clarese, 327
  Sharon, 136
  Sue C., 54
  Unknown, 136
WRIGHT
  Adeline, 178
  Amzie, 178
  Billie J., 178
  Carrie, 178
  Christian, 178
  Dock, 155, 177
  Essie, 177
  Fannie, 178
  Freddie, 178
  Gertrude, 178
  James, 443
  Jessie, 178
  Kenya, 443
  Mitchell, 178

Princess Monica, 244
Rose, 178
Silas D., 178
Suegene, 155, 177
Sylvia, 363
Unknown, 363
Viola, 178
YATES
　Emma, 431
　Shirley Jean, 431
YOUNG
　Carol, 240, 261
　Dora Luzetta, 244
　Linda (Carol), 261
　Marcus, 261
　Neal, 240, 261
　Yolanda, 261
ZOLICOFFER
　Clara, 194, 228, 229
ZOLLICOFFER
　Melinda, 111, 112

Made in the USA
Columbia, SC
29 September 2024